The DICTIONARY of OPERA

KT-457-701

The DICTIONARY of OPERA

Charles Osborne

Macdonald & Co
London & Sydney

A MACDONALD BOOK

Copyright © Charles Osborne 1983

First published in Great Britain in 1983 by
Macdonald & Co (Publishers) Ltd
London & Sydney

A member of BPCC plc

All rights reserved

No part of this publication may be
reproduced, stored in a retrieval system,
or transmitted, in any form or by any
means without the prior permission in
writing of the publisher, nor be
otherwise circulated in any form of
binding or cover other than that in
which it is published and without
a similar condition including this
condition being imposed on the subsequent
purchaser.

ISBN: 0 356 09700 5

This book was designed and produced by
The Rainbird Publishing Group,
40 Park Street,
London, W1Y 4DE

Picture researchers; Tomás Graves and Susan Haskins

Text filmset by Text Processing, Ireland
Printed and bound by Oxford University Press, Oxford

Macdonald & Co (Publishers) Ltd,
Maxwell House,
74 Worship Street, London EC2A 2EN

To Dominic
with love from
Emma

25th March
1985

Foreword

The first operas were composed in Florence, around the year 1600. In 1666 the first reference book concerned with the new art form was published in Rome. This was a list of dramatic works of all kinds, including opera libretti, which had been published in Italy. It was entitled *Drammaturgia*, and it was compiled by Leone Allacci, a Greek theologian and scholar who had come to Italy as a child, had written extensively on a wide range of subjects and, in 1661, had become chief curator of the Vatican Library.

Since the seventeenth century, there have been a great many reference books entirely devoted to opera. They include attempts at a complete listing of all operas, both alphabetically and chronologically; dictionaries containing biographical information concerning composers of opera; synopses of the plots of the most popular operas; books listing famous singers of the past and present.

Among these volumes is a number of works of great interest and use to scholars and specialists in the field of opera. These include the *Dictionnaire Lyrique, ou Histoire des Opéras* by Félix Clément and Pierre Larousse, published in Paris, 1867-9, and subsequently revised and added to by others up to 1905 (photographically reprinted in 1969); *Opera e operisti: Dizionario lirico, 1541-1902* by Carlo Dassori (Genoa, 1903); *Dictionary-Catalogue of Operas and Operettas which have been performed on the public stage* by John Towers (Morgantown, 1910); *Annals of Opera: 1597-1940* by Alfred Loewenberg; and the *Enciclopedia dello spettacolo* (Rome, 1954-1966), a ten-volume work whose index volume lists more than 100,000 entries of plays, films and ballets as well as operas. For those whose interest is in the singer rather than the opera, there are such books as *Unvergangliche Stimmen: ein Sängerlexikon* by K. J. Kutsch and Leo Riemens (second edition published in Berne and Munich, 1982), and for those who prefer opera on record to opera in the opera house there is a plethora of reference works and guides.

The Dictionary of Opera has drawn much of its information from such volumes as these, though it has been written not for specialists but for that ever-increasing opera audience whose interest may not be deeply knowledgeable but is clearly more than casual. *The Dictionary of Opera* is, then, not a working tool for scholars but a reference book for the opera enthusiast, a kind of mini-Grove for opera lovers. It contains entries on nearly 300 composers, and 800 singers, conductors, producers and designers of opera, and librettists. It also includes brief synopses of the plots of 570 operas, in each case adding such information as the date and place of the first performance, and the provenance of the libretto. It differs from most of its predecessors among popular dictionaries or encyclopaedias of opera in two respects: it is illustrated (there are 150 pictures, chosen not for decoration but for their relevance to the text), and it is the work not of an editorial team but of one author.

At this point it is appropriate that the author should make use of the first person singular pronoun, in order to present his credentials to the reader. He feels the need to do so because *The Dictionary of Opera* is not merely a vast repository of facts: it also contains his own opinions and evaluations of many operas, composers and performers. The facts are as accurate as assiduous research, checking, and repeated rechecking can make them: the opinions are informed, but his readers have a right to know something about the person whose informed opinions they are being invited to accept.

Details of my public career, including a list of the books I have written, can be found in *Who's Who* and similar biographical reference books, in *The New Grove Dictionary of Music and Musicians* and on the dust-jacket of this volume. What will not be found in any of those places is that books, plays and music have been my passionate interests since I was a child and that I first heard opera on gramophone records in the 1930s, when the earliest of my several collections of records included Leo Slezak singing 'Celeste Aida' in German, Peter Dawson singing 'Il Balen' from *Il Trovatore* in English, and Maria Galvany singing the Queen of Night's second aria from *Die Zauberflöte* in Italian. I seemed to specialize in opera sung in the wrong language, and to this day can still uselessly remember the words of 'Di quella pira' in German, the final scene of *Salome* in French, and Valentin's aria from *Faust* in Italian.

There was a Bösendorfer piano in the house, and I taught myself to play it, after a fashion, at the age of five, years before anyone taught me to play it properly: I accompanied myself in childish imitations of those singers on the gramophone records a good ten years before entrusting my voice to a singing teacher.

The first singers I heard in the flesh, in concerts, were among the finest of their time: Lotte Lehmann, Elisabeth Schumann, Richard Crooks, Lawrence Tibbett, Ezio Pinza, Elisabeth Rethberg; and, later, Marjorie Lawrence, John Charles Thomas, Ninon Vallin, Erna Berger, Georges Thill, Joan Hammond and Todd Duncan. But there were few opportunities, in the outpost of empire where I grew up, to see and hear real opera performances. I already knew the score of *Rigoletto* by heart when I finally managed to see a production of it, in

1948, with Mario Basiola in the title-role.

It was then that I determined to live and work in a place where opera would be on tap all the time. Five years later, in the summer of 1953, I attended my first European performances of opera: an open-air *Madama Butterfly* in Milan, and *Cav. and Pag.* at the Opéra-Comique in Paris. The Canio in *Pagliacci* was Georges Thill, making his farewell appearance and singing with much more confidence and ease than when I had heard him in recital seven years earlier. Also in Milan that summer I went to a concert at which a number of students each sang an aria. I was impressed by only one of them, a chubbily attractive lyric soprano who sang 'Un bel dì', from *Madama Butterfly*, and I made a note against her name in my programme: she was Renata Scotto.

I began to write and to broadcast about opera, and to review performances in Great Britain and Europe for British newspapers and also for the *New York Times*. I had been a regular reader of the monthly magazine, *Opera*, since it began publication in 1950, and I first appeared in its pages as a reviewer in 1957, writing about opera performances at the Bolshoi Theatre, Moscow. Since 1970 I have been a member of *Opera*'s Editorial Board.

As often as possible, I attend performances in the United States whose regional companies have developed so amazingly in the last thirty years. I first began going to the old Met, that splendid and most atmospheric of opera houses at 39th and Broadway, nearly thirty years ago, and in the autumn of 1962 spent many hours there as the guest of Lotte Lehmann, watching her rehearse her re-staging of *Der Rosenkavalier*, with Régine Crespin. Though I am proud to number one or two of today's great opera singers as my personal friends, I have generally over the years avoided making the acquaintance of singers and conductors whose performances I might find myself having to criticize in print.

I consider, in chronological order, Mozart, Wagner, Verdi, Puccini, and Strauss to be the greatest composers of opera, with Rossini, Bellini, Donizetti, Tchaikovsky, Massenet and Britten the best of the second division. I think that opera production has become both better and worse during the last half-century, and I accept that the 'golden age' of singing will always be that time which one can only just remember from one's childhood. I believe opera to be the highest form of theatrical art, combining as it does, music, drama and décor. It is sometimes said that opera is no longer a living art form, that its masterpieces are all eighteenth- and nineteenth-century works. This is not so. We are constantly being told that the novel, too, is dying, yet new novels – and very good ones – continue to appear. It is true that for the last three decades most art forms have been in a state of flux. Creativity has been at a relatively low ebb, as a quick glance at what is happening (and not happening) in painting, poetry, the theatre and music will confirm. But there are signs that the arts are about to embark upon a period of consolidation. If there is to be a future, all the arts will share it, and our own era will, in retrospect, be seen to have played its part in their development. The opera of the future will be different from that of the past and, hopefully, superior to much of that of the present.

In choosing items for inclusion in this volume I have been guided by practical considerations. I have been generous in my selection of operas, for many works of the past which are currently neglected may find, as indeed some are already finding, their way back into the repertoire. I have adopted a different policy regarding performers, and have concentrated upon those who can be heard today: singers of the present who are now appearing in opera, and singers of the past whose voices have been preserved on gramophone records. A number of operettas are included, because the distinction between opera and operetta is not one that is rigorously insisted upon in most countries. No opera house today turns its nose up at *Die Fledermaus*; Joan Sutherland appears in *The Merry Widow* in Sydney; Gilbert and Sullivan operettas are in the repertoires of opera companies in Austria, Germany and the United States of America; and *Sweeney Todd* is accepted as a classic of modern music theatre.

1983   C.O.

NOTE

The synopses of opera plots are brief. More detailed descriptions of plot may be found elsewhere. The list of roles sung by performers is not intended to be exhaustive, though major roles are included.

Entries are listed in alphabetical sequence; the opera *Don Giovanni* appears under 'D', Don Giovanni the character under 'G'.

Abbreviations that are used are as follows: Met: Metropolitan Opera House; (sop.): soprano; (mezzo-sop.): mezzo-soprano; (contr.): contralto; (ten.): tenor; (bar.): baritone. Dates are shown in full with two exceptions: months are abbreviated in the biographical note at the beginning of entries; and dates relating to centuries are abbreviated, e.g. 20th c. for twentieth century.

Most operas are listed under their names in the language in which they were written, with an English translation in brackets. Where the original title is unlikely to be familiar to English-speaking readers, the opera appears under its English translation and is followed by the title in its original language.

A

Abbado, Claudio, b. Milan, 26 June 1933. Italian conductor. After studying in Milan and in Vienna with Hans Swarowsky, he began to conduct both concerts and opera with great success in Austria and Italy. He made his Covent Garden début with *Don Carlos* in 1968, and has since acquired a particular reputation as a Verdi conductor. He became musical director of La Scala in 1971 (and in the same year principal conductor of the Vienna Philharmonic). He has shown himself willing and able to perform 20th-c. works with the same persuasive vitality which he brings to 19th-c. Italian opera.

Abbott, Emma, b. Chicago, 9 Dec 1850; d. Salt Lake City, 5 Jan 1891. American soprano. She made her début as Maria in *La Figlia del Reggimento* at Covent Garden in 1876, and her American début the following year in the same role. In 1878, with her husband, Eugene Wetherell, as manager, she formed a small touring company of three singers, a pianist and a cornet player, to take abridged versions of popular operas to small towns in the west and mid-west of the United States.

Abencérages, Les, ou L'Étendard de Grenade (*The Abenceragi or The Standard of Granada*). Opera in 3 acts by Cherubini. Libretto by V. J. Étienne de Jouy, based on the novel *Gonzalve de Cordove* by Jean-Pierre Florian. Napoleon attended the première at the Paris Opéra on 6 Apr 1813. The first modern revival was at the Maggio Musicale, Florence, 1957, under Giulini.

The Moorish Abenceragi warriors under their chieftain, Almansor, are defeated at Granada in 1492.

Abigaille (sop.). Daughter of Nabucco, in Verdi's *Nabucco*.

Abraham, Paul [Pál], b. Apatin, Hungary, 2 Nov 1892; d. Hamburg, 9 May 1960. Hungarian composer. After studying at the Budapest Academy of Music, he had some success with his orchestral and chamber music, and became conductor at the Budapest Operetta Theatre in 1927. His first

Claudio Abbado is one of the most gifted of the new generation of Italian conductors.

operetta, *Viktoria und ihr Husar*, which blended elements of the old Viennese operetta with the newer sounds of jazz and the dance music of the late 1920s, was produced with great success in Vienna in 1930. He wrote operettas for the German theatres—*Die Blume von Hawaii* (Leipzig, 1931) and *Ball im Savoy* (Berlin, 1932)—until the advent of Hitler forced him to leave the country. The operettas he composed for Vienna between 1934-7 failed to achieve success and, when Austria was annexed to Germany, Abraham escaped, first to Cuba where he worked as a pianist, and then to New York. *The White Swan* was staged there in 1950, after Abraham had recovered from a mental breakdown in 1946. In the 1950s, he returned to Europe to live in Hamburg.

Abreise, Die (*The Departure*). Comic opera in 1 act by d'Albert. Libretto by Ferdinand von Sporck, after a play by August von Steigentesch. First performed Frankfurt, 20 Oct 1898.

A would-be lover's attempts to arrange for the departure of the woman's husband end in failure.

Abu Hassan. Singspiel in 1 act by Weber. Libretto by Franz Karl Hiemer, after a tale in Antoine Galland's 18th-c. French edition of the Arabic collection, *A Thousand and One Nights*. First performed Munich, 4 June 1811.

Abu Hassan's devious attempts to evade payment of his debts are exposed, but all ends happily.

Acis and Galatea. Pastoral opera in 3 acts by Handel. Libretto by John Gay, based on the legend in Ovid's *Metamorphoses*. Originally written as a masque, then adapted and first performed complete in a public theatre, London, 28 May 1732.

The shepherd Acis (ten.), lover of the nymph Galatea (sop.), is slain by his rival, the giant Polyphemus (bass). The flowing blood of Acis is transformed into a spring.

Lully also used the subject for an opera, *Acis et Galatée* (1686).

Ackté, Aïno, b. Helsinki, 23 Apr 1876; d. Nummela, 8 Aug 1944. Finnish soprano. After making her début as Marguerite in *Faust* at the Paris Opéra in 1897, she sang for some years in Paris, London and New York. She received great acclaim when she sang Salome in the first British production of Richard Strauss's opera, conducted by Beecham in 1910. In 1938-9 she was Director of the Finnish Opera, which she had helped to found in 1911.

Adalgisa (sop. though frequently sung by mezzo-sop.). Druid priestess in love with Pollione in Bellini's *Norma*.

Adam, Adolphe, b. Paris, 24 July 1803; d. Paris, 3 May 1856. French composer. He studied composition at the Paris Conservatoire with Boïeldieu, and began his career with the composition of 1-act comic operas. Among the more than eighty works he composed for the stage, ballet scores as well as operas, the most lasting proved to be *Le Postillon de Longjumeau*, an *opéra-comique* staged in Paris in 1836, and the ballet *Giselle*

Title-page of Adam's *Giralda*. He wrote, 'my only aim is to write music which is...amusing'.

which was first produced at the Paris Opéra in 1841. Adam opened his own opera house in Paris in 1847, but the venture collapsed when revolution broke out there in February, 1848, and the composer was financially ruined. He turned to journalism and the academic life to earn a living, but continued to compose. One of his finest *opéras-comiques*, *Si J'étais Roi*, was written for the Théâtre-Lyrique, where it was staged in 1852.

Adam, Theo, b. Dresden, 1 Aug 1926. German bass-baritone. He made his début in Dresden in 1949 as the Hermit in *Der Freischütz*, and joined the Berlin Staatsoper in 1952. He has sung most of the leading Wagnerian baritone roles at Bayreuth, and was first heard at Covent Garden in 1967 as Wotan. His first appearance at the Met was as Hans Sachs in 1963. With a vocal range and timbre which allow him to include both bass (Baron Ochs, King Philip) and baritone (Scarpia) roles in his repertoire, he has proved an intelligent and resourceful dramatic performer.

Adami, Giuseppe, b. Verona, 4 Feb 1878; d. Milan, 12 Oct 1946. Italian librettist. A successful playwright, he was introduced to Puccini by the publisher Ricordi, and furnished Puccini with libretti for *La Rondine*, *Il Tabarro* and, in collaboration with Renato Simoni, *Turandot*. After the composer's death, Adami published a collection of his letters. He also wrote libretti for two other composers, Vittadini and Zandonai.

Adams, Suzanne, b. Cambridge, Mass., 28 Nov 1872; d. London, 5 Feb 1953. American soprano. After studying in Paris with Mathilde Marchesi, she made her début there in 1895 as Juliette, a role which, like that of Marguérite, she had studied with its composer, Gounod. She created the role of Hero in Stanford's *Much Ado About Nothing* in 1904 at Covent Garden. She sang mainly at Covent Garden and the Met between 1895-1904, in which year her husband's death caused her to retire from the stage.

Adele (sop.). Rosalinde's maid in Johann Strauss's *Die Fledermaus*.

Adelson e Salvini. Opera in 3 acts by Bellini. Libretto by Andrea Leone Tottola, which may have been based on a comedy performed at Esterháza in 1778. Bellini's first opera, produced in Naples, Feb 1825.

At Lord Adelson's castle in 18th-c. Ireland, the Roman painter Salvini (ten.) falls in love with his host's fiancée. The melodramatic plot ends with Salvini transferring his affections to his pupil, Fanny (contr.), and with the marriage of Adelson (bar.) to Nelly (sop.).

Adina (sop.). The beautiful young landowner loved by the peasant, Nemorino, in Donizetti's *L'Elisir d'Amore*.

Adler, Kurt Herbert, b. Vienna, 2 Apr 1905. Austrian, now American, conductor. After conducting at the Volksoper, Vienna, and other European opera houses, and assisting Toscanini at Salzburg, he emigrated to the USA in 1938, and was engaged first in Chicago and then, from 1943, in San Francisco. He became artistic director of the San Francisco Opera, and continued to conduct there after his retirement in 1981.

Admeto, Re di Tessaglia (*Admetus, King of Thessaly*). Opera in 3 acts by Handel.

Libretto by Aurelio Aureli, adapted (probably) by Nicola Francesco Haym. First performed London, 31 Jan 1727. First modern revival, Abingdon, 1964.

The plot is that of Gluck's *Alceste*.

Adriana Lecouvreur. Opera in 4 acts by Cilea. Libretto by Arturo Colautti, based on the play, *Adrienne Lecouvreur*, by Eugène Scribe and Ernest Legouvé. First performed Milan, 6 Nov 1902.

Romantic drama of back-stage intrigue, involving the famous 18th-c. Comédie Française actress (sop.), whose rival for the love of Maurice (ten.) kills her by sending violets sprinkled with a poisonous scent.

Aennchen (sop.). Agathe's cousin and companion in Weber's *Der Freischütz*.

Africaine, L' (*The African Girl*). Opera in 5 acts by Meyerbeer. Libretto by Eugène Scribe. First performed Paris, 28 Apr 1865.

The adventures of the Portuguese navigator, Vasco da Gama (ten.), who in 1498 had discovered the sea route to India. From a later voyage he has brought back two natives, presumed to be Africans, one of whom, Selika (mezzo-sop.), falls in love with him. She sacrifices her life, realizing that he still loves the Portuguese Inez (sop.).

Agathe (sop.). The heroine of Weber's *Der Freischütz*.

Agnes von Hohenstaufen. Opera in 3 acts by Spontini. Libretto by Ernst Raupach. First performed Berlin, 12 June 1829. First modern revival, Florence, 1954.

A tale of love and political intrigue, in which attempts are made to prevent the marriage of Agnes (sop.) to Henry of Brunswick (ten.).

Agrippina. Opera in 3 acts by Handel. Libretto by Vincenzo Grimani. First performed Venice, 26 Dec 1709. First modern revival, Hallé, 1943.

During the absence of the Emperor Claudio (bass) in Britain, the Empress Agrippina (sop.) intrigues in Rome to secure the accession to the throne for her son, Nerone (sop.).

Ägyptische Helena, Die (*The Egyptian Helen*). Opera in 2 acts by Richard Strauss.

Placido Domingo as Radames in Verdi's *Aida* at Covent Garden in January 1974. *Aida* was first performed at the recently opened Cairo Opera House in 1871.

Libretto by Hugo von Hofmannsthal. First performed Dresden, 6 June 1928. Revised and shortened for performance at the 1933 Salzburg Festival.

Menelaus (ten.) returns home from the Trojan war determined to kill his faithless wife, Helen (sop.), but eventually forgives her, after the intervention of an Egyptian sorceress, Aithra (sop.).

Aida. Opera in 4 acts by Verdi. Libretto by Antonio Ghislanzoni from a French text by Camille du Locle, which in turn was based on a synopsis by Auguste Mariette. First performed Cairo, 24 Dec 1871.

In Ancient Egypt, Aida (sop.), daughter of Amonasro (bar.), King of Ethiopia, has been captured by the Egyptians and is a slave at the court of the Pharaoh in Memphis, where she and Radames (ten.), a captain in the Egyptian army, have fallen in love with each other. Radames is chosen to lead the army against the Ethiopians, and during his absence the Pharaoh's daughter, Amneris (mezzo-sop.), discovers their attachment and is roused to a jealous fury as she herself loves Radames.

Radames returns, covered with glory, and bringing many prisoners, among them Amonasro, Aida's father. All of the prisoners except Amonasro are released, and the Pharaoh announces that Amneris is to marry their country's saviour, Radames.

Amonasro persuades his daughter, Aida, to trick Radames into revealing the present position of the Egyptian troops. However, Amneris overhears their talk, and Radames is placed under arrest while Aida and her father escape.

Amneris offers to save the life of Radames if he will abandon Aida, but he refuses. He is denounced as a traitor and condemned to be buried alive. When his tomb is sealed, he discovers that Aida has concealed herself there so that she may die with him. As the lovers prepare for their slow death, above the tomb Amneris prays to the gods for repose for the soul of Radames.

Aiglon, L' (*The Eaglet*). Opera in 5 acts by Honegger, who wrote the central acts, and Ibert, who wrote Acts 1 and 5. Libretto by Henri Cain, based on the play of that name by Edmond Rostand about the tragic career of Napoleon's son and heir, whom Victor Hugo called *l'aiglon*. First performed Monte Carlo, 11 Mar 1937. A projected Naples staging in 1939 was cancelled after the dress rehearsal at Mussolini's instructions. The opera was revived in Paris in 1952.

Aladdin. Opera in 3 acts by Bishop. Libretto by George Soane. First produced at Drury Lane, London, 29 Apr 1826, and intended as a counter-attraction to Weber's *Oberon* at Covent Garden which had been hugely successful. *Aladdin*, described as a fairy opera, was a complete failure and had to be withdrawn after a few nights. In 1830 it was produced in Philadelphia.

Albanese, Licia, b. Bari, 22 July 1913. Italian, now American, soprano. She made her début in Parma as Butterfly in 1935, and appeared in the same role at the Met in 1940. She was a member of the company at the Met for twenty-five years, with a repertoire of more than forty roles, among them Violetta in *La Traviata*, Mimi in *La Bohème*, and Tosca.

Albani, (Dame) Emma, b. Chambly, nr. Montreal, 1 Nov 1847; d. London, 3 Apr 1930. Canadian soprano. Born Marie Lajeunesse, she adopted Albani as her stage name when she made her début as Amina in *La Sonnambula* in Messina in 1870. Two years later she triumphed in the same role at Covent Garden. Later, she added Wagnerian roles to her repertoire, and also sang Desdemona in the first British and American productions of *Otello*. She retired in 1911, and was made a Dame of the British Empire in 1925.

Dame Emma Albani. She was married to the opera impresario, Ernest Gye.

Alberich (bass-bar.). The dwarf who lives under the Rhine in Wagner's *Ring*, and who steals the gold from the Rhinemaidens.

Albert, Eugen d', b. Glasgow, 10 Apr 1864; d. Riga, 3 March 1932. French composer. Of mixed French-British parentage, he studied piano in London, took up a career as pianist, and married another pianist, Teresa Carreño. He adopted German nationality, and composed twenty operas, most of them to German texts. He is remembered chiefly for *Tiefland* and *Die Abreise*, the former being often compared favourably with better-known operas of the realist school of Mascagni or Leoncavallo.

Albert Herring. Opera in 3 acts by Britten. Libretto by Eric Crozier, after the story *Le Rosier de Madame Husson* (1888) by Guy de Maupassant. First produced at Glyndebourne, 20 June 1947. The first American performance was at Tanglewood, Mass., 8 Aug 1949.

A Suffolk village, having failed to find a virtuous maiden to be May Queen, elects a supposedly virtuous youth, Albert Herring. (ten.), as May King, with unexpected consequences. The title-role was composed for, and first performed by, Peter Pears.

Alboni, Marietta [Maria Anna Marzia], b. Città di Castello, 6 Mar 1823; d. Ville d'Avray, 23 June 1894. Italian contralto. She studied in Bologna, and was coached by Rossini in the principal contralto roles in his operas. She sang in the operas of Rossini, Donizetti and Bellini throughout Europe, and at Covent Garden in 1847 undertook the baritone role of Don Carlo in Verdi's *Ernani*. She was said to have a voice of great beauty and flexibility.

Alceste. Opera in 3 acts by Gluck. Libretto by Ranieri da' Calzabigi, after the drama by Euripides. First performed Vienna, 26 Dec 1767. Revised by Gluck, with French text by François du Roullet, staged in Paris, 23 Apr 1776.

Alcestis (sop.) voluntarily descends to Hades in order to ensure that her husband, Admetus (ten.), King of Pherae, is restored to life. With the intervention of, at first Hercules (bass), and then the god, Apollo (bar.), the opera is brought to a happy conclusion.

Among the many operas based on the *Alcestis* of Euripides are those by Lully (1674), Handel (1734), Lampugnani (1745), Rutland Boughton (1922) and Egon Wellesz (1924).

Alcina. Opera in 3 acts by Handel. Libretto by Antonio Marchi, based on *Orlando Furioso* (1516) by Lodovico Ariosto. First performed London, 16 Apr 1735. Joan Sutherland sang the title-role in a number of 20th-c. revivals in London (1957 and 1962), Venice (1960), Dallas (1960) and elsewhere.

The sorceress Alcina (sop.), in love with Ruggiero (mezzo-sop.), holds him captive. Eventually, with the help of Bradamante (contr.), he escapes, and Alcina's magic realm is overthrown.

Alda [Davies], Frances, b. Christchurch, 31 May 1883; d. Venice, 18 Sept 1952. New Zealand soprano. She was raised in Australia and made her first appearances in light opera there. After studying with Marchesi in Paris, she changed her name and made her début as Manon at the Opéra-Comique in 1904. She sang at the Met from 1908 until her retirement in 1930, and married the company's director, Gatti-Casazza, in 1910. She was highly regarded in several of the Verdi and Puccini roles.

Aleko. Opera in 1 act by Rachmaninov. Libretto by Vladimir Nemirovich-Danchenko, after the poem, 'The Gipsies' (1824) by Pushkin. First performed Moscow, 27 Apr 1893.

Aleko (bass), in love with the gipsy Zemfira (sop.), has joined a wandering troupe of gipsies. When Zemfira is unfaithful to him, he kills her.

Alessandro. Opera in 3 acts by Handel. Libretto by Paolo Antonio Rolli. First performed London, 5 May 1726. The Alessandro of the title is Alexander the Great. The opera was revived, in a German edition, at Stuttgart in 1959.

Alessandro Stradella. Opera in 3 acts by Flotow. Libretto by W. Friedrich (pseudonym of Friedrich Wilhelm Riese). The work is based on a French *comédie mêlée de chant* by Philippe Pittaud de Forges and Paul Duport, originally produced, with some new songs by Flotow, in Paris, 4 Feb 1837. The opera, which deals with episodes in the life of the 17th-c. Italian composer, Alessandro Stradella, was first performed in Hamburg, on 30 Dec 1844. After *Martha*, it was Flotow's most successful opera, and was produced throughout Europe.

Alexander, John, b. Meridian, Miss., *c.* 1925. American tenor. He made his début as Faust in Cincinnati in 1952, and later sang with the New York City Opera and the Met. In the late 1960s, he also appeared in Vienna and London. A reliable artist and sound musician, he sang Pollione in *Norma* with the leading Normas of his time: Joan Sutherland, Beverly Sills and Montserrat Caballé.

Alfano, Franco, b. Posillipo, nr. Naples, 8 March 1876; d. San Remo, 27 Oct 1954. Italian composer. Although he composed a number of operas which were staged successfully in Italy, foremost among them being *Risurrezione*, Alfano is known outside his native country primarily as the composer who completed *Turandot*, left unfinished at Puccini's death. His other operas include *L'Ombra di Don Giovanni* (1914: revised for a Florence revival in 1941 as *Don Juan de Mañara*) and *Cyrano de Bergerac* (1936).

Alfio (bar.). The Sicilian village teamster who kills Turiddu in Mascagni's *Cavalleria Rusticana*.

Alfonso, Don (bass). The cynical philosopher who makes a wager with Guglielmo and Ferrando in Mozart's *Così Fan Tutte*. Also Alfonso d'Este (bar.) in Donizetti's *Lucrezia Borgia*, and Alfonso XI (bar.), King of Castile in Donizetti's *La Favorite*.

Alfonso und Estrella. Opera in 3 acts by Schubert. Libretto by Franz von Schober. Not produced during its composer's lifetime, the opera was first performed, in a heavily cut version, under the direction of Liszt, at Weimar, 24 June 1854.

Alfonso (ten.), son of the deposed King Troila (bar.), falls in love with Estrella (sop.), daughter of the usurper, Mauregato (bar.). After many complications, Troila forgives Mauregato, Alfonso and Estrella marry, and Alfonso becomes King.

This is the only opera by Schubert which contains no spoken dialogue.

Alfredo (ten.). Violetta's young lover in Verdi's *La Traviata*.

Alice (sop.). Mistress Ford, one of the 'merry wives of Windsor' in Verdi's *Falstaff*.

Allegra, Salvatore, b. Palermo, 13 July 1898. Italian composer. His operas include *Ave Maria*, produced in Perugia in 1934, *I Viadanti* (1936), *Il Medico suo Malgrado* (based on Molière's *Le Médecin Malgré Lui*: 1938) and *Romulus*, staged in Naples, 1952. He is also the composer of a number of operettas.

Allen, Thomas, b. Seaham, 10 Sept 1944. English baritone. He made his début in 1969 with the Welsh National Opera as Rossini's Figaro, and in the 1970s became a much sought-after performer with the leading British companies. In the Verdi and Mozart roles he is a sturdy and useful performer, and he has achieved a particular success as Britten's Billy Budd.

Thomas Allen in the title-role of Britten's *Billy Budd* at Covent Garden in February 1979.

Allin, Norman, b. Ashton-under-Lyne, 19 Nov 1884; d. London, 27 Oct 1973. English bass. After studying in Manchester, he began his career with the Beecham Opera Company in 1916 as the old Hebrew in *Samson et Dalila*, and in 1919 was a distinguished Gurnemanz at Covent Garden. In the 1920s he sang with the British National Opera Company, and remained the leading British bass of his time until his retirement. In the 1940s he sang with the Carl Rosa Opera Company in London and on tour.

Almaviva. The Count of Almaviva who (ten.) successfully woos Rosina in Rossini's *Il Barbiere di Siviglia*, and who (bar.) is unfaithful to her, at least in intention, in Mozart's *Le Nozze di Figaro*.

Almira. Opera in 3 acts by Handel. Libretto by Friedrich Feustking, based on one written by Giulio Pancieri in 1691 for Giuseppe Boniventi. First performed, Hamburg, 8 Jan 1705. Handel's first opera, it was a bi-lingual production, with some arias in German and others in Italian.

Althouse, Paul, b. Reading, Pa., 2 Dec 1889; d. New York, 6 Feb 1954. American tenor. After appearing at the Met from 1913-22, he went to Europe for further study, and returned to the Met as a leading Wagner tenor from 1934-40. He was the first American tenor to sing Tristan. After his retirement he became a successful teacher, his pupils including Richard Tucker and Eleanor Steber.

alto. Though its literal Italian meaning is 'high', the term has come to denote the female voice whose range is lower than that of soprano and whose timbre darker. The solo alto voice is now usually called contralto, alto being used–as in 's-a-t-b' (soprano, alto, tenor, bass)–of singers in a chorus. The male alto is a baritone or bass voice, singing falsetto.

Alva, Luigi, b. Lima, 10 Apr 1927. Peruvian tenor. After singing in operetta in Peru, he studied in Milan and made his opera début as Alfredo in Milan in 1954. Subsequently he sang with most of the leading companies in Europe and the USA. His flexible lyric tenor is heard at its best in

Rossini's 'tenorino' roles: for years he was a greatly admired Almaviva in *Il Barbiere di Siviglia*. He also sang Mozart's Ottavio and Ferrando with elegance and charm.

Alvarez, Marguerite d', b. Liverpool, 1886; d. Alassio, 18 Oct 1953. English contralto of Peruvian descent. After studying in Brussels, she made her début as Dalila in Rouen in 1904, and later appeared in London, New York and Chicago. She spent most of her career as a concert artist in America. In 1954 she published her memoirs, *Forsaken Altars*.

Alvaro (ten.). The Peruvian hero of Verdi's *La Forza del Destino*.

Alvary [Achenbach], Max, b. Düsseldorf, 3 May 1856; d. Gross-Tabarz, 7 Nov 1898. German tenor. The outstanding Wagnerian dramatic tenor of his time, he sang Tristan and Tannhäuser at Bayreuth in 1891, was Siegfried in the first Covent Garden *Ring* conducted by Mahler, and was the first Loge and Siegfried in the USA. He broke with tradition by performing the Wagnerian heroic roles without a beard. He retired prematurely at the age of forty-one, after being injured in a fall while rehearsing in *Siegfried* at Mannheim.

Alyabyev, Alexander, b. Tobolsk, 15 Aug 1787; d. Moscow, 6 Mar 1851. Russian composer. Though remembered today principally for his song 'The Nightingale', in the repertoire of most coloratura sopranos, he was important in his day as one of the founders of Russian opera. His comic opera, *Lunnaya noch* (*The Moonlit Night*) was staged in 1823. Five years later, he was exiled to his native town, having been found guilty of murder. Later, he was able to return to Moscow, after spending some time in the Caucasus. Two of his operas are based on Shakespeare: *Burya* (*The Tempest*) *c.* 1835 and *Volshebnaya Noch* (*A Midsummer Night's Dream*) 1838-9.

Alzira. Opera in a prologue and 2 acts by Verdi. Libretto by Salvatore Cammarano, after Voltaire's tragedy, *Alzire, ou les Américains* (1730). First performed Naples, 12 Aug 1845.

Alzira (sop.), an Inca princess is forced into marriage with the Spanish governor, Gusman (bar.). Zamoro (ten.), to whom she was betrothed and who was believed dead, stabs Gusman at the wedding ceremony. Before he dies, the governor forgives his assassin.

A failure at its first performance, the opera was not heard after 1858 until a broadcast performance in Vienna on 18 Sept 1936. Its first modern stage revival was in Rome in 1967.

Amadis. Opera in a prologue and 5 acts by Lully. Libretto by Philippe Quinault, based on the 14th-c. romance *Amadis de Gaule*. First performed Paris, 18 Jan 1684. Among other operas on the subject are those by Handel (1715), Johann Christian Bach (1779) and Massenet (composed in 1902 but not staged until 1922 in Monte Carlo).

Amahl and the Night Visitors. Opera in 1 act by Menotti. Libretto by the composer, inspired by the Hieronymus Bosch painting, *Adoration of the Magi*. The first opera expressly written for television, it was transmitted by NBC TV on 24 Dec 1951. Its first stage production was at Indiana University, 21 Feb 1952.

A crippled boy (boy sop.) offers his crutches to the wise men as a gift to the infant Christ, and is miraculously healed.

Amalia (sop.). The heroine of Verdi's *I Masnadieri*.

Amara [Armaganian], Lucine, b. Hartford, Conn., 1 Mar 1927. American soprano of Armenian descent. She studied in San Francisco and sang in the chorus of the opera company there in 1945-6. Her solo début was as the Heavenly Voice in *Don Carlos* at the Met in 1950. Although she sang at Glyndebourne in the 1950s, her career has been confined chiefly to the Met, where she was a useful member of the company for more than a quarter of a century. Her roles include Aida, Butterfly, Donna Anna, Leonora in *Il Trovatore* and Ellen Orford in *Peter Grimes*.

Amato, Pasquale, b. Naples, 21 Mar 1878; d. Jackson Heights, N.Y., 12 Aug 1942. Italian baritone. One of the leading Italian baritones of his day, he was highly regarded in the Verdi roles and also in the *verismo* repertory. He made his début in Naples in 1900 as Germont *père* in *La Traviata*, a role which he sang with great success through-out his career. He created the' role of Jack Rance in Puccini's *La Fanciulla del West* at the Met in 1910.

Amelia (sop.). The hero's lover but the villain's wife in Verdi's *Un Ballo in Maschera*. Also the name by which Maria Grimaldi is known in Verdi's *Simon Boccanegra*; and the heroine of Menotti's *Amelia Goes to the Ball*.

Amelia al Ballo (*Amelia Goes to the Ball*). Comic opera in 1 act by Menotti. Libretto by the composer. First performed Philadelphia (at the Curtis Institute where the composer had graduated four years previously) on 1 Apr 1937. In Italian, as *Amelia al Ballo*, it was produced at San Remo on 4 Apr 1938. On 3 Mar 1938, it became the first comic opera by an American composer to be staged at the Met.

Ameling, Elly, b. Rotterdam, 8 Feb 1938. Dutch soprano. A distinguished concert singer, she has sung only one operatic role, that of Ilia in *Idomeneo*, first with the Nederlandse Opera in 1973 and subsequently in Washington, D.C., the following year.

Amfiparnasso, L'. *Comedia harmonica*, or madrigal comedy, by Vecchi. Probably first sung in 1594 at Modena. Printed in Venice, 1597. An immediate predecessor of opera rather than a full-blown opera, though various attempts have been made to perform it scenically, it is a collection of songs in a mixture of vocal forms with dramatic continuity provided by the *commedia dell' arte* characters who appear in the songs. The title derives from the composer's aesthetic view that the Parnassus of music was surmounted by a twofold summit representing tragedy and comedy.

Amfortas (bar.). The Keeper of the Grail in Wagner's *Parsifal*.

Amico Fritz, L' (*Friend Fritz*). Opera in 3 acts by Mascagni. Libretto by P. Suardon (pseudonym of Nicolo Daspuro), after a novel, *L'Ami Fritz* (1864) by Erckmann-Chatrian. First performed Rome, 31 Oct 1891.

Fritz (ten.), a rich landowner and confirmed bachelor, falls in love with Suzel (sop.), the daughter of one of his tenants. It is, however, only through the machinations of his friend, Rabbi David (bar.), that Fritz is made to declare his love.

Amneris (mezzo-sop.). The Pharaoh's daughter and Aida's rival for the affections of Radames in Verdi's *Aida*.

Amonasro (bar.). King of Ethiopia, and Aida's father, in Verdi's *Aida*.

Amore dei Tre Re, L' (*The Love of the Three Kings*). Opera in 3 acts by Montemezzi. Libretto by Sem Benelli, from his play of the same title (1910). First performed Milan, 10 Apr 1913.

King Archibaldo (bass), having murdered his daughter-in-law, Fiora (sop.), because of her infidelity to his son, poisons the dead woman's lips so that the farewell kiss of her lover will prove fatal to him. It does, but also to her husband, Manfredo (bar.), when he kisses the lips of his dead wife.

Ancona, Mario, b. Livorno, 28 Feb 1860; d. Florence, 22 Feb 1931. Italian baritone. After making his début in Trieste in 1889 in *Le Roi de Lahore*, he was heard as Tonio in *Pagliacci* at Covent Garden and at the Met. He was popular in London and New York in a large number of roles ranging from Mozart through Verdi to Wagner.

Anders, Peter, b. Essen, 1 July 1908; d. Hamburg, 10 Sept 1954. German tenor. He made his début in Max Reinhardt's production of *La Belle Hélène* in Berlin in 1931. After some years with the companies in Hanover, Cologne and Munich, he became principal tenor with the Berlin Staatsoper from 1936-49. At first he specialized in the lyric tenor roles of Mozart, but in his later years he undertook dramatic roles such as Lohengrin and Florestan. He died as the result of a car accident.

Anderson, Marian, b. Philadelphia, 17 Feb 1902. American contralto. Described by Toscanini as having 'the voice that comes once in a hundred years', she was a much-loved concert singer for most of her career. Her only opera role, Ulrica, was undertaken at the age of fifty-three when she became the first black singer to be engaged in a leading role by the Met. She continued to give recitals until well into her sixties.

Andrea Chénier. Opera in 4 acts by Giordano. Libretto by Luigi Illica. First performed Milan, 28 Mar 1896.

The poet Andrea Chénier, born in Constantinople, was educated in Paris. The French Revolution was at its height, and being a worshipper of liberty and opposed to the French monarchy, Chénier supported the Revolution whose victim, however, he became. He was guillotined on 25 July 1794.

Illica's fictional plot supposes Chénier (ten.) to be in love with an aristocrat, Madeleine de Coigny (sop.). Chénier is denounced to a revolutionary tribunal by Charles Gérard (bar.), one of her family's servants who is in love with Madeleine. Though Gérard repents and attempts to testify on the poet's behalf, Chénier is sentenced to death. By bribing a gaoler, Madeleine manages to join Chénier in his cell, and when the tumbril arrives, she goes with Chénier to the guillotine.

Andrésen, Ivar, b. Oslo, 27 July 1896; d. Stockholm, 26 Nov 1940. Norwegian bass. His career, after a début in Stockholm, was mainly in Germany. He sang all the major Wagnerian bass roles at Bayreuth from 1927-36, and also in London and at the Met. His fine, resonant voice was well produced, and he was a sound musician. He was admired at Glyndebourne in 1935 as Sarastro.

Angélique. Opera in 1 act by Ibert. Libretto by Nino (presumably a pseudonym). First performed Paris, 28 Jan 1927.

Boniface (ten.), owner of a china shop in Paris, is persuaded by his friend, Charlot (bar.), to rid himself of his shrewish wife, Angélique (sop.), by putting her up for sale.

Aniara. Opera in 2 acts by Blomdahl. Libretto by Erik Lindegren, based on a Swedish epic poem (1956) by Harry Martinson. First performed Stockholm, 31 May 1959.

A spaceship on its way to Mars carrying refugees from a world devastated by atomic warfare, is knocked off course when it collides with an asteroid, and is destined to travel for ever through space.

Anna Bolena. Opera in 2 acts by Donizetti. Libretto by Felice Romani. First performed Milan, 26 Dec 1830.

King Henry VIII of England (bass), in love with Giovanna or Jane Seymour (sop.), contrives to have his queen Anna Bolena or Ann Boleyn (sop.) tried on a charge of adultery. Anna is found guilty and executed.

The opera was popular in its early years, but was not heard in the 20th c. until 1948, in Barcelona. Callas sang Anna at La Scala in 1957.

Anna, Donna (sop.). The daughter of the Commendatore, assaulted by Giovanni in Mozart's *Don Giovanni.*

Anselmi, Giuseppe, b. Catania, 16 Nov 1876; d. Zoagli, 27 May 1929. Italian tenor. He began his career as a violinist at the age of thirteen, and then sang in operetta before making his opera début in Athens in 1896 as Turiddu. His warm voice and impassioned delivery made him well suited to the *verismo* repertory. In 1901 he sang with Melba in *La Bohème* at Covent Garden. In Madrid, he was preferred to Caruso. He left his heart to Madrid where it is preserved in a theatrical museum.

Ansermet, Ernest, b. Vevey, 11 Nov 1883; d. Geneva, 20 Feb 1969. Swiss conductor. He made his début as a conductor in 1911, and most of his career was spent giving concerts. On the recommendation of Stravinsky he became principal conductor of the Diaghilev Ballets Russes in 1915, and also conducted the first performance of *L'Histoire du Soldat* in 1918. He conducted the première of Britten's *The Rape of Lucretia* at Glyndebourne in 1946, as well as a number of operas in Geneva and elsewhere.

Ansseau, Fernand, b. Boussu-Bois, 6 Mar 1890; d. Brussels, 1 May 1972. Belgian tenor. After his début in Dijon in 1913, his career was interrupted by World War I. He sang in Brussels and London in 1919, and was soon in demand in the French lyric tenor repertory. Later in his career, he undertook the heavier roles of Tannhäuser and Lohengrin. He retired in 1939 and taught in Brussels during World War II.

antefatto. Literally 'antecedent fact', it is the collection of facts which an audience must have in order to understand the plot of an opera. Usually a paragraph or two attached by way of preface to the libretto, it can, as in *Il Trovatore*, be a piece of narration contained at or near the beginning of the opera.

Antheil, George, b. Trenton, N.J., 8 July 1900; d. New York, 12 Feb 1959. American composer. He studied composition with Bloch and became known as a composer of jazz-influenced *avant-garde* music. His opera, *Transatlantic*, written to his own libretto about an American presidential election, was staged at Frankfurt in 1930. He wrote another six operas, all of which were produced once, unsuccessfully, and never revived. He published in London in 1930 a murder mystery, *Death in the Dark*, under the pseudonym Stacey Bishop, and his autobiography, *Bad Boy of Music* (1945).

Antigone. Opera in 3 acts by Honegger. Libretto by Jean Cocteau, based on the tragedy of that title by Sophocles. First performed Brussels, 28 Dec 1927.

In defiance of Creon's (bar.) decree, Antigone (mezzo-sop.) gives her dead brother a token burial, and is herself condemned to be buried alive.

More than thirty operas have been based on the Sophocles play, among them works by minor 18th-c. composers such as Orlandini (1718) and Zingarelli (1790), and, in the 20th c., Alberto Ghislanzoni (1929) and Carl Orff (1949). Gluck's *Antigono* (1756), not based on Sophocles, is about King Antigono of Asia.

Antonia (sop.). One of Hoffmann's three loves in *Les Contes d'Hoffmann* by Offenbach.

Antony and Cleopatra. Opera in 3 acts by Samuel Barber. Libretto by Franco Zeffirelli, based on the play by Shakespeare. First performed to open the new Metropolitan Opera House, New York, 16 Sept 1966. The production and the libretto, both by Zeffirelli, were generally held to be largely responsible for the failure of the opera. When it was revived by the Juilliard School of Music, New York, in the 1974-5 season, the libretto was revised by Gian Carlo Menotti.

Apollo et Hyacinthus. Musical intermezzo in 1 act by Mozart. Libretto by Rufinus Widl, partly derived from Ovid's *Meta-morphoses*. First performed Salzburg, 13 May 1767, between the acts of a play in Latin by Widl, at the University.

The god Apollo interferes in the affairs of mortals, announces his betrothal to Melia, and transforms the dead youth Hyacinthus into a flower. A bowdlerized, or rather 'widlized' version of the myth as recounted by Ovid.

Mozart composed this, his second work for the stage, at the age of eleven. There have been several performances in modern times. During the Salzburg Festival of 1935, the work was staged with puppets.

Appia, Adolphe, b. Geneva, 1 Sept 1862; d. Lyon, 29 Feb 1928. Swiss stage designer. He became fascinated by the problems of opera production, especially production of the operas of Wagner, when he visited Bayreuth in 1882. He set out his ideas in such books as *La Mise-en-Scène du Drame Wagnérien* (1895) and *Die Musik und die Inszenierung* (1899). His theories of space and light influenced a generation of stage designers, but his opportunities to put them into practice were few. After experiments in a private theatre in Paris in 1903, he had no further practical experience until Toscanini invited him to design *Tristan und Isolde* at La Scala in 1923. In the following two years, he designed the first two *Ring* operas in Basle. His ideas were rejected by Cosima Wagner, and his influence reached Bayreuth only through the productions of Wieland Wagner from 1951 onwards.

Arabella. Opera in 3 acts by Richard Strauss. Libretto by Hugo von Hofmannsthal. First performed Dresden, 1 July 1933.

Set in late-19th-c. Vienna, the opera tells of the attempts of the impecunious Count Waldner (bass) and his wife to bring up their two daughters, Arabella (sop.) and Zdenka (sop.), in Viennese society. The course of the true love of Arabella and Mandryka (bar.), a landowner from an eastern European outpost of empire, runs smooth only after certain complications, caused partly by the fact that Zdenka is forced by her parents to masquerade as a young man for financial reasons, have been unravelled.

Aragall, Giacomo [Jaime], b. Barcelona, 6 June 1939. Spanish tenor. He made his début at La Scala in *L'Amico Fritz* in 1964, and has since been in demand for many of the lyric tenor roles of Verdi and Puccini. His first Covent Garden appearance was as the Duke in *Rigoletto* in 1966, the role of his Met début the following year. He has an attractive, well-produced and agreeable voice, though somewhat introverted stage personality.

Araia, Francesco, b. Naples, 25 June 1709; d. Italy, *c.* 1770. Italian composer. He was one of the many minor 18th-c. Italian composers who wrote operas for the Russian court. His *Cephalus and Procris* (1755) is the first opera to have been composed to a Russian text. He wrote at least fourteen operas, most of which were first performed in St Petersburg.

Arakishvili, Dimitri, b. Vladikavkaz, 23 Feb 1873; d. Tbilisi, 13 Aug 1953. Georgian composer. Teacher, ethnomusicologist and one of the founders of modern Georgian music, he studied for seven years in Moscow before returning to Georgia where he took part in four expeditions, collecting and classifying folksongs. He composed two operas: *Tkmuleba Shota Rustavelze* (*The Legend of Shota Rustaveli*), 1919, the earliest Georgian national opera; and *Sitsotskhle Sikharulia* (*Life is a Joy*), 1926, a comic opera.

Arangi–Lombardi, Giannina, b. Marigliano, 20 June 1890; d. Milan, 9 July 1951. Italian soprano. She first made her début in Rome as a mezzo-soprano in 1920, and then, after further study, reappeared in the soprano role of Helen of Troy in *Mefistofele* at La Scala in 1924. She sang with the Scala company, and throughout Europe, in the 1920s in many of the leading dramatic roles, such as Aida, La Gioconda, Donna Anna and the *Trovatore* Leonora. In 1928 she toured Australia with Melba's company. The size and beauty of her voice was generally thought to be more than adequate compensation for her lack of acting ability.

argomento. The 'argument' is usually a summary of the plot of an opera, set forth as a preface to the libretto. It is found in libretti of the 17th and 18th c.

aria. The Italian word for 'air' is used to describe a solo which is a form of self-contained song. The early operas, in which the dialogue was sung in recitative, did not contain arias. However, as solo passages of reflection began to emerge in the operas of the 17th c., these took on the aspect of song, and became more lyrical in utterance than the surrounding recitative or dialogue. The nature and style of the aria has changed over the centuries, and arias by Handel and by Puccini have little in common beyond the fact that they are lyrical or dramatic utterances of a solo singer. A very simple aria is often referred to as an arietta, or even a song. In Mozart's *Die Zauberflöte*, for example, the Queen of Night's two solos are elaborate arias while Papageno's two solo numbers are songs.

Ariadne auf Naxos (*Ariadne on Naxos*). Opera in a prologue and 1 act by Richard Strauss. Libretto by Hugo von Hofmannsthal. First performed Vienna, 4 Oct 1916. (An earlier version of the opera in 1 act, without prologue, was composed to be performed after Molière's play, *Le Bourgeois Gentilhomme*. This version was first staged in Stuttgart, 25 Oct 1912.)

A *nouveau riche* Viennese engages both an opera company and a *commedia dell'arte* troupe to entertain his guests on the same evening. At the last moment, the performers are told that the entertainments must be given simultaneously. The comedienne Zerbinetta (sop.) and her troupe cleverly insert themselves into the opera about Ariadne (sop.) and Bacchus (ten.). (The prologue introduces the young composer (sop.) of the opera who momentarily falls under the spell of Zerbinetta.)

Ariane et Barbe-Bleue (*Ariadne and Bluebeard*). Opera in 3 acts by Dukas. Libretto by Maurice Maeterlinck. First performed Paris, 10 May 1907.

Dukas's only opera, it presents a Bluebeard (bass) who has not killed his earlier wives, but merely imprisoned them. His new wife, Ariane (mezzo-sop.), attempts to free them but when Bluebeard is wounded and brought before them for punishment, they are solicitous. Ariane leaves, but the other wives prefer to remain with Bluebeard.

Arianna, L'. Opera in a prologue and 8 scenes by Monteverdi. Libretto by Ottavio Rinuccini. First performed Mantua, 28 May 1608. All of the music of this, Monteverdi's

A scene from the prelude of Strauss's *Ariadne auf Naxos* performed at the 1979 Salzburg Festival. It was conducted by Karl Böhm just before his eighty-fifth birthday.

second opera, has been lost, except for one lament, sung by Arianna.

Arié, Raphael, b. Sofia, 22 Aug 1920. Bulgarian bass. He studied in Sofia, and began his career there, first appearing abroad at La Scala in 1947 in Prokofiev's *Love of Three Oranges*. At the Fenice, Venice, in 1951 he created the role of Trulove in *The Rake's Progress*. He sang Boris Godunov in a number of European opera houses, and also the Verdi bass roles.

arietta. A small aria. Less elaborate than the aria, the arietta was sung in 18th-c. operas frequently by a character less highly born than the noble protagonists: sometimes by a servant or a rustic.

Ariodante. Opera in 3 acts by Handel. Libretto by Antonio Salvi, from Ariosto's poem *Orlando Furioso* (1516). First performed London, 19 Jan 1735.

Ariodante (mezzo-sop.) is betrothed to Ginevra (sop.), daughter of the King of Scotland. His rival, Polinesso, Duke of Albania (contr.), plots against them, but all ends happily.

arioso. A passage of arioso is one, usually for a solo singer, which is half-way between recitative and aria. It possesses more melodic interest than the recitative, without having the formal shape of the aria. In a large solo scena, a character might well progress from recitative through arioso to aria.

Arkel (bass). The blind King of Allemonde in Debussy's *Pelléas et Mélisande*.

Arkhipova, Irina, b. Moscow, 2 Dec 1925. Russian mezzo-soprano. She made her début at the Bolshoi in 1956 as Carmen, and has been a member of the Bolshoi company since then. In Western Europe and the USA she has distinguished herself in the Verdi mezzo roles, by virtue of her rich voice and commanding presence. It was as Azucena that she was first heard at Covent Garden in 1975.

Arkor, André d', b. Liège, 23 Feb 1901; d. Brussels, 19 Dec 1971. Belgian tenor. After making his début in Liège in 1924 as Gerald in *Lakmé*, he sang in Belgium and France, and was principal lyric tenor at the Théâtre de la Monnaie, Brussels, until 1945. He then

21

became Director of the Théâtre Royal, Liège, until 1967.

Arlecchino. Opera in 1 act by Busoni. Libretto by the composer, based on themes from the *commedia dell' arte*. First performed (together with Busoni's *Turandot*) Zurich, 11 May 1917.

Described by its composer as a 'theatrical caprice', the opera places Harlequin (speaking role) and other characters from the *commedia dell' arte* in 19th-c. Bergamo. The work is in four parts, each corresponding to an aspect of Harlequin, who is seen as rogue, soldier, husband and conqueror.

Arlesiana, L' (*The Girl from Arles*). Opera in 3 acts by Cilea. Libretto by Leopoldo Marenco, based on the play *L'Arlésienne* (1872) by Alphonse Daudet. First performed Milan, 27 Nov 1897, when it was in 4 acts. Cilea reduced it to 3 acts for its revival in Milan the following October.

Dissuaded from marrying the girl he loves when he discovers she is someone else's mistress, Federico (ten.) agrees to marry a childhood sweetheart, but kills himself on the eve of his wedding.

Arme Heinrich, Der (*Poor Henry*). Opera in 3 acts by Pfitzner. Libretto by James Grun, after a medieval legend. First performed Mainz, 2 Apr 1895. The first of Pfitzner's four operas, it reveals a strong Wagnerian influence both in text and in music.

Armida. Opera in 3 acts by Rossini. Libretto by Giovanni Schmidt, after the poem *Gerusalemme Liberata* (1581) by Torquato Tasso. First performed Naples, 11 Nov 1817.

A tale of sorcery displaying, to quote Rossini's biographer Giuseppe Radiciotti, 'Armida's palace and enchanted garden, appearances and disappearances of demons, furies, spectres, chariots pulled by dragons, dances of nymphs and cherubs, characters swept up into the sky and descending from artificial clouds.'

The opera was only moderately successful when first staged. A 20th-c. revival in Florence in 1952, conducted by Tullio Serafin and with a cast headed by Maria Callas, failed to re-establish *Armida* in the repertory.

In addition to Gluck's *Armide*, other operas based on the same narrative from Tasso's poem include those by Lully (1686), Handel (1711), Haydn (1784), and Dvorak (1904).

Armide. Opera in 5 acts by Gluck. Libretto by Philippe Quinault (written for Lully's opera), after the poem *Gerusalemme Liberata* (1581) by Torquato Tasso. First performed Paris, 23 Sept 1777.

Enchanted by Armide (sop.), the crusader Renaud (Rinaldo) (ten.) eventually is recalled to a sense of duty. When he leaves her, Armide destroys her palace and herself in despair.

Arminio. Opera in 3 acts by Handel. Libretto by Antonio Salvi. First performed London, 12 Jan 1737. Not generally regarded as one of Handel's finest operas, it has nevertheless been revived twice in Germany, in Leipzig (1935) and Oldenburg (1963).

Armstrong, Sheila, b. Ashington, 13 Aug 1942. English soprano. After studying at the Royal Academy of Music, she made her début as Despina at Sadler's Wells Theatre in 1965. She subsequently sang other Mozart roles, Pamina and Zerlina, at Glyndebourne, and made her Covent Garden début in 1973 as Marcellina in *Fidelio*.

Arne, Thomas, b. London, 12 Mar 1710; d. London, 5 Mar 1778. English composer. After the success of his first opera, *Rosamund*, staged at Lincoln's Inn Fields Theatre, he embarked upon a career as a composer of English opera and of music for plays, especially those of Shakespeare, and masques. His music for the masque, *The Judgment of Paris* (1740), included the 'Ode in Honour of Great Britain' now known as 'Rule, Britannia'. (He may also have been the composer of 'God Save the King'.) Two of his most attractive light operas, *Thomas and Sally* or *The Sailor's Return* (1760) and *Love in a Village* (1762) (a 'pasticcio' with music by other composers as well as Arne), were written in collaboration with the librettist Isaac Bickerstaffe.

Arnold (ten.). Swiss patriot in love with the Austrian princess, Mathilde, in Rossini's *Guillaume Tell*.

Aroldo. Opera in 4 acts by Verdi. Libretto by Francesco Maria Piave, based on his libretto for Verdi's *Stiffelio* (1850). First performed Rimini, 16 Aug 1857.

The opera is a revision of *Stiffelio*, using the same plot but transporting the characters from 19th-c. Germany to England and Scotland at the beginning of the 13th c. Musically the differences between *Stiffelio* and *Aroldo* are slight, except for Act IV of *Aroldo* which is completely new.

Arroyo, Martina, b. New York, 2 Feb 1937. American soprano. After winning the Metropolitan Opera Auditions in 1958, she made her début in a concert performance of Pizzetti's *L'Assassinio nella Cattedrale* at Carnegie Hall. She sang with European companies in the 1960s, and was a member of the Zurich opera company from 1963-8.

At the Met, she has sung most of the major Verdi soprano roles, in some of which she has also been heard at Covent Garden. Not the most exciting of dramatic artists, she nevertheless has a sympathetic, voice.

Artaxerxes. Opera in 3 acts by Arne. Libretto translated by the composer from *Artaserse* (1729) by Pietro Metastasio. First performed London, 2 Feb 1762.

Metastasio's libretto was first set by Leonardo Vinci in 1730. It was used by more than forty other composers, among them Gluck (for his first opera in 1741), Paisiello (1771), and Cimarosa (1784).

Artôt, Désirée, b. Paris, 21 July 1835; d. Berlin, 3 Apr 1907. Belgian soprano. She began her career as a mezzo-soprano, and sang Fidés in *Le Prophète* at the Paris Opera

'Riot at Covent Garden in 1793 in consequence of the Managers refusing to admit half-price at the Opera of *Artaxerxes*.' Arne's *Artaxerxes* was the first Italian-style opera to be performed in England.

in 1858 on the recommendation of Meyerbeer. Later, she added soprano roles to her repertory, without ever relinquishing the mezzo territory. The greater part of her career was spent in Germany, but she also appeared in England and in Russia, where Tchaikovsky is - said to have proposed marriage to her. In 1869 she married a Spanish baritone, Mariano Padilla y Ramos (1842-1906) with whom she sang in Italian opera until her retirement in 1887.

Arundell, Dennis, b. London, 22 July 1898. English producer. He has been actor, singer, critic and translator, but is principally remembered as producer of operas in Cambridge, London (at both leading opera houses) and, occasionally, abroad. He is also the composer of two operas, *Ghost of Abel* and *A Midsummer Night's Dream*.

Ascanio in Alba. Opera in 2 acts by Mozart. Libretto by Giuseppe Parini. First performed Milan, 17 Oct 1771.

The action takes place in Italy in mythical times. Ascanio (sop.), descended from the goddess Venus, (sop.), conceals his identity from the nymph Silvia (sop.), in order to test her true feelings.

Mozart composed this, his sixth opera, at the age of fifteen. Its first 20th-c. revival was at the Salzburg Festival in 1967.

Aschenbach (ten.). The famous writer around whom the events of Britten's *Death in Venice* revolve.

Assassinio nella Cattedrale, L' (*Murder in the Cathedral*). Opera in 2 acts by Pizzetti. Libretto by the composer, based on Alberto Castelli's translation of the verse play (1935) by T. S. Eliot. First performed Milan, 1 Mar 1958.

The murder is that of Thomas à Becket (bass) in Canterbury Cathedral in 1170, by four knights at the behest of Henry II.

Astuzie Femminili, Le (*Feminine Tricks*). Opera in 2 acts by Cimarosa. Libretto by Giovanni Palomba. First performed Naples, 16 Aug 1794.

Bellina (sop.), a rich heiress, thwarts her father's will, and marries the man she loves.

At the Boar's Head. Opera in 1 act by Holst. Libretto by the composer, based on Shakespeare's *Henry IV*, parts 1 and 2. First performed Manchester, 3 Apr 1925.

The plot derives from the Falstaff scenes in Shakespeare's play.

Atalanta. Opera in 3 acts by Handel. Libretto, by an unknown hand, based on B. Valeriani's *La Caccia in Etolia*. First performed London, 12 May 1736.

The nymph Atalanta (sop.) is in love with the shepherd king, Meleager. This *pièce d'occasion* was composed for the wedding of Frederick, the Prince of Wales, son of George II, to Princess Augusta of Saxe-Gotha.

Atherton, David, b. Blackpool, 3 Jan 1941. English conductor. He made his début conducting *Ariadne auf Naxos* in Cambridge in 1966, and the following year was engaged by Covent Garden where, in 1968, he became the youngest conductor to appear in that theatre. At Covent Garden, he has conducted a wide range of operas from Mozart and Verdi to Britten and Tippett. Elsewhere, he has achieved a reputation as a persuasive advocate of difficult modern works.

Atlantide, L' (*Atlantis*). Opera in 4 acts by Tomasi. Libretto by François Didelot, based on the novel by Pierre Benoit (1920). First produced Mulhouse, 26 Feb 1954.

Antinea (sop.), ruler of the land of Atlantis, lures two French Foreign Legion officers to her kingdom and to their deaths.

Atlantov, Vladimir, b. Leningrad, 19 Feb 1939. Russian tenor. He has sung at the Kirov Theatre, Leningrad since 1963, and at the Bolshoi since 1967. Possessor of a strong dramatic tenor voice, he has specialized in the Italian as well as the Russian repertory, and has made guest appearances with a number of European companies. Though continuing to sing tenor roles, he has since 1977 also sung as a baritone.

Atterberg, Kurt, b. Göteborg, 12 Dec 1887; d. Stockholm, 15 Feb 1974. Swedish composer. Of his five operas, the earliest, *Härvard Harpolekare* (*Harvard the Harpist*) (1919) and *Bäckahästen* (*The White Horse*) (1925), have proved most successful. *Stormen* (1948) is based on Shakespeare's *The Tempest*.

Attila. Opera in a prologue and 3 acts by Verdi. Libretto by Temistocle Solera, based on the play *Attila, König der Hunnen* by Zacharias Werner (1808). First performed Venice, 17 Mar 1846.

Attila the Hun (bass) invades Italy, but is turned back before entering Rome. He is stabbed to death by Odabella (sop.) whose father he has defeated and killed.

A number of minor composers also wrote operas about Attila. They include Johann Wolfgang Franck (1682), Giuseppe Farinelli (1806), Pietro Generali (1807), Giuseppe Mosca (1818), Giuseppe Persiani (1827) and Francesco Malipiero (1847).

Auber, Daniel, b. Caen, 29 Jan 1782; d. Paris, 12 May 1871. French composer. After studying with Cherubini, he achieved success with the second of his *opéra-comique*, *La Bergère Châtelaine* (1820). He then met the librettist Scribe and began a collaboration which continued until the death of Scribe in 1861. He composed more than forty operas, most of them in light vein, of which the best-known today is *Fra Diavolo* (1830) which is still frequently performed. *Gustave III* is remembered as the work whose libretto Verdi chose for the opera which he composed as *Un Ballo in Maschera. Le Cheval de Bronze* (1835), *Le Domino Noir* (1837) and *Les Diamants de la Couronne* (1841) were among the most elegant of Auber's *opéra-comique* scores; with *La Muette de Portici* (or *Masaniello*) (1828), he turned to a serious political subject, and a grander musical style. The Brussels première of this opera in 1830 is said to have sparked off the Belgian revolt. From 1842-70 Auber was Director of the Paris Conservatoire.

Auden, Wystan Hugh, b. York, 21 Feb 1907; d. Vienna, 29 Sept 1973. English, later American, poet and librettist. One of the leading English-language poets of his time, Auden was drawn to music from an early age. His friendship with Benjamin Britten led to their collaboration on several works, among them *Paul Bunyan*, which was first performed at Columbia University, N.Y., in 1941. In collaboration with Chester Kallman, Auden wrote the libretti for a number of operas, of which the most important was Stravinsky's *The Rake's Progress* (1951). The others were *Elegy for Young Lovers* and *The Bassarids*, both by Henze, and *Love's Labour's Lost* by Nicolas Nabokov.

Audran, Edmond, b. Lyon, 12 Apr 1840; d. Tierceville, 17 Aug 1901. French composer. He composed more than thirty operettas, most of which were first produced in Paris, and several of which proved popular when staged in London in English versions. They include *La Mascotte* (1880) and *La Poupée* (1896). In his last years Audran suffered a mental and physical collapse.

Aufstieg und Fall der Stadt Mahagonny (*Rise and Fall of the City of Mahagonny*). Opera in 3 acts by Weill. Libretto by Bertolt Brecht. First performed Leipzig, 9 Mar 1930.

Jimmy Mahoney (ten.) and his friends found the city of Mahagonny, devoted to the pleasure principle, in a mythical America. The work is a satire on modern capitalist society.

Austin, Frederic, b. London, 30 Mar 1872; d. London, 10 Apr 1952. English baritone. He sang with the Beecham Opera Company from 1915-20, but achieved his greatest success when he arranged Gay's *Beggar's Opera* for performance at the Lyric Theatre, Hammersmith, in 1920. He sang Peachum in the production, which played for 1,463 performances, by far the longest run of any Opera Company.

Austral [Wilson], Florence, b. Melbourne, 26 Apr 1894; d. Newcastle N.S.W., 15 May 1968. Australian soprano. Before she adopted her stage name, she was generally known by that of her stepfather, Favaz. She made her début at Covent Garden as Brünnhilde in 1922 with the British National Opera Company, and went on to become a leading dramatic soprano in Wagner and Verdi operas. She had a voice of great purity and warmth, and was much admired as Brünnhilde and Isolde. In the late 1930s she sang with the Sadler's Wells Opera, and returned to Australia in 1940 to teach. Her husband was the flautist, John Amadio, with whom she made concert appearances.

Azucena (mezzo-sop.). The gipsy, thought to be Manrico's mother, in Verdi's *Il Trovatore.*

25

B

Baccaloni, Salvatore, b. Rome, 14 Apr 1900; d. New York, 31 Dec 1969. Italian bass. He made his début in Rome (1922) as Bartolo in *Il Barbiere di Siviglia*. On the advice of Toscanini, who engaged him for La Scala, he specialized in comic roles which he sang in Italy, England and America until he retired from opera in 1962, after which he appeared in films.

Between 1936-9, he appeared at Glyndebourne in all of his Mozart roles. Leporello, Bartolo, Osmin and Don Alfonso, and also in the title-role of Donizetti's *Don Pasquale*. He appeared at the Met every season between 1940-1962.

Bacchus (ten.). The God of wine appears as a character in Strauss's *Ariadne auf Naxos*. Under his Greek name of Dionysus he appears in Szymanowski's *King Roger* and Henze's *The Bassarids*.

Bach, Johann Christian, b. Leipzig, 5 Sept 1735; d. London, 1 Jan 1782. German composer. The youngest son of Johann Sebastian Bach, he produced his first operas in Italy. Arriving in London in 1762, he began to write operas for the King's Theatre. *Orione* (1763), his first, was a triumphant success, and Bach eventually became the leading composer of Italian operas for London theatres. *Zanaida* (1763) and *Adriano in Siria* (1765) were followed by *Carattaco* (1767) whose choral numbers were particularly admired.

After composing two operas for Mannheim in the 1770s, Bach produced one of his finest works, *La Clemenza di Scipione*, for the Theatre Royal, Haymarket, in London in 1778. For Paris in the same year he composed *Amadis des Gaules*, which contained some of his most beautiful music but failed to please the Parisians.

Bacquier, Gabriel, b. Béziers, 17 May 1924. French baritone. He began his career in Nice in 1950, and only began to make his name internationally after singing in the French provinces and in Paris for several years. He first appeared in Great Britain as the Count in *Figaro* at Glyndebourne (1962), and subsequently undertook a variety of

Gabriel Bacquier as Scarpia in *Tosca* at the Paris Opéra in 1960, one of his most successful roles.

roles at Covent Garden: Sir Richard Forth in *I Puritani*, Malatesta in *Don Pasquale*, Scarpia in *Tosca*, and Golaud in *Pelléas et Mélisande*, the last role as recently as 1982. He has sung at the Met since 1964. His voice is not of outstanding quality, but he is an intelligent artist and an actor of forceful personality.

Bahr-Mildenburg, Anna, b. Vienna, 29 Nov 1872; d. Vienna, 27 Jan 1947. Austrian soprano. After making her début in Hamburg in 1895 as Brünnhilde she became a leading Wagner soprano at Bayreuth, and in 1898 was engaged by Mahler for the Vienna Opera. In 1906 she sang Isolde at Covent Garden, and in 1909 married the Viennese author, Hermann Bahr, with whom she wrote *Bayreuth und das Wagner-Theater* (1910). After her retirement in 1917, she taught, though she sang Klytemnestra in Augsburg in 1930.

Bailey, Norman, b. Birmingham, 23 Mar 1933. English baritone. He studied in Vienna, one of his teachers being the distinguished tenor Julius Patzak, and made his début in Vienna in 1959 in Rossini's *La Cambiale di Matrimonio*. For the next eight years, he was a member of several German and Austrian companies, singing mainly in the Italian repertory, but also Wagner roles. He joined the Sadler's Wells company in 1967, and made his London début with them in 1968 as Hans Sachs, a role he sang the following year in Hamburg, Brussels and Munich. In the 1970s he became one of the most sought-after exponents of the Wagner Heldenbariton roles. He has sung at Bayreuth, and was the Wotan in the English *Ring* cycle at the London Coliseum in the early 1970s. A compelling actor, he is heard at his best as Wagner's Dutchman. He is less well suited to those Italian roles, such as Di Luna and Scarpia, which he still occasionally undertakes.

Baker, (Dame) Janet, b. Hatfield, Yorks, 21 Aug 1933. English mezzo-soprano. Although she has always thought of herself primarily as a concert singer, in the 1960-70s, she appeared in various operas, among them Britten's *The Rape of Lucretia*, Purcell's *Dido and Aeneas*, and several works by Handel. She preferred not to sing in opera outside Great Britain, but concentrated on those roles she felt most suited to her, which she could perform in congenial surroundings. An affecting Composer in *Ariadne auf Naxos* with Scottish Opera (1975), she was also a memorable Penelope in Monteverdi's *Ritorno d'Ulisse in Patria* at Glyndebourne (1972). Her Covent Garden début in 1966 was as Hermia in Britten's *A Midsummer Night's Dream*, and she returned to Covent Garden in 1969 as Berlioz's Dido, Vitellia in *La Clemenza di Tito* (1974) and Gluck's *Alceste* (1981), as well as Kate, the role written for her by Britten in *Owen Wingrave* (1973). With the English National Opera, she sang Mary Queen of Scots in Donizetti's *Maria Stuarda* (1973), Charlotte in *Werther* (1976) and Caesar in Handel's *Giulio Cesare* (1979). She retired from opera in 1982, her last appearance being in Gluck's *Orfeo ed Euridice* at Glyndebourne in the summer of that year, but continues as a recitalist.

Balfe, Michael, b. Dublin, 15 May 1808; d. Rowney Abbey, Hertfordshire, 20 Oct 1870. Irish composer and baritone. A violinist as well as singer, he began his career in the orchestra at Drury Lane, and made his début in 1824 as a singer in the role of Kaspar in Weber's *Der Freischütz* in Norwich. After studying in Italy, he sang Rossini's Figaro in Paris in 1827, to the approval of the composer. In 1829, he became principal baritone of the company in Palermo where, the following year, the first of his twenty -nine operas, *I Rivali di se Stesso*, was staged.

Balfe returned to London in 1835, where he began a very successful career as a composer of English opera. *The Siege of Rochelle* was produced at Drury Lane in 1835 to great acclaim, and *The Maid of Artois* (1836) was an even greater success. By far the best-known of his operas is *The Bohemian Girl* (1843). A graceful melodic gift is more in evidence in his operas than flair for drama or characterization.

For a few years in the 1850s Balfe travelled widely in Europe and Russia. His *Pittore e Duca*, its libretto by Verdi's librettist Piave, was a failure in Trieste in 1854, but on his return to England he regained his best form

Dame Janet Baker in the title-role of Gluck's *Alceste* at Covent Garden in 1981.

with *The Rose of Castile* (1857), *Satanella* (1858) and *The Puritan's Daughter* (1861). The last years of his life were spent revising *The Bohemian Girl* for its production in Paris as *La Bohémienne* (1869), and writing his final opera, *The Knight of the Leopard*, which was produced posthumously in 1874 in Italian as *Il Talismano*.

Ballad of Baby Doe, The. Opera in 2 acts by Douglas Moore. Libretto by John Latouche. First performed Central City, Colorado, 7 July 1956.

The opera is based on fact. In Leadville, Colorado, during the gold-rush days, Horace Tabor (bar.) divorces his wife to marry the beautiful Baby Doe (sop.). After his death, Baby Doe lives on for thirty-six years in loneliness and squalor, and is eventually found, frozen to death.

ballad opera. A form of popular opera which flourished for a decade or two in 18th c. England. The spoken dialogue was interrupted by simple songs or ballads which were usually existing folk or popular tunes adapted to a new text. The earliest and most famous example is *The Beggar's Opera*. Another ballad opera, Charles Coffey's *The Devil to Pay* (1731), translated into German in 1743 as *Der Teufel ist Los*, was largely instrumental in the creation of the German genre of *Singspiel*. By the middle of the 18th c. the popularity of the ballad opera was on the decline. Among dramatists who wrote such works are John Gay (author of *The Beggar's Opera* and its sequel *Polly*), Colley Cibber, and Henry Fielding.

ballet in opera. An important element in the masque, which was one of the forerunners of opera, ballet continued to play a part in the new art-form, opera. There are dances in the finales of the earliest Italian operas, and by the end of the 17th-c. France had evolved the *opéra-ballet* of Campra and Lully. It was in France that ballet continued to flourish in 19th c. opera, to the extent that foreign composers writing for Paris had to include a self-contained ballet in each opera. Dance, as distinct from ballet, was often an integral part of the dramatic structure of an opera, as in Tchaikovsky's *Eugene Onegin* with its two ballroom scenes: one a modest country affair, and the other an elegant ball in a town palace.

Ballo in Maschera, Un (*A Masked Ball*). Opera in 3 acts by Verdi. Libretto by Antonio Somma, based on Eugène Scribe's libretto for Auber's *Gustave III ou Le Bal Masqué*. First performed Rome, 17 Feb 1859.

Though Verdi and Somma had set out to write about the assassination of the historical King Gustav III of Sweden, censorship difficulties led to the characters being fictionalized. Thus, the opera as performed in Rome in 1859 deals with the assassination of one Riccardo, Governor of Boston. In recent years, productions have begun to revert to the original historical characters and the 1792 Stockholm setting.

Riccardo (ten.), Governor of Boston at the end of the 17th-c., falls in love with Amelia (sop.), wife of Renato (bar.), his secretary and intimate friend. His love is returned, but Amelia's conscience troubles her and she consults Ulrica (mezzo-sop.), a black sorceress, who sends her to gather at midnight a certain herb which will cause her to forget Riccardo. Overhearing Amelia's conversation with Ulrica, Riccardo follows her to the spot. Renato, who has come in search of Riccardo to warn him of the approach of conspirators, is requested by the Governor to escort the veiled lady to the town without attempting to learn her identity. Riccardo leaves, but Renato and Amelia find themselves surrounded by the conspirators, and Amelia's identity is revealed. Renato swears vengeance on his friend, and joins the plot to assassinate him.

At a grand masked ball, Riccardo is stabbed by Renato. As he lies dying, Riccardo declares the innocence of Amelia, and forgives Renato.

Baltsa, Agnes, b. Lefkas, 19 Nov 1944. Greek mezzo-soprano. An accomplished pianist by the age of seven, she later studied singing in Athens and Munich. She began her career in Frankfurt in 1968 as Cherubino, and was soon taken up by Berlin and Vienna. She impressed Herbert von Karajan, who engaged her for the Salzburg Festival, where she has become a popular favourite. Her roles include Mozart's Dorabella and Sextus (in *La Clemenza di Tito*), Strauss's Octavian and Composer, and Rossini's Rosina and Cenerentola. She was a musically delightful and dramatically credible Cherubino at Covent Garden in

1977, and in 1980 was a much admired Adalgisa there, to the Norma of Sylvia Sass. She returned to sing Carmen in 1983 to great acclaim. She now sings regularly in Vienna and Berlin.

Bampton, Rose, b. Cleveland, Ohio, 28 Nov 1908. American soprano. After studying at the Curtis Institute in Philadelphia, she made her début there as a contralto, and first appeared at the Met in 1932 in the mezzo role of Laura in *La Gioconda*. In 1937 at the Met she sang her first soprano role, Leonora in *Il Trovatore*, though for a time she also continued in mezzo parts: in 1937, for example, she sang Amneris at Covent Garden. She remained at the Met until 1950, a reliable and always musically accurate dramatic soprano, at her best as Donna Anna, Alceste, Kundry and Sieglinde. In 1937 she married Wilfred Pelletier. After her retirement she taught in New York and Montreal.

banda. Literally 'band', the *banda* was the stage band, as often as not mainly composed of brass instruments, used in 19th-c. Italian opera either behind the scenes or to take part in the action on stage. There are numerous instances of its use in the operas of Rossini, Donizetti and Verdi.

Bánk Bán. Opera in 3 acts by Erkel. Libretto by Béni Egressy based on the play (1814) by József Katona. First performed Budapest, 9 Mar 1861. The composer's most popular work, it is still regularly performed in Hungary, though it has never achieved success abroad.

Bantock, (Sir) Granville, b. London, 7 Aug 1868; d. London, 16 Oct 1946. English composer. He wrote his first opera, *Caedmar*, a 1-act piece, while he was still a student: it was produced at the Crystal Palace in 1893. He accepted conducting and academic posts while continuing to compose. Attracted to oriental and Celtic subjects for operas and choral works, but also for orchestral tone-poems, he completed only two more operas. *The Pearl of Iran* (1894) appears not to have been staged, but *The Seal-Woman*, a Celtic folk opera in 2 acts, with libretto by Marjorie Kennedy-Fraser, was produced at the Birmingham Repertory Theatre in 1924.

Barber, Samuel, b. Westchester, Pa., 9 Mar 1910. American composer. A nephew of the contralto Louise Homer, and himself a baritone, Barber has shown a particular interest in vocal music throughout his career. An early work, his setting of Matthew Arnold's *Dover Beach* for voice and string quartet (1931), caused his name to be known outside the United States. It was, however, not until the 1950s that he composed his first opera, *Vanessa*, which was staged at the old New York Met in 1958. When the Metropolitan Opera Company moved to its new home in Lincoln Center, a second opera, *Antony and Cleopatra*, was commissioned from Barber to open the new theatre.

Barber's late-romantic musical style is agreeable and assured, though perhaps not strongly individual.

Barbier, Jules, b. Paris, 8 Mar 1822; d. Paris, 16 Jan 1901. French librettist. He collaborated with Michel Carré on a number of libretti, among them those for Gounod's *Faust*, *Roméo et Juliette* (and five other Gounod operas), Offenbach's *Contes d'Hoffmann* (based on a play by Barbier and Carré, which in turn was derived from Hoffmann's stories), and Thomas's *Mignon* and *Hamlet*.

Barbier von Bagdad, Der (*The Barber of Bagdad*). Opera in 2 acts by Cornelius. Libretto by the composer, based on a story in *The Arabian Nights' Entertainments* (or *A Thousand and One Nights*). First performed Weimar, 15 Dec 1858.

Nureddin, helped by the barber, wins the hand of Margiana, daughter of the Caliph.

Barbiere di Siviglia, Il (*The Barber of Seville*). 1. Opera in 2 acts by Rossini. Libretto by Cesare Sterbini, after the play, *Le Barbier de Séville* (1775) by Beaumarchais. First performed Rome, 20 Feb 1816. 2. Opera in 4 acts by Paisiello. Libretto by Giuseppe Petrosellini, after the play, *Le Barbier de Séville* by Beaumarchais. First performed St Petersburg, 26 Sept 1782.

Count Almaviva (ten.) loves Rosina (mezzo-sop. in Rossini; sop. in Paisiello), the ward of Dr Bartolo (bass), a crusty old bachelor who plans to marry her himself. Almaviva persuades the town barber and general factotum, Figaro (bar.), to arrange a meeting for him, and gains entrance to

Bartolo's house disguised as a soldier seeking a billet. When this attempt fails, he returns, disguised as a substitute for Don Basilio (bass), the priest who is Rosina's music master, whom Almaviva claims is ill. When the real Don Basilio arrives, he is bribed to leave again, and Almaviva makes plans for an elopement.

Bartolo finally arouses Rosina's jealousy by pretending that Almaviva loves someone else, and she promises to forget him and marry her guardian. When the time for the elopement arrives, she reproaches her lover, whom she knows only as Lindoro, but he convinces her of his sincerity and reveals his true identity. When Bartolo arrives with officers to arrest Almaviva, he finds that the lovers have, a few moments earlier, been married, and he has to accept the situation.

Barbieri, Fedora, b. Trieste, 4 June 1920. Italian mezzo-soprano. After studying in Trieste, she made her début in 1940 in Florence, as Fidalma in Cimarosa's *Il Matrimonio Segreto*. She sang at most of the leading Italian houses and, after World War II, at Covent Garden, the Met, and the Teatro Colón, Buenos Aires. Much admired in Italy as Carmen and as Gluck's Orfeo, she was known abroad principally for her firmly and dependably sung Verdi roles. Her first role at the Met in 1950 was Eboli, and her first London appearances in the same year were with the Scala company as Mistress Quickly and in the Verdi *Requiem*. In 1970 she created the role of the Wife in Chailly's *L'Idiota* at the Rome Opera. After she had ceased to sing the more demanding roles, she sang in small parts.

Geraint Evans as Dr Bartolo and Joseph Rouleau as Don Basilio in *Il Barbiere di Siviglia* at Covent Garden in 1967. Rossini's opera supplanted in popularity Paisiello's opera on the same theme.

Barbieri-Nini, Marianna, b. Florence, *c.* 1820; d. Florence, 27 Nov 1887. Italian soprano. After a disastrous first appearance at La Scala in Donizetti's *Belisario* in 1840, due apparently as much to her unprepossessing appearance as to any deficiencies in her performance, she successfully appeared the following season in Florence as Lucrezia Borgia in Donizetti's opera, when the fact that the character appears masked in the first act allowed her audience to concentrate on Barbieri-Nini's considerable vocal and dramatic gifts. She became one of the leading dramatic sopranos of her day, and was chosen by Verdi to create the leading soprano roles in three of his operas: *I Due Foscari* (Rome, 1844), *Il Corsaro* (Trieste, 1848) and, the most important role of her career and the one which keeps her name alive, Lady Macbeth in *Macbeth* (Florence, 1847). She retired in 1856.

Barbirolli, (Sir) John, b. London, 2 Dec 1899; d. London, 29 July, 1970. English conductor, of Italian parentage. He began his career as a cellist, later formed and conducted his own string orchestra, and was invited by the British National Opera Company in 1926 to conduct opera. He conducted frequently at Covent Garden between 1928-33, achieving particular success with the operas of Puccini. In the late 1930s he conducted the Philharmonic Symphony Orchestra of New York, and returned to England to become conductor of the Hallé Orchestra in 1943. Though he was impressive in Italian opera, he conducted infrequently in the opera house. He appeared at the Vienna Opera, Covent Garden and the Rome Opera in the post-World War II years.

barcarolle. An Italian boating song, usually in a lilting 6/8 rhythm, the barcarolle has been introduced into opera by several composers. The most famous barcarolle is that sung in the Venetian act of Offenbach's *Tales of Hoffmann*, though Offenbach originally wrote it for a different work.

baritone. From the Greek, meaning 'of heavy tone', the term is used now to indicate the middle category of male voice, between bass and tenor. The Germans tend to sub-divide baritones into various types, and even use 'bass-baritone' to describe a voice somewhat lighter and higher than a true bass, but not as high as a lyric baritone. The Italian baritone voice is generally higher and lighter of timbre than the German-trained voice, with top notes (up to G sharp) of tenor-like quality.

Barnaba (bar.). A spy for the Inquisition in Ponchielli's *La Gioconda*.

Barnett, John, b. Bedford, 15 July 1802; d. Leckhampton, 16 Apr 1890. English composer, born of a Prussian father (Joseph Beer) and Hungarian mother. He began his career as a composer of music for farces. His first opera, *The Mountain Sylph*, produced at the Lyceum Theatre in 1834 was acclaimed as one of the finest new English operas in many years. It was popular enough to be satirized, much later, by Gilbert and Sullivan in *Iolanthe*. Barnett composed two operas for Drury Lane, *Fair Rosamund* (1837) and *Farinelli* (1839). In 1839 he opened the St James's Theatre with the intention of founding a house for English opera, but this proved a failure and he moved to Cheltenham where he taught singing.

Sir John Barbirolli who made a welcome return to conduct at Covent Garden from 1951-4.

Barraud, Henry, b. Bordeaux, 23 Apr 1900. French composer. He studied composition in Paris with Dukas, and during World War II was Director of the French Radio. His first opera, *La Farce de Maître Pathelin*, was composed in the late 1930s but not staged until 1948. *Numance*, its libretto written by Salvador de Madariaga after Cervantes, was composed in 1950 and staged in 1955. The comic opera, *Lavinia*, followed in 1961, and an opera for radio, *La Fée aux Miettes*, was broadcast in 1968.

Barrault, Jean-Louis, b. Vésinet, 8 Sept 1910. French actor and director. A distinguished stage and film actor, Barrault has also directed opera and operetta. In Paris in 1958, he directed Offenbach's operetta, *La Vie Parisienne*, and undertook the role of the Brazilian. His first opera production was *Wozzeck* at the Paris Opéra in 1963, while at the Met he was engaged to direct French operas: *Faust* in 1965 and *Carmen* in 1967. He also staged *Faust* at La Scala in 1966.

Barrientos, Maria, b. Barcelona, 10 Mar 1883; d. Ciboure, Basses-Pyrénées, 8 Aug 1946. Spanish soprano. She is said to have made her début in Barcelona aged fifteen. She then went to Milan where she appeared at La Scala, and sang Rosina in *Il Barbiere di Siviglia* at Covent Garden in 1903. Her voice was both attractive and agile, and she specialized in roles in which her skill in coloratura could be displayed. At the Met, between 1916-20, she triumphed as Elvira in *Il Puritani*, as Lakmé, as Amina in *La Sonnambula* and especially as Donizetti's Lucia di Lammermoor.

Barstow, Josephine, b. Sheffield, 27 Sept 1940. English soprano. Her début was made in 1964 with a small-scale touring company, Opera for All, as Mimi. After advanced study at the London Opera Centre, she joined the Sadler's Wells company in 1967, her first role being Cherubino. An intelligent artist and convincing actress, she has a voice of individual quality which is heard at its best in such roles as Emilia Marty in *The Makropoulos Affair* and Natasha in *War and Peace*, both of which she has sung with the English National Opera. At Covent Garden she has created roles in operas by Tippett, but has also appeared in roles for which she is less than ideally suited, such as Mascagni's Santuzza, and Salome in Strauss's opera. She appears frequently in Europe and the United States, and in 1982 in San Diego succeeded through intelligence rather than vocal suitability as Amelia in *Un Ballo in Maschera*.

Bartered Bride, The (Original Czech title, *Prodaná Nevěsta*). Opera in 3 acts by

A scene from Smetana's *The Bartered Bride* at the National Theatre in Prague, May 1971.

Smetana. Libretto by Karel Sabina. First performed Prague, 30 May 1866.

Czechoslovakia's most popular national opera, tells a story of Bohemian village life. Jenik (ten.) and Mařenka (sop.) are in love, but the girl's father is determined that she shall marry Vašek (ten.), a stuttering half-wit, and son of his friend·Mícha. The marriage-broker Kecal (bass) offers Jenik 300 crowns to give up Mařenka, which he agrees to do provided that she marry no one but the son of Mícha. Mařenka is confused and distressed when she learns of her beloved's apparently heartless behaviour, and agrees to marry Vašek. Events reach a happy conclusion for the young lovers only when Jenik is revealed to be the long-lost son of Mícha, and therefore elder brother of Vašek. Jenik gains both his bride and the 300 crowns, and all are delighted except the marriage-broker.

Bartoletti, Bruno, b. Sesto Fiorentino, 10 June 1926. Italian conductor. He studied in Florence and made his début there in 1953, conducting *Rigoletto*. He made his American début with the Chicago Lyric Opera in 1956, and has been principal conductor there since 1964, though he has also found time to conduct in Rome and Florence regularly. An excellent interpreter of the 19th-c. Italian repertory, he has been largely responsible for the high standard in recent years of the musical (as opposed to dramatic) aspects of Chicago Lyric Opera.

Bartók, Béla, b. Nagyszentmiklós, 25 Mar 1881; d. New York, 26 Sept 1945. Hungarian composer. Though a prolific composer, Bartók was not primarily interested in the stage. He composed two ballet scores, but only one opera. The opera, *Duke Bluebeard's Castle*, is a powerful and original dramatic work, which continues to be staged in a number of countries and languages.

Bartolo, Don (bass). Rosina's guardian in Rossini's *Il Barbiere di Siviglia*, and physician to the Almaviva household in Mozart's *Le Nozze di Figaro*.

Basilio, Don (bass). Rosina's singing teacher in Rossini's *Il Barbiere di Siviglia* and, as a tenor, music tutor to the Almaviva household in Mozart's *Le Nozze di Figaro*.

bass. Derived from the Italian 'basso' (low), the term is used for the lowest category of male voice. There are various types of bass voice: the *basso profondo* is a deep voice able to sustain a legato line in the lowest part of its register, while the *basso buffo*, or comic bass, does not need this ability. The *basso cantante* is a less deep type of *basso profondo*. The bass-baritone usually combines baritone range with bass timbre.

Bassarids, The. Opera in 1 act, with intermezzo, by Henze. Libretto by W.H. Auden and Chester Kallman, based on *The Bacchae* of Euripides. First performed (in German translation) Salzburg, 6 Aug 1966. First performed in the original English, Santa Fe, New Mexico, 7 Aug 1968.

Pentheus (bar.), King of Thebes, attempts to suppress the Dionysiac side of his nature, and is torn to pieces by his own mother Agave (mezzo-sop.) and the Bacchantes or Bassarids during a bacchanalian orgy.

Bassi, Amadeo, b. Montespertoli, nr Florence, 29 July 1874; d. Florence, 15 Jan 1949. Italian tenor. He made his début in 1897 in Castelfiorentino in Marchetti's *Ruy Blas*, and was Radames in the performance of *Aida* which opened the Teatro Colón, Buenos Aires, in 1908. He sang Dick Johnson in the first London performances of *La Fanciulla del West* (1911) and was with the Met in 1910 and 1911. During Toscanini's regime at La Scala from 1921–6 he sang such Wagner roles as Siegfried and Parsifal. Retiring from the stage in 1926, he taught for many years, but also continued to appear in concerts until 1940.

Bastianini, Ettore, b. Siena, 24 Sept 1922; d. Sirmione, 25 Jan 1967. Italian baritone. He made his début as a bass in Ravenna, in the role of Colline (*La Bohème*) in 1945, and sang bass roles for some years before becoming a baritone with Germont in *La Traviata* in 1951. His voice was of fine quality, with an individual, somewhat burnished timbre, and he was at his most impressive in the bel canto repertory and the Verdi roles. He sang in all the major opera houses, achieving some of his greatest successes in Verdi: Germont at his Met début in 1953, the Count of Luna at Salzburg in 1960, and Renato in *Un Ballo in Maschera* at Covent Garden in 1962. He died prematurely, of cancer, at the peak of his career.

Bastien und Bastienne. Opera (Singspiel) in 1 act by Mozart. Libretto by Friedrich Wilhelm Weiskern (with additional verses by Johann Müller), after the parody with music, *Les Amours de Bastien et Bastienne* by Charles Simon Favart, Marie Justine Favart and Harny de Guerville. First performed (probably) Vienna, October 1768. The first proven performance was given in Berlin, 2 Oct 1890.

The village soothsayer, Colas (bass), helps to patch up a quarrel between the two young lovers, Bastien (ten.) and Bastienne (sop.).

This little 1-act pastorale was composed by Mozart at the age of twelve.

Battaglia di Legnano, La (*The Battle of Legnano*). Opera in 4 acts by Verdi. Libretto by Salvatore Cammarano. First performed Rome, 27 Jan 1849.

In northern Italy in the year 1176, the fighters of the Lombard League defeat the Emperor Barbarossa (bass) and his invading army. Two of the Lombardian leaders, Arrigo (ten.) and Rolando (bar.), quarrel over Lida (sop.) who, formerly Arrigo's fiancée, has during his absence married Rolando.

Battistini, Mattia, b. Rome, 27 Feb 1856; d. Colle Baccaro, nr Rieti, 7 Nov 1928. Italian baritone. He made his début at the Teatro Argentina, Rome, in *La Favorita*, first sang at Covent Garden in 1883 as Riccardo in *I Puritani*, and at La Scala in 1888, in which year his international fame began. Possessor of a mellifluous high baritone, and a superb sense of style, he soon established himself as the leading baritone of his day, lionized throughout Europe and in Russia where he sang each season from 1888–1914. He never sang in the United States, and is said to have had a dread of the Atlantic crossing. He had a wide repertoire of roles which included Wagner's Wolfram, the usual Verdi and Puccini characters, Tchaikovsky's Eugene Onegin, Rossini's Barber, and Mozart's Giovanni. His records are referred to by more recent singers as models of style and technique. In his later years, he sang more frequently in concerts than in opera, but was performing until within a year of his

death, giving his last concert in Graz in October 1927 aged nearly seventy-two.

Baylis, Lilian, b. London, 9 May 1874; d. London, 25 Nov 1937. English musician and theatre manager. At the age of sixteen she went with her parents to South Africa where she taught singing, and founded a ladies' orchestra. She returned to London in 1898 to manage the Old Vic Theatre which she did until her death. In 1931, at the rebuilt Sadler's Wells Theatre, she established a separate home for the Vic-Wells Opera which in due course became the Sadler's Wells Opera Company. Her chief concern was to make opera (and drama) available at prices popular audiences could afford.

Beatrice di Tenda. Opera in 2 acts by Bellini. Libretto by Felice Romani, based on the play of the same title by Carlo Tedaldi Fores. First performed Venice, 16 Mar 1833.

A melodramatic plot of love and intrigue involves Filippo Visconti, Duke of Milan (bar.), and his wife Beatrice (sop.) who is in love with Orombello (ten.), who is also loved by Agnese (mezzo-sop.) with whom the Duke himself is in love. Agnese denounces Beatrice and Orombello to the Duke, who orders the execution of Beatrice.

Béatrice et Bénédict. Opera in 2 acts by Berlioz. Libretto by the composer, after Shakespeare's *Much Ado About Nothing*. First performed Baden-Baden, 9 Aug 1862. The libretto is a simplification of the Shakespeare comedy, omitting a number of characters and replacing Dogberry with Somarone, a pedantic conductor.

Bechi, Gino, b. Florence, 16 Oct 1913. Italian baritone. He made his début at Empoli in 1936 as Germont, and from the late 1930s to around 1950 was generally considered the leading Italian dramatic baritone. In those years he sang mainly in Italy and South America. By the time of his first London appearance with the Scala company in 1950, his voice had already deteriorated, and he was a disappointment as Iago and Falstaff. He continued to appear in opera until 1961.

Beckmesser (bar.). The Town Clerk who loses the singing contest (and the hand of Eva) in Wagner's *Die Meistersinger*.

Sir Thomas Beecham whose influence on opera in 20th-c. Great Britain has been incalculable.

Beecham, (Sir) Thomas, b. St Helens, Lancs, 29 Apr 1879; d. London, 8 Mar 1961. English conductor. A wealthy amateur with no formal musical education, he was able to indulge his taste for opera by mounting his own seasons. He introduced Strauss's *Elektra* and *Salome* to London in 1910, and before World War I had staged in London several other operas by Strauss, one of his favourite composers. He also had a great love for, though perhaps not so great an understanding of, Mozart. The Beecham Opera Company flourished between 1915 and 1920, and in the 1930s Beecham was artistic director and chief conductor for the international seasons at Covent Garden. After World War II he was disappointed at not being invited to resume these functions, and conducted only two operas at Covent Garden, both in 1951: *Die Meistersinger* and Balfe's *The Bohemian Girl*.

Beethoven, Ludwig van, b. Bonn, probably 16 Dec 1770, baptized 17 Dec; d. Vienna, 26 Mar 1827. German composer. Generally regarded as the greatest composer of all, Beethoven composed only one opera, *Fidelio*. Though it is in many ways unsatisfactory as an opera, *Fidelio* transcends categorization, and is an immensely moving affirmation of the power of the human spirit. Viewed more narrowly, it is an expression of faith in liberty and in love.

Beethoven contemplated other subjects for operas, and actually began to make sketches for *Vestas Feuer*, to a libretto by Schikaneder.

Beggar's Opera, The. Ballad opera in 3 acts, its music arranged and in part composed by Pepusch. Libretto by John Gay. First performed London, 9 Feb 1728.

The highwayman, Macheath (bar.), is betrayed by harlots and sentenced to be hanged. He is saved in order to provide a satirically happy end to the opera, which has been ostensibly written by a beggar.

The opera was extremely popular until the late 19th c., after which it was not performed until revived in a new edition by Frederic Austin at the Lyric Theatre, Hammersmith, London, in 1920 when it had a run of 1,463 performances. A later version, with the music arranged by Benjamin Britten, was first performed in 1948 in Cambridge.

Béjart, Maurice, b. Marseilles, 1 Jan 1927. French choreographer and director. Primarily a choreographer of ballet, in which capacity he was engaged to stage the bacchanale in *Tannhäuser* at Bayreuth in 1961, Béjart has also occasionally directed opera. At the Théâtre de la Monnaie in Brussels he has staged, amongst other works, Offenbach's *Contes d'Hoffmann* and Lehár's *Merry Widow*. His 1973 production of *La Traviata* was generally regarded as an extreme example of producer's licence.

bel canto. Though it means simply 'beautiful singing', the term has come to be applied to a style of singing in which a pure, firm legato line is emphasized, perhaps at the expense of dramatic expression, and also to be used more generally to indicate the Italian operas of the first half of the 19th-c., e.g. those of Rossini, Donizetti, Bellini and the early Verdi, which are thought to require that style of performance.

Belcore (bar.). The sergeant who almost marries the heroine of Donizetti's *L'Elisir d'Amore*.

Belisario. Opera in 3 acts by Donizetti. Libretto by Salvatore Cammarano, after Luigi Marchionni's Italian adaptation of Eduard von Schenk's play, *Belisarius* (Munich, 1820). First performed Venice, 4. Feb 1836.

When Belisario (ten.), General in Justinian's army, returns to Byzantium in triumph after defeating the Bulgarians, his jealous wife Antonina (sop.), believing he is responsible for the death of their son, denounces him as a traitor. Belisario is blinded and sentenced to exile, but is then reunited with his son who is, after all, alive. After another battle in which Belisario is fatally wounded, Antonina confesses her guilt to her dying husband.

Belle Hélène, La (*The Beautiful Helen*). Operetta in 3 acts by Offenbach. Libretto by Henri Meilhac and Ludovic Halévy. First performed Paris, 17 Dec 1864.

A satire on the morals and manners of the French Second Empire, the operetta makes use of the story of Paris (ten.) and Helen of Troy (sop.).

Bellezza, Vincenzo, b. Bitonto, Bari, 17 Feb 1888; d. Rome, 8 Feb 1964. Italian conductor. He made his début with *Aida* in Naples in 1908, conducted operetta in Italy during World War I, and then for several years alternated between the Teatro Colón, Buenos Aires, and various European houses. His first Covent Garden appearance was in 1926, when he conducted Boito's *Mefistofele* in which Chaliapin sang the title-role. The following year he conducted the first English *Turandot*. He was with the Met from 1926 to 1935. A skilful and authoritative conductor of Italian opera, he made his final London appearances conducting an *ad hoc* season at the Theatre Royal, Drury Lane, in 1958.

Bellincioni, Gemma, b. Como, 18 Aug 1864; d. Naples, 23 Apr 1950. Italian soprano. The child of singers, she studied first with her father, and later with the tenor Roberto Stagno, whom she met in 1886 and lived with until his death in 1897. Verdi praised her Violetta in *La Traviata* for

'giving new life to the old sinner', but it is as a singing actress of the *verismo* repertory that she is remembered. She created the role of Santuzza in *Cavalleria Rusticana* in Rome (1890) with Stagno as Turiddu. She also created the title-role in Giordano's *Fedora* (Milan, 1898) with the young Caruso as Loris. In Turin in 1906, she was the first Italian Salome. The performance was conducted by Strauss himself, who praised her in the role, which she sang over 100 times, and in which she appeared on stage, ostensibly for the last time, in Paris in 1911. After World War I, she taught, but emerged from her retirement as a singer to appear in Holland as Santuzza, Tosca and Carmen at the age of sixty.

Bellini, Vincenzo, b. Catania, 3 Nov 1801; d. Puteaux, 23 Sept 1835. Italian composer. The son of an organist and composer, Bellini showed evidence of talent at an early age, and with the aid of a grant from the Decurionato, or City Council of Catania, was enabled to study in Naples at the Real Collegio di Musica. His first opera, *Adelson e Salvini* (1825), was produced at the College while he was still a student. This led to Bellini's being offered a commission to compose an opera for the Teatro San Carlo, Naples. *Bianca e Gernando* was produced there in 1826. From then on, the young composer's success was assured. Barbaia, the impresario of the Teatro San Carlo, also managed La Scala, Milan, for which he commissioned Bellini to write an opera. The librettist was the celebrated Romani, with whom Bellini was to continue to collaborate until they quarrelled in 1833. Their first work together was *Il Pirata*, produced at La Scala in 1827. It was also the first of Bellini's operas to become known outside Italy, its success being due perhaps as much to the elegant singing of Rubini, the tenor for whom Bellini had written the title role, as to the intrinsic merits of the work itself.

The following two operas, *La Straniera*, produced at La Scala in February, 1829, and *Zaira*, written in a hurry (and Bellini was not normally a quick worker) for production at the Teatro Nuovo, Parma, in May of the same year, were less successful. But Bellini's professional fortunes revived again with *I Capuleti e i Montecchi*, composed for the Teatro La Fenice, Venice, where it was staged in March, 1830. Two undisputed masterpieces now followed in reasonably quick succession: *La Sonnambula*, first performed at the Teatro Carcano, Milan, in March 1831, and *Norma*, staged at La Scala in December of that year. During their collaboration on the following opera, *Beatrice di Tenda*, Bellini and Romani quarrelled. For what was to be his last opera, *I Puritani*, Bellini chose another librettist, Carlo Pepoli. *I Puritani* was produced at the Théâtre des Italiens, Paris, in January, 1835. It was while he was staying at the villa of an English friend, at Puteaux near Paris, that Bellini died later that year, some weeks short of his thirty-fourth birthday. The cause of his death was an acute inflammation of the large intestine, aggravated by an abcess of the liver.

Together with his elder contemporaries, Rossini and Donizetti, both of whom outlived him by many years, Bellini was one of the three great composers of 19th-c. Italian opera before Verdi. He differed from Rossini in preferring a less adorned simplicity of utterance, and a limpidity of style which some critics claim to have influenced Chopin and in which others claim to detect the influence of Chopin. (The two composers were friends in Paris, and the likelihood is that they influenced each other.) Bellini differed, too, from Donizetti, in lacking the latter's almost manic facility, and in substituting a concern for the sheer craft of composition and a seriousness of purpose which anticipate the great reformer of Italian opera, Giuseppe Verdi.

Bellini's individuality of style and temperament are evident even in his early, and patently immature operas. *Adelson e Salvini* is understandably Rossinian: it is the work of a twenty-three year old who could hardly have escaped the influence of the most successful opera composer of the time. But already, the delicate Chopinesque vocal line had made its appearance, in at least one of the arias. Even more characteristically Bellinian touches are to be found in *Bianca e Gernando* ('Gernando' became 'Fernando' when the opera was extensively revised for production in Genoa.)

Until fairly recent years, Bellini's popularity rested almost entirely on three of his ten operas: *La Sonnambula*, *I Puritani* and, above all, *Norma*; but the appearance on the international scene of singers such as Maria

Vincenzo Bellini. With Donizetti and Rossini he was one of the founders of modern Italian opera

Callas, Joan Sutherland, Renata Scotto and Montserrat Caballé, all of whom brought different qualities to the performance of the Bellini heroines, led to the lesser-known works being reassessed. As a result, among the earlier operas *Il Pirata* and *La Straniera* have been found perfectly viable, and the penultimate *Beatrice di Tenda* has taken on a new lease of life. Nevertheless, it remains true that the greatness of Bellini is most evident in *Norma*, which combines elements of romantic and classical art in fine proportions; in *La Sonnambula* whose elegiac-pastoral tone of voice is completely its own, and whose influence on Donizetti's *L'Elisir d'Amore* (composed some months later), is unmistakable and strong; and above all, perhaps, in Bellini's final opera, *I Puritani* which, though undoubtedly imperfect, points to the directions its composer might have taken had he lived.

Belmonte (ten.). The Spanish nobleman who effects the rescue of Constanze in Mozart's *Die Entführung aus dem Serail*.

Benda, Jiří, b. Staré Benátky, 30 June 1722; d. Köstritz 6 Nov 1795. Czech composer. He composed a number of Singspiele, among them *Der Dorfjahrmarkt* (1775), but it is for having mastered a new stage form, that of the 'duodrama', that he is remembered. These works, with spoken texts accompanied by music, include *Ariadne auf Naxos* and *Medea* (both 1775). Mozart, in 1778, wrote enthusiastically to his father of one of these works, 'I…was absolutely delighted. Indeed, nothing has ever surprised me more, for I had always imagined that this kind of piece would be quite ineffective. I expect you know that there is no singing in these works, only declamation with the music acting as a kind of *recitativo obbligato*. From time to time the actors speak while the music is being played, which creates the most wonderful effect.'

Benedict. (Sir) Julius, b. Stuttgart, 27 Nov 1804; d. London, 5 June 1885. German, later British, composer and conductor. He was a pupil of Weber who took him to Vienna where he became conductor at the Kärntnertor Theater in 1823. Later he conducted at the San Carlo in Naples, where his first opera, *Giacinta ed Ernesto*, was staged in 1827. Two more operas followed, all of them in the florid Italian style of Rossini. In 1835, after a period in Paris, he moved to London and spent the rest of his life there. From 1838 to 1848 he was musical director of Drury Lane Theatre, where he joined the attempts being made to establish English opera. As well as staging operas by such composers as Balfe and Wallace, Benedict produced three English-language operas of his own: *The Gypsy's Warning* (1838), *The Brides of Venice* (1844) and *The Crusaders* (1846). His most popular opera, however, was *The Lily of Killarney*, staged at Covent Garden in 1862. Benedict was also an accomplished pianist, and composed a great deal of music for the piano, including a number of fantasias on themes from the operas of Balfe, Bellini, Donizetti, Gounod, Verdi and others.

Benjamin, Arthur, b. Sydney, 18 Sept 1893; d. London, 10 Apr 1960. Australian composer. He studied with Stanford in London, and after a period in which he taught piano at the Sydney conservatorium, he returned in 1921 to London where he lived for the rest of his life. He composed tuneful and agreeable music in all forms. His first opera, *The Devil Take Her*, a 1-act comic opera, was produced at the Royal College of Music in 1931. Eighteen years later, he produced a companion 1-act piece, *Prima Donna* (1949). His only full-length completed opera, *A Tale of Two Cities*, was produced by the New Opera Company in 1957. He had not orchestrated his final opera, *Tartuffe*, before his death. *Tartuffe* was orchestrated by A. Boustead and produced at Sadler's Wells in 1964. His *Mañana*, the first opera to be commissioned by BBC Television, was transmitted in 1956.

Bennett, Richard Rodney, b. 29 Mar 1936. English composer and pianist. A fluent composer of orchestral and chamber music and film scores, Bennett has composed five operas: *The Ledge* (1961), a 1-act piece to a text by Adrian Mitchell; *The Mines of Sulphur* (1965); *Penny for a Song* (1967) after the play by John Whiting; *All the King's Men* (1969), a children's opera with libretto by Beverley Cross; and *Victory* (1970), its libretto by Beverley Cross after the novel by Joseph Conrad. *Victory* was staged at Covent Garden, but was a failure and has not been revived. Though Bennett's music is euphonious, his operas lack musical personality and dramatic strength.

Benois, Alexandre, b. St Petersburg, 21 Apr 1870; d. Paris, 9 Feb 1960. Russian designer. He began his career as a designer with *Götterdämmerung* at the Maryinsky Theatre in 1903, and was engaged by Diaghilev to design *Boris Godunov* for performance in Paris in 1908. He worked mainly as a designer of ballets for Diaghilev until 1938, though he also designed the first production of Stravinsky's *The Nightingale* in 1914. He returned to opera when invited to join his son Nicola in 1938 at La Scala, where he designed sets for *Faust*, *Eugene Onegin*, *Lucia di Lammermoor* and several other works.

Benois, Nicola, b. St Petersburg, 2 May 1901. Russian designer. The son of

Alexandre Benois, he worked with his father on a number of ballets before being invited by Toscanini in 1925 to design opera sets at La Scala. In 1936 he became head of design at La Scala, a position he retained until 1970.

Benoît, Peter, b. Harlebeke, 17 Aug 1834; d. Antwerp, 8 Mar 1901. Belgian composer. An activist in the cause of Flemish culture, Benoît was principally a composer of vocal music to Flemish texts. His lyric dramas, plays in which the actors speak in strict rhythm accompanied by the orchestra, include *Charlotte Corday* (1876) and *De Pacificatie van Gent* (1876). *Le Roi des Aulnes* (1859) is an opera which Benoît wrote in his twenties to a French text.

Benucci, Francesco, b. *c.* 1745; d. Florence, 5 Apr 1824. Italian bass. He is remembered as the singer who created two important Mozart roles, Figaro and Guglielmo. After making his name in Italy in the 1770s, he became a leading member of the Italian company in Vienna in 1784, and was described by Mozart as 'particularly good'. The first Figaro (in 1786) and Guglielmo (1790), he did not sing in the première of *Don Giovanni* in Prague, but was the Leporello in the first Vienna production (1788) when Mozart composed an extra duet for Zerlina and Leporello (which is now rarely included in performances of the opera). Benucci sang in London in 1788-9, in operas of Paisiello and Gazzaniga, and in Vienna in 1792 created the role of the Englishman, Count Robinson, in Cimarosa's *Il Matrimonio Segreto*.

Benvenuto Cellini. Opera in 2 acts by Berlioz. Libretto by Léon de Wailly and Auguste Barbier, based on the autobiography of Benvenuto Cellini. First performed Paris, 10 Sept 1838.
Cellini (ten.) plans to elope with Teresa (sop.), daughter of the Papal Treasurer (bass), but at the same time is attempting to finish the casting of his masterpiece, the statue of Perseus. Threatened with arrest for murder if the work is not finished on time, Cellini succeeds in casting the statue.

Berenice. Opera in 3 acts by Handel. Libretto by Antonio Salvi. First performed London, 18 May 1737.

Berenice, Queen of Egypt (sop.), faces a number of difficulties. Under political pressure to marry Alessandro (sop.), she is in love with Demetrio (mezzo-sop.) who in turn loves Berenice's sister, Selene (mezzo-sop.). The opera ends with Berenice allowing the marriage of Selene and Demetrio. She herself marries Alessandro.

Berg, Alban, b. Vienna, 9 Feb 1885; d. Vienna, 24 Dec 1935. Austrian composer. Berg, his teacher Schoenberg, and his friend Webern together make up the trio of Viennese composers of twelve-tone music who were the leaders of the 'second Viennese school' of composition (the first presumably stretching from Gluck and Haydn to Mahler and Bruckner). Though Berg composed only two operas, and left the second unfinished, they are among the most powerful and influential operas of the 20th c. *Wozzeck* (1925), his masterpiece, is a drama of great compassion and can be profoundly affecting in performance. *Lulu*, first staged in incomplete form in 1937, has only in recent years come to be known in its full 3 acts. Musically fascinating, it is less compelling as drama than *Wozzeck*.

Berg, Natanael, b. Stockholm, 9 Feb 1879; d. Stockholm, 14 Oct 1957. Swedish composer. He studied in Stockholm, and was offered a large sum of money by a patron, provided he insured his future by taking up a non-musical profession in addition to composition. He therefore became a veterinary surgeon, and worked as such in the Swedish army for thirty-seven years. He composed five operas in a neo-romantic style, all to his own libretti: *Leila* (after Byron's *The Giaour*:1912), *Engelbrekt* (1929), *Judith* (after Hebbel: 1936), *Birgitta* (1942), and *Genoveva* (after Hebbel: 1947). All were staged in Stockholm.

Berganza, Teresa, b. Madrid, 16 Mar 1935. Spanish mezzo-soprano. After studying piano and singing in Madrid, she made her opera début at Aix-en-Provence in 1957 as Dorabella in *Così Fan Tutte*. Though she was heard at Dallas singing Neris in Cherubini's *Médée* (with Callas in the title-role), her greatest successes, due as much to her charm of manner as to her pure, evenly produced voice, have been in Mozart

Teresa Berganza as Rosina in Rossini's *The Barber of Seville*.

and Rossini roles. Her first British appearances were at Glyndebourne, as Cherubino (1958) and Cenerentola (1959). At Covent Garden in 1960 she sang Rosina in *Il Barbiere di Siviglia*. Her Carmen at the Edinburgh Festival in 1977 was thought to suffer from an excess of good taste: it is as Rossini's Cenerentola that she had few if any equals in the 1960-70s. She frequently gives recitals, mainly of Spanish songs, in which she is accompanied by her husband, Felix Lavilla.

Berger, Erna, b. Cossebaude, nr Dresden, 19 Oct 1900. German soprano. She studied in Dresden, and made her début there in 1925 as the First Boy in *Die Zauberflöte*. From 1929-33 she appeared at Bayreuth as the Shepherd in *Tannhäuser*, the Woodbird in *Siegfried* and a Flowermaiden in *Parsifal*, but went on to become Germany's leading lyric-coloratura soprano in the 1930-40s. Constanze in *Die Entführung aus dem Serail*

and the Queen of Night were roles in which she was unequalled for the beauty and agility of her voice, and they were the roles for which she was most admired in London in 1938, when she also sang Sophie in *Der Rosenkavalier*. In Germany she was also a famous Gilda in *Rigoletto*, a role which she sang with conspicuous success at the Met in 1950. She retired from the stage in 1955, but continued to give recitals until 1968, and to teach. Rita Streich and Erika Köth were among her pupils.

Berglund, Joel, b. Torsåker, 4 June 1903. Swedish bass-baritone. He made his début in Stockholm in 1929 as Monterone in *Rigoletto*, and sang leading roles in Stockholm and elsewhere for the next thirty years. Specializing in Wagner roles, he appeared as Hans Sachs, Wotan and the Flying Dutchman in Europe in the 1930s, and was the Bayreuth Dutchman in 1942. He first appeared at the Met in 1946, as Sachs. From 1949-52 he was director of the Stockholm Opera, and continued to make occasional appearances in opera until 1970.

Bergonzi, Carlo, b. Polisene, nr. Parma, 13 July 1924. Italian tenor. After studying in Parma, he made his début in Lecce in 1948 as Rossini's Figaro, and continued to sing as a baritone until 1951 when he made a second début at Bari as a tenor in the title-role of *Andrea Chénier*. For his first appearance at La Scala in 1953, he created the title-role in Napoli's *Masaniello*, and in the same year came to London to sing Alvaro in *La Forza del Destino* at the Stoll Theatre (since demolished). He has sung in the United States, principally in Chicago and New York, since 1955. Though his acting is rudimentary, Bergonzi is a most persuasive performer by virtue of the quality of his voice and, more importantly, the style and taste with which he uses it, especially in the middle-period operas of Verdi. He is also an admired Turiddu, and an engaging Nemorino.

Berio, Luciano, b. Oneglia, 24 Oct 1925. Italian composer. Though several of Berio's works contain elements of drama, none can properly be described as an opera, with the possible exception of *Opera*, a piece of *avant-garde* self-indulgence involving a number of musicians as well as a company of actors. It proved to be a fiasco when staged at Santa Fé in 1970. *Amores*, a chamber play, scored for sixteen solo voices and fourteen instruments, was performed at the Holland Festival in 1972. Several of Berio's concert works have been given staged performances.

Berkeley, (Sir) Lennox, b. Oxford, 12 May 1903. English composer. He studied in Paris with Nadia Boulanger for six years. Berkeley is not primarily an operatic composer: his first opera, *Nelson*, its libretto by Alan Pryce-Jones, was unsuccessful when produced at Sadler's Wells in 1953, and the composer's later three operas were all 1-act pieces. *A Dinner Engagement* (1954) is generally considered the best of them. The others are *Ruth* (libretto by Eric Crozier: 1956) and *The Castaway* (libretto by Paul Dehn: 1967).

Sir Lennox Berkeley.

Berlioz, Hector, b. La Côte-Saint-André, 11 Dec 1803; d. Paris, 8 Mar 1869. French composer. Berlioz's great gifts as a composer were always more impressively deployed in the concert hall than the opera house. Despite this, his lifelong ambition, fired by the success of Meyerbeer, was to succeed as a composer of opera. When *Benvenuto Cellini*, performed at the Paris Opéra in 1838, proved a failure, Berlioz turned for a time to works, like *La Damnation de Faust* and *L'Enfance du Christ*, which might be described as concert music yearning for the stage. With *Les Troyens*, composed in the 1850s, he returned to the opera house but with a work so vast that it could be performed complete only if spread over two evenings. Though full of musical felicities, the work lacks dramatic shape, and its music veers uneasily between a Gluckian classicism and the inflated grand opera style of Meyerbeer. For his final attempt to conquer the operatic stage, Berlioz turned to Shakespeare and fashioned from *Much Ado About Nothing* an oddly attractive though eccentric piece, *Béatrice et Bénédict*.

Bernauerin, Die (*The Bernauer Girl*). 'A Bavarian piece' (so described by its composer) in 1 act by Orff. Libretto by the composer in old Bavarian dialect, based on a 17th-c. Bavarian ballad. First performed Stuttgart, 15 June 1947.

Agnes Bernauer is accused of witchcraft. The work is essentially a spoken play with music, rather than an opera.

Bernstein, Leonard, b. Lawrence, Mass., 25 Aug 1918. American composer and conductor. Predominantly a man of the theatre, though he has written symphonic music as well, Bernstein has produced scores for opera, ballet and the peculiarly American genre of the musical. His first opera was a 1-act comedy, *Trouble in Tahiti* (1952) for which, thirty years later, he composed a sequel and companion piece, *A Quiet Place*. The operetta *Candide* (1956; revised and revived 1974), its plot based on Voltaire, contains much attractive music, but Bernstein's most successful work is his Broadway musical, *West Side Story*, whose libretto by Stephen Sondheim places the plot of *Romeo and Juliet* in a modern New York community of Puerto Ricans. First

41

staged in New York in 1957 it has been frequently revived and produced in many countries.

Bernstein has conducted a number of highly successful performances of opera, among them *La Sonnambula* with Callas at La Scala (1955), *Falstaff* at the Met (1964) and *Der Rosenkavalier* and *Fidelio* in Vienna.

Berry, Walter, b. Vienna, 8 Apr 1929. Austrian bass-baritone. He studied at the Vienna Academy of Music, and made his début with the Vienna Staatsoper in 1950, singing only small roles in his first three seasons. After his Masetto in 1953, he became a principal singer with the company, and has remained a member of the Staatsoper since then. In addition to such Mozart roles as Figaro, Leporello and Guglielmo, he has successfully undertaken Ochs in *Rosenkavalier*, and is a moving Barak in *Die Frau ohne Schatten*. It was as Barak that he made his Covent Garden début in 1976. Though he has sung abroad, his career is firmly based on Vienna, where his other roles include Escamillo, Pizarro and Wozzeck, which he has sung with Christa Ludwig, to whom he was married from 1957-71, as Marie. He is also a successful concert singer.

Bertati, Giovanni, b. Martellago, 10 July 1735; d. Venice, 1815. Italian librettist. He wrote more than seventy libretti, most of them composed in the style of Goldoni, the best known today being those for Cimarosa's *Il Matrimonio Segreto* and Gazzaniga's *Don Giovanni*. His *Don Giovanni* libretto influenced Da Ponte when he came to collaborate with Mozart on the same subject. Among the composers for whom Bertati provided libretti are Galuppi, Paisiello, Paer and Bianchi.

Besch, Anthony, b. London, 5 Feb 1924. English director. He assisted Carl Ebert at Glyndebourne in the early 1950s and staged *Der Schauspieldirektor* there in 1957. He has directed a number of operas for Sadler's Wells and English National Opera, and has also worked in Australia. His production of *La Clemenza di Tito* at Covent Garden in 1974 was exemplary, and his general approach to the staging of opera is agreeably free from any desire to promote himself in place of the work to be produced.

Besuch der Alten Dame, Der (*The Old Lady's Visit*). Opera in 3 acts by Einem. Libretto by Friedrich Dürrenmatt, after his play of the same title. First performed Vienna, 23 May 1971.

Now the richest woman in the world, Claire Zachanassian (mezzo-sop.) returns to her native town to be avenged upon her former lover (bar.), the father of her illegitimate child. She offers the town an immense sum of money if he is killed, and, though at first the town expresses its revulsion at her proposal, the offer is in fact accepted.

Bettelstudent, Der (*The Beggar Student*). Operetta in 3 acts by Millöcker. Libretto by F. Zell (Camillo Walzell) and Richard Genée. First performed Vienna, 6 Dec 1882.

Laura (sop.) is tricked into marrying Symon (ten.), a penniless student, thinking that he is a Prince and a millionaire. The operetta is set in Cracow in 1704, at a time when the ancient Polish capital was occupied by Saxon troops.

Bettinelli, Bruno, b. Milan, 4 June, 1913. Italian composer. He studied at the Milan Conservatorium and later taught there, becoming professor of composition in 1957. His three operas, all of which have been produced only in Italy, are *La Smorfia* (1959), *Il Pozzo e il Pendolo* (1967), its libretto based on Edgar Allan Poe's *The Pit and the Pendulum*, and *Count Down* (1970).

Bianca e Fernando. Opera in 2 acts by Bellini. Libretto by Domenico Gilardoni, based on the play *Bianca e Fernando alla Tomba di Carlo IV Duca di Agrigento* by Carlo Roti (1820). First performed Naples, 30 May 1826 (when it was called *Bianca e Gernando*).

Bianca (sop.) and Fernando (ten.), brother and sister, rescue their father the Duke of Agrigento (bar.) from the usurper, Filippo (bass).

Billy Budd. Opera in 2 acts (originally in 4) by Britten. Libretto by E. M. Forster and Eric Crozier, after Herman Melville's unfinished novel of the same title. First performed London, 1 Dec 1951.

Billy Budd (bar.), a handsome and innocent young sailor pressed into service during the Napoleonic wars, is falsely accused of treachery by the master-at-arms, Claggart (bass). Captain Vere (ten.) is unable to save Billy from being hanged at the yard-arm.

Bishop, (Sir) Henry, b. London, 18 Nov 1786; d. London, 30 Apr 1855. English composer and conductor. He was music director at Covent Garden from 1810 to 1824, and then became music director at Drury Lane. His first opera, *The Circassian Bride*, had been performed at Drury Lane in 1809, the night before the theatre was destroyed by fire, and the score of Bishop's opera with it. He made adaptations of operas by Mozart and Rossini for performance in the London opera houses, and composed a vast number of songs and other vocal pieces for insertion in plays and other composers' operas. Among these is the song by which he is remembered today, 'Home, Sweet Home', the tune of which Bishop first published, identifying it as Sicilian, in a volume, *National Airs*, which he edited in 1821. He then used it as a song in his opera, *Clari* or *The Maid of Milan* (1823: libretto by the American poet John Howard Payne), in which form the tune soon became known throughout Europe, even making its way into Donizetti's *Anna Bolena* (1830) and Verdi's *Nabucco* (1842).

The list of Bishop's works for the stage is long, but only *Aladdin* (1826) can properly be described as an opera. The majority of his stage works are plays into which one or more musical numbers have been inserted.

Bispham, David, b. Philadelphia, 5 Jan 1857; d. New York, 2 Oct 1921. American baritone. He studied in Florence and Milan, and made his début in London in 1891 at the Royal English Opera House (now the Palace Theatre) in Messager's *La Basoche*. The following year he sang Kurwenal at Drury Lane, and in 1893 appeared at Covent Garden where he sang Fiorenzo in Mascagni's *I Rantzau*. He continued to appear at Covent Garden during the following decade, and also at the Met, where his first role was Beckmesser. He sang most of the Wagner baritone roles, and was a great advocate of opera in English. After 1902, he devoted himself mainly to recitals and to teaching. Something of Bispham's style, and indeed his nasal resonance which was thought by some to verge on the excessive, could be heard in the performances of his best-known pupil, the baritone Nelson Eddy.

Bittner, Julius, b. Vienna, 9 Apr 1874; d. Vienna, 9 or 10 Jan 1939. Austrian composer. Mainly self-taught in music, he composed in his spare time, while pursuing a career first as a lawyer and later as a judge. He composed about twenty operas, as well as chamber music and symphonies. Many of his operas remain unperformed, but several were produced, mainly in Vienna. These include *Der Musikant* (1910), *Der Bergsee* (1911; revised version produced in Vienna 1939) and *Das Veilchen* (1934). He wrote his own libretti, often using Austrian dialect. The simplicity and charm of both words and music made his operas popular for a time in Vienna, but they have failed to survive.

Bizet, Georges, b. Paris, 25 Oct 1838; d. Bougival, nr Paris, 3 June 1875. French composer. He studied composition at the Paris Conservatoire with Halévy, and was also strongly influenced by Gounod. Opera was the branch of composition in which he was most interested. His 1-act *opéra comique*, *Le Docteur Miracle* (1857) won a prize offered by Offenbach, and was produced in Offenbach's theatre. Having won the *Prix de Rome* in 1857 Bizet spent nearly three years in Rome and there composed *Don Procopio*, a 2-act comic opera in the style of Donizetti.

Bizet's earliest mature and individual work for the stage is *Les Pêcheurs de Perles* (1863), which was followed by *La Jolie Fille de Perth* (1867). Other stage works were either unsuccessful or remained unperformed. Bizet finally achieved lasting success with what proved to be his final opera, *Carmen*, composed in 1873-4, and staged only a few weeks before his death.

Bjoner, Ingrid, b. Kråkstad, nr Oslo, 8 Nov 1927. Norwegian soprano. After studying in Oslo and Frankfurt, she was engaged by Kirsten Flagstad for the Norwegian National Opera, with whom she made her début in 1957 as Donna Anna. She then began to appear in Germany, and made her Bayreuth début in 1960 as Freia. In the 1960s she became a leading Wagner dramatic soprano, singing throughout Europe and at the Met. Senta and Isolde are among her most successful Wagner roles, and she was also a distinguished Strauss soprano, especially as Ariadne and as the Empress in *Die Frau ohne Schatten*.

Björling, Jussi, b. Stora Tuna, 5 Feb 1911; d. Stockholm, 9 Sept 1960. Swedish tenor. As a child he was a member of the Björling family quartet of singers with his father and two brothers. After studying at the Stockholm Conservatorium, he made his début in 1930 with the Royal Swedish Opera in Stockholm, in the small role of the Lamplighter in *Manon Lescaut*, when he was only nineteen. His beautiful and securely placed voice quickly won him renown. Within weeks of his début he was singing leading roles, the first of which was Ottavio in *Don Giovanni*, and he was soon in demand in other European cities. He first sang in Vienna in 1936, and in the United States, in Chicago, the following year. His Covent Garden début was in 1939, as Manrico, but

Jussi Björling as Roméo in Gounod's *Roméo et Juliette* in Stockholm.

although he gave recitals in London in the 1950s he did not appear again at the Royal Opera House until he sang Rodolfo, within weeks of his death in 1960. Rodolfo had also been the role of his Met début in 1939, and he sang regularly at the Met thereafter, except between 1941-5 when he remained in Sweden. Despite his inability or unwillingness to act, he was greatly in demand in the popular Verdi and Puccini roles in which, as a singer, he was unequalled in his prime. The timbre of his voice may not have been Italianate; but his singing was always in the best of musical taste.

Björling, Sigurd, b. Stockholm, 2 Nov 1907; d. Helsingborg, 8 April 1983. Swedish baritone. He studied in Stockholm, and made his début there in 1934 in the small role of Billy Jackrabbit in *La Fanciulla del West*. Later he specialized in Wagner roles, sang Wotan in the first post-World War II *Ring* at Bayreuth, and was active in the 1950s at Covent Garden, the Met and several European houses, usually in Wagner. His active career in Stockholm continued until the mid-1970s.

Blacher, Boris, b. Niu-chang, China, 19 Jan 1903; d. Berlin, 30 Jan 1975. German composer. He studied, and later taught, in Berlin. His first opera, *Fürstin Tarakanova*, was produced in Wuppertal in 1941. *Romeo und Julia* (1943) was composed during World War II but not staged until 1947. *Preussisches Märchen* (*Prussian Fairytale*) is a ballet-opera, composed in 1949, based on the famous story of the Captain of Köpenick who mocks German veneration for authority. With *Zweihunderttausend Taler*, Blacher combined fantasy and social criticism, while in *Abstrakte Oper no.1* (1953), its libretto by his fellow-composer Werner Egk, he moved into the area of abstract art which was so fashionable in the 1950s.

Blacher's operas are not known outside Germany. His international reputation is as a composer of orchestral and instrumental works.

Blachut, Beno, b. Ostrava-Vitkovice, 14 June 1913. Czech tenor. He studied in Prague, made his début in Olomouc in 1939 as Jenik in *The Bartered Bride*, and in 1941 became a member of the Prague National Theatre company. The leading Czech tenor of his time, he graduated from lyric to dramatic tenor roles, and was renowned in the title-role of Smetana's *Dalibor*. Though he occasionally made guest appearances abroad, he sang mainly in Czechoslovakia. In the latter part of his career he turned to buffo parts. In addition to his Czech roles, he was much admired in Prague as Radames and Florestan.

Blanc, Ernest, b. Sanary, 1 Nov 1923. French baritone. After studying in Toulon and Paris, he joined the Marseilles Opéra in 1950 and the Paris Opéra in 1954. Rigoletto and Scarpia were two of the roles in which he was particularly successful. He sang Telramund at Bayreuth in 1958 and 1959, and at Glyndebourne in 1960 he appeared as Don Giovanni and in *I Puritani* as Riccardo. He was also well received in San Francisco and Chicago, and failed to have an important international career only because he lacked the necessary ambition, preferring to sing in his own country.

Blech, Leo, b. Aachen, 21 Apr 1871; d. Berlin, 24 Aug 1958. German conductor and composer. He began his conducting career in Aachen at the Stadttheater in 1893, and became conductor of the Berlin Hofoper in 1906 and music director there in 1913. He continued to work mainly in Berlin until 1937 when, being Jewish, he was forced to leave. He spent the war years in Stockholm, but returned to conduct in Berlin in 1949. He was an excellent conductor with a wide repertory. In his younger days he composed several operas with which he achieved success in Germany. The most popular were *Das War Ich*, staged in Dresden in 1902, and *Versiegelt* (Hamburg, 1908).

Blegen, Judith, b. Missoula, Mont., 27 Apr 1941. American soprano. After study at the Curtis Institute, Philadelphia, and an apprenticeship with the Santa Fe Opera Festival, she began her European career in 1966 at Nuremberg. The success of her Mélisande at Spoleto in 1966 led to engagements in Vienna, Salzburg and with several American companies. Her lyric soprano is particularly suited to such Mozart roles as Despina, Zerlina and Susanna; she was a charming and accomplished Sophie in *Der Rosenkavalier* at the Met, and in Menotti's *Help, Help, the Globolinks!* at Santa Fe in 1969 she not only sang but also played the violin.

Bliss, (Sir) Arthur, b. London, 2 Aug 1891; d. London, 27 Mar 1975. English composer. A prolific composer of orchestral, choral and chamber music, Bliss composed only two operas. His first, *The Olympians*, was staged at Covent Garden in 1949, since when it has not been heard. His second, *Tobias and the Angel* (libretto by Christopher Hassall), was composed for BBC Television in 1960, and later adapted for the stage.

Blitzstein, Marc, b. Philadelphia, 2 Mar 1905; d. Martinique, 22 Jan 1964. American composer. He studied with Nadia Boulanger in Paris and with Arnold Schoenberg in Berlin. His earliest works employed a modern experimental style; but after attending lectures by Hanns Eisler in New York on 'The Crisis in Music' he began to feel the need to express his own social awareness through his music, and from then on adopted a simpler musical language, especially for his theatre works. *The Cradle Will Rock* (1937) reflected his enthusiasm for left-wing causes.

His attitude perhaps modified by World War II, during which he served with the US Air Force in England and composed music for propaganda purposes, Blitzstein's return to opera was with a non-political drama, *Regina*, based on Lillian Hellman's play, *The Little Foxes*. His translation and adaptation of the Brecht-Weill *Dreigroschenoper* ran for several years in New York in the 1950s as *The Threepenny Opera*. At his death, he left several operatic projects incomplete, among them *Saccho and Vanzetti*, commissioned by the Met, and two 1-act pieces based on stories by Bernard Malamud.

Bloch, Ernest, b. Geneva, 24 July 1880; d. Portland, Oregon, 15 July 1959. Swiss, later American composer. Known specifically as a Jewish composer because so many of his orchestral and instrumental works are inspired by Jewish themes, Bloch composed only one opera. *Macbeth*, staged at the Opéra-Comique, Paris, in 1910, owes something in style to Debussy's *Pelléas et Mélisande* but is at the same time an original and arresting work. It was revived in Geneva in the 1968-9 season, and given in concert form in London in 1975.

Blockx, Jan, b. Antwerp, 25 Jan 1851; d. Kapellenbos, nr Antwerp, 26 May 1912. Belgian composer. He was the most highly regarded Flemish composer of his day, and his seven operas with their romantic attitude to folklore were immensely popular in Belgium. His first major opera was his most successful: *Herbergprinses* (*The Princess of the Inn*). When it was staged in Antwerp in 1896, it was thought to herald the beginning of Flemish national opera. *De Bruid der Zee* (*The Bride of the Sea*: 1901) was equally successful. It was revived in Brussels in 1958.

Blomdahl, Karl-Birger, b. Växjö, 19 Oct 1916; d. Växjö, 14 June 1968. Swedish composer. A composer whose styles changed to keep pace with international fashion, Blomdahl began in the manner of Sibelius, and ended as a purveyor of electronic music. His first opera, *Aniara* (1959), was highly successful; his second, *Herr von Hancken* (1965), less so. At his death he was working on a third opera, *Sagan om den Stora Datan*.

Blonde [or Blondchen] (sop.). Constanze's maid in Mozart's *Die Entführung aus dem Serail*.

Blow, John, b. Newark, Notts, Feb, 1649, baptized 23 Feb; d. London, 1 Oct 1708. English composer. A leader of the school of composition of which Henry Purcell was the most brilliantly gifted, Blow composed only one work for the stage, *Venus and Adonis* (*c.* 1684), a predecessor of Purcell's *Dido and Aeneas* and thus a piece which can claim to be the earliest English opera.

Boatswain's Mate, The. Opera in 1 act by Smyth. Libretto by the composer, based on a story by W. W. Jacobs. First performed London, 28 Jan 1916.

Mrs Waters (sop.), landlady of the Beehive, thwarts Harry's (ten.) plot to trick her into marriage, and expresses a preference for Harry's friend, Ned (bar.).

Boccaccio. Operetta in 3 acts by Suppé. Libretto by F. Zell (Camillo Walzell) and Richard Genée. First performed Vienna, 1 Feb 1879.

A complicated fictional plot involves the 14th-c. Italian prose writer and poet,

Boccaccio (bar.), and ends with his betrothal to Fiametta (sop.), adopted daughter of a grocer but really the daughter of the Duke of Tuscany (bass).

Bockelmann, Rudolf, b. Bodenteich, 2 Apr 1892; d. Dresden, 9 Oct 1958. German bass-baritone. He made his début in Leipzig in 1921 as the Herald in *Lohengrin*, and until 1945 appeared regularly at the leading German opera houses. In the 1930s he also sang in London and Chicago. Primarily a Wagner singer, he was an admired Hans Sachs and Wotan, and in Leipzig in 1930 he created the title-role of Křenek's *Leben des Orest*. His known Nazi sympathies prevented him from resuming his singing career after 1945, but he taught in Hamburg until 1954 and then became professor of singing at the High School for Music in Dresden.

Bodanzky, Artur, b. Vienna, 16 Dec 1877; d. New York, 23 Nov 1939. Austrian conductor. He studied the violin in Vienna and began his career as a violinist in the orchestra of the Vienna Hofoper. In 1903 he became assistant to Gustav Mahler who was at that time the Director of the Opera. He conducted the first English performance of *Parsifal* at Covent Garden in 1914, made his Met début with *Götterdämmerung* in 1915, and conducted regularly at the Met for the rest of his life. Though he was best known as a Wagner specialist, he conducted much of the German 19th-c. repertory at the Met and some 20th-c. works, including the American première of Křenek's *Jonny Spielt Auf*.

Boero, Felipe, b. Buenos Aires, 1 May 1884; d. Buenos Aires, 9 Aug 1958. Argentinian composer. After studying in Paris with Fauré he returned to Argentina and played an important role in musical politics. Six of his operas were staged at the Teatro Colón, Buenos Aires. *Tucumán* (1918) was the first Argentinian nationalist opera in Spanish, and *Raquela* (1923) the first to incorporate regional folk dances into its score. *El Matrero* (*The Rogue*: 1929), based on the symbolist play by Yamandú Rodríguez, is one of the most popular of operas in Argentina.

Bohème, La (*Bohemian Life*). Opera in 4 acts by Puccini. Libretto by Giuseppe

Marilyn Zschau as Musetta, Neil Shicoff as Rodolfo, Ileana Cotrubas as Mimi and Thomas Allen as Marcello in Puccini's *La Bohème* at Covent Garden in 1982.

Giacosa and Luigi Illica, based on the novel, *Scènes de la Vie de Bohème* by Henry Murger. First performed Turin, 1 Feb 1896.

In the Latin Quarter of Paris in 1830, four young Bohemians share a studio: Rodolfo (ten.), a poet; Marcello (bar.), a painter; Colline (bass), a philosopher; and Schaunard (bar.), a musician. The opera's main concern is with the love of one of them, Rodolfo, for Mimi (sop.), a seamstress, fatally ill with consumption. On the evening when Rodolfo and Mimi first meet, Marcello recovers his ex-lover, Musetta (sop.), from a wealthy admirer. Some months later, unable to bear Rodolfo's irrational jealousy, Mimi leaves him, to return only when she is brought in, dying, by Musetta. The Bohemians try to save her, but it is too late.

An opera of the same title, also based on Murger's novel, was composed by Leoncavallo (who wrote his own libretto) at the same time that Puccini was at work on his opera. Leoncavallo's *La Bohème*, also in 4 acts, was first performed in Venice, 6 May 1897. Though it follows more closely the events in the novel, it has never achieved the immense popularity of Puccini's opera.

Bohemian Girl, The. Opera in 3 acts by Balfe. Libretto by Alfred Bunn, based on the ballet-pantomime, *La Gipsy*, by Jules-Henri Vernoy de Saint-Georges, produced in Paris in 1839, and itself based on Cervantes' story *La Gitanella*. First performed London, 27 Nov 1843.

A tale of love, intrigue and mistaken identity, set in Poland. The characters

47

include the Queen of the Gipsies (contr.), a gipsy chief named Devilshoof (bass), and Arline (sop.), a Count's daughter stolen and brought up by gipsies.

Böhm, Karl, b. Graz, 28 Aug 1894; d. Salzburg, 14 Aug 1981. Austrian conductor. After studying in Graz and Vienna, he made his début in Graz in 1917 with Nessler's *Der Trompeter von Säckingen*. He was engaged by various German opera houses, eventually making his way to Dresden where he was Music Director from 1934-42. He then began to conduct regularly in Vienna, and was for a brief period in charge of the newly re-opened Vienna Opera in 1955. He continued to conduct, mainly in Vienna, though with frequent guest appearances at the Met and elsewhere, until his death. He was, together with his chief rival, Herbert von Karajan, a mainstay of the Salzburg Festival for several years, specializing in the operas of Mozart and Strauss. He was also a greatly admired Wagner conductor at Bayreuth. He was the last survivor of a great generation of Austro-German conductors of the Viennese classics, and his death really did signify the end of an era.

Böhme, Kurt, b. Dresden, 5 May 1908. German bass. He studied in Dresden and made his début in 1929 in Bautzen (near Dresden) as Caspar in *Der Freischütz*. He sang with the Dresden company from 1930-50, and then joined the Bavarian State Opera at Munich. In Dresden in 1935 he created the small role of Vanuzzi in Strauss's *Die Schweigsame Frau*, and in the post-World War II years became a noted interpreter of the leading role of Morosus in the same opera. From 1942 for a good thirty years he was one of the two or three singers most associated with the role of Baron Ochs, a role for which his ebullient stage personality was well suited. He first sang at Covent Garden with the Dresden Opera in 1936 as the Commendatore in *Don Giovanni*, and returned to London in Wagner roles in the 1950s. He made his Met début in 1954. He was still singing in opera, mainly in Munich, in 1982.

Bohnen, Michael, b. Cologne, 2 May 1887; d. Berlin, 26 Apr 1965. German bass-baritone. He made his début in Düsseldorf in 1910 as Caspar in *Der Freischütz*, and made his way via Wiesbaden to Berlin. He sang at the Deutsches Opernhaus, Berlin (later the Städtische Oper) from 1933-45, and then became administrator of the company until 1947. He sang in London in 1914, both at Drury Lane (as Ochs and Sarastro) and at Covent Garden (as King Henry in *Lohengrin*). He appeared at the Met on many occasions between 1922-33. Bohnen's wide vocal range allowed him to undertake both bass and baritone roles: Scarpia and Amonasro were among the latter. After 1933, he confined his appearances to Germany.

Boïeldieu, Adrien, b. Rouen, 16 Dec 1775; d. Jarcy, 8 Oct 1834. French composer. The leading French composer of *opéra comique* during the first quarter of the 19th c., he composed his first opera, *La Fille Coupable*, at the age of eighteen. His first work to be performed in Paris was *La Famille Suisse* (1797) which was favourably received. *Le Calife de Bagdad* (1800) was enormously successful at the Opéra-Comique, but it is upon his later works that Boïeldieu's reputation now securely rests. *Jean de Paris* (1812) and his masterpiece, the charming and tuneful *La Dame Blanche* (1825), were composed after he had spent several years in Russia. *Les Deux Nuits* (1829), a fascinating work in which Boïeldieu changed and developed his style, proved too unfamiliar to be successful. It awaits rediscovery.

Boito, Arrigo, b. Padua, 24 Feb 1842; d. Milan, 10 June 1918. Italian composer and librettist. Boito experienced considerable difficulty in sustaining his creative impulses as a composer, and was much more active as a librettist. When his first opera, *Mefistofele*, failed at La Scala in 1868, he made a number of revisions to it on several occasions in later years, but concentrated his energies on writing libretti for other composers, and on translating foreign operas into Italian. He worked on and off for the rest of his life on his second opera, *Nerone*, but never completed it. It was performed posthumously in an edition made by Toscanini and Vincenzo Tommasini.

Boito wrote libretti for Catalani, Ponchielli (*La Gioconda*) and Franco Faccio, but it is as Verdi's librettist that he is remembered. He first collaborated with Verdi on a revision of *Simon Boccanegra*, for

Arrigo Boito. He greatly prized his friendship with Verdi.

performance in 1881, and later was instrumental in persuading the elderly composer to work on *Otello* (1887) and *Falstaff* (1893), the libretti of which, based on Shakespeare, were written by Boito.

Bolivar. Opera in 3 acts by Milhaud. Libretto by Madeleine Milhaud and Jules Supervielle. First performed Paris, 12 May 1950. The opera is based on events in the life of Simón Bolívar (1783-1830), the Venezuelan revolutionary leader and statesman.

Bomarzo. Opera in 2 acts by Ginastera. Libretto by Manuel Mujica Láinez, after his novel of the same title (1962). First performed Washington D.C., 19 May 1967.
  The opera takes place in 16th-c. Italy, its hero a hunchback Duke (ten.) who is sexually impotent and the victim of persecution, either real or imagined.

Bonci, Alessandro, b. Cesena, 10 Feb 1870; d. Viserba, 9 Aug 1940. Italian tenor. He studied for some years in Pesaro and Paris before making his début in Parma, in 1896, as Fenton. By the following year he had appeared at La Scala in *I Puritani*, and was soon acclaimed throughout Italy and, by the turn of the century, abroad, as the only serious rival to Caruso. He sang in London for the first time in *La Bohème* in 1900, and first appeared in the USA in 1906 in *I Puritani* at the opening of Hammerstein's new Manhattan Opera House. He continued to sing until 1925, and then taught. His voice was a lighter instrument than Caruso's, a sweet lyric tenor which he deployed with more elegance than his rival was wont to display.

Bondeville, Emmanuel, b. Rouen, 29 Oct 1898. French composer. The artistic director of the Monte Carlo Opera from 1945-9, he then became director first of the Paris Opéra-Comique (1949) and then of the Opéra, from which post he retired in 1970. His first opera, *L'École des Maris*, a comedy based on Molière, first performed at the Opéra-Comique in 1935, was popular in France in the 1930s. In 1951 it was followed by *Madame Bovary*, based on Flaubert's novel, and in 1972 by *Antoine et Cléopatre*, after Victor Hugo's translation of the Shakespeare play.

Boninsegna, Celestina, b. Reggio Emilia, 26 Feb 1877; d. Milan, 14 Feb 1947. Italian soprano. After very little training, she made her début in Reggio Emilia at the age of fifteen, as Norina in *Don Pasquale*. She then studied at the Conservatorium in Pesaro, and in 1897 sang Marguerite in Bari. A dramatic soprano of great range and volume, she appeared at the leading theatres of Europe, as well as Covent Garden and the Met, until 1920, and then began to teach. She was considered to be at her best in the operas of Verdi: with the exception of *Cavalleria Rusticana* and *Tosca* she tended to ignore the modern repertory of her time.

Bonisolli, Franco, b. Rovereto, *c.* 1935. Italian tenor. After winning an Italian singing competition in 1961, he made his début at Spoleto in 1962 as Ruggero in *La Rondine*. During the 1960s he sang at many of the leading opera houses in Europe, and made his New York début at the Met in 1971, when he sang Gounod's Faust and

Donizetti's Nemorino. He was first heard at Covent Garden in 1981 as Vasco da Gama in *L'Africaine*. An exciting if ill-disciplined singer, with a fine dramatic voice, his style is more'suited to *verismo* than to the Verdi roles he undertakes. He appeared in a film version of *La Traviata* with Mirella Freni.

Bononcini, Giovanni, b. Modena, 18 July 1670; d. Vienna, 9 July 1747. Italian composer. He worked in a number of countries, moving from Italy to Austria and then to England, and by his thirties was famous as a composer throughout Europe. His first operas were produced in Rome and in Vienna, but his career at its height was based on London where he arrived in 1720. Many of his operas were produced there beginning with *Erminia* at the Haymarket Theatre in 1723. During the 1720s his popularity in London rivalled that of Handel, the supporters of each composer deriding the abilities of the other. This led to the emergence of a third opinion, expressed in a verse which went the rounds:

Some say, compared to Bononcini,
That Mein Herr Handel's but a ninny.
Others aver that he to Handel
Is scarcely fit to hold a candle.
Strange that this difference should be
'Twixt Tweedledum and Tweedledee.

Eight operas by Bononcini were produced at the Haymarket, before public taste turned decisively in Handel's favour. Bononcini eventually returned to Vienna where he died in obscurity.

Bonynge, Richard, b. Sydney, 29 Sept 1930. Australian conductor and pianist. He studied piano in Sydney and London, and gave a successful recital at the Wigmore Hall, London, in 1954. In that year he married the soprano Joan Sutherland, whom he had been advising and coaching in the dramatic coloratura repertoire, and in due course their careers progressed jointly. He has frequently acted as his wife's accompanist, and made his début as a conductor in Vancouver in 1963 when she sang Marguerite in *Faust*. He first appeared at Covent Garden with *I Puritani* in 1964, and at the Met in 1970 conducting *Norma* with Joan Sutherland, and Gluck's *Orfeo* with Grace Bumbry and Graziella Tucci. He has been music director of Australian Opera since 1975, but continues to conduct abroad.

In addition to operas, he has also made first-rate recordings of ballet music. Though it can hardly be denied that his career as a conductor was initially helped by his association with Joan Sutherland, it is equally true that his special gifts in bel canto opera have sometimes received less than their due because of that association.

Borg, Kim, b. Helsinki, 7 Aug 1919. Finnish bass. He studied in Helsinki, and made his début in 1951 in Århus, Denmark. He sang at Glyndebourne in 1956 as Don Giovanni, and later as Gremin in *Eugene Onegin*, and made his Met début in 1959, but his career was based mainly on Helsinki, Copenhagen, Hamburg and Stockholm. His voice was mellifluous, and used with fine musicianship, but his stage personality was too pallid for the world of opera. He was, however, an admired Boris Godunov in Scandinavia.

Borgatti, Giuseppe, b. Cento, 17 Mar 1871; d. Reno, Lago Maggiore, 18 Oct 1950. Italian tenor. He made his début in 1892 as Faust, at Castelfranco Veneto, created the title-role of *Andrea Chénier* at La Scala in 1896, and went on to become the leading Italian exponent of the Wagner heroic tenor roles. He sang Tristan and Siegfried under Toscanini at La Scala. His career was confined mainly to Italy and South America: after he sang Parsifal at La Scala in 1914, failing eyesight forced his premature retirement from the stage. In 1923 he became completely blind. His voice was of more beguiling quality than is normally to be expected from a Heldentenor.

Borgioli, Armando, b. Florence, 19 Mar 1898; d. nr Bologna, 20 Jan 1945. Italian baritone. He made his début in Milan in 1925 as Amonasro, and sang at Covent Garden and the Met as well as the leading Italian theatres during the 1930s. He was greatly admired in the Verdi baritone roles. During World War II he made guest appearances in Germany and Holland. He was killed when the train in which he was travelling from Milan to Bologna suffered an air attack.

Borgioli, Dino, b. Florence, 15 Feb 1891; d. Florence, 12 Sept 1960. Italian tenor. After studying in Florence, he made his début in Milan in 1917, in *La Favorita*. An elegant stylist with a lyric tenor voice of moderate size but pleasant timbre, he was admired in Milan especially in Rossini. His Covent Garden début in 1925 was as Edgardo in *Lucia di Lammermoor*, and he continued to appear at Covent Garden throughout the 1930s. The Duke in *Rigoletto* was the heaviest role he undertook. At Glyndebourne, he sang Ernesto in *Don Pasquale* and Ottavio in *Don Giovanni* between 1937-9. He settled in London as a teacher (his pupils including Joan Hammond), and produced operas for the seasons at the Cambridge Theatre, London, in the immediate post-World War II years.

Bori, Lucrezia, b. Valencia, 24 Dec 1887; d. New York, 14 May 1960. Spanish soprano. She made her début in Rome in 1908 as Micaëla in *Carmen*, and in 1910 in Paris sang in *Manon* opposite Caruso. She first sang at the Met in 1912 as Puccini's Manon, and was a popular favourite at the Met until 1936 when she retired. She then became the first woman to serve on the Met's board of directors. She never sang in England. Her voice was an appealing lyric soprano, and she was at her best in such roles as Massenet's Manon and Puccini's Mimi.

Boris Godunov. Opera in a prologue and 4 acts by Mussorgsky. Libretto by the

A scene from Mussorgsky's *Boris Godunov*, staged in Estonia with Tiit Kuuzik as Boris.

composer, based on Pushkin's drama, *The Comedy of the Distress of the Muscovite State, of Tsar Boris, and of Grishka Otrepiev* (1826), and also on Nicolai Karamzin's *History of the Russian Empire* (1829). First performed complete, St Petersburg, 8 Feb 1874. Revised after the composer's death by Rimsky-Korsakov, and performed St Petersburg, 10 Dec 1896.

Having murdered Dmitry, the heir to the Russian throne, Boris Godunov (bass) is crowned as Tsar. The old monk, Pimen (bass), is concluding his history of Russia. With him is the novice, Grigory (ten.), who flees from the monastery and escapes into Poland whence he returns, having won the love of the Polish princess Marina (mezzo-sop.) and proclaims himself to be Dmitry. By now racked with guilt, Boris Godunov begins to have hallucinations. The false Dmitry marches upon Moscow. In the Council Hall, an edict against the Pretender is being read when Boris breaks in, in a state of mental and physical collapse, and falls dead. Grigory, the Pretender, advances inexorably towards Moscow, while a Simpleton (ten.) sings mournfully of the plight of the country.

Borkh, Inge, b. Mannheim, 26 May 1917. Swiss-Austrian soprano. Born of a Swiss father and an Austrian mother, she studied acting in Vienna and made her début as an actress there at the Burgtheater. After taking voice lessons in Vienna and Milan, she made her début as a singer in Lucerne in 1941. She sang in Swiss opera houses until 1951, when her success as Magda in *The Consul* in Basle led to engagements in Germany and Austria. In the 1950-60s she was a leading dramatic soprano, her greatest successes being as Strauss's Elektra, the role of her US début at San Francisco in 1953, and Lady Macbeth, which she sang there two years later. London first heard her as Elektra in 1953, as Salome in 1959 and as the Dyer's Wife in *Die Frau ohne Schatten* in 1967. She was a compelling actress, and a singer of great dramatic power.

Borodin, Alexander, b. St Petersburg, 12 Nov 1833; d. St Petersburg, 27 Feb 1887. Russian composer. His first opera was a farce, *The Bogatirs* (1867), composed to a libretto by Victor Krylov. This was the only opera which Borodin actually completed, and it was only partly original, much of its score being arranged from themes of Rossini, Meyerbeer, Offenbach, Verdi and others. It was a failure when produced at the Bolshoi Theatre, and disappeared until the 1930s when it was revived in Moscow, only to be withdrawn again, this time due to government rather than public disapproval.

Borodin began a second opera, *The Tsar's Bride*, based on the play by L. A. Mey, but did not progress beyond a few sketches. When the critic Vladimir Stasov sent him the scenario for an opera based on a 12th-c. epic, the composer enthusiastically turned his attention to it, and worked on *Prince Igor*, though intermittently, for some years. He did not, however, complete the opera. His only other work for the stage was his contribution of the fourth act to the collective opera, *Mlada*, a project which was abandoned. (*Mlada* was eventually composed by Rimsky-Korsakov alone.)

Boué, Geori, b. Toulouse, 16 Oct 1918. French soprano. She made her début in Toulouse in 1935 and, after studying in Paris with Reynaldo Hahn, sang in operetta in the French provinces before coming to the Opéra-Comique in Paris in the title-role of Gounod's *Mireille*. One of the finest French lyric sopranos of the 1940s, she continued to sing in operetta in Paris, after a certain hardening of her timbre had led to her relinquishing her operatic roles. She was married to the baritone Roger Bourdin (b. Paris, 1900; d. Paris, 1973) who sang in both Paris opera houses from 1922-52, and who was heard at Covent Garden in 1930 as Pelléas.

Boughton, Rutland, b. Aylesbury, 23 Jan 1878; d. London, 24 Jan 1960. English composer. In 1914 he went to live at Glastonbury, and devoted himself to an attempt to create there an English Bayreuth where his own operas and those of other English composers could be performed under festival conditions. He envisaged his own Arthurian cycle as an English counterpart of the *Ring*; but neither *The Birth of Arthur* nor *The Round Table* succeeded at Glastonbury, while much later operas in the cycle, *Galahad* and *Avalon*, written in the 1940s, remained unperformed.

Boughton's one successful opera was *The Immortal Hour*, first staged at Glastonbury in

1914, and revived in Birmingham and London in 1921-2 when it became widely popular. *Alkestis*, based on Gilbert Murray's translation of Euripides (Glastonbury, 1922), reached Covent Garden in 1924.

Bouilly, Jean-Nicolas, b. La Coudraye, 23 Jan 1763; d. Paris, 14 Apr 1842. French librettist. He wrote libretti for a number of composers, among them Auber, Boïeldieu and Méhul, achieving his greatest success with his libretto for Cherubini's *Les Deux Journées* in 1800. He is historically important for having written the text of an opera, *Léonore, ou L'Amour Conjugale* (1798) by a now forgotten composer, Pierre Gaveaux. The libretto of *Léonore* was taken up, adapted and translated by other composers, among whom was Beethoven who created *Fidelio* from it.

Boulevard Solitude. Opera in 7 scenes by Henze. Libretto by the composer and Grete Weil. First performed Hanover, 17 Feb 1952.

The opera is a modern retelling of the plot of Prévost's *Manon Lescaut*, set in Paris in the 1940s, in which Des Grieux (ten.), a drug addict, is killed by Manon (sop.).

Boulez, Pierre, b. Montbrison, 26 Mar 1925. French composer and conductor. A leading composer of his generation, Boulez conducts mainly in the concert hall and principally his own music. Though he once gave it as his view that all conventional opera houses should be destroyed, he has occasionally been tempted to conduct in them. His *Wozzeck* at the Paris Opéra in 1965 was highly regarded, as was his *Pelléas et Mélisande,* a performance of unusual clarity, at Covent Garden in 1969. In 1976 he conducted the *Ring* at Bayreuth in a highly controversial production by his friend Patrice Chéreau, and in 1979 he returned to the Paris Opéra and to Berg with the first complete, 3-act, performance of *Lulu*.

Bovy, Vina, b. Ghent, 22 May 1900. Belgian soprano. She studied in Ghent, and made her début there in 1918 in Poise's *Les Deux Billets*. After three seasons at the Théâtre de la Monnaie, Brussels, she was encouraged by Toscanini to undertake further study in Milan. She sang in Italy and South America and, from 1936-8, at the Met, where her roles included Gounod's Juliet and all four soprano parts in *Les Contes d'Hoffmann*. During World War II her appearances were confined mainly to Paris. From 1947-55 she was director of the Royal Opera, Ghent, and made her last appearance as a singer at Ostend in 1964. She had a fine coloratura technique, and a voice whose timbre was well suited to the French lyric soprano roles.

Bowman, James, b. Oxford, 6 Nov 1941. English countertenor. A boy chorister at Ely Cathedral, he made his stage début at the Aldeburgh Festival in 1967, as Oberon in Britten's *A Midsummer Night's Dream*, a role which he subsequently sang on the continent and in San Francisco. Most of his other opera appearances have been in works by baroque composers such as Monteverdi, Purcell and Handel. At Covent Garden in 1972 he created the role of the Priest Confessor in Maxwell Davies's *Taverner*.

Brandt, Marianne, b. Vienna, 12 Sept 1842; d. Vienna, 9 July 1921. Austrian mezzo-soprano. She studied in Vienna and with Pauline Viardot in Baden-Baden, and made her début in 1867 in Olomouc (then Olmütz) as Rachel in Halévy's *La Juive*. In Berlin she first appeared as Azucena in 1868, and sang there regularly until 1882. Able to sing both soprano and mezzo roles, she made her Covent Garden début in 1872 in the title-role of *Fidelio*. She was Waltraute in the first Bayreuth *Ring* in 1876, and Kundry in the second Bayreuth performance of Parsifal in 1882. Her other Wagner roles included Brangäne and Ortrud, but at the Met between 1884-8 she was also heard as Siebel in *Faust* and Eglantine in the first American performance of Weber's *Euryanthe*. After 1890 she taught in Vienna.

Brangäne (mezzo-sop.). Isolde's attendant in Wagner's *Tristan und Isolde*.

Brannigan, Owen, b. Annitsford, Northumberland, 10 Mar 1908; d. Annitsford, 9 May 1973. English bass. After studying at the Guildhall School of Music, he made his début with the Sadler's Wells company on tour in Newcastle in 1943 as Sarastro. He was a member of the company until 1949, and again from 1952-8 specializing in Mozart roles such as Leporello and Bartolo.

53

He created the role of Swallow in Britten's *Peter Grimes* at Sadler's Wells Theatre in 1945, and Britten subsequently wrote other roles for him, among them Collatinus in *The Rape of Lucretia*, Superintendent Budd in *Albert Herring* and Bottom in *A Midsummer Night's Dream*. Brannigan's voice was of fine quality, and his diction was a model of clarity.

Branzell, Karin, b. Stockholm, 24 Sept 1891; d. Altadena, Calif., 15 Dec 1974. Swedish mezzo-soprano. She made her début in Stockholm in 1912 in d'Albert's *Izeÿl*, and sang with the Royal Swedish Opera until 1918, when she joined the Berlin Staatsoper. She sang the Nurse in *Die Frau ohne Schatten* in Berlin in 1920, under the composer's baton. She left Berlin in 1923, and was heard regularly at the Met from 1924-44, though she made guest appearances elsewhere. She was at Bayreuth in 1930 and 1931, and later in the 1930s sang under Beecham at Covent Garden where she was greatly admired as Brangäne and Ericka. After retiring from the stage in 1944, she gave concerts for three years, and then taught in the United States. A number of excellent singers, among them Mignon Dunn, Jean Madeira and Nell Rankin, were her pupils. Branzell had a voice of rich beauty, and a dignified stage bearing.

Braun, Victor, b. Windsor, Ontario, 4 Aug 1935. Canadian baritone. He made his début with the Canadian Opera Company in 1961 as Escamillo, and from 1963-8 sang with German opera companies. He made his Covent Garden début in 1969 in the title-role of Humphrey Searle's *Hamlet*, and was later heard at Covent Garden in other roles, among them Onegin, the Count in *Figaro* and Germont in *La Traviata*. He has a soft-grained baritone voice of pleasant quality.

Brecht, Bertolt, b. Augsburg, 10 Feb 1898; d. Berlin, 15 Aug 1956. German playwright and poet. He collaborated with Kurt Weill in a number of works for the stage, the best known of which are *Die Dreigroschenoper* (known in English as *The Threepenny Opera*) in 1928, and *Aufstieg und Fall der Stadt Mahagonny* (1930). The other Brecht-Weill stage works are *Happy End* (1929), *Der Jasager* (1930) and *Die Sieben Todsünden*

(1933). Both Roger Sessions, in 1947, and Paul Dessau, in 1951, composed operas based on Brecht's play, *Die Verurteilung des Lukullus*, and Dessau also set Brecht's *Puntila* (1966).

Brecknock, John, b. Long Eaton, Derbyshire, 29 Nov 1937. English tenor. He joined the Sadler's Wells company in 1966, as a member of the chorus, and began to sing principal roles the following year. His healthy and flexible lyric tenor is best suited to the Mozart and Rossini repertory, and his most successful roles with the company, and later with English National Opera, have included Ottavio, Almaviva and Count Ory. He is also an excellent Alfredo in *La Traviata*. He makes guest appearances in Europe and with American companies, but continues to base his career upon English National Opera. His first Covent Garden appearance was in 1974 as Fenton in *Falstaff*.

Bretón, Tomás, b. Salamanca, 29 Dec 1850; d. Madrid, 2 Dec 1923. Spanish composer. He devoted himself to the cause of Spanish opera, though he had little success with his own works. *Los Amantes de Teruel* (1889) and *La Dolores* (1895) proved more popular than his other operas, but he found his greatest popularity with a zarzuela, *La Verbena de la Paloma*, produced in Madrid in 1894. He became professor of composition at the Madrid Conservatorium, and was one of the teachers of Pablo Casals.

Bréval, Lucienne, b. Berlin, 4 Nov 1869; d. Neuilly-sur-Seine, 15 Aug 1935. Swiss, later French soprano. Born of Swiss parents, she studied in Geneva, and made her début at the Paris Opéra in 1892 as Selika in *L'Africaine*. She was a leading singer at the Opéra until well after the end of World War I. In Paris she created leading roles in two Massenet operas, *Grisélidis* (1901) and *Ariane* (1906), and in Monte Carlo the title-role of Fauré's *Pénélope* (1913). She made several appearances at Covent Garden and at the Met around the turn of the century, but was happiest singing in Paris. She even refused an invitation to sing the *Walküre* Brünnhilde at Bayreuth.

Brilioth, Helge, b. Växjö, 7 May 1931. Swedish tenor. He studied in Stockholm,

Rome and Salzburg, originally intending to take up a career as a pianist and organist. He made his singing début as a baritone in 1958 at Drottningholm, near Stockholm, as Bartolo in Paisiello's *Il Barbiere di Siviglia*, and it was only after six years, the last three spent at Bielefeld where his roles included Germont in *La Traviata* and Beckmesser in *Die Meistersinger*, that he retrained and emerged as a tenor in Stockholm in 1965, singing Don José in *Carmen*. He subsequently specialized in the Wagner Heldentenor roles, appearing at Bayreuth for the first time in 1969 as Siegmund, the role of his Covent Garden début the following year. He was first heard at the Met in the 1970-71 season as Parsifal. By the end of the 1970s he had relinquished such roles, and was appearing in smaller character parts.

Brindisi. From the Italian *far brindisi*, (to drink one's health), the term has come to mean a drinking song, or a song used as a toast. There are famous examples in *Cavalleria Rusticana* (sung by Turiddu), *Macbeth* (sung, in the banquet scene, by Lady Macbeth) and, best-known of all, near the beginning of *La Traviata*, sung by Violetta and Alfredo. A refrain is usually repeated by the chorus of revellers or guests.

Britten, Benjamin (Lord Britten of Aldeburgh), b. Lowestoft, 22 Nov 1913; d. Aldeburgh, 4 Dec 1976. English composer. The leading British composer of his time, Britten composed music in most forms but was primarily interested in vocal music and especially opera. He made a false start with an operetta, *Paul Bunyan*, written in New

Benjamin Britten rehearsing his church parable, *Curlew River* for the 1964 Aldeburgh Festival where many of his works both orchestral and operatic were first performed.

York in collaboration with the poet W. H. Auden and first performed there at Columbia University in May 1941. His first real opera was *Peter Grimes* (1945) with which the mid-20th-c. English operatic renaissance can fairly be said to have begun. Many of Britten's operas after *Peter Grimes* were scored for a small orchestra of twelve, and some of them were given their first performances at the Aldeburgh Festival which Britten had helped to found. The leading tenor roles were invariably written for the composer's close friend Peter Pears. *The Rape of Lucretia* (1946) and *Albert Herring* (1947) were first given at Glyndebourne, but *The Little Sweep*, a 1-act work which formed part of an entertainment called *Let's Make an Opera*, was performed at the Aldeburgh Festival in 1949.

Britten reverted to larger orchestral resources for his next two operas, both of which were commissioned by and first staged at the Royal Opera House, Covent Garden. *Billy Budd* (1951) has over the years established itself as one of the composer's most popular works, but *Gloriana* in 1953 suffered from being underestimated as a mere *pièce d'occasion* (the occasion being the coronation of Elizabeth II) and had to wait until its revival by the English National Opera in 1966 to be properly appreciated. *The Turn of the Screw* and *A Midsummer Night's Dream* (Aldeburgh, 1960) are among Britten's most highly regarded operas. Three 1-act operas or 'church parables' written for church performance, *Curlew River* (1964), *The Burning Fiery Furnace* (1966) and *The Prodigal Son* (1968), are perhaps admired more than they are loved. *Owen Wingrave* (1971) was composed for television and later staged. Britten's last opera, *Death in Venice*, was first performed at the 1973 Aldeburgh Festival, and was subsequently taken up by a number of foreign opera houses.

Brook, Peter, b. London, 21 Mar 1925. English director. Primarily a director of plays, he has made occasional forays into the world of opera. In 1948, with no previous experience of the specialized field of opera production, he was appointed director of productions at the Royal Opera House, Covent Garden, and not surprisingly failed to impress. His production there of *Salome* in 1949 marked the end of his association with that opera house, but he was subsequently engaged by the Met to produce *Faust* (1953) and *Eugene Onegin* (1958). He later staged a potted version of *Carmen* in Paris, but devotes most of his time now to experimenting with a group of actors, with no practical aim of public performance in view.

Brouwenstijn, Gré, b. Den Helder, 26 Aug 1915. Dutch soprano. She studied in Amsterdam and made her début there as one of the Ladies in *Die Zauberflöte* in 1940. She joined the Netherlands Opera in 1946, and remained a leading member of the company throughout her career. Her first successes were as Tosca in 1947 and Santuzza. In 1951 she made her Covent Garden début as Aida, and appeared regularly in London in Verdi roles until 1964, being greatly admired for her style and for the dignity of her characterizations. She was Elisabetta in the famous 1958 Visconti production of *Don Carlos* at Covent Garden, and a moving Fidelio at Glyndebourne in 1959, 1961 and 1963. It was as Fidelio that she gave her farewell performances with the Netherlands Opera in 1971.

Brownlee, John, b. Geelong, 7 Jan 1900; d. New York, 10 Jan 1969. Australian baritone. He studied in Melbourne, and was heard by Dame Nellie Melba who introduced him to Covent Garden at her farewell appearance in 1926, when he sang Marcello in Acts 3 and 4 of *La Bohème*. After further study in Paris, he sang with the Paris Opéra from 1927–36, his début role being Athanael in Massenet's *Thaïs*. He was Golaud in the 1930 performances of *Pelléas et Mélisande* at Covent Garden, and was leading baritone in the Glyndebourne opening season of 1935, when he sang Don Alfonso in *Così Fan Tutte*. The following year he was Glyndebourne's Don Giovanni. He first appeared at the Met in 1937 as Rigoletto, and remained a prominent member of the Met company until his retirement in 1958, when he became head of the opera department at the Manhattan School of Music. His voice was more than adequate to the demands placed upon it, and he was a reliable performer and tasteful musician.

Bruch, Max, b. Cologne, 6 Jan 1838; d. Friedenau, nr Berlin, 2 Oct 1920. German composer. Bruch was much more successful as a composer of orchestral music than of opera. The first of his three works for the stage, none of which was more than moderately successful, was a comic opera, *Scherz, List und Rache*, a setting of Goethe's libretto performed at Cologne in 1858. The libretto of *Die Loreley* was by Emanuel Geibel and was written for Mendelssohn who left his opera unfinished. Bruch's *Die Loreley* was staged in Mannheim in 1863 and was well enough received to be performed in several other European cities. Bruch's final opera, *Hermione*, based on Shakespeare's *A Winter's Tale*, was given its première in Berlin in 1872.

By the end of the century, the tide of fashion had turned against Bruch's kind of romanticism. Although the first of his two violin concertos has remained in the concert repertory, it is highly unlikely that Bruch's operas will be successfully revived.

Bruneau, Alfred, b. Paris, 3 Mar 1857; d. Paris, 15 June 1934. French composer and critic. His style a curious amalgam of Wagner and Massenet, Bruneau produced his first opera, *Kérim*, in 1887. He then became strongly attracted to the novels of Emile Zola, and began to base his operas on Zola's novels. *Le Rêve*, a huge success at the Opéra-Comique in 1891, was followed by *L'Attaque du Moulin* (1893). The novelist himself provided original libretti for Bruneau's next four operas, one of which, *Messidor* (1897), suffered somewhat from being produced at the height of the Dreyfus affair. After Zola's death, Bruneau continued to use the novelist's plots for his operas until 1916 when he turned to verse libretti by other authors. In 1932 he published a memoir of Zola.

Brünnhilde (sop.). A Valkyrie, and Wotan's favourite daughter in 3 of the *Ring* operas of Wagner: *Die Walküre*, *Siegfried* and *Götterdämmerung*.

Bruscantini, Sesto, b. Porto Civitanova, 10 Dec 1919. Italian baritone. He made his début at Civitanova in 1946 as Colline in *La Bohème*, and was first heard at La Scala in 1949. In the 1950s he sang frequently at Glyndebourne, mainly in Rossini and Mozart. He made his American début in Chicago in 1961, and in the 1960s began to add heavier roles to his repertoire, among them Rigoletto and Iago. His Germont was much admired at Covent Garden, and also, in 1974, his Malatesta in *Don Pasquale*. He has a voice of pleasant quality, and is a most accomplished actor, especially in elegant comedy roles such as Rossini's Dandini, which he was still singing in 1983, or Mozart's Don Alfonso. For some years he was married to the soprano Sena Jurinac.

Bruson, Renato, b. Este, nr Padua, 13 Jan 1936. Italian baritone. He studied in Padua, and made his début in 1961 in Spoleto as Count di Luna in *Il Trovatore*. After singing for some years in provincial Italian opera houses, he made his first appearance at La Scala in 1972 in *Linda di Chamounix*. Covent Garden heard him in 1976 in *Un Ballo in Maschera*, since when he has returned in other Verdi roles, most notably in the title-role of *Falstaff* in 1982. Although his voice lacks individuality, he is highly regarded in Donizetti and Verdi roles by virtue of his technique and musicianship. He was highly acclaimed as Verdi's Macbeth at the Verona Arena in 1982.

Bucchi, Valentino, b. Florence 29 Nov 1916; d. Rome, 9 May 1976. Italian composer. Also active as teacher and critic, he composed six operas which, with the exception of the first, *La Vergine dei Veleni* (composed in 1939 but not produced), have been performed in his native Florence though not elsewhere. *Il Giuoco del Barone* (1944), *Il Contrabasso* (1954) and *Una Notte in Paradiso* (1960) are 1-act pieces, but *Il Coccodrillo* (1970) is a full-length opera in 4 acts, based on an unfinished story by Dostoevsky. In 1966, Bucchi's realization of Monteverdi's *Orfeo* was broadcast by Italian radio.

Buckman, Rosina, b. Blenheim, New Zealand, c. 1880; d. London, 30 Dec 1948. New Zealand soprano. After studying in Birmingham, she returned to New Zealand and made her stage début there at Wellington in 1906, in *A Moorish Maid* by the New Zealand composer Alfred Hill. In 1911 in Australia she joined the Melba Grand Opera Company, and then returned to London where she made her Covent Garden début as a Flower Maiden in the first English performance of *Parsifal* in 1914. In

Grace Bumbry as Amneris at Covent Garden.

the following ten years she undertook a number of leading roles in Great Britain, her Isolde with the Beecham Opera Company being especially admired.

buffo. The buffoon or comic, in Italian opera, is referred to as the *buffo* role. The *basso buffo*, for example, is a comic bass. An *opera buffa* is a comic opera.

Bülow, Hans von, b. Dresden, 8 Jan 1830; d. Cairo, 12 Feb 1894. German conductor and pianist. A virtuoso pianist and one of the leading conductors of his day, at the beginning of his career he came under the spell of Wagner after hearing *Lohengrin* conducted by Liszt at Weimar in 1850. He studied with Wagner and after becoming chief conductor at Munich he conducted the premières there of *Tristan und Isolde* in 1865 and *Die Meistersinger von Nürnberg* in 1868. He remained faithful to the Wagnerian cause even after his wife Cosima, Liszt's illegitimate daughter, deserted him in 1869 to live with Wagner.

Bumbry, Grace, b. St Louis, Miss., 4 Jan 1937. American mezzo-soprano and soprano. She studied in Boston, Chicago and, under Lotte Lehmann, from 1955-8 at the Music Academy of the West, Santa Barbara, California. Lehmann took her to London where she gave a highly successful recital at the Wigmore Hall. She made her stage début at the Paris Opéra in 1960 as Amneris, and then joined the Basle Opera in order to extend her repertory. In 1961, as Venus, she became the first black singer to appear at Bayreuth. Her first appearances at Covent Garden (1963) and the Met (1965) were as Eboli, and her rich timbre and impressive command of the stage led to her being acclaimed as a Verdi mezzo of rare quality. Like so many mezzo-sopranos she began to desire soprano roles, and has achieved success as Strauss's Salome, Santuzza in *Cavalleria Rusticana* (her first soprano role, which she undertook in Vienna in 1966), and Tosca, which she first sang at the Met in 1971. Lady Macbeth in Verdi's *Macbeth* is one of her finest parts.

Buona Figliuola, La (*The Good Daughter*). Opera in 3 acts by Piccinni. Libretto by Carlo Goldoni, after the novel *Pamela* (1740) by Samuel Richardson. First performed Rome, 6 Feb 1760.

La Cecchina (sop.), a servant and orphan, loves her master the Marchese (ten.). All ends happily when it is discovered that the girl is really a Baroness.

Burghauser, Jarmil, b. Písek, 21 Oct 1921. Czech composer. One of the best-known contemporary composers in his own country, Burghauser has composed three operas, none of which has been performed abroad. They are *Lakomec* (1950: after Molière's *L'Avare*), *Karolinka a Lhář* (*Caroline and the Liar*: 1955, after a play by Goldoni), and *Most* (*The Bridge*: 1967, libretto by J. Pávek), the last-named described by the composer as an anti-opera.

Burian, Emil František, b. Plzeň, 11 June 1904; d. Prague, 9 Aug 1959. Czech composer and producer. In the period between the two world wars he was active as a producer in musical theatre and cabaret. He composed a number of operas which were performed in Czechoslovakia, the most important of which is *Maryša*, which he staged in Brno in 1940, and whose libretto he wrote. He spent most of World War II in a concentration camp, and after the war continued to work in musical theatre though his earlier *avant garde* enthusiasms had by then solidified into the conservative socialist realism required by communism. He was a nephew of the tenor, Karel Burian.

Burian, Karel, b. Rousinov, 12 Jan 1870; d. Senomaty, 25 Sept 1924. Czech tenor, known abroad as Carl Burrian. After studying in Brno and Prague, he made his début in 1891 in Brno as Jenik in *The Bartered Bride*. He subsequently joined the National Theatre in Prague, but was soon engaged by a number of German companies to sing the Wagner Heldentenor roles. He was with the Hamburg Opera from 1898-1902 and then at Dresden for the following ten years. In Dresden he created the role of Herod in *Salome* in 1905, making a tremendous impression as much by his acting as by his singing. In the decade before World War I he sang Tristan, Tannhäuser and Lohengrin at Covent Garden and at the Met. A talented writer, Burian translated opera texts, wrote poetry, and published a volume of memoirs.

He was the uncle of the composer, Emil František Burian.

Burkhard, Paul, b. Zurich, 21 Dec 1911; d. Zell, 6 Sept 1977. Swiss composer. Active also in Switzerland as a conductor, mainly of operetta, Burkhard composed a number of operettas and musical comedies between the mid-1930-50s. They include *Das Paradies der Frauen* (1938), *Casanova in der Schweiz* (1942) and *Die Pariserin* (1957). He achieved great international success with a song, 'O mein Papa'.

Burkhard, Willy, b. Évilard-sur-Bienne, 17 Apr 1900; d. Zurich, 18 June 1955. Swiss composer. Primarily a composer of orchestral and instrumental music in an advanced musical language, Burkhard wrote only one opera, *Die Schwarze Spinne*, based on a story by Jeremias Gotthelf. It was considered successful when first produced in Zurich in 1948, and was later revised by the composer.

Burning Fiery Furnace, The. Church parable (so described by the composer) in 1 act by Britten. Libretto by William Plomer, based on the Old Testament story of Shadrach, Meshach and Abednego. First performed Orford, Suffolk, 9 June 1966.

The opera tells how Nebuchadnezzar (ten.) is moved to worship Jehovah by seeing Shadrach, Meshach and Abednego survive the fiery furnace.

Burrowes, Norma, b. Bangor, Northern Ireland, 24 Apr 1944. Irish soprano. She studied in London, and made her professional début with Glyndebourne Touring Opera in 1970 as Zerlina. A lyric soprano with a secure coloratura technique, she excels in Mozart, and was an excellent Blonde in *Die Entführung aus dem Serail* at Salzburg in 1971. Her first Covent Garden appearance was in 1970 as Fiakermilli in *Arabella*. At Glyndebourne in 1975 she sang the title-role in Janáček's *The Cunning Little Vixen*.

Burrows, Stuart, b. Pontypridd, 7 Feb 1933. Welsh tenor. He began his career as a schoolteacher, and became a professional singer after winning a prize at the 1959 National Eisteddfod. He made his début as Ismaele in *Nabucco* with Welsh National Opera in 1963, and first sang at Covent

Garden as Beppe in *Pagliacci* in 1967. A sweet-voiced lyric tenor, he excels in the Mozart roles. Tamino was the role in which he made his American (San Francisco, 1967) and Vienna (1970) débuts. He triumphs over an unprepossessing stage appearance and a lack of dramatic ability by virtue of his musicianship and vocal technique.

Bury, John, b. Aberystwyth, Wales, 27 Jan 1925. British designer. Though he is primarily a designer of plays, working frequently in collaboration with the director Peter Hall, he has also designed operas for production by Hall, among them *Moses und Aron* and *Tristan und Isolde* at Covent Garden, and, at Glyndebourne, works by Cavalli, Monteverdi and Mozart.

Busch, Fritz, b. Siegen, Westphalia, 13 Mar 1890; d. London, 14 Sept 1951. German conductor. After making his way up through the smaller German companies, he became music director at Dresden in 1922. As an anti-Nazi he was dismissed in March 1933 and two months later left for Buenos Aires where he conducted opera for three years, and again during the war. With the director Carl Ebert he helped to establish opera at Glyndebourne in 1934, and conducted at Glyndebourne every summer until the outbreak of war. He conducted at the Met in 1945, and returned to Glyndebourne in 1950. He was a sound musician and a competent conductor, and his Mozart performances at Glyndebourne were much admired.

Busenello, Giovanni Francesco, b. Venice, 24 Sept 1598; d. Legnaro, Venice, 27 Oct 1659. Italian librettist. The earliest of the great librettists, he wrote the text of Monteverdi's *L'Incoronazione di Poppea* (1642) and four libretti for Cavalli: *Gli Amori d'Apollo e di Dafne* (1640), *Didone* (1641), *La Prosperità Infelice di Giulio Cesare Dittatore* (1646) and *Statira, Principessa di Persia* (1655). A sixth drama by Busenello, which was not set to music, survives in manuscript.

Bush, Alan, b. 22 Dec 1900. English composer. As a communist living in a non-communist country, Bush has found it necessary to inject more of his socialism into his music than would probably have been the case had he been a citizen of a communist country. But if his political beliefs have influenced, in the direction of over-simplification, his opera scores, they have also unfairly influenced the reception of his work in his own country. Of his seven operas, the libretti of six of which are by his wife Nancy Bush, most are of considerable musical interest. It is, perhaps, the lack of dramatic subtlety in their libretti which has occasionally inhibited the composer's imagination. *Wat Tyler*, completed in 1950, had to wait until 1974 for its first British production, by which time it had been given a number of performances in Eastern Europe. *Men of Blackmoor* (1955), *The Sugar Reapers or Guyana Johnny*, (1966) and *Joe Hill* (1970), have all been produced in East Germany, though not in Great Britain.

Busoni, Ferruccio, b. Empoli, 1 Apr 1866; d. Berlin, 27 July 1924. German-Italian composer and pianist. Primarily a composer of orchestral and piano music he wrote four operas which, though they have not achieved great popularity, are admired by the discerning opera-lover. (A fifth, the early *Sigune*, remained unperformed and unpublished.) *Die Brautwahl* (1912) was based on a story by E.T.A. Hoffmann, and *Turandot* (1917) on the Gozzi play which Puccini used some years later for his *Turandot*. The adaptations were made by Busoni himself, and he also provided his own libretti for the 1-act *Arlecchino* (1917) and for his operatic masterpiece, *Doktor Faust*, which was first staged at Dresden in 1925. The composer's philosophical, un-dramatic approach militated against the opera's popular success, but the work continues to be revived from time to time in European opera houses.

Busser, Henri, b. Toulouse, 16 Jan 1872; d. Paris, 30 Dec 1973. French composer and conductor. He composed a number of works for the stage, conservative in idiom but accomplished in craftsmanship. *Colomba* met with great success at its première in Nice (1921), and *Le Carrosse du Saint-Sacrement* (1948) was also admired. Both operas are based on works by Prosper Mérimée. Busser was active as a conductor, mainly of opera, from 1902, when he made his début at the Opéra-Comique with Lalo's *Le Roi d'Ys*, until well after World War II.

Bussotti, Sylvano, b. Florence, 1 Oct 1931. Italian composer. He has composed a number of works for the stage in a modern idiom, some of which could be described as operas, although this is a term their composer prefers to avoid. *La Passion selon Sade*, first performed complete in Stockholm in 1969, after an earlier version had been staged in Palermo, is a 'chamber mystery-play', while *Lorenzaccio*, a 5-act work based on Musset's play and staged in Venice in 1972, is a 'romantic melodrama'. Bussotti has also composed stage works for marionettes to perform: these were produced in Florence and Aix-en-Provence in the mid-1950s.

Butt, (Dame) Clara, b. Southwick, 1 Feb 1873; d. North Stoke, 23 Jan 1936. English contralto. She studied in Bristol and at the Royal College of Music in London, and while a student in 1892 sang Gluck's Orpheus at the Lyceum Theatre, London. The possessor of an impressive contralto voice with an almost baritone-like quality in her lower register, she became a great favourite in oratorio and on the concert platform in Great Britain and throughout what was then the British Empire. Though she recorded arias, among them a stunning account of the Brindisi from Donizetti's *Lucrezia Borgia*, her only appearance in opera after her student days was a return to the role of Orpheus at Covent Garden in 1920 under Sir Thomas Beecham.

C

cabaletta. The term has several meanings, and these have varied at different periods. It is most frequently used to indicate the fast, concluding section of an aria or ensemble in 19th-c. Italian opera. In the early part of that century, in the operas of Rossini and Donizetti, for example, the cabaletta was, as often as not, a separate aria in a lively tempo, following an aria or cavatina in a slower tempo, and linked with it by way of recitative or declamatory arioso. The cabaletta survived into middle-period Verdi, the most famous of all being the tenor aria, 'Di quella pira' in *Il Trovatore*, which is actually the cabaletta to the preceding aria, 'Ah si, ben mio'.

Caballé, Montserrat, b. Barcelona, 12 Apr 1933. Spanish soprano. She studied in Barcelona, and in 1956 joined the Basle Opera, remaining a member of that company for three years during which time she built up a wide repertory of roles, including many, such as Pamina, Eva, Elisabeth, Arabella and Salome, which she did not sing again after she began to specialize in the bel canto roles of the 19th c. It was when she replaced another singer at short notice in a New York concert performance of Donizetti's *Lucrezia Borgia* in 1965 that she became internationally famous. She had sung at Glyndebourne as early as 1965 as the Marschallin, and as the Countess in *Le Nozze di Figaro*, and in the same year made her Met début as Gounod's Marguerite. Covent Garden first heard her in 1972 as Violetta. She has a voice of character and fine quality, and an assured technique, but is an indifferent and apparently lazy musician. She has nevertheless, at her best, given fine performances of a number of Bellini and Donizetti roles. Her husband, Bernabe Marti has sung with her in Spain, though rarely in opera abroad.

Caccini, Giulio, b. Rome, *c.* 1545; d. Florence on or shortly before 10 Dec 1618. Italian composer, singer and lutenist. A member of the Florentine Camerata, the group of poets and musicians whose discussions and experiments led to the creation of opera as a new form of musical drama, Caccini composed some of the music for *Euridice* (1600), most of which is by Peri, and also composed his own *Euridice* which was performed in 1602. His recitative-like settings for solo voice and instruments, which he himself performed, influenced his fellow composers of the earliest operas. His daughter Francesca (b. Florence, 18 Sept 1587; d. probably in Florence in 1640) was a singer, and his pupil, and also the first woman known to compose an opera. Her *Liberazione di Ruggiero dall' Isola d'Alcina* was performed in Florence in 1625 to celebrate the visit of the future King Wladislaw IV of Poland.

cadenza. Until after the end of the 18th c., singers as well as instrumentalists were often expected to improvise a cadenza or passage in free time before the final bars of a movement or aria. This could be as simple as a flourish of notes or as lengthy and complex as the performer's ability would allow. After the time of Rossini, it became the practice for the composer himself to write out the cadenzas, perhaps as a safeguard against vain and incompetent singers. Eventually, the practice died out. 19th c. singers and teachers of singing used to edit or compose volumes of cadenzas for interpolation into appropriate arias.

Cadman, Charles Wakefield, b. Johnstown, Penn., 24 Dec 1881; d. Los Angeles, 30 Dec 1946. American composer. From an early age he was interested in the music of the American Indians, and made recordings of tribal songs as well as composing his own songs on Indian subjects. His first opera, *The Land of the Misty Water*, remains unperformed, but *Shanewis or The Robin Woman*, based on events in the life of the Princess Redfeather, was highly acclaimed when first performed at the Met in 1918. He wrote a number of other operas in the 1920-30s, two of which, *The Garden of Mystery* (performed in New York in 1925) and *A Witch of Salem* (Chicago, 1926) achieved some success. His music utilized Indian themes, arranged and harmonized in a 19th-c. European style.

Cahill, Teresa, b. Maidenhead, 25 Sept 1946. English soprano. She made her début at Glyndebourne in 1970 as First Lady in *Die Zauberflöte*, and won the John Christie Award that year. She has since appeared with most of the British opera companies, and made her American début at Santa Fe in 1972 as Donna Elvira. Her voice is an attractive lyric soprano, heard at its best in the Mozart soubrette roles or as Strauss's Sophie. In 1982 at Covent Garden she sang Lisa in *La Sonnambula*.

Calaf (ten.). The Unknown Prince whose name Turandot seeks to discover in Puccini's opera.

Caldara, Antonio, b. Venice, *c.* 1670; d. Vienna, 28 Dec 1736. Italian composer. The composer of nearly 100 operas, the earlier ones produced in various Italian cities and the later ones, after 1714, usually first staged in Vienna, Caldara was court composer to the Austrian Emperor Charles VI from 1714 onwards. In Vienna he set libretti mainly by

Zeno and Metastasio, in an agreeably rococo style somewhat lacking in dramatic impetus. His Viennese operas include *Scipione nelle Spagne* (1722; libretto by Zeno), *Adriano in Siria* (1732; libretto by Metastasio) and a setting of Metastasio's *La Clemenza di Tito* in 1734, which was to be set more memorably in 1791 by Mozart.

Calderón de la Barca, Pedro, b. Madrid, 17 Jan 1600; d. Madrid, 25 May 1681. Spanish dramatist and poet. The author of more than 120 plays and, after he became a priest in 1651, some 70 religious dramas, he was a typical writer of the baroque period in style, though increasingly pessimistic in his philosophy. He wrote the text of the first known *zarzuela*, *El Jardín de Falerina*, which was performed in Madrid in 1648. Among operas based on his plays are Egk's *Circe*, Richard Strauss's *Friedenstag*, Godard's *Pédro de Zalaméa*, Malipiero's *Vita è Sogno* (which derives from Calderón's best-known play in English, *Life is a Dream*), Schubert's *Fierrabras* and Weingartner's *Dame Kobold*.

Calife de Bagdad, Le. Opera in 1 act by Boïeldieu. Libretto by Claude Godard d'Aucour de Saint-Just, after a story in the Arabian Nights. First performed Paris, 16 Sept 1800.

Though it is rarely performed today, *Le Calife de Bagdad* was the earliest of Boïeldieu's successful comic operas, remaining in the repertoire of the Opéra-Comique for thirty-six years. Its Parisian musical style makes no concessions to its Oriental theme.

Calisto, La. Opera in 3 acts by Cavalli. Libretto by Giovanni Battista Faustini, drawn from Ovid's *Metamorphoses*. First performed Venice, autumn 1651. First modern performance, in an edition by Raymond Leppard, Glyndebourne, 26 May 1970.

Jove (bass) has decreed that Calisto (sop.), daughter of the King of Pelasgia, should be given immortality as one of the stars in the sky. He descends to earth, to discover that Calisto has become a nymph of Diana (mezzo-sop.). Disguising himself as Diana, the god attempts to seduce Calisto. Juno (bass) changes Calisto into a little bear. Taken to Mount Olympus by Jove, she is transmogrified into the constellation Ursa Minor.

Callas, Maria, b. New York, 3 Dec 1923; d. Paris, 16 Sept 1977. Greek soprano. Born of Greek parents, she was taken to Greece at the age of fourteen, and studied in Athens with Elvira de Hidalgo. She sang Santuzza in 1938 as a student, when she can have been no more than fifteen, and made her professional début the following year in *Boccaccio* with the Athens Royal Opera. Her Italian début at Verona in 1947 in *La Gioconda* was the beginning of her international career. At first she sang heavy dramatic roles, but was led by the conductor Tullio Serafin to concentrate on the bel canto repertoire in which she made her greatest successes. In the 1950s she was the leading exponent of such roles as Norma,

Maria Callas in the title-role in Act 1 of Puccini's *Tosca* at the Paris Opéra in February 1965.

Medea, Anna Bolena and Lucia. Her faulty technique led to a vocal crisis, and her performances began to deteriorate in the early 1960s, though her intuitive dramatic and musical intelligence helped her to survive in the vocally easy role of Tosca until 1965. She then retired, at the comparatively early age of forty-two, but made an ill-judged return to public performance in a concert tour in 1972-3 with the tenor Giuseppe di Stefano. She was an artist of strong personality and, at her best, of exceptional dramatic power.

Calvé, Emma, b. Décazeville, 15 Aug 1858; d. Millau, 6 Jan 1942. French soprano. After studying with, among other teachers, Mathilde Marchesi, she made her début in Brussels in 1881 as Marguerite. Her first great success was as Ophelia in Thomas's *Hamlet* at La Scala in 1890. From the early 1890s until 1904 she was active at the Met and Covent Garden, acclaimed especially as Santuzza and as Carmen, the latter generally considered to be her finest role. She created two roles in operas by Massenet: Anita in *La Navarraise* at Covent Garden in 1894, and Fanny in *Sapho* at the Opéra-Comique, Paris, in 1897. Her appearances were infrequent after 1904, though she continued to give occasional concerts until after World War I.

Calzabigi, Raniero de', b. Livorno, 23 Dec 1714; d. Naples, July, 1795. Italian librettist. He published the works of Metastasio in Paris in 1755, and in 1761 moved to Vienna where he began to collaborate with Gluck. Their first project was the ballet, *Don Juan*, to a scenario by Calzabigi. He is remembered for those three of his ten libretti which were set by Gluck: *Orfeo ed Euridice*, *Alceste* and *Paride ed Elena*. These were thought, in their day, to constitute a move away from the artificialities of *opera seria* to a new directness and simplicity, qualities which today are more readily apparent in *Orfeo ed Euridice* than in the other two works.

Cambert, Robert, b. Paris, *c.* 1627; d. London, Feb or Mar 1677. French composer. He wrote a stage work called *Pastorale* in 1659 which is sometimes described as the earliest French opera, though in fact it was preceded by *Le Triomphe de l'Amour* (1655) by Michel de la Guerre. His *Pomone*,

performed at the Académie Royale de Musique, Paris, in 1671 was, however, the first French opera of any importance. When he was supplanted in royal favour by Lully, Cambert went to London, but composed no new operas there.

Cambiale di Matrimonio, La (*The Marriage Contract*). Opera in 1 act by Rossini. Libretto by Gaetano Rossi, based on the comedy (1790) by Camillo Federici. First performed Venice, 3 Nov 1810.

Rossini's first performed opera. Fanny (sop.), in love with Edoardo (ten.), outwits the attempts of her father, Sir Tobias Mill (bass), an English merchant, to force her to marry Slook (bar.), his Canadian colleague.

Camerata. Literally a group or an association, the Camerata was the assembly of poets, musicians and philosophers who met in the houses of the Florentine noblemen, Giovanni de' Bardi and Jacopo Corsi in the late years of the 16th c. Their discussions gave rise to the experiments which eventually led to the creation, out of the performances of madrigals and choruses, of the new art form of opera. The group's aim was to revive Greek tragedy, with its ideal of the word supported by music.

Cammarano, Salvatore, b. Naples, 19 Mar 1801; d. Naples, 17 July 1852. Italian librettist. He worked as a scene painter and stage manager at the Teatro San Carlo, Naples, before beginning to write plays and libretti. He provided libretti for operas by Mercadante, Pacini and Donizetti; those for the last-named including *Lucia di Lammermoor* (1835), *Roberto d'Evereux* (1837) and *Maria di Rohan* (1843). His fruitful collaboration with Verdi began in 1845 when he adapted a Voltaire play which became the opera *Alzira*, and continued with *La Battaglia di Legnano* (1849), *Luisa Miller* (1849) and *Il Trovatore* (1853). He died while at work on *Il Trovatore*. A sound craftsman, he had an instinct for theatrical effect.

Campana Sommersa, La (*The Sunken Bell*). Opera in 4 acts by Respighi. Libretto by Claudio Guastalla, based on Gerhard Hauptmann's play, *Die Versunkene Glocke* (1896). First performed, in German, Hamburg, 18 Nov 1927. First performance in Italian, New York, 24 Nov 1928.

Heinrich (ten.), a bell-maker, loses a bell he has cast when it falls into a lake. Bewitched by the elf Rautendelein (sop.), he deserts his wife who throws herself into the lake and rings the bell to remind him of his guilt.

Campanello di Notte, Il (*The Night Bell*). Opera in 1 act by Donizetti. Libretto by the composer, based on a French *vaudeville*, *La Sonnette de Nuit* by Brunswick, Troin and Lhérie (1835). First performed Naples, 1 June 1836.

When Don Annibale Pistacchio (bass), an elderly chemist, marries the young Serafina (sop.), her former lover Enrico (ten.) interrupts their wedding night by ringing the night-bell and presenting himself in various disguises with prescriptions for the bridegroom to dispense.

Campo, Conrado del, b. Madrid, 28 Oct 1878; d. Madrid, 17 Mar 1953. Spanish composer. He composed twelve operas and twenty-two *zarzuelas*, the earlier operas being somewhat Straussian in style. Most of his operas were staged in Madrid, the most successful among them being *El Final de Don Alvaro* (1911), *Fantochines* (1924) and *La Tragedia del Beso* (1915).

Campra, André, b. Aix-en-Provence, 4 Dec 1660; d. Versailles, 29 June 1744. French composer. A leading figure in French musical theatre in the early 18th c., he was the composer of more than twenty operas and *opéras-ballets*, which formed an important link between Lully and Rameau. His main contribution to the French lyric stage was in the development of the *opéra-ballet*. His *L'Europe Galante* (1697) provided Lully with a pattern for *Les Indes Galantes*. Among his later works for the stage are *Alcine* (1705), *Idoménée* (1712), *Camille* (1717) and *Achille et Deidamie* (1735). The librettist in every case was Antoine Danchet (whose *Idoménée* was later reworked by Giambattista Varesco for Mozart's *Idomeneo*), and the first performances were all at the Paris Opéra.

Candide. Operetta by Bernstein. Lyrics by Richard Wilbur, John Latouche and Dorothy Parker; book by Lillian Hellman,

Bernstein's *Candide* in New York. John Lankston as Dr Pangloss and David Eisler as Candide.

after Voltaire's novel, *Candide.* First performed New York, 1 Dec 1956. Revised version with new lyrics by Stephen Sondheim and book by Hugh Wheeler, first performed New York, 8 Mar 1974. A further revision was performed by the New York City Opera in 1982.

Caniglia, Maria, b. Naples, 5 May 1905; d. Rome, 15 Apr 1979. Italian soprano. After studying in Naples, she made her début in Turin in 1930 as Chrysothemis in *Elektra*. She sang at La Scala regularly from 1930-45, appearing also at Covent Garden and the Met in the late 1930s. She was one of the finest interpreters of middle-period Verdi soprano roles in the 1930-40s and was also a greatly admired Tosca. She married Pino Donati, composer and arts administrator, who was artistic director of the Chicago Lyric Opera until his death in 1975.

Canio (ten.). The leader of the strolling players in Leoncavallo's *Pagliacci*.

Canterbury Pilgrims, The. Opera in 3 acts by Stanford. Libretto by Gilbert Arthur A'Beckett, after Chaucer's *Canterbury Tales*. First performed London, 28 Apr 1884.

The American composer Reginald de Koven (1859-1920) wrote a 4-act opera with the same title, also based on Chaucer, with a libretto by Percy Mackaye. It was produced at the Met on 8 Mar 1917.

cantilena. Originally that part of a choral composition with the main tune, the term was later used to describe any smoothly flowing passage of melody. It is now also applied to a short song or aria of lyrical character. It is used, in the same sense, to describe instrumental solo passages.

canzone. More often used to indicate a short composition for instrumental ensemble, the word, of Provençal origin, also describes a song sung in an opera by a character who is rendering it for other characters in the opera. Cherubino's song, 'Voi che sapete' in *Le Nozze di Figaro*, is a well-known example.

Capecchi, Renato, b. Cauro, 6 Nov 1923. Italian baritone. He studied violin and singing in Milan, and made his stage début in Reggio Emilia in 1949 as Amonasro. He

has since sung nearly 300 roles. His first Met appearance was as Germont in *La Traviata* in 1952, but he is best known for comedy roles such as Melitone in *La Forza del Destino*. It was as Melitone that he made his Covent Garden début in 1962: at Glyndebourne he was a superb Falstaff. A singer of musical intelligence and rare dramatic ability, he has created roles in operas by Malipiero and Ghedini, and in recent years has become known as a teacher.

Capobianco, Tito, b. La Plata, Argentina, 28 Aug 1931. Argentinian producer. After beginning his career by working in theatres in Argentina and Mexico, he became producer at the Teatro Colón, Buenos Aires, in 1959. He left in 1962 to go to the United States as artistic director of the Cincinnati Summer Opera, and in 1965 began to direct opera for the New York City Opera. He has directed opera in Europe and Australia, and has been artistic director of San Diego Opera since 1977. Under him the San Diego company has developed, and its annual summer Verdi Festival has acquired an enviable reputation.

Cappuccilli, Piero, b. Trieste, 9 Nov 1929. Italian baritone. He studied in Trieste where he appeared in small roles, making his official début in Milan in 1957 as Tonio in *Pagliacci*. The possessor of a baritone voice of attractive timbre, and a superb technique, he became the leading Italian baritone after Tito Gobbi and until the emergence of Renato Bruson. Like Bruson, but unlike the singing-actor Gobbi, he does not project a strong personality on stage, but is a reliable musician. He has achieved his greatest successes in the operas of Verdi, among them *La Traviata*, in which he made his Covent Garden début in 1967, *Simon Boccanegra* and *Don Carlos*.

Capriccio. Opera in 1 act by Richard Strauss. Libretto by Clemens Krauss. First performed Munich, 28 Oct 1942.

Set in a château near Paris, in the 18th c. at the time of Gluck's operatic reforms, the opera dramatizes the question of whether words or music are of the greater importance in opera. The Countess

Agnes Baltsa and José Carreras in Bizet's *Carmen* at Covent Garden in 1983.

Madeleine (sop.), during the course of an evening, is asked to decide which of two suitors she prefers, a poet (Olivier, bar.) or a composer (Flamand, ten.). The work ends with a solo scene for the Countess in which she addresses the question, without arriving at a definite answer.

Capuleti e i Montecchi, I (*The Capulets and the Montagues*). Opera in 2 acts by Bellini. Libretto by Felice Romani, a reworking of his libretto for Vaccai's *Giulietta e Romeo* (1825) which had been indirectly derived from Shakespeare's play (*c*. 1595). First performed Venice, 11 Mar 1830.

In the 19th c., the final scene of Vaccai's opera was often substituted for the corresponding scene by Bellini. Bellini composed the role of Romeo for a young mezzo-soprano: in 1960 a performing version by Claudio Abbado, first staged at La Scala, assigned the role to a tenor.

Carafa, Michele, b. Naples, 17 Nov 1787; d. Paris, 26 July 1872. Italian composer. He composed nearly forty operas. His early works were usually produced in Naples or Rome, while the later ones, composed after his move to Paris, were as often as not written to French texts and first performed in Paris. His earliest successful opera was *Gabriella di Vergy* (Naples, 1816), and the most popular of his works for Paris were *Jeanne d'Arc à Orléans* (1821) and *Le Nozze di Lammermoor* (1829). He contributed some music to two operas by his life-long friend Rossini: *Adelaide di Borgogna* and *Mosè in Egitto*.

Cardillac. Opera in 3 acts by Hindemith. Libretto by Ferdinand Lion, based on E.T.A. Hoffmann's story, *Das Fräulein von Scuderi* (1818). First performed Dresden, 9 Nov 1926. A revised version, with the score unchanged but a new libretto provided by the composer, was first performed in Zurich, 20 June 1952.

Cardillac (bar.), a goldsmith and master jeweller, cannot bear to part with his creations, and murders each customer after a sale.

Carlo, Don (bar.). Brother of the heroine in Verdi's *La Forza del Destino*, he avenges the death of their father.

Carlos, Don (ten.). Son of Philip II of Spain, in Verdi's *Don Carlos*.

Carlyle, Joan, b. Upton-on-the-Wirral, Cheshire, 6 Apr 1931. English soprano. She made her début at Covent Garden in 1955 as Frasquita in *Carmen*, and sang at Covent Garden frequently for the next fifteen years. Her roles ranged widely from Mozart's Countess through Verdi (Desdemona and Oscar) and Puccini (Mimi) to Zdenka in *Arabella*. She made a few appearances abroad, in Vienna, Munich and Buenos Aires, but her career remained centred upon London.

Carmen. Opera in 4 acts by Bizet. Libretto by Meilhac and Halévy, after the novel by Prosper Mérimée (1845). First performed Paris, 3 Mar 1875. When the opera was performed in Vienna some months later, on 23 Oct 1875, the spoken dialogue was replaced by recitatives composed by Ernest Guiraud. It is only in recent years that the original version has begun to oust Guiraud from the stage.

The opera is set in and near Seville in 1820. Act 1 takes place in a square, where a young corporal, Don José (ten.) is on guard. He is visited by Micaëla (sop.), his village sweetheart and who brings him news of his mother. When the girls who are employed at a nearby cigarette factory emerge from their place of work, one of them, the gipsy Carmen (mezzo-sop.), throws him a flower. Minutes later, following a fight with another girl, Carmen is arrested and José prepares to escort her to prison. Carmen persuades José to allow her to escape.

Act 2 takes place in the tavern of Lillas Pastia, a haunt of smugglers. Escamillo (bar.), a toreador, offers his homage to Carmen, while she awaits José, who has spent some time in prison for having allowed her to escape. Carmen attempts to persuade José to join her and a band of smugglers who have an escapade afoot. He is on the point of refusing when the arrival of his Captain (bass) with whom he fights over Carmen, decides the issue. José deserts his regiment for Carmen and the smugglers.

In Act 3, set in the smugglers' hideout in the mountains, José becomes jealous of Escamillo who visits Carmen. When Micaëla brings him a message that his mother is dying, José leaves with her, but vows to return. The fourth act takes place outside the bull ring in Seville. Carmen arrives to watch her new lover, Escamillo, triumph in the bull fight. When a desperate José blocks her path and demands that she return to him, she replies scornfully. In a jealous fury, José stabs her, and then allows himself to be arrested, as the crowd inside the stadium is heard acclaiming the triumph of Escamillo.

Carmen Jones. Musical, which makes use of much of the music of Bizet's *Carmen*, with a new English text by Oscar Hammerstein II, and the characters American blacks during World War II. Carmen Jones (mezzo-sop.), who works in a parachute factory, deserts Corporal Joe (ten.) for Husky Miller (bar.), a prizefighter. *Carmen Jones* was first performed in New York on 2 Dec 1943. A film version, directed by Otto Preminger, was made in 1954, for which the singing voice of Carmen Jones was provided by Marilyn Horne.

Carmina Burana (*Songs of Benediktbeuren*, a Bavarian monastery). Opera in 3 parts by Orff, with a text drawn by the composer and Michel Hofmann from poems in Latin, old German and old French, in a 13th-c. Latin codex in the monastery of Benediktbeuren. First performed, Frankfurt, 8 June 1937.

Carosio, Margherita, b. Genoa, 7 June 1908. Italian soprano. She studied in Genoa, and in 1927 made her début at nearby Novi Ligure as Lucia. The following year she sang Feodor in *Boris Godunov* at Covent Garden, and appeared regularly in the bel canto roles at La Scala throughout the 1930-40s. She returned to London in 1946 with the Naples San Carlo company, as Violetta, and again in 1950 with the Scala company, as Adina in *L'Elisir d'Amore*. An attractive lyric coloratura, she was also an actress of considerable charm.

Carré, Michel, b. Paris, 1819; d. Argenteuil, 27 June 1872. French librettist. A prolific writer and translator, he furnished libretti for most of the French composers of his time, either alone or in collaboration with Jules Barbier. Those he wrote with Barbier include *Les Contes d'Hoffmann* for Offenbach, *Faust* for Gounod, *Dinorah* for Meyerbeer and *Mignon* for Thomas. With Eugène Cormon he wrote *Les Pêcheurs de Perles* for Bizet, and alone he provided Gounod with *Mireille*.

Carreras, José, b. Barcelona, 5 Dec 1946. Spanish tenor. He studied in Barcelona, where he made his début in 1969 as Ismaele in *Nabucco*. He first appeared in the US with the New York City Opera as Pinkerton in 1972, having sung in London the previous year in a concert performance of *Maria Stuarda* with Montserrat Caballé who was instrumental in helping him at the outset of his career. He sings in the leading international houses, and has enjoyed particular success as Alfredo, Pinkerton and Rodolfo. His essentially lyrical voice is of attractive quality, though he occasionally strains it in attempting roles too heavy for him.

cartellone. Literally a huge playbill, the cartellone is the list of operas which a company plans to perform during the season. This is usually a preliminary list, drawn up in advance before the full details of casting are known.

Caruso, Enrico, b. Naples, 27 Feb 1873; d. Naples, 2 Aug 1921. Italian tenor. The most famous tenor of his time, he was born of poor parents and, as a child, sang in churches. After studying in Naples, he sang in a number of small theatres in southern Italy. His international career dates from the première of Giordano's *Fedora* (Milan, 1898) when he created the role of Loris. He first appeared at Covent Garden in 1902, as the Duke in *Rigoletto*, but the theatre with which he is most associated is the old Metropolitan Opera House, where he was engaged for most seasons from 1902-20. His voice, not of exceptional range, was of superb quality, from its dark, baritone base, which became even darker in later years, to the brilliance of his high notes. The warmth and immediacy of his phrasing made him one of the most popular of singers on record, in Italian song as well as in opera.

Casella, Alfredo, b. Turin, 25 July 1883; d. Rome, 5 Mar 1947. Italian composer. He studied in Paris with Fauré, and then returned to Italy where he became one of the most influential figures in Italian musical life

Enrico Caruso as the Duke of Mantua in Verdi's *Rigoletto*, a role he sang at Covent Garden in 1902.

in the 1920-30s. He composed music for a number of ballets, and three operas: *La Donna Serpente*, based on the fable by Carlo Gozzi, and first performed in Rome in 1932; *La Favola d'Orfeo*, a chamber opera staged in Venice, also in 1932; and a 1-act piece, *Il Deserto Tentato*, described as 'a mystery', produced in Florence in 1937. By the time he came to compose his operas, Casella's style was neo-classical.

Caspar [or Kaspar] (bass). A young huntsman in Weber's *Der Freischütz*.

Cassilly, Richard, b. Washington D.C., 14 Dec 1927. American tenor. He studied in Baltimore, and made his stage début in 1954

in New York in Menotti's *The Saint of Bleeker Street*. He sang with the New York City Opera and Chicago Lyric Opera, before going to Europe where his first appearance was in Geneva in 1965 as Raskolnikoff in Sutermeister's opera of that name, based on Dostoevsky's *Crime and Punishment*. A dramatic tenor of imposing voice and physique, he has proved a useful exponent of the Wagner roles which he sang in a number of European opera houses in the 1960-70s, and into the early 1980s.

Castagna, Bruna, b. Bari, 15 Oct 1905. Italian contralto. She made her début in Mantua in 1925 as the Nurse in *Boris Godunov*, and sang in Italy and at the Met until 1945. She had a huge success at La Scala in 1933 as Isabella in *L'Italiana in Algeri*, and was also a distinguished Adalgisa, Azucena, and Amneris. After her retirement she taught in Milan for many years.

Castelnuovo-Tedesco, Mario, b. Florence, 3 Apr 1895; d. Los Angeles, 17 Mar 1968. Italian composer. One of the leading Italian composers of the 1920-30s, as a Jew he left Italy in 1939, and lived for the rest of his life in the USA. He showed a marked predilection for English subjects in his mature operas, which include *The Merchant of Venice* (first performed in Florence, 1961), *All's Well That Ends Well* (composed between 1955-8; unperformed), and a chamber opera based on Oscar Wilde's play, *The Importance of Being Earnest* (performed on Italian radio in 1972).

Casti, Giovanni Battista, b. Acquapendente, 29 Aug 1724; d. Paris, 5 Feb 1803. Italian poet, dramatist and librettist. For a time he was court poet to Francis II in Vienna, and also travelled in Russia where he provided libretti for Italian operas performed at the Russian court. Among the libretti he wrote in Vienna for Salieri is that for *Prima la Musica e Poi le Parole*, a satire on the low status of the librettist which Clemens Krauss remembered when he came to write the libretto of *Capriccio* for Richard Strauss in the 20th c.

Castor et Pollux. Opera in a prologue and 5 acts by Rameau. Libretto by Pierre Joseph Bernard. First performed Paris, 24 Oct 1737.

The story from Greek mythology of Castor and Polydeuces (or Pollux, as Latinized), the twins who in later myth were identified with the constellation Gemini. When Castor (ten.), son of Leda and Tyndareus, is killed, Pollux (bar.), son of Leda and Jupiter and thus immortal, offers himself in Castor's place. Eventually Jupiter (bass) decrees that both shall be taken up to Olympus.

castrato. Literally a castrated male, the castrato was the male soprano whose unbroken voice had been preserved by pre-pubertal castration. Such voices were in demand in church choirs in the Catholic countries, and in the 17th-18th c. they began to be heard in opera. A number of male roles in the operas of such composers as Handel and Haydn are written for the castrato voice. The last composers to write such roles were Rossini and Meyerbeer at the beginning of the 19th c. The castrato survived in the choir of the Sistine Chapel until the turn of the century, the last professional castrato being Alessandro Moreschi, who made gramophone records in the early years of the 20th c., and who died in 1922 in his sixties.

Castro, Juan José, b. Avellareda, 7 Mar 1895; d. Buenos Aires, 5 Sept 1968. Argentinian composer and conductor. One of four brothers, all of them musicians, he conducted at the Teatro Colón between 1928-68. He composed eight operas, none of which is known outside Argentina, although one, *Proserpina y el Extranjero* (based on Lorca), was awarded the Verdi Prize by La Scala, Milan, in 1951.

Catalani, Alfredo, b. Lucca, 19 June 1854; d. Milan, 7 Aug 1893. Italian composer. The libretto of his first opera, *La Falce* (1875), was written by Boito. A 1-act student work, it was performed at the Milan Conservatorium. His first full-length opera, *Elda*, written before 1876, was not performed until 1880, and only became successful when, ten years later, it was revised and re-titled *Loreley*. Catalani's only opera to have endured, albeit tenuously, is *La Wally*, a piece of high romanticism first performed at La Scala in 1892, and championed by Toscanini (who named his daughter Wally after the opera's heroine). It is still performed in Italian opera houses.

Caterina Cornaro. Opera in a prologue and 2 acts by Donizetti. Libretto by Giacomo Sacchero, after Vernoy de St Georges's libretto for Halévy's *La Reine de Chypre* (1841). First performed Naples, 12 Jan 1844.

The wedding of Caterina (sop.) to a French knight, Gerardo (ten.), is postponed when Mocenigo (bass) brings word that Lusignano, King of Cyprus (bass), wishes to marry her. Gerardo and Lusignano later meet, and Gerardo helps Lusignano defend Cyprus against the Venetians. Lusignano is killed in battle but before he dies entrusts his people to Caterina's care.

Catulli Carmina. Scenic cantata by Orff. Libretto by the composer after verses by Catullus. First performed, Leipzig, 6 Nov 1943.

Elders interrupt the love-making of boys and girls by reminding them of the fate of the poet Catullus, who died of love. The story of Catullus and his love for Lesbia who betrays him with his friend Caelus is mimed, as a warning to the young people, while a hidden chorus sings poems by Catullus. At the end, the young people return, undeterred, to their expressions of everlasting passion.

Cavalieri, Lina, b. Viterbo, 25 Dec 1874; d. Florence, 7 Feb 1944. Italian soprano. She made her début in Lisbon in 1900 as Nedda, and later sang leading roles in a number of European opera houses. A woman of great beauty, she enjoyed a successful career although her vocal ability was not exceptional. Violetta, Manon and Tosca were among her most admired characterizations. She was married four times; one of her husbands was the tenor Lucien Muratore.

Cavalleria Rusticana. Opera in 1 act by Mascagni. Libretto by Guido Menasci and Giovanni Targioni-Tozzetti, based on the play of that name (1884) by Giovanni Verga which in turn was an adaptation of Verga's story (1880). First performed Rome, 17 May 1890.

Turiddu (ten.), a young Sicilian peasant, returns from war to find his sweetheart Lola (mezzo-sop.) married to Alfio (bar.), a carter. For consolation, he turns to Santuzza (sop.), who is distraught when, tiring of her, he becomes interested again in Lola who encourages him. When Turiddu refuses to return to Santuzza, she informs Alfio of his wife's infidelity with Turiddu. Alfio challenges Turiddu to a duel and kills him.

The entire action takes place in a Sicilian village square, on the morning of Easter Sunday. The famous 'Easter Hymn' is sung by a congregation within the church (off-stage) and by Santuzza and others in the square.

Cavalli, Pietro Francesco, b. Crema, 14 Feb 1602; d. Venice, 14 Jan 1676. Italian composer. A popular and prolific composer of opera in Venice in the quarter-century following Monteverdi, he sang at St Mark's as a boy soprano, and at the age of eighteen became organist there. He composed at least thirty-three operas, most of which were performed in Venice at the Teatro San Cassiano. Though they suffered neglect after his death, and are thought generally to possess less dramatic strength than those of Monteverdi, several operas by Cavalli have been revived in recent years. *Ormindo* (1644) and *Calisto* (1651) were staged at Glyndebourne in new performing editions by Raymond Leppard, and other operas have been taken up at Santa Fe (*Egisto* in 1974), Drottningholm (*Scipione Africano* in 1973) and elsewhere.

Cavaradossi (ten.). The artist hero of Puccini's *Tosca*.

cavatina. Supposedly a short solo song, the term has been used to describe such widely differing types of song or aria that it is now virtually meaningless. In the 18th-19th c., it was usually the singer's first solo number in an opera. Thus, the Countess's gently melancholy 'Porgi amor' in *Le Nozze di Figaro* is a cavatina, but so too is Figaro's ebullient 'Largo al factotum' in *Il Barbiere di Siviglia*. The term is occasionally used for instrumental music, such as the famous cavatina of Beethoven's String Quartet op. 130.

Cebotari, Maria, b. Kishinev, Bessarabia, 10 Feb 1910; d. Vienna, 9 June 1949. Austrian soprano of Russian birth. She studied in Berlin, and made her début in Dresden in 1931 as Mimi. She remained with the Dresden company until 1936,

creating the role of Aminta in Strauss's *Die Schweigsame Frau* there in 1935, and then sang at the Berlin Staatsoper from 1936-44. From 1946-9 she was a member of the Vienna Staatsoper. A lyric soprano with a fine voice and an attractive presence, she appeared in six films in Germany in the 1930s.

Cellier, Alfred, b. London, 1 Dec 1844; d. London, 28 Dec 1891. English composer and conductor. He conducted at several theatres, among them the Prince's Theatre, Manchester (from 1871-5) and the Criterion and St James's Theatres in London. He conducted the first performances of a number of Gilbert and Sullivan operas as well as the première of Sullivan's opera, *Ivanhoe* (1891), and also composed a number of comic operas and operettas, achieving his greatest success with *Dorothy* in London in 1888. He was the composer of the overture for Sullivan's *The Sorcerer* and assisted Sullivan with the composition of the overture for *The Pirates of Penzance*.

Cenerentola, La. Opera in 2 acts by Rossini. Libretto by Jacopo Ferretti, based on a French libretto by Charles Guillaume Étienne (written for the opera *Cendrillon* by Isouard, performed in 1810), which was in turn derived from the fairy story in Charles Perrault's *Mother Goose Tales* (1697). First performed Rome, 25 Jan 1817.

Angelina (mezzo-sop.), known as Cenerentola (Cinderella), is ill-treated by her father Don Magnifico (bass) and her two step-sisters (sop. and mezzo-sop.). The Prince Ramiro (ten.), posing as his valet Dandini (bar.) falls in love with Angelina, and his tutor Alidoro (bass) helps Angelina to attend the ball at the palace. The plot follows that of the familiar children's tale, with the element of magic removed by the substitution of a purely human agent, Alidoro (bass), for the fairy godmother of Perrault.

Cerquetti, Anita, b. Macerata, 13 Apr 1931. Italian soprano. She studied in Perugia, and made her début in 1951 in Spoleto as Aida. She became famous when, in 1958, she replaced Callas in *Norma* at the Rome Opera. Her dramatic soprano was well suited to such roles as Abigaille and Amelia but after an illness she retired.

Cesti, Antonio, b. Arezzo, 5 Aug 1623; d. Florence, 14 Oct 1669. Italian composer. The most famous Italian musician of his time, he became a monk of the Franciscan order while in his teens. He was, for a time, organist of Volterra Cathedral, and was later known as a tenor. His earliest opera, *Orontea*, was performed in Venice in 1649, and achieved great popularity throughout Italy in the following decades. Opera became his principal interest; even before he was released from his vows he became court composer to the Austrian Archduke Ferdinand Carl at Innsbruck and later was resident in Vienna. His most famous opera, *Il Pomo d'Oro*, a spectacular baroque production, was staged in Vienna in 1668.

Chabrier, Emmanuel, b. Ambert, Puy-de-Dôme, 18 Jan 1841; d. Paris, 13 Sept 1894. French composer. The libretti of his first two stage works, the unfinished operettas *Fisch-Ton-Kan* and *Vaucochard et Fils Ier* of

Title-page of *Le Roi Malgré Lui* by Emmanuel Chabrier. It was Chabrier's most successful *opéra comique*.

THÉÂTRE NATIONAL DE L'OPÉRA-COMIQUE

Le ROI MALGRÉ LUI

Opéra-Comique en 3 Actes

PAROLES DE MM. EMILE DE NAJAC & PAUL BURANI

Musique de EMMANUEL CHABRIER

ENOCH FRÈRES & COSTALLAT, ÉDITEURS 27, Boulevard des Italiens, PARIS

1863-4, were provided by the poet, Paul Verlaine. The works did not reach the stage until 1941 when they were produced by students in Paris. *L'Étoile*, a comic opera staged in Paris in 1877, was his first successful work for the stage, and it was followed two years later by the 1-act piece, *Une Education Manquée*. His best-known operas were written after his experience of hearing *Tristan und Isolde* in Munich. *Gwendoline*, staged in Brussels in 1886, is Wagnerian in its use of the *leitmotif*, while *Le Roi Malgré Lui* reverts to the vein of elegant comedy which appears to have been Chabrier's real métier.

Chailly, Luciano, b. Ferrara, 19 Jan 1920. Italian composer. He studied in Milan and under Hindemith in Salzburg, and took up several administrative positions in Italy. Between 1968-71 he was artistic director of La Scala, Milan. He has also taught composition at the Milan Conservatorium. His first opera, *Ferrovia Sopraelevata*, was staged at Bergamo in 1955, and he has since written several others. They include *Il Canto del Cigno* (Bologna, 1957), its libretto based on Chekhov; *Era Proibito* (Milan, 1963); and *L'Idiota*, based on Dostoevsky's novel, produced in Rome in 1970. Chailly's son, Riccardo (b. Milan, 20 Feb 1953) is a conductor of opera.

Chaliapin, Feodor, b. Kazan, 11 Feb 1873; d. Paris, 12 Apr 1938. Russian bass. He began his career with touring opera companies in Russia, and by the mid-1890s was singing in St Petersburg. He first appeared at the Bolshoi, Moscow, in 1899, and continued to sing there until 1920. His voluminous voice and great acting ability made him a famous Boris Godunov, and he was also much admired as Gounod's Méphistophélès. He made his first appearance outside Russia at La Scala in 1901 as Boito's Mefistofele. His Met début was in 1907, but he was less successful there than in London where he was a favourite for many years. Even after his voice had lost much of its power and freshness, his powerful acting (though some critics thought it over-acting) stood him in good stead as Boris, the role he chose for his final stage appearance in Monte Carlo in 1937. In 1932 he played the title-role in a film, *Don Quichotte*, for which Ibert composed the score.

Luigi Cherubini.

Chapi, Ruperto, b. Villena, 27 Mar 1851; d. Madrid, 25 Mar 1909. Spanish composer. Though he composed a 1-act opera, *Las Naves de Cortés*, which was staged in Madrid in 1874 with the famous tenor Enrico Tamberlik in the role of Cortés, it is as the composer of more than 100 *zarzuelas* that he became popular. Many of them are still performed in Spanish theatres.

Charlotte (mezzo-sop.). The heroine of Massenet's *Werther*.

Charpentier, Gustave, b. Dienze, 25 June 1860; d. Paris, 18 Feb 1956. French composer. He studied composition with Massenet, and in 1887 was awarded the Prix de Rome for his dramatic cantata, *Didon*. It was in Rome that he began the composition of his opera, *Louise*, for which he wrote his own libretto based to some extent on a Paris adventure of his student days. It was to take him ten years to achieve a production of *Louise* which, when it was eventually staged at the Paris Opéra-Comique in 1900, was a triumphant success. The work was acclaimed as a masterpiece of social realism which offered a new direction to French opera. In 1902 Charpentier founded a Conservatoire to give free musical instruction to working-girls like his heroine, Louise. The institution functioned until the outbreak of war in 1914. Charpentier was unable, however, to follow up the success of *Louise*. He produced a sequel, *Julien*, in 1913, but it failed to hold the stage. Though he lived on until the age of ninety-six, Charpentier never managed to complete any of his other operatic projects.

Charpentier, Marc-Antoine, b. Paris, *c.* 1640; d. Paris, 24 Feb 1704. French composer. Widely considered during his lifetime to be the equal of his more famous contemporary, Lully, he studied with Carissimi in Rome for several years, and then returned to Paris where he made a reputation for himself primarily as a composer of sacred music, both vocal and instrumental. He wrote the music for approximately thirty theatre pieces, which range from small-scale pastorals and chamber operas to full-scale lyric tragedies. His two major operas are *Medée* (1693) and *David et Jonathan* (1688), in the style of Lully.

Chausson, Ernest, b. Paris, 20 Jan 1855; d. Limay, 10 June 1899. French composer. At first he studied law, and it was only after he had obtained his degree and been sworn in as a barrister that he began seriously to study composition under Massenet and Franck. He composed in many forms, but was especially drawn to vocal music. In addition to a number of songs, he wrote three operas. Two, *Les Caprices de Marianne* (1884) and *Hélène* (1884) were not performed, but *Le Roi Arthus*, a somewhat Wagnerian work whose libretto the composer himself provided, was performed in Brussels in 1903, eight years after its composition.

Cherubini, Luigi, b. Florence, 8 or 14 Sept 1760; d. Paris, 15 Mar 1842. Italian composer. Though Italian, Cherubini lived for most of his life in Paris, and was a dominant figure in French musical (especially operatic) life in the first forty years of the 19th c.

He had already composed fifteen Italian operas before establishing himself in Paris, but it was only with the first of his operas to a French text, *Démophon* (1788), that his individuality became readily apparent. *Lodoïska* (1791), his first *opéra comique*, influenced a number of his younger contemporaries, and was followed by several other operas which are important in the development of *opéra comique* and of 19th-c. romantic opera. These include *Medée* (1797), a classical tragedy which has been revived in the mid-20th c.; *Les Deux Journées* (1800), a work which influenced Beethoven in the composition of *Fidelio*; *Anacréon* (1803); and *Les Abencérages* (1813). In his later years, Cherubini's interest in the stage lessened. He was Director of the Paris Conservatoire from 1821 until his death twenty-one years later.

Cherubino (sop.). The Countess Almaviva's young page in Mozart's *Le Nozze di Figaro*.

Cheval de Bronze, Le (*The Bronze Horse*). Opera in 3 acts by Auber. Libretto by Eugène Scribe. First performed Paris, 23 Mar 1835.

When Tsing Sing (bass), a mandarin, is turned to stone by one of his wives, another wife, Peki (sop.), flies off on a magic bronze horse to enlist the aid of Stella (sop.), a fairy princess. The spell is broken, on the understanding that, in return, Tsing Sing will divorce Peki and allow her to marry her true love, a young farmer.

Chiara, Maria, b. Oderzo, 24 Nov 1939. Italian soprano. She studied in Venice and made her début there in 1965 as Desdemona. She was first heard at Covent Garden as Liù in 1973. She is a sensitive artist, with a lyric soprano voice of great warmth. One of her best roles is Butterfly in Puccini's *Madama Butterfly*.

Chlubna, Osvald, b. Brno, 22 June 1893; d. Brno, 30 Oct 1971. Czech composer. Though he had a few lessons with Janáček, he earned his living as a bank clerk until his retirement in 1953. His music is essentially lyrical but, despite his lack of aptitude for opera, he continued throughout his life to compose works for the stage. He wrote nine operas, among them *Pomsta Catullova* (*Catullus's Revenge*; 1917) and *Kolébka* (*The Cradle*; 1952). An excellent orchestrator, he scored the final act of Janáček's *Sárka* and helped to prepare Janáček's *From the House of the Dead* for its posthumous première in 1930.

chorus. The chorus is both the group of singers and the music they sing. The chorus in opera usually consists of groups of citizens or slaves or soldiers or guests who observe and comment upon the action. In the earlier operas the chorus played a subsidiary role in the drama, but since Gluck in the 18th-c., and Wagner in the 19th-c., it has come to assume a more important dramatic function.

Christoff, Boris, b. Sofia, 18 May 1918. Bulgarian bass. He studied in Rome and Salzburg, and made his first appearance in opera in Reggio Calabria as Colline in *La Bohème*. He first sang Boris Godunov at Covent Garden in 1949: he became the leading Boris of the post-war years, and was still singing the role more than thirty years later. He was also a superb Philip II in *Don Carlos*, and showed an unexpected gift for comedy as Basilio in *Il Barbiere di Siviglia*. His voice had a highly individual timbre, and his acting a power and intensity which made him unrivalled in the great Russian and Italian bass roles.

Christophe Colomb. Opera in 2 parts (27 scenes) by Milhaud. Libretto by Paul Claudel. First performed Berlin, 5 May, 1930 (in German translation).

A narrator (speaking role) announces the work as 'The Book of the Life and Voyages of Christopher Columbus, who discovered America'. The opera recounts events in the life of Columbus (bar.), the main protagonist of the plot being the Chorus, which takes on the role of interpreter. Pantomime, ballet and even a filmed episode, are introduced, and the action takes place on varying levels of consciousness, with no straightforward dramatic development.

Boris Christoff in the title-role of *Boris Godunov* at Covent Garden in 1965. He is one of the leading interpreters of this role in the postwar years and is an outstanding Philip II in *Don Carlos*.

Chrysothemis (sop.). Elektra's sister in Strauss's *Elektra*.

Ciboulette. Operetta in 3 acts by Hahn. Libretto by Robert de Flers and Francis de Croisset. First performed Paris, 7 Apr 1923.

Set in the Paris of the Second Empire, the typically complicated operetta plot tells of the adventures of a country girl, Ciboulette (sop.), who becomes involved with Antonin (ten.), a Parisian aristocrat.

Cid, Le. Opera in 4 acts by Massenet. Libretto by Adolphe D'Ennery, Louis Gallet and Édouard Blau, based on the play by Corneille (1637). First performed Paris, 30 Nov 1885.

The plot is based on the exploits of Ruy Díaz de Bivar (*c.* 1043-99) who was known as El Cid (from the Arabic, *sidi* or 'lord'), and who fought both for and against the Moorish rulers who at that time controlled much of the Iberian peninsula.

Cigna, Gina, b. Paris, 6 Mar 1900. Italian soprano of French birth. She studied singing in Paris, and also piano with Cortot, and made her début at La Scala in 1927 as Freia, under the name of Genoveffa Sens (having married the tenor Maurice Sens). She returned in 1929 as Gina Cigna, and sang at La Scala until 1943, establishing herself as the leading Italian dramatic soprano of her time. She appeared at Covent Garden and the Met in the 1930s, and also sang in Chicago and San Francisco. After a motor accident in 1947 she gave up her stage career and devoted herself to teaching.

Cikker, Ján, b. Banska Bystrica, 29 July 1911. Slovak composer. He studied in Prague and Vienna, and then taught in Bratislava for some years. He has composed five operas in a post-romantic idiom, all of which have been successfully produced in Czechoslovakia. The best-known outside his own country is *Vzkriesenie (Resurrection)*, based on Tolstoy. Composed in 1962, it is the first of Cikker's operas in which twelve-tone serial techniques begin to replace, or at least to be heard alongside his earlier style.

Cilea, Francesco, b. Palmi, 26 July 1866; d. Varazze, 20 Nov 1950. Italian composer. His first opera, *Gina*, was composed while he was still a pupil at the Naples Conservatorium in 1889, and created a sufficiently favourable impression for Cilea to be taken up by the publishing firm of Sonzogno. *La Tilda*, produced in Florence in 1892, was generally considered disappointing, but Sonzogno persevered with the young composer who, discouraged by the reception of *La Tilda*, took the first of several teaching posts he was to have throughout his life. With his third opera, *L'Arlesiana* (Milan, 1897), based on Daudet's tragedy *L'Arlesienne*, Cilea achieved a certain measure of success, due in large part to the fact that the tenor role of Federico was sung by Enrico Caruso. The composer continued to revise and alter *L'Arlesiana*, even supplying a new prelude as late as 1937. It was, however, with *Adriana Lecouvreur*, staged in Milan in 1902 with Angelica Pandolfini and (again) Caruso, that Cilea achieved his only real success in Italy. The opera is still performed in Italy, though it has never been popular abroad. *Gloria* was staged in Milan in 1907 but dropped after two performances, and a final opera, *Il Matrimonio Selvaggio*, composed in 1909, was never performed.

Cimarosa, Domenico, b. Aversa, 17 Dec 1749; d. Venice, 11 Jan 1801. Italian composer. An important composer of comic opera in the late-18th c., he studied in Naples where his first opera, *Le Stravaganze*

del Conte, was produced. Within a few years he had achieved a reputation as the leading Neapolitan opera composer of his generation, and his operas began to be produced elsewhere. In 1787 he accepted an invitation to become composer to the court of Catherine II (Catherine the Great) at St Petersburg, and spent four years in Russia, during which time three new works were produced in St Petersburg: *La Felicità Inaspettata* (1788), *Le Vergine del Sole* (1789) and *La Cleopatra* (1789). He then moved to Vienna where he succeeded Salieri as Court Kapellmeister. *Il Matrimonio Segreto*, his most famous opera, and the only one to be regularly performed today, was staged in Vienna in 1792. Its first performance was such a success that the Emperor Leopold II ordered a second performance the same evening. After the death of Leopold, Cimarosa returned to his native Naples. The most important of his serious operas, *Gli Orazi ed I Curiazi*, was produced in 1796 in Venice. His composition of a patriotic hymn during the period when Naples was briefly occupied by French republicans in January 1799 led to his arrest and imprisonment when the monarchy was re-established some months later. At the intercession of friends he escaped a death sentence, was released, and made his way to Venice where he died while at work on a new opera, *Artemisia*.

Cio-Cio-San (sop.). The real name of the eponymous heroine of Puccini's *Madama Butterfly*.

Ciro in Babilonia (*Cyrus in Babylon*). Opera in 2 acts by Rossini. Libretto by Francesco Aventi. First performed Ferrara, 14 Mar 1812.

Rossini's fifth opera, its première was regarded by the composer as a fiasco, and he showed little further interest in it. It was given a few other performances in Italy for about fifteen years, since when it has not been revived.

claque. The French word for 'smack' or 'slap' is used to describe a group of regular opera-goers who organize themselves together for the purposes of leading the applause for a performer. Their leader receives a fee from the singer or conductor, and the members of the group may share in this or simply be given free tickets to performances. They then applaud at appropriate moments, and demand encores. In the 19th c. and earlier 20th c. the claque was an accepted fact of life in most opera houses, especially in Latin countries. A tariff quoted in Italy in 1919 offered applause for a gentleman's entry at 25 lire, applause for a lady's entry at 15 lire, insistent applause at 15 to 17 lire, and so on, leading up to 'wild enthusiasm' for which special arrangements had to be made. As recently as the late 1950s and early 1960s at La Scala, the rival claques of Maria Callas and Renata Tebaldi have clashed, and on one occasion the resulting brawl led to the arrest of two *claqueurs*. The claque in Rome is also by no means inactive.

Claudel, Paul, b. Villeneuve, 6 Aug 1868; d. Paris, 23 Feb 1955. French dramatist, poet, and librettist. His poetic drama, *L'Annonce Faite à Marie* (1910, revised in 1948) was used by Renzo Rosselini for his opera of the same name (1972). Claudel himself wrote the libretti of Milhaud's *Christophe Colomb* and *Orestie*, and of Honegger's stage oratorio, *Jeanne d'Arc au Bûcher*.

Clément, Edmond, b. Paris, 28 Mar 1867; d. Nice, 24 Feb 1928. French tenor. He studied in Paris, and made his début there at the Opéra-Comique in 1889 as Vincent in Gounod's *Mireille*. He became the leading French lyric tenor of his time, and made a number of appearances abroad. His Met début was in 1909 as Werther. An elegant stylist, he was at his best in French roles.

Clemenza di Tito, La *(The Clemency of Titus)*. Opera in 2 acts by Mozart. Libretto by Pietro Metastasio, revised by Caterino Mazzolà. (Metastasio's libretto, originally in 3 acts, had first been set by Antonio Caldara, whose *Clemenza di Tito* was produced in Vienna in 1734.) First performed, Prague, 6 Sept 1791.

Mozart's penultimate opera, composed when he had already written the greater part of his final opera, *Die Zauberflöte*, it is set in Rome, in AD 80. The Emperor Tito (ten.) is plotted against by Vitellia (sop.) who incites her admirer Sesto (mezzo-sop.) to murder him. The plot is unsuccessful, and the conspirators are brought before the Emperor who forgives them.

Cleva, Fausto, b. Trieste, 17 May 1902; d. Athens, 6 Aug 1971. Italian, later American, conductor. He studied in Trieste and Milan, and made his début while still in his teens, conducting *La Traviata* at the Teatro Carcano in Milan. In 1920 he emigrated to the United States (and later became an American citizen), and was immediately engaged by the Met as an assistant conductor. He conducted at the Met for the rest of his life, specializing in the 19th-c. Italian repertory. He also conducted in Chicago, San Francisco and Cincinnati. He died while conducting an open-air performance of Gluck's *Orfeo* in Athens.

Cloches de Corneville, Les *(The Bells of Corneville)*. *Opéra comique* in 3 acts by Planquette. Libretto by 'Clairville' (i.e. Louis François Nicolaie) and Charles Gabet. First performed Paris, 19 Apr 1877.

Planquette's most popular comic opera, it is set in Normandy at the time of Louis XV, and tells of the love of Henri, Marquis of Valleroi (bar.) for his servant, Germaine (mezzo-sop.) who, in due course, is discovered to be a Marchioness in her own right. This tuneful work is still performed in France, though it is little-known abroad.

Cluytens, André, b. Antwerp, 26 Mar 1905; d. Paris, 3 June 1967. Belgian, later French, conductor. He studied in Antwerp, and made his début conducting Bizet's *Les Pêcheurs de Perles* at the Royal Theatre in Antwerp in 1927. In the 1930s he conducted at several French opera houses, and became music director of the Opéra-Comique, Paris, in 1947. In 1955 he conducted *Tannhäuser* at Bayreuth, the first Belgian or French conductor to be engaged there. He also conducted regularly at the Vienna Staatsoper after 1959. He was at his best in the operas of 19th-c. French composers.

Coates, Albert, b. St Petersburg, 23 Apr 1882; d. Cape Town, 11 Dec 1953. Anglo-Russian conductor and composer. He studied in Leipzig, and conducted in German towns before becoming chief conductor and artistic director of the St Petersburg Opera from 1909-17. He then left Russia and between 1917-38 frequently conducted in England. He composed two operas. *Samuel Pepys* was produced in Munich in 1929, and *Pickwick* was staged at

Covent Garden in 1936 during a season mounted by the short-lived British Music Drama Opera Company, whose guiding spirits were Coates and the Russian tenor Vladimir Rosing.

Coates, Edith, b. Lincoln, 31 May 1908; d. Worthing, 7 Jan 1983. English mezzo-soprano. She studied at Trinity College of Music, London, and after a period in the chorus, made her opera début at the Old Vic, as Giovanna in *Rigoletto*. When the company moved to Sadler's Wells Theatre in 1931, she became its principal mezzo, and remained with the company until 1946, when she joined the newly formed ensemble at the Royal Opera House. She created the role of Auntie in *Peter Grimes* in 1945, and towards the end of her career was a striking Countess in Tchaikovsky's *Queen of Spades*. She was an enthusiastic, if over-colourful actress.

Coates, John, b. Girlington, 29 June 1865; d. Northwood, 16 Aug 1941. English tenor. He was in his late twenties when he decided to become a professional singer, and sang as a baritone for five years with the D'Oyly Carte company. After further study, he made his début in opera at Covent Garden in the tenor role of Claudio in Stanford's *Much Ado About Nothing*. He went on to become the finest English oratorio tenor of his time, but also sang the Wagner tenor roles, both at Covent Garden and abroad. He was much admired as Tristan and as Siegfried, both of which roles he sang under Sir Thomas Beecham. He sang very little opera after 1914.

Cocteau, Jean, b. Maisons-Laffitte, 5 July, 1889; d. Paris, 12 Oct 1963. French poet, playwright and novelist. Involved to some extent with almost every experimental artistic movement of his time, Cocteau allowed several of his plays to be used for operatic purposes, among them *Antigone* (Honegger), and *La Voix Humaine* (Poulenc). He wrote the libretto of *Le Pauvre Matelot* for Milhaud and adapted *Oedipus Rex* from Sophocles for Stravinsky.

Coertse, Mimi, b. Durban, 12 June 1932. South African soprano. She studied in Johannesburg and with Josef Witt in Vienna, and then joined the company of the Vienna

Staatsoper. A lyric coloratura of great agility, she excelled in such roles as Mozart's Queen of Night, Zerbinetta in *Ariadne auf Naxos* and Olympia in *Tales of Hoffmann*. She made guest appearances at Covent Garden in the mid-1950s, but in recent years has sung mainly in South Africa.

Colas Breugnon. Opera in 3 acts by Kabalevsky. Libretto by V. G. Bragin after the play by Romain Rolland. First performed Leningrad, 22 Feb 1938; revised version performed Moscow, 20 Mar 1971.

A satirical tale of a sculptor, Colas Breugnon (bar.) who outwits the tyrannical Duke (ten.).

Colbran, Isabella, b. Madrid, 2 Feb 1785; d. Bologna, 7 Oct 1845. Spanish soprano. She studied in Madrid, and after singing in concerts in Paris made her way to Italy, where she became a leading singer in Naples. Her extensive range of almost three octaves and her dramatic power led Rossini to compose roles for her in a number of operas, among them *Elisabetta, Regina d'Inghilterra* (1815), *Otello* (1816) and *La Donna del Lago* (1819). She lived with Rossini for some years and in 1822 married him. The final opera Rossini composed for her was *Semiramide* (1823), and she retired from the stage the following year, her voice having seriously declined. She and Rossini legally separated in 1837. Colbran was the composer of four volumes of songs.

Collier, Marie, b. Ballarat, 16 Apr 1926; d. London, 8 Dec 1971. Australian soprano. She studied in Melbourne, and began her career there in operetta. After appearing in Offenbach's *La Belle Hélène* with Max Oldaker as Paris, she undertook a tour of Australia as Magda Sorel in Menotti's *The Consul*. She made her London début at Covent Garden in 1956 as Musetta, and sang at Covent Garden regularly until her death. She was at her best as Puccini's Butterfly, Tosca and Manon. At the Met in 1967 she created the role of Christine Mannon in Levy's *Mourning Becomes Electra*. She was an antipodean Callas, with much of the Greek soprano's vibrant stage personality and flawed vocalism.

Colline (bass). A philosopher, one of the four bohemians in Puccini's *La Bohème*.

coloratura. Literally 'colouring', the term refers musically to passages of elaborate ornamentation, more properly known in Italian as *fioritura*. The word is also used as an adjective to describe the type of singer who specializes in roles requiring great agility of voice, and containing a significant number of passages of brilliant and elaborate vocalism. Such voices are usually of necessity light, lyric voices, but occasionally a dramatic voice will exhibit the same degree of agility.

Coltellini, Marco, b. Livorno, 13 Oct 1719; d. St Petersburg, Nov 1777. Italian librettist. For a time he worked in Vienna as court poet, but in 1772 moved to St Petersburg in a similar capacity. He wrote more than eighteen libretti, among them *La Finta Semplice*, a revision of Goldoni, for Mozart; *La Finta Giardiniera*, a revision of Calzabigi, also for Mozart; and *L'Infedeltà Delusa* for Haydn.

Combattimento di Tancredi e Clorinda, Il (*The Combat of Tancredi and Clorinda*). Dramatic cantata by Monteverdi. Libretto from Tasso's *Gerusalemme Liberata* (1575). First performed Venice, in the carnival season of 1624.

Tancredi, a Christian knight in love with a Saracen maiden, Clorinda, fights and defeats a Saracen in armour who has burnt a Christian castle. The Saracen is revealed to be Clorinda. Not strictly an opera, the work is performed by actors, with a narrator who sings.

comprimario. Literally 'with the principal', the term refers to the singer of small roles, and to those roles. Examples of comprimario roles are the countless confidantes, servants and messengers who utter no more than a line or two, or who may have larger roles but without any solo arias or important parts in ensembles, e.g. Goro in *Madama Butterfly*, Spoletta in *Tosca*, Marullo in *Rigoletto*. Some singers begin their careers in comprimario roles before graduating to leading parts, but others, whose voices may not be attractive enough for leading roles, make their careers as comprimario artists.

Comte Ory, Le (*Count Ory*). Opera in 2 acts by Rossini. Libretto by Eugène Scribe and Charles Gaspard Delestre-Poirson. First performed Paris, 20 Aug 1828.

When her brother leaves to go on one of the Crusades, the Countess Adèle (sop.) retreats with her ladies-in-waiting to her castle. The licentious Count Ory (ten.) makes attempts upon her virtue, by disguising himself first as a hermit and then, when this fails, as the Mother Superior of a group of nuns, who are really his own men in female attire. Ory's plans are thwarted by the young page, Isolier (mezzo-sop.) who is in love with the Countess, and also by the return of the Crusaders at a crucial moment.

Rossini's penultimate stage work, and his only comic opera in French, *Le Comte Ory* makes use of much of the music of an earlier Rossini opera, *Il Viaggio a Reims* (1825). Twelve numbers, however, were newly written.

Constanze (sop.). The heroine of Mozart's *Die Entführung aus dem Serail*.

Consul, The. Opera in 3 acts by Menotti. Libretto by the composer. First performed Philadelphia, 1 Mar 1950.

In a police state, 'somewhere in Europe', Magda Sorel (sop.) attempts to obtain an exit visa for herself and her husband John (bar.), a revolutionary who is being pursued by the secret police. Her attempts to see the Consul are frustrated by a secretary (sop.). When her husband is arrested, Magda kills herself.

Contes d'Hoffmann, Les (*The Tales of Hoffmann*). Opera in 3 acts by Offenbach. Libretto by Jules Barbier and Michel Carré, based on their play of the same title (1851), which in turn was based on stories by E.T.A. Hoffmann, from his volumes *Nachtstücke* (1817), *Fantasiestücke in Callots Manier* (1814) and *Die Serapionsbrüder* (1819). Left incomplete by the composer, the opera was revised, given recitatives and (in part) orchestrated by Ernest Guiraud.

A prologue and epilogue are set in a wine-cellar under the opera house in Nuremberg, where the drunken poet, Hoffmann (ten.), is regaling students with tales of his three great loves. Act I tells of his infatuation for Olympia (sop.) who is revealed to be a mechanical animated doll, and is destroyed by one of her creators, Coppelius (bar.). In Act II, he is involved with the singer Antonia (sop.), a consumptive who has been forbidden, for health reasons, to sing, but who is forced to do so by Dr Miracle (bar.). Act III, set in Venice, introduces the courtesan, Giulietta (sop.), who, at the instigation of Dapertutto (bar.), steals Hoffmann's reflection (soul) from him. Coppelius, Miracle and Dapertutto are all manifestations of the poet's evil genius, and are intended to be performed by one singer.

There is no definitive performing edition of the opera. Productions occasionally reverse the order of Acts II and III, and Guiraud's recitatives are sometimes replaced by the original dialogue. An edition by Dr Fritz Oeser, first performed in Miami in January, 1980, conducted by Antonio de Almeida, with Nicolai Gedda as Hoffmann, would seem most closely to represent the composer's intentions.

contralto. The contralto has the lowest range of any female voice. Formerly, the contralto and the soprano were the only classifications, but in modern times a number of singers who earlier would have been classified as contraltos are described as mezzo-sopranos, the upper part of their range being developed to give them one or two notes beyond the usual contralto range. The really deep contralto voice has become rare.

Copland, Aaron, b. Brooklyn, NY, 14 Nov 1900. American composer. The son of Russian Jews who had emigrated to the United States, he is the most distinguished American composer of our time. Prolific in many forms of music, he has composed only two operas, the first of which was a school-play opera, *The Second Hurricane*, performed at a high school in 1937. His major opera, *The Tender Land*, began as a 2-act piece in 1954, and was revised by the composer and presented again the following year in 3 acts. A melodious and colourfully scored opera set in the mid-west in the depression years, it is one of Copland's most enjoyable works which has not received the acclaim it deserves.

Copley, John, b. Birmingham, 12 June 1933. English producer. He studied at the National School of Opera, London, and became a stage manager at Sadler's Wells

Theatre before producing *Il Tabarro* there in 1957. He later became resident producer with The Royal Opera, Covent Garden, and has staged a large number of operas for the company. He has also worked in America and Australia. His style is conventional and competent, in the best sense. He directed the 1982 Covent Garden production of Handel's *Semele* which commemorated the 150th anniversary of the theatre.

Corelli, Franco, b. Ancona, 8 Apr 1921. Italian tenor. He studied in Pesaro and made his début in 1951 at Spoleto as Don José. By 1954 he was appearing at La Scala, where he was heard frequently throughout the following decade. His first Covent Garden appearance was in 1957 as Cavaradossi, and his Met début was in 1961 as Manrico. He

Aaron Copland, composer of *The Tender Land*, an attractive modern American opera.

sang at the Met for a number of seasons, and was greatly admired in the heavier Italian tenor roles, and also as Werther. His voice was a fine instrument, and his handsome stage presence enhanced his appeal. His acting was, at best, casual.

Corena, Fernando, b. Geneva, 22 Dec 1916. Swiss bass. He had intended to take holy orders, but turned to singing after winning an amateur contest. He then studied in Milan, but returned to Zurich during the war years, singing occasionally at the Municipal Theatre. His post-war début was in Trieste in 1947 as Varlaam in *Boris Godunov*. He soon began to specialize in the buffo bass roles such as Leporello, the role of his Met début in 1953, Rossini's Bartolo, which he sang at his first appearance at Covent Garden in 1960, Osmin and Dulcamara. He sang the title-role in *Falstaff* for the first time at the Edinburgh Festival in 1955.

Cornelius, Peter, b. Mainz, 24 Dec 1824; d. Mainz, 26 Oct 1874. German composer. At the age of 16 he was a violinist in the Mainz theatre orchestra, after which he became an actor for some years. In Weimar he met Liszt who recognized his talents as a composer, and introduced him to the musicians and poets of his circle. Through Liszt he also met Wagner, to whose ideals he thereafter devoted his life. Primarily interested in the composition of Lieder, Cornelius spent three years composing his first opera, *Der Barbier von Bagdad* which was produced by Liszt in Weimar in 1858. It proved a fiasco and led to Liszt's leaving Weimar, but slowly made its way to other German theatres. Cornelius moved to Vienna, where he wrote both the libretto and the music of his second opera, *Der Cid*, which was produced in Weimar in 1865. At Wagner's instigation, Cornelius then took up residence in Munich where he became one of Wagner's close friends. His third opera, *Gunlöd*, which promised to be rather more Wagnerian than the earlier two, was begun in 1866 but never finished.

Corregidor, Der (*The Magistrate*). Opera in 4 acts by Wolf. Libretto by Rosa Mayreder, after the story *El Sombrero de Tres Picos* by Pedro Antonio de Alarcón (1874). First performed Mannheim, 7 June 1896.

In early 19th-c. Andalusia, the magistrate (ten.) of a small town attempts to seduce Frasquita (mezzo-sop.), the wife of the miller (bar.), but merely brings comic disaster upon himself.

Into this, his only completed opera, Wolf introduced two of his finest songs, 'In dem Schatten meiner Locken', sung by Frasquita to the magistrate, and 'Herz, verzage nicht geschwind', sung by the magistrate.

Corsaro, Il (*The Corsair*). Opera in 3 acts by Verdi. Libretto by Francesco Maria Piave, based on the poem *The Corsair* by Byron (1814). First performed Trieste, 25 Oct 1848.

This early Verdi opera tells of the exploits of the pirate or corsair, Corrado (ten.), who leaves his mistress, Medora (sop.), on his Aegean island while he leads his followers against the Pasha Seid (bar.) in the Turkish city of Coron. Taken prisoner by Seid, he is helped to escape by the Pasha's favourite slave, Gulnara (sop.), who accompanies him back to his island where they arrive to find Medora dying. In despair, Corrado throws himself into the sea.

Though it was neglected for many years, *Il Corsaro*, like other early Verdi operas which are coming back into favour, has recently been staged in several countries.

Cortez, Viorica, b. Bucium, 26 Dec 1935. Romanian mezzo-soprano. She studied in Bucharest, and began her career as a concert singer. She first sang in opera as Dalila in Toulouse in 1965, and the following year became a member of the Bucharest Opera. It was as Carmen that she was first heard at Covent Garden, in 1968, and in the United States (Philadelphia) in 1970. She is a useful performer in the Verdi mezzo roles.

Cortis, Antonio, b. on a ship between Oran and Altea, Spain, 12 Aug 1891; d. Valencia, 2 Apr 1952. Spanish tenor. He studied in Madrid and sang small roles there before beginning to assume larger ones, such as Cavaradossi and Don José, in Barcelona and Valencia. His Italian career began in 1919, and from 1924-32 he was heard regularly in Chicago. His only Covent Garden appearances were in 1931 as Calaf and as Ippolito in Romani's *Fedra* opposite Rosa Ponselle. After 1935 he sang only in Spain. His splendid voice and faultless technique caused him to be known as 'the Spanish Caruso'.

Così Fan Tutte (*All Women Are Like That*). Opera in 2 acts by Mozart. Libretto by Lorenzo da Ponte. First performed Vienna, 26 Jan 1790.

In 18th-c. Naples, two young officers, Ferrando (ten.) and Guglielmo (bar.), enter into a wager with their friend Don Alfonso (bar.) that their lovers, the sisters Fiordiligi (sop.) and Dorabella (mezzo-sop.) will remain faithful during the absence of the two men. They test this by pretending to be called away to join their regiment, and then re-appear in disguise. Gaining admission to the sisters' villa with the help of the maid, Despina (sop.), Ferrando pays court to Guglielmo's sweetheart, Fiordiligi, and Guglielmo to Dorabella. In due course, both

Agnes Baltsa as Dorabella, Thomas Allen as Guglielmo, Daniela Mazzucato as Despina, Kiri Te Kanawa as Fiordiligi and Stuart Burrows as Ferrando in Mozart's *Così Fan Tutte* at Covent Garden.

girls agree to marry their new lovers, and a marriage is arranged at which Despina impersonates a notary. At the last moment, Ferrando and Guglielmo return as themselves, and the repentant and chastened Fiordiligi and Dorabella embrace their original lovers who magnanimously forgive them.

Cossotto, Fiorenza, b. Crescentino, 22 Apr 1935. Italian mezzo-soprano. She studied in Turin, and made her début in 1957 at La Scala as Sister Mathilde in Poulenc's *Les Dialogues des Carmélites*. In the 1960s she became the leading Italian mezzo of her day, after the retirement of Giulietta Simionato, singing most of the Verdi mezzo roles and Bellini's Adalgisa. She first appeared at Covent Garden in 1959 as Neris in Cherubini's *Medea* with Callas. A forceful and full-blooded singer with a healthy voice, she is a reliable performer though not an especially interesting or subtle artist. She is married to the Italian bass, Ivo Vinco.

Cossutta, Carlo, b. Trieste, 8 May 1932. Italian tenor. He studied in Buenos Aires, and made his début there in 1958 as Cassio in *Otello* at the Teatro Colón. After singing at the Colón for several seasons, he was engaged by Chicago Lyric Opera, and in 1964 made his European début at Covent Garden as the Duke in *Rigoletto*. He returned to Covent Garden frequently to sing other Verdi roles, and in recent years has been admired as Otello, a role he first sang at Covent Garden in 1974. He has sung at the Met since 1973, and appears regularly in Berlin and Vienna as well as the leading Italian theatres.

Costa, Michael, b. Naples, 4 Feb 1808; d. Hove, Sussex, 29 Apr 1884. Italian, later English, conductor and composer. After studying in Naples, he went to England at the age of twenty-one to fulfil a professional engagement. He remained in England for the rest of his life. He had composed four operas while he was still a student in Naples, but in England he made his career as a conductor, and in due course became music director of the Royal Italian Opera at Covent Garden. In 1871 he conducted at Her Majesty's in the Haymarket until its amalgamation ten years later with the Covent Garden company. His opera, *Don Carlos*, was produced at Her Majesty's in 1844.

Cotogni, Antonio, b. Rome, 1 Aug 1831; d. Rome, 15 Oct 1918. Italian baritone. After studying in Rome, he made his début there in 1852 as Belcore in *L'Elisir d'Amore*. He sang at La Scala from 1860, and at Covent Garden for twenty-two seasons from 1867-89. Verdi was said to have been moved to tears by his singing. After his retirement, he taught successfully, his pupils including Jean de Reszke, Battistini, Lauri-Volpi and Gigli.

Cotrubas, Ileana, b. Galati, 9 June 1939. Romanian soprano. After studying in Bucharest, she made her début there in 1964 as Yniold in *Pelléas et Mélisande*. In 1967 she undertook further study at the Vienna Music Academy, and the following year she joined the Frankfurt Opera where her roles included Sophie, Pamina, Gilda and Mélisande. She made her Covent Garden début in 1971 as Tatiana in *Eugene Onegin*, in which she gave a most affecting performance. She returned to Covent Garden in a number of roles, becoming a great favourite there, especially as Norina in *Don Pasquale*, Susanna and Gilda. She has some facility in coloratura, but hers is essentially a lyric soprano capable of expressing deep feeling. She was acclaimed at La Scala in 1975 when at short notice she replaced Mirella Freni as Mimi.

Count, Countess. The characters thus familiarly referred to are the Count (bar.) and Countess (sop.) Almaviva in Mozart's *Le Nozze di Figaro*.

countertenor. Opinions of specialists differ as to whether the countertenor voice is a normal tenor singing falsetto, or whether it is merely a high tenor voice of such lightness that in its highest register it shades off into tones which sound distinctly soprano. The countertenor voice is distinguishable from that of the tenor singing falsetto only by its ease and flexibility, presumably acquired by practice. Countertenors are in demand in opera for those baroque roles which were written for the male soprano or castrato. Occasionally, however, a contemporary composer writes specifically for this type of voice. Britten wrote the role of Oberon in *A Midsummer Night's Dream* for such a voice.

Cox, Jean, b. Gadsden, Ala., 14 Jan 1922. American tenor. He studied in Alabama, in Boston and in Rome, and made his début with the New England Opera Theatre in Boston in 1951 as Lensky in *Eugene Onegin*. He first sang in Europe as Rodolfo at Spoleto in 1954, but after his 1956 Bayreuth début as the Steersman in *Der fliegende Holländer* he began to specialize in the Wagner Heldentenor roles, most of which he sang at Bayreuth. He was still singing Siegfried in the 1970s, not only in Bayreuth but also at Covent Garden, Vienna, Chicago and, in 1981, Florence.

Cox, John, b. Bristol, 12 Mar 1935. English producer. After directing the British stage première of Ravel's *L'Enfant et les Sortilèges* at Oxford in 1958, he became assistant to Günther Rennert at Glyndebourne in 1959. He was appointed director of productions at Glyndebourne in 1972. Though most of his productions have been at Glyndebourne, he has also worked abroad. He is an intelligent and imaginative director, who always seeks to reveal the essence of a work rather than to impose his own ideas upon it.

Crabbé, Armand, b. Brussels, 23 Apr 1883; d. Brussels, 24 July 1947. Belgian baritone. He studied in Brussels and Milan, and made his début in Brussels in 1904 as the Nightwatchman in *Die Meistersinger*. From 1906-14 he appeared in every Covent Garden season, where his roles included Valentin in *Faust*, Silvio in *Pagliacci*, and Ford in *Falstaff*. From 1907 he sang in New York, and in 1915 was La Scala's Rigoletto. One of his finest roles was the title-role of *Mârouf*, which the composer, Rabaud, transposed for him from tenor to baritone. In the 1930-40s he sang mainly in Belgium, and after his retirement taught in Brussels.

Craig, Charles, b. London, 3 Dec 1920. English tenor. He was in the chorus at Covent Garden when, in 1947, he came to the attention of Sir Thomas Beecham who was impressed by the quality of his voice and paid for his tuition for two years. He made his solo début as a concert singer with Beecham in 1952, and then joined the touring Carl Rosa Company as principal

tenor. Rodolfo in *La Bohème* was his first role, and he achieved a particular success as Benvenuto Cellini. He joined Sadler's Wells Opera in 1956, and first appeared at Covent Garden in 1959 as Pinkerton in *Madama Butterfly*. A forthright singer with a sturdy dramatic tenor voice, he has sung a wide variety of roles in England and in a number of European opera houses, and in the early 1980s was still an authoritative Otello for English National Opera.

Crespin, Régine, b. Marseilles, 23 Mar 1927. French soprano. After studying in Paris, she made her début in Mulhouse in 1950 as Elsa in *Lohengrin*, the role of her first appearance at the Paris Opéra later that year. Throughout the 1950s she sang the lighter dramatic soprano roles in Paris and in the French provinces, and sang at Bayreuth for the first time in 1958 as Kundry. She excelled in Wagner, and was an especially appealing Sieglinde. In 1962 she made a successful Met début as the Marschallin, under the direction of that role's most famous exponent, Lotte Lehmann. Unwisely, at Salzburg in 1967, she allowed herself to be persuaded by Herbert von Karajan to undertake the role of Brünnhilde which was too heavy for her. She has a voice of warmth and beauty and a stage personality of great charm.

Crimi, Giulio, b. Paterno, nr Catania, 10 May 1885; d. Rome, 29 Oct 1939. Italian tenor. He made his début in Rome in 1910, in Catalani's *La Wally*. At the Met in 1918 he created the roles of Luigi in *Il Tabarro* and Rinuccio in *Gianni Schicchi*. He sang in Italy until the late 1920s, and then taught in Rome. His pupils included Tito Gobbi.

Crociato in Egitto, Il (*The Crusader in Egypt*). Opera in 2 acts by Meyerbeer. Libretto by Gaetano Rossi. First performed Venice, 7 Mar 1824.

The last and most successful of Meyerbeer's early Italian operas, it tells of Armando d'Orville (mezzo-sop.; originally sung by a castrato), a Knight of Rhodes who, assumed to have died in Egypt during the Sixth Crusade, has become the confidant of the Sultan, Aladino (bass), and has taken the name Elmireno. In love with the Sultan's daughter Palmide (sop.), he secretly converts her to Christianity and marries her.

When his uncle, Adriano (ten.) arrives to sue for peace, Armando's identity is discovered, and he and the other captured Christians are sentenced to death. However, when Armando saves the Sultan's life, a peace treaty is signed and Armando and Palmide are reunited.

Crooks, Richard, b. Trenton, N.J., 26 June, 1900; d. Portola Valley, Calif., 1 Oct 1972. American tenor. He began his career as soloist in a Presbyterian·church in New York, and then became a successful concert singer. His opera début was as Cavaradossi in *Tosca* in Hamburg in 1927, after which he sang with the Berlin Staatsoper and other European companies. He first appeared in opera in the USA as Cavaradossi in Philadelphia in 1930, and at the Met in the 1930s specialized in the French and Italian lyric roles. A fine musician with a voice of beautiful timbre, he was forced by poor health to abandon his international careér in 1946.

Cross, Joan, b. London, 7 Sept 1900. English soprano. She studied in London at the Trinity College of Music, and in 1924 joined the chorus of the opera company at the Old Vic. She soon graduated to solo parts, the first of which was Cherubino, and when the opera company was separately established at Sadler's Wells Theatre in 1931 she became its leading soprano, remaining there until 1946. She also sang at Covent Garden, her début role being Mimi in 1931. She was a much admired Countess in *Figaro* and Marschallin at Sadler's Wells, and in 1943 became director of the company. In 1945 she created the role of Ellen Orford in Britten's *Peter Grimes* at Sadler's Wells, and in 1953 sang Elizabeth I in the première of Britten's *Gloriana*. Other roles which she created in Britten operas are Lady Billows in *Albert Herring* at Glyndebourne in 1947, and Mrs Grose in *The Turn of the Screw* at the Fenice, Venice, in 1954. After 1955, she turned to directing opera, in Great Britain and Norway, and in that year a singing school she had helped to establish became the National School of Opera in London.

Crosse, Gordon, b. Bury, 1 Dec 1937. English composer. He studied at Oxford with Egon Wellesz and, briefly, with Petrassi in Rome. The composer of much orchestral and instrumental music, he has also produced four operas, the earliest of which, *Purgatory* (1966), a 1-act opera based on the play of that title by W.B. Yeats, is a superb piece of melodrama. *The Grace of Todd*, a comedy, was composed as a companion-piece to *Purgatory*, and first staged in 1969. Crosse's only full-length opera to date is *The Story of Vasco*, composed to a libretto by Ted Hughes and produced at the London Coliseum in 1974.

Crozier, Eric. b. London, 14 Nov 1914. English producer and librettist. He was a co-founder, with Benjamin Britten and John Piper, of the English Opera Group, directed the first productions of Britten's *Peter Grimes* at Sadler's Wells in 1945 and *The Rape of Lucretia* at Glyndebourne in 1946, and wrote the libretti of *Albert Herring*, *Let's Make an Opera* and (with E.M. Forster) *Billy Budd* for Britten. For Lennox Berkeley he wrote the libretto of *Ruth*.

Cuénod, Hugues, b. Vevey, 26 June 1902. Swiss tenor. After studying in Basle and Vienna, he made his stage début in Paris in 1928 in *Jonny Spielt Auf*, and the following year appeared in the first New York production of Noël Coward's *Bitter Sweet*. In the late 1930s he sang 17th-c. music with Nadia Boulanger's ensemble, and during World War II was a professor at the Geneva Conservatorium. He created the role of Sellem in Stravinsky's *The Rake's Progress* in Venice in 1951, and sang the Astrologer in Rimsky-Korsakov's *The Golden Cockerel* at Covent Garden in 1954. From 1954 until the 1980s he appeared at Glyndebourne in a number of small roles in operas by Mozart, Cavalli, Strauss and others. As late as November, 1982, he sang the role of the Emperor of China in a concert performance of *Turandot* at the London Barbican.

Cui, César, b. Vílna, Lithuania, 18 Jan 1835; d. St Petersburg 26 Mar 1918. Russian composer and critic, of French descent. Together with Balakirev, he was one of the founders of the nationalist group of Russian composers known as 'the mighty handful'. (The other members were Borodin, Mussorgsky and Rimsky-Korsakov.) He composed twelve operas, some of which were successfully staged during his lifetime, though none appears to have continued to

A scene from the 1979 production of Janáček's *The Cunning Little Vixen* at the Erkel Theatre, Budapest. The opera was produced by Lázzló Vámos.

hold the stage, even in Russia. His finest opera is generally thought to be *William Ratcliff*, its libretto a Russian translation of Heine's play. It was first performed in 1869 in St Petersburg. Cui contributed the first act to a projected collaborative venture, *Mlada*, which proved abortive. His other operas include *Angelo* (1876), *The Saracen* (1899) and *The Captain's Daughter* (1911). He also made a performing edition of Mussorgsky's unfinished *Sorochinsky Fair*.

Cunning Little Vixen, The (Czech title, *Příhody Lišky Bystroušky*). Opera in 3 acts by Janáček. Libretto by the composer, after Rudolf Těsnohlídek's *Liška Bystrouška* (1920). First performed Brno, 6 Nov 1924.

The adventures of Sharpears, the vixen (sop.) who escapes from the Forester (bar.) who has brought her up as a pet, are recounted in this opera in which humans play the animal characters such as the dog, Lapák (mezzo-sop. or ten.), the hen (sop.), the fox, Goldenmane (sop. or ten.). When Sharpears escapes, she marries the fox Goldenmane, but later is shot by Harašta, the poacher (bass). The Forester's sadness at the loss of the vixen is linked with his longing for a gipsy girl who marries the poacher. When, awakening from a sleep in the forest, he sees a young foxcub exactly like her mother, Sharpears, the Forester derives consolation from the idea of nature perpetually renewing herself.

Curlew River. Church parable in 1 act by Britten. Libretto by William Plomer, after the 15th-c. Noh play, *Sumidagawa* (The Sumida River) by Juro Motomasa. First performed Orford Parish Church, Suffolk, 13 June 1964.

The first of Britten's three 'church parables', 1-act operas intended for performance in churches rather than theatres, it tells of a Madwoman (ten.) who arrives at a ferry, seeking her son who proves to have died. The Ferryman (bar.) takes her across the river to a shrine established in the child's memory, for he remembers the boy who crossed the river to escape robbers, only to die of exhaustion on the other side.

Curtin, Phyllis, b. Clarksburg, W. Va., 3 Dec 1922. American soprano. She began her career as a concert singer, and then joined the New England Opera Theatre in Boston, with whom she appeared as Lisa in *The Queen of Spades* in 1946. In 1953 she made her début with the New York City Opera in Einem's *Der Prozess*. She created the title-role in Carlisle Floyd's *Susannah* and Cathy in the same composer's *Wuthering Heights*. She was Cressida in the New York première of Walton's *Troilus and Cressida*, and Ellen Orford in the first American *Peter Grimes*. Though she sang with European companies in the 1960s, her career has been based principally in the USA.

Czerwenka, Oscar, b. Linz, 5 July 1924. Austrian bass. He made his début at Graz in 1947 as the Hermit in *Der Freischütz*, and joined the Vienna Staatsoper in 1951, remaining a member of the company throughout his career, while making guest appearances with other companies. His most famous role was Baron Ochs in *Der Rosenkavalier*, which he sang at the Met and Glyndebourne as well as in Vienna.

D

Dafne. Opera in a prologue and 6 scenes by Peri. Libretto by Ottavio Rinuccini. First performed in Jacopo Corsi's house in Florence during the Carnival season of 1597.

The music of this, the first opera to be written, is now lost. The earliest German-language opera was a setting of the same libretto, translated by Martin Opitz, composed by Heinrich Schütz. It, too, is lost.

Daland (bass). Senta's father in Wagner's *Der fliegende Holländer* who, for purely venal reasons, encourages his daughter's betrothal to the Dutchman.

Dalayrac, Nicolas-Marie, b. Muret, Haute Garonne, 8 June 1753; d. Paris, 26 Nov 1809. French composer. He composed about sixty *opérascomiques*, the first of which, *Le Petit Souper*, was performed privately in 1781. His most famous work, *Nina ou La Folle par Amour*, first staged in Paris in 1786, is not, however, a comedy but a sentimental romance. His music has a *galant* charm and some dramatic strength.

Dalibor. Opera in 3 acts by Smetana. Libretto by Josef Wenzig, translated from German into Czech by Ervin Spindler. First performed Prague, 16 May 1868.

Dalibor (ten.), imprisoned for having killed a man to avenge a friend's death, is rescued by Milada (sop.) who gains access to him in prison by disguising herself as a youth. She is wounded in the rescue operation, and dies in the arms of Dalibor who then kills himself. The similarity to the plot of *Fidelio* has often been remarked, and indeed *Dalibor* is invested in Czechoslovakia with the same significance for national liberty as Beethoven's opera in other countries.

Dalila (mezzo-sop.). The Philistine temptress of Samson in Saint-Saëns's *Samson et Dalila*, she was killed when Samson destroyed the temple.

Dalis, Irene, b. San Jose, Calif., 8 Oct 1929. American mezzo-soprano. She studied in Milan, and made her début in Oldenburg in 1953 as Eboli. She was first heard at the Met in 1957 in the same role, but later specialized in Wagner parts. Covent Garden heard her in 1958 as Brangäne, and she made her Bayreuth début in 1961 as Ortrud. In 1962 she became the first American to sing Kundry at Bayreuth. She is an intelligent interpreter with a voice of rich timbre.

Dallapiccola, Luigi, b. Pisino, Istria, 3 Feb 1904; d. Florence, 19 Feb 1975. Italian composer. He studied in Graz and Florence, and began his musical career in 1926 as a pianist. He later began to compose, earning his living by teaching, and became one of the leading Italian composers of his time, writing in a style which evolved from his enthusiasm for Mahler, Schoenberg and Berg. His first opera, *Volo di Notte*, an imaginative work, though rather mixed in style, was composed in the late 1930s and first performed in 1940. *Il Prigioniero* (1950) subordinates the composer's musical prowess to his concern for modern man and his predicament. *Job* (1950), its text derived by the composer from the Bible, reveals the strong influence of Webern whom Dallapiccola had met in Austria in 1942. His final opera was *Ulisse*, based on Homer, which was performed in Berlin in 1968. A long, slow-moving work, it is Dallapiccola's largest and most ambitious composition.

Dalla Rizza, Gilda, b. Verona, 12 Oct 1892; d. Milan, 4 July 1975. Italian soprano. She studied in Bologna, and made her début there in 1912 as Charlotte in *Werther*. Puccini admired her, and wrote for her the role of Magda in *La Rondine* which she sang at the Monte Carlo première of that opera in 1917. She was the first Italian Lauretta (*Gianni Schicchi*) and Suor Angelica, and also sang these roles at Covent Garden in 1920. After hearing her sing the role of Minnie in *La Fanciulla del West* in 1921, Puccini said: 'At last I've seen my Fanciulla.' He wrote the role of Liu in *Turandot* for her, though she did not in fact sing in that opera's posthumous première. She was a distinguished Violetta in *La Traviata* at La Scala in 1923, and the first Italian Arabella in Strauss's opera in Genoa in 1936. A beautiful woman, she was generally considered a great singing actress.

Dal Monte, Toti, b. Mogliano Veneto, nr Treviso, 27 June 1893; d. Treviso, 26 Jan 1975. Italian soprano. She studied piano in Venice but after an injury to her hand took up singing, making her début in Milan in 1916 as Biancafiore in Zandonai's *Francesca da Rimini*. In 1922 she sang Gilda under Toscanini at La Scala, after which she embarked upon a highly successful career in the coloratura repertory. She sang in Chicago between 1924-8, at the Met in 1924, and made her only Covent Garden appearances in 1926 as Lucia and Rosina. She was also an affecting Butterfly in Puccini's opera. She retired in 1949 and taught for several years.

Damase, Jean-Michel b. Bordeaux, 27 Jan 1928. French composer. He began to compose at the age of nine by setting some poems by Colette after meeting the writer. At the age of twelve he became a pupil of Alfred Cortot, and made his début as a pianist while at the same time studying composition. He has composed a number of ballet scores, and seven operas which include *Colombe* (1958), based on Anouilh's play; *Madame de...* (1969), its libretto by Cocteau based on a story by Louise de Vilmorin; and *L'Heritière* (1974), which derives from Henry James's *Washington Square*.

Damnation de Faust, La. Dramatic legend in 4 parts by Berlioz. Libretto by the composer, after Goethe's *Faust* (part I) in Gérard de Nerval's French version. First performed in concert form in Paris, 6 Dec 1846.

Berlioz did not expect his *légende dramatique* to be staged in the form in which he left it, though it was his intention to rewrite it for stage production. Since its first staging at Monte Carlo on 18 May 1893, adapted for this purpose by the impresario Raoul Gunsbourg, the work has frequently been presented as an opera. As in Gounod's *Faust*, the role of Faust is assigned to a tenor, Marguerite is a soprano, and Méphistophélès a bass.

Danco, Suzanne, b. Brussels, 22 Jan 1911. Belgian soprano. She studied in Prague, and made her début in Genoa in 1941 as Fiordiligi in *Così Fan Tutte*. She was Ellen Orford in the first Italian production of *Peter Grimes* at La Scala in 1947. She sang in a number of Italian houses, and also at

Glyndebourne, specializing in Mozart and in modern roles.

Dantons Tod *(Danton's Death)*. Opera in 2 parts by Einem. Libretto by Boris Blacher and the composer, after the play by Georg Büchner (1835). First performed Salzburg, 6 Aug 1947.

After speaking against the French Revolution, Danton (bar.) is arrested by Robespierre (ten.) and sentenced to death by the revolutionary tribunal.

Dapertutto (bar.). The sorcerer in the Giulietta act of Offenbach's *Les Contes d'Hoffmann*.

Daphne. Opera in 1 act by Richard Strauss. Libretto by Josef Gregor after the classical legend. First performed Dresden, 15 Oct 1938.

Daphne (sop.), daughter of Peneios (bass) and Gaea (mezzo-sop.), attracts the love of Apollo (ten.) who comes to earth disguised as a shepherd. Leukippos (ten.), a shepherd, who also loves Daphne, is killed by Apollo who reveals himself as the god and has transformed Daphne into a tree.

Da Ponte, Lorenzo, b. Ceneda, 10 Mar 1749; d. New York, 17 Aug 1838. Italian librettist. Son of a converted Jewish family, he originally studied for the priesthood, but later settled in Vienna as court poet to the Emperor Joseph II. He provided libretti for Salieri, Martín y Soler, and Mozart for whom he wrote *Le Nozze di Figaro, Don Giovanni* and *Così Fan Tutte*. In 1792 he left Vienna and worked for a time in London before emigrating to the United States in 1805 where he became a teacher of Italian language and literature in New Jersey, Pa. and New York. In 1825 he helped to found what was to become Columbia University. He was responsible for the production of *Don Giovanni* in New York in 1825.

Darclée, Hariclea, b. Braila, 10 June 1860; d. Bucharest, 10 Jan 1939. Romanian soprano. After studying in Bucharest and Paris, she made her début at the Paris Opéra in 1888 as Marguerite in *Faust*. Her career reached its peak when she created the role of Tosca in Puccini's opera in Rome in 1900. She was also the first Iris in Mascagni's opera of that name. She retired in 1918.

Dargomyzhsky, Alexander, b. Troitskoye, Tula district, 14 Feb 1813; d. St Petersburg, 17 Jan 1869. Russian composer. Together with Glinka one of the pioneers of Russian national opera, he is an important precursor of such major opera composers as Mussorgsky and Tchaikovsky, rather than a first-rate creative artist in his own right. His first opera, *Esmeralda*, was performed at the Bolshoi Theatre, Moscow in 1847 but was not particularly successful. A 1-act opera-ballet, *The Triumph of Bacchus*, though written in 1848, did not reach the stage until 1867 at the Bolshoi. *Rusalka*, a 4-act opera based on Pushkin's tale, was performed in St Petersburg in 1856, but again with little success, although it is still occasionally performed in the Soviet Union. Dargomyzhsky's most important work for the stage was *The Stone Guest*, composed in a kind of melodic recitative which was to influence much later 19th-c. Russian opera. (It has been described as the most influential failure in the history of opera.) When the composer died, he had not orchestrated *The Stone Guest*, which existed only in piano score. Completed and orchestrated by Cui and Rimsky-Korsakov, it was first performed in St Petersburg in 1872.

David (ten.). Hans Sachs's apprentice in Wagner's *Die Meistersinger von Nürnberg*.

David, Félicien, b. Cadenet, 13 Apr 1810; d. St-Germain-en-Laye, 29 Aug 1876. French composer. His great interest in exotic oriental subjects was a strong influence on generations of later French opera composers, among them Gounod, Bizet and Delibes. David travelled widely in the Middle East, living for two years in Cairo where he gave music lessons. His first opera, *La Perle du Brésil*, staged in Paris in 1851, had a vogue for some years, more by virtue of its orchestral colouring than its dramatic strength which is negligible. *Herculanum* (1859) was an opera of more substance, and *Lalla-Roukh* (1862), based on the work of an Irish poet, Thomas Moore, quickly established itself as David's most popular opera, and one in which his talents were best suited to the subject and scale of the composition.

Davies, Peter Maxwell, b. Manchester, 8 Sept 1934. English composer. He studied at the Royal Manchester College of Music, in Rome with Petrassi and in Princeton N.J. with Roger Sessions. His first dramatic works were pieces of music theatre written for his own group, Pierrot Players, later called Fires of London, and performed in concert halls. These were *Revelation and Fall* (1968), a setting of a prose poem by Georg Trakl; *Eight Songs for a Mad King* (poems by Randolph Stow: 1969) and *Miss Donnithorne's Maggot* (Stow: 1974). His chamber opera, *The Martyrdom of St Magnus*, was performed in St Magnus Cathedral, Orkney, in 1977, and a children's opera, *The Two Fiddlers* (1978), has proved successful with a number of youthful audiences. His full-length opera, *Taverner*, a study of the 16th-c. composer John Taverner, failed to please adult audiences when staged at Covent Garden in 1972.

Davies, Ryland, b. Cwm, Ebbw Vale, 9 Feb 1943. Welsh tenor. After studying at the

Royal Manchester College of Music, he joined the Glyndebourne chorus in 1964, and was the first winner of the John Christie Award. He sang Nemorino in *L'Elisir d'Amore* with the Glyndebourne Touring company, and has sung frequently at Glyndebourne. He made his Covent Garden début in 1969 as Hylas in *Les Troyens*, and his United States début in San Francisco in 1970 as Ferrando in *Così Fan Tutte*. His light-textured lyric tenor is heard at its best in the Mozart roles.

Davis, (Sir) Colin, b. Weybridge, 25 Sept 1927. English conductor. He studied clarinet at the Royal College of Music in London, and conducted concert performances of opera with the Chelsea Opera Group, before conducting his first stage performances at Sadler's Wells Theatre (*Die Entführung aus dem Serail*, 1958) and at Glyndebourne (*Die Zauberflöte*, 1960). He was music director of Sadler's Wells Opera

Sir Colin Davis. He became director of The Royal Opera House, Covent Garden in 1971.

from 1961–4, made his Met début with *Peter Grimes* in 1966, and succeeded Solti as music director of The Royal Opera House, Covent Garden, in 1971. At Covent Garden he has been especially admired for his performances of the Mozart operas, and also for those of Berlioz, a composer of whom he is a firm advocate. He has also been associated with the operas of Tippett. In 1977 he became the first British conductor to appear at Bayreuth, when he conducted *Tannhäuser*. He was knighted in 1980.

Dean, Stafford, b. Kingswood, Surrey, 20 June 1937. English bass. He studied at the Royal College of Music, and privately with Howell Glynne and Otakar Kraus. At Glyndebourne in 1964 he sang Lictor in Monteverdi's *L'Incoronazione di Poppea*, and in the same year joined Sadler's Wells Opera. He remained a member of the Sadler's Wells company for a number of years, and made his Covent Garden début in 1969 as Masetto. Abroad, he is best known for his two major Mozart roles, Leporello and Figaro, which he has sung in Europe and the United States. It was as Figaro that he first appeared at the Met in 1976.

De Angelis, Nazareno, b. Rome, 17 Nov 1881; d. Rome, 14 Dec 1962. Italian bass. As a boy, he sang in the Sistine Chapel Choir. He made his opera début in 1903 at Aquila in *Linda di Chamounix*, and by 1906 was appearing at La Scala. He sang at La Scala and other leading Italian theatres until the mid-1930s, and in South America between 1909–25. His North American début was made with Chicago Opera in 1910. Generally considered the leading Italian bass of his time, his major successes were in the Verdi bass roles, as Rossini's Moses, and as Boito's Mefistofele.

Death in Venice. Opera in 2 acts by Britten. Libretto by Myfanwy Piper, based on Thomas Mann's story, *Der Tod in Venedig* (1911). First performed Snape, Suffolk, 16 June 1973.

Mann's symbolic story of the distinguished writer, Gustav von Aschenbach, whose obsession with a beautiful Polish boy whom he observes on the Lido leads to self-awareness but also to death, is closely followed by composer and librettist. The role of Aschenbach is assigned to a tenor, the

Sir Peter Pears as Aschenbach in Britten's *Death in Venice* at Covent Garden.

boy Tadzio is portrayed by a dancer, and various subsidiary male roles are all sung by one baritone in various disguises.

Debussy, Claude, b. St-Germain-en-Laye, 22 Aug 1862; d. Paris, 25 Mar 1918). French composer. He studied at the Paris Conservatorium and won the Prix de Rome in 1884. A master of orchestral impressionism, and arguably the most influential composer of his time, he completed only one opera though he contemplated setting various other subjects, among them the Tristan and Isolde legend and Shakespeare's *As You Like It*. His opera *Pelléas et Mélisande* (1902) accurately parallels in music the shadowy symbolist world of the Maeterlinck play on which it is based. A highly original work, it at first aroused hostility but eventually found its admirers.

Debussy made more than one attempt to begin a second opera, *La Chute de la Maison Usher* (*The Fall of the House of Usher*), based on the Edgar Allan Poe story. What exists of the work was given a performance in New Haven, Conn. in 1977 and in London in 1981 conducted by Simon Rattle.

Decembrists, The. (Russian title: *Dekabristy*). Opera in 4 acts by Shaporin. Libretto by Vsevolod Rozhdestvensky. First performed Moscow, 23 June 1953. (Two scenes only, under the title *Paulina Goebbel*, had been performed in Leningrad in 1925.)

The opera is set at the time of the December uprising in Russia in 1825, and presents a love-story involving Dmitri (ten.) and Elena (sop.) against the events of the unsuccessful revolution, led by Ryleyev (bar.).

De Fabritiis, Oliviero, b. Rome, 13 June 1902; d. Rome, 12 Aug 1982. Italian conductor. He studied in Rome, and made his début there at the age of eighteen. After conducting throughout Italy, he began in 1934 an association with the Rome Opera which continued until 1961. He conducted the inaugural performance of *Lucia di Lammermoor* at the Terme di Caracalla, Rome in 1938, and the first Covent Garden *Simon Boccanegra* in 1965. He was engaged widely throughout Germany, Austria, and the United States, but never conducted at La Scala, the leading opera house in his own country. He was an excellent interpreter of the 19th-c. Italian repertory, and continued to conduct impressive performances until shortly before his death.

Delibes, Léo, b. St-Germain-du-Val, 21 Feb 1836; d. Paris, 16 Jan 1891. French composer. A pupil of Adam at the Paris Conservatorium, Delibes possessed much of the earlier composer's gift for agreeable melody and sparkling orchestration, qualities which made him an ideal composer for the theatre. Best-known for his ballet scores, of which the finest is *Coppélia*, he also wrote a number of operettas beginning with *Deux sous de charbon* (1856), 1-act piece which he described as an 'asphyxie lyrique'. After nearly a score of these had been produced, he turned to writing somewhat more serious operas for the Paris Opéra-Comique. *Le Roi l'a Dit* (1873) and

Jean de Nivelle (1880) were followed by his masterpiece, *Lakmé* (1883), a charming piece of pastiche Oriental confectionary. He began another opera, *Kassya*, which was completed after Delibes's death by Massenet, and performed in Paris in 1893. In his last years, Delibes taught composition.

Delius, Frederick, b. Bradford, 29 Jan 1862; d. Grez-sur-Loing, France, 10 June 1934. English composer. All of Delius's operas were written in the early part of his career, and some were never performed during his lifetime. *Irmelin*, composed in the 1890s, was first staged in Oxford in 1953 when it was conducted by the composer's friend and champion, Sir Thomas Beecham. *The Magic Fountain*, also written in the 1890s, has been performed only on radio. *Koanga* (1895-7) was produced in Elberfeld, Germany, in 1904, while *Margot la Rouge* (1902) remains unstaged. Delius's most successful operas are *A Village Romeo and Juliet*, first staged in Berlin in 1907, and *Fennimore and Gerda* (composed in 1910, staged in Frankfurt am Main, 1919). These last two works have had other productions in recent years.

Della Casa, Lisa, b. Burgdorf, nr Berne, 2 Feb 1919. Swiss soprano. She studied in Zurich, and made her début in 1941 in Solothurn-Biel as Puccini's Butterfly. From 1942-50 she sang leading roles with the company at the Stadttheater, Zurich, and first appeared abroad in 1947 at the Salzburg Festival as Zdenka in Strauss's *Arabella*. She first sang the title-role in *Arabella* in 1951 in Munich, and immediately made the role her own. In the 1950-60s in Vienna, Salzburg and Munich, she was the most admired Strauss soprano since Lotte Lehmann, especially as the Marschallin and Octavian in *Der Rosenkavalier*, the Countess in *Capriccio*, and Ariadne in *Ariadne auf Naxos*. Her beauty of voice and person, and her cool and relaxed stage manner were also well suited to a number of Mozart roles. She made her British début in 1951 at Glyndebourne as the Countess in *Le Nozze di Figaro*, and her American début at the Met in 1953. She sang Eva in *Die Meistersinger* at Bayreuth in 1952.

Del Monaco, Mario, b. Florence, 27 July 1915; d. Mestre, nr Venice, 16 Oct 1982. Italian tenor. After six months' study in Rome, he decided to rely on self-teaching from gramophone record. He made his début at Pesaro in 1939 as Turiddu, and in 1941 sang Pinkerton in *Madama Butterfly* at La Scala. In the 1950s he was the leading Italian dramatic tenor, greatly admired in such Verdi roles as Alvaro, Radames and, above all, Otello. He was also a famous Andrea Chénier. His Covent Garden début in 1946 was as Cavaradossi, and he was extremely popular at the Met from 1951-9. Though not the most subtle of interpreters, he possessed the advantages of a large and impressive voice, and a good appearance.

De Luca, Giuseppe, b. Rome, 25 Dec 1876; d. New York, 26 Aug 1950. Italian baritone. He studied in Rome, and made his début in Piacenza in 1897 as Valentin in *Faust*. He created the role of Michonnet in *Adriana Lecouvreur* in Milan in 1902, and Sharpless in *Madama Butterfly* in Milan in 1904. He was immensely popular at the Met from the time of his début in 1915 as Rossini's Figaro to his final appearance in opera there in 1951. He made about 700 appearances in eighty operas at the Met where, in 1918, he created the title-role in *Gianni Schicchi*. His fine voice, relaxed stage manner and superb bel canto style were admirably suited to the Verdi and Mozart roles in which he specialized.

De Lucia, Fernando, b. Naples, 11 Oct 1860; d. Naples, 21 Feb 1925. Italian tenor. After studying in Naples, he made his début there at the Teatro San Carlo in *Faust* in 1885. He first made his reputation as an exponent of the early 19th-c. repertory, in such lyric tenor roles as Rossini's Almaviva, Elvino in *La Sonnambula* and Nemorino in *L'Elisir d'Amore*, but he later began to undertake the heavier roles of the *verismo* school, and became an admired Turiddu in *Cavalleria Rusticana* and Canio in *Pagliacci*. He was the original interpreter of the title role in Mascagni's *L'Amico Fritz* in Rome in 1891, and in its first Covent Garden and Met productions. He retired in 1917, and taught in Naples. His pupils included Maria Nemeth and Georges Thill.

De Reszke, Édouard, b. Warsaw, 22 Dec 1853; d. Garnek, Poland, 25 May 1917. Polish bass, brother of the tenor Jean De Reszke. He studied in Warsaw, and later in Italy, and made his début as the King in the first Paris production of *Aida* in 1876. With his brother Jean he sang frequently at the Paris Opéra, at Covent Garden and at the Met during the last decade of the 19th c. He was a famous Méphistophélès in *Faust*, and was also admired in such Wagner roles as Hans Sachs, King Mark and Kurwenal. He had a voice of great volume and an imposing stage presence.

De Reszke, Jean, b. Warsaw, 14 Jan 1850; d. Nice, 3 Apr 1925. Polish tenor, brother of the bass Édouard De Reszke. He studied in Milan, made his début as a baritone in 1874 and, after restudying, as a tenor in 1879 in Meyerbeer's *Robert Le Diable* in Madrid. He created the title-role in Massenet's *Le Cid* in Paris in 1885, and made his first appearance in England at Drury Lane as Radames in *Aida* in 1887. He sang in London nearly every season until 1900, and at the Met from 1891-1901. His principal roles included Roméo, Faust, Lohengrin, Walther, Tristan and Siegfried. He was renowned both for the beauty of his voice and for his superb musicianship.

Dermota, Anton, b. Kropa, 4 June 1910. Yugoslav tenor. After studying in Ljubliana and Vienna, he made his début in Vienna in 1936 as the First Armed Man in *Die Zauberflöte*. He was immediately invited to join the Vienna State Opera, and was still a member in 1983. He sang a wide number of lyric tenor roles, specializing in Mozart, and was also greatly admired as Pfitzner's Palestrina and as David in *Die Meistersinger*. In recent years he has undertaken smaller roles, and since 1966 has taught at the Academy of Music in Vienna.

Dernesch, Helga, b. Vienna, 3 Feb 1939. Austrian soprano, later mezzo-soprano. She studied in Vienna, and made her début in Berne in 1961 as Marina in *Boris Godunov*. Her Bayreuth début in 1965 was as Wellgunde in *Das Rheingold*, and by the late 1960s she was singing such leading Wagner roles as Eva and Sieglinde. She began to undertake heavier roles in Salzburg, among them Brünnhilde and Isolde, and this led to a vocal crisis. In recent years she has deployed her still beautiful voice of great warmth and her charming appearance and personality as a mezzo-soprano. She appears frequently in Vienna.

De Sabata, Victor, b. Trieste, 10 Apr 1892; d. Santa Margherita Ligure, 11 Dec 1967. Italian conductor. He studied in Milan, and became conductor of the Monte Carlo Opera in 1919, remaining there for the next ten years. There in 1925 he conducted the première of Ravel's *L'Enfant et les Sortilèges*. In 1929 he was engaged by La Scala, and remained with that theatre until 1953. Before World War II he appeared mainly in Italy, though he conducted *Tristan und Isolde* at Bayreuth in 1939, but after 1950 he began to conduct abroad more widely. He was especially admired in Verdi, and many thought him a fine Wagner conductor. He was also a composer: his only opera, *Il Macigno*, was produced at La Scala in 1917.

Desdemona (sop.). Otello's wife, in both Verdi's and Rossini's *Otello*.

Des Grieux (ten.). The lover of Manon in Massenet's *Manon* and Puccini's *Manon Lescaut*.

Despina (sop.). The maid, adept at comic disguise, in Mozart's *Così Fan Tutte*.

Destinn, Emmy, b. Prague, 26 Feb 1878; d. České Budějovice, 28 Jan 1930. Czech soprano. Her real name was Ema Kittlovà: for professional purposes she adopted the name of her teacher, Marie Loewe-Destinn, and in the later part of her career used the name in its Czech form, Ema Destinnovà. She made her début in Berlin in 1898 as Santuzza, and became one of the leading dramatic sopranos of her time, excelling in Wagner and Puccini as well as in Czech operas. Between 1904-16 she sang frequently at Covent Garden and the Met, was the first Bayreuth Senta in 1901, and created the role of Minnie in Puccini's *La Fanciulla del West* at the Met in 1910. She was a fine tragic actress with a highly individual voice.

Destouches, André, b. Paris, Apr 1672; d. Paris, 7 Feb 1749. French composer. He composed a number of operas which were staged in Paris around the beginning of the 18th c., among them *Amadis de Grèce* (1699), *Omphale* (1701) and *Le Carnaval et la Folie* (1703). None was more successful than the first, *Issé*, in 1699. He was Director of the Paris Opéra from 1728-31, and was greatly admired by Louis XIV. His later operas

include *Télémaque et Calypso* (1714) and *Sémiramis* (1718).

Destouches, Franz von, b. Munich, 21 Jan 1772; d. Munich, 9 Dec 1844. German composer. He studied in Vienna with Haydn, and wrote three operas, *Die Thomasnacht* (1792), *Das Missverständnis* (1805) and an unperformed work, *Der Teufel und der Schneider*.

Deutekom, Cristina, b. Amsterdam, 28 Aug 1932. Dutch soprano. She studied at the Amsterdam Conservatorium and made her début in Amsterdam in 1962 as the Queen of Night, a role which brought her immediate fame. It was with this role that she introduced herself to the Met in 1967 and Covent Garden in 1968. She has since added a number of other dramatic coloratura roles to her repertory, among them Lucia, Norma and Abigaille. She has also been successful in a number of early and middle-period Verdi operas, among them *I Lombardi* and *Les Vêpres Siciliennes*.

Devil and Daniel Webster, The. Opera in 1 act by Douglas Moore. Libretto by the composer, after a story by Stephen Vincent Benét (1937). First performed New York, 18 May 1939.
    In 19th-c. New Hampshire, when Jabez Stone (ten.) sells his soul to the devil, he is extricated from his predicament by Daniel Webster (bar.) who summons up a jury of historical villains to acquit Jabez.

Devil and Kate, The (original Czech title, *Čert a Káča*). Opera in 3 acts by Dvořák. Libretto by Adolf Wenig, after a folk-tale in the collection *Fairy Tales* by Božena Němcová (1845). First performed Prague, 23 Nov 1899.
    Since no one wants to dance with her at the country fair, the unattractive Kate (mezzo-sop.) says she would dance with the Devil himself. The Devil, Marbuel (bass) promptly appears, and carries her off to Hell. She is rescued from Hell without difficulty, for Lucifer is glad to be rid of her. When the Lady of the Manor (sop.) hears that the Devil is coming for her, the shepherd Jirka (ten.) who had rescued Kate, takes her to the Manor House. Marbuel appears at the Manor, but is frightened off by the sight of Kate.

Devils of Loudun, The (Polish title, *Diably z Loudun*). Opera in 3 acts by Penderecki. Libretto by the composer based on John Whiting's play, *The Devils of Loudun* (1961) which, in turn, is based on the book by Aldous Huxley. First performed Hamburg, 20 June 1969.

The priest Urbain Grandier (bar.) is accused of devilish practices by a group of hysterical Ursuline nuns, led by the prioress Jeanne des Anges (sop.). He is tortured and burned at the stake.

Dexter, John, b. Derby, 2 Aug 1925. English director. He began his career as a director of plays, turning to opera with *Benvenuto Cellini* at Covent Garden in 1966. He directed operas in Hamburg from 1969-73, staged the British première of Penderecki's *The Devils of Loudon* for the English National Opera in 1973, and has been director of productions at the Met since 1974.

Dialogues des Carmélites, Les (*The Carmelites*). Opera in 3 acts by Poulenc. Libretto by Ernest Lavery, after the play by Georges Bernanos, which was in turn based on Gertrude von le Fort's novel, *Die letzte am Schafott* (1931) and a film scenario by Raymond Brückberger and Philippe Agostini. First performed Milan, 26 Jan 1957.

The opera tells of the martyrdom of a group of Carmelite nuns during the French revolution.

Díaz, Justino, b. San Juan, Puerto Rico, 29 Jan 1940. American, Puerto Rican, bass. He sang Ben in Menotti's *The Telephone* in Puerto Rico in 1957, and after further study at the New England Conservatory made his Met début in 1963 as Monterone. In 1966 at the opening of the new Met he created the role of Antony in Barber's *Antony and Cleopatra*. He first appeared at La Scala in 1969 as Mahomet II in Rossini's *Assedio di Corinto*. He has appeared in Vienna, Salzburg and other European houses, was in the inaugural production at the Kennedy Center Opera House in Washington D.C., and made his Covent Garden début in 1976 as Escamillo. He continues to sing regularly at the Met.

Dibuc, Il (*The Dybbuk*). Opera in a prologue and 3 acts by Rocca. Libretto by Renato Simoni, after the play *The Dybbuk* (1916) by Shelomoh Anski. First performed Milan, 24 Mar 1934.

Anski's play about the Yiddish legend of the Dybbuk, a spirit which enters into the body of another, was also the basis of *The Dybbuk*, an opera in 3 acts by David Tamkin, composed *c.* 1931 and first performed in New York on 4 Oct 1951. George Gershwin began an opera on the same subject, but abandoned it when he learned that the rights at that time belonged to Rocca. Also based on the play is the opera, *Dybuk,* by Karl Heinz Füssl, first performed in 1970 in Karlsruhe.

Dick Johnson (ten.) The pseudonym adopted by the outlaw, Ramerrez, in Puccini's *La Fanciulla del West.*

Dido and Aeneas. Opera in a prologue and 3 acts by Purcell. Libretto by Nahum Tate, after Book IV of Virgil's *Aeneid.* First performed Chelsea, London, 1689.

Set in ancient Carthage, the opera tells of the love of Queen Dido (sop.) for Aeneas (ten.) who leaves her to travel on to Italy to fulfil his destiny. Dido then takes her own life. *Dido and Aeneas* is the earliest English opera which is still performed to, and appreciated by, non-specialist audiences.

Di Luna (bar.). The Count, brother of Manrico, in Verdi's *Il Trovatore.*

D'Indy, Vincent, b. Paris, 27 Mar 1851; d. Paris, 2 Dec 1931. French composer. A disciple of Wagner, D'Indy composed six operas, after having made a number of false starts with stage projects which he left unfinished during his teens and twenties. His first completed and performed opera was the 1-act comic piece, *Attendez-moi sous l'orme*, performed at the Opéra-Comique in 1882. *Le Chant de la Cloche*, a stage version of a choral work composed between 1879-83, was produced in Brussels in 1912. His most important opera, *Fervaal* (1897), uses a vast orchestra and Wagnerian *leitmotifs*, while *L'Étranger* (1903) has more in common with the earlier Wagner of *Der fliegende Holländer.* In *La Légende de Saint Christophe* (1920) D'Indy attacked the politics of the Third Republic. He ended his operatic career with a disappointingly slight musical comedy, *Le Rêve de Cinyras*, staged in Paris in 1927.

Dinorah (Alternative title, *Le Pardon de Ploërmel.*) Opera in 3 acts by Meyerbeer. Libretto by Jules Barbier and Michel Carré. First performed Paris, 4 Apr 1859.

The peasant-girl Dinorah (sop.), believing that her lover, the goatherd Hoël (bar.), has deserted her, loses her reason. Hoël, whose odd behaviour was caused by his having been sworn to silence concerning the location of buried treasure, saves Dinorah from drowning, abandons his quest for the treasure, and returns to her.

Di Stefano, Giuseppe, b. Motta Santa Anastasia, nr Catania, 24 July 1921. Italian tenor. He studied with Luigi Montesanto in Milan, and made his début in 1946 in Reggio Emilia as Des Grieux in *Manon*. His first Met appearance was as the Duke in *Rigoletto* in 1948. He sang frequently at the Met, La Scala, Vienna and elsewhere, and established himself as a lyric tenor with a beautiful vocal quality though a less than ideal bel canto technique. After 1953 he began to accept roles which were too heavy for his voice, and by the end of that decade his appearances had become sporadic and uncertain, and his performances stylistically coarse. In 1973, by which time his voice had lost its earlier beauty of timbre and much of its range, he undertook a concert tour with Maria Callas in which neither artist was heard to advantage.

Mattiwilda Dobbs, American soprano popular at Covent Garden in the 1950s.

Dittersdorf, Karl Ditters von, b. Vienna, 2 Nov 1739; d. Neuhof, 24 Oct 1799. Austrian composer. Of his approximately forty operas, the first twelve were written to Italian texts while the remainder are German Singspiels written for and staged in Vienna (1786-90) and the Ducal Theatre in Oels (*c.* 1794-9). The Singspiels are of historical importance, for they are among the earliest examples of a genre which was to persist in Vienna until the middle of the 19th c., and which was to lead to the Viennese operetta of the late-19th c. Only *Doktor und Apotheker*, the earliest of the Singspiels first staged in Vienna in 1786, is sometimes revived.

Dmitri (ten.). The young Pretender (at first known as the novice, Grigori) in Mussorgsky's *Boris Godunov*.

Dobbs, Mattiwilda, b. Atlanta, Ga., 11 July 1925. American soprano. She studied

with Lotte Leonard in New York, and made her début in Amsterdam in 1952 in Stravinsky's *Le Rossignol*, and was the first black singer to appear at La Scala, when she sang Elvira in *L'Italiana in Algeri* in 1953. In the summer of that year she appeared at Glyndebourne as Zerbinetta in *Ariadne auf Naxos*, and was much admired at Covent Garden in the 1953-4 season as Gilda in *Rigoletto* and the Queen of Shemakhan in Rimsky-Korsakov's *The Golden Cockerel*. She first appeared at the Met in 1957, and at the Wexford Festival in 1965 in the title-role of Mozart's *La Finta Giardiniera*. She was a member of the Stockholm Royal Opera from 1957-73, since when she has taught at the University of Texas.

Dobrowen, Issay, b. Nizhny-Novgorod, 27 Feb 1894; d. Oslo, 9 Dec 1953. Russian conductor. He studied in Moscow, and made his début there in 1919 with *Les Contes* *d'Hoffmann.* He was then engaged in Dresden, Berlin, Vienna and other towns as a conductor of opera, specializing in Russian works. During World War II he conducted at the Stockholm Royal Opera, and between 1948–53 conducted Russian operas at La Scala. He made his Covent Garden début in 1952 with *Boris Godunov.*

Docteur Miracle(bass). Evil doctor in Offenbach's *Les Contes d'Hoffmann.*

Docteur Miracle, Le. Operetta in 1 act by Bizet. Libretto by Léon Battu and Ludovic Halévy. First performed Paris, 9 Apr 1857.

Bizet's operetta shared with a setting by Lecocq of the same libretto the first prize (of 12,000 francs) in a competition arranged by Offenbach, for a short work with no more than four characters, a small orchestra, and a duration of no more than 45 minutes. There were seventy-eight entrants, and the judges included Jacques François Halévy, Scribe, Auber, Thomas and Gounod.

Dodon (bass). The King in Rimsky-Korsakov's *The Golden Cockerel.*

Dohnányi, Christoph von, b. Berlin, 8 Sept 1929. German conductor. He studied in Berlin and Munich, and also in the United States with his grandfather, the composer Ernst von Dohnányi. In 1952 he became chorus master and conductor with the Frankfurt Opera, and later became music director of the companies at Lübeck (1957–62) and Kassel (1962–4). From 1968–75 he was music director of the Frankfurt company, and then accepted a similar post at Hamburg. He conducted the premières of Henze's operas *Der Junge Lord* (Berlin, 1965) and *The Bassarids* (translated in German as *Die Bassariden*) (Salzburg, 1966). He first appeared at Covent Garden in 1974 to conduct *Salome.*

Doktor Faust. Opera in 2 prologues, an interlude, and 3 scenes by Busoni (completed by his pupil Philipp Jarnach). Libretto by the composer, based on the Faust legend and specifically upon Christopher Marlowe's play, *Dr Faustus* (1589). First performed Dresden, 21 May 1925.

After making his contract with Mephistopheles (ten.) and regaining his lost youth, Faust (bar.) elopes with the Duchess of Parma (sop.). The Duchess dies, but Faust subsequently encounters a beggar woman who appears to be the Duchess, clasping the corpse of a child. Faust offers his own life for that of the child, and as he dies a youth arises from the dead body.

Domingo, Placido, b. Madrid, 21 Jan 1941. Spanish tenor. The son of *zarzuela* singers who emigrated to Mexico when he was a child, he made his first stage appearances there in a *zarzuela*, and then joined the Mexican National Opera as a baritone. His first major role as a tenor was Alfredo in *La Traviata* in 1960. He made his American

Placido Domingo about to go on stage as Dick Johnson in Verdi's *La Fanciulla del West.*

début in Dallas the following year with Joan Sutherland in *Lucia di Lammermoor*, and then joined the Israel National Opera for three years. Since 1968 he has sung frequently at the Met, Covent Garden and the principal European houses, and is widely regarded as one of the two or three leading tenors of his generation. He possesses a fine *spinto* voice and attractive appearance, and has been successful in a wide repertoire which is based on the great Verdi and Puccini roles. His Otello has been much admired. He is also a proficient conductor, and in recent years has conducted opera in several theatres.

Don Carlos. Opera in 5 acts by Verdi. Libretto by Joseph Méry and Camille du Locle, based on Friedrich Schiller's play, *Don Carlos* (1787). First performed Paris, 11 Mar 1867. A revised version, omitting Act 1, and with the libretto translated into Italian by Achille de Lauzières and Angelo Zanardini, was first performed in Milan, on 10 Jan 1884.

In order to secure peace between Spain and France, Philip II of Spain (bass) marries Elisabeth de Valois (sop.) who was engaged to his son, the Infante Don Carlos (ten.). Carlos is urged by his friend Rodrigue, Marquis of Posa (bar.) to try to secure freedom from Spanish misrule for the Netherlands, and this leads Carlos to confrontation with the King who orders his arrest. The Princess Eboli (mezzo-sop.), a former mistress of the King, but now in love with Carlos, is led by jealousy to intrigue against him and Elisabeth. Rodrigue sacrifices his life in order to effect the escape of Carlos, but when Carlos and Elisabeth meet secretly to say farewell, they are spied upon by the King and the Grand Inquisitor (bass), and Carlos is saved from the Inquisition only by the apparition of his grandfather, Charles V, who leads him to safety.

The opera is now more frequently performed in Italian, as *Don Carlo*, than in its original French version. However, in some productions of the 5-act version, material which had been cut during rehearsals before the Paris première (but recently found in Paris archives) is added to the score.

Don Giovanni. Opera in 2 acts by Mozart. Libretto by Lorenzo da Ponte, based on several earlier sources, among them Giovanni Bertati's libretto for Gazzaniga's opera, *Il Convitato di Pietra* (1787). First performed Prague, 29 Oct 1787.

Leporello (bass) keeps watch outside the Seville house of the Commendatore (bass) while his master Don Giovanni (bar.) is inside attempting the seduction of the Commendatore's daughter, Donna Anna (sop.). Giovanni emerges, pursued by Anna. When her father challenges him, he is killed by Giovanni, who escapes. Anna and her betrothed, Don Ottavio (ten.), swear vengeance on the masked intruder whose identity they do not suspect. Elvira (sop.) a discarded mistress of Giovanni, arrives in Seville in search of him. At the wedding of a peasant couple, Masetto (bar.) and Zerlina (sop.), Giovanni attempts to seduce the bride but, at a party in his palace, he is unmasked by Ottavio, Anna and Elvira.

Giovanni again escapes, and in Act II is to be found serenading Elvira's maid, having bullied Leporello into disguising himself as his master and luring Elvira away. Giovanni, in turn, has to disguise himself as Leporello in order to evade a beating at the hands of a group of peasants led by Masetto. In a cemetery, the statue of the dead Commendatore speaks, denouncing Giovanni who, in a fit of bravado, invites the statue to supper. The invitation is accepted, and the statue of the Commendatore arrives that evening at Giovanni's palace, to drag him, unrepentant, down to Hell. In an epilogue pointing the moral of the tale, the survivors express their satisfaction at what they regard as a just punishment.

Donizetti, Gaetano, b. Bergamo, 29 Nov 1797; d. Bergamo, 8 Apr 1848. Italian composer. He studied with Mayr in Bergamo and with Stanislao Mattei in Bologna. His gift for comic opera was discovered while he was still a student. His first success, *Enrico di Borgogna* (Venice, 1818), led to commissions from other Italian theatres, and he quickly embarked upon a career as a composer of sub-Rossinian comic operas, but was also capable of setting serious dramatic texts. Among his early serious operas are *L'Esule di Roma* (1828) and *Il Paria* (1829). It was with *Anna Bolena* in 1830 that he found both his mature style and the beginnings of his international success. The tragic story of Henry VIII and Anne

Boleyn was followed by four relatively undistinguished pieces, but in 1832, to a libretto by Romani based on Scribe, Donizetti composed *L'Elisir d'Amore*, a delightful sentimental comedy whose gaiety and melodic charm have earned it a permanent place in the repertoire.

Donizetti's most famous opera, *Lucia di Lammermoor*, was staged in Naples in 1835. Together with *Lucrezia Borgia* (1833) and *Roberto Devereux* (1836) it forms the apex of his dramatic achievement. He continued to compose to order, both comedies and tragedies, and from 1840 wrote for the Paris opera houses as well as for Italian theatres. Two of his finest and most successful comic operas are *La Fille du Régiment* (Paris, 1840) and *Don Pasquale* (Paris, 1843). An interesting hybrid work, *Linda di Chamounix*, which combines elements of Italian *opera seria* and French *opéra comique*, was produced in Vienna in 1842.

After the death of Bellini, Donizetti was the undisputed leading Italian composer of his day until the emergence of Verdi. Undoubtedly prolific, with nearly seventy operas to his credit, he was nevertheless to some extent a victim of the theatrical conditions of his time, for he wrote far too quickly and, on occasions, carelessly. Originality and triviality are disconcertingly juxtaposed even in some of his finest operas. Many of his operas faded into obscurity after his death, and he was remembered for no more than a handful of works. It was not until the middle of the 20th c., with the arrival on the operatic scene of a number of dramatic coloratura sopranos such as Callas, Sutherland and Gencer, that Donizetti's serious operas other than *Lucia di Lammermoor* began to be revived. He is now firmly established as one of the geniuses of Italian 19th-c. opera.

Donna del Lago, La. Opera in 2 acts by Rossini. Libretto by Andrea Leone Tottola, based on Sir Walter Scott's narrative peom, *The Lady of the Lake* (1810). First performed Naples, 24 Sept 1819.

Giacomo (King James V of Scotland: ten.) loses his way during a hunt and seeks shelter in the house of his enemy Douglas (bass) whose daughter Elena (sop.) is being forced to marry the rebel chief Roderigo (ten.). When Roderigo is killed in the uprising, Elena successfully pleads with the King both for the life of her father and for permission to marry the man she really loves, Malcolm (mezzo-sop.).

Donna Diana. Opera in 3 acts by Rezniček. Libretto by the composer, based on the comedy, *El Lindo Don Diego* (1654) by Moreto y Cavaña. First performed Prague, 16 Dec 1894.

Though the opera is now hardly ever performed, its overture has remained popular as a concert piece.

Don Pasquale. Opera in 3 acts by Donizetti. Libretto by Giacomo Ruffini, after Angelo Anelli's libretto for Pavesi's *Ser Marc' Antonio* (1810). First performed Paris, 3 Jan 1843.

When the crusty old bachelor Don Pasquale (bass) decides to marry in order to spite his nephew Ernesto (ten.), of whose fiancée, Norina (sop.), he disapproves, Ernesto and Norina concoct a plot, with the aid of Doctor Malatesta (bar.), by which Pasquale is tricked into a mock marriage with one Sofronia, a demure maid fresh from a convent, who is, in fact, Norina in disguise. After the ceremony, Sofronia begins to behave so shrewishly that Pasquale is only too anxious to be rid of her. He is made to admit he acted foolishly, and agrees to the marriage of Ernesto and Norina.

Don Quichotte. Opera in 5 acts by Massenet. Libretto by Henri Cain, after the play *Le Chevalier de la Longue Figure* which in turn is based on the novel, *Don Quixote* (1605, 1615) by Cervantes. First performed Monte Carlo, 19 Feb 1910.

The opera presents episodes from the famous novel in which the knight Don Quixote (bass) and his squire Sancho Panza (bar.) ride forth to redress the wrongs of the world, and Quixote attempts to win the love of Dulcinea (contr.).

Dorabella (sop. or mezzo-sop.). One of the two sisters in Mozart's *Così Fan Tutte*.

Dosifei (bass). The leader of the religious sect of Old Believers in Mussorgsky's *Khovanshchina*.

Downes, Edward, b. Birmingham, 17 June 1924. English conductor. He studied in Birmingham and London, and began his

Gabriel Bacquier as Malatesta and Geraint Evans in the title-role of *Don Pasquale* at Covent Garden.

career as a horn player. After further study under the conductor Hermann Scherchen in Zurich, he joined the Carl Rosa company as a coach, and in 1952 was taken on by the Covent Garden company in the same capacity. He first conducted the Covent Garden company on tour in Rhodesia (now Zimbabwe) in 1953 (*La Bohème*), and since then has conducted an impressively wide range of works for The Royal Opera. From 1971-5 he was music director of the Australian Opera. He has translated a number of Russian operas into English.

Dreigroschenoper, Die (*The Threepenny Opera*). Opera in a prologue and 8 scenes by Weill. Libretto by Bertolt Brecht, a modern reworking of the plot of Gay's *The Beggar's Opera*. First performed Berlin, 31 Aug 1928.

A satire on capitalist economic theory, the work takes some of the characters and elements of the plot of *The Beggar's Opera*, setting the action in Soho, London at the end of the reign of Queen Victoria. An adaptation in English by the American composer Marc Blitzstein was first performed at Brandeis University, Mass. on 14 June 1952, and in 1953 began a run of several years on Broadway.

Drei Pintos, Die (*The Three Pintos*). Opera in 3 acts, begun by Weber in 1821, and completed by Mahler in 1887. Libretto by Theodor Hell, after the novel *Der Braut-*

101

kampf (1819) by C. Seidel. First performed Leipzig, 20 Jan 1888.

A complicated comic plot, in which first Don Gaston (ten.) and then Gomez (ten.) pass themselves off as Don Pinto (bass), in order to prevent Don Pinto from marrying Clarissa (sop.), was arranged in its present form by Mahler and Carl von Weber, the grandson of the composer.

Duca di Mantua [Duke of Mantua] (ten.). The rakish anti-hero of Verdi's *Rigoletto*.

Due Foscari, I *(The Two Foscari)*. Opera in 3 acts by Verdi. Libretto by Francesco Maria Piave, after the play *The Two Foscari* (1821) by Byron. First performed Rome, 3 Nov 1844.

Jacopo Foscari (ten.), son of the Doge of Venice, has been unjustly condemned to exile in Crete. Despite the protests of Jacopo's wife, Lucrezia (sop.), the Doge (bar.) is forced to uphold the verdict of the Council of Ten. At the moment of his departure, Jacopo suddenly falls dead. When the Doge is forced to abdicate, he too collapses and dies as the bells of St Mark's are heard tolling to acclaim his successor.

Duenna, The, or The Betrothal in a Monastery. (Russian title, *Obrucheniye v Monastyre*). Opera in 4 acts by Prokofiev. Libretto by the composer, with verses by Mira Mendelssohn, based on the libretto by Sheridan for Linley's *The Duenna* (1775). First performed Leningrad, 3 Nov 1946.

Louisa (sop.), the daughter of the Seville nobleman Don Jerome (ten.) frustrates her father's plan that she should marry the elderly Don Mendoza (bass). Mendoza is tricked into marrying the Duenna (contr.) and all ends happily for Louisa and her beloved Antonio (ten.).

Sheridan's text was originally written for the comic opera, *The Duenna* or *The Double Elopement*, composed by Thomas Linley and

A scene from Prokofiev's *La Duenna* performed at the Bolshoi Theatre, Moscow, in December 1982 as part of the 'Russian Winter' Arts Festival. It was conducted by Rozhdestvensky.

his nineteen-year-old son, also Thomas Linley, and first performed in London, 21 Nov 1775. The opera was highly popular in its day, but is now hardly ever performed.

A 3-act opera, *The Duenna*, by Roberto Gerhard, whose libretto by the composer was also based on Sheridan, was composed in the mid-1940s, given in concert form at Wiesbaden in 1951, and performed on BBC radio in 1959.

Dukas, Paul, b. Paris, 1 Oct 1865; d. Paris, 17 May 1935. French composer. Although he made modern editions of operas by Rameau, Dukas composed only one opera, *Ariane et Barbe-Bleue*, which was the first major work to be influenced by Debussy's *Pelléas et Mélisande*. Based, like *Pelléas*, on a play by Maeterlinck, it was staged in Paris in 1907. Dukas is best known for his orchestral tone-poem, *L'Apprenti Sorcier*.

Duke Bluebeard's Castle. (Hungarian title, *A Kékszakállú Herceg Vára*). Opera in 1 act by Bartók. Libretto by Béla Balázs. First performed Budapest, 24 May 1918.

An intellectual re-working of the Mother Goose fairy-tale, the opera deals with the relationship of Bluebeard (bass) and his fourth wife, Judith (sop.). Judith makes Bluebeard unlock his seven secret doors, one by one, and when the final door reveals his three former wives, she takes her place with them, leaving him alone and in despair.

Dulcamara (bass). The itinerant peddler of panaceas and patent medicines in Donizetti's *L'Elisir d'Amore*.

Du Locle, Camille, b. Orange, 16 July 1832; d. Capri, 9 Oct 1903. French librettist. He was a director of the Opéra-Comique, Paris, from 1870 to 1876. With Joseph Méry he was responsible for the libretto of Verdi's *Don Carlos*. He wrote the original French draft libretto of *Aida* which was then translated into Italian verse for composition, and translated *Simon Boccanegra* and (with Charles Nuittier) *La Forza del Destino* into French. He also wrote the libretti of Reyer's *Sigurd* and *Salammbô*.

Duni, Egidio, b. Matera, nr Naples, 9 Feb 1709; d. Paris, 11 June 1775. Italian composer. Though his works are no longer performed, he was one of the most important composers of *opéra comique* in the second half of the 18th c. His early Italian operas are considered of less interest than the twenty or more works he composed after 1756 for Paris, in which he blended Italian and traditional French elements to create a livelier and to some extent more realistic type of comic opera. Among his most successful operas are *La Fille Mal Gardée* (1758), *Nina et Lindor* (1758) and *La Clochette* (1766). The best-known of his Italian operas is *La Buona Figliuola*, staged in Parma in 1756.

Duprez, Gilbert, b. Paris, 6 Dec 1806; d. Passy, 23 Sept 1896. French tenor. After study in Paris and an unsuccessful début there, he went to Italy for further study, where he sang from 1829-35. In 1835 he created the role of Edgardo in *Lucia di Lammermoor* in Naples, and then returned to Paris where he created the title-role in Berlioz's *Benvenuto Cellini* (1838) as well as the tenor roles in two more Donizetti operas, *La Favorite* (1840) and *Les Martyrs* (1840). He later became a successful teacher, and wrote two books on singing.

Duval, Denise, b. Paris, 23 Oct 1921. French soprano. She made her début in Bordeaux in 1941 as Lola in *Cavalleria Rusticana*, and first sang at the Paris Opéra in 1947 as Salome in Massenet's *Hérodiade*. She continued to sing at the Opéra and the Opéra-Comique in Paris until 1965 in a wide repertoire. Abroad, she was principally known for her French roles, especially those in Poulenc operas. She created two roles in Poulenc works: Thérèse in *Les Mamelles de Tirésias* (1947) and Elle in *La Voix Humaine* (1959), and also sang Blanche in the first Paris production of *Les Dialogues des Carmélites* (1957). At Glyndebourne in 1962 she was an affecting Mélisande in Debussy's *Pelléas et Mélisande*.

Dvořák, Antonin, b. Nelahozeves, Bohemia, 8 Sept 1841; d. Prague, 1 May 1904. Czech composer. One of the two leaders of the 19th-c. nationalist movement in what is now Czechoslovakia (the other being Smetana), Dvořák composed thirteen operas which, though many of them are still popular in Czechoslovakia, have not found wide acceptance abroad. Of them, only *Rusalka* (1901) is to be quite frequently

Antonin Dvořák. An important Czech composer, Brahms and Tchaikovsky were among his friends.

encountered in foreign opera houses, though *The Jacobin* (1889) and *The Devil and Kate* (1899) are occasionally performed. Dvořák was not naturally drawn to the stage: his musical stature is only properly revealed in his symphonic and chamber music. His earliest stage works are comic pieces. With the operas mentioned, *Armida* (1904) is still performed in Czechoslovakia.

Dvořáková, Ludmila, b. Kolín, nr Prague, 11 July 1923. Czech soprano. She studied in Prague, made her début in Ostrava in 1949 as Káťya Kabanová, and sang in Bratislava and Prague for some years. She joined the Berlin Staatsoper in 1960 as Octavian in *Der Rosenkavalier*, and from 1965-71 appeared in a number of Wagner roles at Bayreuth, among them Brünnhilde, Venus and Kundry. She made her first Covent Garden and Met appearances in 1966, her début roles being Leonore in *Fidelio* at the Met

and Brünnhilde in a complete *Ring* cycle at Covent Garden. An attractive woman with an impressively rich voice, she was never technically the most proficient of singers.

Dyer's Wife (sop.). The wife of Barak, the dyer, in Strauss's *Die Frau ohne Schatten*, she is, in fact, the *Frau* of the opera's title.

Dzerzhinsky, Ivan, b. Tambov, 9 Apr 1909; d. Leningrad, 18 Jan 1978. Russian composer. He composed ten operas and two musical comedies, none of which has been performed outside the Soviet Union. He became known abroad when his first opera, *Quiet Flows the Don*, based on Sholokhov's novel of that name, was produced in Leningrad in 1935, to be praised by Stalin who recognized its propaganda value as a work upholding the Cossack virtues of strength and courage. The opera was officially proclaimed the model of Soviet realism in music, and its composer was awarded a Stalin prize. None of Dzerzhinsky's subsequent operas attracted much critical attention or public interest.

E

Eames, Emma, b. Shanghai, 13 Aug 1865; d. New York, 13 June 1952. American soprano. She studied in Boston and Paris, and made her début in Paris in 1889 when Gounod chose her to sing Juliette in his revised version of *Roméo et Juliette*. She created the role of Colombe in Saint-Saëns's *Ascanio* in Paris in 1890, and first sang at Covent Garden and at the Met in 1891, her début role on both occasions being Juliette. For many years she appeared regularly at Covent Garden and the Met, continuing at the Met until shortly before her retirement from opera in 1912. She was an admired Tosca, Desdemona and Aida. She published her memoirs, *Some Memories and Reflections*, in 1927.

Ebert, Carl, b. Berlin, 20 Feb 1887; d. Santa Monica, Calif., 14 May 1980. German director. He began his career as an actor in Germany with Max Reinhardt, later became a stage director, and in 1931 was appointed general director of the Berlin Städtische Oper. He left Germany in 1933, and the following year helped Fritz Busch to found Glyndebourne Festival Opera. He directed opera at Glyndebourne regularly both before and after World War II, until 1959. He was engaged at the Met between 1959-62. His productions of Mozart and Verdi operas were admired for their fidelity to the intentions of composer and librettist. His son, Peter Ebert (b. Frankfurt, 6 Apr 1918), has directed operas in a number of countries, but has been most closely associated with Scottish Opera.

Eboli (mezzo-sop.). The ex-mistress of Philip II in Verdi's *Don Carlos*, whose love for Carlos is unrequited.

Eddy, Nelson, b. Providence, R.I., 29 June 1901; d. Miami, 9 Mar 1967. American baritone. He studied under David Bispham, and made his opera début with the Philadelphia Opera Society in 1924 as Amonasro. His success was immediate, and when the company played at the Met later in the same year Eddy was assigned the role of Tonio in *Pagliacci*. He visited Europe in 1927, auditioned for Fritz Busch at the Dresden Opera and was offered a contract as leading baritone. He chose, however, to return to the USA where he sang in the first American performances of Strauss's *Feuersnot* in 1927 and *Ariadne auf Naxos* (as Harlequin) in 1928, both with Philadelphia Civic Opera. He sang in the first American performances of *Wozzeck* under Stokowski in Philadelphia in March, 1931, and subsequently at the Met in November of the same year. Under the baton of the composer, he sang in the première of Respighi's *Maria Egiziaca* in New York in 1932. After a recital which he gave in Los Angeles in place of Lotte Lehmann who had cancelled due to illness, he was engaged by M-G-M, and went on to make a series of musical films in the 1930-40s, in most of which he was teamed with Jeanette MacDonald. Though he continued his concert career until his death, he never again appeared in opera.

Edgar. Opera in 4 acts by Puccini. Libretto by Ferdinando Fontana, based on Alfred de Musset's play, *La Coupe et les Lèvres* (1832). First performed Milan, 21 Apr 1889.

Edgar (ten.), torn between his love for the gentle Fidelia (sop.) and his infatuation with the gipsy Tigrana (mezzo-sop.), leaves his village with Tigrana, but tires of her and joins a military expedition led by Fidelia's brother Frank (bar.). Fidelia is stabbed to death by the jealous Tigrana.

Edgardo (ten.). The hero of Donizetti's *Lucia di Lammermoor*, in love with Lucia.

Egk, Werner, b. Auchsesheim, nr Donauwörth, 17 May 1901. German composer. He studied in Munich with Orff, and wrote his first opera, *Columbus*, for performance on Bavarian Radio in 1933. (It was later adapted for the stage, and produced in Frankfurt in 1942.) His first opera for the stage, *Die Zaubergeige*, proved highly popular at its Frankfurt première in 1935, and when the composer conducted it at the Berlin State Opera in 1937. *Peer Gynt*, staged in Berlin the following year, was admired by Hitler, and Egk remained at the Berlin State Opera as guest conductor until 1941. His post-war operas include *Circe* (1948), *Irische Legende* (staged in Salzburg in 1955), *Der Revisor* (1957) and his best-known work, *Die Verlobung in San Domingo* (1963). His style, though individual, owes something to Stravinsky, and he has an innate feeling for the stage. His operas have made little impression abroad, but are popular in Germany.

Ehrling, Sixten, b. Malmö, 3 Apr 1918. Swedish conductor. After studies at the Royal Academy of Music in Stockholm and under Karl Böhm in Dresden, he became a coach at the Royal Opera, Stockholm, in 1939, made his conducting début there the following year, and in 1953 became principal conductor and music director of the company. He has conducted widely in Europe and America, and was for many years a frequent guest at the Met. He brought his Stockholm company to the Edinburgh Festival in 1959 and to Covent Garden the following year, on both occasions including in the repertoire Blomdahl's opera *Aniara* whose première he had conducted in Stockholm in 1959.

Einem, Gottfried von, b. Berne, 24 Jan 1918. Austrian composer. Primarily a composer of opera, von Einem had a pronounced success with his first work for the stage, *Dantons Tod*, performed at the

Salzburg Festival in 1947, and subsequently produced frequently both in Austria and abroad. *Der Prozess*, first performed at the 1953 Salzburg Festival, is a compelling piece based on Kafka's novel, *The Trial*. With *Der Zerrissene* (1964), von Einem temporarily forsook the world of abnormal psychology for that of 19th-c. Viennese farce, but his next opera, *Der Besuch der alten Dame*, based on Friedrich Dürrenmatt's novel of that title, was more characteristic of the composer, and has proved to be his most popular work. First staged in Vienna in 1971, it has since been produced in a number of countries. It was performed in English at Glyndebourne in 1973. *Kabale und Liebe* (1976) was the last of von Einem's collaborations with his friend the composer Boris Blacher, who had written the libretti of all the operas except *Der Besuch der alten Dame* for which Dürrenmatt himself provided the adaptation. (Blacher died in 1975.) A highly eclectic composer, von Einem has nevertheless forged from his eclecticism a personal style which has made his operas attractive and accessible to the present-day opera-going public.

Eisenstein (ten.). The husband of Rosalinde in Johann Strauss's *Die Fledermaus*.

Eléazar (ten.). The Jewish goldsmith, father of Rachel, in Halévy's *La Juive*.

Elegy for Young Lovers. Opera in 3 acts by Henze. Libretto by W.H. Auden and Chester Kallman. First performed (in German translation) Schwetzingen, 20 May 1961. First performance in the original English, Glyndebourne, 19 July 1961.

The opera describes the relationship between the great poet Gregor Mittenhofer (bar.) and those on whom he feeds for literary inspiration: Hilda (sop.) and the young lovers Toni (ten.) and Elisabeth (sop.). Mittenhofer is responsible for the death of Toni and Elisabeth in the Alps, an event which inspires him to write his greatest poem, an elegy for young lovers.

Elektra. Opera in 1 act by Richard Strauss. Libretto by Hugo von Hofmannsthal, after the tragedy by Sophocles (*c.* 450 BC). First performed Dresden, 25 Jan 1909.

Elektra (sop.) mourns the death of her father Agamemnon, murdered by her mother Klytemnestra (mezzo-sop.), and tries to persuade her sister Chrysothemis (sop.) to help her avenge him. Their brother Orest (bar.) whom they had believed dead returns home and kills both Klytemnestra and her lover Aegisth (ten.). Elektra dances dementedly and falls dead.

Elias, Rosalind, b. Lowell, Mass., 13 March, 1929. American mezzo-soprano. She studied at the New England Conservatorium and in Italy, and sang with the New England Opera Company from 1948-52. She joined the Met in 1954, where she created roles in two operas by Barber, Erika in *Vanessa* (1958) and Charmian in *Antony and Cleopatra* (1966), and was much admired as Carmen, Cherubino and Octavian. Her first appearance in Britain was in the title-role of Rossini's *Cenerentola* with the Scottish Opera in Glasgow in 1970.

Elisabeth (sop.). Daughter of the Landgrave in *Tannhäuser*, and in love with Tannhäuser.

Elisabeth de Valois (sop.). In love with Don Carlos, she is forced for reasons of state into marriage with his father, Philip II of Spain, in Verdi's *Don Carlos*.

Elisabetta, Regina d'Inghilterra *(Elizabeth, Queen of England)*. Opera in 2 acts by Rossini. Libretto by Giovanni Schmidt, after a play by Carlo Federici (1814). First performed Naples, 4 Oct 1815.

Queen Elizabeth I (sop.) learns from the Duke of Norfolk (ten.) that Leicester (ten.), whom she loves, is secretly married to Mathilde (sop.). She has Leicester imprisoned, but when Norfolk's intrigues against her are revealed, she pardons Leicester.

(The opera is sometimes said by commentators, following Stendhal in his life of Rossini, to be based on Sir Walter Scott's *Kenilworth*. This is incorrect. *Kenilworth* was not published until six years after the première of *Elisabetta*.)

Elisir d'Amore, L' *(The Elixir of Love)*. Opera in 2 acts by Donizetti. Libretto by Felice Romani, based on Scribe's libretto for Auber's *Le Philtre* (1831). First performed Milan, 12 May 1832.

The young peasant Nemorino (ten.) is in love with the rich young landowner Adina

Geraint Evans as Dulcamara in Donizetti's *L'Elisir d'Amore* at Covent Garden in 1976.

(sop.) who pays no attention to him. In despair he purchases from the itinerant 'quack' Dulcamara (bass) what he is told is a love-potion. It is, in fact, a bottle of red wine. Unfortunately, the newly found confidence which the wine gives to Nemorino so puzzles and irritates Adina that she agrees to marry Sergeant Belcore (bar.). In despair, Nemorino earns the money to purchase another bottle of the 'elixir' by joining Belcore's regiment. News of the death of his rich uncle makes Nemorino suddenly desirable to all the village girls, and Adina's jealousy causes her to realize that she really loves him. The opera ends happily for Adina and Nemorino, and for Dulcamara who points out that his love potion is clearly efficacious. Belcore accepts the situation philosophically.

Elsa (sop.). The heroine of Wagner's *Lohengrin* who is falsely accused of witchcraft and murder.

Elvino (ten.). The young Swiss farmer, in love with Amina, in Bellini's *La Sonnambula*.

Elvira (sop.). A discarded mistress of the eponymous hero of Mozart's *Don Giovanni*, and also the heroine of Verdi's *Ernani*, betrothed to one man, in love with another, and desired by a third.

Emperor Jones, The. Opera in 2 acts by Gruenberg. Libretto by Kathleen de Jaffa, from the play of the same title by Eugene O'Neill (1921). First performed New York, 7 Jan 1933.

Brutus Jones (bar.), a black ex-Pullman porter and escaped convict, rules his Caribbean island in the style of an absolute monarch. When he is warned by Henry Smithers (ten.) that his people are about to revolt, Jones flees into the jungle. He imagines he is confronted by past victims of his cruelty, and as his terror strips him of his superficial sophistication he reverts to a state of superstition. He kills himself with a silver bullet.

Enfant et les Sortilèges, L' *(The Child and the Enchantments)*. Opera in 2 acts by Ravel. Libretto by Colette. First performed Monte Carlo, 21 Mar 1925.

A naughty child (mezzo-sop.) who has ill-used his toys is frightened when they come to life to torment him. He flees into the garden but the animals and trees are equally hostile to him. It is only when he bandages the paw of a wounded squirrel that they relent. The child, having learned his lesson, runs back to the arms of his mother.

Enrico (bar.). The brother of Lucia in Donizetti's *Lucia di Lammermoor*.

Entführung aus dem Serail, Die *(The Abduction from the Harem)*. Opera in 3 acts by Mozart. Libretto by Gottlieb Stephanie Jnr, based on Christoph Friedrich Bretzner's libretto for André's *Belmont und Constanze* (1781). First performed Vienna, 16 July 1782.

Belmonte (ten.) arrives at the palace of the Pasha Selim (speaking role) who has captured his beloved Constanze (sop.), her maid Blonde (sop.) and Belmonte's servant Pedrillo (ten.). The Pasha's steward Osmin (bass), who is in love with Blonde, foils their plans to escape, and they are brought before the Pasha whose approaches have been haughtily rejected by Constanze. When the Pasha discovers that Belmonte is the son of his old enemy, the situation looks gloomy for the Europeans, but the Pasha magnanimously sets both pairs of sweethearts free.

entr'acte. Any piece of orchestral music played between the acts or between the scenes of an opera.

Enzo (ten.). The lover of the eponymous heroine of Ponchielli's *La Gioconda*.

Erb, Karl, b. Ravensburg, 13 July 1877; d. Ravensburg, 13 July 1958. German tenor. He made his début in Stuttgart in 1907 in Kienzl's *Der Evangelimann*, and in 1912 joined the Munich Opera, remaining with that company until 1925. In Munich in 1917 he created the title-role in Pfitzner's *Palestrina*. He was a fine exponent of the

Mozart tenor roles. After an injury received in an accident in 1930 he confined himself to concerts and recitals, and was highly regarded as a singer of Lieder. From 1920-31 he was married to the soprano Maria von Ivogün.

Erda (contr.). The earth-goddess, and mother of the Valkyries, in Wagner's *Ring*.

Erede, Alberto, b. Genoa, 8 Nov 1909. Italian conductor. After studying piano and cello in Genoa, composition in Milan, and conducting with Weingartner in Basle and Fritz Busch in Dresden, he joined Glyndebourne Festival Opera in its first season in 1934 as Busch's assistant, returning there each summer until 1939, and conducting *Don Giovanni* and *Le Nozze di Figaro* in the last two pre-war seasons. In 1939 in the United States he conducted the radio première of Menotti's *The Old Maid and the Thief*. During World War II he conducted opera in Italy, and returned to England in 1946 to become music director of the New London Opera Company. He conducted at the Met between 1950-5, and made his Bayreuth début with *Lohengrin* in 1968. He is a reliable conductor of the standard Italian repertory, and an excellent trainer of singers.

Erhardt, Otto, b. Breslau, 18 Nov 1888; d. San Carlos de Bariloche, Argentina, 18 Jan 1971. German director. He staged the first German performance of Monteverdi's *Orfeo* in Breslau in 1913, and directed opera in Düsseldorf (1918-20), Stuttgart (1920-7) and Dresden (1927-1933). In Dresden in 1928 he directed the première of Strauss's *Die Agyptische Helena*. He was forced to leave Germany in 1933, and worked at Covent Garden until 1935, where his Wagner productions were greatly admired. From 1939-60 he directed productions at the Teatro Colón, Buenos Aires, and was engaged by New York City Opera in 1954-6 and again in 1967.

Erkel, Ferenc, b. Gyula, 7 Nov 1810; d. Budapest, 15 June 1893. Hungarian composer. He began his career as a pianist, and as a conductor of opera, but achieved immediate success with his first composition for the stage, *Bátori Mária* (1840), and thenceforth devoted himself to writing operas. *Hunyadi*

László, staged at the Budapest National Theatre in 1844, was even more successful, and is generally considered to be the work which brought a genuinely Hungarian style of opera into existence. It was several years later that Erkel produced his operatic masterpiece, *Bánk Bán*, staged in 1861. His later operas, some of them slight comic pieces and others nationalistic historical dramas, lacked the sureness of touch of *Hunyadi László* and *Bánk Bán*, and in the last of them, *István Király* (1885), the composer's individuality became submerged under a torrent of Wagnerism. His two major operas have kept their place in the repertory in Hungary as the foundation pieces of Hungarian national opera. They are occasionally performed abroad.

Ernani. Opera in 4 acts by Verdi. Libretto by Francesco Maria Piave, after Victor Hugo's play, *Hernani* (1830). First performed Venice, 9 Mar 1844.

The opera is set in Spain in 1519. Donna Elvira (sop.), though about to marry her elderly guardian, Don Ruy Gomez de Silva (bass), is in love with the bandit Ernani (ten.). When she is abducted from Silva's castle by Don Carlo, King of Spain (bar.), Ernani and Silva join forces to rescue her and to plot against the King. Spanish concepts of honour lead Ernani to consider his life forfeit to Silva, so he gives Silva a hunting horn and tells him that whenever Silva chooses to sound the horn, he, Ernani, will take his own life.

The conspirators' plot against the King is discovered, but Carlo, at the moment of his election to the throne of the Holy Roman Empire, pardons them. It is then discovered that Ernani is of noble rank.

The wedding festivities of Elvira and Ernani are interrupted by a sombre figure in a black mask who sounds a hunting-horn. Ernani fulfils his pledge, stabs himself, and dies in Elvira's arms.

Ernesto (ten.). The lover of Norina and nephew of Pasquale in Donizetti's *Don Pasquale*.

Ero the Joker (Serbian title, *Ero s onoga svijeta*). Opera in 3 acts by Gotovac. Libretto by Milan Begović, based on a Dalmatian folk-tale. First performed Zagreb, 2 Nov 1935.

Though seldom performed abroad, this is one of the most popular of Yugoslav operas. The opera tells of the love of Micha (ten.) for Jula (sop.), the daughter of a rich peasant. Micha pretends that he has come from heaven, and calls himself 'Ero from the other world' (which is the Serbian title of the opera). He answers all the questions put to him by the villagers about their relatives who have passed to the other world. All ends happily for the lovers.

Erwartung *(Expectation)*. Opera or monodrama in 1 act by Schoenberg. Libretto by Marie Pappenheim. First performed Prague, 6 June 1924.

A half-hour piece for solo soprano and orchestra, in which the soprano portrays a woman searching for her lover in a dark forest, and finally stumbling across his dead body.

Escamillo (bar.). The toreador who entices Carmen away from Don José in *Carmen*.

Étoile du Nord, L' *(The North Star)*. Opera in 3 acts by Meyerbeer. Libretto by Eugène Scribe, based on Ludwig Rellstab's libretto for *Ein Feldlager in Schlesien* (the earlier version of Meyerbeer's opera, staged in Berlin, 7 Dec 1844) which in turn was based on an episode in the life of Frederick the Great. First performed Paris, 16 Feb 1854.

The Russian Tsar, Peter the Great (bass), is in love with a village girl, Katherine (sop.) who takes the place of her brother Georges (ten.) in the Russian army. In the disguise of a carpenter, the Tsar successfully woos her and makes her his Tsarina.

Eugene Onegin. Opera in 3 acts by Tchaikovsky. Libretto by the composer and Konstantin Shilovsky, after the narrative poem by Pushkin (1831). First performed Moscow, 29 Mar 1879.

At the country house of Madame Larina (mezzo-sop.), her daughters Olga (mezzo-sop.) and Tatiana (sop.) are visited by Olga's fiancé Lensky (ten.) and his friend, the Byronic Onegin (bar.). The young and inexperienced Tatiana falls in love with Onegin, and writes him an indiscreet letter. Onegin addresses her in avuncular tones, rejecting her. Out of boredom, at a ball at Madame Larina's house he flirts with Olga,

A scene from the last act of Tchaikovsky's *Eugene Onegin* at the Bolshoi Theatre.

and is challenged to a duel by the jealous Lensky. In the duel Lensky is killed, and Onegin flees abroad.

Six years later, having returned to Russia, Onegin attends a ball in St Petersburg and is introduced to the poised and elegant wife of Prince Gremin (bass). He is disconcerted to recognize her as Tatiana and to realize that he now loves her. He urges Tatiana to leave her husband for him, but, although she confesses that she still loves Onegin, she refuses to be unfaithful to her husband. She dismisses Onegin, and in despair he realizes that he has lost her for ever.

Euridice. (sop.). Orfeo's wife in many operas on the theme.

Euridice. Opera in a prologue and 6 scenes by Peri. Libretto by Ottavio Rinuccini. First performed Florence, 6 Oct 1600.

The earliest opera of which the music is extant, it is a version of the Orpheus and Euridice legend. Rinuccini's libretto was also set by Caccini, whose *Euridice* was first performed in Florence in 1602.

Euryanthe. Opera in 3 acts by Weber. Libretto by Helmine von Chezy, based on a mediaeval French romance. First performed Vienna, 25 Oct 1823.

Lysiart (bar.) makes a wager with Adolar (ten.), who is in love with Euryanthe (sop.), that he, Lysiart, can seduce her. Because of the machinations of the evil Eglantine (mezzo-sop.), it appears that Adolar is to lose the wager, and consequently his lands and possessions. Adolar leads Euryanthe, whom he now believes unfaithful to him, into the desert and leaves her to die. She is rescued by the King and his hunting party, the falsehood of Eglantine is revealed, and Adolar is reunited with Euryanthe.

Eva. Opera by Foerster. Libretto by the composer, after the play, *The Innkeeper's Daughter* by Gabriela Preisová. First performed Prague, 1 Jan 1899.

The opera is still occasionally produced in Czechoslovakia. *Eva* is also the title of an operetta by Franz Lehár, which was first performed in Vienna, 24 Nov 1911.

Eva (sop.). The daughter of Pogner, and heroine of Wagner's *Die Meistersinger von Nürnberg*.

Evangelimann, Der *(The Evangelist).* Opera in 2 acts by Kienzl. Libretto by the composer, based on a story (1894) by Leopold Florian Meissner. First performed Berlin, 4 May 1895.

Although the opera is hardly ever performed outside the German-speaking countries, it remains popular in Kienzl's own country, Austria. It tells the story of Matthias (ten.), unjustly imprisoned for arson who, on his release, becomes an evangelist. Many years later, Matthias's brother Johannes (bar.) on his death-bed confesses to the crime for which Matthias had been imprisoned. He calls for the evangelist to hear his confession, the brothers recognize each other, and after a great inner struggle Matthias forgives Johannes.

Evans, (Sir) Geraint, b. Pontypridd, South Wales, 16 Feb 1922. Welsh baritone. He studied in London, Hamburg and Geneva, and joined the company at the Royal Opera House, Covent Garden, in 1948, making his début as the Nightwatchman in *Die Meistersinger*. Excelling in the lighter baritone roles of Mozart, such as Leporello, Guglielmo (*Così Fan Tutte*), Figaro and Papageno, he was soon in demand abroad in these roles, as well as Verdi's Falstaff. He was much appreciated in Salzburg for his Mozart performances, and has over the years made many appearances in the United States, especially with San Francisco Opera. At Covent Garden, he created a number of roles in operas by Britten and Walton. He is also a renowned Beckmesser in *Die Meistersinger*. Knighted in 1969, he announced his retirement from opera in 1983.

Everding, August, b. Bottrop, Westphalia, 31 Oct 1928. German director. He studied philosophy and drama in Bonn and Munich, and became a theatre director in Munich where he also staged his first operas in the mid-1960s. His production of *Tristan und Isolde* in Vienna in 1967 led to engagements in Hamburg, where he directed the première of Humphrey Searle's *Hamlet* in 1968, and Bayreuth (*Der fliegende Holländer*, 1969). He made his Covent Garden début with *Salome* in 1970, and in 1971 directed *Tristan und Isolde* at the Met. He is generally regarded as one of the finest present-day directors of Wagner and Strauss operas.

Excursions of Mr Brouček, The (Czech title, *Vylety pana Broučka*). Opera in 2 parts by Janáček. Libretto by the composer, after the novels by Svatopluk Čech (1888-9). First performed Prague, 23 Apr 1920.

A satirical fantasy in which Mr Brouček, a bourgeois citizen, journeys first to the moon and then back through time to the 15th c.

Fafner (bass). One of the two giants in *Das Rheingold*. He also appears in *Siegfried*, in the guise of a dragon, guarding the gold for which he had killed Fasolt.

Fairy Queen, The. Masque in a prologue and 5 acts by Purcell. Libretto by (probably) Elkanah Settle, based on Shakespeare's *A Midsummer Night's Dream* (1595). First performed London, Apr 1692.

Sometimes described as a 'semi-opera', but really a succession of masques, the score of the work was lost for 200 years, 20 guineas being offered for its recovery in 1700. It was found in 1901 in the library of the Royal Academy of Music in London, and was given a concert performance in London in June of that year. The first modern stage performance was in England, at Cambridge, in 1920.

Fall, Leo, b. Olmütz, Moravia, 2 Feb 1873; d. Vienna, 16 Sept 1925. Austrian composer. He studied in Vienna, and after conducting in Germany for several years settled in Vienna in 1904 and began a highly successful career as a composer of operetta. Among the most successful of his operettas, works which combine gaiety and a wistful charm, are *Der Fidele Bauer*, first performed in Mannheim in 1907, *Die Dollarprinzessin* (Vienna, 1907), *Die geschiedene Frau* (Vienna, 1908), *Der liebe Augustin* (Berlin, 1912), *Die Rose von Stamboul* (Vienna, 1916) and *Madame Pompadour* (Vienna, 1922). All of these were popular abroad, and were performed in London and New York in English versions shortly after their premières. Except in Austria, however, they have been revived less often than the operettas of Lehár, the leading Viennese operetta composer of Fall's generation.

Falla, Manuel de, b. Cádiz, 23 Nov 1876; d. Alta Gracia, Argentina, 14 Nov 1946. Spanish composer. His first works for the stage were five *zarzuelas*, only one of which, *Los Amores de la Inés*, was performed, and that with only moderate success. It was with the opera, *La Vida Breve*, composed in 1904-5 but not performed until 1913, that his mature personality as a composer emerged. His second opera, *El Retablo de Maese Pedro*, based on an incident in *Don Quixote*, was written to be performed with puppets. It was first staged in Paris, privately, in 1923. Apart from ballets, Falla's only other known work in a theatrical format is *Atlántida*, a 'scenic cantata' which he left unfinished at his death and which was completed by Ernesto Halffter. Though Falla probably did not intend it to be staged, it was in fact produced as an opera at La Scala, Milan, posthumously, in 1962.

Falstaff. Opera in 3 acts by Verdi. Libretto by Arrigo Boito, based on Shakespeare's *The Merry Wives of Windsor* (1600) and several passages concerning Falstaff in Shakespeare's *Henry IV* (1597-8). First performed Milan, 9 Feb 1893.

The plot is a simplification of that of *The Merry Wives of Windsor* in which the rascally old knight, Falstaff (bar.), sends identical love letters to two respectable married women, Alice Ford (sop.) and Meg Page (mezzo-sop.). The women dispatch a go-between, Mistress Quickly (mezzo-sop.), to Falstaff with messages accepting his favours, and arranging an assignation with Alice. Ford (bar.), apprised of Falstaff's interest in his wife by two of the knight's disaffected hangers-on, makes plans to thwart him. Ford also plans to marry off his daughter, Nannetta (sop.) to Dr Caius (ten.), although she is in love with Fenton (ten.). In due course, the wives are revenged not only on Falstaff but also on Ford, and Nannetta is enabled to marry the man of her choice.

Fanciulla del West, La *(The Girl of the West)*. Opera in 3 acts by Puccini. Libretto by Guelfo Civinini and Carlo Zangarini, based on David Belasco's play, *The Girl of the Golden West* (1905). First performed New York, 10 Dec 1910.

Minnie (sop.), owner of a saloon in a miners' camp in California during the days of the gold rush, falls in love with a stranger,

Placido Domingo and Carol Neblett in *La Fanciulla del West* at Covent Garden in 1977.

Dick Johnson (ten.) who visits her saloon. Johnson is really the bandit Ramerrez, the initial purpose of whose visit was to rob the saloon, a purpose put aside when he finds himself attracted by Minnie. The sheriff, Jack Rance (bar.), also in love with Minnie, tracks the wounded bandit to her cabin in the hills, but she bargains with him. Minnie and Rance play poker. If Minnie wins, Rance will let the bandit go free; if Rance wins, he may claim Minnie as his bride. Minnie wins by cheating, and Rance leaves, but Johnson–Ramerrez is later captured. He is about to be hanged when he is saved by Minnie who pleads with the miners for his life. Minnie and Johnson leave California to find a new life together elsewhere.

Faninal (bar.). The *nouveau riche* merchant who is the father of Sophie, in Strauss's *Der Rosenkavalier*.

Farrar, Geraldine, b. Melrose, Mass., 28 Feb 1882; d. Ridgefield, Conn., 11 Mar 1967. American soprano. After studying in America and Germany, she made her début in Berlin in 1901 as Marguerite in Gounod's *Faust*. She then became a pupil of Lilli Lehmann, and in 1906 made her first appearance at the Met as another Gounod heroine, Juliette. She remained a leading soprano at the Met until her retirement in 1922. She was considered an outstanding Butterfly and Carmen. She appeared in silent films, and in 1938 published her memoirs, *Such Sweet Compulsion*.

Fasolt (bass). One of the two giants in *Das Rheingold*, he is killed by the other giant, Fafner.

Fassbaender, Brigitte, b. Berlin, 3 July 1939. German mezzo-soprano. Daughter of Willi Domgraf-Fassbaender, a German baritone of the 1920-30s, she studied with her father, and made her début in Munich in 1961 as Nicklausse in *The Tales of Hoffmann*. Since then, she has remained a member of the Munich Staatsoper, and has made guest appearances throughout Europe as well as in London and the United States. Her first Covent Garden appearance was in 1971 as Octavian, and in the same year she made her US début in San Francisco as Carmen. Dorabella in *Cosi Fan Tutte* is a role for which she is also much admired.

Fauré, Gabriel, b. Pamiers, 12 May 1845; d. Paris, 4 Nov 1924. French composer. Though not primarily a composer for the stage, he did in fact write four operas of one kind or another. His earliest, *Barnabé*, described as an *opéra comique,* remains unperformed and unpublished. *Prométhée* (1900), a lyric tragedy with spoken interludes, reveals a strong Wagnerian influence. It was with *Pénélope* (1913) that Fauré found his individual voice and style for the stage. Composed in a series of short lyrical passages, linked by arioso or recitative, *Pénélope* is an interesting and stylistically unique work.

Faure, Jean-Baptiste, b. Moulins, 15 Jan 1830; d. Paris, 9 Nov 1914. French baritone. He studied at the Paris Conservatoire, and made his début at the Opéra-Comique in 1852 as Pygmalion in Massé's *Galathée*. In 1865 he created the role of Nelusko in Meyerbeer's *L'Africaine* and in 1867 Rodrigue in *Don Carlos*. His Covent Garden début in 1860 was as Hoël in Meyerbeer's *Dinorah*. He was greatly admired as Don Giovanni and Rossini's *William Tell*.

Faust. Opera in 5 acts by Gounod. Libretto by Jules Barbier and Michel Carré, based on pt I of Goethe's *Faust* (1808). First performed Paris, 19 Mar 1859.

Faust (ten.), an aged scholar in mediaeval Germany, sells his soul to Méphistophélès (bass) in exchange for the return of his youth. Now young again, he meets and seduces Marguerite (sop.) and later kills her brother Valentin (bar.). When Marguerite is imprisoned and awaiting execution for having killed the child she has borne to Faust, he attempts to rescue her, but she refuses to go with him. She dies, and her soul ascends to Heaven, while Faust is dragged down to Hell by Méphistophélès.

Favero, Mafalda, b. Portomaggiore, near Ferrara, 6 Jan 1905; d. Milan, 3 Sept 1981. Italian soprano. She studied in Bologna and made her début in Cremona in 1906 as Lola in *Cavalleria Rusticana*, under the name of Maria Bianchi. Under her own name the following year she sang Liù in *Turandot* in Parma, and then was engaged by Toscanini for La Scala, where she sang regularly until 1943. She continued to appear in Italy until 1950. An attractive lyric soprano, she sang at Covent Garden in 1937 and again in 1939 as Norina (*Don Pasquale*), Liù and Zerlina (*Don Giovanni*), and in 1938 made her only American appearances in San Francisco and New York, making her Met début as Mimì.

Favola d'Orfeo, La *(The Legend of Orpheus)*. Opera in a prologue and 5 acts by Monteverdi. Libretto by Alessandro Striggio. First performed Mantua, Feb 1607.

Monteverdi's version of the legend of Orpheus (ten.) and Eurydice (sop.) recounts their nuptials, her death, his journey to the underworld in search of her, and their return. Eurydice dies again because Orpheus has turned to look at her. The god Apollo (bass) promises Orpheus that he will be granted immortality with Eurydice.

Favorite, La *(The Favourite)*. Opera in 4 acts by Donizetti. Libretto by Alphonse Royer and Gustave Vaëz, reworked by Eugène Scribe, after François Baculard d'Arnaud's play, *Le Comte de Commingues* (1764). First performed Paris, 2 Dec 1840.

Set in 14th-c. Spain, the opera tells of the love of Ferdinand, a young novice (ten.), for Leonore (mezzo-sop.), mistress of Alphonse (bar.), King of Castile. Ferdinand becomes an Officer in the King's forces. He is not aware of Leonore's identity or situation until Alphonse, under threat of excommunication, bestows Leonore on him. Ferdinand returns to his monastery, but Leonore follows him in male disguise, only to die in his arms.

In its Italian translation as *La Favorita*, the opera is still quite frequently performed in Italy.

Fedora. Opera in 3 acts by Giordano. Libretto by Arturo Colautti after the play *Fédora* (1882) by Victorien Sardou. First performed Milan, 17 Nov 1898.

Princess Fedora Romanov (sop.) discovers that the assassin of her fiancé is Count Loris Ipanov (ten.), with whose wife the dead man had carried on an intrigue. Fedora falls in love with Loris, but too late to save his family from the consequences of her plotting against him. Fedora takes poison and dies.

Fedra. Opera in 3 acts by Pizzetti. Libretto by Gabriele D'Annunzio based on Euripides's *Hippolytus*. First performed Milan, 20 Mar 1915.

Phaedra (sop.), wife of Theseus (bar.) falls in love with her stepson, Hippolytus (ten.). When she is rejected by him she kills herself, leaving a letter falsely accusing Hippolytus of having been her lover.

Another *Fedra*, a 1-act opera, by Romano Romani, its libretto by Alfredo Lanzoni, was staged in Rome in 1915, having been awarded first prize in a competition. Its composer also taught singing, and numbered among his pupils the soprano Rosa Ponselle who was responsible for the opera's revival at Covent Garden in 1931 when she sang the title-role. Critical opinion regretted that the soprano had chosen to waste her talents on the work.

Feen, Die *(The Fairies)*. Opera in 3 acts by Wagner. Libretto by the composer, based on Carlo Gozzi's play, *La Donna Serpente* (1762). First performed (posthumously) Munich, 29 June 1888.

Prince Arindal (ten.) marries the fairy Ada (sop.), but loses her when he asks about her origin. Under a curse, she is turned to stone. Eventually, Arindal succeeds in effecting her return to the fairy world, and is allowed fairy status and remains with her for ever.

Felsenstein, Walter, b. Vienna, 30 May 1901; d. Berlin, 8 Oct 1975. Austrian producer. He studied in Graz and Vienna, and after working as an actor began to produce opera in provincial German theatres. In 1947 he became the Intendant of the Komische Oper in East Berlin, where his meticulously rehearsed productions brought international acclaim to the company. He remained the head of the Komische Oper until his death, and helped to train a younger generation of producers, two of whom, Götz Friedrich and Joachim Herz, subsequently pursued important international careers.

Fenton (ten.). The young man in love with Nannetta in Verdi's *Falstaff*.

Ferrando (ten.). The young officer in Mozart's *Così Fan Tutte* who is in love with Dorabella.

Ferretti, Jacopo, b. Rome, 16 July 1784; d. Rome, 7 Mar 1852. Italian librettist. He is best known for the version of the Cinderella story he provided for Rossini's *Cenerentola* (1817). For Rossini he also wrote the libretto of *Matilde di Shabran* (1821), based on earlier French works, and for Donizetti *Torquato Tasso* (1833). He was an elegant versifier, who also wrote libretti for Mayr, Mercadante, Pacini and many other Italian composers of his time.

Ferrier, Kathleen, b. Higher Walton, Lancs, 22 Apr 1912; d. London, 8 Oct 1953. English contralto. She studied with Roy Henderson in London, and made her career primarily as a concert and oratorio singer. Her opera début was as Lucretia in the world première of Britten's *The Rape of Lucretia* at Glyndebourne in 1946. Her only other role in opera was Orpheus in Gluck's *Orfeo ed Euridice* which she sang at Glyndebourne in 1947, in Holland in 1949 and at Covent Garden for two performances in 1953, the second of which was her last public appearance. She possessed a voice of sympathetic warmth and an attractive and dignified stage presence.

Kathleen Ferrier by Fayer.

Feuersnot *(Fire Famine)*. Opera in 1 act by Richard Strauss. Libretto by Ernst von Wolzogen, based on a Flemish legend recounted in J.W. Wolf's *Sagas of the Netherlands* (1843). First performed Dresden, 21 Nov 1901.

Furious at his public rejection by Diemut (sop.), the alchemist Kunrad (bar.) causes the extinction of all fire. He allows fire to exist again only when he is accepted by the repentant Diemut.

Février, Henry, b. Paris, 2 Oct 1875; d. Paris, 8 July 1957. French composer. He studied at the Paris Conservatoire with Massenet and privately with Messager, and composed four operettas and five operas. His first opera, *Le Roi Aveugle*, based on a Norwegian legend, was only moderately successful when staged in Paris in 1906, but *Monna Vanna* (after Maeterlinck), first performed in Paris in 1909, proved highly popular and was subsequently produced in a number of countries. *Gismonda* was first given in Chicago in 1919, with Mary Garden in the title-role. Février's later operas, which combined uneasily the charm of Massenet with the vigour of the Italian *verismo* school, were not sufficiently successful to survive after their initial productions.

Fibich, Zdeněk, b. Všebořice, 21 Dec 1850; d. Prague, 15 Oct 1900. Czech composer. A prolific composer whose works number more than 600, he wrote seven operas and a trilogy of melodramas, as well as a further six or seven operas which were either lost, destroyed or left incomplete. None of his operas made any headway abroad, but the best of them is generally considered to be *Šárka*, based on a popular Czech legend, first performed in 1897.

Fidelio, oder Die eheliche Liebe. Opera in 2 acts by Beethoven. Libretto by Josef Sonnleithner and Georg Friedrich Treitschke, after Jean-Nicolas Bouilly's libretto, *Léonore, ou L'Amour Conjugal*, set by Pierre Gaveaux (1798), and in Italian translation by Ferdinando Paer (1804) and Johann Simon Mayr (1805). First performed Vienna, 23 May 1814.

Leonore (sop.) whose husband Florestan (ten.) has been unjustly accused and imprisoned by Pizarro (bass-bar.), gains employment at the prison disguised as a youth, in order to rescue Florestan. As the youth, Fidelio, she attracts the love of Marzelline (sop.), daughter of the gaoler, Rocco (bass), to the annoyance of Marzelline's fiancé, Jacquino (ten.), Rocco's assistant.

Learning that an inspection of the prison by a Minister of State is imminent, Pizarro, who is Governor of the prison, orders Florestan's grave to be dug, and is about to kill him when he is prevented by Leonore with a pistol. The Minister (bass) arrives, Leonore and Florestan are reunited, and Pizarro is arrested. A chastened Marzelline returns to her Jacquino.

Beethoven's final (1814) version of *Fidelio* was preceded by two earlier versions. As *Leonore*, the opera was first performed in Vienna in 1805, when it was in 3 acts. Revised and reduced to 2 acts, it was staged again in Vienna in 1806, still as *Leonore*. The Leonore Overtures nos 1, 2, and 3 were composed for the 1804 version (Leonore No. 2), the 1805 version (Leonore No. 3) and for a projected performance in Prague (Leonore No. 1). The overture to *Fidelio* was composed for the 1814 première of the definitive version of the opera.

Fidès (mezzo-sop.). Mother of the prophet, John of Leyden, in Meyerbeer's *Le Prophète*.

Fiery Angel, The (Russian title, *Ognenny Angel*). Opera in 5 acts by Prokofiev. Libretto by the composer, after a story by Valery Bryusov, first published in the magazine *The Scales* (1907-8). First performed complete, in concert form, Paris, 25 Nov 1954 (though there had been a performance on Paris Radio, 15 Jan 1954). First stage performance, Venice, 14 Sept 1955.

The composer's libretto is confused and confusing. Renata (sop.) mistakes Ruprecht (bass) for her former lover, Heinrich (bar.). Ruprecht, in love with Renata, nevertheless effects a meeting between Renata and Heinrich. Renata, repulsed by Heinrich, urges Ruprecht to fight him. Now finding Ruprecht repulsive, Renata throws a knife at him, accusing him of being possessed by the Devil. Later, Renata who is now a nun is accused by the Inquisitor of having dealings with the Devil, and is sentenced to be burned alive.

Prokofiev composed his opera between 1920-7. It was not produced during his lifetime, and he may have supposed it would never be staged, for he used in his Third Symphony, composed in 1928, material taken from the opera.

Fiesco (bass). The Genoese nobleman who is the implacable enemy of Simon in Verdi's *Simon Boccanegra*.

Figaro (bar.). The barber who, in Rossini's *Il Barbiere di Siviglia*, (and Paisiello's opera of the same name) helps Count Almaviva to win the hand of Rosina; and who, in Mozart's *Le Nozze de Figaro*, is employed in the Almaviva household.

Figner, Medea, b. Florence, 4 Apr 1859; d. Paris, 8 July 1952. Italian, later Russian, soprano. Born Medea Mei, she married the Russian tenor Nicolai Figner. After studying in Florence, she made her début in Sinalunga in 1874 in the mezzo-soprano role of Azucena. She sang as a mezzo-soprano until 1886, when she began to undertake soprano roles. She married Figner in 1889, and appeared with him in St Petersburg until several years after their divorce in 1904. In St Petersburg she created two Tchaikovsky roles: Lisa in *Queen of Spades* (1890) and the title-role in *Iolanta* (1892). She retired from the stage in 1923, although she continued to make gramophone recordings until 1930.

Figner, Nicolai, b. Nikoforovka, nr Kazan, 21 Feb 1857; d. Kiev, 13 Dec 1918. Russian tenor. He studied in St Petersburg and Naples, and made his début in Gounod's *Philémon et Baucis* in Naples in 1882. After singing in other Italian towns, he travelled with a touring company in Brazil. He made his Covent Garden début as the Duke in *Rigoletto* in 1897. With his wife, Medea Figner, he sang in St Petersburg for several years, and created the role of Hermann in the première of Tchaikovsky's *Queen of Spades* in which his wife sang Lisa. They were also both in the première of Tchaikovsky's *Iolanta* in 1892. After his divorce he remarried, and from 1915 taught singing.

Fille de Madame Angot, La *(Madame Angot's Daughter)*. Operetta in 3 acts by Lecocq. Libretto by Paul Siraudin, Louis François Clairville and Victor Koning, based on the *vaudeville, Madame Angot ou La Poissarde Parvenue* (1796) by A.F. Eve Maillot. First performed Brussels, 4 Dec 1872.

Lecocq's most popular operetta, it had a run of 500 performances when first produced in Brussels. It was subsequently staged throughout Europe, as well as in England and the United States, but is now rarely performed outside France.

Fille du Régiment, La *(The Daughter of the Regiment).* Opera in 2 acts by Donizetti. Libretto by Jules-Henri Vernoy de St-Georges and Jean François Alfred Bayard. First performed Paris, 11 Feb 1840.

Marie (sop.) has been brought up since childhood by Sulpice (bass) and his regiment, and is regarded as their mascot. She and Tonio (ten.), a mountaineer, are in love and, in order to be near Marie, Tonio enlists in the regiment. When it is

discovered that Marie is the niece of the Marquise de Berkenfeld (mezzo-sop.) she is made to leave her friends of the regiment, take up residence with the Marquise, and receive an education more in keeping with her new station in life. In the palace of the Marquise, Marie pines for her Tonio and for her other friends. Suddenly, the regiment arrives at the palace. Sulpice learns from the Marquise that Marie is really her daughter, born out of wedlock. He passes this information on to Marie who had intended to elope with Tonio but now feels she cannot defy her mother, who wishes her to marry a nobleman. Finally, however, Marie's obvious misery touches the Marquise's heart, and she consents to the union of her daughter with Tonio.

Finta Giardiniera, La *(The Feigned Garden Maid).* Opera in 3 acts by Mozart. Libretto by Raniero de' Calzabigi, originally written

Joan Sutherland as Marie and Spiro Malas as Sulpice in *La Fille du Régiment* at Covent Garden in 1966.

for Anfossi's opera of the same title (1774), and revised by Marco Coltellini. First performed Munich, 13 Jan 1775.

The opera is set in 18th-c. Italy. The Countess Violante, having been wounded by her lover Count Belfiore (ten.) in a jealous quarrel, and thought by him to be dead, goes in search of him. Calling herself Sandrina (sop.), she takes employment as a gardener's maid in the house of the Mayor (ten.) whose niece Arminda (sop.) is now being courted by Belfiore. Other characters in an extremely complicated plot include Ramiro (a role written for a male soprano, and now usually sung by a young soprano or mezzo-soprano), a cavalier in love with Arminda who has abandoned him; Serpetta (sop.), chamber-maid of the Mayor with whom she is in love; and Violante's servant Roberto (bass), posing as Nardo, the gardener. Eventually all ends happily, with only the Mayor left without a romantic partner.

Finta Semplice, La *(The Feigned Idiot-girl)*. Opera in 3 acts by Mozart. Libretto by Carlo Goldoni, originally written for Perillo's opera of the same title (1764), and revised by Marco Coltellini. First performed Salzburg, 1 May 1769.

The officers Fracasso (ten.) and Simone (bass) are billeted on the estate of two wealthy bachelors, Don Cassandro (bass) and Don Polidoro (ten.). Fracasso enlists the aid of his sister, Rosina, a Hungarian baroness (sop.), in his attempt to gain permission to marry the brothers' sister, Donna Giacinta (sop.). After a series of comical and complicated incidents, all ends happily for Fracasso and Giacinta, for Simone and Giacinta's maid Ninetta (sop.) whom he has been courting, and for Rosina and one of the brothers, Cassandro, who decide to marry. Only Polidoro is left alone.

Fiordiligi (sop.). One of the two sisters in Mozart's *Così Fan Tutte*.

Fischer-Dieskau, Dietrich, b. Berlin, 28 May 1925. German baritone. One of the leading German baritones of his time, he is primarily a singer of Lieder, though he has also had a considerable career in opera, especially in Germany. He made his opera

Kiri Te Kanawa as Rosalinde and Hermann Prey as Eisenstein in *Die Fledermaus* at Covent Garden.

début as Rodrigo in *Don Carlos* in Berlin in 1948, and has been a leading baritone at the Deutsche Oper for many years. Here he has sung many of the Verdi baritone roles, although abroad he prefers to restrict himself to German-language opera. At Bayreuth in the mid-1950s he sang Wolfram, Amfortas and Kothner. In 1965 he made his Covent Garden début in one of his finest roles, Mandryka in Strauss's *Arabella*. He is also a greatly admired Dutchman in *Der fliegende Holländer*. Among roles he has created are Mittenhofer in Henze's *Elegy for Young Lovers* (1961) and the title-role in Aribert Reimann's *Lear* (1978).

Fisher, Sylvia, b. Melbourne, 18 Apr 1910. Australian soprano. She studied in Melbourne and made her début there in 1932 as Hermione in Lully's *Cadmus et Hermione*. This remained her only stage performance until she moved to London in 1947, although she sang Aida and Donna Anna for Australian Radio. She made her Covent Garden début in 1948 as Beethoven's Leonore, and remained with the company as a leading dramatic soprano for the following ten years. She was especially successful in the Wagner roles such as Isolde and Sieglinde, and also as Strauss's Marschallin in *Der Rosenkavalier*, her radiant voice and warmly appealing stage personality reminding many of Lotte Lehmann. She continued to sing until well into her sixties, creating the role of Miss Wingrave in Britten's *Owen Wingrave* in 1971. She was also an imposing Elizabeth I in Britten's *Gloriana* at its 1966 revival by the Sadler's Wells company in London.

Flagstad, Kirsten, b. Hamar, Norway, 12 July 1895; d. Oslo, 7 Dec 1962. Norwegian soprano. She made her début in Oslo in 1913 as Nuri in D'Albert's *Tiefland*, and sang only in Scandinavia until 1933 when she was recommended to Bayreuth. There she sang small parts in 1933 and Sieglinde and Gutrune the following year. Her success at Bayreuth led to an engagement at the Met, where she made her first appearance in 1935 as Sieglinde. She sang most of the major Wagner soprano roles at the Met until 1941 when she returned to Norway to be with her husband, whose sympathies were with the Nazi regime. Her return to the Met after World War II aroused much controversy. At Covent Garden she sang Isolde, Brünnhilde and Senta in 1936 and 1937, and returned in 1948 as Isolde. Her last appearances in opera were as Dido in Purcell's *Dido and Aeneas* in the little Mermaid Theatre in the garden of Sir Bernard Miles's house in St John's Wood, London, in 1951 and 1952. She had a voice of great beauty, size and firmness. Her operatic portrayals suffered somewhat from her placidity of temperament.

Fledermaus, Die *(The Bat).* Operetta in 3 acts by Johann Strauss. Libretto by Carl Haffner and Richard Genée, based on *Le Réveillon* (1872) by Henri Meilhac and Ludovic Halévy, which was in turn based on Roderich Bendix's comedy, *Das Gefängnis* (1851). First performed Vienna, 5 Apr 1874.

When her husband, Gabriel von Eisenstein (ten.) leaves their house ostensibly to go to prison to serve a short sentence, Rosalinde (sop.) is visited by the opera singer Alfredo (ten.), a former admirer. However, Eisenstein has in fact gone to a party in the company of his old friend Dr Falke (bar.), and when Frank (bar.) the Governor of the prison arrives at the house to escort Eisenstein to gaol, he arrests instead Alfredo whom he naturally assumes to be Rosalinde's husband. The party to which Eisenstein and Falke have gone is given by the bored young Prince Orlofsky (mezzo-sop.). Falke, who is plotting an elaborate revenge for a joke played on him by Eisenstein, has arranged for Rosalinde and her maid Adele (sop.) also to appear at the party. A complicated series of encounters based on mistaken identities culminates in a final scene in Frank's prison, in which Falke has his revenge, but all agree to blame everything on the champagne they have been drinking.

Fleta, Miguel, b. Albalate de Cinca, 28 Dec 1893; d. La Coruña, 30 May 1938. Spanish tenor. He studied at the Barcelona Conservatorium and then in Italy with Luisa Pierrich whom he married. He made his début in Trieste in 1919 as Paolo in Zandonai's *Francesca da Rimini*, and quickly became a leading tenor in other Italian towns, in Vienna, Madrid and Buenos Aires. He was engaged at the Met and at La Scala 1923-6, and at La Scala in 1926 created the role of Calaf in *Turandot*. His misuse of an intrinsically beautiful voice caused his career to decline while he was still in his thirties.

Fliegende Holländer, Der. *(The Flying Dutchman).* Opera in 1 act (or in 3 acts) by Wagner. Libretto by the composer, based on an old legend as recounted in Heinrich Heine's *Aus den Memoiren des Herren von Schnabelewopski* (1831). First performed Dresden, 2 Jan 1843.

For having sworn that he would round the Cape of Good Hope, even if he had to keep on sailing forever, the Dutchman (bar.) is doomed to sail the seas for eternity, landing only once every seven years, until redeemed by the love of a faithful woman. He lands on the Norwegian coast, and bribes a sea-captain, Daland (bass) to allow him to marry Daland's daughter, Senta (sop.). Senta, to the distress of her suitor Erik (ten.) is already obsessed by the legend of the Dutchman, and pledges her faith to the stranger whom her father brings home to meet her. However, the Dutchman overhears Erik pleading his cause with Senta and, thinking himself betrayed, rushes off to his vessel. He proclaims his true identity, and puts out to sea in order that Senta shall not be condemned to everlasting damnation with him. Senta cries out that she will be faithful to him until death, and flings herself from a cliff into the sea. The Dutchman's phantom ship sinks, and the spirits of the Dutchman and Senta are seen arising towards the heavens, clasped in an embrace.

Wagner originally intended his opera to be performed in 1 continuous act, but practical considerations dictated its being split into 3 acts at its première. Until the end of the 19th c. it was always given in 3 acts. The original 1-act version was first performed at Bayreuth in 1901, and the opera is now quite frequently staged in 1 act, without intervals.

Florestan (ten.). The wrongfully imprisoned husband of Leonore, who rescues him as he is about to be murdered by Pizarro, in Beethoven's *Fidelio*.

Flotow, Friedrich von, b. Teutendorf, 27 Apr 1812; d. Darmstadt, 24 Jan 1883. German composer. Though he is known today primarily for *Martha* (1847) which was also Flotow's most popular opera in his own time, he composed more than thirty operas and a number of ballet scores. His musical education took place in Paris, and his earlier works for the stage are essentially French in style, most of them having their premières in Paris. *Alessandro Stradella* (1844), first performed in Hamburg, was Flotow's earliest great success. Like *Martha*, it was a revision in German of an earlier French work. None of his later operas achieved the popularity of these two works. *Martha*, Flotow's masterpiece, is a work of considerable period charm, and agreeable and fluent melody, combined with just sufficient dramatic flair to enable the opera to survive, at least in the German-speaking countries. The tenor aria, 'Ach, so fromm', is widely known because a number of tenors, from Caruso onwards, have made recordings of it, often in Italian, as 'M'appari tutt' amor!'.

Floyd, Carlisle, b. Latta, South Carolina, 11 June 1926. American composer. He studied at Syracuse University where his first work for the theatre, a 1-act piece, *Slow Dusk*, was performed. His earliest full-length opera, *Susannah* (1955) was well received. *Wuthering Heights*, commissioned by Santa Fe Opera, was first staged at Santa Fe in 1958, and has since been performed by other American companies. Floyd's next three operas, *The Passion of Jonathan Wade* (1962), *The Sojourner and Mollie Sinclair* (1963) and *Markheim* (1966) were not successful, but *Of Mice and Men*, first performed at Seattle in 1970, has been taken up by other American companies, and shows every sign of surviving. *Bilby's Doll* had its première at Houston in 1976, but has not since been performed. Houston Grand Opera also commissioned and staged, in 1981, Floyd's most recent opera, *Willie Stark*, whose libretto by the composer (who always writes his own libretti) is based on Robert Penn Warren's novel, *All the King's Men*. Its musical language is an amalgam of grand opera and the Broadway musical, *Willie Stark* was received with great enthusiasm. It is Floyd's most interesting opera to date, as well as his most accessible, written in an agreeable, lyrical style.

Flying Dutchman, The. (bar.). The eponymous leading character of Wagner's *Der fliegende Holländer*.

Foerster, Josef Bohuslav, b. Prague, 30 Dec 1859; d. Nový Vestec, 29 May 1951. Czech composer. He studied in Prague, and worked as a music critic in Hamburg and Vienna. An impressive composer of symphonic and choral music, he also composed six operas, only one of which, *Eva* (1899), is still occasionally performed in Czechoslovakia. The others, as well as *Eva*, were all first performed in Prague: the earliest, *Debora*, in 1893, and the last, *Bloud (The Fool)* in 1936. Though his musical language is conventional, Foerster's operas contain more of metaphysics than of dramatic conflict.

Fontana, Ferdinando, b. Milan, 30 Jan 1850; d. Lugano, 12 May 1919. Italian librettist. A journalist and playwright, he is remembered mainly as the librettist of Puccini's first two operas, *Le Villi* (1884) and *Edgar* (1889). He was also the Italian translator of *The Merry Widow*. His libretti for Puccini were mediocre, and the composer turned to others for his texts from *Manon Lescaut* onwards.

Ford (bar.). The citizen of Windsor whose wife Alice is courted by Falstaff in Verdi's *Falstaff.*

Forrester, Maureen, b. Montreal, 25 July 1930. Canadian contralto. She began her career as a concert singer. Her first opera role was Orpheo in Gluck's *Orfeo ed Euridice* in Toronto in 1961. She was Cornelia in the production of Handel's *Giulio Cesare* with which the New York City Opera opened the State Theater in Lincoln Center in 1966, and in 1974 she sang Erda in Wagner's *Ring* at the Met. In recent years she has taught at the Philadelphia Academy of Music, though in 1982 she sang the Countess in *Queen of Spades* at Houston.

Fortner, Wolfgang, b. Leipzig, 12 Oct 1907. German composer. His first opera, *Cress Ertrinkt*, a 1-act piece intended for performance in schools, was composed in 1930. His two most successful operas, *Bluthochzeit* (1957) and *In Seinem Garten Liebt Don Perlimplin Belisa* (1962) are both based on plays by the Spanish poet Lorca. In *Elisabeth Tudor* (1972) he dealt, as so many other composers before him had done, with the struggle between Elizabeth I and Mary Queen of Scots.

Sena Jurinac, David Poleri and Hervey Alan in Verdi's *La Forza del Destino* at Edinburgh in 1955.

Forza del Destino, La *(The Force of Destiny).* Opera in 4 acts by Verdi. Libretto by Francesco Maria Piave, based on the play *Don Alvaro o la Fuerza del Sino* (1835) by Angel Saavedra, Duke of Rivas, and on a scene from the play *Wallensteins Lager* (1799) by Friedrich Schiller. First performed St Petersburg, 10 Nov 1862.

When the Marquis of Calatrava (bass) attempts to prevent the elopement of his daughter Leonora (sop.) with Don Alvaro (ten.) who is the son of an Inca princess, Alvaro accidentally kills him. Cursed by her father as he dies, Leonora seeks the help of the Father Superior (bass) of a monastery, who arranges for her to live the life of a hermit in a retreat close to the monastery. Leonora's brother, Don Carlo (bar.) pursues Alvaro in search of vengeance. The two men meet as fellow-officers in the army, but when his true identity is revealed to Carlos, Alvaro refuses to fight him and decides to enter a monastery. Eventually, he is found by Carlo, who taunts him to such an extent that Alvaro forgets his Christian vows and the two men rush out of the monastery to fight. Their duel takes place close to Leonora's retreat. Alvaro mortally wounds Carlo, and calls to the hermit for aid to the dying man. When the hermit appears, Alvaro is astonished to discover that it is Leonora. Before he dies, Carlo stabs his sister. As she dies, her prayer for Alvaro's redemption is answered.

The ending of the opera is usually performed as revised by Verdi for its first Italian production in 1869. In the original St Petersburg version (and in the Duke of Rivas's play), Alvaro curses earth and heaven and flings himself over a cliff. Some productions of the opera revert to this ending which is dramatically superior but musically inferior to Verdi's second and apparently final thoughts.

Forzano, Giovacchino, b. Borgo San Lorenzo, 19 Nov 1883; d. Rome, 18 Oct 1970. Italian librettist. Originally intending to become a singer, he began his career as a baritone in the Italian provinces. He wrote the libretti of two of the three operas of Puccini's *Trittico* (1918): *Suor Angelica* and *Gianni Schicchi*. He also collaborated with other composers, among them Leoncavallo for whom he provided the libretto of *Edipo Re* (1920). He became a producer of opera, and was responsible for the staging of the premières of Boito's *Nerone* (1924) and Puccini's *Turandot* (1926). He later produced operas abroad, in Vienna and London.

Foss [originally Fuchs], Lukas, b. Berlin, 15 Aug 1922. American composer of German birth. He began his musical studies in Berlin, moved to the United States with his family at the age of fifteen, and continued his studies in Philadelphia, at the Berkshire Music Center with Koussevitsky, and at Yale with Hindemith. His first opera, *The Jumping Frog of Calaveras County* (1950), based on the story by Mark Twain, revealed a marked talent for the stage. A second opera, *Griffelkin*, was composed in 1955 for television performance. *Introductions and Goodbyes*, a 9-minute opera with a libretto by Menotti, and Foss's only other operatic work, was produced at the Spoleto Festival in 1960.

Four Saints in Three Acts. Opera in 4 acts by Virgil Thomson. Libretto by Gertrude Stein. First performed on the stage, Hartford, Conn., 8 Feb 1934. (A concert performance had been given in Ann Arbor, Mich., 20 May 1933.)

The allegorical action of the opera takes place in Spain, with Saint Theresa and Saint Ignatius among the characters. The libretto is a confusing and pointless word-game which is not without charm. The singers at the première were all black Americans.

Fra Diavolo *(Brother Devil).* Opera in 3 acts by Auber. Libretto by Eugène Scribe. First performed Paris, 28 Jan 1830.

The bandit Fra Diavolo (ten.), calling himself the Marquis of San Marco, is involved in a plan to steal the jewels of Lady Pamela (mezzo-sop.), wife of the English Lord Cockburn (bar.). A sub-plot involves the young lovers Zerlina (sop.) and Lorenzo (ten.). The opera ends happily for the lovers but Fra Diavolo is shot by dragoons.

Françaix, Jean, b. Le Mans, 23 May 1912. French composer. Primarily a composer of orchestral and instrumental music (he has written a number of film scores), Françaix has composed five operas: *Le Diable Boiteux*, a comedy in 1 act (1937); *L'Apostrophe*, based on Balzac (1940); *La Main de Gloire*, after Gérard de Nerval (1945); *Paris à nous deux*, (libretto by the composer, 1954); and *La Princesse de Clèves*, after Mme de la Fayette (1965). His music has an ironic sharpness and wit, which is heard at its best in the last-named opera.

Francesca da Rimini. Opera in 4 acts by Zandonai. Libretto by Tito Ricordi based on Gabriele D'Annunzio's play of the same title (1902). First performed Turin, 19 Feb 1914.

The story, which derives ultimately from Canto V of Dante's *Inferno*, tells how Francesca (sop.), about to be married to Gianciotto (bar.) whom she has never seen, falls in love with his brother Paolo (ten.) whom she assumes to be Gianciotto. A third brother, Malatestino (ten.), betrays the lovers to Gianciotto who, discovering them *in flagrante delicto*, kills Paolo.

Franchetti, Alberto, b. Turin, 18 Sept 1860; d. Viareggio, 4 Aug 1942. Italian composer. A wealthy nobleman, he was able to afford a prolonged period of musical study in Italy and Germany, and also able to subsidize the stage productions of nine of his operas. (A further three remained unperformed.) Both Wagnerian and Meyerbeerian traces can be found in abundance in his earliest opera, *Asrael* (1888), which nevertheless attracted the favourable comment of Verdi, who recommended that Franchetti be entrusted with the composition of *Cristoforo Colombo* (1892), the opera generally considered to be the composer's finest. Franchetti's reputation did not travel beyond Italy, and his later operas did not add to his fame even in his own country. From 1926-8 he was director of the Florence Conservatorium.

Franck, César, b. Liège, Belgium, 10 Dec 1822; d. Paris, 8 Nov 1890. French composer. Of French-German parentage, he became one of the leading French composers and musical figures in the second half of the 19th c. Opera did not play an important part in his *oeuvre*: he completed only three works for the stage, none of which is reckoned to be among his major compositions. Neither *Stradella*, composed in the mid-1840s, nor the 1-act comic opera *Le Valet de Ferme* (1851-3), was performed. *Hulda*, written between 1882-5, was produced in Monte Carlo in 1894. A 4-act opera, *Ghisèle*, was begun by Franck, but after working on it for a year, he abandoned the work, having orchestrated Act I. The orchestration was completed by a number of his pupils, among them D'Indy and Chausson, and the opera was produced posthumously in Monte Carlo in 1896.

Frantz, Ferdinand, b. Kassel, 8 Feb 1906; d. Munich, 25 May 1959. German bass-baritone. He made his début at Kassel in 1927 as Ortel in *Die Meistersinger*, sang with the companies at Halle and Chemnitz, and in 1938 joined the Hamburg Opera where he remained until 1943 when he became a member of the Bavarian State Opera in Munich. He stayed with the Bavarian State Opera until his death, specializing in the Wagner baritone roles such as Wotan, Hans Sachs and the Dutchman, and also such bass roles as King Mark in *Tristan und Isolde* and Daland in *Der fliegende Holländer*. He sang at the Met between 1949-51 and again in the

1953-4 season when he was also engaged at Covent Garden. After Hans Hotter, he was considered to be the most notable Wotan of the post-World War II years.

Frau ohne Schatten, Die *(The Woman without a Shadow)*. Opera in 3 acts by Richard Strauss. Libretto by Hugo von Hofmannsthal. First performed Vienna, 10 Oct 1919.

An allegorical fantasy in which the Empress (sop.) of an enchanted realm, whose husband the Emperor (ten.) will be turned to stone if she does not find a shadow (which is understood as the ability to bear children), travels down to the world of humans in the company of her faithful Nurse (mezzo-sop.) in search of a shadow. They visit the hovel of a Dyer (bar.) and his wife (sop.) and trick the wife into selling her shadow. The Empress, however, finds that she cannot deprive the woman of her right to bear children, and at the last moment refuses to accept the shadow. For this she is rewarded: the Emperor is released from his spell, the Dyer and his wife are reunited, and the Empress gains her longed-for shadow.

Freia (sop.). Goddess of youth and keeper of the golden apples in *Das Rheingold*.

Freischütz, Der *(The Free Shooter)*. Opera in 3 acts by Weber. Libretto by Friedrich Kind, based on a story in the *Gespensterbuch* (1811) of Johann Apel and Friedrich Laun. First performed Berlin, 18 June 1821.

In love with Agathe (sop.), daughter of the head ranger, Max (ten.) enters a shooting competition the winning of which will confirm his eligibility to marry her. He accepts the help of Caspar (bass) who has sold his soul to the evil spirit Samiel (speaking role), and accompanies Caspar to the dreaded Wolf's Glen where, with Samiel's aid, seven magic bullets are forged. Unknown to Max, the last bullet will go where it is directed by Samiel. Although Max wins the contest, his seventh bullet, which he aims at a dove, wounds Agathe. A Hermit (bass) intercedes, Agathe recovers, and Caspar dies. Max confesses and is given a year in which to atone.

Fremstad, Olive, b. Stockholm, 14 Mar 1871; d. Irvington, N.Y., 21 Apr 1951. Swedish, later American, soprano. An illegitimate child, she was adopted by a Scandinavian couple who took her to America. She studied piano and singing in Minnesota and New York, and then became a pupil of Lilli Lehmann in Berlin. Her début was in the mezzo-soprano role of Azucena, in Cologne in 1895. She sang Ortrud and Venus at Covent Garden in 1903, and in the same year made her Met début as Sieglinde. She remained at the Met for eleven consecutive seasons, singing Wagner's Isolde, Kundry and Brünnhilde, but also achieving success with such roles as Carmen, Tosca and Santuzza. Her final stage appearance was as Tosca in Chicago in 1918. She was a stage personality of exciting temperament with a sumptuous voice.

Freni, Mirella, b. Modena, 27 Feb 1935. Italian soprano. She studied in Bologna, and made her début in Modena in 1955 as Micaëla in *Carmen*. She first appeared in Great Britain at Glyndebourne in 1960 as Zerlina, and made her Covent Garden début in 1961 as Nannetta in *Falstaff*. She has sung frequently at Covent Garden, where she was especially admired as Susanna in *Le Nozze di Figaro*. She has also appeared regularly at the Met since 1965, and at the Salzburg Festival under Herbert von Karajan she has undertaken heavier Verdi roles than her essentially lyrical soprano might be expected to attempt. She is an actress of great charm, and an elegant and musical singer.

Frick, Gottlob, b. Olbronn, Württemberg, 28 July 1906. German bass. He studied in Stuttgart, sang in the chorus of the Stuttgart Opera from 1927-31, and made his solo début at Coburg in 1934 as Daland in *Der fliegende Holländer*. From 1941-52 he was a member of the Dresden Staatsoper. He made his first Covent Garden appearance in 1951, and sang there frequently until 1967 in the Wagner bass roles and as Rocco in *Fidelio*. He made his Met début in 1962. Although he officially retired in 1970, he was still making occasional appearances in Munich and Vienna several years later. He possessed a dark-hued voice of considerable volume. One of his finest roles was Gurnemanz in *Parsifal*, which he came back to sing at Covent Garden in 1971.

Fricka (mezzo-sop.). The wife of Wotan in *Der Ring des Nibelungen*.

Fricsay, Ferenc, b. Budapest, 9 Aug 1914; d. Basle, 20 Feb 1963. Hungarian conductor. He studied with Bartók and Kodály in Budapest, and at the age of nineteen became conductor of the opera company at Szeged. Six years later, in 1939, he became principal conductor of the Budapest Opera, a post he held until 1945 when his international career began. He took over the première of Einem's *Dantons Tod* in Salzburg in 1947 from an indisposed Otto Klemperer, and conducted frequently in Munich and Berlin in the 1950s. From 1961-3 he conducted at the rebuilt Deutsches Opernhaus in West Berlin. He conducted the premières of Martin's *Le Vin Herbé* (1948) and Orff's *Antigonae* (1949), both in Salzburg, and was admired for his Mozart performances.

Friedenstag *(Day of Peace)*. Opera in 1 act by Richard Strauss. Libretto by Joseph Gregor, based on a scenario by Stefan Zweig which was in turn based on Calderón's *La Redención de Breda* (1625). First performed Munich, 24 July 1938.

The Commandant (bar.) of a city besieged in 1648 during the Thirty Years' War intends to blow up the citadel rather than surrender. Only when his wife Maria (sop.), who is willing to die with her husband, persuades him to accept peace does he relent. The opera ends with a hymn in praise of peace.

Friedrich, Götz, b. Naumburg, 4 Aug 1930. German producer. He studied stagecraft at Weimar, and was engaged as an assistant by Walter Felsenstein at the Komische Oper in 1953. He remained at the Komische Oper for nine years, becoming a producer under the tutelage of Felsenstein. He was invited to stage productions in other German cities, and made his Bayreuth début in 1972 with a controversial production of *Tannhäuser*. He contrives to stage most works from a rigidly communist viewpoint, and in consequence some of his productions are more successful than others. He was appointed principal producer at Covent Garden in 1976, after he had staged the *Ring* for The Royal Opera, but the appointment proved congenial neither to Friedrich nor to The Royal Opera.

Friml, Rudolf, b. Prague, 7 Dec 1879; d. Los Angeles, 12 Nov 1972. American composer, of Czech birth. He studied composition with Dvořák in Prague, and first visited the United States as accompanist to the violinist Jan Kubelik. In 1906 he settled in the US, and in the same year performed his First Piano Concerto with the New York Symphony Orchestra. He wrote instrumental music and songs under the pseudonym Roderick Freeman, but is chiefly remembered as the composer of some thirty operettas, of which the best-known are *The Firefly* (1912), *Rose Marie* (1924), *The Vagabond King* (1925) and *The Three Musketeers* (1928). His works of the 1920s were the last of the old-style American operettas. In the 1930s, as the operetta genre gave way to musical comedy, Friml's style began to be considered outdated. He then worked in Hollywood, writing music for films, but also remained active as pianist and conductor.

Froh (ten.). One of the Gods in Wagner's *Das Rheingold*.

Fuchs, Marta, b. Stuttgart, 1 Jan 1898; d. Stuttgart, 22 Sept 1974. German soprano. She studied in Stuttgart, Munich and Milan, and made her début as a mezzo-soprano in Aachen in 1928. In 1930 she was engaged by the Dresden Staatsoper, her roles there including Octavian in *Der Rosenkavalier*, Amneris and Azucena. Gradually she began to assume higher roles, and became a leading dramatic soprano at Bayreuth, where she sang Kundry, Brünnhilde and Isolde with great success. She retired in 1945. Her career was confined largely to Germany, though she appeared at Covent Garden with the Dresden company in 1936 in Mozart and Strauss roles.

Fugère, Lucien, b. Paris, 22 July 1848; d. Paris, 15 Jan 1935. French baritone. He began his stage career in Paris in 1874 in Offenbach's *Mme L'Archiduc*, and in 1877 was engaged by the Opéra-Comique where he remained until 1910, singing more than 100 roles of which several were in world premières of operas by French composers. He created the role of the Father in Charpentier's *Louise* (1900), and was the leading French exponent of such Mozart roles as Figaro, Leporello and Papageno. He continued to sing after his retirement from the Opéra-Comique, and celebrated his eightieth birthday in 1928 by appearing in Messager's *La Basoche* at Le Touquet.

Furtwängler, Wilhelm, b. Berlin, 25 Jan 1886; d. Baden-Baden, 30 Nov 1954. German conductor. He studied in Munich, and was chief conductor at Mannheim from 1915-20. His performances with the Berlin Staatsoper in 1924 attracted great attention, and he became a leading Wagner conductor at Bayreuth in the 1930s and throughout World War II, during which period he was also active in Berlin. He conducted regularly in Salzburg and Vienna as well. His equivocal position with regard to the Nazi regime made it impossible for him to conduct in America after World War II, though he continued to conduct opera in Germany and concerts throughout Europe and in London. His performances were highly idiosyncratic: at his best he was a powerful interpreter of Wagner.

Wilhelm Furtwängler, a great conductor of Wagner and Mozart operas in the 1930-40s.

Fux, Johann Joseph, b. Hirtenfeld, near Graz, 1660; d. Vienna, 13 Feb 1741. Austrian composer. Composer to the Austrian Court in Vienna from 1698, he was primarily a composer of music for the church. Even his operas were considered to be more ecclesiastical than theatrical in style. Of his twenty operas, most of which were first performed at the Hoftheater, Vienna, the later ones were baroque spectacles on an especially grand scale. These include *Elisa* (1719), performed at the palace of Laxenburg, near Vienna; *Le Nozze di Aurora* (1722); and *Costanza e Fortezza*, composed for the coronation of Charles VI in Prague (1723).

G

Gadski, Johanna, b. Anklam, 15 June 1872; d. Berlin, 22 Feb 1932. German soprano. She studied in Stettin and made her début (apparently when only seventeen) in 1889 in Berlin in Lortzing's *Undine*. Her first American appearance was as Elsa in *Lohengrin* at the Met in 1895, and her career was from then on centred around her Met performances. She continued to appear with the company until 1917, singing at Covent Garden only between 1898-1901. She specialized in the Wagner dramatic soprano roles, but was also an admired Aida, Leonora (in *Il Trovatore*) and Amelia (in *Un Ballo in Maschera*). When the United States entered World War I in 1917 she returned to Germany, and was not heard in North America again until 1929 when she was past her prime. She had a voice of great beauty, and brought something of the pure bel canto style to her performances of even the heaviest Wagner roles.

Galli-Curci, Amelita, b. Milan, 18 Nov 1882; d. La Jolla, Calif., 26 Nov 1963. Italian soprano. She studied in Milan, and made her début at Trani in 1906 as Gilda in *Rigoletto*, a role well suited to her limpid lyric soprano voice and sympathetic personality. She sang the lyric coloratura repertory throughout Italy, Spain, Russia and in Central and South America, and made her North American début in 1916 in Chicago, achieving a spectacular success, again as Gilda. She appeared with the Chicago company for

eight consecutive seasons, and sang at the Met for the first time in 1921 as Violetta in *La Traviata*. After a throat operation, her Mimi in *La Bohème* in Chicago in 1936 was unsuccessful, and she retired. In England she appeared only in concerts.

Galuppi, Baldassare, b. Burano, 18 Oct 1706; d. Venice, 3 Jan 1785. Italian composer. He composed nearly one hundred operas, and is regarded as an important figure in the development of opera buffa in the 18thc. Most of his works were first performed in Venice, though he also composed for the King's Theatre in the Haymarket, London, from 1741-3, and was active in St Petersburg between 1765-8. He was the first composer of comic opera to become internationally famous: his fame now rests mainly on those of his operas composed to libretti by Goldoni, among them *Il Mondo della Luna* (1750), *Il Mondo alla Roversa* (1750) and *Il Filosofo di Campagna* (1754). In recent years Galuppi's serious operas have begun to receive scholarly attention.

Gambler, The (Russian title, *Igrok*). Opera in 4 acts by Prokofiev. Libretto by the composer, after Dostoevsky's novel, *The Gambler* (1866). First performed Brussels (in French translation) as *Le Joueur*, 29 Apr 1929. (The projected première in St Petersburg, or Petrograd, in 1917 did not take place due to the Russian Revolution. A second projected production in 1927 in the same city, by this time known as Leningrad, was also postponed.)

At the German spa of Roulettenburg, the Russian General (bass), having gambled away most of his money, is in debt to a French Marquis (ten.), to whom he considers marrying off his daughter Polina (sop.). The General's grandmother (mezzo-sop.), whose fortune he hopes eventually to receive, turns up at the casino and proceeds to lose her fortune at the tables. Alexei (ten.), the General's servant who is in love with Polina, gambles in order to help the General out of his dilemma. He succeeds in breaking the bank, but when he presents his winnings to Polina she flings the money in his face in a fit of hysteria.

Gardelli, Lamberto, b. Venice, 8 Nov 1915. Italian conductor and composer. He

Alexander Ognivtsev as the General and Alexei Maslennikov as Alexei in Prokofiev's *The Gambler* at the Bolshoi Theatre in April 1974.

studied piano and composition in Pesaro and Rome, and worked as an assistant to Tullio Serafin in Rome where, in 1944 he made his début as a conductor of opera, with *La Traviata*. From 1946-55 he was resident conductor in Stockholm with the Swedish Royal Opera. His Met début was with *Andrea Chénier* in 1966. He first appeared in Great Britain at Glyndebourne in 1964, conducting *Macbeth*, and made his Covent Garden début in 1969 with *Otello*. He is one of the finest Verdi conductors of his generation. He has composed four operas, among them *Alba Novella* (1937) and *Il Sogno* (1942).

Garden, Mary, b. Aberdeen, 20 Feb 1874; d. Inverurie, 3 Jan 1967. Scottish soprano. Taken to the United States as a child, she studied singing in Chicago, and made her

début in Paris at the Opéra-Comique in 1900 when called on to replace an ailing soprano half-way through a performance of Charpentier's *Louise*. In 1902 in Paris she created the role of Mélisande in Debussy's *Pelléas et Mélisande*. Massenet wrote *Chérubin* (1905) for her, and Erlanger the role of Aphrodite in *Camille* (1906). She made her American début in New York in 1907 as Massenet's *Thaïs*. From 1910-31 she sang regularly with the Chicago Opera, and was the company's director for the 1921-2 season. Her final appearance in opera was at the Paris Opéra-Comique in 1934 in Alfano's *Risurrezione*.

Gavazzeni, Gianandrea, b. Bergamo, 27 July 1909. Italian conductor, composer and critic. He studied piano in Rome and composition in Milan, and until 1949 was

127

mostly engaged in composition. His opera, *Paolo e Virginia* (1935), was well received. At the age of forty he gave up composing, refusing to allow any further performances of his works, and began to accept more engagements as a conductor. He has appeared regularly at La Scala since 1949, and between 1965-8 was artistic director of that theatre. He made his first English appearance conducting *Anna Bolena* at Glyndebourne in 1965, and he has also conducted opera at the Met, the Bolshoi and at Chicago's Lyric Opera House. He has written critical studies of several composers, among them Bellini, Donizetti, Pizzetti, and Mussorgsky.

Gay, John, b. Barnstable, 16 Sept 1685; d. London, 4 Dec 1732. English librettist, poet and theatre manager. Best known as the librettist of *The Beggar's Opera* (1728), he also wrote its sequel, *Polly*. However, its performance was not allowed by the government, and *Polly* was not staged until forty-five years after Gay's death. He was the librettist of Handel's *Acis and Galatea* (1731) and was responsible for the building of the first Covent Garden Theatre in 1732.

Gay, Maria, b. Barcelona, 13 June 1879; d. New York, 29 July 1943. Spanish mezzo-soprano. Self-taught, she made her début as Carmen in Brussels in 1902, the role in which she first appeared at Covent Garden (1906). She sang at the Met in 1908 and in Chicago in 1910, continuing to appear regularly in Chicago until 1927. Carmen was her most famous role, but she was also successful as Amneris in *Aida* and as Saint-Saëns's Dalila. In 1913 she married the tenor Giovanni Zenatello with whom, in the same year, she was jointly responsible for initiating the regular summer seasons of opera in the Roman arena at Verona.

Gazza Ladra, La *(The Thieving Magpie).* Opera in 2 acts by Rossini. Libretto by Giovanni Gherardini, based on the play *La Pie Voleuse* (1815) by Jean Marie Théodore Baudouin d'Aubigny and Louis Charles Caigniez. First performed Milan, 31 May 1817.

Ninetta (sop.), a servant-girl engaged to Giannetto (ten.), the son of the farmer in whose household she is employed, is accused of stealing silverware from her employer. The Mayor (bass), whose amorous advances Nanetta has repulsed, insists that she be brought to trial, and she is found guilty and condemned to death. It is only when Ninetta is being led to execution that the real thief is discovered to be a magpie.

Gazzaniga, Giuseppe, b. Verona, 5 Oct 1743; d. Crema, 1 Feb 1818. Italian composer. One of the last of the Italian 18th-c. opera buffa composers, he studied in Naples with Porpora and Piccinni, and in the 1770s wrote operas for various Italian theatres. In 1778 he composed *La Contessa di Nuovaluna* for Dresden, and in 1786 *Il Finto Cieco*, its libretto by Lorenzo da Ponte, was produced at the Burgtheater in Vienna. He achieved a wider fame with a 1-act opera, *Don Giovanni Tenorio o sia Il Convitato di Pietra (Don Giovanni Tenorio or The Stone Guest)*, which was first staged in Venice in 1787 and subsequently in other Italian cities, in Paris, Lisbon and London. Giovanni Bertati's libretto for this opera was known to and made use of by Lorenzo da Ponte when he came to write *Don Giovanni* for Mozart, also in 1787. Whether Mozart took an opportunity to study Gazzaniga's score is not known. As a composer of opera, Gazzaniga provides a link between Paisiello, Cimarosa and the old Italian buffa composers on the one hand, and the young Rossini on the other.

Gedda, Nicolai, b. Stockholm, 11 July 1925. Swedish tenor. He studied in Stockholm and made his début there in 1952 while still a student, in Adam's *Le Postillion de Longjumeau*. His success led immediately to engagements with the leading European companies, and he embarked upon a distinguished career in which his versatility and gift for languages led him to become the leading interpreter of the French and Russian lyric tenor roles, a stylish Mozart singer, and an exponent of the difficult and high-lying bel canto roles of Bellini. He first appeared at Covent Garden in 1954 as the Duke in *Rigoletto*, and began a long association with the Met in 1957, celebrating his twenty-fifth anniversary with the company in a gala recital in December, 1982. His repertoire is huge, ranging from Gluck's *Orfée* through the French, Italian, German and Russian 19th-c. roles to

Nicolai Gedda and Reri Grist in *L'Elisir d'Amore* in Vienna in 1973.

Viennese operetta and contemporary opera. At the Met in 1958 he created the role of Anatol in Barber's *Vanessa*.

Gencer, Leyla, b. Istanbul, 10 Oct 1924. Turkish soprano. She studied in Istanbul, and made her début at Ankara in 1950 as Santuzza. Her Italian career began with the same role in Naples in 1953, but she later began to specialize in the bel canto dramatic coloratura repertory. Her individual style and timbre and her dramatic temperament have brought her success in such roles as Donizetti's Anna Bolena, Maria Stuarda and Lucrezia Borgia, Verdi's Lady Macbeth, Rossini's Elisabetta and Bellini's Norma. She sang the Countess in *Le Nozze di Figaro* at Glyndebourne in 1962, and Elisabeth de Valois in *Don Carlos* at Covent Garden in the same year. In Italy she has also sung in a number of early Verdi operas.

Genée, Richard, b. Danzig, 7 Feb 1823; d. Baden, nr Vienna, 15 June 1895. German librettist, conductor and composer. In collaboration with F. Zell (the pseudonym of Camillo Walzel), he wrote the libretti of several operettas, among them Millöcker's *Der Bettelstudent* (1882) and *Gasparone* (1884), Johann Strauss's *Cagliostro in Wien* (1875) and *Eine Nacht in Venedig* (1883), and Suppé's *Boccaccio* (1879). With Carl Haffner he wrote the libretto of Johann Strauss's *Die Fledermaus* (1874). He conducted opera and operetta in a number of German towns, and was conductor at the Theater an der Wien, Vienna, from 1868-78. He also composed operettas, the most successful of which, *Der Seekadett*, was first performed in Vienna in 1876 and was soon afterwards translated into several other languages and staged in Stockholm, Budapest, London, Naples, Brussels, Zagreb and elsewhere. His *Nanon*, first performed in Vienna in 1877, was almost equally popular.

Gentele, Göran, b. Stockholm, 20 Sept 1917; d. Sardinia, 19 July 1972. Swedish producer and administrator. He began his career as an actor, and then directed plays at the Stockholm Dramatic Theatre from 1946-52. In 1952 he directed Menotti's *The Consul* at the Royal Opera, Stockholm, and continued to direct opera productions there until 1963 in which year he succeeded Set Svanholm as artistic director of the company. In 1971 he was engaged by the Met as general manager, but was killed in a car crash weeks before the opening of his first season.

Gérard (bar.). The servant who becomes a revolutionary leader in Giordano's *Andrea Chénier*.

Gerhard, Roberto, b. Valls, Catalonia, 25 Sept 1896; d. Cambridge, 5 Jan 1970. Spanish (later, British) composer, of Franco-Swiss descent. Primarily a composer of orchestral and instrumental music, he wrote five ballet scores and one opera, *The Duenna*. Based on Sheridan's libretto for the 1775 opera of the same title by Thomas Linley, father and son, Gerhard's *The Duenna* was composed in the mid-1940s, broadcast by the BBC in 1959, and given a concert performance in Wiesbaden in 1951. It is an agreeable and tuneful work.

German, (Sir) Edward, b. Whitchurch, Shropshire, 17 Feb 1862; d. London, 11 Nov 1936. English composer. He studied at the Royal Academy of Music, London, and first began to compose music for the theatre when he became conductor at the Globe Theatre in 1888. He had composed an operetta, *The Two Poets*, while still a student, and upon the death of Sir Arthur Sullivan in 1900 he was commissioned to complete *The Emerald Isle*, a comic opera left unfinished by Sullivan. Its success at the Savoy Theatre in 1901 led to his being invited to compose a new work with the same librettist, Basil Hood. *Merrie England*, staged at the Savoy in 1902, achieved such immediate popularity that German was acclaimed as the natural successor to the Sullivan of the Savoy operas. *A Princess of Kensington* (1903) was less successful, but *Tom Jones* (1907) with new librettists, Alexander M. Thomson and Robert Courtneidge, rivalled the popularity of *Merrie England*. German collaborated with Sullivan's old partner, W. S. Gilbert, to create *Fallen Fairies*, which had no more than a moderate success when produced at the Savoy in 1909. Finding himself unsympathetic to modern trends in music, German wrote no more for the theatre.

Germont (bar.). Alfredo's father, who opposes his son's liaison with Violetta, in Verdi's *La Traviata*.

Gershwin, George, b. Brooklyn, 26 Sept 1898; d. Hollywood, 11 July 1937. American composer. One of the most gifted American composers of musical comedy, songs, and light orchestral music, Gershwin composed two operas. *Blue Monday Blues* (1922), a 1-act piece in the style of jazz, was first performed as part of a Broadway revue, *George White's Scandals of 1922. Porgy and Bess* (1935) is a mixture of jazz and more conventional modern operatic styles, composed to be sung by an all-black cast. A unique work which has come to be regarded as the most successful American contribution to 20th-c. opera, it contains a wealth of melody and reveals in many of its songs a strong influence of traditional jazz.

Gershwin's most popular Broadway musicals include *Lady, Be Good* (1924), *Strike Up the Band* (1927), *Rosalie* (1928), *Girl Crazy* (1930) and *Of Thee I Sing* (1931).

Ghedini, Giorgio, b. Cuneo, 11 July 1892; d. Nervi, 25 Mar 1965. Italian composer. He studied in Turin and began his career as a conductor. Of his eight operas, two early works, written in 1915 and 1921, remain unpublished and unperformed. *Maria D'Alessandria* (1937) attracted little attention, but *Rè Hassan*, staged in Venice in 1939, was more successful, as was *La Pulce d'Oro* (Genoa, 1940). *Le Baccanti*, first performed at La Scala in 1948, is generally thought to be Ghedini's finest opera. His *Billy Budd* (Venice, 1949) has suffered by comparison with Benjamin Britten's musically and dramatically more compelling opera based on the same Herman Melville novella. *Lord Inferno*, a radio opera (1952), was rewritten for the stage as *L'Ipocrita Felice* and performed in Milan in 1956.

Ghiaurov, Nicolai, b. Velingrad, 13 Sept 1929. Bulgarian bass. He studied in Sofia, Leningrad and Moscow, and made his début in Sofia in 1935 as Basilio in *Il Barbiere di Siviglia*. He was soon in demand internationally, in such leading roles as Boris Godunov in Mussorgsky's opera and Philip II in Verdi's *Don Carlos* (both at La Scala, 1959), and Padre Guardiano in *La Forza del Destino* (Covent Garden, 1962). He has sung a number of roles in Paris, Vienna and New York. He has a large voice of fine timbre and excels in roles of grave dignity.

Ghislanzoni, Antonio, b. Lecco, 25 Nov 1824; d. Caprino Bergamasco, 16 July 1893. Italian librettist. He began his career as an operatic baritone, and sang in a number of minor Italian theatres before being arrested for revolutionary activity and deported to Corsica. After his release in 1851 he began to write libretti, and provided more than eighty libretti for such composers as Petrella, Ponchielli, Gomez and Catalani. He is best remembered, however, as the librettist of Verdi's *Aida*. He was responsible for translating the French text by Camille du Locle into Italian verse for Verdi to set.

Ghazarian, Sona, b. Beirut, 2 Sept 1945. Armenian soprano. She studied in Beirut, Siena and Rome, and began her career at the Vienna Staatsoper where her first important role was Oscar in *Un Ballo in Maschera* in 1972.

She remains a member of the Vienna ensemble, and makes guest appearances elsewhere in Europe and America. One of her best roles in Vienna is Lucia di Lammermoor, and she was also greatly admired there as Juliet in Bellini's *I Capuleti ed i Montecchi* in 1977. Her most successful Covent Garden appearances have been as Musetta, in 1979, and as Zdenka in *Arabella* in 1981.

Giacosa, Giuseppe, b. Colleretto Parella, nr Turin, 21 Oct 1847; d. Colleretto Parella, 2 Sept 1906. Italian librettist and playwright. He was famous in Italy as a playwright of romantic historical dramas as well as modern problem plays when he was invited to work on the libretto of Puccini's *Manon Lescaut* (1893). He enlisted the aid of Luigi Illica, and with Illica also provided Puccini with the libretti of *La Bohème* (1896), *Tosca* (1900) and *Madama Butterfly* (1904).

Gianni Schicchi. Opera in 1 act by Puccini. Libretto by Giovacchino Forzano, based on some lines in Canto XXX of Dante's *Inferno*. The third opera in Puccini's *Trittico*, first performed New York, 14 Dec 1918.

In 13th-c. Florence the relatives of the recently deceased Buoso Donati consider ways in which they can alter in their own favour Donati's will which leaves his fortune to a monastery. Rinuccio (ten.), nephew of the dead man, suggests that they enlist the aid of the rascally Gianni Schicchi (bar.) whose daughter Lauretta (sop.) he hopes to marry. Schicchi is called for, and in the presence of a notary impersonates the deceased, dictating a new will which, while it offers something to the greedy relatives, leaves the most coveted items to Gianni Schicchi. The relatives are unable to expose Schicchi, as they have connived in forging a will, the penalties for which are severe. They are forced to accept the situation rather than go to prison.

Giannini, Dusolina, b. Philadelphia, 19 Dec 1902. American soprano of Italian parentage. She studied in New York, and made her début in Hamburg in 1925 as Aida, which was also the role of her Covent Garden début in 1928. She sang such dramatic soprano roles as Donna Anna, Tosca and Santuzza in the leading European theatres, and was active at the Met between 1936-41. In 1938 in Hamburg she created the role of Hester in *The Scarlet Letter*, an opera composed by her brother, Vittorio Giannini (1903-66). After her retirement in 1962 she became a noted teacher.

Gigli, Beniamino, b. Recanati, 20 Mar 1890; d. Rome, 30 Nov 1957. Italian tenor. He studied in Rome, and made his début in Rovigo in 1914 as Enzo in *La Gioconda*. His first successes abroad were in Spain, in South America, and at the Met where, in 1920, his beautiful lyric tenor was so greatly admired when he sang Faust in Boito's *Mefistofele* that he returned to New York for twelve consecutive seasons, in twenty-eight roles. He was generally regarded as Caruso's heir in the lyric tenor roles. In 1930 he made his Covent Garden début in the title-role of *Andrea Chénier*. During the 1930s he sang mainly in Europe and South America: his post-war career suffered from his having been a favourite of Mussolini, though he

Beniamino Gigli as Canio in Leoncavallo's *Pagliacci* in Milan (1953).

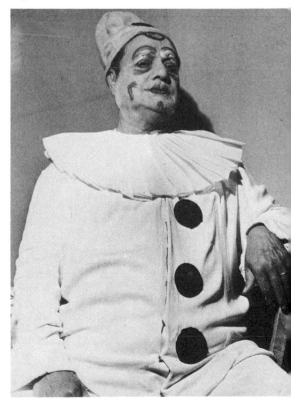

was acclaimed when he reappeared at Covent Garden in 1946 with his daughter, Rina Gigli, in *La Bohème*. He continued to appear in opera in Rome and Naples until 1953. The outstanding quality of Gigli's singing was the sweetness of his tone. His style tended towards the lachrymose, and he was not a convincing actor.

Gilbert, (Sir) William Schwenk, b. London, 18 Nov 1836; d. Harrow, 29 May 1911. English poet, playwright and librettist. His success as a playwright with, among other works, *Pygmalion and Galatea* (1871) was eclipsed when he began to collaborate with the composer Sir Arthur Sullivan on the series of immensely successful operettas which became known as the Savoy Operas, most of them being first staged at the Savoy Theatre, London. The partnership of Gilbert and Sullivan began with the 1-act operetta, *Trial by Jury* (1875) and ended with *The Grand Duke* (1896). *The Gondoliers, The Mikado, H.M.S. Pinafore, The Pirates of Penzance* and *Iolanthe* are among Gilbert's finest libretti.

Gilda (sop.). Daughter of Rigoletto, in love with the Duke of Mantua, in Verdi's *Rigoletto*.

Ginastera, Alberto, b. Buenos Aires, 11 Apr 1916; d. Geneva, 25 June 1983. Argentinian composer. He studied in Buenos Aires, and aged twenty-five became professor of composition at the National Conservatorium. He has continued to pursue an academic career simultaneously with that of composer. His first opera, *Don Rodrigo*, was staged in Buenos Aires in 1964. He has stated that he regards sex, violence and hallucination as three of the basic elements of opera, and his second opera, *Bomarzo*, which was first performed in Washington D.C. in 1967, certainly bears witness to these preoccupations. *Beatrix Cenci* was commissioned by the Washington Opera, and performed to open the Opera House in the new Kennedy Center, Washington D.C., in 1971.

Gioconda, La *(The Joyful Girl)*. Opera in 4 acts by Ponchielli. Libretto by 'Tobia Gorrio' (an anagram of Arrigo Boito), based on Victor Hugo's play, *Angelo, Tyran de Padoue* (1835). First performed Milan, 8 Apr 1876.

La Gioconda (sop.), a street-singer in Venice, is in love with Enzo Grimaldo (ten.) who loves Laura (mezzo-sop.), wife of the nobleman Alvise (bass). La Gioconda is loved by Barnaba (bar.), a government spy whose advances she rejects. In revenge, Barnaba orders the arrest of La Cieca (contr.), La Gioconda's mother, accusing her of witchcraft. Laura helps to save La Cieca, and in return La Gioconda helps Laura to escape from Venice with Enzo. Rather than submit to Barnaba, whose aid she has had to enlist in this enterprise, La Gioconda kills herself.

Gioielli della Madonna, I *(The Jewels of the Madonna)*. Opera in 3 acts by Wolf-Ferrari. Libretto by Enrico Golisciani and Carlo Zangarini. First performed Berlin, 23 Dec 1911, in a German translation by Hans Liebstöckl, as *Der Schmuck der Madonna*. First performance in Italian, Chicago, 16 Jan 1912.

Gennaro (ten.) steals the jewels from a statue of the Madonna, to give to Maliella (sop.) who had expressed a desire for them. When she confesses to Raffaele (bar.) who had hoped to prove his love for her by stealing the jewels himself, Raffaele is enraged. Maliella drowns herself, and Gennaro returns the jewels before stabbing himself.

After a performance in Genoa in 1913, the opera was not performed in Italy again until 1953, being considered blasphemous.

Giordano, Umberto, b. Foggia, 28 Aug 1867; d. Milan, 12 Nov 1948. Italian composer. He studied in Naples, and composed his first operas in the early days of Italian enthusiasm for *verismo* immediately after the success of Mascagni's *Cavalleria Rusticana. Mala Vita* (1892), a crude work about a labourer who offers to reform a prostitute if the Virgin Mary will cure his tuberculosis, was quite popular when first performed, but has failed to survive. Giordano reverted to an old-fashioned romantic style for *Regina Diaz* (Naples, 1894), but the failure of this opera caused him to compose his next work, *Andrea Chénier* (Milan, 1896), in the popular realistic style of the day, and was rewarded with a resounding success. *Fedora* (1898) and *Siberia* (1903), both first produced in Milan, have proved less enduring than *Andrea*

Chénier which is still popular in Italian theatres. Giordano's later operas, among them *Madame San-Gêne* (New York, 1915), *La Cena della Beffe* (Milan, 1924) and *Il Rè* (Milan, 1929), are stronger dramatically than musically. At its best, Giordano's music has an emotive power and a theatrical effectiveness.

Giorgetta (sop.). Wife of the barge-owner, Michele, in Puccini's *Il Tabarro*.

Giorno di Regno, Un *(A One-Day Reign)*. Opera in 2 acts by Verdi. Libretto by Felice Romani, originally written for the opera *Il Finto Stanislao* by Adalbert Gyrowetz (1818), and based on the play *Le Faux Stanislas* (1808) by Alexandre Vincent Pineu-Duval. First performed Milan, 5 Sept 1840.

Belfiore (bar.), en route to Poland, posing as King Stanislaus, successfully persuades Baron Kelbar (bass) to allow his daughter Giulietta (mezzo-sop.) to marry Edoardo (ten.), the man of her choice, instead of La Rocca (bass) whom her father had wished to force upon her. At the same time, Belfiore effects a reconciliation with his former mistress, the Marchesa del Poggio (sop.).

Giovanna d'Arco *(Joan of Arc)*. Opera in a prologue and 3 acts by Verdi. Libretto by Temistocle Solera, based on Friedrich Schiller's play, *Die Jungfrau von Orleans* (1801). First performed Milan, 15 Feb 1845.

The plot of the opera is not based on history but is a simplification of Schiller's fictionalized account of the life of Joan of Arc. Giovanna (sop.) is loved by Carlo (ten.), the Dauphin. Denounced by her father, Giacomo (bar.), at the Dauphin's coronation, she is imprisoned. However, Giacomo repents and helps her escape in order to lead the French forces. Giovanna dies not at the stake but from wounds received in battle.

Giovanni, Don (bar.). The licentious Spanish nobleman who is the eponymous hero of Mozart's *Don Giovanni*.

Giuditta. Operetta in 3 acts by Lehár. Libretto by Paul Knepler and Fritz Löhner. First performed Vienna, 20 Jan 1934.

Sometimes wrongly described as an opera, perhaps because it was first presented in the Vienna State Opera House, *Giuditta*, Lehár's final operetta, is rather more serious in tone than some of his earlier, lighter works. Giuditta (sop.), a married woman seduced by Octavio (ten.), an army officer, follows him to North Africa. He is forced to leave her when his regiment is called away, and Giuditta supports herself by becoming a night-club entertainer. She accepts the attention of wealthy admirers, and although in due course Octavio returns from fighting, it is too late for the lovers to be reconciled.

Giulini, Carlo Maria, b. Barletta, 9 May 1914. Italian conductor. He studied at the

Carlo Giulini, superb Verdi conductor.

Santa Cecilia Academy in Rome, and after early experience as a viola player became a conductor and, in 1946, music director of Italian Radio. He conducted at La Scala regularly between 1951-6, and made his first Covent Garden appearance as conductor of the Visconti production of *Don Carlos* in 1958. In 1967, after conducting *La Traviata* at Covent Garden, he announced his intention to withdraw from opera and concentrate on the concert repertory. It was not until 1982 that he returned to opera with a production of *Falstaff* in Los Angeles which was also seen in London and, the following year, in Florence. He is a conductor of authority, especially in Verdi.

Giulio Cesare in Egitto *(Julius Caesar in Egypt).* Opera in 3 acts by Handel. Libretto by Nicola Francesco Haym. First performed London, 20 Feb 1724.

One of Handel's most successful operas, it deals with the exploits of Julius Caesar (castrato; now sung by mezzo-sop.) in Egypt. A complicated plot involves Tolomeo (bass) who plots against Caesar, and Tolomeo's sister Cleopatra, who charms Caesar into supporting her in her battle with her brother. The opera ends with Caesar crowning Cleopatra as Queen.

Glinka, Mikhail, b. Novospasskoye, 1 June 1804; d. Berlin, 15 Feb 1857. Russian composer. He was the father of the 19th-c. Russian nationalist school of composers, and a pioneer in Russian opera. Though he made sketches for several more, he completed only two operas. Both, however, are not only important in the history of Russian opera but are also full of musical riches. *A Life for the Tsar* (1836) is now known in the Soviet Union as *Ivan Susanin*, the name of its leading character, and the title which Glinka originally intended to give the opera. A tuneful work, it could almost be regarded as a Russian contribution to the predominantly Italian bel canto era. *Ruslan and Lyudmila* (1842), though dramatically unsatisfactory, is musically even superior to the earlier opera. A seminal work, it profoundly influenced such later composers as Balakirev, Rimsky-Korsakov and Tchaikovsky.

Gloriana. Opera in 3 acts by Britten. Libretto by William Plomer, after Lytton Strachey's historical study, *Elizabeth and Essex* (1928). First performed London, 8 June 1953.

The opera was commissioned by The Royal Opera to celebrate the coronation of Queen Elizabeth II in 1953. It deals with events in the life of Elizabeth I (sop.), and in particular with her relationship with the Earl of Essex (ten.). Other characters include Essex's sister, Penelope (sop.), Lord Mountjoy (bar.) and Sir Robert Cecil (bar.).

Glossop, Peter, b. Sheffield, 6 July 1928. English baritone. He studied in Sheffield, joined the Sadler's Wells chorus in 1952, and sang principal roles with the company from 1953-62, among them Rigoletto, Scarpia, and Gérard in *Andrea Chénier*. In 1961 he made his Covent Garden début as Demetrius in Britten's *A Midsummer Night's Dream*, and subsequently sang a number of Verdi roles with The Royal Opera. He sang Rigoletto at La Scala in 1965. In 1970 he was Iago in Karajan's production of *Otello* at Salzburg.

Gluck, Alma, b. Bucharest, 11 May 1884; d. New York, 27 Oct 1938. American soprano of Romanian birth. She was taken to the United States as an infant, studied in New York, and made her début there in 1909 as Sophie in Massenet's *Werther*. She sang at the Met with great success for three seasons, after which she devoted her career almost exclusively to concerts. She had a voice of great purity, and an impeccable technique.

Gluck, Christoph Willibald von, b. Erasbach, 2 July 1714; d. Vienna, 15 Nov 1787. German composer. Gluck's importance as a composer of opera lies in the fact that, although he began as a composer of the old *opera seria*, he effected a reform by striking a new balance between music and drama in his later works. Though few of his forty-three operas are now regularly performed, his greatest works have remained in the repertory. His first opera, *Artaserse*, was performed in Milan in 1741. He composed a further eight operas for Italy before visiting London in 1746 and writing two operas, *La Caduta de' Giganti* and *Artemene*, for performance at the Theatre Royal, Haymarket, in that year. In 1750 he settled in Vienna where he composed to both Italian and

French texts. The first of his great 'reform' operas was *Orfeo ed Euridice*, performed in Vienna in 1762, and subsequently rewritten for Paris in 1774. His other major operas are *Alceste* (Vienna, 1767; Paris, 1776), *Paride ed Elena* (Vienna, 1770), *Iphigénie en Aulide* (Paris, 1774), *Armide* (Paris, 1777), and *Iphigénie en Tauride* (Paris, 1779; German version, Vienna, 1781). In these later works, the conventional flourishes of *opera seria* gave way to a dramatic directness and musical simplicity of style. In his search for dramatic truth in opera, Gluck can be said to have paved the way for Wagner.

Glückliche Hand, Die *(The Favoured Hand)*. Opera in 1 act by Schoenberg. Libretto by the composer. First performed Vienna, 14 Oct 1924.

An expressionistic work with one singing role for a man (bar.), a chorus of twelve, and two mimed roles for man and woman. The man expresses his longing for the unattainable.

Gobbi, Tito, b. Bassano del Grappa, 24 Oct 1913. Italian baritone. He studied in Rome, and made his début in Gubbio in 1935, as Rodolfo in *La Sonnambula*. The following

Tito Gobbi as Falstaff, painted by Max Moreau in 1958.

135

year he won an international singing competition in Vienna, and joined the Rome Opera as principal baritone. He sang in Rome for several seasons in the leading Verdi and Puccini roles, and was acclaimed in the title-role of Berg's *Wozzeck* in that opera's first Italian performance in 1942. In that year he made his first appearance at La Scala, as Belcore in *L'Elisir d'Amore*, the role in which he first appeared at Covent Garden in 1950. He was a favourite of Covent Garden audiences in the 1950-60s as Rigoletto, Iago, Rodrigo (in *Don Carlos*), Falstaff, Macbeth, Boccanegra, Scarpia and several other roles. His American début was in San Francisco in 1948, and he began a long association with Chicago Lyric Opera both as singer and director in 1954. He sang Don Giovanni under Karajan at Salzburg in 1952, and was much admired in that role, and as the Count in *Le Nozze di Figaro*, at Covent Garden. The leading Italian baritone of his generation, he possessed a voice capable of conveying dramatic irony and was a remarkably fine actor. He appeared in twenty-six films, and published his memoirs, *My Life*, in 1979.

Godard, Benjamin, b. Paris, 18 Aug 1849; d. Cannes, 10 Jan 1895. French composer. He studied composition in Paris with Vieuxtemps and Henri Reber, and achieved success as a composer of chamber music and instrumental works before turning his attention to opera. Six of his seven operas were performed, the earliest being *Les Guelfes* which was composed in the early 1880s though not staged until 1902 in Rouen. *Jocelyn*, first performed in Brussels in 1888, is remembered only for a *Berceuse* or cradle song which is still popular with singers. The most successful of his operas in Godard's lifetime was *La Vivandière*, staged in Paris in 1895. None of these works have achieved successful revival.

Goehr, Alexander, b. Berlin, 10 Aug 1932. English composer of German birth. The son of Walter Goehr, an excellent conductor who moved from his native Germany to England at the advent of Naziism, Alexander Goehr studied composition in Paris with Messiaen. His first opera, *Arden Must Die*, was first performed in German as *Arden Muss Sterben* at Hamburg in 1967. His subsequent works for the stage have not

been conventional operas, but pieces of 'music theatre' scored for comparatively small forces. They include *Naboth's Vineyard* (1968), *Shadowplay* (1970) and *Sonata about Jerusalem* (1971).

Goetz, Hermann, b. Königsberg, 7 Dec 1840; d. Hottingen, nr Zurich, 3 Dec 1876. German composer. He completed only one opera, *Der widerspenstigen Zähmung*, based on Shakespeare's *The Taming of the Shrew*, first produced in Mannheim in 1874, and still occasionally performed in German opera houses. It is generally regarded as one of the finest German comic operas of the 19th c., and one completely free from any trace of Wagnerian influence. Goetz began a second opera, *Francesca von Rimini*, but died before finishing it. The opera was completed by Ernest Frank and produced, unsuccessfully, in Mannheim in 1877.

Golaud (bar.). Half-brother of Pelléas, and husband of Mélisande in Debussy's *Pelléas et Mélisande*.

Golden Cockerel, The (Russian title: *Zolotoy Petushok*). Opera in 3 acts by Rimsky-Korsakov. Libretto by Vladimir Ivanovich Belsky, based on a satirical fairy tale (1834) by Pushkin. First performed Moscow, 7 Oct 1909.

A golden cockerel (sop.) presented to King Dodon (bass) by an Astrologer (ten.), crows to warn the King whenever danger is imminent. Returning from the wars, Dodon brings with him the Queen of Shemakhan (sop.), whom the Astrologer claims as payment for the cockerel. Dodon strikes the Astrologer dead with his sceptre, and is in turn killed by the cockerel. The Queen and the cockerel disappear. In an epilogue, the Astrologer addresses the audience, assuring them that it was only a fairy tale.

Goldmark, Karl, b. Keszthely, 18 May 1830; d. Vienna, 2 Jan 1915. Austro-Hungarian composer. He studied in Vienna, where he worked for a time as violinist in theatre orchestras, and also supported himself by giving piano lessons. Although he first achieved prominence as a composer of orchestral and instrumental music, his importance is due mainly to his six operas, all but one of which were first performed in

Vienna, to which city Goldmark's fame was largely confined. His first opera, *Die Königin von Saba* (1885), an immediate success, was followed by *Merlin* (1886) and *Das Heimchen am Herd* (1896), a charming work based on Charles Dickens's *The Cricket on the Hearth*. Of Goldmark's later operas, the most interesting is his last, *Ein Wintermärchen* (1908), based on Shakespeare's *A Winter's Tale*.

Goldoni, Carlo, b. Venice, 25 Feb 1707; d. Paris, 6 Feb 1793. Italian dramatist. His comedies provided libretti for such 18th-c. composers as Galuppi, Haydn, Paisiello, Piccinni, Vivaldi and Sarti. Wolf-Ferrari, Malipiero and others have made use of plays by Goldoni in the 20th c.

Gomes, Carlos, b. Campinas, 11 July 1836; d. Belém, 16 Sept 1896. Brazilian composer. His first two operas were performed in Rio de Janeiro, after which he received a government scholarship to study in Italy. His earliest Italian works for the stage were two musical comedies, but it was with the production of his opera, *Il Guarany*, at La Scala, Milan, in 1870, that Gomes achieved international fame. Verdi referred to it as the work of a 'truly musical genius' and, like the other operas of Gomez, it reveals a strong Verdian influence. *Fosca*, first performed in Milan in 1873, was less successful, but *Salvator Rosa* (Genoa, 1874) and *Maria Tudor* (Milan, 1879) were highly acclaimed. His next opera, *Lo Schiavo*, had a Brazilian theme and was first staged in Rio de Janeiro in 1889. A final opera, *Condor*, which bows in the direction of Italian *verismo*, was staged in Milan in 1891. *Il Guarany* and *Lo Schiavo* are still performed in South America.

Gondoliers, The. Operetta in 2 acts by Sullivan. Libretto by W.S. Gilbert. First performed London, 7 Dec 1889.
   The gondoliers Marco (ten.) and Giuseppe (bar.) are under consideration as heirs to the throne of Barataria, until, after a series of complications involving the Duke of Plaza-Toro (bar.), his Duchess (contr.) and their daughter Casilda (sop.), the rightful heir is identified as the Duke's servant Luiz (ten.), in love with Casilda.

Goodall, Reginald, b. Lincoln, 13 July 1905. English conductor. He studied piano and conducting at the Royal College of Music in London, and began his career in the opera house at Covent Garden in the late 1930s as assistant to Albert Coates. In 1944 he joined Sadler's Wells Opera, and in 1945 conducted the first performance of Britten's *Peter Grimes*. After conducting some performances of Britten's *The Rape of Lucretia* at Glyndebourne in 1946 he joined the music staff at Covent Garden. Until 1961 he conducted a wide range of operas at Covent Garden and on tour, but after 1961, under Georg Solti's directorship, he was used only as a coach. He re-emerged as a conductor when, in 1968, he conducted *Die Meistersinger* for Sadler's Wells Opera. Since then he has been acclaimed as a Wagner specialist, and has conducted the *Ring* for English National Opera, and for Welsh National Opera *Tristan und Isolde* (1979).

Goossens, (Sir) Eugene, b. London, 26 May 1893; d. Hillingdon, Middlesex, 13 June 1962. English composer of Belgian descent. A member of the third generation of the Goossens family to distinguish themselves musically, Eugene Goossens III pursued a professional career as conductor. He composed two operas, both to libretti by Arnold Bennett. The first, *Judith*, a 1-act piece, was performed at Covent Garden in 1929, and the second, a 4-act opera, *Don Juan de Mañara*, was also performed at Covent Garden in 1937. In 1947 Goossens became director of the New South Wales Conservatorium of Music in Sydney where Joan Sutherland, as a student, made her operatic début in the title-role of Goossens' *Judith* in 1951.

Gorr, Rita, b. Zelzaete, 18 Feb 1926. Belgian mezzo-soprano. She studied in Ghent and Brussels, and made her début in 1949 in Antwerp as Fricka in *Die Walküre*. She sang at Strasbourg until 1952 when she won the Lausanne International Singing Competition, which led to her joining the Paris Opéra. She made her Bayreuth début in 1957 as Fricka, and first appeared at Covent Garden in 1959 as Amneris, and at the Met in 1962. An artist of lively temperament with a rich and powerful voice, she has been acclaimed in a number of Wagner and Verdi roles, notably Ortrud in *Lohengrin* and Azucena in *Il Trovatore,* and Eboli in *Don Carlos*.

The end of Valhalla from the Bayreuth production of Wagner's *Ring* shown on BBC TV in 1982.

Gossec, François, b. Vergnies, 17 Jan. 1734; d. Passy, 16 Feb. 1829. French composer of Belgian descent. One of the most prolific of composers in 18th-c. France, he wrote more than twenty operas most of which were produced in Paris. They include *Les Pêcheurs* (1766), *Toinon et Toinette* (1767), both comic operas, and *Sabinus* (1773), a 5-act tragedy. His operatic gifts were no more than modest, his importance lying not only in his instrumental compositions but also in his influence on French musical life as an organizer and administrator.

Gotovac, Jakov, b. Split, 11 Nov 1895; d. Zagreb, 16 Oct 1982. Yugoslav composer. He studied in Split and with Joseph Marx in Vienna, and was a conductor at the Zagreb Opera from 1923-57. Of his five operas, only one, *Ero s Onoga svijeta* (literally *Ero from the Other World*, though known in English usually as *Ero the Joker*), is known outside Yugoslavia. *Ero* has been performed in more than eighty European opera houses. *Dalmaro*, first performed in Zagreb in 1964, has proved popular within Yugoslavia.

Götterdämmerung *(Twilight of the Gods)*. Opera in a prologue and 3 acts by Wagner. Libretto by the composer. First performed Bayreuth, 17 Aug 1876.

The fourth and final part of Wagner's tetralogy, *Der Ring des Nibelungen*. In a prologue, the three Norns (contr., mezzosop. and sop.) are seen winding the skein of life. They recount events of the past, and then foretell the future and the downfall of the gods as the skein breaks. In Act I, Siegfried (ten.) leaves Brünnhilde, after giving her the fated ring. He journeys down the Rhine to the Hall of the Gibichung tribe where Hagen (bass), son of Alberich (bass-bar.) lives with his half-brother Gunther (bar.) and half-sister Gutrune (sop.). Hagen schemes to make Siegfried forget Brünnhilde by means of a potion which will also induce in him desire for Gutrune. Siegfried is then dispatched to fetch Brünnhilde from her mountain-top to be the bride of Gunther. Waltraute (mezzosop.) attempts to persuade Brünnhilde to return the ring to the Rhine and thus lift the curse from the gods, but Brünnhilde refuses. Siegfried arrives, disguised by the magic Tarnhelm, tears the ring from her finger, and carries her off to Gunther.

In Act II, Hagen summons the vassals to attend a double wedding ceremony. When Brünnhilde sees the ring on Siegfried's finger, she accuses him of treachery. He, still under the influence of the potion, cannot remember ever having seen her before. With Gunther and Hagen, Brünnhilde plans the death of Siegfried.

In Act III, Hagen spears Siegfried in the back. The hero's body is borne to the Hall of the Gibichungs where Hagen and Gunther quarrel over the ring, and Gunther is killed. When Hagen approaches the dead body to seize the ring, Siegfried's arm rises warningly. Brünnhilde, now remorseful, orders a funeral pyre to be constructed for Siegfried. When it is lit, she mounts her horse, Grane, and rides into the flames. As Hagen tries to snatch the ring from Brünnhilde, the Rhine overflows its banks and he is dragged into the depths of the river by the Rhinemaidens. Valhalla, the home of the gods, is seen burning in the distance.

Gounod, Charles, b. Paris, 17 June 1818; d. St Cloud, 18 Oct 1893. French composer. Believing that the basis of a successful career in composition was through opera, Gounod completed twelve operas, revealing a distinct talent for the theatre with his earliest work for the stage, *Sapho*, first performed at the Paris Opéra in 1851. *La Nonne Sanglante* (1854) was a failure, but the small-scale pieces, *Le Médecin Malgré Lui* (1858) and *Philémon et Baucis* (1860), were well received. Gounod's masterpiece, *Faust*, an engaging trivialization of pt I of Goethe's play, was performed in Paris in 1859. Neither *La Reine de Saba* (1862) nor *Roméo et Juliette* was especially successful, though the latter work has been staged frequently in recent years. *Mireille* (1864) still holds the stage in France. Gounod exercised a strong influence on the operas of Bizet and Massenet. At its best, his music possesses a gentle charm and an agreeable melodic flow.

Goyescas *(Scenes from Goya)*. Opera in 3 scenes by Granados. Libretto by Fernando Periquet. First performed New York, 28 Jan 1916.

When his beloved, the highborn Rosario (sop.), is invited to a ball by the toreador

Paquiro (bar.), Fernando (ten.), a young officer, is jealous. Both men attend the ball, and later fight a duel. Fernando is fatally wounded, and dies in Rosario's arms.

The characters and setting of the opera in Spain in 1800 are suggested by the paintings of Goya, and the music of the opera is expanded from that of a suite of piano pieces of the same title which Granados had composed in 1911.

Graf, Herbert, b. Vienna, 10 Apr 1904; d. Geneva, 5 Apr 1973. Austrian, later American, producer. He directed opera in a number of German opera houses before leaving Europe at the advent of the Nazis. He emigrated to the United States in 1934, staged operas in Philadelphia, and was engaged at the Met between 1936-60, in which year he returned to Europe to become director of the Zurich Opera. From 1965 until his death he was director of the Geneva company. A traditional stage director of the highest standard, he also wrote about opera. His *Opera for the People* was published in 1951.

Graf von Luxemburg, Der *(The Count of Luxembourg)*. Operetta in 3 acts by Lehár. Libretto by Alfred Maria Willner and Robert Bodansky. First performed Vienna, 12 Nov 1909.

In Paris, early in the 20th c., the profligate René, Count of Luxembourg (ten.) agrees, for a sum of money, to marry the singer Angèle Didier (sop.), a commoner, thus raising her to noble rank and making her eligible for a subsequent marriage in earnest to Prince Basil Basilovich (bass). René and Angèle marry in a curious ceremony in which matters are so arranged that they do not actually see each other. Subsequently they fall in love, and it is only after a series of complications that all ends happily for them when Prince Basil receives orders from the Tsar to marry Stasa Kokozoff (contr.).

Graham, Colin, b. Hove, Sussex, 22 Sept 1931. English producer. He studied acting at the Royal Academy of Dramatic Art in London, became a stage manager for the English Opera Group in 1954, and staged the première of Britten's *Noyes Fludde* at Aldeburgh in 1958. He has produced a wide range of operas for most of the British opera companies, and has also held a number of administrative posts. He has been especially associated with the operas of Britten.

Granados, Enrique, b. Lérida, 27 July 1867; d. at sea in the English Channel, 24 Mar 1916. Spanish composer. He composed a number of *zarzuelas*, the most successful of which was *Maria del Carmen*, staged in Madrid in 1898, before embarking upon his operatic masterpiece, *Goyescas*, whose music included material based upon his piano suite of the same title. *Goyescas* was given its première at the Met in Jan 1916. It was when he was returning to Spain some weeks later that the composer was killed. His ship was torpedoed, and Granados dived into the sea in an unsuccessful attempt to save his wife.

grand opera. In French, *grand opéra* is that form of opera which flourished in Paris in the first half of the 19th c., which did not involve the use of dialogue but was composed throughout. A grand opera was usually in 5 acts, and invariably included an important ballet sequence. Meyerbeer is a typical example of a French composer of grand opera, and among foreign composers who provided grand operas for Paris are Rossini (*Guillaume Tell*) and Verdi (*Les Vêpres Siciliennes* and *Don Carlos*).

Grande Duchesse de Gérolstein, La *(The Grand Duchess of Gerolstein)*. Operetta in 3 acts by Offenbach. Libretto by Henri Meilhac and Ludovic Halévy. First performed Paris, 12 Apr 1867.

A satire on militarism. The Grand Duchess (sop.) is attracted by Private Fritz (ten.) whom she promotes eventually to the rank of General. Eventually Fritz is allowed to marry his sweetheart Wanda (sop.), and the Grand Duchess marries Prince Paul (ten.).

Grandi, Margherita, b. Hobart, Tasmania, 4 Oct 1894. Australian soprano. Born Margaret Garde, she studied in Paris and Milan, and made her début in Paris in 1921 under the name Djema Vecla (Vecla being an anagram of Calvé, her Paris teacher). At Monte Carlo in 1922 she created the title-role in Massenet's *Amadis* at its posthumous première. She married the scene designer Giovanni Grandi, and after some years away from the stage resumed

her career in 1932 in Milan as Aida. Her English début was at Glyndebourne in 1939 as Verdi's Lady Macbeth, a role which she returned to sing with the Glyndebourne company at the Edinburgh Festival in 1947. She spent the years of World War II in Italy, and sang Maria in the first Italian performance of Strauss's *Friedenstag* (Venice, 1940). She was a flamboyant and convincing Tosca at the Cambridge Theatre, London, in 1947, and in 1949 created the role of Diana in Bliss's *The Olympians* at Covent Garden.

Graun, Karl Heinrich, b. Wahrenbrück, 1703 or 1704; d. Berlin, 8 Aug 1759. German composer. The composer of approximately thirty-five operas, most of them written to Italian libretti and first performed in Berlin, he was considered, after Hasse, to be the most important composer of Italian opera in Germany. His *Cesare e Cleopatra* opened the opera house in the Unter den Linden which is today the Berlin Staatsoper. *Montezuma* (1755) was written to a libretto by Frederick the Great. The libretti of other operas by Graun, among them *I Fratelli Nemici* and *La Merope* (both 1756), were also written by Frederick the Great (Frederick II).

Gregor, Joseph, b. Czernowitz, 26 Oct 1888; d. Vienna, 12 Oct 1961. Austrian librettist. He wrote the libretti of three operas by Richard Strauss: *Friedenstag* (1938), *Daphne* (1938) and *Die Liebe der Danae* (1944). He was also known in Austria and Germany as a writer on theatre, and for many years was theatre archivist of the Austrian National Library in Vienna.

Greindl, Josef, b. Munich, 23 Dec 1912. German bass. He studied in Munich, and made his début in Krefeld in 1936 as Hunding in *Die Walküre*. He was a member of the Düsseldorf company from 1938-42 and was then engaged by the Berlin Staatsoper, with whom he appeared until 1949. He later moved to the Städtische Oper (now the Deutsche Oper) in West Berlin. His first Bayreuth performance was as Pogner in *Die Meistersinger* in 1943. He subsequently sang Hans Sachs in the same opera, and continued to appear frequently at Bayreuth until 1969. He was an admired Boris Godunov in Berlin in the 1950s, but is known abroad mainly for his Wagner roles, and as Rocco in *Fidelio*. In 1973 he became a professor of singing at the Hochschule für Musik in Vienna.

Gretel. One of the two children who become lost in the forest in Humperdinck's *Hänsel und Gretel*.

Grétry, André, b. Liège, 8 Feb 1741; d. Paris, 24 Sept 1813. French composer of Walloon descent. He was the dominating force in French *opéra comique* in the late-18th c. He composed more than sixty operas over a period of thirty-five years, most of them first performed in Paris. *Zémire et Azor* (1771) is the best known of them. Among his few serious operas, *Richard Coeur-de-Lion* (1784) stands out, together with *Guillaume Tell* (1791), as an interesting anticipation of 19th-c. romantic opera. His music is graceful and charming, but not of sufficient individuality to have survived into the 20th c.

Grisélidis. Opera in a prologue and 2 acts by Massenet. Libretto by Paul Armand Silvestre and Eugène Morand, based on a tale by Boccaccio which also occurs in Chaucer's *Canterbury Tales* as 'The pleasant comedy of patient Griselidis'. First performed Paris, 20 Nov 1901.

The Devil (bar.) makes a wager with the Marquis de Saluces (bar.) that the Marquis's wife Grisélidis (sop.) will be unfaithful to him while he is away fighting the Saracens. Grisélidis resists the Devil's wiles even when he kidnaps her child. The Marquis returns from the wars, the child is rescued by the power of prayer, and all ends happily.

Grist, Reri, b. New York, *c.* 1932. American soprano. She studied in New York, and began her career as a singer and dancer in musicals (she was in the first cast of *West Side Story* in 1957), before making her operatic début at Santa Fe in 1959 as Blonde in Mozart's *Die Entführung aus dem Serail*. Her first European appearances were in 1960 in Cologne as the Queen of Night in *Die Zauberflöte* and at Zurich as Zerbinetta in Strauss's *Ariadne auf Naxos*, a role which she has sung with great success in Vienna and Salzburg. She made her Covent Garden début in 1962 in Rimsky-Korsakov's *The Golden Cockerel* and her Met début in 1966 as Rosina in *Il Barbiere di Siviglia*. In Vienna in

Reri Grist as Queen of Shemakhan in *The Golden Cockerel* at Covent Garden in 1962.

1973 she delighted audiences when she sang opposite Nicolai Gedda in a Festival production of *L'Elisir d'Amore*. She is a performer of great charm, with a lyrical voice of wide range and coloratura agility.

Grob-Prandl, Gertrude, b. Vienna, 11 Nov 1917. Austrian soprano. She studied in Vienna and made her début in 1938 at the Volksoper, Vienna, as Santuzza. She remained with the Volksoper company until 1945, sang in Zurich from 1945-7, and then joined the Vienna Staatsoper as a leading dramatic soprano. She sang in Vienna until 1964, making guest appearances throughout Europe. She was first heard at Covent Garden in 1951 as Turandot, and was also a notable Donna Anna in *Don Giovanni*, Isolde and Ortrud.

Groves, (Sir) Charles, b. London, 10 Mar 1915. English conductor. He studied piano and organ at the Royal College of Music in London, and in 1944 became conductor of

141

the BBC Northern Orchestra. He is primarily a concert conductor, and had had virtually no operatic experience when he became musical director of English National Opera in 1978. In 1979 he resigned from that post to resume his concert career.

Gruberová. Edita, b Bratislava, 23 Dec 1946. Czech soprano. She studied in Prague and Vienna, and made her début in Bratislava in 1968 as Rosina in *Il Barbiere di Siviglia*. In 1970 she sang the Queen of Night in Vienna as a guest, and in 1972 joined the ensemble of the Vienna Staatsoper. In Vienna her roles include Lucia (which she sang for the first time in 1978), Zerbinetta, Gilda and Violetta, and in Salzburg since 1974 she has been greatly acclaimed, especially as the Queen of Night and as Zerbinetta. In the latter role she triumphed at the Met in 1979.

Gruenberg, Louis, b. Brest-Litovsk, 3 Aug 1884; d. Beverly Hills, Calif., 10 June 1964. American composer of Russian origin.

Taken to the United States by his parents at the age of two, he studied in New York and Berlin. Two early operas, *The Witch of the Brocken* and *The Bride of the Gods*, were composed in 1912-13, and were followed by two operas composed for children, *The Sleeping Beauty* (1922) and *Jack and the Beanstalk* (1929). His most successful opera was *The Emperor Jones*, which was produced at the Met in 1933 with Lawrence Tibbett in the title-role. It was revived in Chicago (1946) and Rome (1950). *Green Mansions*, a radio opera, was broadcast in 1937.

Grümmer, Elisabeth, b. Niederjeutz, Alsace-Lorraine, 31 Mar 1911. German soprano. She began her career as an actress in Aachen, and was persuaded by Herbert von Karajan, then musical director of the Aachen Opera, to study singing. She made her opera début in Aachen in 1940 as the First Flowermaiden in *Parsifal*. Between 1942-4 she was engaged as leading lyric soprano in Duisberg, and in 1946 was engaged by the Städtische Oper, Berlin, where her subsequent career was based. Her purity of style and voice of radiant beauty made her a greatly admired Eva in *Die Meistersinger* and Elsa in *Lohengrin*. She sang these roles and others at Bayreuth, was first heard at Covent Garden in 1951 as Eva, and

in 1953 made her first appearances in Salzburg and Vienna. The Marschallin in *Der Rosenkavalier*, Desdemona and Pamina were among her other successful roles.

Gueden, Hilde, b. Vienna, 15 Sept 1917. Austrian soprano. She studied in Vienna, made her stage début in Vienna in 1939 in Robert Stolz's operetta, *Servus, Servus*, and first appeared in opera in Zurich some months later as Cherubino in *Le Nozze di Figaro*. In 1941-2 she sang with the Munich company, and at the suggestion of the composer himself studied the role of Sophie in Strauss's *Der Rosenkavalier* which she sang in Munich and, in 1942, in Rome in an Italian translation. In 1946 she sang Zerlina at the Salzburg Festival, and was immediately offered an engagement with the Vienna Staatsoper with which company she remained until her retirement a quarter of a century later. It was with the Vienna Staatsoper company that she first appeared in London in 1947. Known abroad for her Mozart and Strauss roles, she sang a much wider repertory in Vienna, including Verdi and Puccini roles and works by contemporary composers. She appeared at the Met frequently between 1951-60, and sang Anne Truelove in the first American production of Stravinsky's *The Rake's Progress* at the Met in 1953. In 1964 she was greatly acclaimed for her performance in the title-role of Strauss's *Daphne* in Vienna.

Guelfi, Giangiacomo, b. Rome, 21 Dec 1924. Italian baritone. After studying in Florence, he made his début in Spoleto in 1950 as Rigoletto. He first appeared in the United States in Chicago in 1954, and in Great Britain at Covent Garden in 1957 as Scarpia. At the Theatre Royal, Drury Lane, in 1958 he sang Gérard in *Andrea Chénier*. A vigorous, unsubtle performer with a superb voice, he was at his best in the *verismo* repertory.

Guglielmo (bar.). One of the two young officers who wager on the fidelity of their sweethearts, in Mozart's *Così Fan Tutte*.

Guglielmo Ratcliff. Opera in 4 acts by Mascagni. Libretto by Andrea Maffei, translated from Heinrich Heine's tragedy, *William Ratcliff* (1822). First performed Milan, 16 Feb 1895.

William Ratcliff (ten.) swears to kill anyone who attempts to marry Maria (sop.), daughter of MacGregor (bass). In consequence, he is forced to challenge Count Douglas (bar.) to a duel. Ratcliff is the loser, but Douglas spares his life. Ratcliff who, unknown to himself is acting out an old family curse, kills Maria. He, too, dies, and Count Douglas kills himself.

Gui, Vittorio, b. Rome, 14 Sept 1885; d. Florence, 17 Oct 1975. Italian conductor and composer. He studied in Rome, and made his début there in 1907 conducting *La Gioconda*. He became a leading conductor in Italy, was active at La Scala in the 1920-30s and conducted regularly at the Florence Maggio Musicale from 1933. Between 1952-65 he conducted regularly at Glyndebourne, and was especially admired for his performances of the operas of Rossini. He first conducted at Covent Garden in 1938 and returned there in 1952 to conduct *Norma* with Maria Callas. He composed two operas, *David*, staged in Rome in 1907, and *Fata Malerba*, staged in Turin in 1927. Neither of them proved successful.

Guillaume Tell. Opera in 4 acts by Rossini. Libretto by Étienne de Jouy, and Hippolyte Louis Florent Bis, based on the play, *Wilhelm Tell* (1804) by Schiller. First performed Paris, 3 Aug 1829.

Rossini's final opera, it tells the story of the 13th-c. Swiss patriot William Tell (bar.), and the uprising of the Swiss against their Austrian overlords. A fictional plot concerns the love of Arnold (ten.), a Swiss follower of Tell, for the Austrian Mathilde (sop.), sister of the tyrant Gessler (bass). The incident in which Tell is forced to shoot an apple from the head of his son Jemmy (sop.) is included.

Guiraud, Ernest, b. New Orleans, 23 June 1837; d. Paris, 6 May 1892. French composer. Although he composed nine operas, most of which were performed in Paris, he is remembered today mainly for having added recitatives to Bizet's *Carmen* for its production in Vienna in 1875, and for having orchestrated Offenbach's *Les Contes d'Hoffmann*. His own operas include *Sylvie* (1864), *Le Kobold* (1870), and *Frédégonde* which was completed by Saint-Saëns and Dukas and staged posthumously in 1895.

Gunther (bar.). Hagen's half-brother, the leader of the Gibichung tribe, in Wagner's *Götterdämmerung*.

Guntram. Opera in 3 acts by Richard Strauss. Libretto by the composer. First performed Weimar, 10 May 1894.

Strauss's first opera, it was a failure when first staged, and has rarely been revived. The action takes place in 13th-c. Germany, and involves Guntram (ten.) and Friedhold (bass), members of a secret society.

Gurnemanz (bass). The elderly Knight of the Grail in Wagner's *Parsifal*.

Gutheil-Schoder, Marie, b. Weimar, 10 Feb 1874; d. Bad Ilmenau, 8 Oct 1935. German soprano. After studying in Weimar, she made her début there in 1891 as First Lady in *Die Zauberflöte*. She was engaged for the Vienna Opera by Gustav Mahler in 1900, and remained a member of the company until 1926 when she retired. A dramatic soprano of great power and authority, she was a famous Elektra and Carmen. Her only London appearance was as Octavian in *Der Rosenkavalier* at Covent Garden in 1913.

Guthrie, (Sir) Tyrone, b. Tunbridge Wells, 2 July 1900; d. Newbliss, 15 May 1971. British producer. He produced plays at the Old Vic in London from 1933, and in 1941 became director of the Sadler's Wells Opera. He made his Covent Garden début directing Britten's *Peter Grimes* in 1947, and his Met début with *Carmen* in 1952. He was generally thought to be more successful as a director of plays than as a director of operas.

Gutrune (sop.). The sister of Gunther, in Wagner's *Götterdämmerung*.

Gyrowetz, Adalbert, b. České Budějovice, 20 Feb 1763; d. Vienna, 19 Mar 1850. Bohemian composer. Most of his twenty-five operas were staged in Vienna, among them the successful *Der Augenarzt* (1811), and *Hans Sachs im Vorgerückten Alter* (1834). The subject of the latter opera was that which Wagner was later to deal with in *Die Meistersinger*. *Il Finto Stanislao* (1818) is remembered because its libretto, by Felice Romani, was later used by Verdi for *Un Giorno di Regno* in 1840.

H

H.M.S. Pinafore. Operetta in 2 acts by Sullivan. Libretto by W.S. Gilbert. First performed London, 25 May 1878.

Josephine (sop.), daughter of the Captain (bar.) of H.M.S. Pinafore loves Ralph (ten.), a member of her father's crew, but is in danger of being wedded to the First Lord of the Admiralty, Sir Joseph Porter (bar.). Little Buttercup (contr.) reveals that, as babies, the Captain and Ralph were switched, and that Ralph is the more highly born of the two. Ralph becomes Captain and wins the hand of Josephine.

Habañera. A slow dance which originated in Havana, Cuba, after which city it is named. A famous example in opera is the *Habañera* in Bizet's *Carmen*, which is sung and danced by Carmen.

Hagen (bass). Son of Alberich, and half-brother of Gunther, in Wagner's *Götterdämmerung*.

Hahn, Reynaldo, b. Caracas, 9 Aug 1875; d. Paris, 28 Jan 1947. French composer of Venezuelan origin. He was taken to Paris at the age of three. He studied piano, harmony, and (under Massenet) composition at the Paris Conservatoire, and quickly made a reputation with his songs and salon pieces. His most famous song, 'Si mes vers avaient des ailes', was written when he was thirteen. He composed at least fifteen operas, operettas and musical comedies, most of which were first staged in Paris. Exquisitely orchestrated, and full of melodies of elegance and charm, they range from the operas, *La Carmélite* (1902) and *Le Marchand de Venise* (1935) to the delightful operetta *Ciboulette* (1923), which is still popular in France, and the musical pastiche *Mozart* (1925). Hahn also achieved a reputation as a conductor of opera, especially Mozart, and conducted several Mozart performances as director of the Paris Opéra in 1945-6.

Haitink, Bernard, b. Amsterdam, 4 Mar 1929. Dutch conductor. He studied in Amsterdam, and made his début there in 1963 conducting *Der fliegende Holländer* for the Holland Festival. After 1966, when he conducted *Don Carlos*, he was not involved with opera until his Glyndebourne début in 1976 with *The Rake's Progress*. He made his first appearance at Covent Garden with *Don Giovanni* in 1976, and became music director at Glyndebourne in 1978. He has proved an excellent Mozart and Wagner conductor and a skilful interpreter of modern works.

Halévy, Fromental, b. Paris, 27 May 1799; d. Nice, 17 Mar 1862. French composer. Born into a Jewish family which changed its name from Levy when he was eight, he became a pupil of Cherubini in Paris at the age of twelve. Winning the Conservatoire's Prix de Rome in 1819, he travelled to Rome where he composed, among other works, the finale of an opera in Italian, *Marco Curzio*. Opera was his chief interest, and from 1826-45 he held advisory posts in Paris at the Théâtre-Italien and the Opéra. His first successful opera, *Clari*, was performed at the Théâtre-Italien in 1828, and his most famous work, *La Juive*, was given its première at the Opéra in 1835. *La Juive* was admired even by the anti-semitic Wagner who referred to it and to a later opera by Halévy, *La Reine de Chypre* (1841), as 'two monuments in the history of the art of music'. Another grand opera, *Charles VI* (1843), was successful, but later operas, many of them lighter works, were less well received. In 1850, *La Tempesta* was first performed at Her Majesty's Theatre, London. Based on Shakespeare's play, with a libretto written by Scribe in French and then translated into Italian to be set by Halévy, it was, perhaps not surprisingly, a failure. Only *La Juive* has survived to be staged occasionally in the 20th c.

Halévy, Ludovic, b. Paris, 31 Dec 1833; d. Paris, 3 May 1908. French librettist. In collaboration with Henri Meilhac he wrote the libretti of a number of Offenbach operettas, among them *La Belle Hélène* (1864), *Barbe-Bleue* (1866), *La Vie Parisienne* (1866), *La Grande Duchesse de Gérolstein* (1867), *La Périchole* (1868) and *Les Brigands* (1870). With Meilhac he also wrote the libretto of Bizet's *Carmen* (1875). His co-librettist for Offenbach's *Orphée aux Enfers* (1858) was Hector Crémieux. He was the nephew of the composer, Fromental Halévy.

Halka *(Helen)*. Opera in 4 acts by Moniuszko. Libretto by Wlodzimierz Wolski, based on the story *Góralka* by Kazimierz Wladyslaw Wójcicki. First performed by amateurs in a 2-act version, in Wilno, 20 Dec 1847. First professional performance, still in 2 acts, Wilno, 16 Feb 1854. First performance of definitive 4-act version, Warsaw, 1 Jan 1858.

A story of unhappy love, seduction and suicide, this is Poland's most popular national opera.

Hall, (Sir) Peter, b. Bury St Edmunds, 22 Nov 1930. English producer. He began his career as a producer of plays, and had become one of the leading British theatre directors when he was invited to join the Royal Opera, Covent Garden in 1971, as joint artistic director with Colin Davis. Although in that year he directed *Tristan und Isolde* at Covent Garden with Davis conducting. Hall decided not to take up the appointment. His earlier productions at Covent Garden had included Schoenberg's *Moses und Aron* with which he made his Royal Opera début in 1965. *Die Zauberflöte* (1966) and Tippett's *The Knot Garden* (1970). At Glyndebourne in the 1970s his Mozart productions were particularly successful, but his staging of Verdi's *Macbeth* for the Met in 1982 was adversely criticized.

A scene from the Peter Hall production of Schoenberg's *Moses und Aron* at Covent Garden in 1965.

He is, in general, one of the most imaginative, intelligent and meticulous contemporary producers of opera.

Hamilton, Iain, b. Glasgow, 6 June 1922. Scottish composer. He studied at the Royal Academy of Music in London, taught in London from 1951-61 and then took up the first of several teaching posts in the United States. Between 1967-9 he worked simultaneously on two operas, *Agamemnon*, which has not been performed, and *The Royal Hunt of the Sun* (after the play by Peter Shaffer), which was staged in London in 1977. A third opera, *The Catiline Conspiracy*, was first performed in Glasgow in 1974, having been composed in 1972-3 and *Anna Karenina* (1981) commissioned by English National Opera, was staged in 1982. All four operas reveal a keen dramatic sense.

Hammerstein, Oscar II, b. New York, 12 July 1895; d. Doylestown, Penn., 23 Aug 1960. American librettist, lyricist and producer. He began his career in 1917 as a stage manager in New York theatres, and went on to write the libretti (in Broadway parlance, 'books') and lyrics for a number of musical comedies, working with such leading composers as Vincent Youmans (*Wildflower*, 1923), Rudolf Friml (*Rose Marie*, 1924), Sigmund Romberg (*The Desert Song*, 1926) and Jerome Kern (*Showboat*, 1927). His long-lasting partnership with Richard Rodgers began with *Oklahoma* in 1943, and was responsible for *South Pacific* (1949), *The King and I* (1951) and *The Sound of Music* (1959). His grandfather, Oscar Hammerstein (b. Stettin, which was then in Germany, 8 May 1846; d. New York, 1 Aug 1919) was an opera impresario in the late-19th and early 20th c. who built opera houses in New York and London.

Hammond, (Dame) Joan, b. Christchurch, 24 May 1912. New Zealand, later Australian, soprano. She studied in Sydney, London, and Vienna, and made her début in Vienna in 1939 as Nedda in *Pagliacci*. The outbreak of World War II prevented a continuation of her career in Vienna, and she joined the Carl Rosa company, touring Great Britain. She first appeared at Covent Garden in 1948 as Leonora in *Il Trovatore*, and was greatly admired as a leading Verdi

and Puccini soprano. Aida and Tosca were among her finest roles. She made guest appearances in opera in New York, Lisbon, Moscow and Leningrad. She had a voice of individual quality and appealing warmth and was a fine Verdi stylist. In 1960 she sang Salome in Strauss's opera with great success in Australia.

Hammond-Stroud, Derek, b. London, 10 Jan 1929. English baritone. He studied in London and with Gerhard Hüsch in Munich, and joined Sadler's Wells Opera in 1961. He has sung a wide range of mostly comic roles, from Melitone in *La Forza del Destino* to Faninal in *Der Rosenkavalier*, and is an outstanding Beckmesser in *Die Meistersinger*, and an engaging Papageno. He has made guest appearances at Covent Garden and at the Met.

Handel, George Frideric, b. Halle, 23 Feb 1685; d. London, 14 Apr 1759. German, later English composer. The first two of his forty-four operas, *Almira* and *Nero*, were composed when he was in his teens, and were produced in Hamburg in 1705. Parts of the music of *Almira*, and all of *Nero* are lost. In 1706 Handel left for Italy, where he began to write Italian operas. *Rodrigo* was produced in Florence in 1707, and *Agrippina* in Venice in 1709. His career as a composer of opera flourished when he took up residence in London in 1712, after a visit there in 1710-11 when *Rinaldo* (1711) was staged with such success that it ushered in an era in which Italian opera became the fashion in London. *Il Pastor Fido* (1712), *Teseo* (1713) and *Amadigi di Gaula* (1715) are among Handel's other early successes in London. In 1720 he became a director of the Royal Academy of Music which presented annual seasons of opera. Between 1720-8 when the Academy collapsed, a number of Handel operas were successfully presented, among then. *Radamisto* (1720), *Floridante* (1721), *Giulio Cesare in Egitto* (1724), *Tamerlano* (1724), *Rodelinda* (1725), *Admeto, Rè de Tessaglia* (1727), *Riccardo Primo, Rè d'Inghilterra,* (1727) and *Tolomeo, Rè de Egitto* (1728).

After 1728, Handel continued to produce his operas in London at the King's Theatre, in association with the impresario John Heidigger. *Partenope* (1730), *Poro Rè dell'Indie.* (1731), *Sosarme, Rè di Media* (1732) and

Orlando (1733) were among the most successful. In 1734, he began an association with Covent Garden where such works as *Ariodante* (1735), *Alcina* (1735), *Berenice* (1737) and *Serse* (1738) were staged. *Serse* contains the serenade to a tree, 'Ombra mai fù', now famous in countless spurious religious adaptations as 'Handel's Largo'.

After *Imeneo* (1740) and *Deidamia* (1741), both produced at Lincoln's Inn Fields, Handel wrote no more operas but turned his attention to oratorio. First performed as concert works, several of these have, since Handel's day, been staged as operas. *Semele*, for example, performed at Covent Garden as an oratorio in 1744, was produced again in the present opera house at Covent Garden in 1982 as an opera, to celebrate the bicentenary of opera at Covent Garden.

Hans Heiling. Opera in a prologue and 3 acts by Marschner. Libretto by Eduard Devrient, based on a story by Karl Theodor Körner. First performed Berlin, 24 May 1833.

An opera on the tragic consequences of the love of Hans (bar.), son of the Queen of Earth Spirits (sop.), for Anna (sop.) a mortal girl, it is generally regarded as Marschner's finest opera.

Hans Sachs (bass-bar.). The cobbler-poet of Wagner's *Die Meistersinger von Nürnberg*, Sachs was a real-life figure in 16th-c. Nuremberg. He is also the leading character in Lortzing's *Hans Sachs*.

Hänsel und Gretel. Opera in 3 acts by Humperdinck. Libretto by Adelheid Wette, after the fairy story by the Grimm brothers in *Kinder- und Hausmärchen* (1812-14). First performed Weimar, 23 Dec 1893.

Hänsel (mezzo-sop.) and Gretel (sop.) are sent by their mother into the woods to pick strawberries. Consoled by the Sandman (sop.) and the Dew Fairy (sop.) when they find themselves lost, they are later captured by a Witch (mezzo-sop.) who attempts to turn them into gingerbread. They outwit the Witch, and free a number of other children who have been transformed by her into gingerbread, a fate which is now meted out to the Witch.

Hanson, Howard, b. Wahoo, Nebr., 28 Oct 1896. American composer. He studied in New York and Rome, and was Director of the Eastman School of Music, in Rochester, N.Y., from 1924-64. A neo-romantic composer, his only opera was *Merry Mount* which was produced by the Met in 1933.

Harmonie der Welt, Die *(The Harmony of the World).* Opera in 5 scenes by Hindemith. Libretto by the composer. First performed Munich, 11 Aug 1957.

Its plot drawn from the life and work of the astronomer Johannes Kepler, the opera deals with the relationship of the artist or scientist to the society of his time.

Harper, Heather, b. Belfast, 8 May 1930. Irish soprano. She studied in London, and made her début as Lady Macbeth in 1954 with Oxford University Opera Society. She sang Anne in the Sadler's Wells production of Stravinsky's *The Rake's Progress* in 1959, and made her first Covent Garden appearance in 1962 as Helena in Britten's *A Midsummer Night's Dream*. An accomplished Mozart singer, she was also a fine Eva in *Die Meistersinger* at Covent Garden. She made her Bayreuth début in 1967 as Elsa. Her characterizations as Ellen Orford in Britten's *Peter Grimes* and as the Governess in *The Turn of the Screw* were greatly admired.

Hartmann, Rudolf, b. Ingolstadt, 11 Oct 1900. German producer. In 1924 he was engaged as resident producer of opera in Altenberg, and made his way via Nuremberg (1928-34) and Berlin (1934-8) to Munich where he worked as chief producer of the Bavarian State Opera for many years. After World War II he produced opera at Covent Garden, where he staged the first post-war *Elektra* in 1953. He was a close associate of Richard Strauss, and staged the premières of *Friedenstag* (1938), *Capriccio* (1942) and *Die Liebe der Danae* (1952). He is a fine traditional producer of the Strauss and Wagner operas.

Harwood, Elizabeth, b. Barton Seagrave, Northamptonshire, 27 May 1938. English soprano. She studied at the Royal Manchester College of Music, and then sang in the chorus at Glyndebourne, making her solo début there as Second Boy in *Die Zauberflöte* in 1960. In 1961 she joined Sadler's Wells Opera, and successfully undertook a number of Mozart roles, as well as Gilda in *Rigoletto* and Zerbinetta in Strauss's *Ariadne auf Naxos*. In 1965 she toured Australia with a company headed by Joan Sutherland, and alternated the title-role of *Lucia di Lammermoor* with Sutherland. At Salzburg since 1970 she has been acclaimed as Constanze in *Die Entführung aus dem Serail*, Fiordiligi in *Così Fan Tutte*, Donna Elvira, and the Countess Almaviva. She made her Met début as Fiordiligi in 1975, and later proved a fine Marschallin in *Der Rosenkavalier* at Glyndebourne. She has a voice of silvery beauty, and an attractive appearance.

Háry János. Opera in a prologue, 5 parts and an epilogue by Kodály. Libretto by Béla Paulini and Zsolt Harsányi, based on a poem by János Garay. First performed Budapest, 16 Oct 1926.

A fantasy about János Háry (bass), a figure in Hungarian folklore who is a prodigious liar, the opera deals with his love for the wife of Napoleon and for Orzse (mezzo-sop.), the peasant girl whom he eventually marries.

Hasse, Johann, b. Bergedorf, nr Hamburg, baptized 25 Mar 1699; d. Venice, 16 Dec

A scene from Kodaly's *Háry János* given at the Erkel Theatre in November 1979. A tremendous success in Hungary, it is seldom performed elsewhere.

1783. German composer. His first opera, *Antioco*, was produced in Brunswick in 1721, after which he went to Italy where he studied with Porpora and Alessandro Scarlatti and soon established a reputation as a composer of Italian opera. *Il Sesostrate*, performed in Naples in 1726, was followed by twenty other operas, all first performed in Italian cities. From 1731-59 Hasse was in charge of the opera in Dresden, where he established the supremacy of Italian opera, and where at least fourteen of his operas were given their first performances. After the siege of Dresden in 1760 he moved to Vienna and subsequently to Venice. He composed more than 100 operas, conservative in style but rich in melody.

Hauer, Josef, b. Wiener Neustadt, 19 Mar 1883; d. Vienna, 22 Sept 1959. Austrian composer. He taught himself musical theory and composition, and developed a theory of atonal music independently of, and to some extent in advance of, Schoenberg. He composed two operas. *Salambo*, based on Flaubert's historical novel, was given in an incomplete concert performance conducted by Klemperer in Berlin in 1930, but *Die schwarze Spinne*, composed in 1932, was not performed until 1966 when it was staged in Vienna, with considerate success.

Haydn, Joseph, b. Rohrau, 31 Mar 1732; d. Vienna, 31 May 1809. Austrian composer. Although Haydn's great achievements are not in opera but in the symphony, the string quartet and religious music, he composed as many as twenty-five operas, of which the earliest (those composed between 1751-66) are lost. Most of those from *Lo Speziale* (1768) onwards were composed while Haydn was in the employ of Prince Esterházy, and were first performed in the private theatre on the Esterházy estate. They include *Le Pescatrici* (1770), *L'Infedeltà Delusa* (1773), *Il Mondo della Luna* (1777), *La Vera Costanza* (1779), *L'Isola Disabitata* (1779) and *Armida* (1784). Haydn's talents as a dramatic composer were limited, and as a result his operas fail to come to life on the stage despite the beauty of individual arias and choruses. Several have been revived during the 20thc. under special festival conditions, though none seems likely to attract the wider public for opera.

Heger, Robert, b. Strasbourg, 19 Aug 1886; d. Munich, 14 Jan 1978. German conductor and composer. He studied in Strasbourg, Zurich and Berlin and began his career as a conductor of opera in Strasbourg in 1907. He was engaged by the opera companies of Ulm, Barmen, Vienna (the Volksoper), Nuremberg and Munich, until he reached the height of his career at the Vienna Staatsoper in 1925. He remained a leading conductor, appearing frequently in Vienna, Munich and Berlin, until the late 1960s. He conducted at Covent Garden in the 1920-30s, and returned in 1953 with the Bavarian State Opera to conduct the British première of Strauss's *Capriccio*.

Heinrich (bass). Henry the Fowler, King of Saxony, in Wagner's *Lohengrin*.

Heldy, Fanny, b. Ath, nr Liège, 29 Feb 1888; d. Paris, 13 Dec 1973. Belgian soprano. She studied in Liège and Brussels, and made her début in Brussels in 1910 as Elena in Gunsbourg's *Ivan le Terrible*. After singing Violetta in Paris in 1917, she became highly popular there and appeared regularly at both Paris opera houses until 1939. She was the leading Manon of her day, and was chosen by Toscanini to sing Mélisande and Charpentier's Louise at La Scala.

Hempel, Frieda, b. Leipzig, 26 June 1885; d. Berlin, 7 Oct 1955. German soprano. She studied in Berlin and made her début there in 1905 as Frau Fluth in Nicolai's *Die Lustigen Weiber von Windsor*. A superb Mozart soprano, she sang the Queen of Night at Drury Lane in 1914, as well as the Marschallin in Strauss's *Der Rosenkavalier*. She first sang at the Met in 1912 as the Queen in *Les Huguenots*, and appeared regularly in New York until 1919. After 1921, she sang only in concerts.

Hendricks, Barbara, b Stephens, Arkansas, 20 Nov 1948. American soprano. She studied in New York, and made her début there in the première of Virgil Thomson's *Lord Byron* in 1972. She sang the title-role in Cavalli's *La Calisto* at Glyndebourne in 1974, was the Vixen in the Santa Fe production of *The Cunning Little Vixen* in 1975, a charming Susanna at the Deutsche Oper in West Berlin in 1978, an accomplished Pamina at Orange in 1981, and a highly praised Nannetta in the Giulini *Falstaff* in 1982 in Los Angeles and London.

Henze, Hans Werner, b. Gutersöh, 1 July 1926. German composer. The most important German composer of his generation, he has written fourteen operas or works of one kind or another for the theatre. The earliest, *Das Wundertheater*, a 1-act piece described by the composer as an opera for actors, was first performed in Heidelberg in 1949. Revised for singers fifteen years later, it was given again in Frankfurt in 1965. *Ein Landarzt*, an opera for radio based on a story by Kafka, was broadcast from Hamburg in 1951. The composer revised it for stage performance and in 1964, and the following year it was produced in Frankfurt in a triple-bill with *Das Wundertheater* and *Das Ende einer Welt*, originally written for radio in 1953. His first major opera for the stage, *Boulevard Solitude*, a modern version of the Manon Lescaut story, was an instant success at its première in Hanover in 1952, and has often been revived. *König Hirsch* (1956) and *Der Prinz von Homburg* (1960) advanced Henze's reputation as a composer of opera, and *Elegy for Young Lovers* (1961) also attracted favourable critical attention. Henze's subsequent operas include *Der Junge Lord* (1965), *The Bassarids* (1966), and *We Come to the River*, a failure at its first performance at Covent Garden in 1976.

Herbert, Victor, b. Dublin, 1 Feb 1859; d. New York, 26 May 1924. Irish, later American, composer. After studying in Stuttgart, he began his career as a cellist, and played his First Cello Concerto in Stuttgart in 1885. In 1886 he married an opera soprano and travelled with her to America, where he began to compose operettas. *Babes in Toyland* (1903) is still occasionally revived in the United States, and such later operettas as *The Red Mill* (1906), *Naughty Marietta* (1910) and *Sweethearts* (1913), have also remained popular. Herbert's two operas, the somewhat Wagnerian *Natoma*, produced in Philadelphia in 1911, and the 1-act *Madeleine*, staged at the Met in 1914, have fared less well, although they are as attractive and tuneful works as any of the operettas.

Herincx, Raimund, b. London, 23 Aug 1927. English bass-baritone. He studied in Belgium and Italy, made his début with Welsh National Opera in 1950 as Mozart's Figaro, and in 1957 joined Sadler's Wells Opera, singing over forty roles with the company. In 1968 he sang King Fisher in Tippett's *A Midsummer Marriage* at Covent Garden, and in 1974 returned to the former Sadler's Wells company, now English National Opera, to sing Wotan. He is an excellent musician and a capable actor.

Hermann (ten.). The young officer in Tchaikovsky's *Queen of Spades* whose obsession with gambling leads to tragedy.

Hérodiade. Opera in 4 acts by Massenet. Libretto by Paul Milliet and Henri Grémont (pseudonym of Georges Hartmann), based on Flaubert's *Hérodias* (1877). First performed Brussels, 19 Dec 1881.

A version of the Biblical story of Salome and John the Baptist in which Herodias (contr.), at first unaware that Salome (sop.) is her daughter, realizes that her husband Herod (bar.) lusts after the younger woman. Salome, in turn, desires John the Baptist (ten.). John and Salome are imprisoned by command of Herod when he realizes that it is John whom Salome loves. John admits his love for Salome and urges her to save herself. She refuses. John is executed, and Salome stabs herself.

Hérold, Ferdinand, b. Paris, 28 Jan 1791; d. Paris, 19 Jan 1833. French composer. One of the most successful composers of 19th-c. French *opéra comique*, he travelled to Italy after winning the Prix de Rome, and had his first opera, *La Gioventù di Enrico Quinto*, produced in Naples in 1815 with great success. For Paris he wrote twenty-seven operas, the majority of them light and tuneful comic operas which were popular with Paris audiences. His earliest success in Paris was with *Les Rosières* (1817), but his more original works are those written in the last seven years of his short life. *Marie* (1826), *Zampa* (1831) and *La Pré aux Clercs* (1832) are generally regarded as his finest works for the theatre, and the last-named is of sufficient stature to suggest that, had he lived, Hérold might have gone on to fulfil his ambition to compose grand opera.

Herz, Joachim, b. Dresden, 14 June 1924. German producer. He studied conducting and production in Dresden, and became an assistant to Walter Felsenstein at the Komische Oper, Berlin, in 1953. He produced a number of operas for the Komische Oper, before moving first to Cologne and then, in 1957, to Leipzig, where he remained as director until 1976, when he succeeded Felsenstein at the Komische Oper. He has also produced operas abroad. His productions tend to be politically slanted towards a socialist concept of music theatre.

Heuberger, Richard, b. Graz, 18 June 1850; d. Vienna, 28 Oct 1914. Austrian composer and critic. A well-known music critic in Vienna, he wrote a number of operas and operettas which were successfully staged in Vienna. The opera *Manuel Venegas* (1889) and the operetta *Mirjam* (1894) are among his finest works. His masterpiece, the operetta *Der Opernball*, was staged in Vienna in 1898, and is frequently revived in Austria, although it is less well-known abroad.

Heure Espagnole, L' *(The Spanish Hour).* Opera in 1 act by Ravel. Libretto by Franc-Nohain (pseudonym of Maurice Legrand), based on his comedy of the same title, 1904. First performed Paris, 19 May 1911.

In 18th-c. Toledo, the clockmaker Torquemada (ten.) goes off to attend to the town clocks, leaving a customer, the muleteer Ramiro (bar.) in the shop to await his return. This annoys Torquemada's wife, Concepción (sop.), who likes to use her hour of freedom to entertain her lovers. The plot concerns two of her lovers, Gonsalve (ten.), a poet, and Don Inigo Gomez (bass) a banker, who are concealed from Torquemada by being carried from room to room in grandfather clocks by the virile young muleteer whom, finally, Concepción decides she prefers.

Hindemith, Paul, b. Hanau, 16 Nov 1895; d. Frankfurt, 28 Dec 1963. German composer. The foremost German composer of his generation, he composed three 1-act operas which were unsuccessful, before creating a stir with *Cardillac* (1926), a dramatically compelling work which Hindemith revised considerably for a revival in 1952. *Hin und Zurück* (1927) and *Neues vom Tage* (1929) were lighter pieces. His best-known opera, *Mathis der Maler*, was composed in 1933-4 but its production was banned by the Nazis, and it was not staged until 1938 in Zurich, by which time Hindemith had emigrated to the United States. *Die Harmonie der Welt*, produced in Munich in 1957, deals with the relationship of the artist or scientist to the society of his time, as *Mathis der Maler* (Mathis being the painter Matthias Grünewald) had done. Hindemith's only English-language opera was a 1-act piece, *The Long Christmas Dinner*, based on a play by Thornton Wilder. It was first performed in Mannheim in 1961, in a German translation made by the composer.

Hines, Jerome, b. Hollywood, 8 Nov 1921. American bass. He studied in Los Angeles, and made his début in San Francisco in 1941 as Monterone in *Rigoletto*. He joined the Met in 1947, and has sung many of the major bass roles with that company. He first appeared in England with Glyndebourne Opera in 1953 as Nick Shadow in Stravinsky's *The Rake's Progress*, made his Bayreuth début in 1958 as Gurnemanz, and in 1962 sang Boris Godunov at the Bolshoi. He composed an opera on the life of Christ, *I am the Way*, which has been performed in a number of American cities. His memoirs appeared in 1968, and in 1982 he published an excellent book, *Great Singers on Great Singing*, in which he interviewed a number of singers on the subject of vocal technique.

Hislop, Joseph, b. Edinburgh, 5 Apr 1884; d. Upper Largo, Fife, 6 May 1977. Scottish tenor. He studied in Stockholm, and made his début there in 1916 as Faust. He sang a number of Verdi and Puccini roles at Covent Garden between 1920-8, and made his first American appearance in Chicago in 1921, after which he toured the United States and Canada with Antonio Scotti's Grand Opera Company. In London in 1931 he sang in *Frederica* (an English translation of Lehár's *Friederike*.) From 1936-48 he taught in Stockholm, where his pupils included Jussi Björling and Birgit Nilsson. He later taught in London.

Hoengen, Elisabeth, b. Gevelsberg, 7 Dec 1906. German mezzo-soprano. She studied in Berlin and made her début in Wuppertal in 1933, after which she was engaged in

Düsseldorf (1935–40) and Dresden (1940–3), becoming a principal mezzo-soprano with the Vienna State Opera in 1943. She was an admired Lady Macbeth in Vienna. She made her British début at Covent Garden with the Vienna Opera in 1947 as Dorabella in *Così Fan Tutte*, and her New York début in 1951 as Strauss's Herodias. A superb singing-actress, she was an impressive Klytemnestra in *Elektra* in Vienna, New York and London.

Hoffman, François Benoît, b. Nancy, 11 July 1760; d. Paris, 25 Apr 1828. French librettist. Between 1786 and 1828 he wrote a number of libretti for French composers, among them Méhul and Cherubini. His best-known work is his libretto for Cherubini's *Medée* (1797).

Hoffman, Grace, b. Cleveland, 14 Jan 1925. American mezzo-soprano. She studied in New York, Milan and Stuttgart, and made her début with a touring company in the United States in 1951 as Lola in *Cavalleria Rusticana*. From 1953–5 she was leading mezzo-soprano with the Zurich Opera, and was then engaged by Stuttgart. Her Covent Garden début was as Eboli in *Don Carlos* in 1959. Between 1957–70 she appeared at Bayreuth in a number of Wagner roles, most successfully as Fricka and Brangäne.

Hoffmann, E.T.A., b. Königsberg, 24 Jan 1776; d. Berlin, 25 June 1822. German writer and composer. He wrote a number of Singspiels, or operas with dialogue, of which the most successful, *Undine* (1816),

A scene from the English National Opera's *The Tales of Hoffman* at the London Coliseum in 1977.

anticipates much in later German romantic opera. It is, however, as the writer of the stories on which Offenbach's *Les Contes d'Hoffmann (Tales of Hoffmann)* is based that his name is of operatic importance. A number of other composers based operas on stories by Hoffmann, most of which are now forgotten. They include, however, Busoni's *Die Brautwahl* (1912), based on an 1820 story of that title; and Hindemith's *Cardillac* (1926), based on Hoffmann's *Das Fräulein von Scuderi* (1819).

Hofmannsthal, Hugo von, b. Vienna, 1 Feb 1874; d. Rodaun, 15 July 1929. Austrian librettist, poet and playwright. A leading literary figure in Austria at the turn of the 20th c. he wrote all but one of his libretti for Richard Strauss. Their collaboration began with *Elektra* (1903) for which Hofmannsthal adapted his already written play, and continued with *Der Rosenkavalier* (1911), *Ariadne auf Naxos* (first version 1912; second version 1916), *Die Frau ohne Schatten* (1919), *Die Agyptische Helena* (1928) and *Arabella* (staged, after the librettist's death, in 1933). Hofmannsthal's only other libretto was written for Egon Wellesz's *Alkestis* (1924). His play *Die Hochzeit der Sobeide* was used as the basis of Tcherepnin's opera of that title, staged in Vienna in 1933, and another play, *Das Bergwerk zu Falun*, was used by Wagner-Regény for his opera of that title, staged in Salzburg in 1961.

Holbrooke, Josef, b. Croydon, 5 July 1878; d. London, 5 Aug 1958. English composer. Commissioned by Lord Howard de Walden, he composed a trilogy of operas based on Walden's vast epic poem, 'The Cauldron of Annwyn'. The operas were *The Children of Don* (1912), *Dylan* (1914) and *Bronwen* (whose performance was delayed until 1929). The trilogy, influenced by Wagner's *Ring*, is not likely to be revived, though *The Children of Don* was staged successfully in Vienna in 1923. Holbrooke composed three other operas, only two of which were performed: *The Enchanter* (Chicago, 1915) and *The Stranger* (Liverpool, 1924).

Holm, Richard, b. Stuttgart, 3 Aug 1912. German tenor. He studied in Stuttgart, and sang with companies in Kiel, Nuremberg and Hamburg before being engaged in 1948 by the Bavarian State Opera in Munich. His roles included David in *Die Meistersinger*, Flamand in Strauss's *Capriccio*, Loge in *Das Rheingold* and Belmonte in *Die Entführung aus dem Serail*. Though he remained a member of the Munich company until his retirement, he made several guest appearances abroad, in London, New York, Vienna, and Salzburg.

Holst, Gustav, b. Cheltenham, 21 Sept 1874; d. London, 25 May 1934. English composer. Four early operas remain unpublished. It is with *Savitri*, composed in 1908 and staged in London in 1916, that Holst first attracted attention as a composer of opera. Using only three voices, a wordless chorus and twelve instruments, it achieves a great intensity. Holst's later operas failed to maintain the interest aroused by *Savitri*. All 1-act pieces, they are *The Perfect Fool* (1923), which suffers from an inadequate libretto by the composer; *At the Boar's Head* (1925), a quite skilful setting of the tavern scenes from Shakespeare's *Henry IV*; and *The Wandering Scholar* (1934), an attractive but slight work based on an incident in Helen Waddell's *The Wandering Scholars* (1927).

Homer, Louise, b. Pittsburgh, 28 Apr 1871; d. Winter Park, Fla., 6 May 1947. American contralto. Born Louise Beatty, she married the composer Sidney Homer who took her to Paris where she studied. She made her début in Vichy in 1898 as Leonora in Donizetti's *La Favorite*. At Covent Garden in 1899 she sang Lola in *Cavalleria Rusticana* and Amneris in *Aida*, and made her American début with the Met on tour in San Francisco in 1900 as Amneris. She was a leading singer with the Met from 1900-19, singing a number of Wagner roles. She returned to the Met in 1927, and ended her long association with the company as Azucena in *Il Trovatore* in 1929.

Honegger, Arthur, b. Le Havre, 10 Mar 1892; d. Paris, 27 Nov 1955. Swiss composer. He studied in Zurich and Paris, and became a member of the group of composers in Paris known as 'Les Six'. *Le Roi David*, staged at Mézières in 1921, is often performed as a concert piece. His biblical opera, *Judith*, had its première at Monte Carlo in 1926 and *Antigone*, with a libretto by Cocteau, was produced in Brussels in 1927. *L'Aiglon*, after the play by

Rostand, was composed in collaboration with Ibert, and first performed at Monte Carlo in 1937. Honegger's best-known work for the stage is *Jeanne d'Arc au Bûcher*, staged in Basle in 1938. Described as a 'dramatic oratorio', it is a work of great emotional impact. The role of Joan of Arc is written for an actress who is not required to sing. Honegger's three later stage works have proved of less interest.

Hopf, Hans, b. Nuremberg, 2 Aug 1916. German tenor. He studied in Munich and made his début there in 1936 as Pinkerton in *Madama Butterfly*. He sang with a number of German companies, specializing in the Wagner dramatic tenor repertory, and appeared in London and New York in the 1950s in Wagner roles. Between 1961-6 he sang Siegfried, Tannhäuser and Parsifal at Bayreuth. In Germany he was also an admired Otello.

Horne, Marilyn, b. Bradford, Penn. 16 Jan 1929. American mezzo-soprano. She studied in California, taking part in Lotte Lehmann's master classes, and first came to public attention when she provided the singing voice for Dorothy Dandridge in the title role of *Carmen Jones (1954)*, the film based on Bizet's *Carmen*. From 1957-60 she sang with the opera company at Gelsenkirchen, making her début as Giulietta in *Les Contes d'Hoffmann*. She first appeared at Covent Garden in 1964 as Marie in Berg's *Wozzeck*, and made her Met début as Adalgisa to the Norma of Joan Sutherland in 1970. She has in recent years specialized in the bel canto repertory, to which her voice of great power, range and flexibility is admirably suited.

Hotter, Hans, b. Offenbach-am-Main, 19 Jan 1909. Austrian bass-baritone of German birth. He began his career as organist and

Marilyn Horne (right) and Joan Sutherland in *Norma*.

choir-master, and made his opera début in Opava in 1929 as the Speaker in *Die Zauberflöte*. After engagements in Prague, Breslau and Hamburg, he became a member of the Munich company in 1938, and based the remainder of his opera career on Munich and Vienna. In those cities he sang a number of Verdi and Puccini baritone roles, such as Iago, Amneris and Scarpia, as well as German roles, but abroad he became known, after World War II, as a Wagner specialist, and as the finest Wotan of his time. An intelligent artist, a fine musician and a compelling actor, he was greatly admired in the title-role of *Der fliegende Holländer*. He sang at the Met from 1950-4, and regularly at Covent Garden from 1947 (when he was first heard there as Don Giovanni with the Vienna Opera) to 1967. He created three roles in operas by Richard Strauss: the Kommandant in *Friedenstag* (Munich, 1938), Olivier in *Capriccio* (Munich, 1942) and Jupiter in *Die Liebe der Danae* at the unofficial première in Salzburg in 1944.

Howell, Gwynne, b. Gorseinon, 13 June 1938. Welsh bass. He studied in Manchester, and in 1968 joined Sadler's Wells Opera, making his début as Monterone in *Rigoletto*. His first appearance at Covent Garden was in 1970 as First Nazarene in *Salome*. He has a rich and voluminous voice, and a dignified stage presence, and has sung a wide range of roles with the leading British companies.

Howells, Anne, b. Southport, 12 Jan 1941. English mezzo-soprano. She studied in Manchester and made her début in 1966 with Welsh National Opera as Flora in *La Traviata*. The following year she made her first appearance at Covent Garden in the same role, but was soon singing leading mezzo roles with both London companies. Cherubino, Dorabella and Annius in *La Clemenza di Tito* are among her most successful Mozart roles, and she has also sung Rosina in *Il Barbiere di Siviglia*, Octavian in *Der Rosenkavalier* and the Composer in *Ariadne auf Naxos*, in Britain and abroad. She made her American début in 1972 in Chicago as Dorabella, and in 1975 first sang at the Met in the same role.

Hugh the Drover. Opera in 2 acts by Vaughan Williams. Libretto by Harold Child. First performed London, 14 July 1924.

In a small town in the Cotswolds at the time of the Napoleonic wars, Hugh the Drover (ten.) defeats John the Butcher (bar.) in a boxing match to decide which of the two shall marry Mary (sop.), the constable's daughter. John then accuses Hugh of being a French spy. The officer who arrives to arrest Hugh recognizes him as an old comrade, and takes John away instead, to make a soldier of him. Hugh and Mary leave the town, determined to find a new life together elsewhere.

Huguenots, Les. Opera in 5 acts by Meyerbeer. Libretto by Eugène Scribe and Émile Deschamps. First performed Paris, 29 Feb 1836.

The opera is set in France in 1572. The Huguenot nobleman Raoul de Nangis (ten.) spurns Valentine (sop.), believing her to be the mistress of the Catholic Comte de Nevers (bar.). From the Queen, Marguerite de Valois (sop.), who is betrothed to Henry IV, Raoul learns that Valentine was innocent, and risks his life to visit her in her home, after she has married the Comte de Nevers. He overhears a Catholic plot to slaughter the Huguenots, but is powerless to stop it. In the final scene of the opera, Valentine embraces Raoul's faith, a Catholic mob breaks into the church, and the lovers are slaughtered. The leader of the mob, St Bris (bass), Valentine's father, is horrified to discover that he has been responsible for the death of his daughter.

Humperdinck, Engelbert, b. Siegburg, 1 Sept 1854; d. Neustrelitz, 27 Sept 1921. German composer. He assisted Wagner in the preparation of *Parsifal* for its first performance at Bayreuth. Ten years later, his first opera *Hänsel und Gretel* (1893) imposed a Wagnerian style upon a simple fairy-tale. Humperdinck's most popular work, it is still revised frequently, often at Christmas, in the belief that it is enjoyed by children. Humperdinck composed a further seven operas, the best of which, *Königskinder* (1897), is occasionally still performed in Germany. His other operas failed to achieve success.

Hunding (bass). The husband of Sieglinde in Wagner's *Die Walküre*.

Hunter, Rita, b. Wallasey, 15 Aug 1933. English soprano. She studied in Liverpool and London, and began her career in 1954 as a member of the chorus of Sadler's Wells Opera. After singing a number of small roles, she became a principal with the company in 1960, appearing as Marcellina in *Le Nozze di Figaro*, Senta in *Der Fliegende Holländer* and Odabella in Verdi's *Attila*. It was in 1970 when she sang Brünnhilde in the Sadler's Wells *Ring* in English that she suddenly became famous as a Wagner dramatic soprano. She sang Brünnhilde at the Met in 1972, and Norma in San Francisco in 1975, and has made guest appearances with Australian Opera in Sydney and Melbourne. She has a voice of great size, and fine attack, as well suited to the Verdi dramatic soprano roles as to Wagner. In 1983 she took up a four year contract with Australian opera.

Huon (ten.). A mediaeval knight, the hero of Weber's *Oberon*.

Hüsch, Gerhard, b. Hanover, 2 Feb 1901. German baritone. He made his début in Osnabrück in 1923 in Lortzing's *Der Waffenschmied*, and by 1930 had become leading lyric baritone in Berlin. He continued to sing in Berlin until 1942, and was a delightful Papageno, an authoritative Count in *Le Nozze di Figaro* and an admired Verdi baritone. At Bayreuth in 1930 and 1931 he was acclaimed as Wolfram in *Tannhäuser*, and sang Falke in the 1930 Covent Garden production of *Die Fledermaus* under Bruno Walter. He was also a famous Lieder singer: his only post-war appearances were in recitals. Since the early 1960s he has been active as a teacher.

I

Iago (bar.). Otello's Ensign in Verdi's *Otello*, and also (ten.) in Rossini's *Otello*.

Ibert, Jacques, b. Paris, 15 Aug 1890; d. Paris, 5 Feb 1962. French composer. He studied at the Paris Conservatoire, and in 1919 was awarded the Prix de Rome. His seven operas (two of them written in collaboration with Honegger) are light and entertaining works, one of the earliest of which, a 1-act comedy, *Angélique* (1927) has proved the most popular. *Le Roi d'Yvetot* (1930) and *Barbe-bleue* (1943), the latter a comic opera written for radio, are equally delightful works. *L'Aiglon* (1937) and *Les Petites Cardinales* (1939), composed jointly with Honegger, were less successful.

Ice Break, The. Opera in 3 acts by Tippett. Libretto by the composer. First performed, London, 7 July 1977.

Lev (bass) arrives to join his wife Nadia (sop.) in the United States, after having spent seven years in prison camps. The plot of the opera is confused, confusing and naive, and the message which it was intended to convey does not clearly emerge. It was the least successful of Tippett's operas, and one in which the composer's creative fire burns only fitfully.

Idomeneo, Rè di Creta. Opera in 3 acts by Mozart. Libretto by Giambattista Varesco. based on an earlier libretto by Antoine Danchet, written for Campra's *Idomenée* (1712). First performed Munich, 29 Jan 1781.

The opera takes place in Crete, shortly after the end of the Trojan wars. The King, Idomeneo (ten.), shipwrecked on his way home from the wars, vows to sacrifice the first living being he encounters on shore, should he be saved. Horrified to discover the first person he meets to be his own son, Idamante (sop. but later rewritten by Mozart for ten.), he prevaricates, thus offending the god Neptune who sends a monster to ravage the country. Idamante, loved by Elettra (sop.), is in love with Ilia (sop.), daughter of King Priam of Troy. Idamante kills the monster, and Idomeneo realizes that nothing now will assuage the wrath of Neptune but the blood of the promised victim. Idamante is about to be sacrificed when the god decrees that he should be spared, and that he should rule in place of his father. Idomeneo abdicates, and Idamante ascends the throne with his bride Ilia. All are content with the god's judgment except the jealous Elettra.

Ilia (sop.). A Trojan princess, in love with Idamante, in Mozart's *Idomeneo*.

Illica, Luigi, b. Piacenza, 9 May 1857; d. Piacenza, 16 Dec 1919. Italian librettist.

A scene from Monteverdi's *L'Incoronazione di Poppea* at La Scala in 1952. The conductor was Giulini.

While engaged as a journalist in Milan, he began to write libretti, often in collaboration with others. His first, for Smareglia's *Il Vassallo di Szigeth* (1889), was written in collaboration with Felice Pozza. He was one of several writers to contribute to *Manon Lescaut* (1893) for Puccini, and is best known for having collaborated with Giuseppe Giacosa on three further Puccini operas, *La Bohème* (1896), *Tosca* (1900) and *Madama Butterfly* (1904). Alone, he wrote the libretti of Catalani's *La Wally* (1892), Giordano's *Andrea Chénier* (1896), Mascagni's *Iris* (1898) and *Le Maschere* (1901), and several other operas.

Immortal Hour, The. Opera in 2 acts by Boughton. Libretto by 'Fiona Macleod' (pseudonym of William Sharp). First performed Glastonbury, 26 Aug 1914.

The fairy Etain (sop.), about to be married to Eochaidh, King of Ireland (bar.), is lured by a fairy prince, Midir (ten.), back to the Land of Heart's Desire, whence she had come.

The opera had an extraordinarily successful run of 216 performances in London in 1922-3, followed by a further 160 performances in 1923-4. It failed to repeat this success when revived in London in 1953.

Incoronazione di Poppea, L' *(The Coronation of Poppea).* Opera in a prologue and 3 acts by Monteverdi. Libretto by Giovanni Francesco Busenello. First performed Venice, autumn 1642.

Monteverdi's last opera, and the first to be composed on an historical (rather than a biblical or mythological) subject, it tells of the Emperor Nero's love (ten.: male soprano) for Poppea (sop.). His wife Ottavia (mezzo-sop.), whom he wishes to divorce, plans to have Poppea murdered, but the attempt fails. Ottavia is divorced, and the coronation of Poppea is celebrated.

Inghilleri, Giovanni, b. Porto Empedocle, Sicily, 9 Mar 1894; d. Milan, 10 Dec 1959. Italian baritone. He began his career as a pianist and coach, and made his début as a singer in Milan in 1919 as Valentin in *Faust*. After singing at a number of Italian opera houses, he was invited to Covent Garden in 1928, making his début there as Tonio in *Pagliacci*. He sang in Chicago in 1929-30, and was considered one of the finest Italian baritones active in the 1930s. He continued to sing in opera until 1953, and then taught in Pesaro and Milan.

Intendant. The German term for the administrator or general manager of an opera house.

Intermezzo. Opera in 2 acts by Richard Strauss. Libretto by the composer. First performed Dresden, 4 Nov 1924.

Based on incidents in Strauss's own life, the opera tells of the domestic upheaval when Christine (sop.), wife of the celebrated composer Robert Storch (bar.), wrongly suspects him of a liaison with another woman.

intermezzo. Originally a piece of music played within some larger work, such as Pergolesi's *La Serva Padrona*, which was first performed as comic relief between the acts of the same composer's *Il Prigionier Superbo*. Later the term came to mean simply a short instrumental piece and, in an operatic context, a piece played between scenes or acts or when the stage is empty.

Iolanta. Opera in 1 act by Tchaikovsky. Libretto by Modest Tchaikovsky, based on the Danish story *Kong Renés Datter* by Henrik Hertz. First performed St Petersburg, 18 Dec 1892.

Iolanta (sop.), daughter of King René (bass), does not realize that she is blind, for the King has forbidden anyone to tell her. Ebn-Hakia (bar.), a Moorish physician, informs the King that only if his daughter knows of her blindness is there any possibility of her being cured of it. Count

Vaudémont (ten.) falls in love with Iolanta and makes her aware of her condition. The King decrees that Vaudémont must die if Iolanta remains blind, and this leads to her cure and to her betrothal to Vaudémont.

Iolanthe. Operetta in 2 acts by Sullivan. Libretto by W.S. Gilbert. First performed simultaneously in London and New York, 25 Nov 1882.

In order that Strephon (bar.), who is half-mortal and half-fairy, can marry the shepherdess Phyllis (sop.), the Queen of the Fairies (contr.) turns the entire House of Lords into fairies. An amiable satire on British politics.

Iphigénie en Aulide *(Iphigenia in Aulis)*. Opera in 3 acts by Gluck. Libretto by Bailly du Roullet, based on Racine's play, *Iphigénie* (1674) which in turn is based on Euripides. First performed Paris, 19 Apr 1774.

Agamemnon (bass) is informed that the gods require the sacrifice of his daughter Iphigenia (sop.). She is reprieved at the last moment.

Iphigénie en Tauride. *(Iphigenia in Tauris)*. Opera in 4 acts by Gluck. Libretto by Nicolas François Guillard, based on Euripides. First performed Paris, 18 May 1779.

The plot follows on from that of *Iphigénie en Aulide*. Iphigenia (sop.), now a priestess of Diana in the Scythian capital of Tauris, is expected to officiate at the sacrifice of a shipwrecked Greek, whom she discovers to be her brother, Oreste (bass). Oreste's friend Pylade (ten.) offers to substitute himself as sacrifice, and the goddess Diana is moved by this to reprieve both men.

Ippolitov-Ivanov, Mikhail, b. Gatchina, 19 Nov 1859; d. Moscow, 28 Jan 1935. Russian composer. He studied in St Petersburg, and took up a career as conductor and academic. He was a professor at the Moscow Conservatorium from 1893 until his death, and was also active as a conductor of opera. His operas, heavily influenced by Rimsky-Korsakov who had been one of his teachers, include *Ruth* (1887), *Asya* (1900), *Treachery* (1910), and *Olye the Norseman* (1916). *The Last Barricade*, composed in 1933, remains unperformed and unpublished.

Harold Blackburn as Mustapha and Eric Shilling as Taddeo in a scene from Act I of *L'Italiana in Algeri* at the London Coliseum in November 1982.

Iris. Opera in 3 acts by Mascagni. Libretto by Luigi Illica. First performed Rome, 22 Nov 1898.

In 19th-c. Japan, Osaka (ten.) attempts to win the love of the innocent Iris (sop.). He arranges to have her abducted to a brothel, where she is discovered by her blind father (bass) who curses her. Iris drowns herself in a sewer.

Irische Legende (*Irish Legend*). Opera in 5 scenes by Egk. Libretto by the composer, based on the play, *The Countess Cathleen* (1892) by William Butler Yeats. First performed Salzburg, 17 Aug 1955.

The Devil has caused a famine in Ireland, and people are forced to sell their souls to him in exchange for food. The beautiful Countess Cathleen (sop.) barters her soul for those of everyone else, and is rewarded for her generous act by being rescued from damnation by angels.

Irmelin. Opera in 3 acts by Delius. Libretto by the composer. First performed Oxford, 4 May 1953.

Irmelin (sop.), a princess, rejects three suitors, because she awaits her true love. Nils (ten.), a prince who has become a swineherd, is searching for his ideal woman.

He is told that he will find her if he follows a silver stream. He does so, and there he and Irmelin find each other.

The opera lacks both dramatic action and continuous musical interest. Delius was apparently not very interested in seeing it staged, so it is hardly surprising that *Irmelin* had to wait until nearly twenty years after his death to be performed.

Isabeau. Opera in 3 acts by Mascagni. Libretto by Luigi Illica. First performed Buenos Aires, 2 June 1911.

For her unwillingness to choose a husband, the Princess Isabeau (sop.) is made to ride naked through the streets of the city at noon. It is decreed that anyone who dares to look upon her will be put to death. This edict is disobeyed by Folco (ten.), a young forester. Isabeau falls in love with Folco and, when he is lynched by the mob, she kills herself over his dying body.

Isabella (mezzo-sop.). The heroine of Rossini's *L'Italiana in Algeri*.

Isolde (sop.). The Irish princess who is the heroine of Wagner's *Tristan und Isolde*.

Isolier (mezzo-sop.). The Count's page, in Rossini's *Le Comte Ory*.

Italiana in Algeri, L' *(The Italian Girl in Algiers)*. Opera in 2 acts by Rossini. Libretto by Angelo Anelli, originally written for an opera of the same title by Luigi Mosca (1808). First performed Venice, 22 May 1813.

Isabella (mezzo-sop.), who has been sailing the Mediterranean in search of her lover Lindoro (ten.), is shipwrecked on the coast of Algiers. Taken to the Bey of Algiers, Mustafà (bass), who plans to add her to his harem, she discovers Lindoro to be a slave in the Bey's service. With the aid of Elvira (sop.), a neglected wife of Mustafà, Isabella and Lindoro finally escape, together with Isabella's admirer Taddeo (bar.).

Ivan Susanin. Opera in 4 acts and an epilogue by Glinka. Libretto by Baron Georgy Fyodorovich Rozen. First performed St Petersburg, 9 Dec 1836. (The opera was produced as *A Life for the Tsar*, at the request of Nicholas I. In Russia it has now reverted to its original title.)

The opera is set in 1612 in Russia and Poland. The Polish forces decide to advance on Russia, and compel Susanin (bass), a Russian, to guide them. However, he leads the Poles on a false trail, and is killed. He is praised, posthumously, by the new Tsar.

Ivanhoe. Opera in 5 acts by Sullivan. Libretto by Julian Sturgis after the novel, *Ivanhoe* (1819) by Sir Walter Scott. First performed London, 31 Jan 1891.

Ivanhoe (ten.) returns with King Richard I (bass) from the Third Crusade. Together they rescue the country from the King's enemies, and defeat the wicked Templar (bar.). Ivanhoe wins the hand of Rowena (sop.), ward of Cedric the Saxon (bar.).

Sullivan's only grand opera, *Ivanhoe* had a continuous run of 160 performances when it was first performed to open the Royal English Opera House (now the Palace Theatre), London. Its popularity proved to be short-lived.

Ivogün, Maria, b. Budapest, 18 Nov 1891. Hungarian soprano. She studied in Vienna, and was engaged by Bruno Walter for Munich where she made her début in 1913 as Mimi. In 1917 she created the role of Ighino in the première of Pfitzner's *Palestrina*. She made her Covent Garden début in 1924 as Zerbinetta, appeared regularly in Chicago in the 1920s, and was highly acclaimed in the lyric coloratura repertory. She retired in 1934, due to failing eyesight, and became a distinguished teacher, her pupils including Elisabeth Schwarzkopf and Rita Streich. She was married first to the tenor Karl Erb, and then to the pianist Michael Raucheisen.

J

Jacquino (ten.). Rocco's young assistant, in love with Marzelline, in Beethoven's *Fidelio*.

Jacobin, The (Czech title, *Jakobín*). Opera in 3 acts by Dvořák. Libretto by Marie Červinková-Riegrová. First performed Prague, 12 Feb 1889.

Bohuš (bar.), son of the Count (bass), returns from exile with his wife Julie (sop.), to learn that his father intends to disinherit him. Though Bohuš is arrested because of his political views, Julie and the village schoolmaster Benda (ten.) are able to persuade the Count to change his mind.

Jadlowker, Hermann, b. Riga, 5 July 1877; d. Tel Aviv, 13 May 1953. Latvian tenor. He studied in Vienna and made his début in Cologne in 1899 as Fenton in Nicolai's *Die Lustigen Weiber von Windsor.* He first sang at the Met in 1910 as Gounod's *Faust,* and remained with the company for two seasons, creating the role of the King's son in Humperdinck's *Königskinder* there in 1910. In 1912 Richard Strauss chose him to create Bacchus in *Ariadne auf Naxos* in Stuttgart. Later in his career, he undertook such Wagner roles as Tannhäuser and Parsifal. After 1921 he appeared only rarely in opera, though he created the leading tenor role of Armand in Lehár's operetta, *Frasquita,* in Vienna in 1922. In 1929 he returned to Riga and became a cantor in the synagogue. He emigrated to Palestine in 1938 and taught in Tel Aviv. He had an attractive voice and a superb technique.

Janáček, Leoš, b. Hukvaldy, 3 July 1854; d. Ostrava, 12 Aug 1928. Czech composer. He studied in Brno, Prague, Leipzig and Vienna, and settled in Brno where he was active as a choral conductor and writer on music. His first opera, *Šárka,* (written in the 1880s but not staged until 1925) is an immature work, and his second, *The Beginning of a Romance* (1894), is a slight comedy in folkstyle. Janáček's reputation rests upon the operas of his maturity, the earliest of which is *Jenůfa* (1904). What these works lack in lyrical melody they compensate for in dramatic intensity. *Katya Kabanova* (1921), *The Cunning Little Vixen* (1924), *The Makropulos Case* (1926) and *From the House of the Dead* (1930) made their way slowly into the international repertoire, but in recent years performances have become more frequent, thanks to the advocacy of certain critics and conductors.

Janowitz, Gundula, b. Berlin, 2 Aug 1937. German soprano. She studied in Graz, and at the age of twenty-one was engaged by Herbert von Karajan for the Vienna Staatsoper, making her début in 1960 as Barbarina in *Le Nozze di Figaro.* The following year she sang Pamina, and in 1962 Marzelline in *Fidelio,* revealing a voice of

steely beauty and a firm technique. She has remained with the Vienna Opera as a leading dramatic soprano, while making frequent guest appearances abroad. She first appeared at the Met in 1967 as Sieglinde, and at Covent Garden in 1976 as Donna Anna in *Don Giovanni.* She is also a fine Empress in *Die Frau ohne Schatten* and Ariadne in *Ariadne auf Naxos.*

Janssen, Herbert, b. Cologne, 22 Sept 1895; d. New York, 3 June 1965. German baritone. He studied in Cologne and Berlin, and made his début at the Berlin Staatsoper in 1922 in Schreker's *Der Schatzgräber.* He remained with the company until 1938, as leading lyric baritone, admired in Verdi as well as in the lighter Wagner baritone roles such as Wolfram, Kurwenal and Amfortas, which he sang at Bayreuth each summer between 1930-7. He appeared at Covent Garden every season from 1926-39, making his début there as Kurwenal in *Tristan und Isolde.* In 1938 political events caused him to leave Germany, and from the following year until his retirement he was the leading Wagner baritone at the Met. He had a voice of warm and mellifluous timbre, and was an intelligent interpretative artist.

Jeanne d'Arc au Bûcher. (*Joan of Arc at the Stake*). Dramatic oratorio in a prologue and 10 scenes by Honegger. Libretto by Paul Claudel. First performed Basle, 12 May 1938.

Joan of Arc (a speaking role), tied to the stake, remembers parts of her life and her trial at the moment of her death.

Jenik (ten.). The young villager, in love with Mařenka, in Smetana's *The Bartered Bride.*

Jenůfa. (Czech title, *Její Pastorkyňa,* or 'Her Foster-Daughter'). Opera in 3 acts by Janáček. Libretto by the composer, based on a play (1890) by Gabriela Preissová. First performed Brno, 21 Jan 1904.

Jenůfa (sop.) is pregnant by Števa (ten.) who does not really love her. His half-brother Laca (ten.), jealous because Jenůfa prefers Števa, slashes her face with a knife, and is instantly remorseful. When Jenůfa's child is born, her foster-mother who is known as the Kostelnička or Sextoness (sop.) secretly kills the baby, as

Števa has refused to marry Jenůfa. Jenůfa and Laca marry, but the wedding is interrupted by the discovery of the child's body. The Kostelnička confesses, and is' forgiven by Jenůfa who has now found happiness with Laca.

Jeritza, Maria, b. Brno, 6 Oct 1887; d. Orange, N.J., 10 July 1982. Czech soprano. She studied in Brno and Prague, and made her début in Olomouc in 1910 as Elsa in *Lohengrin*. The following year she sang in Vienna at the Volksoper, and in 1912 joined the Staatsoper, remaining a member of the company for more than two decades. She was a famous Tosca and Turandot, and

Maria Jeritza as Turandot, one of her most admired roles.

Puccini himself admired her as Minnie in his *La Fanciulla del West*. She created the roles of Ariadne (in both versions of *Ariadne auf Naxos*) and the Empress (in *Die Frau ohne Schatten*) and sang other Strauss roles, most notably Salome. She made her début at the Met in 1921 in Korngold's *Die tote Stadt*, and immediately became a Met favourite, appearing in most seasons for the following twelve years. At Covent Garden she sang in only two seasons, as Tosca and the eponymous heroine of Giordano's *Fedora* in 1925, and in *Thaïs, I Gioielli della Madonna* and *Die Walküre* (Sieglinde) in 1926. She retired in 1935, and spent the war years in America, but returned to Vienna to reappear in some of her old roles between 1949-52.

Jerusalem, Siegfried, b Oberhausen, 1940. German tenor. He studied violin and bassoon, and began his career as a bassoonist. From 1961-77 he played in various German orchestras, but began to take voice lessons in 1972, and made his début as a singer with the Stuttgart Opera in 1975 as First Prisoner in *Fidelio*. The following year he sang Lohengrin in Hamburg. Since 1977 he has appeared regularly at Bayreuth, adding Parsifal and Walther to his repertoire.

Jochanaan (bar.). The prophet, known in English as John the Baptist, who is a character in Richard Strauss's *Salome*.

Johnson, Edward, b. Guelph, Ontario, 22 Aug 1878; d. Toronto, 20 Apr 1959. Canadian tenor and opera administrator. He studied in New York and Florence, and made his début in Padua in 1912 as Giordano's Andrea Chénier. He was the first tenor to sing Parsifal in Italy, at La Scala in 1914. He sang in Milan and Rome until 1919, and then returned to North America, making his United States début in Chicago in 1919, and first appearing at the Met in 1922 in Montemezzi's *L'Amore dei Tre Rè*. He continued to sing at the Met until 1935, creating roles in such new American operas as Deems Taylor's *The King's Henchman* and *Peter Ibbetson* and Howard Hanson's *Merry Mount*. He was also an admired Pelléas in *Pelléas et Mélisande*. In 1935 he became general manager of the Met, remaining in that capacity until 1950 when he joined the Music Faculty of Toronto University.

Gwyneth Jones as Brünnhilde in the production of the *Ring* shown on BBC TV in 1982.

Jolie Fille de Perth, La *(The Fair Maid of Perth)*. Opera in 4 acts by Bizet. Libretto by Jules-Henri Vernoy de St-Georges and Jules Adenis, based on the novel, *The Fair Maid of Perth* (1832) by Sir Walter Scott. First performed Paris, 26 Dec 1867.

Only loosely based on Scott's novel, the opera tells of the love of Henry Smith (ten.), an armourer, for Catherine Glover (sop.), daughter of Simon (bass), a glovemaker of Perth.

Jommelli, Niccolò, b. Aversa, 10 Sept 1714; d. Naples, 25 Aug 1774. Italian composer. He studied in Naples, and had his first operatic success with *L'Errore Amoroso*, which was performed in Naples in 1737. He soon became recognized as one of the leading opera composers of the Neapolitan school, and received commissions to compose operas for the leading Italian cities and for Vienna. From 1753-68 he was in the service of the Duke of Württemberg, in Stuttgart, where his most important opera, *Fetonte* was staged in 1768. Of his more than eighty operas, fifty-three are known to survive, but are rarely staged nowadays.

Jones, Gwyneth, b. Pontnewynydd, 7 Nov 1936. Welsh soprano. She studied in London, Siena and Geneva as a mezzo-soprano, and was engaged by Zurich Opera whose musical director, Nello Santi, persuaded her to undertake soprano roles. She made her British début as Verdi's Lady Macbeth with Welsh National Opera in 1963, and then sang with the Covent Garden company on tour and, as Beethoven's *Fidelio*, in London. She first attracted international attention when, at short notice, she replaced Leontyne Price in a new production of *Il Trovatore* at Covent Garden in November, 1964. Her sympathetic voice and personality were also greatly admired when she sang Sieglinde in London in 1966. She made her Bayreuth and Vienna débuts in that year, and made her first appearance at the Met as Sieglinde, in 1972. For some years her vocal production was afflicted by an uncontrolled vibrato, familiarly known as 'wobble', but she had managed largely to eliminate this by the 1980s. She remains an uneven vocalist, but is nonetheless an impulsive and dramatically exciting performer.

Jongleur de Notre-Dame, Le *(The Juggler of Our Lady)*. Opera in 3 acts by Massenet. Libretto by Maurice Léna, based on a story by Anatole France in the volume *L'Étui de Nacre* (1892). First performed Monte Carlo, 18 Feb 1902.

In 14th-c. Burgundy, Jean (ten.), the tumbler or juggler of the title, offers to the image of the Virgin Mary in the monastery his only gift, his talent for dancing and juggling. The monks are horrified, but the statue of the Virgin is seen to incline its head in blessing, and Jean falls dead in a state of religious ecstasy.

Jonny spielt auf *(Johnny Strikes Up)*. Opera in 2 parts by Křenek. Libretto by the composer. First performed Leipzig, 10 Feb 1927.

Jonny (bar.), the black leader of a jazz-band, steals a violin from Daniello (bar.). He hides it first in the room of the singer, Anita (sop.) and then in that of Max (ten.), the composer. With the violin he becomes immensely successful as a jazz musician: the new world has conquered the old.

Joplin, Scott, b. Texarkana, Ark., 24 Nov 1868; d. New York, 1 Apr 1917. Black American composer and pianist. Known in his lifetime as the King of Ragtime, he wrote mainly for the piano. He composed the first ragtime opera, *A Guest of Honor*, which may have been performed in St Louis in 1903 but which is now lost. His only other opera, also based on ragtime music, was *Treemonisha*, which he himself published in 1911. Its only performance during Joplin's lifetime was given in 1915, without scenery, and with the composer accompanying on the piano. The opera was not fully staged until 1975, in Houston, Texas.

José, Don (ten.). The officer in love with Carmen, in Bizet's *Carmen*.

Journet, Marcel, b. Grasse, 25 July 1867; d. Vittel, 7 Sept 1933. French bass. He studied at the Paris Conservatoire, and made his début in Béziers in 1891 in Donizetti's *La Favorite*. From 1894–1900 he sang at the Théâtre de la Monnaie, Brussels, and made his Covent Garden début in 1897 in D'Erlanger's *Inez Mendo*. He made his Met début as Ramfis in *Aida* in 1900, and in the first decade of the 1900s was active regularly in London and New York. He also sang in most seasons at the Paris Opéra until 1932, and at La Scala in 1924 created the role of Simon Mago in the posthumous première of Boito's *Nerone*. His huge range allowed him to sing certain baritone roles, such as Tonio in *Pagliacci* and Scarpia in *Tosca*.

Juive, La *(The Jewess)*. Opera in 5 acts by Halévy. Libretto by Eugène Scribe. First performed Paris, 23 Feb 1835.

In 15th-c. Constance, the Jews are persecuted by Cardinal Brogni (bass). Rachel (sop.), the supposed daughter of the goldsmith Eléazar (ten.), is arrested for having attracted the love of a Christian, Prince Léopold (ten.). She exonerates Léopold, but she and her father are condemned to death. The Cardinal offers to spare Rachel if her father will renounce the Jewish faith. He refuses, as does Rachel, and only when Rachel has been led to her death in a cauldron of boiling water does Eléazar reveal that she was not his daughter but that of Cardinal Brogni.

Julietta. Opera in 3 acts by Martinů. Libretto by the composer, based on the play *Juliette ou La Clé des Songes* (1930) by Georges Neveux. First performed Prague, 16 Mar 1938.

Michel (ten.) has returned from Paris to a small coastal town, haunted by the memory of Julietta (sop.) whom he saw only once. The inhabitants of the town, however, appear to remember nothing of her, and memory, fantasy and reality all appear to Michel to be equally unsatisfactory.

Juliette (sop.). The heroine of Gounod's *Roméo et Juliette*.

Junge Lord, Der *(The Young Lord)*. Opera in 2 acts by Henze. Libretto by Ingeborg Bachmann, based on a story in *Der Scheik von Alexandria und seine Sklaven* (1827) by Wilhelm Hauff. First performed Berlin, 7 Apr 1965.

When Sir Edgar (a mimed role) introduces his nephew, Lord Barratt (ten.), to the polite society of a small German provincial town, all are snobbishly entranced by the young man's boorish behaviour, until it is finally revealed that he is, in fact, an ape dressed in human clothes.

Jurinac, Sena, b. Travnik, 24 Oct 1921. Yugoslav.soprano. She studied in Zagreb, and made her début there in 1942, her first roles being the First Flowermaiden in *Parsifal* and Mimi in *La Bohème*. She was immediately invited to join the Vienna Staatsoper company, of which she has remained a member ever since. Her Covent Garden début was in 1947, with the visiting Vienna ensemble, as Dorabella in *Così Fan Tutte*. Later she made many guest appearances at Covent Garden, and was a memorable Leonore in the Klemperer production of *Fidelio* in 1961. In *Der Rosenkavalier*, she progressed from the role of Octavian which she sang with great success in Vienna, Salzburg, London and elsewhere, to that of the Marschallin, which became one of her finest roles. At Glyndebourne in the 1950s she was a greatly loved Mozart soprano, especially as the Countess in *Le Nozze di Figaro*, and in Vienna she is as much admired in Verdi and Puccini as in the Mozart and Strauss roles. Her radiant voice and sympathetic portrayals have made her one of the finest opera sopranos of her time.

K

Kabaivanska, Raina, b. Burgas, 15 Dec 1934. Bulgarian soprano. She studied in Sofia, and made her début there in 1957 as Tatiana in *Eugene Onegin*. After further study in Milan, she made her first appearance in Italy (as Raina Kabai) in Fano in 1959 as Nedda in *Pagliacci*, and in 1961 sang Agnese in Bellini's *Beatrice di Tenda* at La Scala, with Joan Sutherland as Beatrice. She has become a leading soprano in the popular Verdi and Puccini roles, making her Covent Garden début in 1962 as Desdemona and her Met début in the same year as Nedda. She is a fine Tosca, an excellent actress with a commanding stage presence.

Kabalevsky, Dmitry, b. St Petersburg, 30 Dec 1904. Russian composer. He studied at Moscow Conservatorium, worked for a time in music publishing, became a professor at the Conservatorium in 1939, and composed seven operas and operettas. His first work for the theatre, *Colas Breugnon* (1938), based on a novel by Romain Rolland, is an opera of lyrical charm and immediate appeal which he has subjected to revision twice, in 1953 and 1969. He joined the Communist party in 1940, and his next opera, *Into the Fire* (1942), a large-scale patriotic work dealing with the Red Army's defence of Moscow against the Germans, reflected a new-found earnestness of purpose. *Into the Fire* was only moderately successful, and Kabalevsky subsequently withdrew it. *The Taras Family* (1947), his next opera, was revised twice in the light of the party's 1948 decree on music, and later works have been light operettas, such as *Spring Sings* (1957) and *The Sisters* (1967).

Kallman, Chester, b. Brooklyn, N.Y., 7 Jan 1921; d. Athens, 17 Jan 1975. American librettist and poet. He wrote the libretto of Carlos Chávez's *Panfilo and Lauretta* (1957) and, in collaboration with W.H. Auden, the libretti of Stravinsky's *The Rake's Progress* (1951), Henze's *Elegy for Young Lovers* (1961) and *The Bassarids* (1966), and Nicolas Nabokov's *Love's Labour's Lost* (1973).

Kálmán, Emmerich, b. Siófok, 24 Oct 1882; d. Paris, 30 Oct 1953. Hungarian composer. He studied at the Budapest Academy of Music, and then wrote music criticism as well as composing so-called 'serious' music, before deciding to concentrate on operetta. His first operetta, *Tatárjárás (The Gay Hussars)*, was produced in Budapest in 1908 and had an extraordinary success throughout Europe and in the United States in the years before World War I. It was especially well received in Vienna, the home of operetta, and Kálmán moved to the Austrian capital where he continued to live until the Anschluss in 1938 forced him to move, first to Paris, and then, in 1939, to the United States. Between 1909-39 he composed twenty operettas, most of which were first staged in Vienna before being translated for productions elsewhere in Europe and in the English-speaking world. Those which have proved most lasting include *Die Czardasfürstin* (1915), produced in London in 1921 as *The Gypsy Princess; Gräfin Mariza (Countess Maritza;* 1924); and *Die Zirkusprinzessin (The Circus Princess,* 1926). *Golden Dawn,* composed in collaboration with Herbert Stothart, was first staged in New York in 1927, and in 1945 Kálmán had another operetta, *Marinka,* staged on Broadway with a run of twenty-one weeks. *Arizona Lady*, which he died before finishing, was completed by his son Charles Emmerich Kálmán (b. Vienna, 17 Nov 1929) and produced in Berne in 1954.

Kálmán's finest operettas are, like those of Lehár, musically and dramatically the equal of many operas composed during the 20th c. They combine the colouring of Hungary with the rhythms of Vienna, and are superbly orchestrated.

Karajan, Herbert von, b. Salzburg, 5 Apr 1908. Austrian conductor and producer. He studied in Salzburg and Vienna and began his career as a conductor with the opera company at Ulm in 1927, having already conducted *Fidelio*, earlier that year, at the Landestheater, Salzburg. He remained at Ulm until 1934 when he was engaged by the company at Aachen where, in 1936, he became music director. He first conducted at the Berlin Staatsoper in 1937 and

Herbert von Karajan rehearsing Anna Tomowa-Sintow in *Lohengrin* at Salzburg.

remained there throughout the war years. From 1956-64 he was artistic director of the Vienna State Opera, since when he has been one of the directors of the Salzburg Festival. In 1963 he established an additional Easter Festival in Salzburg, in which he performs, usually, one of the Wagner operas. He is a superb conductor of Strauss and Wagner, and also of Italian opera, especially Verdi. In recent years, he has preferred to direct, himself, the productions of the operas he conducts.

Katerina Ismailova. Opera in 4 acts by Shostakovich. Libretto by the composer and A. Preys after a novel by Nicolai Lyeskov.. First performed, as *Lady Macbeth of Mtsensk District*, Leningrad, 22 Jan 1934. Revised version first performed Moscow, 26 Dec 1962.

Katerina (sop.), unhappy in her marriage to the weakling Zinovy (ten.), succumbs to the charms of Sergei (ten.), a farm worker. Their affair is discovered by Boris (bar.), her father-in-law, who has himself been planning to seduce Katerina. Boris has Sergei thrashed, and in revenge Katerina kills the old man with rat poison. She and Sergei are then forced to kill her husband. The wedding ceremony of Katerina and Sergei is interrupted by the discovery of Zinovy's body, and the lovers are arrested. In a prison camp, Sergei transfers his affections to Sonyetka (sop.), a young female convict. Katerina attacks her rival, dragging her into the river where both women drown.

Katya Kabanova. Opera in 3 acts by Janáček. Libretto by the composer, based on the play *The Storm* (1859) by Alexander Ostrovsky. First performed Brno, 23 Nov 1921.

Katya (sop.), no longer in love with her husband Tichon (ten.), and hated by her mother-in-law Kabanicha (contr.), has an affair with Boris (ten.). Unnerved by a storm, she confesses her guilt to her family and others. Boris is dispatched to Siberia by his uncle, and Katya throws herself into the Volga.

Kecal (bass). The marriage-broker in Smetana's *The Bartered Bride*.

Keilberth, Joseph, b. Karlsruhe, 19 Apr 1908; d. Munich, 21 July 1968. German conductor. He studied in Karlsruhe, and became music director there in 1935. From 1945-50 he conducted in Dresden, and then was engaged by the Bavarian State Opera in Munich. He became general music director in Munich in 1959, and remained in that post until his death, which occurred while he was conducting a performance of *Tristan und Isolde*. He was a sound musician, and an experienced interpreter of the German repertory.

Kelemen, Zoltán, b. Budapest, 1933; d. Zurich, 9 May 1979. Hungarian bass. He studied in Budapest and Rome, and made his début in Augsburg in 1959. He first appeared at Bayreuth in 1964 as Alberich, the role of his Covent Garden début in 1970. He was an excellent performer of comic roles: he undertook Verdi's Falstaff, Mozart's Osmin and Strauss's Baron Ochs with equal success.

Kempe, Rudolf, b. Niederpoyritz, 14 June 1910; d. Zurich, 11 May 1976. German conductor. He studied in Dresden, began his career as an oboe player, and joined the musical staff of the Leipzig Opera in 1925, making his début as conductor there in 1935 with *Der Wildschütz*. He later conducted in a number of other German towns, and became internationally known after World War II. He first appeared at Covent Garden conducting performances by the Munich company in 1953, and made his Met début in 1954. He was a first-rate interpreter of Wagner and Strauss. His *Ring* at Covent Garden was admired for the beautiful playing he obtained from his orchestra and for his grasp of dramatic structure.

Kern, Patricia, b. Swansea, 14 July 1927. Welsh mezzo-soprano. She studied in London and made her début with the Arts Council's Opera for All touring company in 1952 in Rossini's *Cenerentola*. In 1959 she joined Sadler's Wells Opera, where her performances in the Mozart and Rossini mezzo roles were much admired. She made her Covent Garden début in 1967 as Zerlina, and later sang with the New York City Opera, and with companies in Dallas and Washington D.C. She had a voice of warm timbre and great agility, qualities which made her an attractive Isabella in Rossini's *L'Italiana in Algeri*.

Kertész, István, b. Budapest, 28 Aug 1929; d. Herzlia, Israel, 17 Apr 1973. Hungarian conductor. He studied in Budapest and Rome, became an assistant conductor at the opera in Budapest in 1954, making his début there in that year with *Die Entführung aus dem Serail*, and became music director in Augsburg in 1958. In 1964 he moved to Cologne in the same capacity, and remained in that post until his death by drowning off the coast of Israel. He made his Covent Garden début in 1966 with *Un Ballo in Maschera*, but was generally regarded as a Mozart specialist.

Khovanshchina. *(The Khovansky Affair).* Opera in 5 acts by Mussorgsky, completed and orchestrated by Rimsky-Korsakov. Libretto by the composer and Vladimir Stasov. First performed St Petersburg, 21 Feb 1886.

The opera is set in Russia at the time of the accession of Peter the Great in 1682, and concerns the political and religious strife between various factions. Prince Khovansky (bass) and his followers are opposed by Prince Galitsyn (ten.) and his party. An important role is played by the religious sect of Old Believers, led by Dosifei (bass) and the Princess Marfa (sop.).

Kienzl, Wilhelm, b. Waizenkirchen, 17 Jan 1857; d. Vienna, 3 Oct 1941. Austrian composer. He studied in Graz, and became an enthusiast for the music of Wagner when, as a nineteen-year-old student, he travelled to Bayreuth for the first performance of the *Ring*. His ten operas include *Heilmar der Narr* (1892), *Das Testament* (1916) and *Hans Kipfel* (1926), but the only two to have become known outside Austria and Germany are *Der Evangelimann* (1895) and *Der Kuhreigen* (1911). *Der Evangelimann*, his most popular work, is still to be found in the repertoire of the Vienna Volksoper.

Kiepura, Jan, b. Sosnowiec, 16 May 1902; d. Harrison, N.Y., 15 Aug 1966. Polish tenor. He studied in Warsaw, and made his début in Lvov in 1924 as Faust. In 1926 he sang Cavaradossi in Vienna, and became very popular in Austria and Germany. In 1938 he left Europe and sang at the Met until 1941, making his début as Rodolfo in *La Bohème*. He made a number of films in Europe in the 1930s, with his wife, Marta

A scene from Mussorgsky's *Khovanshchina* at Covent Garden in November 1982.

Eggerth, a Hungarian soprano (b. 1912) with whom he also appeared in Europe and America in *The Merry Widow*.

King, James, b. Dodge City, Kans., 22 May 1925. American tenor. He studied in Cincinnati, began his career as a baritone, went to Europe for further study and made his début as a tenor in Florence in 1961 as Cavaradossi. He then began to undertake heroic tenor roles with some success, appearing at Bayreuth for the first time in 1965 as Siegmund, at the Met in 1966 as Florestan in *Fidelio*, and at Covent Garden in 1967 as the Emperor in *Die Frau ohne Schatten*. He appears frequently in Berlin and Vienna, and in 1974 in San Francisco undertook Verdi's Otello. His voice is serviceable, but he is a somewhat stolid interpreter.

King Mark (bass). King of Cornwall in Wagner's *Tristan und Isolde*.

King Priam. Opera in 3 acts by Tippett. Libretto by the composer, after Homer's *Iliad*. First performed Coventry, 29 May 1962.

The opera re-tells part of the old legend. Priam (bass-bar.) chooses to have his son Paris killed, but the boy (sop.) is spared and grows to manhood (ten.), fetches Helen (mezzo-sop.) from Sparta, and is instrumental in beginning the Trojan wars. Paris and Hector (bar.) quarrel, Hector is killed by Achilles (ten.), Priam is killed by the son of Achilles.

King Roger (Polish title, *Król Roger*). Opera in 3 acts by Szymanowski. Libretto by the composer and Jaroslaw Iwaszkiewicz. First performed Warsaw, 19 June 1926.

Queen Roxane (sop.), wife of King Roger (bar.) of Sicily, falls under the spell of a young shepherd (ten.) from a far distant land. The shepherd is revealed to be the god Dionysus, and the opera ends with a dionysiac bacchanal in a Greek temple.

Kipnis, Alexander, b. Zhitomir, Ukraine, 1 Feb 1891; d. Westport, Conn. 14 May 1978. Russian, later American, bass. He studied in Warsaw and Berlin, and made his début in Hamburg in 1915. In 1919 he joined the Berlin Städtische Oper with whom he sang leading bass roles for eleven years, before moving to the company of the Berlin Staatsoper in 1930. In 1934, as a Jew he was forced to leave Germany, and he became an American citizen. He had already sung a number of roles in Chicago between 1923-32, and now made his Met début in 1940 as Gurnemanz. His most admired performances were as Sarastro, Baron Ochs, Boris Godunov and Philip II in Verdi's *Don Carlos*. His rich, voluminous bass voice was one of the finest of his day.

Kirsten, Dorothy, b. Montclair, N.J., 6 July 1917. American soprano. She studied in New York, received advice and assistance from the soprano Grace Moore who arranged for her to undertake further study in Rome, and made her début in Chicago in 1940 in the minor role of Pousette in *Manon*. She sang with the New York City Opera as Violetta in 1944, and the following year joined the Met, making her first appearance as Mimi, and continuing to sing with the company until 1975. A thoroughly professional artist and a popular performer, she sang a wide range of roles, her most successful including Tosca, Butterfly, Manon, (in both the Puccini and Massenet operas), Minnie (in *La Fanciulla del West*). She appeared in films, among them *The Great Caruso* (1951) with Mario Lanza.

Kiss, The (Czech title, *Hubička*). Opera in 2 acts by Smetana. Libretto by Eliška Krásnohorská based on a story (1871) by Karolina Světlá (pseudonym of Joanna Mužáková). First performed Prague, 7 Nov 1876.

Vendulka (sop.) refuses to let the widower Lukáš (ten.) kiss her before they are married, for it is believed that would arouse the wrath of his deceased first wife. Vendulka and her aunt Martinka (contr.) flee to the mountains, and are followed by Lukáš who, eventually, is allowed his betrothal kiss.

Klebe, Giselher, b. Mannheim, 28 June 1925. German composer. He studied in Berlin and specialized in composing operas, becoming one of the leaders of German opera in the years since World War II. *Die Räuber*, his first opera, was staged in Düsseldorf in 1957, and later works have included *Die Ermordung Cäsars* (Essen, 1959), *Figaro lässt sich scheiden* (Hamburg, 1963), based on the play by Odön von Horváth, and *Jacobowsky und der Oberst* (Hamburg, 1965), based on Franz Werfel's play. His operas in the 1970s, *Ein Wahrer Held* (Zurich, 1975), based on Synge's *The Playboy of the Western World*, and *Das Mädchen aus Domrémy* (Stuttgart, 1976), after Schiller's *Das Jungfrau von Orleans*, have been of less musical interest than his earlier works.

Kleiber, Carlos, b. Berlin, 3 July 1930. German conductor. The son of Erich Kleiber, he studied in Buenos Aires, began his conducting career at the Gärtnerplatz Theater, Munich in 1954, and, after gathering experience in a number of other German theatres, became internationally known in the late 1960s. He first appeared at Bayreuth in 1974 with *Tristan und Isolde*, and made his Covent Garden début in the same year with *Der Rosenkavalier*. He is one of those 'star' conductors who seeks to impose his own personality upon the works he conducts, which for the most part Kleiber impressively succeeds in doing.

Kleiber, Erich, b. Vienna, 5 Aug 1890; d. Zurich, 27 Jan 1956. Austrian conductor. He studied in Prague, began his career in Darmstadt in 1912, and conducted at a number of provincial German opera houses until he became general music director in Berlin in 1923. He resigned in 1934 and left Germany to live in Argentina where he conducted frequently at the Teatro Colón, Buenos Aires, for the rest of his life. He returned to Berlin in 1950, and also conducted at Covent Garden between 1950-3 where his performances of *Tristan* *und Isolde, Der Rosenkavalier, Die Zauberflöte* and the first London production of *Wozzeck* (in 1952) were especially admired.

Klein, Peter, b. Zündorf, nr Cologne, 25 Jan 1907. Austrian tenor of German birth. He studied in Cologne, and began his career as a member of the chorus in the opera company there. In 1937 he was engaged by the Hamburg Opera, and in 1942 he joined the ensemble of the Vienna Opera, specializing in character tenor roles. He was an impressive Mime in the *Ring*, a role he also sang in London and New York, and

proved invaluable in a wide range of small roles, such as Valzacchi in *Der Rosenkavalier*, Pedrillo in *Die Entführung aus dem Serail* and Blind in *Die Fledermaus.*

Klemperer, Otto, b. Breslau, 14 May 1885; d. Zurich, 6 July 1973. German conductor. He studied in Frankfurt and Berlin, and made his début in Berlin in 1906 conducting the Max Reinhardt production of Offenbach's *Orpheus in the Underworld.* On the recommendation of Mahler he was engaged at the German Theatre in Prague from 1907-10, and progressed via Hamburg,

Otto Klemperer, a great 20th-c. conductor of Mozart and Wagner, and exemplary interpreter of *Fidelio*.

Strasbourg, Cologne and Wiesbaden to Berlin where he worked from 1927-33, first at the Krolloper and later at the Staatsoper. In Berlin he conducted the premières and first local performances of a number of important operas, but was forced to leave Germany in 1933. He went to America, and did not conduct opera again until his return to Europe after the war when from 1947-50 he was engaged at the Budapest State Opera. He conducted memorable performances of his own productions of *Fidelio* (1961), *Die Zauberflöte* (1962) and *Lohengrin* (1963) at Covent Garden. He was undoubtedly one of the great conductors of the century, especially of Beethoven and Wagner.

Klingsor (bass). The evil magician in Wagner's *Parsifal*, and he is destroyed by Parsifal in Act II.

Klose, Margarete, b. Berlin, 6 Aug 1902; d. Berlin, 14 Dec 1968. German mezzo-soprano. She studied in Berlin, and made her début in Ulm in 1927 as Manja, the young Gipsy fortune-teller, in Kálmán's *Gräfin Mariza*. She was a leading mezzo-soprano in Berlin from 1932-61, her clear, rich voice being heard at its best as Brangäne in *Tristan und Isolde*, Ortrud in *Lohengrin* and a number of Verdi roles. Her first appearances at Covent Garden in 1935 and Bayreuth in 1936 were as Ortrud. She was also a famous exponent in Germany of Gluck's Orpheus and Bizet's Carmen, and Klytemnestra in Strauss's *Elektra*.

Kluge, Die *(The Clever Girl)*. Opera in 6 scenes by Orff. Libretto by the composer, based on the story, *Die Kluge Bauerntochter*, by the Grimm Brothers. First performed Frankfurt, 18 Feb 1943.

The King (bar.) marries the clever daughter (sop.) of a peasant (bass), but tires of her cleverness, and sends her away, telling her she may take with her only one chest filled with whatever she wants from the treasures at the palace. When the King awakens the next morning, he discovers that his wife has put him in the chest, for it is she whom she most treasures. Delighted, the King takes his wife back.

Klytemnestra (mezzo-sop.). Elektra's mother, and widow of Agamemnon whom she has murdered, in Strauss's *Elektra*.

Knappertsbusch, Hans, b. Elberfeld, 12 Mar 1888; d. Munich, 25 Oct 1965. German conductor. He studied in Cologne, and made his début in Mulheim in 1911, after which he worked in a number of German opera houses. He became general music director in Munich in 1922, resigning in 1936 because of his hostility to Naziism. He conducted in Vienna from 1936-50, and appeared at Bayreuth in 1951. After 1954 he conducted again in Munich. His only Covent Garden performances were of *Salome* in 1937. He was considered a great Wagner conductor, and managed, despite his extreme distaste for rehearsing, to secure excellent performances from his orchestras.

Knot Garden, The. Opera in 3 acts by Tippett. Libretto by the composer. First performed London, 2 Dec 1970.

The knot garden of the title is both symbolic and real. Among the characters whose relationships and attitudes are examined are Faber (bar.), his wife Thea (mezzo-sop.), their ward Flora (sop.), Denise (sop.), who is described as a dedicated freedom-fighter who has suffered torture, and a homosexual couple, the white musician Dov (ten.) and the black poet Mel (bar.). The catalyst is Mangus (bar.), a middle-aged analyst. By the end of the opera, the heterosexual marriage has been strengthened, and the homosexual one destroyed. Mel leaves with Denise, Flora finds independence, and Dov sets off upon a journey of, presumably, self-discovery.

Koanga. Opera in a prologue, 3 acts and an epilogue by Delius. Libretto by Charles Francis Keary, based on the novel *The Grandissimes* (1880) by George Washington Cable. First performed Elberfeld, 30 Mar 1904 in German translation. First performance in English, London, 23 Sept 1935.

On a Mississippi plantation, the mulatto girl Palmyra (sop.) falls in love with the slave Koanga (bar.), an African chieftain. The planter Don José Martinez (bass) allows them to marry, but during the festivities Palmyra is abducted by the slave-driver Simon Perez (ten.) whom she had spurned. Koanga escapes into the forest, and by means of voodoo causes a plague which afflicts Palmyra. Koanga kills Perez, before himself being killed, and Palmyra stabs herself with Koanga's spear.

Zoltán Kodály. He worked with Bartok on collecting and editing Hungarian folk music.

Kodály, Zoltán, b. Kecskemét, 16 Dec 1882; d. Budapest, 6 Mar 1967. Hungarian composer. He studied in Budapest and, with Bartók, helped to create a new style of Hungarian music based on folk song and dance. His three operas are in the form of Singspiels, with musical numbers separated by extensive dialogue. The best-known outside Hungary is *Háry János* (1926), largely based on folk music. *The Transylvanian Spinning Room* (in 1 act, 1932) presents a scene from village life, and *Czinka Panna* (1948) deals with the 1848 national uprising whose centenary it was first performed to commemorate.

Kollo, René, b. Berlin, 20 Nov 1937. German tenor. The grandson of the operetta composer Walter Kollo, and the son of the lyricist and composer of popular songs Willi Kollo, he began his career as a pop singer before graduating to opera via operetta. He made his début in Brunswick in 1965 in Stravinsky's *Oedipus Rex*, first appeared at Bayreuth as the Steersman in *Der fliegende*

Höllander, and went on to undertake leading Wagner roles in Bayreuth and elsewhere. In 1976 he made his New York début at the Met as Lohengrin, and his Covent Garden début as Siegmund. He has an attractive, lyrical voice, and a fine appearance.

Konetzni, Anny, b. Vienna, 12 Feb 1902; d. Vienna, 6 Sept 1968. Austrian soprano, sister of Hilde Konetzni. She studied in Vienna and Berlin, and made her début at the Volksoper in Vienna in 1925 as a contralto. She later became a leading Wagner soprano in Berlin and Vienna, first appeared at Covent Garden as Brünnhilde in 1935, returned every season until the outbreak of war, and sang Brünnhilde again at Covent Garden in 1951. She retired in 1955.

Konetzni, Hilde, b. Vienna, 21 Mar 1905; d. Vienna, 20 Apr 1980. Austrian soprano, sister of Anny Konetzni. She studied in Vienna, and made her début in Chemnitz in 1929, singing Sieglinde to her sister's Brünnhilde. She was a popular Wagner soprano in Vienna, and was also greatly admired there as the Marschallin in *Der Rosenkavalier*, the role in which she made her Covent Garden début in 1938, when she replaced Lotte Lehmann who collapsed ill at the end of Act I. She returned to Covent Garden with the Vienna Opera in 1947 as Leonore in *Fidelio*, and in 1951 sang Sieglinde at Covent Garden, again to the Brünnhilde of her sister Anny. She continued to sing in her later years, undertaking small roles in opera and operetta in Vienna until shortly before her death.

König Hirsch *(The Stag King)*. Opera in 3 acts by Henze. Libretto by Heinz von Cramer, based on the fairy tale, *Il Rè Cervo* (1762) by Carlo Gozzi. First performed Berlin, 23 Sept 1956. Revised and shortened, as *Il Rè Cervo oder Die Irrfahrten der Wahrheit, (The Stag King, or the Vicissitudes of Truth)* it was first performed in Cassel, 10 Mar 1963.

King Leandro (ten.), brought up in the forest by wild animals, returns to claim his throne, but is thwarted by the evil Governor (bass-bar.), and returns to the forest. He assumes the form of a stag. Eventually he is able to return to the city, to resume human form and to see the Governor killed by his own assassins.

Königin von Saba, Die *(The Queen of Sheba)*. Opera in 4 acts by Goldmark. Libretto by Salomon Hermann Mosenthal. First performed Vienna, 10 Mar 1875.

Assad (ten.), favourite courtier of King Solomon (bar.), is struck by the beauty of the Queen of Sheba (mezzo-sop.), and rejects his beloved Sulamith (sop.). His obsession leads to his downfall and his banishment to die in the desert.

Königskinder *(Royal Children)*. Opera in 3 acts by Humperdinck. Libretto by Ernst Rosmer (pseudonym of Elsa Bernstein). First performed New York, 28 Dec 1910.

The Goose-girl (sop.), who lives in the house of a witch (contr.), falls in love with the King's son (ten.) when he comes to the forest disguised as a beggar. They marry, but die after eating the witch's poisoned bread.

Kónya, Sándor, b. Sarkad, 23 Sept 1923. Hungarian tenor. He studied in Budapest, made his début in Bielefeld in 1951 as Turiddu, and became known as a leading Wagner tenor in the 1950s in Berlin and Bayreuth. His most successful role, *Lohengrin*, was the one in which he appeared for the first time at Bayreuth in 1958, at the Met in 1961 and at Covent Garden in 1963. At the Met he has also appeared with success in a number of other roles, among them Parsifal, Max in *Der Freischütz* and Calaf in *Turandot*.

Korjus, Miliza, b. Warsaw, 18 Aug 1912; d. Los Angeles, 18 Aug 1980. Polish, later American, soprano. She studied in Moscow, was engaged by the Berlin State Opera in 1934, making her début as Gilda in *Rigoletto*. She sang leading coloratura roles such as Zerbinetta in *Ariadne auf Naxos* and the Queen of Night in *Die Zauberflöte*, as well as Delibes's Lakmé, Donizetti's Lucia, Violetta in *La Traviata* and Rosina in *Il Barbiere di Siviglia*. She made guest appearances throughout Europe, and in 1938 went to Hollywood to appear in the film, *The Great Waltz*. She remained in America and sang in concerts and recitals until 1946, though she never sang again in opera. Her fame is disproportionate to the extent of her operatic career, not only because of *The Great Waltz* but also as a result of a series of superb gramophone records of arias and songs which she made during her time at the Berlin Staatsoper.

Korngold, Erich Wolfgang, b. Brno, 29 May 1897; d. Hollywood, 29 Nov 1957. Austrian composer. Son of the eminent Viennese music critic Julius Korngold, he was a child prodigy who, at the age of ten, was described as a genius by Mahler. When he was eleven, his ballet *Der Schneemann* was a huge success at the Vienna Opera. He was an extremely prolific composer in most forms of music, and his operas impressed his older contemporaries Strauss and Puccini, to whose styles Korngold's own was not dissimilar. *Der Ring des Polykrates* and *Violanta*, two 1-act works, were first performed together in 1916. His operatic masterpiece, *Die tote Stadt*, composed when Korngold was twenty, had a dual première in Hamburg and Cologne in 1920, and soon afterwards reached Vienna, New York, Prague, Zurich, Berlin, Budapest and Amsterdam. A Viennese newspaper's opinion poll in 1928 returned Korngold and Schoenberg as the two greatest living composers. *Das Wunder der Heliane* was first produced in Hamburg in 1927, and *Die Kathrin* in Stockholm in 1939. Korngold went to Hollywood in 1934 and became a leading composer of film scores. His lush, late-romantic style, after some years in which it was out of fashion, is now back in favour.

Köth, Erika, b. Darmstadt, 15 Sept 1927. German soprano. She studied in Darmstadt, supporting herself by singing with a jazz orchestra, and made her opera début at Kaiserslautern in 1948 as Philine in *Mignon*. She joined the Munich company in 1953, and has remained a member of the company, excelling in high coloratura roles such as Zerbinetta, and in such Mozart roles as the Queen of Night and Constanze. She first appeared in England with the Munich company at Covent Garden in 1953 as the Italian Soprano in *Capriccio* and Fiakermilli in *Arabella*. She was especially successful in the title-role of *Lucia di Lammermoor* in Munich when the opera was revived for her in 1957, and as Susanna in *Le Nozze di Figaro* in Munich and elsewhere in Germany.

Alfredo Kraus as Gennaro with Joan Sutherland as Lucrezia in Donizetti's *Lucrezia Borgia* at Covent Garden in 1980. Kraus is admired in the operas of both the Italian and French repertories.

Kraus, Alfredo, b. Las Palmas, 24 Nov 1927. Austrian-Spanish tenor. He studied in Barcelona and Milan, and made his début in Turin in 1956 as Alfredo in *La Traviata*, the role in which he was first heard in London in 1957. He soon established himself as a stylish lyric tenor, especially in bel canto roles such as Edgardo in *Lucia di Lammermoor*, and Almaviva in *Il Barbiere di Siviglia*, and also as Massenet's Des Grieux and Werther. He made his Met début in 1966 as the Duke in *Rigoletto*, and was still in fine voice when he sang Edgardo opposite the Lucia of Joan Sutherland at the Met in the autumn of 1982.

Kraus, Otakar, b. Prague, 10 Dec 1909; d. London, 28 July 1980. Czech, later British, baritone. He studied in Prague and Milan, and made his début in Brno in 1935 as Amonasro. From 1936-9, when the advent of Hitler forced him to leave the country, he was a member of the Bratislava company. His first British appearance was in *Sorochintky Fair* in London in 1942, alternating as Tcheverick and the Old Crony. In 1943 he joined the touring Carl Rosa Company, and in 1946 created Tarquinius in Britten's *Rape of Lucretia* with the English Opera Group. He was a member of The Royal Opera company at Covent Garden from 1951-73 when he retired, his more than forty roles including Scarpia, Iago, Pizarro, Alberich and Klingsor. He also created the role of Nick Shadow in Stravinsky's *The Rake's Progress* at Venice in 1951. In his later years he became a highly respected teacher.

Krause, Tom, b. Helsinki, 5 July 1934. Finnish baritone. He studied in Vienna, and made his début in Berlin in 1958 as Escamillo. For many years his career was based in Hamburg where he sang the leading Wagner and Verdi baritone roles. He first appeared in England as the Count in *Capriccio* at Glyndebourne in 1963, and made his Met début in 1971 as Malatesta in *Don Pasquale*. He has also appeared frequently at Glyndebourne. He has a firm and well-schooled, though not highly individual voice, and a sound technique.

Krauss, Clemens, b. Vienna, 31 Mar 1893; d. Mexico City, 16 May 1954. Austrian conductor. He studied in Vienna, and made his début in Brno in 1913 with Lortzing's *Zar und Zimmermann*. He directed the Frankfurt Opera from 1924-9, the Vienna State Opera from 1929-35, and after two years in Berlin became general music director in Munich in 1937. A close friend of Richard Strauss, he conducted the premières of *Arabella* (1933), *Friedenstag* (1938), *Capriccio* (1942, for which he wrote the libretto) and *Die Liebe der Danae* (1952). He first appeared at Covent Garden in 1934, and returned with the Vienna Staatsoper company in 1947. He was married to the soprano Viorica Ursuleac.

Křenek, Ernst, b. Vienna, 23 Aug 1900. Austrian, later American, composer. He studied in Vienna and Berlin, and his first opera, the 1-act *Zwingberg*, was staged in Berlin in 1924. He has composed more than twenty operas, though none which has equalled the success or fame of *Jonny spielt auf*, a jazz-opera performed in Leipzig in 1927, which scandalized some and delighted others. It was translated into eighteen languages and performed in more than one hundred cities. Three 1-act operas, one (*Der Diktator*) a satire on Mussolini, were staged in Wiesbaden in 1928. Later operas include *Leben des Orest* (1930), *Karl V* (1938) and *Pallas Athene Weint* (1955). More recent works, written in advanced serial techniques, have been greeted with wary respect rather than with the excitement with which *Jonny spielt auf* burst upon the world.

Kreutzer, Conradin, b. Messkirch, Baden, 22 Nov 1780; d. Riga, 14 Dec 1849. German composer. He composed more than fifty works for the stage, serious as well as comic operas and Singspiels. His earliest successful

opera was *Konradin von Schwaben*, staged in Stuttgart in 1912, but he is remembered mainly for *Das Nachtlager von Granada*, a romantic opera first performed in Vienna in 1834 which was enormously successful in German theatres throughout the 19th c. and which is still occasionally revived in the German-speaking countries.

Krips, Josef, b. Vienna, 8 Apr 1902; d. Geneva, 13 Oct 1974. Austrian conductor. He studied in Vienna, made his début there at the Volksoper in 1921, and then worked in German theatres until joining the conducting staff of the Vienna Staatsoper in 1933. He was dismissed in 1938 when the Germans occupied Austria, and he spent the war years in hiding. He conducted the first post-war opera performance in Vienna in 1945, and was instrumental in bringing the company back to its former high standards. He conducted the Vienna company during its Covent Garden season of 1947, and subsequently conducted The Royal Opera at Covent Garden. He also conducted at the Met between 1966-70. He was a superb interpreter of Mozart and Richard Strauss, and also gave fine performances of *Fidelio* and *Die Meistersinger*.

Krombholc, Jaroslav, b. Prague, 30 Jan 1918. Czech conductor. He studied in Prague, and has conducted there since 1940, becoming chief conductor at the National Theatre in 1963. He has also conducted abroad, and first appeared at Covent Garden in 1959 with *Boris Godunov*. He conducted an excellent *Don Giovanni* for English National Opera in 1978. He is best known for his performances of operas by Smetana, Dvořák and Janáček.

Kubelik, Rafael, b. Bychory, 29 June 1914. Czech conductor and composer. The son of the violinist Jan Kubelik, he studied violin as well as composition and conducting in Prague. He conducted opera in Brno from 1939-41, became music director at Covent Garden in 1955, making his début with *Otello*, and later conducting successful productions of *Jenůfa* and *Les Troyens*. He resigned from Covent Garden in 1958. He was music director of the Met briefly in 1973-4. He conducted the première of his own opera, *Cornelia Faroli*, in Augsburg in 1966.

175

Kubiak, Teresa, b. Lodz, 26 Dec 1937. Polish soprano. She studied in Lodz, and made her début there in 1965 in the title-role of Moniuszko's *Halka*. In 1971 she sang Lisa in *Queen of Spades* at Glyndebourne, and the following year she was heard at Covent Garden for the first time, as Butterfly. She made her Met début in 1972 as Lisa. She is an impressive Tosca and Aida, a fine lyric-dramatic soprano.

Kullman, Charles, b. New Haven, Conn. 13 Jan 1903; d. Bloomington, Ind., 8 Feb 1983. American tenor. He studied in New York, and made his début with the American Opera Company on tour in 1929 as Pinkerton. In 1931 he made his first European appearance, again as Pinkerton, in Berlin. Covent Garden heard him for the first time as Babinsky in Weinberger's *Schwanda, the Bagpiper*, and he was greatly admired at Salzburg in the 1930s as Mozart's Ferrando *(Così Fan Tutte)* and Belmonte *(Die Entführung aus dem Serail)* and also as Walther in *Die Meistersinger*. He first appeared at the Met in 1935 as Faust, and returned every season until his retirement in 1960. He was a versatile artist with an extremely pleasant lyric tenor voice. In 1947, he appeared in a supporting role in *Song of Scheherazade*, a Hollywood film about Rimsky-Korsakov.

Kundry (sop.). The enchantress who tries to seduce Parsifal, in Wagner's opera of that title.

Kunz, Erich, b. Vienna, 20 May 1909. Austrian bass-baritone. He studied in Vienna, and made his début in Troppau in 1933 as Osmin. He sang in the chorus at Glyndebourne in 1936, and on one occasion during the season undertook at short notice the speaking role of Selim in *Die Entführung aus dem Serail*. (His official Glyndebourne début came in 1950, when he sang Guglielmo in *Così Fan Tutte*.) He joined the Vienna Staatsoper in 1940, and in 1983 was still singing in Vienna. He was the ideal Papageno, Figaro (in *Le Nozze di Figaro*), Guglielmo and Leporello of his time, and a famous Beckmesser. In Vienna, he also undertook a number of roles in Italian operas. He first appeared in London in his Mozart roles with the Vienna company in 1947, and made his Met début in 1953.

Kurwenal (bar.) Tristan's retainer in Wagner's *Tristan und Isolde*.

Kurz, Selma, b. Bielitz, 15 Nov 1874; d. Vienna, 10 May 1933. Austrian soprano. She studied in Vienna and Paris, and made her début in Hamburg in 1895 as Mignon. She was engaged for Vienna by Mahler, and the rest of her career was based there. She became a firm Viennese favourite in roles requiring coloratura agility, such as Lucia, but was also greatly admired as Gilda, Violetta, and as Oscar in *Un Ballo in Maschera*. Her great success at Covent Garden in the years between 1904-7 aroused the jealousy of Melba, and she did not reappear there until 1924, when she sang Mimi and Violetta. In 1916 in Vienna she created the role of Zerbinetta in the revised *Ariadne auf Naxos*. She had a beautiful voice with a remarkable trill.

Kusche, Benno, b. Freiburg, 30 Jan 1916. German bass-baritone. He studied in Karlsruhe, and made his début in Coblenz in 1938 as Melitone in *La Forza del Destino*. He sang at Augsburg throughout World War II, and joined the Munich company in 1946. A first-rate character actor with a fine voice, he excelled as Mozart's Figaro, La Roche in *Capriccio*, and as Beckmesser, the role of his Covent Garden début in 1952.

L

Lakmé. Opera in 3 acts by Delibes. Libretto by Edmond Gondinet and Philippe Gille, based on Pierre Loti's novel, *Le Mariage de Loti* (1880). First performed Paris, 14 Apr 1883.

In 19th-c. India, Lakmé (sop), daughter of the Brahmin priest Nilakantha (bass), falls in love with Gérald (ten), a young British officer. Nilakantha stabs Gérald, but Lakmé carries him to safety. Realizing, however, that she will eventually lose him, she takes poison and dies.

Lalo, Édouard, b. Lille, 27 Jan 1823; d. Paris, 22 Apr 1892. French composer. He studied in Lille and Paris, originally intending to be a violinist. His first opera, *Fiesque,* based on a play by Schiller, won only third prize in a government-sponsored competition in 1866, and was never performed. His second, *Le Roi d'Ys,* was completed in 1878 but had to wait until 1888 to be staged, when it proved popular with audiences. He began a third opera, *La Jacquerie,* but had completed only one act when he died. The opera was finished by Arthur Coquard and produced in Monte Carlo in 1895.

Lampugnani, Giovanni Battista, b. Milan, 1706; d. Milan, ?1786. Italian composer. His first operas were produced in Milan. Later works were staged in London as well as Milan. He composed twenty-nine operas, most of them considered in his day to be worthy examples of *opera seria. Alfonso* (1744), first staged in London, and *L'Amor Contadino* (1760), his only surviving comic opera, first staged in Venice, are among his more important operas. His works have been rarely performed in modern times.

Landgraf (bass). Hermann, Landgrave of Thuringia and uncle of Elisabeth, in Wagner's *Tannhäuser.*

Langdon, Michael, b. Wolverhampton, 12 Nov 1920. British bass. He studied in Vienna, Geneva and London, and joined the Covent Garden chorus in 1948, becoming a principal singer in 1951. He sang a large number of roles with the company until his retirement in 1977, and scored a particular success as Baron Ochs in *Der Rosenkavalier,* a role he also sang at the Met, the Paris Opéra and the Vienna Staatsoper. He had an engaging personality and a serviceable voice. In 1978 he became Director of the National Opera Studio in London.

Larsén-Todsen, Nanny, b. Hagby, 2 Aug 1884; d. Stockholm, 26 May 1982. Swedish soprano. She made her début in Stockholm in 1906 as Agathe in *Der Freischütz,* and was a leading soprano there until 1933. She became a renowned Wagner dramatic soprano, and made guest appearances at the Met between 1924-7 and, in 1927, at Covent Garden. From 1927-30 she also sang at Bayreuth. Brünnhilde, Kundry and Isolde were among her most successful roles.

László, Magda, b. Marosvásárhely, ?1919. Hungarian soprano. She studied in Budapest and made her début with the Budapest Opera in 1943. In 1946 she went to Italy, where she created the role of the Mother in Dallapiccola's *Il Prigioniero* on Italian Radio in 1949 and on stage in Florence in 1950. She made her English début at Glyndebourne in 1953 in the title-role of Gluck's *Alceste,* and 1954 created the role of Cressida in Walton's *Troilus and Cressida* at Covent Garden.

Laubenthal, Rudolf, b. Düsseldorf, 10 Mar 1886; d. Pöckling, nr Munich, 2 Oct 1971. German tenor. He studied in Berlin, and made his début there in 1913. He sang in opera in Berlin and Munich until 1923 when he was engaged to sing Walther in *Die Meistersinger* at the Met. He remained at the Met until 1933 and also made guest appearances at Covent Garden where he was admired as Tristan and as the *Götterdämmerung* Siegfried. The chief rival of Lauritz Melchior in the Wagner heroic roles in the 1920-30s, he was an intelligent actor and a forceful personality. He retired in 1937.

Laura (mezzo-sop.). Wife of Alvise, and lover of Enzo, in Ponchielli's *La Gioconda.*

Lauretta (sop.). Daughter of the eponymous hero of Puccini's *Gianni Schicchi.*

Lauri-Volpi, Giacomo, b. Rome, 11 Dec 1892; d. Valencia, 17 Mar 1979. Italian tenor. He studied in Rome and made his début in Viterbo in 1919 as Arturo in *I Puritani.* Engaged by Toscanini to sing the Duke of Mantua in *Rigoletto* at La Scala in 1922, he continued to appear regularly at La Scala until the 1940s. His début role at the Met in 1923 was also the Duke of Mantua, and he appeared frequently at the Met until 1934, taking part in the first American performances of *Turandot* in 1926. He continued to sing, mainly in Italy, until 1959, and in 1972, at the age of eighty, participated in a gala concert at the Teatro Liceo, Barcelona, singing 'Nessun dorma' from *Turandot.* He published his memoirs and in 1955, *Voci parallele.*

Lawrence, Marjorie, b. Dean's Marsh, nr Melbourne, 17 Feb 1909; d. Little Rock, Ark., 10 Jan 1979. Australian soprano. She studied in Melbourne and Paris, and made her début in Monte Carlo in 1932 as Elisabeth in *Tannhäuser.* She was then

She was then engaged by the Paris Opéra where her first role, in 1933, was Ortrud in *Lohengrin*. She was a leading dramatic soprano in Paris for four seasons, singing the important Wagner roles, as well as Salome, Aida, and Valentine in *Les Huguenots*. In 1935 she made her Met début as the *Götterdämmerung* Brünnhilde, and remained with the company until 1941, mainly in the Wagner roles which she shared with Kirsten Flagstad. In 1941 in Mexico City she was suddenly stricken with poliomyelitis during a performance of *Die Walküre,* but was eventually able to continue her career, singing in concerts from a wheelchair. She occasionally appeared in specially staged performances of opera, as Isolde or Venus, and sang a superb Amneris in *Aida* in Melbourne in 1946. She retired in 1952 and taught in the US. She had a dramatic soprano voice of great beauty and power.

Lear, Evelyn, b. Brooklyn, N.Y., 8 Jan 1928. American soprano. She studied in New York and Berlin, and made her début in Berlin in 1959 as the Composer in *Ariadne auf Naxos*. In 1962, in Vienna, she sang *Lulu* in Berg's opera in its local première, and subsequently sang with a number of companies. She appeared at Covent Garden in 1956 as Donna Elvira, and was first heard at the Met when she created the role of Lavinia in Martin David Levy's *Mourning Becomes Electra* at its 1967 première. She is married to the baritone Thomas Stewart. In 1982 in Miani, she and her husband created the roles of Margo and Emil in a new opera, *Minutes Till Midnight,* by Robert Ward.

Lecocq, Charles, b. Paris, 3 June 1832; d. Paris, 24 Oct 1918. French composer. He studied at the Paris Conservatoire, and shared with Bizet the prize offered by Offenbach for a setting of the operetta libretto, *Docteur Miracle* (1857). He composed more than fifty operettas, most of which were first performed in Paris. His earliest success was with *Fleur-de-thé* (1868), which was set in Japan, but he is best remembered for *La Fille de Madame Angot* (1872) and *Giroflé-Girofla* (1874). His last important operetta was *La Belle au Bois Dormant* (1900). His only serious opera, *Plutus,* was a failure when it was staged in 1886. He had a great gift for melody, and for theatrical effect.

Franz Lehár

Legend of the Invisible City of Kitezh, The (Russian title, *Skazaniye o Nevidimom Grade Kitezhe.*) Opera in 4 acts by Rimsky-Korsakov. Libretto by Vladimir Ivanovich Belsky. First performed St Petersburg, 20 Feb 1907.

Fevroniya (sop.), wife of Prince Vsevolod (ten.) is helped to escape from her Tartar captors by the drunken Grishka (ten.), and guided back to Kitezh by the spirit of Vsevolod.

Lehár, Franz, b. Komárom, Hungary, 30 Apr 1870; d. Bad Ischl, 24 Oct 1948. Austrian composer. The leading composer of Viennese operetta in the 20th c., he studied in Prague and then became a Bandmaster in the Austrian army. His first work for the stage was an opera, *Kukuschka* (1896), which was performed in Leipzig. He settled in Vienna when he left military service in 1902, and began to conduct at Viennese theatres and to compose operettas. His first success was with *Wiener Frauen* (1902), but it was with *Die lustige Witwe (The Merry Widow)* (1905) that his name suddenly became known throughout the world. His masterpiece, *The Merry Widow,* was phenomenally successful wherever it was staged. Lehár continued to compose operettas, among them *Der Graf von Luxemburg* (1909), *Frasquita* (1922), *Paganini (1925), Der Zarewitsch* (1927), *Friederike* (1928), and *Das Land des Lächelns* (1929: a reworking of an earlier work, *Die Gelbe Jacke).* After *Frasquita,* his leading tenor roles were written for his friend the opera tenor, Richard Tauber. Lehár's last operetta, *Giuditta,* was produced at the Vienna State Opera, with Jarmila Novotna and Richard Tauber in the leading roles, in 1934. At his best, as in most of *Die lustige Witwe,* and in the second act finale of *The Land of Smiles (Das Land des Lächelns)* Lehár ranks with Johann Strauss II and, when he breaks down the barrier between opera and operetta in *Das Land des Lächelns,* with his operatic contemporaries, Richard Strauss and Puccini.

Lehmann, Lilli, b. Würzburg, 24 Nov 1848; d. Berlin, 17 May 1929. German soprano. Taught singing by her mother, she made her début as First Boy in *Die*

Zauberflöte in Prague in 1865. From 1870–85 she sang lyric soprano roles in Berlin, and in 1876 sang in the première of Wagner's *Ring* at Bayreuth, as Woglinde, Helmwige and the Woodbird. She later undertook dramatic soprano roles, and was heard at Covent Garden in 1884 as Isolde. Her Met début the following year was as Carmen. She continued to sing leading roles in Europe until she was past the age of sixty, after which she sang only in concerts, and taught. She was a prodigious vocalist and a superb artist, with an enormous repertoire. She published her memoirs in 1913, and an important book on singing, *Meine Gesangskunst,* in 1902 (The English edition was called *How to Sing.*)

Lehmann, Lotte, b. Perleberg, 27 Feb 1888; d. Santa Barbara, Calif., 26 Aug 1976. German, later American, soprano. She studied in Berlin, and made her début in Hamburg in 1910 as Third Boy in *Die Zauberflöte*. After her success as Elsa in *Lohengrin,* she was engaged by the Vienna Opera, where her career was to be based until the Nazi invasion caused her to emigrate to the United States. She became a Viennese favourite in a wide variety of roles, and was admired greatly by Puccini, in several of whose operas she sang in Vienna, and by Richard Strauss, who wrote roles with her in mind. For Strauss she created the Composer in *Ariadne auf Naxos,* the Dyer's Wife in *Die Frau ohne Schatten* and Christine in *Intermezzo*. In *Der Rosenkavalier* she became the most beloved Marschallin of her generation, having earlier sung Sophie and Octavian in the same opera. Though she was known abroad principally for her Wagner and Strauss roles, she also sang the Italian and French repertory in Vienna. She was a renowned Leonore in *Fidelio* in Vienna and Salzburg. During the years of World War II she sang at the Met, retiring from opera in 1945, and from concerts in 1951. She then became a noted teacher. The first of her many books on singing, *More Than Singing,* was published in 1945, and the last, *Eighteen Song Cycles,* in 1971. She had a voice of great warmth and beauty, and was considered to be by far the most persuasive operatic actress of her generation.

Leider, Frida, b. Berlin, 18 Apr 1888; d. Berlin, 4 June 1975. German sporano. She studied in Berlin, and made her début in Halle in 1915 as Venus in *Tannhäuser*. From 1923–40 she was leading dramatic soprano at the Berlin Staatsoper, her rich and beautiful voice and the dramatic intensity of her characterizations making her one of the most admired Wagner sopranos of her time, especially as Brünnhilde, Kundry and Isolde. She also sang Verdi and Mozart roles in Berlin. Between 1924–38 she sang often at Covent Garden, her roles including Isolde, Brünnhilde, Senta, Donna Anna, and Leonora in *Il Trovatore.*. Her Met appearances were confined to 1933 and 1934 in Wagner roles. During World War II she sang in Berlin. Her memoirs, *Das War Mein Teil,* appeared in 1959 and, in English translation, as *Playing My Part,* in 1966.

Leinsdorf, Erich, b. Vienna, 4 Feb 1912. Austrian conductor. He studied in Vienna, and assisted Bruno Walter and Arturo Toscanini in the preparation of operas at Salzburg from 1934–7. He was then engaged by the Met, on the recommendation of Lotte Lehmann, and made his début there conducting *Die Walküre* in 1938. From 1939–43 he was chief conductor of the German repertoire at the Met. He has continued to appear occasionally at the Met, and with San Francisco Opera. In recent years he has been more active in concerts than in opera, but in both fields he continues the Viennese tradition which he inherits from Mahler through Bruno Walter. In 1983 he conducted *Arabella* at the Met.

Leitmotiv. German word, meaning 'leading motive'. The term was first used by a writer on Weber to describe the composer's use of a short musical phrase or figure to represent a particular character or idea. It has come to be used specifically to describe Wagner's more developed use of musical ideas or fragments of melody for this purpose, especially in *Der Ring des Nibelungen* and *Tristan und Isolde,* Wagner in writing of this aid to musical characterization, referred to it as a *Grundthema* (basic theme) or *Hauptmotiv* (chief motive).

Leitner, Ferdinand, b. Berlin, 4 Mar 1912. German conductor. He studied in Berlin, and began his career as assistant to Fritz Busch at Glyndebourne in 1934. He made his début as a conductor in Berlin in 1943, conducted at the Hamburg Staatsoper in 1945, and in Munich in 1946-7. He was music director of the Stuttgart Opera from 1947-69, and gave there the first performances of Orff's *Oedipus der Tyrann* (1959) and *Prometheus* (1968). He has been principal conductor of the Zurich Opera since 1969, and has also conducted a number of German operas at the Teatro Colón, Buenos Aires. He is an excellent interpreter of 19th-c. German opera as well as of contemporary works.

Lemnitz, Tiana, b. Metz, 26 Oct 1897. German soprano. She studied in Metz and Frankfurt, and made her début in 1920 in Heilbronn in Lortzing's *Undine.* She became a leading lyric soprano in Berlin, where she sang from 1934-57, her sweet voice being especially suited to such roles as Pamina in *Die Zauberflöte,* Strauss's Arabella, Tatiana in *Eugene Onegin,* and Verdi's Desdemona. She was considered in the 1930s to be one of the finest exponents of the role of Octavian in *Der Rosenkavalier,* and later assumed the role of the Marschallin in the same opera. At Covent Garden she sang Eva in *Die Meistersinger* in 1936, and Octavian to Lotte Lehmann's Marschallin in 1938, but her career was mainly confined to Germany.

Lensky (ten.). Friend of Onegin and fiancé of Olga in Tchaikovsky's *Eugene Onegin,* he is killed by Onegin in a duel.

Leoncavallo, Ruggero, b. Naples, 8 Mar 1857; d. Montecatini, 9 Aug 1919. Italian composer. He studied in Naples, and completed his first opera, *Chatterton,* while still in his teens, though it was not performed until several years later. His first success, and easily his greatest, was with *Pagliacci,* which was staged in Milan in 1892, bringing him immediate fame. *I Medici,* the first part of a projected trilogy, was a failure the following year, and he did not compose the remaining two parts. *La Bohème* (1897) suffered by comparison with Puccini's opera based on the same novel by Murger, and staged only some months earlier, and with the exception of *Zazà* (1900), Leoncavallo produced nothing further of interest. *Der Roland von Berlin,* commissioned by Wilhelm II and produced in Berlin in 1904, was an expensive failure. Even before *Zingari,* staged in London in 1912, Leonca-

vallo had turned his attention to the composition of operetta, for which he had little gift. His operettas include *Are You There?,* produced in London in 1913, and *A Chi la Giarrettiera? (Whose is the Garter?),* performed in Rome in 1919. His fame rests solely but securely upon *Pagliacci,* a masterpiece of Italian *verismo.*

Leonora. This is a popular name with Italian composers and librettists. In Donizetti's *La Favorite,* the favourite of the title is a (mezzo-sop.) Leonora. There are three soprano heroines named Leonora in operas by Verdi: Oberto's daughter in *Oberto;* Donna Leonora di Vargas in *La Forza del Destino;* and, most famous of all, the heroine of *Il Trovatore.*

Leonore (sop.). The heroine of Beethoven's *Fidelio* who disguises herself as a youth in order to rescue her husband from his enemy Pizarro.

Leporello (bass). Servant to Giovanni, in Mozart's *Don Giovanni.*

Leppard, Raymond, b. London, 11 Aug 1927. English conductor. He studied in Cambridge, was a coach at Glyndebourne from 1954-6, and conducted Handel's

Raymond Leppard

Samson at Covent Garden in 1958. At Glyndebourne he conducted his performing editions of *L'Incoronazione di Poppea* (1962), *Ormindo* (1967), *Calisto* (1969) and *Il Ritorno d'Ulisse in Patria* (1972). A specialist in 17th- and 18th-c. opera, he also conducted the première of Nicholas Maw's *The Rising of the Moon* at Glyndebourne in 1970.

Le Sueur, Jean-François, b. Drucat-Plessiel, nr Abbeville, 15 Feb 1760; d. Paris, 6 Oct 1837. French composer. One of the most prominent French composers between the time of the Revolution in 1789 and the restoration of the monarchy in 1814, he wrote eight operas, many of which anticipate 19th-c. grand opera. His most successful works were *Paul et Virginie* (1794), *Télémaque* (1796) and *Ossian, ou Les Bardes* (1804).

Lescaut (bar.). Cousin of the heroine in Massenet's *Manon,* he has become her brother in Puccini's *Manon Lescaut.*

Levine, James, b. Cincinnati, 23 June 1943. American conductor. He made his début as a pianist with the Cincinnati Symphony Orchestra at the age of ten, and later studied in New York, becoming an assistant conductor to George Szell with the Cleveland Orchestra in 1964. He made his Met début in 1971 conducting *Tosca,* was appointed principal conductor in 1973, and since 1975 has been music director of the Met. It was with Welsh National Opera that he made his British début in 1970 with *Aida.* He has conducted regularly at the Salzburg Festival since 1976, and is widely regarded as one of the finest opera conductors of the day. A sensitive interpreter of Mozart and a dramatic exponent of Verdi, he is an extremely versatile musician.

Levy, Marvin David, b. Passaic, N.J., 2 Aug 1932. American composer. He studied in New York, and had his first successes with chamber music works in the mid-1950s. His operas include *Sotoba Komachi,* based on a Japanese Noh play and first performed in New York in 1957, *The Tower* (Santa Fe, 1957), and *Mourning Becomes Electra,* commissioned by the Met, and first performed during the company's initial season at the new opera house in Lincoln Center in 1967.

Lewis, Richard, b. Manchester, 10 May 1914. English tenor. He studied in Manchester and London, and made his first opera appearances in 1947 in operas by Britten, as Male Chorus in *The Rape of Lucretia* at Glyndebourne, and as Peter Grimes at Covent Garden. He was heard at Glyndebourne in a number of Mozart roles between 1950-74, and also as Tom Rakewell in *The Rake's Progress,* Bacchus in *Ariadne auf Naxos,* Florestan in *Fidelio,* and several other roles. He has also sung a wide variety of roles with San Francisco Opera since 1953. His lyric tenor voice is of pleasant quality, and he is a fine musician. He was a superb Captain Vere at Covent Garden.

libretto. Literally 'little book', or booklet, the libretto is the verbal text of an opera, written for the composer to set to music. Although some libretti are original works, the majority are adaptations of existing works: novels, poems or, more usually, plays. Composers have often preferred to continue to collaborate with the same librettist. Famous partnerships of this kind have included Mozart and Da Ponte; Verdi and first Cammarano, then Piave, and finally Boito; Strauss and Hofmannsthal; Puccini and the team of Giacosa and Illica. Wagner preferred to write his own libretti.

Libuše. Opera in 3 acts by Smetana. Libretto translated from the German of Josef Wenzig by Ervin Špindler. First performed Prague, 11 June 1881.

A national Czech opera which deals with the mythical Libuše (sop.), Queen of Bohemia, and with the love of two brothers, Chrudoš (bass) and Šťáhlav (ten.) for the same woman. Unable to effect a reconciliation between the brothers, Libuše defers to her new consort, Přemysl.

Liebe der Danae, Die *(The Love of Danae).* Opera in 3 acts by Richard Strauss. Libretto by Josef Gregor. First performed Salzburg, 14 Aug 1952. (It had been given a public dress rehearsal in Salzburg, on 16 Aug 1944, but the closure of all theatres by Goebbels prevented the première from taking place.)

In order to possess Danae (sop.), the god Jupiter (bar.) assumes the form of King Midas (ten.). However, finally convinced of Danae's devotion to the real Midas, Jupiter gives the couple his blessing.

Christl Goltz as Penelope in the première of Liebermann's *Penelope* at the Salzburg Festival in 1954. Her suitors are (left to right) Peter Klein, Carl Doench and Walter Berry.

Liebermann, Rolf, b. Zurich, 14 Sept 1910. Swiss composer and administrator. His operas include *Leonore 40/45,* which created much interest when it was first produced in Basle in 1952; *Penelope* (1954); and *The School for Wives* (1955). He was the administrative director of the Hamburg Opera from 1959-73, and occupied a similar position with the Paris Opéra from 1973-80 during which time he vastly improved the standard of performance at the Opéra.

Liebesverbot, Das *(The Ban on Love).* Opera in 2 acts by Wagner. Libretto by the composer, based on Shakespeare's *Measure for Measure.* First performed, Magdeburg, 29 Mar 1836.

The plot is only loosely based on Shakespeare, with the action no longer in Vienna but in Sicily. Friedrich (bass), Governor of Sicily, decrees that fornication will be punished by death. Claudio (ten.), awaiting execution for this offence, is interceded for by his sister Isabella (sop.), a novice. Friedrich agrees to reprieve Claudio if Isabella will submit to his advances. By sending Friedrich's estranged wife Mariana (sop.) to take her place at the rendezvous, Isabella outwits the Governor, who is forced to rescind his decree.

Ligendza, Catarina, b. Stockholm, 18 Oct 1937. Swedish soprano. The daughter of singers at the Stockholm opera, she studied

183

in Vienna, and made her début in Linz in 1965 as the Countess in *Le Nozze di Figaro*. She has since specialized in the Wagner dramatic roles, making her Bayreuth début in 1971 as Brünnhilde and appearing at Covent Garden the following year as Senta. She was first heard at the Met in 1971 as Leonore in *Fidelio*. Her Isolde in Vienna in 1973 was highly praised for the beauty of her voice as well as for her convincing characterization.

Ligeti, György, b. Discöszentmárton, Transylvania, 28 May 1923. Austrian composer of Hungarian birth. An *avant-garde* composer, in many of whose works distinct pitch and rhythm play no part, he composed an opera or piece of music theatre, *Le Grand Macabre,* an absurdist work which was first performed in Stockholm in 1978, and has subsequently been seen in other countries. In 1982 it was staged in London by English National Opera.

Lima, Luis, b. Cordoba, 12 Sept 1948. Argentinian tenor. He studied in Buenos Aires and Madrid, and made his début in Lisbon in 1974 as Turiddu in *Cavalleria Rusticana*. The possessor of a lyric tenor voice of fine quality, and a handsome stage presence, he has sung a wide repertoire from Donizetti to Puccini in Europe and the Americas. His Edgardo in *Lucia di Lammermoor* at La Scala in 1977 was highly regarded, as it was in Vienna in 1981. He made his Met début in 1978 as Alfredo.

Limpt, Adriaan van, b. Eindhoven, 30 June 1940. Dutch tenor. He studied in Amsterdam, and sang small roles with the Netherlands Opera until 1977, when he won a television competition and had a great success as Pinkerton in *Madama Butterfly* and Riccardo in *Un Ballo in Maschera* with Netherlands Opera. In 1978 in Amsterdam he sang Pollione in *Norma* opposite Joan Sutherland. He sang Riccardo in the 1982 Verdi Festival in San Diego, Calif., giving a performance of immaculate style, and revealing himself as a fine Verdi tenor.

Lind, Jenny, b. Stockholm, 6 Oct 1820; d. Malvern, England, 2 Nov 1887. Swedish soprano. She studied in Stockholm, and made her début there in 1838 as Agathe in *Der Freischütz*. She soon became one of the leading European prima donnas, her roles including Bellini's Norma, Donizetti's Lucia, and Amalia in Verdi's *I Masnadieri,* the role she sang at the opera's première in London in 1847. She was only twenty-eight when she retired from opera, though she continued to give concerts until she was past sixty. It was as a concert singer that she entered upon her years of greatest fame, becoming known internationally as 'the Swedish nightingale'.

Linda di Chamounix. Opera in 3 acts by Donizetti. Libretto by Gaetano Rossi, based on the play, *La Grâce de Dieu* by Adolphe Philippe d'Ennery and Gustave Lemoine. First performed Vienna, 19 May 1842.

To escape the unwelcome attentions of the Marchese (bass), Linda (sop.), who is in love with Carlo (ten.), flees to Paris where she lives in an apartment belonging to Carlo. Her father (bar.) finds her and refuses to believe that she is not living an immoral life. Linda loses her reason, but regains it when she returns to Chamounix and is reunited with Carlo.

Lindholm, Berit, b. Stockholm, 18 Oct 1934. Swedish soprano. She studied in Stockholm, and made her début there in 1963 as the Countess in *Le Nozze di Figaro*. She subsequently became known as a Wagner soprano, making her Bayreuth début in 1967 as Venus. She first appeared at Covent Garden as Chrysothemis in *Elektra* in 1966, and later was acclaimed for her Brünnhilde, the role of her San Francisco début in 1972. She was still a forceful Brünnhilde in the Covent Garden *Ring* in 1982.

Lindoro (ten.). The name occurs twice in operas by Rossini. Lindoro is Isabella's long-lost fiancé in *L'Italiana in Algeri*. It is also the name which Count Almaviva assumes throughout most of the action of *Il Barbiere di Siviglia*.

Lionel (ten.). The young farmer who falls in love with the eponymous heroine of *Martha,* who is above his social class.

Lisa (sop.). Grand-daughter of the old Countess in Tchaikovsky's *Queen of Spades*. She is in love with Hermann.

Litvinne, Félia, b. St Petersburg, 11 Oct 1860; d. Paris, 12 Oct 1936. Russian soprano. She studied in Paris, making her début there in 1883 in *Simon Boccanegra*. At Covent Garden and the Met, as well as in European opera houses in the last decade of the century, she was an outstanding Wagner dramatic soprano, and also sang in complete cycles of *Der Ring des Nibelungen* in Moscow and St Petersburg between 1900-14. She later became a distinguished teacher in Paris.

Liu (sop.). The slave girl in Puccini's *Turandot* who dies for love of Prince Calaf.

Lloyd, Robert, b. Southend, 2 Mar 1940. English bass. He studied in London, and joined Sadler's Wells Opera in 1969. Since 1972, he has sung a number of roles with The Royal Opera at Covent Garden, among them Monterone in *Rigoletto,* Banquo in *Macbeth,* and Sarastro in *Die Zauberflöte.* He has also made guest appearances abroad. At Covent Garden in 1983 he sang Philip II in Verdi's *Don Carlos* when the original French version of the opera was performed there for the first time.

Loder, Edward, b. Bath, 1813; d. London, 5 Apr 1865. English composer. He studied in Frankfurt, then returned to London where he became a prominent composer of English-language opera. *Nourjahad* opened the new English Opera House, now the Lyceum Theatre, in 1834. His later operas include *The Night Dancers* (1846), *Robin Goodfellow* (1848), and *Raymond and Agnes* (1855). He had an almost Verdian gift for

Anna Tomova-Sintow as Elsa in a scene from Wagner's *Lohengrin* at Covent Garden in 1977. It is one of her best-known roles.

melody and musical characterization which, in a different milieu, might have developed excitingly. *Raymond and Agnes* proved that it still had power to entertain an audience when it was revived at the Arts Theatre, Cambridge, in 1966.

Lodoïska. Opera in 3 acts by Cherubini. Libretto by Claude François Fillette-Loraux. First performed Paris, 18 July 1791.

Lodoïska (sop.) is kidnapped by Dourlinsky (bar.) who desires her. When Dourlinsky's castle is attacked by Tartars, Lodoïska is rescued by her beloved, Florestan (ten.).

Lodoletta. Opera in 3 acts by Mascagni. Libretto by Giovacchino Forzano, after the novel, *Two Little Wooden Shoes* (1874) by Ouida. First performed Rome, 30 Apr 1917.

In love with the artist Flammen (ten.), Lodoletta (sop.) follows him from Holland to Paris, but dies in the snow outside his house.

Loge (ten.). The god of fire in Wagner's *Das Rheingold*.

Lohengrin. Opera in 3 acts by Wagner. Libretto by the composer. First performed Weimar, 28 Aug 1850.

In 10th-c. Antwerp, Elsa (sop.) is accused of the murder of her brother by Telramund (bar.). The German King Henry (bass) calls for a champion to defend her, and the call is answered by a knight in shining armour who arrives in a boat drawn by a swan. The knight (ten.) defeats Telramund in combat and claims Elsa as his bride. He makes Elsa swear never to ask his name or his origin.

Telramund and his wife Ortrud (mezzo-sop.), adherents of the old pre-Christian religion, plot to bring about the downfall of Elsa, and attempt unsuccessfully to stop the wedding procession of Elsa and her champion. Ortrud, however, has succeeded in sowing doubts in Elsa's mind, and when she and the knight are alone in the bridal chamber, Elsa questions him about his name and origin. At that moment, Telramund and four knights rush in to attack the bridegroom, who immediately kills Telramund. He then calls for the King and nobles to be assembled.

Addressing the assembly, the knight reveals that he is Lohengrin, son of Parsifal,

Keeper of the Holy Grail. He bids Elsa a sad farewell, returns her brother, who had been bewitched by Ortrud, to her, and leaves. Elsa falls, lifeless, to the ground.

Lola (mezzo-sop.). Alfio's wife, in love with Turiddu, in Mascagni's *Cavalleria Rusticana*.

Lombard, Alain, b. Paris, 4 Oct 1940. French conductor. He studied in Paris, made his début as a conductor with the Pasdeloup Orchestra in Paris at the age of eleven, became an assistant conductor with the Lyons Opéra in 1961, and later principal conductor. He left Lyons in 1965, conducted Poulenc's *Dialogues des Carmélites* for New York City Opera in 1966, and the following year first appeared at the Met to conduct *Faust*. Since 1974 he has been music director of the Opéra du Rhin, based in Strasbourg.

Lombardi alla Prima Crociata, I *(The Lombards at the First Crusade).* Opera in 4 acts by Verdi. Libretto by Temistocle Solera, based on Tomasso Grossi's poem of the same title (1821-6). First performed Milan, 11 Feb 1843.

Attempting to kill his brother Arvino (ten.), whose wife he desires, Pagano (bar.) kills his father by mistake. To expiate his crime, he becomes a hermit in the Holy Land. Arvino also visits the Holy Land, on the First Crusade. His daughter Giselda (sop.) who has accompanied him is captured by Acciano (bass), tyrant of Antioch, and falls in love with Acciano's son Oronte (ten.). Oronte and Giselda escape but Oronte is mortally wounded. He is baptized before he dies, by the Hermit (Pagano), who then helps the Crusaders to attack Jerusalem. The Hermit dies, forgiven, in the arms of his brother, Arvino.

London, George, b. Montreal, 30 May 1920. Canadian bass-baritone. He studied in Los Angeles, and made his début in Hollywood in 1941 as Dr Grenvil in *La Traviata*. Karl Böhm engaged him for the Vienna Staatsoper in 1949, and he made his début there as Amonasro. He first sang at the Met as Amonasro in 1951, and in the following five seasons returned as Boris Godunov, Scarpia, Don Giovanni and in several other roles. In 1960 he became the

Ilona Tokody and Éva Tihanyi (sitting) in a scene from Verdi's *I Lombardi* at the Erkel Theatre, Budapest in 1979.

first non-Russian to sing Boris Godunov at the Bolshoi. He retired from his singing career in 1967, and became an administrator and producer of opera, most notably in Washington D.C.

Lorengar, Pilar, b. Saragossa, 16 Jan 1928. Spanish soprano. She studied in Madrid and began her career in Spain in *zarzuelas*. She made her operatic début in Aix-en-Provence in 1955 as Cherubino, and enjoyed considerable success, especially in Berlin, in other Mozart roles, among them the Countess Almaviva and Fiordiligi. Donna Elvira was her début role at the Met in 1966. She has an attractive voice with a vibrato which is thought by some to be a shade too prominent for Mozart.

Lorenz, Max, b. Düsseldorf, 10 May 1901; d. Vienna, 12 Jan 1975. German tenor. He studied in Berlin, and made his début in 1927 in the small role of Walther von der Vogelweide in *Tannhäuser*. He became a leading Wagner tenor, singing mainly in Berlin from 1929-44, with frequent appearances in Vienna, Bayreuth and elsewhere. He also appeared occasionally at Covent Garden and the Met in the 1930s, and returned to the Met between 1947-50. He was a notable Tristan and Siegfried, and towards the end of his career created roles in new operas at the Salzburg Festival, among them Einem's *Der Prozess* (1953) and Liebermann's *Penelope* (1954).

Lortzing, Albert, b. Berlin, 23 Oct 1801; d. Berlin, 21 Jan 1851. German composer. An actor and singer, he composed his first opera, *Ali Pascha von Janina,* at the age of twenty-three. It was staged five years later, in 1828, with sufficient success to encourage him to continue writing comic operas. Of his twenty works for the stage, the most successful were *Zar und Zimmermann* (1837) and *Der Wildschütz* (1842). *Undine* (1845) has more in common with German romantic opera than with Lortzing's other lighter pieces, but *Der Waffenschmied* (1846) marked a return to his familiar vein of romantic comedy. *Regina,* an opera on the theme of revolution, was not produced until many years after Lortzing's death, in 1899, but *Die Opernprobe,* his final work, was cordially received. Lortzing died a few hours after its première.

Los Angeles, Victoria de, b. Barcelona, 1 Nov 1923. Spanish soprano. She studied in Barcelona and made her début there in 1941 as Mimi. After the war she soon became internationally known in opera, in such roles as Butterfly, Massenet's Manon, and the Countess in *Le Nozze di Figaro.* Mimi was her first role at Covent Garden in 1950, and Marguerite in *Faust* the role of her Met début in 1951. Since 1970 she has sung mainly in concerts. Her voice at its peak was a most beautiful and pure instrument, and her technique was impeccably unobtrusive.

Victoria de los Angeles as Mimi in Puccini's *La Bohème.*

Louise. Opera in 4 acts by Charpentier. Libretto by the composer. First performed Paris, 2 Feb 1900.

A story of working-class and Bohemian life in Paris. When Louise (sop.) is forbidden by her father (bass) to marry the artist Julien (ten.), she leaves home to live with Julien. She returns home when her father is ill, but after a quarrel he throws her out.

Love for Three Oranges, The. (Russian title, *Lyubov k tryom apelsinam*). Opera in 4 acts by Prokofiev. Libretto by the composer, after Carlo Gozzi's play, *L'Amore delle Tre Melarance* (1761). First performed Chicago, 30 Dec 1921 (in French). First performance in Russian, Leningrad, 18 Feb 1926.

A fantastic plot concerning a prince (ten.) whose melancholy is cured when he laughs at the discomfiture of the sorceress Fata Morgana (contr.). By way of revenge, Fata Morgana makes him fall in love with three oranges and pursue them to the ends of the earth. The oranges, when found, are discovered to contain princesses, two of whom die of thirst. After many strange adventures, all ends happily for the prince and the remaining princess (sop.).

Lubin, Germaine, b. Paris, 1 Feb 1890; d. Paris, 27 Oct 1979. French soprano. She studied in Paris, and made her début there in 1912 as Antonia in *Les Contes d'Hoffmann.* Until 1944 she was a leading dramatic soprano at the Paris Opéra, her principal roles including Sieglinde, Kundry and Isolde, the last two of which she also sang in 1938-9 at Covent Garden and Bayreuth. Collaboration with the Germans during World War II led to her imprisonment for three years, after which she did not resume her opera career.

Luchetti, Veriano, b. Viterbo, 12 Mar 1939. Italian tenor. He studied in Milan and Rome, sang Alfredo in Wexford in 1965, and Fernando in Donizetti's *Il Furioso all'Isola di San Domingo* at Spoleto in 1967. He first appeared at Covent Garden in 1973 as Pinkerton in *Madama Butterfly.* A robust, unsubtle performer, he is much in demand in the popular Verdi and Puccini roles in Italy, though vocal difficulties seemed to beset many of his performances in Venice, Florence and Barcelona in 1982.

Lucia di Lammermoor. Opera in 3 acts by Donizetti. Libretto by Salvatore Cammarano, based on the novel, *The Bride of Lammermoor* (1819) by Sir Walter Scott. First performed Naples, 26 Sept 1835.

Determined to marry his sister Lucia (sop.) to Arturo (ten.), Enrico (bar.) forges letters from her absent lover, Edgardo (ten.) revealing that he no longer loves her. Lucia unwillingly marries Arturo, but the ceremony is interrupted by Edgardo who curses Lucia for having been false to him. Lucia loses her reason and, on her wedding night, kills her bridegroom and falls dead. Mad with grief, Edgardo kills himself.

Lucio Silla. Opera in 3 acts by Mozart. Libretto by Giovanni de Gamerra, revised by Pietro Metastasio. First performed Milan, 26 Dec 1772.

In ancient Rome, the dictator Lucio Silla (ten.) is in love with Giunia (sop.), wife of Cecilio (sop.), a proscribed senator. Cecilio makes an attempt upon Silla's life, but the opera ends happily when Silla pardons both Cecilio and Giunia.

Lucrezia Borgia. Opera in a prologue and 2 acts by Donizetti. Libretto by Felice Romani, based on Victor Hugo's play, *Lucrèce Borgia* (1833). First performed Milan, 26 Dec 1833.

The interest shown by Lucrezia Borgia (sop.) in Gennaro (ten.) is misunderstood by her husband Alfonso (bass) who thinks she is having an affair with the young man. Actually, he is her son whose identity is known only to her. When Gennaro is arrested on Alfonso's orders for having insulted the Borgias, Lucrezia arranges his escape. At a banquet, Lucrezia poisons a number of her enemies, and is horrified to find that Gennaro was among them. He refuses the antidote she offers him, because the amount is insufficient to save the lives of his companions as well. Gennaro dies, and Lucrezia, distraught, also collapses and dies.

Ludwig, Christa, b. Berlin, 16 Mar 1924. German mezzo-soprano. Her parents were both singers at the Vienna Volksoper, and she studied with her mother before making her début in Frankfurt in 1946 as Orlovsky in *Die Fledermaus*. In 1954 she sang Cherubino at the Salzburg Festival, was immediately engaged for the Vienna State

Opera, and has remained a member of the Vienna company, though she has also sung frequently at the Met. Her range is prodigious, from the Verdi mezzo roles, to Carmen, both Octavian and the Marschallin in *Der Rosenkavalier,* Ortrud, Marie in *Wozzeck* and Verdi's Lady Macbeth. Some of these roles could be described as soprano, and she unambiguously ventured into soprano territory with her acclaimed portrayal of the Dyer's Wife in *Die Frau ohne Schatten* in Vienna and Salzburg. She has a voice of creamy richness, and is a powerful actress. At Covent Garden she was heard only as Amneris and Carmen. At Salzburg in 1981, and again the following year, she was a delightful Mistress Quickly in Karajan's production of *Falstaff.*

Ludwig, Leopold, b. Witkowitz, Moravia, 12 Jan 1908; d. Lüneburg, 24 Apr 1979. Austrian conductor. He studied in Vienna, and conducted in provincial Czech towns until becoming music director of the opera at Oldenburg in 1936. He was appointed principal conductor of the Vienna Staatsoper in 1939, and took up a similar post at the Berlin Städtische Oper in 1943. From 1950-71 he was general music director of the Hamburg Staatsoper. He made his American opera début in San Francisco in 1958, and conducted Glyndebourne's first *Rosenkavalier* in 1959. He was a sound conductor of the German opera repertoire.

Luisa Miller. Opera in 3 acts by Verdi. Libretto by Salvatore Cammarano, based on Schiller's play, *Kabale und Liebe* (1784). First performed Naples, 8 Dec 1849.

Luisa (sop.), daughter of an old soldier, Miller (bar.), living on the estate of Count Walter (bass), is loved by the Count's son Rodolfo (ten.). The Count, however, intends that Rodolfo shall marry a noblewoman, Federica (mezzo-sop.), Duchess of Ostheim. The Count has Miller arrested, and sends his follower, Wurm (bass), to force Luisa to write a letter to Rodolfo confessing that she is in love with Wurm. Only if she does so will her father be released. Luisa unwillingly complies. When Rodolfo receives the letter he pretends to agree to marry Federica, but visits Luisa and poisons both her and himself. Luisa, as she dies, tells Rodolfo the truth, and Rodolfo kills Wurm before he himself dies.

Lully, Jean-Baptiste, b. Florence, 28 Nov 1632; d. Paris, 22 Mar 1687. French composer of Italian birth. Taken to France as a child, he became the leading French composer of his day, and was instrumental in the creation and development of French opera. His twenty operas, beginning with *Les Fêtes de l'Amour,* established a pattern which opera in France was to follow for more than a century. The most important of his operas are *Cadmus et Hermione* (1673), *Alceste* (1675), *Amadis* (1684), *Roland* (1685) and *Armide et Renaud* (1686).

Lulu. Opera in 3 acts by Berg. Libretto by the composer, based on the plays *Erdgeist* (1895) and *Die Büchse der Pandora* (1901) by Frank Wedekind. Berg died before completing the third act. The opera was produced in truncated form in Zurich, 2 June 1937. It was only after the death of the composer's widow that permission was granted for Friedrich Cerha to complete Act 3. The complete *Lulu* was first performed in Paris, 24 Feb 1979.

Lulu (sop.), an amoral creature, succeeds in ruining all those who desire her, among them Dr Schön (bar.), his son Alwa (ten.) and the lesbian Countess Geschwitz (mezzo-sop.), the only one of her sex partners who really loves her. Sent to prison for killing Dr Schön, Lulu is helped to escape by the Countess Geschwitz, and makes her way to London where she becomes a prostitute. In the final scene of the opera, she is killed by Jack the Ripper who also kills the Countess Geschwitz when she, once again, attempts to come to Lulu's aid.

Lustige Witwe, Die *(The Merry Widow).* Operetta by Lehár in 3 acts. Libretto by Viktor Léon and Leo Stein, based on the comedy *L'Attaché* by Henri Meilhac. First performed Vienna, 30 Dec 1905.

In an attempt to prevent the fortune of the young widow Hannah Glawari (sop.) from leaving the country, the Pontevedrian Ambassador in Paris, Baron Mirko Zeta (bass), orders his attaché, Count Danilo (ten) to court her. As Danilo had been in love with Hannah before her marriage, but had been forbidden by his uncle to make her his wife, he and Hannah are now at loggerheads. They still love each other, but Danilo swears he will never marry her because of her millions. Eventually, Hannah

Jean-Baptiste Lully

tricks Danilo into proposing to her, and all ends happily for the lovers and for the country of Pontevedro. A sub-plot concerns the Ambassador's wife, Valencienne (sop.), and her flirtation with a young Frenchman, Camille de Rosillon (ten.).

Lustigen Weiber von Windsor, Die *(The Merry Wives of Windsor).* Opera in 3 acts by Nicolai. Libretto by Salomon Hermann Mosenthal, based on Shakespeare's *The Merry Wives of Windsor.* First performed, Berlin, 9 Mar 1849.

The plot is the same as that of Shakespeare's play, and thus also of Verdi's *Falstaff,* though the characters of Bardolph and Pistol are omitted. The episode in Shakespeare's play in which Falstaff is tricked into dressing up as an old woman, omitted in Verdi's opera, is included in Nicolai's.

Luxon, Benjamin, b. Redruth, 24 Mar 1937. English baritone. He studied in London, began his career in small roles with the English Opera Group, and came to prominence when he created the title-role in Britten's *Owen Wingrave* on TV in 1971 and at Covent Garden the following year. He first appeared at Glyndebourne in 1972 as Monteverdi's Ulysses, and was a notable Don Giovanni in Peter Hall's Glyndebourne production of the opera in 1977. At Frankfurt in 1982, he sang the title-role of Handel's *Giulio Cesare* with great success. He has a warm, sympathetic voice, and an engaging stage personality.

M

Maag, Peter, b. St Gallen, 10 May 1919. Swiss conductor. He began his career in Biel-Solothurn in 1943 as coach and chorus master, and became a conductor there in 1945, making his début with *Die Zauberflöte.* He was appointed principal conductor in Düsseldorf in 1952, and was general music director in Bonn from 1952-9. He first appeared at Covent Garden in 1959 to conduct *Die Zauberflöte,* but was not engaged at the Met until 1972. In 1982 he became music director of the Berne City opera. He has specialized in the Mozart operas.

Maazel, Lorin, b. Neuilly-sur-Seine, France, 6 Mar 1930. American conductor. Brought up in Los Angeles and Pittsburgh, he studied piano and violin from the age of five, and conducted the New York Philharmonic when he was nine. With no opera experience, he became the first American to conduct at Bayreuth in 1960 *(Lohengrin),* and in 1962 he made his Met début with *Don Giovanni.* From 1965-71 he was artistic director of the Deutsche Oper, Berlin, and in 1978 appeared at Covent Garden for the first time with *Luisa Miller.* In 1982 when he became the first non-Austrian artistic director of the Vienna State Opera, one of his first actions was to replace the old repertory system with one in which new productions are mounted for a series of performances within a set period.

Macbeth. Opera in 4 acts by Verdi. Libretto by Francesco Maria Piave, after the play by Shakespeare (1605-6). First performed Florence, 14 Mar 1847. Revised version first performed Paris, 21 Apr 1865.

The plot is a simplified adaptation of Shakespeare. Having murdered the king in order to gain the throne of Scotland, Macbeth (bar.) and Lady Macbeth (sop.) are forced to kill Banquo (bass) and to slaughter the family of Macduff (ten.). After the death of Lady Macbeth, Macbeth is killed in battle by Macduff.

McCormack, John, b. Athlone, 14 June 1884; d. Dublin, 16 Sept 1945. Irish tenor. He studied in Milan, and made his début, under the name of Giovanni Foli, in Savona in 1906 in the title-role of Mascagni's *L'Amico Fritz.* He first appeared at Covent Garden in 1907 as Turiddu in *Cavalleria Rusticana,* and sang at Covent Garden every summer until 1914, often opposite Tetrazzini or Melba. In 1909 he made his Met début in *La Traviata,* and appeared regularly at the Met between 1910-18. He became an American citizen in 1917, and after 1923 devoted his career to concerts, becoming one of the most popular concert artists of his time. He possessed a lyric tenor voice of great beauty and an impeccable technique, but was, by his own admission, an indifferent actor.

McCracken, James, b. Gary, Ind., 11 Dec 1926. American tenor. He began his career in the chorus of Broadway musicals, and made his opera début as Rodolfo in *La Bohème* in Central City, Colo. in 1952. The following year he joined the Met, but was given only small roles. He left in 1957 and sang in Bonn, Vienna and Zurich, returning to the United States in 1959 to sing the title-role in Verdi's *Otello* in Washington, D.C. Otello was to become his most celebrated role, and his Covent Garden début in 1964 occurred when he undertook it at short notice to replace an indisposed tenor. He was still an exciting Otello in the early 1980s. He is also a superb Florestan, Calaf and Manrico, as much by virtue of his powerful acting as of his singing.

McIntyre, Donald, b. Auckland, New Zealand, 22 Oct 1934. New Zealand bass-baritone. He studied in London, and made his début in 1959 as Zaccaria in *Nabucco* with the Welsh National Opera in Cardiff. For the Sadler's Wells company between 1960-7 he sang more than thirty roles, and in 1967 he made his first appearances at Covent Garden (as Barak in *Die Frau ohne Schatten*) and Bayreuth (as Telramund). He became a regular performer of leading Wagner roles and continues to appear at Bayreuth, Covent Garden and, since 1974, the Met.

Mackerras, (Sir) Charles, b. Schenectady, N.Y., 17 Nov 1925. Australian conductor.

191

He studied in Sydney and Prague, and made his opera début conducting *Die Fledermaus* at Sadler's Wells, London, in 1948. He remained with the Sadler's Wells company until 1954 as a staff conductor, accepted engagements with a number of European companies, and made his Covent Garden début in 1963 with *Katerina Ismailova*. From 1966–70 he was principal conductor of the Hamburg Staatsoper, and in 1970 became music director of Sadler's Wells Opera (now English National Opera). He remained in that post until 1977, conducting operas by Mozart and Janáček, two composers in whom he has specialized, as well as Puccini and Verdi, whose operas he has also conducted at Covent Garden. He appears frequently at the Met, and most leading European houses, and is generally regarded as one of the finest opera conductors of his generation. He conducted Handel's *Semele* at Covent Garden to great acclaim.

MacNeil, Cornell, b. Minneapolis, 24 Sept 1922. American baritone. He studied in Connecticut, and began his career in 1946 by taking small parts in Broadway musicals. He was Sorel in the première of Menotti's *The Consul* in Philadelphia in 1950, and sang with the New York City Opera (1952–5), San Francisco Opera (1955) and Chicago Lyric Opera (1957). His international career dates from his début at La Scala in 1959 as Carlo in *Ernani,* and his Met début the same year as *Rigoletto*. He is a fine Verdian high baritone, though a less compelling actor than most of his rivals. In 1981 he was a compelling Michele in *Il Tabarro* at the Met.

Madama Butterfly. Opera in 2 acts by Puccini. Libretto by Giuseppe Giacosa and Luigi Illica, based on *Madame Butterfly* (1900), David Belasco's dramatization of a story of the same title (1898) by John Luther Long. First performed Milan, 17 Feb 1904.

Cio-Cio-San (Leona Mitchell) arrives for her marriage to Lieutenant Pinkerton in Puccini's *Madama Butterfly* performed by Houston Grand Opera in 1980.

Revised version first performed Brescia, 28 May 1904.

Lieutenant Pinkerton (ten.), an American Navy officer stationed in Japan, goes through a form of marriage with a teenage geisha girl, Cio-Cio-San (sop.), known as Butterfly. The American Consul, Sharpless (bar.) attempts to warn him of the dangers inherent in the match and, when Pinkerton returns to America, Sharpless has the unenviable task of informing Butterfly that her husband will never return to her. Unknown to Pinkerton, Butterfly has had a child by him after his departure. When Pinkerton's ship returns, Butterfly and her servant Suzuki (mezzo-sop.) eagerly anticipate the Lieutenant's arrival, but it is Pinkerton's American wife Kate (mezzo-sop.) who calls, and only to make arrangements to adopt the child. Grief-stricken, Butterfly kills herself.

Madame Sans-Gêne. Opera in 3 acts by Giordano. Libretto by Renato Simoni, based on the play of the same title by Victorien Sardou and Émile Moreau (1893). First performed New York, 25 Jan 1915.

A realistic comedy in a historical setting, the opera tells of the elevation of Catherine Huebscher (sop.) from laundry-woman to duchess.

Maddalena (mezzo-sop.). Sister of the assassin, Sparafucile, in *Rigoletto*.

Madeira, Jean, b. Centralia, Ill., 14 Nov 1918; d. Providence, R.I., 10 July 1972. American mezzo-soprano. She studied in New York, and made her début at the Chautauqua Summer Opera in 1943 under her maiden name of Jean Browning. In 1947 she married the conductor Francis Madeira, and made her first appearance at the Met in 1948 as the First Norn in *Götterdämmerung*. After 1955 she sang mainly in Europe, her most successful roles including Klytemnestra (Salzburg, 1956) and Carmen (Aix-en-Provence, 1957). In Berlin in 1968 she created Circe in Dallapiccola's *Ulisse*.

Madeleine de Coigny (sop.). The heroine of Giordano's *Andrea Chénier*.

Magdalene (sop.). Eva's nurse, in love with the apprentice David, in Wagner's *Die Meistersinger von Nürnberg*.

Magnifico, Don (bass). Cinderella's father, in Rossini's *La Cenerentola*.

Mahler, Gustav, b. Kalište, 7 Jul 1860; d. Vienna, 18 May 1911. Austrian composer and conductor. The last of the great symphonic composers, Mahler was also one of the most important opera conductors of his time. He made his début with a small summer company at Bad Hall in 1880, and after engagements in various towns in Austro-Hungary and Germany he became artistic director of the Vienna Opera in 1897, remaining in that post for ten years. During that time he was responsible for superb new productions of operas by Mozart and Verdi, which he directed and conducted. He composed three operas which were not performed and which have not survived, and completed and orchestrated Weber's *Die Drei Pintos* (1888). Between 1907-10 he conducted at the Met.

Maid of Orleans, The (Russian title, *Orleanskaya Deva*). Opera in 4 acts by Tchaikovsky. Libretto by the composer, based on Schiller's play, *Die Jungfrau von Orleans* (1801). First performed St Petersburg, 25 Feb 1881.

Though for the most part the plot follows that of Schiller's play (and therefore also of Verdi's *Giovanna d'Arco*), it departs from Schiller by reverting to historical accuracy in its final scene, in which Joan (mezzo-sop.) dies at the stake.

Maid of Pskov, The (Russian title, *Pskovityanka*). Opera in 4 acts by Rimsky-Korsakov. Libretto by the composer, based on the play (1860) by Lev Mey. First performed St Petersburg, 13 Jan 1873. Subsequently revised twice by the composer. Final version first performed St Petersburg, 18 Apr 1895.

Ivan the Terrible (bass), having destroyed Novgorod, approaches the town of Pskov. Olga (sop.), in love with Mikhail Tucha (ten.) is revealed to be the daughter of Ivan. When Tucha attempts to rescue Olga from Ivan's retinue, a shot aimed at him kills Olga.

Maillart, Aimé, b. Montpellier, 24 Mar 1817; d. Moulins-sur-Allier, 26 May 1871. French composer. He studied at the Paris Conservatoire, and in 1841 won the Prix de

Josephine Barstow as Emilia in Janáček's *The Makropoulos Affair* at the Coliseum in 1982.

Rome. His first opera, *Gastibelza, ou Le Fou de Tolède,* produced in Paris in 1847, was followed by five others. By far the most successful was *Les Dragons de Villars,* staged in Paris in 1856. It was first performed in Berlin in 1860 as *Das Glöckchen des Eremiten,* and is still occasionally performed in France and Germany though rarely elsewhere.

Makropoulos Affair, The (Czech title, *Věc Makropulos*). Opera in 3 acts by Janáček. Libretto by the composer, based on the play of the same title by Karel Čapek (1922).

When she intervenes in a lawsuit, it is discovered that the singer Emilia Marty (sop.) is three hundred years old. Weary of eternal life, Emilia dies only when the formula of the elixir which originally prolonged her life is discovered and destroyed.

Malatesta (bar.). Doctor and friend of Pasquale, in Donizetti's *Don Pasquale.*

Malheurs d'Orphée, Les *(The Sorrows of Orpheus).* Opera in 3 acts by Milhaud. Libretto by Armand Lunel. First performed Brussels, 7 May 1926.

A retelling of the myth of Orpheus in modern terms. The chemist Orpheus (bar.) is unable to save Eurydice (sop.), a gipsy girl who has transgressed the law of her own people in marrying him. She dies, and eventually her sisters murder Orpheus.

Malipiero, Gian Francesco, b. Venice, 18 Mar 1882; d. Treviso, 1 Aug 1973. Italian composer. One of the most original composers of his generation, he was prolific in most musical forms. He composed thirty-five operas, the earliest five of which were not produced although one, the 1-act *Sogno d'un Tramonto d'Autunno* (1913), was broadcast in 1963. His first opera to be staged was the trilogy, *L'Orfeide,* performed complete in Düsseldorf in 1925. Among his later works, most of which were first performed in Italy or Germany, are another trilogy, *Il Mistero di Venezia* (1932), *Giulio Cesare* (1936) based on Shakespeare's *Julius Caesar, Mondi Celesti e Infernali* (broadcast in 1950, staged in 1961), and two 1-act pieces, *Uno dei Dieci* and *L'Iscariota,* performed together in 1971. None of Malipiero's operas has made its way into the international repertory.

Mamelles de Tirésias, Les *(The Breasts of Tiresias).* Opera in 2 acts by Poulenc. Libretto by Guillaume Apollinaire. First performed Paris, 3 June 1947.

A surrealist comedy in which a husband (ten.) and wife (sop.) change sexes, and he produces forty thousand children before the couple revert to their normal roles.

Mandryka (bar.). The wealthy landowner in love with the eponymous heroine of Richard Strauss's *Arabella.*

Manon. Opera in 5 acts by Massenet. Libretto by Henri Meilhac and Philippe Gille, based on the novel *L'Histoire du Chevalier des Grieux et de Manon Lescaut* (1731) by Abbé Prévost. First performed Paris, 19 Jan 1884.

The Chevalier des Grieux (ten.) meets and seduces the young Manon (sop.) when she is being escorted by her cousin Lescaut (bar.) to a convent. Manon lives with Des Grieux in Paris, but when she leaves him for a rich friend of her cousin, Des Grieux enters the priesthood. Manon, tiring of her new lover, entices Des Grieux away from his church. At a gambling house, she is arrested, charged with being a prostitute, and subsequently condemned to be transported. Des Grieux attempts to rescue her, but she is too weak to escape, and dies in his arms.

Manon Lescaut. Opera in 4 acts by Puccini. Libretto by Marco Praga, Domenico Oliva, Luigi Illica and Giuseppe Giacosa, based on the novel *L'Histoire du Chevalier des Grieux et de Manon Lescaut* (1731) by Abbé Prévost. First performed Turin, 1 Feb 1893.

Based on the same source as Massenet's *Manon,* the plot of *Manon Lescaut* is generally similar, except that Manon's cousin has become her brother, and the episode of Des Grieux's becoming a priest is omitted. The ending of the opera differs from Massenet's: Manon is deported to Louisiana, and Des Grieux is allowed to accompany her. Attempting to escape, Manon dies in the arms of Des Grieux, in a desert outside New Orleans.

Manrico (ten.). The troubadour hero of Verdi's *Il Trovatore.*

Peter Lindroos as Des Grieux and Nelly Miricioiu as Manon in *Manon Lescaut* in 1982.

Manuguerra, Matteo, b. Tunis, 5 Oct 1924. Italian baritone. The son of Sicilian parents, he worked as an upholsterer before emigrating to Argentina where, at the age of thirty-five, he began to study singing. In 1963 he returned to Europe, became a French citizen and sang at the opera in Lyons as leading baritone for three years. He made his début at the Paris Opéra in 1966, and first sang at the Met in 1971, as Ashton in *Lucia di Lammermoor*. He sings a wide repertory of French and Italian roles. His Nabucco in San Francisco in 1982 was well sung but dramatically featureless.

Marcellina (mezzo-sop.). Housekeeper to the Almavivas, revealed to be the mother of Figaro, in Mozart's *Le Nozze di Figaro*.

Marcello (bar.). The artist, and friend of Rodolfo, in Puccini's *La Bohème*.

Marcoux, Vanni, b. Turin, 12 June 1877; d. Paris, 22 Oct 1962. French bass-baritone. He studied in Turin and made his début

there at the early age of seventeen as Sparafucile in *Rigoletto*. After singing in French provincial theatres he was engaged by Covent Garden in 1905 as Don Basilio in *Il Barbiere di Siviglia,* and returned there each season until 1914, singing a wide variety of baritone and bass roles. His American début was made in Chicago in 1913 as Scarpia. He sang at the Paris Opéra for nearly forty years, making his first appearance as Méphistophélès in 1908, and his last in the title-role of Massenet's *Don Quichotte* in 1947.

Mařenka (sop.). The village girl who is the heroine of Smetana's *The Bartered Bride*.

Marguerite (sop.). The heroine of Gounod's *Faust*.

Marguerite de Valois (sop.). Henry IV's betrothed, in Meyerbeer's *Les Huguenots*.

Maria di Rohan. Opera in 3 acts by Donizetti. Libretto by Salvatore Cammarano, based on the play, *Un Duel sous le Cardinal de Richelieu* (1832) by Édouard Lockroy (pseudonym of Joseph-Philippe Simon). First performed Vienna, 5 June 1843.

Maria (sop.) is secretly married to Chevreuse (bar.) but when her husband kills the nephew of Richelieu in a duel she begs an ex-lover, Riccardo, Count of Chalais (ten.), to intercede for him. Her love for Riccardo is re-awakened, and Chevreuse, led to believe Maria has been unfaithful to him, challenges Riccardo to a duel. Rather than kill Maria's husband, Riccardo turns his pistol upon himself. Maria begs her husband to kill her, but he condemns her to a life of disgrace.

Maria Golovin. Opera in 3 acts by Menotti. Libretto by the composer. First performed Brussels, 20 Aug 1958.

A melodramatic story about a blind youth (ten.) who thinks he has killed his lover, Maria (sop.), who has, however, been saved by his mother (mezzo-sop.).

Maria Stuarda. Opera in 3 acts by Donizetti. Libretto by Giuseppe Bardari, based on Schiller's play, *Maria Stuart* (1800). First performed Naples, 18 Oct 1834, as *Buondelmonte*.

The leading characters are Elizabeth I and Mary Queen of Scots. Elizabeth (sop.), in love with the Earl of Leicester (ten.), is persuaded by him to visit Mary (sop.) who is being held prisoner at Fotheringhay. During the visit, Mary insults Elizabeth, and in due course, Elizabeth signs Mary's death warrant. Leicester, in love with Mary, is ordered to witness her execution.

Marie (sop.). Wozzeck's mistress, in Berg's *Wozzeck*.

Marin(o) Faliero. Opera in 3 acts by Donizetti. Libretto by Emanuele Bidera (with additions by Agostino Ruffini), based on the French play *Marino Faliero* (1829) by Casimir Delavigne which was derived from Lord Byron's play of the same title (1829). (Early playbills refer to the opera as both *Marin Faliero* and *Marino Faliero*.) First performed Paris, 12 Mar 1835.

A tragedy of adultery, intrigue and honour, set in Venice in the time of the Doges, it tells of the love of Elena (sop.), wife of the Doge, Marin Faliero (bass), for the Doge's nephew, Fernando (ten.). The Doge is arrested for having conspired against the council. Before his execution, he forgives Elena.

Marina (mezzo-sop.). The Polish princess who marries the false Dmitri, pretender to the Russian throne, in Mussorgsky's *Boris Godunov*.

Maritana. Opera in 3 acts by Wallace. Libretto by Edward Fitzball, based on the play *Don César de Bazan* by Adolphe-Philippe d'Ennery and Philippe François Dumanoir. First performed London, 15 Nov 1845.

In his attempt to win the love of the Queen of Spain, the young, wealthy courtier Don José (bar.) hatches an extremely complicated plot, which involves him in manipulating Maritana, a gipsy street singer (sop.) and Don Caesar de Bazan (ten.), an impecunious nobleman.

Marmontel, Jean François, b. Bort, 11 July 1723; d. Abloville, 31 Dec 1799. French dramatist and librettist. As a critic, he was active in the debate over the comparative merits of Gluck and Piccinni, siding with the latter for whom he wrote five libretti,

among them *Roland* (1778) and *Didon* (1783). His libretto of *Huron* (1768) for Grétry displays his admiration for Rousseau's ideal of the Noble Savage. Among his numerous other libretti are those of Grétry's *Zémire et Azor* (1771), Rameau's *Acante et Céphise* (1751), and Cherubini's *Démophon* (1788).

Mârouf, Savetier du Caire *(Marouf, Cobbler of Cairo)*. Opera in 4 acts by Rabaud. Libretto by Lucien Népoty, based on a story in *The Arabian Nights' Entertainments*. First performed Paris, 15 May 1914.

The cobbler Mârouf (ten.) escapes his shrewish wife by going to sea. Shipwrecked, he meets an old friend who passes him off to the Sultan (bass) as a wealthy merchant. He marries the Sultan's daughter (sop.), and lives luxuriously at the expense of his father-in-law. When the Sultan becomes suspicious, the pair flee. They are pursued by the Sultan, but are saved by a magic ring which provides them with a palace and all the appurtenances of wealth.

Marriage, The (Russian title, *Zhenitba*). Act I of an unfinished opera by Mussorgsky. Libretto based on Gogol's comedy (1842) of the same title. First performed (with piano accompaniment) St Petersburg 1 Apr 1909. First full performance, St Petersburg, 26 Oct 1917. The remaining three acts were composed by Ippolitov-Ivanov, for a performance in Moscow in 1931.

The marriage broker Fiokla (contr.) experiences difficulty in arranging the marriage of the government clerk, Podkolesin (bar.).

Marschallin, The (sop.). The Field Marshal's wife, the Princess von Werdenberg, a leading character in Richard Strauss's *Der Rosenkavalier*.

Marschner, Heinrich, b. Zittau, 16 Aug 1795; d. Hanover, 14 Dec 1861. German composer. The most important composer of German opera in the generation between Weber and Wagner, he wrote sixteen operas, the earliest of which to be performed was *Heinrich IV und D'Aubigné,* staged by Weber in Dresden in 1820. Marschner's ambition was to develop German romantic opera beyond the point to which it had been brought by Weber, and this he achieved in the most successful of his mature works, *Der Vampyr,* staged in Leipzig in 1828; *Der Templer und die Jüdin* (based on Sir Walter Scott's *Ivanhoe*), staged in Leipzig in 1829; and the opera generally regarded as his masterpiece, *Hans Heiling* (Berlin, 1833). His later works for the stage, some of which reveal the influence of French grand opera, are less interesting. *Hans Heiling* is the only one of his operas which is still occasionally revived.

Martha, oder Der Markt von Richmond

(Martha, or Richmond Market). Opera in 4 acts by Flotow. Libretto by W. Friedrich (pseudonym of Friedrich Wilhelm Riese), based on the 3-act ballet-pantomime *Lady Harriette ou La Servante de Greenwich* (1844) by Jules-Henri Vernoy de St-Georges, for which Flotow had written the music of Act I. First performed Vienna, 25 Nov 1847.

The action takes place in Richmond and the surrounding district in 1700. Bored with court life, Lady Harriet (sop.), Maid of Honour to Queen Anne, visits Richmond Fair with her maid, Nancy (mezzo-sop.). Disguised as country girls, Martha and Julia, they are hired as servants by two young farmers, Lionel (ten.) and Plunkett (bass). Lionel falls in love with Martha, and Plunkett with Julia. The girls make their escape, and Martha (Lady Harriet) later pretends not to recognize Lionel. All ends happily when Martha realizes she loves Lionel, and he is serendipitously revealed to be of noble birth.

Martin, Frank, b. Geneva 15 Sept 1890; d. Naarden, 21 Nov 1974. Swiss composer. Though he composed incidental music for a number of plays, he wrote only two operas, the first of which, *Der Sturm,* based on Shakespeare's *The Tempest,* was produced at the Vienna Staatsoper in 1956. *Monsieur de Pourceaugnac,* based on Molière's *comédie-ballet* of that title, was staged in Geneva in 1963. *Le Vin Herbé* (1942), sometimes described as an opera, and indeed staged in Salzburg in 1948, is actually a secular oratorio for twelve solo voices with an accompaniment of seven strings and piano, which recounts the Tristan and Isolde legend.

Martín y Soler, Vicente, b. Valencia, 2 May 1754; d. St Petersburg, 11 Feb 1806.

Spanish composer. Known also as Vincenzo Martini, he composed a number of comic operas to Italian libretti. His earliest works were produced in Naples between 1779-83, and from 1784-8 he was active in Vienna where he composed three operas to libretti by Lorenzo da Ponte. The most successful, *Una Cosa Rara,* staged at the Burg Theater in Vienna in 1786, gained the distinction of being quoted by Mozart the following year in the supper scene of *Don Giovanni.* In 1788 he travelled to St Petersburg where he became court composer to Catherine II and composed operas to both Italian and Russian texts. In 1794 he settled in London for two years, renewing his collaboration with Da Ponte in two more operas, before returning to St Petersburg. He was one of the most successful composers of comic opera of his day, though without Mozart's genius for musical characterization.

Martinelli, Giovanni, b. Montagnana, 22 Oct 1885; d. New York, 2 Feb 1969. Italian tenor. He studied in Milan and made his début there in 1910 as Verdi's Ernani. He first appeared at Covent Garden in 1912 as Cavaradossi in *Tosca,* and made his Met début the following year in *La Bohème.* He sang with the Met company for the following thirty years, in a total of more than a thousand performances of thirty-six operas. He was especially admired for his style and the clarion ring of his voice in the Verdi dramatic roles such as Alvaro in *La Forza del Destino,* Radames in *Aida,* and, above all, Otello. He was sixty-two when he sang his last Otello in Philadelphia in 1947, and in his eighty-second year when he sang the small role of the Emperor of China in *Turandot* in 1967 in Seattle.

Marton, Eva, b. Budapest, 18 June 1943. Hungarian soprano. She studied in Budapest and made her début in 1968 at the Budapest National Opera as the Queen of Shemakhan in Rimsky-Korsakov's *Golden Cockerel.* She sings in all the leading European opera houses, and is highly regarded in such Verdi roles as Leonora in *La Forza del Destino,* Aida, and Elisabeth in *Don Carlos.* She made a successful début in Chicago in 1980 as Madeleine in Giordano's *Andrea Chénier,* and in 1982 at Salzburg she sang Leonora in *Fidelio,* and in 1983 sang *Turandot* in Harold Prince's production at the Vienna Staatsoper.

Martinů, Bohuslav, b. Polička, 8 Dec 1890; d. Liestal, Switzerland, 28 Aug 1959. Czech composer. One of the most prolific composers of the 20th c., he wrote sixteen operas, the first of which, *The Soldier and the Dancer,* was staged in Brno in 1928. From 1923 until the outbreak of World War II he lived in Paris where he composed, among other works, operas which were not performed. His first successful stage work was *Julietta,* an opera concerning the relationship of dream and reality, which was produced in Prague in 1938. He wrote two operas for radio, and two for television of which the second, *The Marriage,* a setting of Gogol's comedy, was successfully televised in New York in 1953. His final opera for the stage, *The Greek Passion,* based on the novel *Christ Re-crucified* by Nikos Kazantzakis, was produced in Zurich in 1961.

Martyrs, Les. See *Poliuto.*

Marzelline (sop.). Daughter of the gaoler, Rocco, in Beethoven's *Fidelio.*

Mascagni, Pietro, b. Livorno, 7 Dec 1863; d. Rome, 2 Aug 1945. Italian composer, He studied in Milan, and then became a conductor of touring operetta companies. When his 1-act opera, *Cavalleria Rusticana,* which he submitted to a competition organized by the publisher Sonzogno, was awarded first prize, and performed to wildly enthusiastic audiences in Rome in 1890, he quickly became famous. *Cavalleria Rusticana* was produced by opera houses all over the world, and is still one of the most popular works in the international repertory. *Guglielmo Ratcliff,* composed before *Cavalleria Rusticana,* was not staged until 1895. By then, *L'Amico Fritz,* which Mascagni composed immediately after *Cavalleria Rusticana,* had been performed (Rome, 1891) with only moderate success, and *I Rantzau* (Florence, 1892) had been a failure. None of Mascagni's later operas equalled the success of *Cavalleria Rusticana* which can be said to have begun the fashion for *verismo* or realism in Italian opera. *Iris* (1898) was followed by *Le Maschere* which was produced simultaneously in six Italian cities in 1901, and hissed off the stage in most of them. *Il Piccolo Marat* (1921) recaptured some of the old excitement of the early days of *verismo,* but Mascagni's subsequent works were of little musical or dramatic interest. He became the official composer of the Fascist regime, and composed *Nerone* (staged at La Scala, Milan, in 1935) as a tribute to Mussolini.

Mascotte, La. Operetta in 3 acts by Audran. Libretto by Alfred Duru and Henri Charles Chivot. First performed Paris, 28 Dec 1880. Audran's most popular operetta, it reached its thousandth performance in Paris after only five years, and was produced in a number of other countries within months of its première.

The mascot of the title is Bettina (sop.), a country-girl who is sent to the farmer Rocco (bar.) by his brother in the hope that she will bring Rocco the good luck he sorely needs. In due course, Bettina marries Rocco's shepherd, Pippo (ten.).

Masetto (bar.). The peasant, in Mozart's *Don Giovanni,* whose bride attracts the attention of Giovanni.

Maskarade. Opera in 3 acts by Nielsen. Libretto by Vilhelm Andersen, based on a play by Ludvig Holberg. First performed Copenhagen, 11 Nov 1906.

Leander (ten.) rejects the bride chosen for him by his parents, having fallen in love with Leonora (sop.) whom he has met at a masquerade. The young lovers discover that they are, in fact, the choices their respective parents had made for each other.

Masnadieri, I *(The Bandits).* Opera in 4 acts by Verdi. Libretto by Andrea Maffei, based on the play *Die Räuber* (1781) by Friedrich Schiller. First performed London, 22 July 1847.

Carlo (ten.), son of Count Moor (bass) from whose house he has been banished by the intrigue of his brother Francesco (bar.), has formed a band of brigands. His betrothed, Amalia (sop.), repulses Francesco's advances and is reunited with Carlo. Carlo rescues his father from Francesco, and kills his evil brother. When his followers refuse to release him from his oath of loyalty to them, he stabs Amalia to death rather than have her dishonoured by a life with him and his bandits.

masque. A spectacular entertainment of late

Valerie Masterson in the title-role of Handel's *Semele* at Covent Garden.

renaissance and early baroque times, found mainly in England where Ben Jonson wrote masques for the court, but also in France and Italy. Music, text, costumes and elaborate scenery were equally important elements. *Comus* (1634), with a text by Milton and music by Henry Lawes, was a popular masque of its time.

Massé, Victor, b. Lorient, 7 Mar 1822; d. Paris, 5 July 1884. French composer. He composed twenty-three operas and operettas, most of which were first staged at the Opéra-Comique, Paris. *Les Noces de Jeannette* (1853), a 1-act operetta, was one of his earliest successes. His light and tuneful operas were popular in their day, but have not proved durable. *Paul et Virginie* (1876) was his most ambitious work.

Massenet, Jules, b. Montaud, St Etienne, 12 May 1842; d. Paris, 13 Aug 1912. French composer. The leading composer of French opera of his generation, and the most prolific, he studied at the Paris Conservatoire, won the Prix de Rome in 1863 and, after writing two operas which were not performed, had his first opera, a 1-act piece, *La Grand'tante,* staged at the Opéra-

Comique in Paris in 1867. His first major success was the 5-act opera, *Le Roi de Lahore* (1877). Of his thirty-four operas, *Manon* (1884) and *Werther* (1892) have proved the most popular, though in recent years a renewal of interest in French romantic opera has led to the revival of several others, among them *Hérodiade* (1881), *Le Cid* (1885), *Esclarmonde* (1889), *Thaïs* (1894), *Cendrillon* (1899), *Grisélidis* (1901), *Le Jongleur de Notre-Dame* (1902) and *Don Quichotte* (1910). The best of his operas are notable for their melodic charm and gracefulness, though Massenet tended to repeat the same effects from work to work. *La Navarraise,* a 1-act piece written in the style of Italian *verismo* as an answer to the success in 1890 of Mascagni's *Cavalleria Rusticana,* was first performed at Covent Garden in 1894.

Masterson, Valerie, b. Birkenhead, 3 June 1937. English soprano. She studied in Liverpool, London and Milan, and made her début in 1964 at the Landestheater in Salzburg, singing Nannetta in *Falstaff* and Fiorilla in *Il Turco in Italia.* She was engaged by the touring D'Oyly Carte company in England as leading soprano in Gilbert and

Sullivan operettas from 1966-70, and then joined Sadler's Wells (now English National) Opera, for whom she has sung a wide variety of roles, her many successes ranging from Adèle in *Le Comte Ory* to Violetta in *La Traviata* and Manon in Massenet's opera. She made her début at the Paris Opéra in 1978 as Marguerite, and was a greatly admired Cleopatra in Handel's *Giulio Cesare* in London in 1979. She has a beautiful voice, a fine technique, an attractive stage presence and great acting ability. At Covent Garden, she sang the title-role in *Semele* in 1982, and Marguérite in *Faust* in 1983.

Mastilovič, Danica, b. Negotin, Serbia, 7 Nov 1933. Yugoslav soprano. She studied in Belgrade, sang in operetta while still a student, and made her opera début in Frankfurt in 1959 as Tosca. She remained a member of the Frankfurt company for several years, and in 1969 began to undertake the heavier Strauss and Wagner roles. She is an admired Senta, Brünnhilde and Electra in a number of European opera houses. She first sang in the United States in Chicago in 1963 as Abigaille in *Nabucco,* and made her Covent Garden (1973) and Met (1975) débuts as Strauss's Elektra. After Birgit Nilsson, she was the most admired dramatic soprano of the 1970s, not only in the Wagner roles but also as Puccini's Turandot, a role which she sang at Torre del Lago in 1974 to commemorate the fiftieth anniversary of the composer's death.

Matačić, Lovro von, b. Sušak, 14 Feb 1899. Yugoslav conductor. He studied in Vienna where, as a child, he had been a member of the Vienna Boys' Choir, and made his début as conductor in Cologne in 1917. After conducting opera for some years in other Yugoslav towns, he became general music director of the Belgrade Opera in 1938. After the war, he held similar appointments in Dresden, Berlin and Frankfurt, before becoming chief conductor of Monte Carlo Opera. He excels in the German-language operetta and operetta repertory of the 19th c.

Mathis, Edith, b. Lucerne, 11 Feb 1938. Swiss soprano. She studied in Lucerne and made her début there in 1956 as 2nd Boy in *Die Zauberflöte.* She joined Cologne Opera in 1953 and moved to the Deutsche Oper, Berlin, in 1963. A delightful lyric soprano,

her best roles include Susanna in *Le Nozze di Figaro,* in which she made her Covent Garden début in 1970, and Sophie in *Der Rosenkavalier,* which she sang at Glyndebourne in 1965. She first appeared at the Met in 1970, and sings regularly at the Salzburg and Munich Festivals.

Mathis der Maler *(Mathis the Painter).* Opera in 7 scenes by Hindemith. Libretto by the composer. First performed Zurich, 28 May 1938.

The opera recounts incidents from the life of the 16th-c. painter, Matthias Grünewald. Grünewald (bar.) sympathizes with the revolt of the peasants, helps their leader Schwalb (ten.) to escape, and when Schwalb is killed consoles his daughter Regina (sop.). He experiences a vision in which he sees the images he must paint for the altar at Isenheim, comforts the dying Regina, and prepares for his own death.

Matrimonio Segreto, Il *(The Secret Marriage).* Opera in 2 acts by Cimarosa. Libretto by Giovanni Bertati, based on the play, *The Clandestine Marriage* by George Colman and David Garrick (1766). First performed Vienna, 7 Feb 1792.

The rich merchant Geronimo (bass) attempts to find aristocratic husbands for his two daughters. The impecunious English Count Robinson (bass) writes to ask for the hand of Elisetta (sop.) but finds he prefers her sister Carolina (sop.) who is secretly married to Geronimo's clerk, Paolino (ten.). The girls' aunt, Fidalma (mezzo-sop.), unaware of the marriage, is herself in love with Paolino. After a series of comic incidents, Carolina and Paolino confess to their marriage, Count Robinson resigns himself to Elisetta, and Fidalma looks forward to continued spinsterhood.

Matzenauer, Margarete, b. Temesvár, 1 June 1881; d. Van Nuys, Calif., 19 May 1963. Austro-Hungarian soprano and mezzo-soprano. She studied in Graz, Berlin and Munich, and made her début in Strasbourg in 1901 as Fatima in *Oberon.* From 1904-11 she sang in Munich, and then joined the Met, remaining with the company until 1930. She had a voice of exceptional range and power, and was able to sing contralto, mezzo and soprano roles. She made her Met début as Amneris, but was also a notable

Aida. In *Il Trovatore* she sang both Leonora and Azucena. Her Wagner roles included Brünnhilde, Isolde, Ortrud and Fricka.

Maurel, Victor, b. Marseilles, 17 June 1848; d. New York, 22 Oct 1923. French baritone. He studied in Marseilles and Paris, and made his début in Marseilles in 1867 in Rossini's *Guillaume Tell*. After appearances in Paris, St Petersburg, Cairo and Venice, he sang at La Scala in the première of Gomes's *Il Guarany* in 1870. He then sang leading roles at the Paris Opéra for several years. He undertook the title-role in the revised version of Verdi's *Simon Boccanegra* at La Scala in 1881, as a consequence of which the composer chose him to create Iago in *Otello* (1887) and the title-role of *Falstaff* (1893). He sang many of his most successful Wagner and Verdi roles at Covent Garden and the Met, and was the first Tonio in Leoncavallo's *Pagliacci* in Milan in 1892. He was renowned as much for his exceptional acting ability as for his vocal qualities, and, a skilled painter, designed the sets for Gounod's *Mireille* at the Met in 1919. He also wrote a number of books on singing, one on the staging of *Don Giovanni,* and a volume of memoirs.

Mavra. Opera in 1 act by Stravinsky. Libretto by Boris Kochno, after Pushkin's poem, *The Little House at Kolomna* (1830). First performed Paris, 2 June 1922.

Sent by her mother (contr.) to find a new cook, Parasha (sop.) engages her lover, the Hussar Vasily (ten.) who disguises himself as a girl, Mavra, for the purpose. However, he is discovered shaving and is ejected from the house.

Maw, Nicholas, b. Grantham, 5 Nov 1935. English composer. He studied in Paris, and wrote a 2-act comic opera, *One Man Show,* which was produced in London in 1964. *The Rising of the Moon,* a romantic opera commissioned by Glyndebourne Festival Opera was favourably received when it was staged at Glyndebourne in 1970. He writes for the voice with a lyrical warmth which is too seldom encountered in opera since the death of Britten.

Max (ten.). The huntsman who uses a magic bullet in the shooting contest in Weber's *Der Freischütz*.

Maximovna, Ita, b. Pskov, 31 Oct 1914. Russian designer. She studied painting in Paris, and began to design operas in Berlin in 1945. She became one of the leading designers of the post-war period, and her work has been seen in most major opera houses. She often worked in association with the director, Günther Rennert in Munich in the 1960-70s.

May Night (Russian title, *Mayskaya Noch*). Opera in 3 acts by Rimsky-Korsakov. Libretto by the composer after a story of that title in the volume *Evenings on a Farm near Dikanka* (1831-32) by Gogol. First performed St Petersburg, 21 Jan 1880.

In order to outwit his father the Mayor (bass), who will not allow him to marry Hanna (mezzo-sop.), Levko (ten.) enlists the aid of the water-nymph Pannochka (sop.).

Mayr, Richard, b. Salzburg, 18 Nov 1877; d. Vienna, 1 Dec 1935. Austrian bass. A student of medicine, he was persuaded by Mahler to adopt the career of a singer, and studied in Vienna, making his début at Bayreuth in 1902 as Hagen in *Götterdämmerung*. In that same year Mahler engaged him for Vienna, and he remained a member of the company until his death thirty-three years later. His wide vocal range allowed him to undertake such roles as Wotan and Figaro as well as Gurnemanz and Sarastro. He was Baron Ochs in the first Viennese production of *Der Rosenkavalier,* and with his superb acting ability and ripe, voluminous voice he made this role his own. He created Barak in *Die Frau Ohne Schatten* in Vienna in 1919, took part in every Salzburg Festival from 1921-34, and made his Covent Garden début in 1924 as Ochs in the famous production conducted by Bruno Walter, with Lotte Lehmann as the Marschallin, Elisabeth Schumann as Sophie, and Delia Reinhardt as Octavian. His first Met role, in 1927, was Pogner, but he shortly afterwards added Ochs to his New York repertory, and sang at the Met for three seasons.

Mayr, Simon, b. Mendorf, 14 June 1763; d. Bergamo, 2 Dec 1845. German composer. He became a leading composer of Italian opera in the generation before Rossini, after being taken to Italy at the age of twenty-four. His first opera, *Saffo,* was an immediate success when staged in Venice in 1794, and he brought something of the instrumental richness of the Viennese school to Italian opera with the more than seventy works he composed over a period of thirty years. His most celebrated opera, *Medea in Corinto*, was staged in Naples in 1813. *L'Amor Coniugale* (1805) was a setting of the same libretto that Beethoven used, also in 1805, for his *Leonore* (which later became *Fidelio*). Mayr founded a school of music in Bergamo, and from 1806-15 taught the young Donizetti without charge.

Mazeppa. Opera in 3 acts by Tchaikovsky. Libretto by the composer and Viktor Burenin, based on Pushkin's poem *Poltava* (1829). First performed Moscow, 15 Feb 1884.

Mazeppa (bar.) abducts Maria (sop.) when her father, Kochubey (bass), refuses permission for them to marry. Maria's rejected suitor Andrey (ten.) tells the Tsar that Mazeppa is in league with the Swedes, but he is not believed. The Tsar executes Kochubey, Mazeppa kills Andrey, and Maria loses her reason.

Mazurok, Yuri, b. Krasnik, 8 July 1931. Polish baritone, He studied in Moscow, joined the Bolshoi Opera in 1963, and has been a member of the company ever since. He makes frequent guest appearances outside the Soviet Union, in Vienna, London, New York, Geneva and elsewhere. His performance of the title-role in *Eugene Onegin* has been widely admired for the elegance and firmness of his singing, and he is also an impressive interpreter of such Verdi roles as the Count of Luna in *Il Trovatore* and Rodrigue in *Don Carlos*.

Médecin Malgré Lui, Le *(The Doctor in Spite of Himself)*. Opera in 3 acts by Gounod. Libretto by Jules Barbier and Michel Carré, based on Molière's comedy of the same title (1666). First performed Paris, 15 Jan 1858. Gounod's first successful opera, and his only comedy.

The woodcutter, Sgnarelle (bar.), forced by his wife to masquerade as a medical specialist, finds himself involved in a series of adventures.

Médée *(Medea)*. Opera in 3 acts by Cherubini. Libretto by François Benoît

Hoffman, based on Corneille's tragedy of the same title (1635). First performed Paris, 13 Mar 1797.

Medea (sop.), unable to win back the love of Jason (ten.), murders his new bride Glauce (sop.), and their own two sons.

Medium, The. Opera in 2 acts by Menotti. Libretto by the composer. First performed New York, 8 May 1946.

Madame Flora (contr.), a medium, practices fraud upon her clients with the aid of her daughter Monica (sop.) and the mute Toby. Frightened when the world of the occult seems to intervene, she shoots at a ghost, and kills Toby in error.

Mefistofele. Opera in a prologue, 4 acts and an epilogue by Boito. Libretto by the composer, based on Goethe's *Faust*. First performed Milan, 5 Mar 1868. Twice revised. First performance of definitive version, Venice, 13 May 1876.

The libretto is based on both parts of Goethe's play, and the opera thus includes, after the death of Margherita (sop.), the love affair of Faust (ten.) with Elena (sop.) or Helen of Troy. At the end, Faust is redeemed and saved from Mefistofele (bass).

Mehta, Zubin, b. Bombay, 29 Apr 1936. Indian conductor. He studied in Vienna, and

Zubin Mehta, a welcome visiting conductor at Covent Garden

made his opera début with *Tosca* in Toronto in 1964. The following year he conducted *Aida* at the Met, and in 1977 made a successful Covent Garden début with *Otello*. His performances of *La Fanciulla del West* and *Die Fledermaus* at Covent Garden have also been much admired. He has also conducted opera in Salzburg, Vienna and Florence, though his career has been primarily concerned with concerts.

Méhul, Étienne-Nicolas, b. Givet, 22 June 1763; d. Paris, 18 Oct 1817. He composed more than thirty *opéras comiques* which were popular in the Paris of his day. The earliest, *Euphrosine* (1790), contained a duet which became immediately famous, and the opera held the stage for more than forty years. His most important work was *Joseph* (1807), a solemn religious opera which was also his last major success.

Meilhac, Henri, b. Paris, 21 Feb 1831; d. Paris, 6 July 1897. French dramatist and librettist. Most of his libretti were written in collaboration with others. He and Philippe Gille wrote the libretto of Massenet's *Manon,* and he collaborated with Albert Millaud and Ernest Blum on Hervé's *Mam'zelle Nitouche* (1883). His most important partnership was with Ludovic Halévy with whom he wrote the libretto of *Carmen* as well as the libretti of a number of operettas, among them Offenbach's *La Belle Hélène, Barbe-Bleue, La Vie Parisienne, La Grande Duchesse de Gérolstein* and *La Périchole.* The Meilhac and Halévy play, *Le Réveillon,* was the basis of Johann Strauss's *Die Fledermaus,* and Meilhac's comedy, *L'Attaché,* was the basis of Lehár's *Die Lustige Witwe.*

Meistersinger von Nürnberg, Die *(The Mastersingers of Nuremberg).* Opera in 3 acts by Wagner. Libretto by the composer. First performed Munich, 21 June 1868.

In 16th-c. Nuremberg, the young nobleman, Walther von Stolzing (ten.), falls in love with Eva (sop.), daughter of the goldsmith Pogner (bass). He discovers, however, that she is to be betrothed to the winner of a singing contest organized by the tradesmen's Guild of Mastersingers. David (ten.), apprentice and fiancé of Eva's nurse Magdalene (sop.), explains the rules of the Guild to Walther, who applies for mem-

bership so that he may enter the contest. David's master, Hans Sachs (bar.), cobbler and poet, is sympathetic, but the pedantic Town Clerk, Beckmesser (bar.), attempts to veto Walther's admission to the Guild of Mastersingers, for Beckmesser himself hopes to win the contest and Eva.

Eva and Walther decide to elope, but Hans Sachs prevents the elopement and aids Walther in the composition of a song for the contest. Beckmesser steals a copy of the song, but at the contest is unable to perform it accurately, and Walther wins the prize, and the hand of Eva in marriage. When Pogner attempts also to invest him with the insignia of the Guild, Walther brushes him aside, but is rebuked by Sachs who lectures him on the virtues of tradition and on the necessity of keeping German art free from foreign influence by adhering to the rules of the Guild. The opera ends with the acclamation of Sachs by the citizens of Nuremberg.

Melba, (Dame) Nellie, b. Richmond, nr Melbourne, 19 May 1861; d. Sydney, 23 Feb 1931. Australian soprano. She was born Helen Mitchell, and took the name Melba (from Melbourne) for professional purposes. She studied in Melbourne and Paris, and made her début in Brussels in 1887 as Gilda. The following year she appeared at Covent Garden as Lucia. She had a voice of rare beauty and agility, and became one of the most famous sopranos of her time. Lucia was the role of her Met début in 1893, and she made frequent appearances at the Met until 1910 although Covent Garden remained her main base. She excelled in a number of French roles, among them Gounod's Juliette and Marguerite and Thomas's Ophélie. Her Covent Garden farewell appearance in 1926 was followed by occasional appearances in opera in Australia.

Melchior, Lauritz, b. Copenhagen, 20 Mar 1890; d. Santa Monica, Calif., 18 Mar 1973. Danish, later American, tenor. He studied in Copenhagen, and began his career in 1912 as a baritone, with the role of Germont in a touring production of *La Traviata.* In 1918, he made a second début in Copenhagen as a tenor in the title-role of *Tannhäuser.* He became the leading Wagner tenor of his generation, more by virtue of his large, exciting voice than by his musicianship. He

Dame Nellic Melba as Lakmé, one of the many French roles in which she excelled.

made his Covent Garden début in 1924 as Siegmund, and his first Bayreuth appearances the same year, as Siegmund and Parsifal. He first appeared at the Met in 1926 as Tannhäuser, and began an association with that company which continued until 1950 when, at the age of sixty, he appeared at the Met for the last time, as Lohengrin. In the 1940-50s he embarked upon a second career in Hollywood films.

Mélisande (sop.). The heroine of Debussy's *Pelléas et Mélisande*.

Mendelssohn (-Bartholdy), Felix, b. Hamburg, 3 Feb 1809; d. Leipzig, 4 Nov 1847. German composer. Primarily a composer of instrumental and orchestral music, he showed an early gift for opera. As a child, he composed several comic operas, and the only opera he completed as an adult,

Die Hochzeit des Camacho, was in fact written in his seventeenth year. It was a failure when produced in Berlin in 1827 and, although Mendelssohn later made plans to compose an opera on Shakespeare's *The Tempest,* and in 1847 actually began work on *Die Loreley,* he effectively turned away from opera, utilizing his dramatic gifts in oratorio.

Menotti, Gian Carlo, b. Cadegliano, 7 July 1911. American composer of Italian birth. He studied in Milan and, after his family moved to America, in Philadelphia. He is primarily a composer of operas, for all of which he has provided his own libretti. His earliest opera, *Amelia al Ballo,* a 1-act piece in Italian, was given its first performance in English translation in Philadelphia in 1937, as *Amelia Goes to the Ball.* Menotti's subsequent operas have been written in English. *The Medium* (1946) attracted a large following with its journalistically effective music and highly dramatic plot, and had a run of 211 performances on Broadway in 1947-8, together with a 1-act comedy, *The Telephone,* which Menotti wrote to accompany it. His greatest success was with *The Consul* (1950), in which he proved that the *verismo* of Italian opera of fifty years earlier was still a viable musical language when skilfully used. *Amahl and the Night Visitors* (1951) was written for television, and *The Saint of Bleecker Street* (1954) again exploited Menotti's Puccinian style. *Maria Golovin* (1958) was less successful, and since *Le Dernier Sauvage* (first performed in Paris in 1963) the composer seems to have been merely repeating himself. His best works, however, are musically respectable and theatrically effective, and fall easily upon the ear. He founded the Spoleto Festival of Two Worlds in 1958.

Méphistophélès (bass). The Devil of Gounod's *Faust* and, Italianized, of Boito's *Mefistofele.* Also (bass-bar.) a character in *La Damnation de Faust* by Berlioz.

Mercadante, Saverio, b. Altamura, nr Bari, 17 Sept 1795; d. Naples, 17 Dec 1870. Italian composer. He studied in Naples, and composed fifty-nine operas. Active at the same time as Donizetti, Bellini and Verdi, he was during his lifetime considered their equal, though his reputation suffered a rapid decline after his death, and his works are now no longer regularly performed. His first great success was with *Elisa e Claudio* (1821), and his most important subsequent operas include *Il Giuramento* (1837) which is his best-known work, *Le Due Illustri Rivali* (1838), *Il Bravo* (1839), *La Vestale* (1840) and *Orazi e Curiazi* (1846). Occasional 20th-c. revivals of one or other of these works suggest that, at his best, Mercadante was certainly the equal of Donizetti at his less than best.

Merrie England. Opera in 2 acts by German. Libretto by Basil Hood. First performed London, 2 Apr 1902.

Queen Elizabeth I (mezzo-sop.), jealous of one of her Ladies-in-Waiting, Bessie Throckmorton (sop.), who is loved by the Queen's, favourite, Sir Walter Raleigh (ten.), plots to have Bessie murdered, but is thwarted by Raleigh's rival, the Earl of Essex (bar.).

Merrill, Robert, b. Brooklyn N.Y., 4 June 1919. American baritone. He studied in New York, and made his début at the Met in 1945 as Germont in *La Traviata*. (He made a belated Covent Garden début in 1967 in the same role.) He continued to sing leading roles at the Met, especially in the operas of Verdi, for more than thirty seasons.

Merriman, Nan, b. Pittsburgh, 28 Apr 1920. American mezzo-soprano. She studied in Los Angeles, and made her opera début in Cincinnati in 1942 as La Cieca in *La Gioconda*. Her subsequent career was mainly in concerts, but she was a notable Dorabella in *Così Fan Tutte* at Aix-en-Provence in 1953 and later, and at Glyndebourne in 1956. She made her first British appearance as Baba the Turk in Stravinsky's *The Rake's Progress* with the Glyndebourne company at the Edinburgh Festival in 1953. She retired in 1965.

Merry Mount. Opera in 3 acts by Howard Hanson. Libretto by Richard Stokes, based on the story *The May-Pole Lovers of Merry Mount* by Nathaniel Hawthorne. First performed New York, 10 Feb 1934.

Though it has not been revived, this opera about a Puritan pastor, Wrestling Bradford, (bar.) whose attempts to save the soul of Lady Marigold (sop.) lead to disaster for them both, was acclaimed at its Met

première, when the leading role was sung by Lawrence Tibbett.

Messager, André, b. Montluçon, 30 Dec 1853; d. Paris, 24 Feb 1929. French composer and conductor. He studied in Paris, and made his career as a conductor. (He conducted the première of *Pelléas et Mélisande* in Paris in 1902.) His first operettas were successful not only in Paris but also in London, and he was commissioned to write *Mirette* for production at the Savoy Theatre, London, in 1894. His best-known operetta, *Véronique* (1898), a work of engaging charm, is still frequently performed. He continued to compose works for the stage until the end of his life, adapting his style to the new sounds of the post-war world in *Monsieur Beaucaire* (1919) which he wrote, to an English libretto, for the soprano Maggie Teyte, and *L'Amour Masqué* (1923), written for the French operetta star, Yvonne Printemps. He conducted a number of operas at Covent Garden, and was influential in France as a conductor of Wagner.

Messel, Oliver, b. Cuckfield, 13 Jan 1904. English designer. He began to design for the theatre in 1926, and later became renowned as a ballet designer. He first worked in opera with *Die Zauberflöte* at Glyndebourne in 1947, and then designed a number of Mozart and Rossini operas also for Glyndebourne. He designed the 1961 Met production of *Le Nozze di Figaro*.

Metastasio, Pietro, b. Rome, 3 Jan 1698; d. Vienna, 12 Apr 1782. Italian librettist. The foremost librettist in the age of *opera seria,* he wrote his first libretti in Naples, but in 1730 became court poet in Vienna, where he lived for the remainder of his life. He produced libretti for Caldara, Hasse and others, and many of his texts were set subsequently by later composers. His libretti for Caldara's *La Clemenza di Tito* (1734) and Giuseppe Bonno's *Il Rè Pastore* (1751) were later set by Mozart. His *Artaserse* was used by forty composers.

Meyer, Kerstin, b. Stockholm, 3 Apr 1928. Swedish mezzo-soprano. She studied in Stockholm and made her début there in 1952 as Azucena. While remaining a member of the Royal Opera in Stockholm, she embarked upon an international career, appearing in Berlin for the first time in 1959 as Carmen, in New York in 1960 in the same role, at Covent Garden in 1961 as Dido in *Les Troyens,* and at Bayreuth in 1962 as Brangäne. An intelligent actress and musician, she has created a number of roles in new operas, and is also a fine Orfeo in Gluck's *Orfeo ed Euridice.* She created the role of Amando in Ligeti's *Le Grand Macabre* in Stockholm in 1978.

Meyerbeer, Giacomo, b. Vogelsdorf, nr Berlin, 5 Sept 1791; d. Paris, 2 May 1864. German composer. The son of a wealthy Jewish family, he studied in Berlin and Darmstadt, and produced his first two operas to German texts. *Jephtas Gelübde* (Munich, 1812) and *Wirth und Gast* (Stuttgart, 1813) were both equally unsuccessful, and it was not until he visited Italy in 1816 that Meyerbeer's career as a composer of opera began in earnest. Between 1817-24 he composed seven Italian operas which were staged in Padua, Turin, Venice and Milan, and which were all immediately successful. When the last of them, *Il Crociato in Egitto,* was accepted for production in Paris he took up residence there, and began to compose large-scale works in the style of French grand opera, to libretti provided mostly by Eugène Scribe. *Robert le Diable* (1831), a great success, was followed by the even greater success of *Les Huguenots* (1836). He temporarily turned away from French grand opera to compose *Ein Feldlager in Schlesien* for Berlin (1844), though he made use of its music later for *L'Étoile du Nord* (1854). *Le Prophète* (1849) was enthusiastically received, as was *Le Pardon de Ploërmel* (1859), later known as *Dinorah. L'Africaine,* on which he had worked intermittently for nearly twenty-five years, was completed only a month before his death, and performed posthumously in 1865. His lavishly staged operas, in which drama was subordinated to spectacle, were eclipsed by the music dramas of Wagner, but in recent years have been making their way back into fashion.

mezzo-soprano. The middle category of female voice, between contralto and soprano, its timbre has something of the brightness of the soprano, with more fullness and warmth at the bottom of the range.

Giacomo Meyerbeer

Micaëla (sop.), who loses him to Carmen. The village sweetheart of Don José in Bizet's *Carmen.*

Micheau, Janine, b. Toulouse, 17 Apr 1914; d. Paris, 18 Oct 1976. French soprano. She studied in Toulouse and Paris, and made her début in Paris in 1933 as La Plieuse in Charpentier's *Louise.* Though she sang Mélisande in a number of opera houses abroad, her career was mainly based in France. She sang at both Paris opera houses until 1956, her roles including Mireille, Juliette, and Leila in *Les Pêcheurs de Perles,* as well as Verdi's Gilda and Violetta. She sang Micaëla at Covent Garden in 1937, and was Anne Trulove in the first Paris production of *The Rake's Progress* in 1953. A dependable performer, she had a bright soprano voice, characteristically French in timbre.

Michele (bar.). The Seine barge-owner in Puccini's *Il Tabarro.*

Midsummer Marriage, The. Opera in 3 acts by Tippett. Libretto by the composer. First performed London, 27 Jan 1955.

A metaphysical dissertation on the subject of self-knowledge and spiritual and physical fulfilment, the plot concerns two couples, Mark (ten.) and Jenifer (sop.) who exist on a high philosophical level, and Jack (ten.) and Bella (sop.) whose relationship is on a lower, more material plane. King Fisher (bar.), Jenifer's father, represents parental opposition and the commercial world. Ancient myth also plays its part in the person of the seer, Sosostris (contr.)

Midsummer Night's Dream, A. Opera in 3 acts by Britten. Libretto by the composer and Peter Pears, based on Shakespeare's play (*c.*1594). First performed Aldeburgh, 11 June 1960.

The plot follows closely that of the play. The role of Oberon is assigned to a counter-tenor, and Puck is a speaking-role. The other main characters are Tytania (sop.), Helena (sop.), Hermia (mezzo-sop.), Lysander (ten.), Demetrius (bar.) and Bottom (bass-bar.) The performance by Bottom and his friends of their play about Pyramus and Thisbe is turned into an amusing parody of bel canto opera.

Mignon. Opera in 3 acts by Thomas. Libretto by Jules Barbier and Michel Carré, based on the novel *Wilhelm Meisters Lehrjahre* (1795-6) by Goethe. First performed Paris, 17 Nov 1866.

Lothario (bass), a wandering minstrel whose mind is deranged, searches for his daughter who has been stolen by gipsies. When a band of gipsies arrives, and tries to force one of their number, Mignon (mezzo-sop.), to dance, the young Wilhelm Meister (ten.) rescues her by buying her as his servant. After an adventure involving a group of strolling players with one of whom, Philine (sop.), Meister is infatuated, he realizes that he loves Mignon. He saves her from a burning castle and nurses her back to health, aided by Lothario who, his senses restored, identifies himself as a Count and Mignon as his long-lost daughter.

Mikado, The. Operetta in 2 acts by Sullivan. Libretto by W.S. Gilbert. First performed London, 14 Mar 1885.

Nanki-Poo (ten.), son of the Emperor of Japan (bass), escapes from his intended bride, the elderly Katisha (contr.) and falls in love with Yum-Yum (sop.), ward and fiancée of Ko-Ko (bar.), Lord High Executioner of the town of Titipu.

Milanov, Zinka, b. Zagreb, 17 May 1906. Yugoslav soprano. After studying in Zagreb, she made her début in Ljubljana in

Glenys Fowles and William McCue in Britten's *A Midsummer Night's Dream.*

1927 as Leonora in *Il Trovatore,* a role which thirty years later she sang at Covent Garden with great style, authority and vocal poise. From 1928-35 she was leading soprano at the Zagreb Opera, but after her Met début in 1937, again as Leonora, she became a leading Met soprano in the great Verdi and Puccini roles until 1966, giving her final performance there as Madeleine de Coigny in *Andrea Chénier.* Tosca, Leonora in *La Forza del Destino* and Amelia in *Un Ballo in Maschera* were among her other most successful roles, and her performance in the title-role of *La Gioconda* was also highly acclaimed. She had a voice of great beauty, and an intuitive understanding of the vocal requirements of middle-period Verdi which made her one of the finest opera singers of her time.

Milhaud, Darius, b. Aix-en-Provence, 4 Sept 1892; d. Geneva, 22 June 1974. French composer. Son of a wealthy Jewish family in Aix, and one of the group of composers known as 'Les Six', he composed fifteen operas, the first of which, *La Brebis Égarée,* composed between 1910-15, was produced in Paris in 1923. *Le Pauvre Matelot,* a melodically direct and theatrically effective 3-act opera, was successfully staged in 1927, and *Christophe Colomb,* a work on the grandest scale, calling for forty-five solo singers as well as actors and film inserts, was first performed in Berlin in 1930. Among his later operas are *David,* composed for performance in Jerusalem in 1954 in honour of the 3,000th anniversary of King David, and *La Mère Coupable,* a setting of the little-known third play of Beaumarchais's Figaro trilogy, produced in Geneva in 1965.

Miller, Jonathan, b. London, 21 July 1934. English producer. Diverted into the theatre from his chosen profession of medicine because of his ability as a performer, he went on to direct plays and, after 1974, operas. His production of Goehr's *Arden Must Die* in 1974 was followed by a series of productions for Kent Opera and for English National Opera, all imbued with a searching intelligence though some displayed a cavalier disregard for the composer's intentions. His modern-dress production of

Rigoletto (1982), with the 'Duke' as a mafia leader in New York, and Rigoletto as his barman, was widely acclaimed. Shortly after its première, Miller announced his retirement from opera and theatre, in order to devote himself to medicine.

Millöcker, Karl, b. Vienna, 29 Apr 1842; d. Baden, nr Vienna, 31 Dec 1899. Austrian composer. He studied in Vienna, worked as a conductor in theatres in Budapest and Vienna, and composed eighteen operettas. The first two were 1-act pieces, produced at the Thalia Theater in Graz, while he was conductor there. Most of the others were first staged at the Theater an der Wien in Vienna, the most successful being *Der Bettelstudent* (1882), *Gasparone* (1884) and *Der arme Jonathan* (1890). With Strauss and Suppé he was one of the three leading composers of Viennese operetta of his time. *Der Bettelstudent* is still frequently performed in Germany and Austria, but the operetta *Die Dubarry,* attributed to Millöcker, is a pastiche concocted in 1931 by Theo Mackeben from Millöcker's unsuccessful *Gräfin Dubarry* (1879) and other pieces.

Milnes, Sherrill, b. Downers Grove, Ill., 10 Jan 1935. American baritone. After singing in the chorus of the Santa Fe Opera, he made his solo début as Masetto in *Don Giovanni* with Boris Goldovsky's touring company in 1960. He sang Valentin in *Faust* with New York City Opera in 1964 and the following year made his Met début in the same role. He has since appeared in most of the world's leading opera houses, and was first heard at Covent Garden in 1971 as Renato in *Un Ballo in Maschera*. He has specialized in the Italian repertory, with emphasis on the Verdi roles, and is also a forceful Don Giovanni. In 1982, he sang in Australia for the first time, in Sydney, in the title-role of Thomas's *Hamlet*.

Mime (ten.). The Nibelung dwarf, brother of Alberich, in Wagner's *Das Rheingold* and *Siegfried.*

Mimi (sop.). The seamstress, in love with Rodolfo, in Puccini's *La Bohème.*

Minnie (sop.). The saloon-keeper, in love with Dick Johnson, in Puccini's *La Fanciulla del West*. She saves him from being lynched.

Minton, Yvonne, b. Sydney, 4 Dec 1938. Australian mezzo-soprano. She studied in Sydney and London, and made her first appearance in opera as Lucretia in Britten's *The Rape of Lucretia* in London in 1964. The following year she sang the title-role in *Rinaldo* for the Handel Opera Society, and in 1965 joined The Royal Opera, Covent Garden, making her début there as Lola in *Cavalleria Rusticana*. The light quality and weight of her voice have led her to concentrate on Mozart (Dorabella, Cherubino) and Strauss (Octavian) rather than on the Italian repertory, though she has also undertaken such Wagner roles as Waltraute and Brangäne. She made her Met début in 1973 as Octavian, and has sung Sextus in *La Clemenza di Tito* with great success in Cologne and London. In 1982 at Covent Garden she sang Marfa in *Khovanshchina*.

Mireille. Opera in 3 (originally 5) acts by Gounod. Libretto by Michel Carré, based on the poem *Mirèio* (1859) by Frédéric Mistral. First performed Paris, 19 Mar 1864 and, in the revised 3-act version, 15 Dec 1864.

The action takes place in and near the town of Arles, in Provence. Mireille (sop.) and Vincent (ten.) are in love. Ourrias

Sherrill Milnes in the title-role of *Simon Boccanegra* at Covent Garden in 1981

(bar.), also in love with Mireille, makes an unsuccessful attack on Vincent's life. In the 3-act version, Mireille's father, Ramon (bass), finally gives his blessing to the lovers' union. In the longer original version Mireille dies of exhaustion on her way across a desert to meet Vincent.

Mitchell, Leona, b. Enid, Okla., 13 Oct 1949. American soprano. She studied at the University of Oklahoma, and made her first appearances with San Francisco Opera after winning the San Francisco Opera Auditions in 1971. Her first major role there was Micaëla in *Carmen* in 1972, and this was also the role of her Met début in 1974. The following year she sang Mathilde in Rossini's *Guillaume Tell* in Barcelona. She made her début with The Royal Opera on tour in Tokyo as Pamina in 1979, and returned to sing with the company at Covent Garden as Amelia in *Simon Boccanegra,* Antonia in *Les Contes d'Hoffmann* and, in 1983, Micaëla. She has a voice of rare beauty and the potentiality of developing her artistry to match it.

Mitridate, Rè di Ponto (*Mithridates, King of Pontus*). Opera in 3 acts by Mozart. Libretto by Vittorio Amadeo Cigna-Santi, based on Racine's tragedy, *Mithridate* (1673). First performed Milan, 26 Dec 1770.

Mozart's second full-length opera, and his first *opera seria,* composed when he was fourteen, it concerns the rivalry of the half-brothers Sifare (male sop.) and Farnace (male alto) for the affections of Queen Aspasia (sop.), betrothed to King Mitridate (ten.), falsely presumed killed in battle.

Mitropoulos, Dmitri, b. Athens, 1 Mar 1896; d. Milan, 2 Nov 1960. Greek conductor and composer. Though he began his career as a *répétiteur* in Berlin from 1921-5, and had seen his own opera *Soeur Béatrice* produced by students in Athens in 1920, he entered upon a career as a concert conductor, and did not conduct opera until the 1950s when, after successful concert performances in New York of *Wozzeck,* *Elektra* and Schoenberg's *Erwartung,* he came to the Met in 1954 to conduct *Salome,* and remained until 1960, directing taut performances of Verdi and Puccini operas, and the première in 1958 of Barber's *Vanessa.*

Mlada. Opera in 4 acts by Rimsky-Korsakov. Libretto by Viktor Krylov. First performed St Petersburg, 1 Nov 1892. Originally commissioned by the Russian Imperial Theatres in 1872, to be composed jointly by Cui (Act 1), Mussorgsky (Act 2), Rimsky-Korsakov (Act 3) and Borodin (Act 4), with ballet music by Minkus, the project was abandoned because of the expense. In 1889 Rimsky-Korsakov revised Krylov's libretto and composed the entire work.

Mödl, Martha, b. Nuremberg, 22 Mar 1912. German soprano. She studied in Nuremberg, and began her career as a mezzo-soprano with the role of Hänsel in *Hänsel und Gretel* at Remscheid in 1942. With the Düsseldorf Opera from 1945-9 she continued to sing mezzo roles, but found her voice changing and began to assume soprano roles in Berlin in 1950. With a warm and exciting dramatic voice, she soon became a leading Wagner soprano. She was Kundry at the first post-war Bayreuth Festival in 1951, and was a superb Brünnhilde and Isolde at Bayreuth in the 1950s. She first appeared at Covent Garden in 1949, singing Carmen in English, returned in 1953 and 1959 as Brünnhilde, and then reverted to a mezzo role, Klytemnestra, in 1966. Her last Covent Garden appearance was with the Bavarian State Opera in 1973, by which time she was singing small roles, contributing a telling vignette as the Housekeeper in *Die schweigsame Frau.* She continues to be a fine operatic actress, and at her peak was the leading Brünnhilde of her day, between the retirement of Flagstad and the emergence of Birgit Nilsson. At the 1981 Salzburg Festival, she created the role of Baal's mother in Friedrich Cerha's *Baal.*

Moffo, Anna, b. Wayne, Penn., 27 June 1935. American soprano. She studied in Philadelphia and Rome, and made her début in Spoleto in 1955 as Norina in *Don Pasquale.* She made her first appearance at the Met in 1959 as Violetta and in the 1960-70s sang regularly with the company in such roles as Pamina, Gilda, Luisa Miller, Gounod's Marguerite, all four heroines of *Les Contes d'Hoffmann,* and Massenet's *Manon.* She sang Gilda at Covent Garden in 1964. After a vocal breakdown in the mid-1970s, she resumed her career, choosing her roles more carefully. However, her assumption of the role of Katerina in a revival of Vittorio Giannini's 1953 opera *The Taming of the Shrew,* in Vienna, Virginia, in 1979 revealed her voice to be again in a state of premature decline.

Molinari-Pradelli, Francesco, b. Bologna, 4 July 1911. Italian conductor. He studied in Rome, and decided to concentrate on a career in opera, making his début in 1939 with *L'Elisir d'Amore* in Bologna, Bergamo and Brescia. He first appeared at La Scala in 1946, and subsequently conducted at all the leading Italian opera houses, as well as Vienna, Covent Garden, the Met, and San Francisco. An experienced and dependable interpreter of the 19th-c. Italian repertory, he was still active in the early 1980s.

Moll, Kurt, b. Buir, nr Cologne, 11 Apr 1938. German bass. He studied in Cologne, and made his début in Aachen in 1961 as Lodovico in *Otello*. He was a member of the company at Aachen until 1963, and then made his way via other German houses to Hamburg, joining the company there in 1970. He also sings frequently in Vienna, Salzburg, Munich and Paris, appearing in most of the leading bass roles in Wagner, and also as Sarastro in *Die Zauberflöte* and Osmin in *Die Entführung aus dem Serail*. He first sang at Covent Garden in 1977 as Caspar in *Der Freischütz*.

Mond, Der *(The Moon)*. Opera in 3 acts by Orff. Libretto by the composer, after a story by the Brothers Grimm. First performed Munich, 5 Feb 1939.

A Narrator (ten.) describes how four boys once stole the moon, taking a quarter each. After their death many years later, they put the pieces together and hang it up as a lamp, but the light awakens the dead who make such a noise that St Peter (bass) descends to the underworld to investigate, takes the moon away and hangs it up on a star whence, ever since, it has given light to the entire earth.

Mondo della Luna, Il *(The World on the Moon)*. Opera in 3 acts by Haydn. Libretto by Carlo Goldoni, originally written for Galuppi (1750). First performed Esterháza, 3 Aug 1777.

Buonafede (bar.), a rich merchant, is tricked by a pseudo-astrologer, Ecclitico (ten.) into believing that he has been transported to the moon, where he is persuaded to agree to his two daughters Flaminia (sop.) and Clarice (sop.) marrying the men of their choice.

Moniuszko, Stanislaw, b. Ubiel, 5 May 1819; d. Warsaw, 4 June 1872. Polish composer. The most representative composer of the Polish 19th-c. national school of opera, his first works for the stage were operettas, produced in Vilna in 1839-40. His earliest opera, *Halka* (1848; revised in 1858), remains his best known, and has always been regarded in Poland as that country's most important national opera. He composed at least a further nine operas but, with the exception of *The Haunted Manor* (1865), these were less well received.

Monostatos (ten.). The Moorish slave of Sarastro, in Mozart's *Die Zauberflöte*.

Monsigny, Pierre-Alexandre, b. Fauquembergues, 17 Oct 1729; d. Paris, 14 Jan 1817. French composer. His main interest was in the stage, and all of his compositions are comic operas, works of tunefulness and charm rather than great originality. He composed eighteen operas, all but one of which were staged in Paris between 1759-77. Success came with the first of them, *Les Aveux Indiscrets (1759);* the best of his subsequent works, which appeared at approximatly yearly intervals, include *Le Roi et le Fermier* (1762), *Rose et Colas* (1764) and *Le Déserteur* (1769). After the immense success of *Felix, ou L'Enfant Trouvé* (1777) he gave up composition although he lived on for another forty years.

Montarsolo, Paolo, b. Portici, nr Naples, 16 Mar 1925. Italian bass. He studied in Naples, and made his début at La Scala, Milan in 1954. Possessor of an excellent basso-buffo voice, and an engaging stage personality, he has specialized in comic roles, especially those of Rossini, such as Don Magnifico in *Cenerentola,* Don Bartolo in *Il Barbiere di Siviglia* and Mustafà in *L'Italiana in Algeri*. It was in the last-named opera that he appeared at Glyndebourne for

Paolo Montarsolo as Don Magnifico in Rossini's *La Cenerentola* in San Francisco in 1982.

the first time in 1957. He sings in the leading opera houses of Europe and the Americas. In 1983, he was still an engaging Don Magnifico in Barcelona.

Montemezzi, Italo, b. Vigasio, 31 May 1875; d. Vigasio, 15 May 1952. Italian composer. He studied in Milan, and composed eight operas, six of which were staged in Turin, Milan or Verona. The only one to have made its way abroad is *L'Amore dei Tre Rè,* a powerful piece written in a late-romantic style, which was first produced in Milan in 1913, and reached New York, Paris and London the following year. After *La Nave* (Milan, 1918), an uneven work which revealed the influence of Richard Strauss, he wrote little of consequence. His final opera, *L'Incantesimo,* for American radio in 1943, was staged in Verona in 1952.

Monterone (bass). The nobleman who places a curse upon the Duke of Mantua and his jester, in Verdi's *Rigoletto.*

Monteux, Pierre, b. Paris, 4 Apr 1875; d. Hancock, Maine, 1 July 1964. French conductor. Primarily a conductor of concerts, he directed the première of Stravinsky's *Rite of Spring* in Paris in 1913. He was engaged at the Met from 1917-19 as a conductor of French opera, and during this period he also conducted, in 1918, the American première of Rimsky-Korsakov's *The Golden Cockerel.* He returned to the Met between 1953-6, conducting authoritative performances of a number of French operas, including *Manon, Faust, Les Contes d'Hoffmann* and *Samson et Dalila.*

Monteverdi, Claudio, b. Cremona, 15 May 1567; d. Venice, 29 Nov 1643. Italian composer. One of the earliest composers of opera, several of whose works are still performed, his first opera, *L'Orfeo,* staged in Mantua in 1607, was the earliest to reveal the potential of what was still a new genre. (The first opera of all, Peri's *Dafne,* had been given its première only ten years earlier.) Of his second opera, *L'Arianna,* (Mantua, 1608), all of the music except for the famous 'Lament' has been lost. Among later works which have survived there are *Il Combattimento di Tancredi e Clorinda* (1624), *Il Ritorno d'Ulisse in Patria* (1640) and his

masterpiece, *L'Incoronazione di Poppea* (1642), all of them first staged in Venice. *L'Incoronazione di Poppea* brought a vivid humanity into the art form: of all Monteverdi's operas, it is the one which can most easily be appreciated by modern non-specialist audiences.

Moore, Douglas, b. Cutchogue, N.Y., 10 Aug 1893; d. Greenport, N.Y., 25 July 1969. American composer. He studied in New York and, in Paris, with D'Indy and Nadia Boulanger, before taking up an academic career in music. He taught at Columbia University from 1926 until his retirement in 1962, and composed ten operas, the first of which to be successfully staged was *The Devil and Daniel Webster* (New York, 1939) which is still occasionally revived by American opera companies. Even more successful was *The Ballad of Baby Doe,* first produced in Central City, Colo. in 1956. His final opera, *Carrie Nation,* staged at the University of Kansas in 1966, is based on the life of an American proponent of women's rights.

Moore, Grace, b. Jellicoe, Tenn., 5 Dec 1901; d. nr Copenhagen, 26 Jan 1947. American soprano. She studied in New York where she began her career in revue and operetta, before travelling to Europe for further study. She first appeared in opera in Paris in 1928, then returned to the United States and made her Met début later the

Claudio Monteverdi

same year as Mimi. She sang frequently at the Met throughout the 1930s, her attractive voice and charismatic personality making her extremely popular. Her roles included Tosca, Manon, and Charpentier's Louise which she studied with the composer. From 1931 she also began to appear in Hollywood musical films. She sang Mimi at Covent Garden in 1935, and made her last opera appearances in Paris in 1946 as Louise. She died in an aeroplane crash while still at the height of her career.

Mosè in Egitto *(Moses in Egypt).* Opera in 3 acts by Rossini. Libretto by Andrea Tottola, based on the tragedy, *Sara in Egitto* (1747) by Padre Francesco Ringhieri. First performed Naples, 5 Mar 1818. Revised, and staged in 4 acts in French as *Moïse et Pharaon, ou Le Passage de la Mer Rouge,* Paris, 26 Mar 1827.

Because of the plagues visited upon Egypt by the God of the Jews, the Pharaoh (bass) wishes to set Moses (bass) and his people free. He is frustrated by his son Osiris (ten.) who is in love with Elcia (sop.), a young Hebrew woman. Only after Osiris is killed by a stroke of lightning are the Israelites able to leave Egypt. Pursued by the Pharaoh and his forces who swear revenge for the death of Osiris, the Israelites reach the Red Sea which, when touched by the rod of Moses, parts to let them across, and then closes over the pursuing Egyptians.

Moser, Edda, b. Berlin, 27 Oct 1941. Austrian soprano of German birth. She studied in Berlin and made her début there in 1962 as Kate Pinkerton. She has been singing leading roles in Vienna, Salzburg and Hamburg since the late 1960s. Her first appearance at the Met was as one of the Rhinemaidens in *Das Rheingold* in 1968, and she has sung such Mozart roles there as Donna Anna in *Don Giovanni* and Constanze in *Die Entführung aus dem Serail.* She has a fine dramatic coloratura voice, and is an excellent musician. In 1981, she was admired in West Berlin as Electra in *Idomeneo.*

Moses und Aron. Incomplete opera in 3 acts (the music for Act III of which was not composed) by Schoenberg. Libretto by the composer. First performed Zurich, 6 June 1957. (A concert performance had been given in Hamburg on 12 Mar 1954).

Moses (spoken role) receives the word of God, but lacks the gift of communication and uses his brother Aaron (ten.) as spokesman to his people. While Moses is on Mount Sinai, Aaron finds it expedient to allow the Hebrews to erect a Golden Calf, a tangible object of worship. When Moses returns with the Ten Commandments, he orders the destruction of the Golden Calf. Act II ends with Moses in despair at his inability to communicate the true word of God to his people. (Act III was to have ended with the death of Aaron and Moses's assurance to his people that their future would be secure if they trusted God's word.)

Mother of Us All, The. Opera in 3 acts by Virgil Thomson. Libretto by Gertrude Stein. First performed New York, 7 May 1947.

The opera is about Susan B. Anthony, the 19th-c. American feminist agitator.

Mottl, Felix, b. Unter-St Veit, nr Vienna, 24 Aug 1856; d. Munich, 2 July 1911. Austrian conductor and composer. He studied in Vienna under Bruckner, helped with the musical preparation for the first Bayreuth Festival in 1876, and from 1886-1902 conducted frequently at Bayreuth. He was one of the foremost early conductors of Wagner, all of whose operas he performed at Karlsruhe between 1881-1903. He conducted the *Ring* at Covent Garden in 1898. Though he prepared the first American performances of *Parsifal* at the Met in 1903, he declined to conduct them, not wishing to be involved in altercation with the Wagner family over copyright. In 1903 he relinquished his post as music director at Karlsruhe, to take up a similar position in Munich where, in 1911, he collapsed while conducting *Tristan und Isolde,* and died a few days later. He composed two operas, one of which, *Agnes Bernauer,* was staged in Weimar in 1880.

Mourning Becomes Electra. Opera in 3 acts by Levy. Libretto by Henry Butler, based on the dramatic trilogy of the same title (1931) by Eugene O'Neill. First performed New York, 16 Mar 1967.

The *Oresteia* of Aeschylus transferred to New England at the time of the American Civil War. Agamemnon is represented by Ezra Mannon (bass), a general returning

from the war, Electra by his daughter, Lavinia (sop.), Orestes by his son, Orin (bar.). The modern Clytemnestra is Mannon's wife, Christine (sop.), and her lover, Aegisthus, is Adam Brant (bar.).

Mozart, Wolfgang Amadeus, b. Salzburg, 27 Jan 1756; d. Vienna, 5 Dec 1791. Austrian composer. One of the greatest composers in most forms of music, Mozart was interested in opera from an early age, and began to compose for the stage while he was being displayed throughout Europe as a child prodigy by his father. His earliest efforts were the music for part 1 of a 3-part sacred Singspiel, *Die Schuldigkeit des ersten Gebots* and for *Apollo et Hyacinthus,* an intermezzo performed between the acts of a Latin comedy, both of which he composed at the age of eleven, for performance in Salzburg in 1767. He was twelve before he wrote his first full-length opera, *La Finta Semplice,* for performance at the Court of the Archbishop of Salzburg in 1769. The delightful one-act Singspiel, *Bastien und Bastienne,* was probably given its first performance by amateurs in Vienna in 1768. He entered the world of *opera seria* with *Mitridate, Rè di Ponto,* composed at the age of fourteen for performance in Milan in 1770, where his next opera, the pastoral *Ascanio in Alba* was also produced in 1771. After *Il Sogno di Scipione* (Salzburg, 1772) and *Lucio Silla* (Milan, 1772), he composed the most successful of his teenage works for the stage, the comic opera, *La Finta Giardiniera* (Munich, 1775). *Il Rè Pastore* (1775) was followed by *Thamos, König in Aegypten,* a play for which Mozart provided choruses and entr'actes (1779), and by *Zaide* which he began to compose in 1779 but did not complete, probably because he had received a commission to compose *Idomeneo* for Munich. First performed in 1781, *Idomeneo* is (with the exception of *La Clemenza di Tito* ten years later) Mozart's last *opera seria,* and a masterpiece of that genre. It is generally regarded as the first of his mature works, a series of great operas of various kinds, which continued with the Singspiel, *Die Entführung aus dem Serail* (1782), but was interrupted by two works *(L'Oca del Cairo* and *Lo Sposo Deluso)* which he began, only to abandon, perhaps because he had

Wolfgang Amadeus Mozart

artistically outgrown that type of opera buffa. *Der Schauspieldirektor* (1786), a 1-act comedy for which Mozart provided an overture, two arias, a trio and a quartet-finale, was another interlude on the way to the trio of great operas which Mozart composed in collaboration with the librettist Lorenzo da Ponte: *Le Nozze di Figaro* (1786), *Don Giovanni* (1787) and *Così Fan Tutte* (1790). In the last year of his life, 1791, he composed two operas, the unclassifiable serious pantomime, *Die Zauberflöte,* and an *opera seria* which did not fully engage his genius, *La Clemenza di Tito.* Together with Verdi and Wagner, Mozart is one of the three greatest composers of opera, and the earliest to inject humanity into a form which, a century and a half after its invention, had been in danger of succumbing to formula despite the reforms of Gluck and other earlier masters. The operas he wrote, with Da Ponte are in the repertoire of opera houses all over the world.

Mozart and Salieri (Russian title, *Motsart i Salyeri*). Opera in 1 act by Rimsky-Korsakov. Libretto derived from Pushkin's dramatic poem of the same title (1830). First performed Moscow, 7 Dec 1898.

The composer Salieri (bass), jealous of the genius of his rival Mozart (ten.), decides to poison him.

Much Ado About Nothing. Opera in 4 acts by Stanford. Libretto by Julian Russell Sturgis, after the play (1598-9) by Shakespeare. First performed London, 30 May 1901.

The plot of the opera is a simplification of that of Shakespeare's comedy.

Muck, Karl, b. Darmstadt, 22 Oct 1859; d. Stuttgart, 3 Mar 1940. German conductor. He studied in Leipzig, and conducted opera in Salzburg, Graz and Brno, before being engaged in Prague in 1886. He appeared regularly in Berlin from 1892-1912, and became one of the leading Wagner interpreters of his day, appearing at Bayreuth where from 1901-30 he conducted *Parsifal* every season.

Muette de Portici, La *(The Dumb Girl of Portici).* Opera in 5 acts by Auber. Libretto by Eugène Scribe and Germaine Delavigne. First performed Paris, 29 Feb 1828.

Based on historical events in Naples in 1647, the opera tells how Masaniello (ten.), moved to anger by the oppression of his people and the betrayal of his sister Fenella (a mute) by Alfonso (ten.), Viceroy of Naples, leads a revolt of the fishermen against their Spanish overlords. The opera ends with the defeat of Masaniello and the suicide of Fenella. A performance in Brussels on 22 Aug 1830, sparked off the Belgian revolt against the Dutch. The opera was staged under other titles, among them *Masaniello* (London, 1829), *Die Stumme, oder Untreue und Edle Rache* (Vienna, 1829), *Manfredi Primo, Rè di Napoli* (Naples, 1836) and *Il Pescatore di Brindisi* (Rome, 1847).

Müller, Maria, b. Teresienstadt, 29 Jan 1898; d. Bayreuth, 13 Mar 1958. Austrian soprano. She studied in Vienna and made her début in Linz in 1919 as Elsa in *Lohengrin*. After engagements in Prague and Munich, she appeared at the Met in 1925 as Sieglinde and remained with the company until 1935, singing not only the Wagner roles for which she was especially admired but also a number of roles in American premières of operas, among them Alfano's *Madonna Imperia* (1928), Pizzetti's *Fra Gherardo* (1929) and Weberger's *Shvanda the Bagpiper* (1931). She sang in Berlin throughout the 1930s and until 1943, and at Salzburg between 1930-9. She made her first Covent Garden appearance in 1934 as Eva in *Die Meistersinger* and returned in 1937 as Sieglinde. She had a large voice of warm and sympathetic timbre, heard to particular advantage in her Wagner roles.

Müller, Wenzel, b. Tyrnau, 26 Sept 1767; d. Baden nr Vienna, 3 Aug 1835. Austrian composer and conductor. The most successful of the early 19th-c. Viennese composers of popular theatre pieces, he was engaged for most of his life as a conductor in Viennese theatres. He is thought to have written music for more than two hundred plays, and his scores for the comedies and parodies of Ferdinand Raimund are still frequently performed in Vienna. He and Raimund wrote a number of *Zauberpossen,* popular plays with a magical element (a peculiarly Viennese genre of which Mozart's *Die Zauberflöte* might be said to be an early example). Müller's joint works with Raimund include *Der Barometermacher*

auf der Zauberinsel (1823), *Die Gefesselte Phantasie* and *Der Alpenkönig und der Menschenfeind* (both 1828), all of which contain melodies of a simple and sentimental charm which Viennese audiences continue to find beguiling.

Mullings, Frank, b. Walsall, 10 May 1881; d. Manchester, 19 May 1953. English tenor. He studied in Birmingham and made his début in Coventry in 1907 as Faust. He later sang with Sir Thomas Beecham's company and made his first Covent Garden appearance in 1919. As principal dramatic tenor with the British National Opera Company from 1922-9, he sang a number of Wagner roles in English, and was also admired as a fiercely dramatic Otello. He sang only in England and in English, but many who heard him considered him to be the finest Tristan and Otello of his time.

Munsel, Patrice, b. Spokane, Washington, 12 May 1925. American soprano. She studied in New York and made her début at the Met in 1943, at the age of eighteen, as Philine in *Mignon*. A lyric soprano with coloratura agility, she sang such roles as Adele in *Die Fledermaus,* Rosina in *Il Barbiere di Siviglia* and Despina in *Così Fan Tutte,* with considerable success at the Met for a number of seasons. In 1953 she played the role of Dame Nellie Melba in the film, *Melba,* and in 1963, after some years in which she appeared mainly in operetta, she sang in Monteverdi's *L'Incoronazione di Poppea* in Dallas.

Muratore, Lucien, b. Marseilles, 29 Aug 1876; d. Paris, 16 July 1954. French tenor. He began his career as an actor, then studied in Paris and made his opera début in Hahn's *La Carmélite* in Paris in 1902. He created roles in three of Massenet's later and lesser operas: Thésée in *Ariane* (1906), the title-role in *Bacchus* (1909) and Lentulus in *Roma* (1912). From 1913-22 he sang in the United States in Boston and Chicago, returning to France in 1923. He was a notable interpreter of the 19th-c. French tenor roles, such as Faust, Des Grieux and Don José. After his retirement in the mid-1930s he became a distinguished teacher, and between 1943-5 was manager of the Opéra-Comique, Paris. He was married to the soprano Lina Cavalieri from 1913-27.

Lonette McKee as Julie, Karla Burns as Queenie and Sheryl Woods as Magnolia in Kern and Hammerstein's musical *Show Boat* on tour in the United States in 1982-3.

Musetta (sop.). The mistress of the painter, Marcello, in Puccini's *La Bohème*.

Musgrave, Thea, b. Edinburgh, 27 May 1928. Scottish composer. She studied in Edinburgh and with Nadia Boulanger in Paris, and has composed five operas, the first of which, a 1-act chamber opera, *The Abbot of Drimock,* was staged by students in London in 1962. Her major operas are *The Voice of Ariadne,* first performed at Aldeburgh in 1974, *Mary Queen of Scots* (Edinburgh,1977), and *A Christmas Carol,* first staged in Norfolk, Va., by Virginia Opera, in 1979.

music drama. An alternative name for opera, the term first came into use with reference to the operas of Wagner which the composer claimed were different from earlier operas in that they gave equal importance to the drama and the music.

music theatre. A term used to describe certain kinds of modern small-scale opera, in an attempt to differentiate between them and, on the one hand, Wagnerian music drama and, on the other, conventional earlier opera. Among British composers of the post-war generation, Peter Maxwell Davies and Harrison Birtwistle have written works in this genre. Music theatre pieces are usually of shorter duration than conventional operas, are written for smaller resources, and can be staged without the facilities of a fully-equipped opera house. Although not designated as such, Britten's three church parables could be considered examples of music theatre, along with Maxwell Davies's *Eight Songs for a Mad King* or Birtwistle's *Down by the Greenwood Side.*

musical, musical comedy. Musical comedy is a form of light opera, derived from operetta, which developed in the United

States early in the 20th c. George M. Cohan's *Little Johnny Jones* (1904), with its hit tune, 'Give My Regards to Broadway', is an early popular example, and in the 1920-30s such composers as Vincent Youmans *(No, No, Nanette),* Cole Porter *(Anything Goes),* Irving Berlin *(As Thousands Cheer),* George Gershwin *(Lady Be Good)* and Jerome Kern *(Roberta)* made important contributions. In the late 1940s, comedy became a less important ingredient, and the American musical began to emerge. Richard Rodgers's *Oklahoma!* pointed in the new direction, as did the same composer's *South Pacific,* Leonard Bernstein's *West Side Story,* and works by many other composers, among them Frederick Loewe *(My Fair Lady)* and Frank Loesser *(Guys and Dolls).* The most successful of the current generation of composers of the Broadway musical is Stephen Sondheim, whose *Sweeney Todd* has the stature of opera as well as the broad appeal of the musical.

Mussorgsky, Modest, b. Karevo, 21 Mar 1839; d. St Petersburg, 28 Mar 1881. Russian composer. Though he began or contemplated beginning ten operatic projects, he managed to complete, after a fashion, only one, *Boris Godunov,* which is, more frequently than not, performed in the orchestration made by Rimsky-Korsakov who was also called on to complete and orchestrate the only other opera which Mussorgsky almost finished, *Khovanshchina.* Other hands completed *Sorochinsky Fair,* but the remainder of Mussorgsky's attempts at composing operas did not progress far enough to be brought to completion by others. These include *The Marriage,* of which the first act was composed, *Salammbo,* and *Pugachovshchina.* In *Boris Godunov,* however, Mussorgsky revealed himself to be a composer whose lack of stage technique was rendered irrelevant by the unique richness of his imagination and his conception of the work as a vast, panoramic national opera.

Mustafà (bass). The Bey of Algiers, enamoured of Isabella, in Rossini's *L'Italiana in Algeri.*

Muti, Riccardo, b. Naples, 28 July 1941. Italian conductor. He studied in Naples and Milan, and made his opera début with *I*

Claudia Muzio

Puritani in Florence in 1961. Especially admired for his Verdi performances, he conducts frequently in Vienna, Salzburg and London. Since 1977 he has been artistic director of the Florence Maggio Musicale Festival. His first Covent Garden appearance was in 1977 with a highly impressive *Aida,* and in the same year he was acclaimed in Vienna for his performance of Bellini's *Norma.* His *Così Fan Tutte* at the 1982 Salzburg Festival was considered superb.

Muzio, Claudia, b. Pavia, 7 Feb 1889; d. Rome, 24 May 1936. Italian soprano. She studied in Turin and Milan and made her début in Arezzo in 1910 in Massenet's *Manon.* She appeared at Covent Garden only in 1914 as Desdemona, Margherita in *Mefistofele,* Tosca and Mimi, but after her Met début as Tosca in 1916 she returned to sing there every season until 1922. She also appeared regularly in Chicago between 1922-31. She had a beautiful voice and an affecting stage personality, and was generally regarded as one of the finest operatic artists of her day.

N

Nabokov, Nicolas, b. Lyubcha, nr Minsk, 17 Apr 1903; d. New York, 6 Apr 1978. Russian, later American, composer. He studied in Russia and Germany, and lived in the United States after 1933. He composed two operas, the first of which, *The Holy Devil,* was produced in Louisville, Kentucky, in 1958. *Love's Labour's Lost,* to a libretto by Auden and Kallman based on Shakespeare, was first performed in Brussels in 1973.

Nabucco (properly, *Nabucodonosor*). Opera in 4 acts by Verdi. Libretto by Temistocle Solera, based on the play *Nabucodonosor* (1836) by Auguste Anicet-Bourgeois and Francis Cornu. First performed Milan, 9 Mar 1842.

In Jerusalem in 586 BC, the Hebrews have been defeated by Nebuchadnezzar or Nabucco (bar.), King of Babylon. The Hebrew prophet and leader, Zaccaria (bass), has captured Nabucco's daughter, Fenena (sop.), the lover of a young Hebrew officer, Ismaele (ten.). Nabucco's other daughter, Abigaille (sop.), helps her father to invade and desecrate the holy temple of the Jews. Later, Abigaille discovers that she is only the adopted daughter of Nabucco. When Nabucco blasphemes, he is struck down by Jehovah, and his reason deserts him. He is imprisoned by Abigaille who seizes the crown from him. It is only when Nabucco prays to Jehovah that he recovers his senses, in time to save Fenena from execution. A dying and repentant Abigaille implores forgiveness of Jehovah, and with her last breath blesses the union of Fenena and Ismaele.

Nacht in Venedig, Eine *(A Night in Venice).* Operetta in 3 acts by Johann Strauss II. Libretto by F. Zell (pseudonym of Camillo Walzel) and Richard Genée. First performed Berlin, 3 Oct 1883.

A complicated plot, set in Venice at Carnival time. The plan of Senator Delacqua (bass) to protect his wife Barbara (sop.) from the amorous advances of the Duke of Urbino (ten.) goes astray. Others involved include the Duke's barber, Caramello (ten.), his fiancée the fishseller,

Annina (sop.), and another engaged couple, Pappacoda (bar.), a macaroni-seller, and Ciboletta (sop.), a cook.

Nachtlager von Granada, Das *(The Night Camp of Granada).* Opera in 2 acts by Kreutzer. Libretto by Karl Johann Braun, based on the play of the same title by Friedrich Kind. First performed Vienna, 13 Jan 1834.

A popular work in the 19th c., now seldom performed, its plot concerns the disguised Crown Prince of Spain (bar.) and his involvement with the young lovers Gomez (ten.) and Gabriela (sop.).

Nadir (ten.). The fisherman in love with the Brahmin priestess Leïla, in Bizet's *Les Pêcheurs de Perles.*

Nannetta (sop.). Ford's daughter, in love with Fenton, in Verdi's *Falstaff.* (In Shakespeare's play, *The Merry Wives of Windsor,* she is Anne Page.)

Nash, Heddle, b. London, 14 June 1896; d. London, 14 Aug 1961. English tenor. He studied in Milan, and made his début there in 1924 as Almaviva in *Il Barbiere di Siviglia.* He sang in London and Glyndebourne in the 1920-30s, his finest roles being the Duke in *Rigoletto,* Ottavio in *Don Giovanni* and David in *Die Meistersinger.* An elegant lyric tenor, he continued to sing at Covent Garden until 1948, and in 1957 at Sadler's Wells Theatre created the character role of Dr Manette in Arthur Benjamin's *A Tale of Two Cities.*

Navarraise, La *(The Girl from Navarre).* Opera in 2 acts by Massenet. Libretto by Jules Claretie and Henri Cain, based on Claretie's story, *La Cigarette.* First performed London, 20 June 1894.

In order to acquire money for a dowry so that she may marry Araquil (ten.), Anita (sop.) decides to help the enemy General Garrido (bar.). Attempting to stop her, Araquil is killed, and Anita loses her reason.

Neblett, Carol, b. Modesto, Calif., 1 June 1946. American soprano. She studied with Lotte Lehmann in Santa Barbara, and made her début in New York in 1969 as Musetta in the City Opera's production of *La Bohème.* With the same company in 1975 she had a great success as Marietta in Korngold's *Die tote Stadt*. A dramatic soprano with a fine voice and beautiful appearance, she has sung in most of the leading opera houses of the United States and Europe, her roles including Chrysothemis in *Elektra,* the Countess in *Le Nozze di Figaro* and Minnie in *La Fanciulla del West.* It was as Minnie that she made her Covent Garden début in 1977. In 1981 her performance in the title-role of *La Wally* was highly acclaimed.

Nedda (sop.). Canio's unfaithful wife in Leoncavallo's *Pagliacci.*

Neher, Caspar, b. Augsburg, 11 Apr 1897; d. Vienna, 30 June 1962. German designer. He began to design operas during Klemperer's regime at the Kroll Oper, Berlin, in 1924, and later worked with the opera companies in Frankfurt and Hamburg until 1947. He has also designed for Salzburg, Covent Garden, Glyndebourne and the Met.

Neidlinger, Gustav, b. Mainz, 21 Mar 1910. German bass-baritone. He studied in Frankfurt, and made his début in 1931 in Mainz, remaining with the Mainz company until 1934. He sang leading roles in Hamburg from 1936-50, and was heard at Bayreuth frequently between 1952-75 as Alberich, Klingsor, Kurwenal, and Hans Sachs. He also appeared regularly in Vienna during the 1950-60s, but did not make his Met début until 1972 when he appeared as Alberich in *Der Ring des Nibelungen.* An excellent actor, he sang the Wagner character parts with a rare mellifluousness of tone.

Nelusko (bar.). The slave, in Meyerbeer's *L'Africaine.*

Nemeth, Maria, b. Körmend, 13 Mar 1897; d. Vienna, 28 Dec 1967. Hungarian soprano. After studying in Budapest, Naples, Milan and Vienna, she made her début in Budapest in 1923 as Sulamith in Goldmark's *Die Königin von Saba.* Possessor of a fine dramatic soprano voice with coloratura agility, and an exciting stage personality, she sang at the Vienna Staatsoper from 1924-46, her roles ranging from the Queen of Night in *Die Zauberflöte,* through the Verdi and Puccini repertory to the

Carol Neblett as Chimene in Massenet's *Le Cid* in San Francisco in 1981.

Siegfried Brünnhilde. Considered one of the finest Turandots of her time, she appeared in this role at Covent Garden in 1931.

Nemirovich-Danchenko, Vladimir, b. Ozurgety, Georgia, 23 Dec 1858; d. Moscow, 25 Apr 1943. Georgian producer. He studied in Moscow, and in 1898 with Stanislavsky founded the Moscow Art Theatre. After some years of producing plays he brought his production ideas to opera, founding the Moscow Art Theatre Musical Studio out of which grew, in 1926, the Nemirovich-Danchenko Musical Theatre. His productions of opera and operetta, highly stylized, placed an emphasis always upon social relevance, to the extent of altering scores and libretti where he thought this necessary. In his production of *Carmen,* for instance, the role of Micaëla was eliminated, while in *La Traviata* a new chorus was inserted to provide a running social commentary. He produced a number of new Soviet operas, among them Shostakovich's *Katerina Ismailova.*

Nemorino (ten.). The young peasant in love with Adina, in Donizetti's *L'Elisir d'Amore.*

Nerone. Opera in 4 acts by Boito. Libretto by the composer. The words of a fifth act were written, but remained unset at the composer's death. The scoring of the four existing acts was completed by Vincenzo Tommasini and Arturo Toscanini. First performed Milan, 1 May 1924.

The opera portrays incidents in the life of the Emperor Nero (ten.), including the burning of Rome.

Nessler, Victor, b. Baldenheim, Alsace, 28 Jan 1841; d. Strasbourg, 28 May 1890. Alsatian composer. Son of a Protestant parson, he studied theology as well as music, and decided on composition as a career only when he was expelled from the theology faculty of Strasbourg University because of his musical activities. His first opera, *Fleurette,* was successfully staged in Strasbourg in 1864, after which he became a conductor in Leipzig where several more of his operas were performed, among them *Der Rattenfänger von Hameln* (1879) and, in 1884, the work which became enormously popular throughout Germany where it is still occasionally performed: *Der Trompeter von Säckingen,* an innocuously sentimental opera of melodic charm.

Nesterenko, Evgeny, b. Moscow, 8 Jan 1938. Russian bass. He studied in Leningrad, and made his début there in 1963 as Prince Gremin in *Eugene Onegin.* He sang leading bass roles in Leningrad until 1971 when he joined the Bolshoi company in Moscow, where his roles include Boris Godunov, Dosifei in *Khovanshchina* and Khan Konchak in *Prince Igor.* He made his Met début with the Bolshoi company in *Boris Godunov* in 1975, and first appeared at Covent Garden in 1978 as Don Basilio in *Il Barbiere di Siviglia.* He has a typically Russian deep bass voice, and is an imposing actor. Gounod's Méphistophélès and Verdi's Philip II in *Don Carlos* are among his

finest roles. His Khovansky in *Khovanshchina* at Covent Garden in 1982 was highly acclaimed.

Nestroy, Johann, b. Vienna, 7 Dec 1801; d. Graz, 25 May 1862. Austrian playwright, actor, singer and director. He made his stage début in Vienna at the age of twenty, as Mozart's Sarastro, but later became popular in comedy roles. He wrote, in association with a number of Viennese composers, most notably Adolf Müller, a series of comedies with music which are still performed regularly in Vienna, though rarely elsewhere. They include *Lumpazivagabundus* (1833), *Das Mädl aus der Vorstadt* (1841) and *Einen Jux Will Er Sich Machen* (1842), all with music by Müller. He also composed operatic parodies, among them *Tannhäuser* (1857, music by Karl Binder) and *Lohengrin* (1859, music by Binder).

Neues vom Tage *(News of the Day).* Opera in 3 parts by Hindemith. Libretto by Marcellus Schiffer. First performed Berlin, 8 June 1929.

The opera satirizes modern popular journalism. The employees (mezzo-sop. and ten.) of an international press agency exploit a young married couple (sop. and bar.) in order to provide sensational copy.

Neway, Patricia, b. Brooklyn, N.Y., 30 Sept 1919. American soprano. She studied in New York, and made her début at the Chautauqua Festival in 1946 as Fiordiligi in *Così Fan Tutte.* She is best known for having created the role of Magda Sorel in Menotti's *The Consul,* which she performed for nearly a year on Broadway and subsequently elsewhere in the United States and Europe. In 1952 she joined the Paris Opéra-Comique for two years, and in 1958 she created another Menotti role, the Mother in *Maria Golovin.*

Nicklausse (mezzo-sop.). Young friend of Hoffmann, and also his Muse in disguise, in Offenbach's *Les Contes d'Hoffmann.*

Nicolai, Otto, b. Königsberg, 9 June 1810; d. Berlin, 11 May 1849. German composer and conductor. At the age of sixteen he ran away from an unhappy home, was helped by a protector to study in Berlin, and eventually became a distinguished conductor, and founder of the Vienna Philharmonic concerts. His first four operas, among them *Enrico II* (Trieste, 1839) and *Il Templario* (Turin, 1840), were commissioned by Italian opera houses and composed to Italian texts, but it is for his fifth and final opera, *Die lustigen Weiber von Windsor,* produced in Berlin in 1849, that Nicolai is remembered. One of the finest examples of early romantic German opera, it is still popular in the German-speaking countries where its melodic facility and high-spirited charm seem almost to be preferred to the sharper musical wit of Verdi's *Falstaff,* a setting of the same Shakespeare play.

Nielsen, Carl, b. Sortelung, 9 June 1865; d. Copenhagen, 3 Oct 1931. Danish composer. Though his major contribution to music was as a composer of symphonies, he also composed two operas, both comparatively early works. *Saul og David* (1902) is rather static, but *Maskarade* (1906) is a popular comedy in a livelier theatrical style. Both operas are occasionally performed in Denmark, though rarely elsewhere.

Nightingale, The (Russian title, *Solovey*). Opera in 3 acts by Stravinsky. Libretto by the composer and Stepan Mitusov, after the story by Hans Andersen. First performed Paris, 26 May 1914.

The song of the nightingale (sop.) has become so famous that the Imperial Court arrives in search of the bird who agrees to sing for the Emperor (bar.) but disappears when a mechanical nightingale is installed by the Emperor's bedside. Death (contr.) promises to grant the Emperor a reprieve if the nightingale should return and sing. This the bird does, and the Emperor is saved.

Nilsson, Birgit, b. Karup, 17 May 1918. Swedish soprano. She studied in Stockholm, and made her début there in 1946 as Agathe in *Der Freischütz*. She became a leading soprano with Stockholm Royal Opera, her roles including Lady Macbeth, the Marschallin, Tosca, Senta in *Der fliegende Holländer* and Lisa in Tchaikovsky's *Queen of Spades*. Her first important appearance abroad was as Electra in *Idomeneo* at Glyndebourne in 1951, but it was in 1954 when she sang in Vienna and Bayreuth for the first time that her international fame as a Wagner soprano

began. She became the leading exponent of the roles of Brünnhilde and Isolde in Bayreuth, Vienna, London and New York, and continued to sing these and other Wagner roles, as well as Puccini's Turandot and a number of Strauss roles, until the late 1970s. She first appeared at Covent Garden in 1957 in Wagner's *Ring,* and at the Met in 1959 as Isolde. Her voice is a ringing soprano of extraordinary volume, and though her acting has always been something less than commanding she has had, in vocal terms, few equals as Brünnhilde, Turandot, and Strauss's Elektra. She was still in good voice as the Dyer's Wife in *Die Frau ohne Schatten* at the Met in 1981.

Noble, Dennis, b. Bristol, 25 Sept 1899; d. Javea, Alicante, Spain, 14 Mar 1966. English baritone. He studied in Bristol, and made his Covent Garden début in 1923 as Silvio in *Pagliacci*. He sang regularly at Covent Garden until 1938, and returned for the first post-war season in 1947. His well-produced voice and forthright characterizations made him the leading baritone of his day in England, especially in Italian opera. He created roles in English operas, including Sam Weller in Albert Coates's *Pickwick* (1936) and Don José in Gossens's *Don Juan de Mañara* (1937).

Norina (sop.). The heroine of Donizetti's *Don Pasquale.*

Norma. Opera in 2 acts by Bellini. Libretto by Felice Romani, after the play by Louis Alexandre Soumet (1831). First performed Milan, 26 Dec 1831.

Norma (sop.), a Druid priestess in love with a Roman Proconsul, Pollione (ten.), by whom she has had two children, discovers that Pollione has transferred his affections to another priestess, Adalgisa (mezzo-sop.). When she fails to persuade Pollione to return to her, Norma publicly confesses her guilt, and is condemned to be burned alive. Moved by her courage, Pollione also confesses and dies with her.

Norman, Jessye, b. Augusta, Georgia, 15 Sept 1945. American soprano. After winning a Bavarian Radio competition in 1968, she made her opera début the following year in Berlin as Elisabeth in *Tannhäuser*. She sang Aida at La Scala in 1972, and made her

Birgit Nilsson as Isolde in *Tristan und Isolde* at the Opera House, Stockholm in 1976, in celebration of the thirtieth anniversary of her début.

first appearance at Covent Garden in the same year as Cassandra in Berlioz's *Les Troyens*. Her ample figure has militated against her effectiveness as a singing actress, but she is admired for the beauty of her voice and the sensitivity of her musicianship. In September 1983, she sang in *Les Troyens* at the Met.

Nose, The (Russian title, *Nos*). Opera in 3 acts by Shostakovich. Libretto by A. Preis, A. Zamyatin, G. Yonin and the composer, after a story (1835) by Gogol. First performed Leningrad, 12 Jan 1930.

A satirical fantasy in which Yakovlevich (bass-bar.) finds in his bread roll, a nose (ten.) which belongs to Kovalyov (bar.). The nose escapes from the bread roll and leads an independent life of its own. But it is eventually arrested by the police inspector (high ten.) and he then returns it to its owner.

Noyes Fludde. Opera in 1 act by Britten. Libretto taken from the medieval Chester Miracle Play. First performed Orford, Suffolk, 18 June 1958.

The biblical story of the flood and of Noah's Ark. The voice of God (speaking role) tells Noah (bar.) to build an Ark in which his wife (sop.) and family will be safe from the coming flood. The animals enter the Ark in pairs, and leave again after the flood waters recede. The score, written to be performed by a children's orchestra, incorporates three well-known hymns in the performance of which the audience is invited to participate.

Nozze di Figaro, Le *(The Marriage of Figaro)*. Opera in 4 acts by Mozart. Libretto by Lorenzo da Ponte, based on the play *La Folle Journée ou Le Mariage de Figaro* (1778) by Pierre Augustin Caron de Beaumarchais. First performed Vienna, 1 May 1786.

The opera takes place on the day on which Figaro (bar.) and Susanna (sop.), two of the servants of the Count (bar.) and Countess (sop.) Almaviva, are to be married. The Count, desirous of reviving the old 'droit de

225

seigneur' by which he may enjoy the favours of Susanna before her marriage, attempts to postpone the ceremony, and is aided by the existence of a contract Figaro has signed, promising that he will marry Marcellina (contr.), the housekeeper, if he cannot repay the money he has borrowed from her. Irritated by the flirtatious young page, Cherubino (sop.), the Count orders him away to join his regiment.

In order to help the Countess regain the love of her husband, Susanna and Figaro concoct a plan to expose the Count's amorous pursuit of the female servants on the estate. This involves Susanna in pretending to agree to a rendezvous with the Count, and in the Countess and Susanna impersonating each other. After a series of complications, in the course of which Figaro discovers Marcellina to be his mother, Figaro and Susanna are married, and the Count's intended infidelity is exposed. He is forgiven by the Countess, and the 'folle journée' ends happily.

Nucci, Leo, b. 1942, Castiglione dei Pepuli, nr Bologna. Italian baritone. Winner of a competition in Spoleto, he made his début there in 1967 as Figaro in *Il Barbiere di Siviglia*. He joined the chorus at La Scala in 1969, remaining there for six years. His success dates from his performance of Rossini's Figaro in Padua in 1975. He was invited to sing the same role at La Scala the following year which he did with great success. In 1978 when he undertook at short notice the role of Miller in *Luisa Miller* at Covent Garden, he was greatly acclaimed, and he has since returned in other roles. In 1982 he sang Ford in *Falstaff* in Los Angeles and London, under Giulini's baton.

number opera. The term is used to describe an opera written in separate 'numbers' or self-contained pieces of music (arias, duets, trios, ensembles, choruses, orchestral interludes), separated either by spoken dialogue or by recitative. Until the middle of the 19th c. most operas could be so described. The later operas of Wagner and Verdi tended to dispense with recitative, replacing it with arioso, and the separate numbers therefore disappeared, although even in late Wagner passages of greater melodic interest might still be identified which could be described as separate arias or 'numbers'. Two such passages in Act I of *Die Walküre* are Siegmund's 'Winterstürme' and Sieglinde's 'Du bist die Lenz'. In his neo-classical opera, *The Rake's Progress* (1951), Stravinsky reverted to the use of separate numbers, though they are usually to be found now only in musicals, but not invariably.

A scene from Sir Peter Hall's 1976 production of *Le Nozze di Figaro* at Glyndebourne.

Oberon. Opera in 3 acts by Weber. Libretto by James Robinson Planché, based on Wieland's poem, *Oberon* (1780), which in turn is based on the 13th-c. *Huon de Bordeaux*. First performed London, 12 Apr 1826.

Oberon (ten.), King of the Elves, has quarrelled with his Queen, Titania. They cannot meet until he has found a pair of lovers who are eternally faithful to each other. Oberon chooses Sir Huon (ten.) and Reiza (sop.), and Huon is dispatched to rescue Reiza, which he does with the aid of his squire, Sherasmin (bar.) who rescues Reiza's attendant, Fatima (sop.). Weber's only English-language opera, it is infrequently performed because of its cumbersome plot.

Oberto, Conte di San Bonifacio. Opera in 2 acts by Verdi. Libretto by Antonio Piazza, revised by Temistocle Solera. First performed Milan, 17 Nov 1839.

Preparations for the marriage of Cuniza (mezzo-sop.) and Riccardo (ten.) are interrupted by the arrival of Leonora (sop.) whom Riccardo had seduced, and Leonora's father, Count Oberto (bass), who challenges Riccardo to a duel. Oberto is killed, and Riccardo flees the country. Verdi's first opera to be performed, it was fairly successful but has had few revivals in the 20th c.

Obratsova, Elena, b. Leningrad, 7 July 1937. Russian mezzo-soprano. She studied in Leningrad, and made her début at the Bolshoi, Moscow, in 1963 as Marina in *Boris Godunov*. She has been a member of the Bolshoi company since then, appearing with success not only in the Russian repertoire but also in the Verdi mezzo roles and as Carmen. She first appeared at the Met with the Bolshoi company in 1975, and in the same year sang Azucena in *Il Trovatore* in San Francisco. Possessor of a vibrant voice and an exciting stage personality, she has been particularly admired outside the Soviet Union in the Verdi roles.

Ochs, Baron (bass). Cousin of the Marschallin, his plan to marry Sophie is thwarted by Octavian, in Strauss's *Der Rosenkavalier*.

Octavian (sop. or mezzo-sop.). The young nobleman who falls in love with Sophie in *Der Rosenkavalier*.

Oedipus Rex *(King Oedipus)*. Opera-oratorio in 2 acts by Stravinsky. Libretto by Jean Cocteau, after the tragedy by Sophocles. First performed Paris, 30 May 1927, as an oratorio. First staged, Vienna, 23 Feb 1928.

A Narrator (speaking role) tells the story of Oedipus (ten.), fated to kill a stranger who is later revealed to have been his father, and to marry his own mother, Jocasta (mezzo-sop.). The plot is acted out by the singers and a chorus.

Of Mice and Men. Opera in 3 acts by Floyd. Libretto by the composer, based on the novel of the same title (1937) by John Steinbeck. First performed Seattle, 20 Jan 1970.

Two farm-workers, George (bar.) and Lennie (ten.), hope to acquire a ranch of their own. When the mentally retarded Lennie accidentally kills a girl who has tried to seduce him, his friend George shoots him, rather than have him face the horror of execution by an angry lynch mob.

Offenbach, Jacques, b. Cologne, 20 June 1819; d. Paris, 5 Oct 1880. German, later French, composer. Son of a synagogue cantor, he studied in Cologne and Paris, became a cellist in the orchestra of the Opéra-Comique in Paris, and began to write light pieces for the stage. He became the most famous composer of operetta of his day, and wrote more than a hundred pieces ranging from 1-act sketches to full-length operettas. His most successful works, satirizing the Paris of the Second Empire, were written in the 1860s. The earliest of his internationally successful works, *Orphée aux Enfers,* was staged in 1858, and was followed by *La Belle Hélène (1864), La Vie Parisienne* (1866), *La Grande-Duchesse de Gérolstein* (1867), and *La Périchole* (1868). After the Franco-Prussian war in 1870-1, his frivolous style went out of fashion, though he remained popular abroad, especially in Vienna. (It was Offenbach who encouraged Johann Strauss II to compose operettas.) His opera, *Les Contes d'Hoffmann,* was complete only in piano score at his death, and it was at the request of Offenbach's family that it was

A caricature by T. Thomas of the composer Jacques Offenbach.

orchestrated by Ernest Guiraud. First performed in Paris in 1881, it has established a firm place in the international repertory as a work of unique imaginative power.

Olczewska, Maria, b. Ludwigsschwaige, nr Donauwörth, 12 Aug 1892; d. Klagenfurt, 17 May 1969. German mezzo-soprano. She studied in Munich, began her career in operetta, and made her opera début in Krefeld in 1915. She sang in Munich and Vienna in the 1920-30s, and was greatly admired in Wagner roles, and as Verdi's Amneris and Bizet's Carmen. She first appeared at Covent Garden in 1924 and at the Met in 1933. She had a beautiful voice and was acclaimed as an intelligent dramatic artist. From 1947 until her death she taught in Vienna.

Olivero, Magda, b. Saluzzo, nr Turin, 25 Mar 1913. Italian soprano. She studied in Turin and made her début there in 1933 as Lauretta in Puccini's *Gianni Schicchi*. In Cilea's *Adriana Lecouvreur* she became the composer's preferred interpreter. She retired when she married in 1941, but when urged to sing Adriana Lecouvreur again by Cilea shortly before his death, she returned to the stage in that role in 1951, though too late for the composer to hear her. At the age of seventy, she was still singing, her successes as Tosca, Fedora, Minnie in *La Fanciulla del West* and Medea in Cherubini's opera being due as much to her superb acting as to her singing. She appeared in London in 1952 at the Stoll Theatre as Mimi, and made a Met début in 1975 as Tosca.

Olympia (sop.). The doll who is Hoffmann's first love, in Offenbach's *Les Contes d'Hoffmann*.

Olympians, The. Opera in 3 acts by Bliss. Libretto by J.B. Priestley. First performed London, 29 Sept 1949.

The story concerns the Olympian gods and goddesses, now merely a company of strolling players, but restored to their former glory for one night of each year.

Olympie. Opera in 3 acts by Spontini. Libretto by Michel Dieulafoy and Charles Brifaut, after the play by Voltaire (1762). First performed Paris, 22 Dec 1819.

Olympie (sop.), daughter of Alexander the Great, desires to marry Cassandre (ten.), but is opposed by her mother Statire (mezzo-sop.) who believes that Cassandre was the murderer of her husband. When Antigone (bass), another suitor for the hand of Olympie, is wounded in a battle with Cassandre's troops, he dies confessing that it was he who killed Alexander. Olympie and Cassandre are reunited, and Statire succeeds to the throne of Alexander.

O'Mara, Joseph, b. Limerick, 16 July 1864; d. Dublin, 5 Aug 1927. Irish tenor. He studied in Milan, and made his début in London in 1891 in the title-role of Sullivan's *Ivanhoe*. He sang such roles as Lohengrin and Walther on tour in Great Britain, created the role of Mike in Stanford's *Shamus O'Brien* in London in 1896, and sang at Drury Lane and Covent Garden until 1912 when he founded the O'Mara Grand Opera Company with which he sang until 1924.

Oncina, Juan, b. Barcelona, 15 Apr 1925. Spanish tenor. He studied in Barcelona, and made his début there in 1946 as Des Grieux in *Manon*. He sang a number of bel canto roles in Italy, and from 1951-62 sang regularly at Glyndebourne, with particular success in the Rossini roles of Ramiro, Lindoro *(L'Italiana in Algeri)*, Almaviva and Count Ory. He later undertook somewhat heavier roles, and appeared frequently in Vienna.

Onegin, Sigrid, b. Stockholm, 1 June 1889; d. Magliaso, Switzerland, 16 June 1943. Swedish contralto and mezzo-soprano, of French and German parentage. She studied in Munich and Milan, and made her début in Stuttgart in 1912 as Carmen. She created the small role of Dryade in *Ariadne auf Naxos* in Stuttgart in 1912, and appeared in the same role in the opera's British première in London the following year. She made her Met début in 1922 as Amneris, and in London in 1927 sang Amneris and a number of Wagner mezzo roles. In the 1930s she sang in Berlin, Zurich, Bayreuth, and Salzburg where in 1931 and 1932 she was a celebrated Orfeo in Gluck's *Orfeo ed Euridice*. She had an impressive voice of great range and flexibility.

opéra-ballet. A form of opera which arose in France, in the period between Lully and Rameau. Ballet had already been introduced into French opera by Lully, and in *opéra-ballet* the balletic elements were all-important, the drama being advanced more by dance than by the voice. The creator of the form was Campra, whose *L'Europe Galante* (1697) was highly popular. A famous later *opéra-ballet* is Rameau's *Les Indes Galantes* (1735).

opera buffa. The term is used to describe Italian comic operas of the 18th c. with recitative rather than spoken dialogue between the numbers. The equivalent term in French, *opéra bouffe,* was applied to light operas or operettas with dialogue between the numbers. The operettas of Offenbach are examples of *opéra bouffe*.

opéra comique. Though it literally means, and originally was used to describe, comic opera, the term was used from the early 18th c. onwards to refer specifically to works

with spoken dialogue interspersed with songs or other musical numbers, whether or not the dramatic content was comical. The term was associated especially with the Paris theatre, and with the Opéra-Comique Theatre itself, where such works were performed. *Opéra comique* embraces not only comedies but also romantic works such as Boieldieu's *La Dame Blanche* and even tragedies such as Bizet's *Carmen* (in its original form with dialogue, but not when performed with Guiraud's recitatives which transform the work into a quasi-grand opera).

opera seria and semiseria. *Opera seria* is a term used to describe 18th c. Italian operas on heroic or tragic subjects, often from mythological or classical times. The form persisted until the early 19th c. Gluck was a master of *opera seria,* and the young Mozart composed operas in this form, culminating in what is probably the masterpiece of *opera seria, Idomeneo. Opera semiseria* was a term which originated in the second half of the 18th c. to describe works which did not fall completely into either of the classical genres of tragedy or comedy, but combined elements of both. Both terms, *opera seria* and *opera semiseria,* were used more frequently in retrospect as the genres began to be replaced. In the middle of the 18th c., it was more usual to refer to *dramma per musica* than *opera seria,* and to *dramma tragicomico* or *dramma di sentimento* than *opera semiseria*.

operetta. The term used to describe a light opera with spoken dialogue, songs and dances, in English, French *(opérette)* or German *(operette)*. Operetta grew from the French *opéra comique* of the first half of the 19th c., though its German-language equivalent in Austria also had its antecedents in the *Zauberpossen* of which Mozart's *Die Zauberflöte* was an early example. The operettas of Offenbach, Messager and others in France, and of Johann Strauss II, Lehár and their followers in Vienna led, in due course, to musical comedy and to the musical as composers from central Europe made their way to the New World.

Opernball, Der *(The Opera Ball)*. Operetta in 3 acts by Heuberger. Libretto by Viktor Léon and Heinrich von Waldberg, based on the farce *Les Dominos Roses* by Alfred

Delacour and Maurice Hennequin. First performed Vienna, 5 Jan 1898.

Two young wives put the fidelity of their husbands to the test in a complicated plot involving the disguise of a pink domino to be worn at the annual Opera Ball at the Paris Opéra. Act II takes place at the ball, and includes the well-known duet, 'Gehen wir ins chambre séparée'.

Orest (bar.). Elektra's brother (Orestes), in Strauss's *Elektra*.

Orfeo ed Euridice. Opera in 3 acts by Gluck. Libretto by Raniero Calzabigi. First performed Vienna, 5 Oct 1762. Revised, with libretto in French and the title-role re-written for high tenor, the opera was performed as *Orphée et Eurydice* in Paris, 2 Aug 1774. In 1859 a version was prepared by Berlioz, in which the role of Orfeo was assigned to a female contralto voice, and this is the version now most frequently performed. Modern German productions of the opera have given the role to a baritone.

Orfeo descends into the underworld in search of his wife Euridice (sop.) who has died. He is allowed to bring her back on condition that he should not turn to look on her during the journey. He is unable to fulfil the condition, and Euridice collapses, to be revived again by the god, Amor (sop.), who has been moved by the devotion of Orfeo to Euridice.

Orff, Carl. b. Munich, 10 July 1895; d. Munich, 29 Mar 1982. German composer. His earliest works for the stage were versions of Monteverdi, but he first came to wide notice with *Carmina Burana* (1937), a sequence of medieval Latin lyrics set to brutally primitive musical rhythms. He went on to set other Latin texts, as well as fairy-tales in Bavarian dialect. *Der Mond* (1939), *Catulli Carmina* (1943), *Die Kluge* (1943) and *Trionfo di Afrodite* (1953) are among the best known of these. His later works, which have attracted less attention, include *Oedipus der Tyrann* (1959), *Ein Sommernachtstraum* (1964) and *De Temporum Fine Comoedia* (1973).

Orlovsky (contr., sometimes sung by tenor). The eccentric young Russian prince whose party is the scene of Act II of Johann Strauss's *Die Fledermaus*.

ornamentation. The art of decorating or embellishing a melody, which was expected of singers by composers of the 17-18th c. By the time of Rossini, composers were beginning to write out in full the notes they required to be sung, rather than leave this to singers who had tended to overdo the decoration and to indulge in tasteless displays of what were frequently inappropriate virtuosity.

Oroveso (bass). High priest of the Druids and Norma's father in Bellini's *Norma*.

Orphée aux Enfers *(Orpheus in the Underworld)*. Operetta in 4 (originally 2) acts by Offenbach. Libretto by Hector Crémieux and Ludovic Halévy. First performed Paris, 21 Oct 1858 (in 2 acts). 4-act version first performed Paris, 7 Feb 1874.

A parody on the Orpheus myth, in which Orpheus (ten.), a music teacher in Thebes, is in love with the shepherdess Chloe (sop.), and is happy to leave Euridice (sop.) in the underworld with Pluto (ten.) and Jupiter (bass).

Ortrud (mezzo-sop.). Pagan wife of Telramund, in Wagner's *Lohengrin*.

Oscar (sop.). The page to Gustavus (or Riccardo) in Verdi's *Un Ballo in Maschera*.

Osmin (bass). Steward to the Pasha Selim in Mozart's *Die Entführung aus dem Serail*.

Osten, Eva von der, b. Heligoland, 19 Aug 1881; d. Dresden, 5 May 1936. German soprano. She studied in Dresden, and made her début there in 1902 as Urbain in *Les Huguenots*. She was a leading soprano in Dresden until 1927, and created the role of Octavian in *Der Rosenkavalier* in 1911, making her London début as Octavian in 1913. She toured the United States with the German Opera Company (1922-4).

Otello. Opera in 3 acts by Rossini. Libretto by Francesco Berio di Salsa, after the play (1604-5) by Shakespeare. First performed Naples, 4 Dec 1816.

Rossini's *Otello,* like Verdi's, omits the

Placido Domingo as Otello and Mirella Freni as Desdemona in Verdi's *Otello* at La Scala, Milan in 1982.

first act of Shakespeare, setting the entire action in Cyprus. It held the stage during the 19th c. until supplanted by Verdi's masterpiece. Otello, Iago and Rodrigo are all tenor roles; Desdemona is written for soprano and Emilia for mezzo-soprano.

Otello. Opera in 4 acts by Verdi. Libretto by Arrigo Boito, based on the play (1604-5) by Shakespeare. First performed Milan, 5 Feb 1887.

Otello, Rodrigo and Cassio are tenor roles, Iago is written for baritone, Desdemona for soprano and Emilia for mezzo-soprano. The plot is a simplification of that of the play, omitting Act I so that the entire action takes place in Cyprus.

Ottavio, Don (ten.). Donna Anna's betrothed, in Mozart's *Don Giovanni.*

Otto, Teo, b. Remschied, 4 Feb 1904; d. Frankfurt, 9 June 1968. German designer. He was engaged by Klemperer to design operas for the Kroll Oper in Berlin in 1927, and worked in opera in Berlin until leaving Germany in 1933. After 1945, he designed opera productions in Salzburg, Vienna, Zurich and elsewhere. He designed *Tristan und Isolde* for the Met in 1960, and *Le Nozze di Figaro* for Covent Garden in 1963. At the time of his death he had been for some years Professor of Stage Design at the Academy of Fine Arts in Düsseldorf.

Our Man in Havana. Opera in 3 acts by Williamson. Libretto by Sidney Gilliat, based on the novel of the same title (1958) by Graham Greene. First performed London 2 July 1963.

A British vacuum-cleaner salesman (ten.) in Cuba is persuaded to become a secret agent, although he has no access to any secret information and is forced to pass on plans which are, in fact, nothing more than designs for vacuum-cleaner components.

overture. A piece of music played by the orchestra before the opera begins, the overture may be based on, or may quote from, themes in the opera, or may be a completely independent composition. The term is usually reserved for a movement of some stature, a shorter piece being referred to as a prelude. Many 20th-c. composers dispense with both overture and prelude, taking the curtain up on the action after a few introductory bars of music or even simultaneously with the first bar of music. Operettas and musicals usually are still given overtures, but these are more often than not merely a *pot-pourri* of tunes from the work itself.

Owen Wingrave. Opera in 2 acts by Britten. Libretto by Myfanwy Piper, based on the story (1892) by Henry James. Originally written for television, and first transmitted 16 May 1971. Revised for the stage

Jon Vickers as Canio and Diana Soviero as Nedda in a scene from Leoncavallo's *Pagliacci* at Houston in 1982.

and first performed London, 10 May 1973.

Owen (bar.), pacifist son of a military family, is dared by his betrothed, Kate (mezzo-sop.) to spend a night in the haunted room of his family's house. Next morning, he is found dead.

P

Pacini, Giovanni, b. Catania, 17 Feb 1796; d. Pescia, 6 Dec 1867. Italian composer. He studied singing and composition in Bologna, and composed his first opera buffa at the age of seventeen. An amazingly fast and prolific composer, he modelled his early works on Rossini, and became one of the most successful composers in Italy. By the age of thirty-four he had composed and staged more than forty operas. After 1833 he composed nothing for five years, in the belief that he had been overtaken by Bellini and Donizetti; but he returned to the stage with *Furio Camillo* (Rome, 1839), and thereafter composed his finest operas, among them *Saffo* (Naples, 1840), *La Fidanzata Corsa* (Naples, 1842), *Medea* (Palermo, 1843) and *Bondelmonte* (Florence, 1845). His later operas were less successful, the rise to fame of Verdi being to some degree responsible. His last major success was *Il Saltimbanco* (Rome, 1858). He was to a certain extent a victim of the operatic conditions of his time, and lacked Verdi's genius and energy to rise above them. His best operas, however, are no less worthy of consideration than many by Donizetti.

Padmâvatî. Opera-ballet in 2 acts by Roussel. Libretto by Louis Laloy. First performed Paris, 1 June 1923.

As one of the conditions of an alliance with Ratan-sen (ten.), the Mogul Sultan Alaouddin (bar.) demands Ratan-sen's wife, Padmâvatî (mezzo-sop.). The opera ends with Padmâvatî killing her husband for reasons of honour, and being condemned to die on his funeral pyre.

Paer, Ferdinando, b. Parma, 1 June 1771; d. Paris, 3 May 1839. Italian composer. He studied in Parma, and had his earliest successes in Italian cities with such operas as *Circe* (Venice, 1792), *Ero e Leandro* (Naples, 1794) and *Griselda* (Parma, 1798). In 1797 he assumed the direction of the Kärntnertor Theater in Vienna, where he came to know Beethoven. Between 1801-6 he was composer to the court in Dresden, where he composed, among other operas, *Leonora* (1804), based on the story which Beethoven was to take up the following year as *Leonore* and, eventually, as *Fidelio*. Paer's music was admired by Napoleon who appointed him *maître de chapelle* in Paris which, after 1807, became the composer's permanent home. He composed, in all, fifty-five operas, whose fluent melody and dramatic efficiency were much admired.

Pagliacci *(Clowns).* Opera in 2 acts by Leoncavallo. Libretto by the composer. First performed Milan, 21 May 1892.

In a prologue sung before the curtain, Tonio (bar.) informs the audience that the events they are about to see portrayed are true. The story that follows is about Canio (ten.), the leader of a group of strolling players, whose wife, Nedda (sop.), is unfaithful to him with Silvio (bar.), a young villager. Tonio, a member of the company, overhears Nedda and Silvio planning to run away together and, having himself been rejected by Nedda, informs Canio of their liaison. That evening, during the performance, Canio in a fit of jealous rage stabs his wife on stage. When Silvio rushes up from the audience to her aid, Canio kills him as well.

Pagliughi, Lina, b. Brooklyn, N.Y., 27 May 1907; d. Rubicone, 2 Oct 1980. Italian soprano. She studied in San Francisco and Milan, and made her début in Milan in 1927 as Gilda in *Rigoletto*. Though her stage appearance was unimpressive, her limpid voice and assured coloratura technique caused her to become a leading lyric soprano in Italian theatres throughout the 1930s, her most successful roles being Donizetti's Lucia, Elvira in Bellini's *I Puritani,* and the Queen of Night in Mozart's *Die Zauberflöte.* She appeared at Covent Garden in 1938 as Gilda. After World War II she continued to sing in opera on the Italian radio until 1957 when she retired and taught in Milan.

Paisiello, Giovanni, b. Roccaforzata, nr Taranto, 9 May 1740; d. Naples, 5 June 1816. Italian composer. One of the most influential and successful opera composers in the second half of the 18th-c. he studied in Naples where he soon established himself as a leading composer of comic opera. The earliest of his more than eighty operas were produced in Italy between 1764-76, in which year the composer travelled to Russia to become *maestro di capella* at the court of Catherine the Great. He returned to Italy in 1783 where he was based in Naples until he fell out of favour with the Bourbon rulers. His Beaumarchais opera, *Il Barbiere di Siviglia,* first performed in St Petersburg in 1782, became immensely popular in Italy, until Rossini's superior version of the same play in 1816 ousted it from the stage. Almost equally popular was his sentimental comedy, *Nina, o sia La Pazza per Amore,* first performed in 1789.

Palestrina. Opera in 3 acts by Pfitzner. Libretto by the composer. First performed Munich, 12 June 1917.

The 16th-c. composer Palestrina (ten.), commissioned by Cardinal Borromeo (bar.) to compose a mass to uphold the old traditions of church music, is at first reluctant, but is moved by a vision of nine great composers of the past to attempt the task. He composes the Missa Papae Marcelli which, when it is performed in the Sistine Chapel, creates a profound impression. Palestrina is blessed by the Pope (bass) and appointed director of the chapel. Apparently unmoved by such honours, the composer sits quietly at the organ while his son Ighino (sop.) and friends celebrate outside in the street.

Pamina (sop.). Heroine of Mozart's *Die Zauberflöte,* she is the daughter of the evil Queen of Night.

Panerai, Rolando, b. Campi Bisenzio, nr Florence, 17 Oct 1924. Italian baritone. He studied in Florence and Milan, and made his début in Naples in 1947 as the Pharaoh in Rossini's *Mosè.* After 1951 he sang regularly at La Scala, becoming one of the leading Italian baritones of the 1950-60s. He was an engaging Figaro in *Il Barbiere di Siviglia* and a sympathetic Germont in *La Traviata,* and made a number of successful appearances at the Salzburg Festival, especially as Ford in *Falstaff* and as Guglielmo in *Così Fan Tutte.* He made his Covent Garden début in 1960 as Rossini's Figaro. He is a sensitive musician

and an appealing stage personality, with a voice of attractively distinctive timbre. In 1983 he scored a personal success in the title-role of *Gianni Schicchi* in Munich.

Panizza, Ettore, b. Buenos Aires, 12 Aug 1875; d. Milan, 27 Nov 1967. Argentinian conductor and composer of Italian descent. First taught by his father, principal cellist in the orchestra of the Teatro Colón, Buenos Aires, he later studied in Milan. From 1907-14 he conducted regularly at Covent Garden. After 1921 he conducted at the Teatro Colón frequently until his retirement in 1954, and between 1934-42 he was in charge of the Italian repertory at the Met. He composed four operas: *Il Fidanzato del Mare,* produced in Buenos Aires in 1897; *Medioevo Latino* (Genoa, 1900); *Aurora* (Buenos Aires, 1908); and *Bisanzio* (Genoa, 1939).

Papageno (bar.). The birdcatcher who unwillingly accompanies Tamino on his quest in *Die Zauberflöte,* and is rewarded by finding a mate, Papagena (sop.).

Paride ed Elena *(Paris and Helen).* Opera in 5 acts by Gluck. Libretto by Raniero de' Calzabigi. First performed Vienna, 3 Nov 1770.

Paris (ten.) arrives to claim the fairest woman in Greece, having been promised her as a reward for choosing Venus in his famous Judgment. Helen (sop.) at first resists his approaches, but eventually confesses her love for him.

parlando. Literally 'speaking', this is a direction to the singer to let the tone of voice approximate to that of speech, usually for the purpose of clarity, in passages of rapid patter, or in recitative.

Parsifal. Opera in 3 acts by Wagner. Libretto by the composer, based on the early 13th-c. poem, *Parzifal,* by Wolfram von Eschenbach. The work was described by Wagner as a *Bühnenweihfestspiel* or sacred festival stage play. First performed Bayreuth, 26 July 1882.

In a castle in Spain in the Middle Ages, a band of knights preserve and worship the Grail, the cup in which blood from the side of the crucified Christ was caught, and the spear which wounded him. In Act I, the leader of the knights, Amfortas (bar.), is suffering from a wound which will not heal. He had taken the holy spear with him to fight the evil Klingsor (bass), but had been seduced by Kundry (sop.), had lost the spear to Klingsor and been wounded by it. The aged knight Gurnemanz (bass) tells two young novices that Amfortas's wound will heal only when a guileless fool, made wise by pity, is found. A young man, Parsifal (ten.), appears, having killed one of the sacred swans. At first Gurnemanz thinks Parsifal may be the promised saviour, but when Parsifal fails to understand the significance of the communion service in the Temple of the Grail, the old knight angrily dismisses him. In Act II, Parsifal visits Klingsor's magic garden, withstands the blandishments of Kundry, and wrests the spear back from Klingsor. Years later, Parsifal returns to the knights of the Grail, re-encounters and forgives Kundry who had been under the spell of Klingsor, who heals Amfortas's wound, gives the spear back to its rightful protectors, orders the Grail to be unveiled and blesses the knights.

Pasatieri, Thomas, b. New York, 20 Oct 1945. American composer. After three 1-act pieces had been produced by college workshops between 1965-7, he achieved a wider success with *Calvary,* a setting of the play by W.B. Yeats, which was performed in a number of churches throughout the United States. In 1972, *The Trial of Mary Lincoln,* an opera commissioned by and composed for television, was transmitted, and in 1974, *The Seagull,* based on Chekov's play, was produced by Houston Grand Opera. In the American bicentennial year, 1976, two more operas were commissioned: *Inez de Castro,* performed by Baltimore Opera; and *Washington Square,* based on the Henry James novel, performed by the Michigan Opera Theater, Detroit. Pasatieri composes in a conservative, neo-romantic idiom which is appreciated both by audiences and by singers. *Before Breakfast,* a 1-act piece for soprano and orchestra, commissioned by New York City Opera, was first performed in New York in 1980.

Pasero, Tancredi, b. Turin, 11 Jan 1893; d. Milan, 17 Feb 1983. He made his début in Vicenza as Count Rodolfo in *La Sonnambula* in 1919, appeared at La Scala in *Don Carlos* in 1926, and sang as a leading bass regularly at

La Scala until 1952. His only Covent Garden appearance was in 1931 as Guardiano in *La Forza del Destino,* but he was heard at the Met between 1929-33. He excelled in the Verdi bass roles, and in Italy was an admired Boris Godunov. Possessor of a sonorous voice of wide range, he was also an excellent actor.

Paskalis, Kostas, b. Levadia, Boeotia, 1 Sept 1929. Greek baritone. He studied in Athens, and made his début there in 1951 as Rigoletto. In 1958 he became a member of the Vienna State Opera, and has sung much of the Italian baritone repertory with that company. He made a notable British début as Macbeth at Glyndebourne in 1964, and in the following year first appeared at the Met as Don Carlos in *La Forza del Destino.* He excels in the Verdi operas for which his warm timbre, wide vocal range and sense of style are ideally suited.

Pasta, Giuditta, b. Saronno, nr Milan, 28 Oct 1797; d. Blevio, nr Lake Como, 1 Apr 1865. Italian soprano. She studied in Como and Milan, and made her début in Milan in 1815 in *Le Tre Eleonore,* an opera by her teacher, Giuseppe Scappa. She became one of the most famous singers of her time, and was the creator of such roles as Donizetti's Anna Bolena, and Bellini's Amina *(La Sonnambula),* Norma, and Beatrice di Tenda. By 1840, when she was engaged to sing in St Petersburg, her voice had virtually left her. Always an uneven vocalist, perhaps the Callas of her day, she triumphed by virtue of the forcefulness and conviction of her characterizations. Her vocal and dramatic style influenced Bellini in the composition of those operas in which she appeared.

pasticcio. A stage work whose music has been partly or wholly borrowed from existing works of various composers. Such works were popular in the 18th c., and enabled audiences to hear a selection of their favourite arias, strung together with a new libretto. The practice died out before the end of the century.

Patanè, Giuseppe, b. Naples, 1 Jan 1932. Italian conductor. Son of an opera conductor, Franco Patanè, he studied in Naples and then made his début there in 1951 with *La Traviata.* He was engaged as assistant conductor in Naples until 1956, and in the 1960s worked mainly in Austria and Germany. He made his American début in 1967 in San Francisco with *La Gioconda,* and first appeared at Covent Garden in 1973 with *La Forza del Destino.* He has given exciting performances of 19th-c. Italian operas, especially those of Verdi. In Rome in 1982, his production of *La Gioconda* was greatly admired.

Patience. Operetta in 2 acts by Sullivan. Libretto by W.S. Gilbert. First performed London, 25 Apr 1881.

An amiable satire on the aesthetic movement in which poets of two rival schools, the fleshly Bunthorne (bar.) and the aesthetic Grosvenor (bar.) compete with each other for the affections of the milkmaid, Patience (sop.).

patter song. A comic song in which the humour derives from having the greatest possible number of words delivered at the fastest possible tempo, the tune being of the simplest variety whose purpose is simply to support the articulation of the words. Sometimes, as in Bartolo's 'La Vendetta' in Mozart's *Le Nozze di Figaro* or the same character's 'A un dottor della mia sorte' in Rossini's *Il Barbiere di Siviglia,* the patter element will be confined to one part of a song or aria. Gilbert and Sullivan tended to write complete patter songs, such as 'I am the very model of a modern major-general' in *The Pirates of Penzance,* or 'When you're lying awake with a dismal headache' in *Iolanthe.*

Patti, Adelina, b. Madrid, 19 Feb 1843; d. Craig-y-Nos Castle, nr Brecon, Wales, 27 Sept 1919. Italian soprano. The daughter of singers, she was taught to sing by a half-brother, and toured as a child prodigy in the United States. She made her opera début in New York at the age of seventeen as Lucia, and first appeared in Europe when she sang Amina in *La Sonnambula* at Covent Garden in 1861. She quickly became a leading lyric-coloratura soprano in European opera houses, and sang in twenty-five consecutive seasons at Covent Garden. Though she was vocally ill-suited to the role, she was London's first Aida in 1876. She retired from opera in 1897, but continued to sing in concerts until 1914. She was renowned for the purity of her tone and for her technique, rather than for any musical or dramatic qualities.

Pattiera, Tino, b. Ragusa, 27 June 1890; d. Cavtat, nr Dubrovnik, 24 Apr 1966. Yugoslav tenor. He studied in Vienna and made his début in Dresden in 1916 as one of the Armed Men in *Die Zauberflöte.* His first leading role was Manrico in *Il Trovatore.* He became a leading dramatic tenor in the Italian repertory which he sang mainly in Germany and Austria, though in 1921-2 he appeared in Chicago. He had a voice of Italianate brilliance and a fine sense of Verdian style. In 1950 he became a professor at the Academy of Music in Vienna where he taught until shortly before his death.

Patzak, Julius, b. Vienna, 9 Apr 1898; d. Rottach-Egern, Bavaria, 26 Jan 1974. Austrian tenor. He studied conducting in Vienna, and was largely self-taught as a singer. He made his début in Reichenberg in 1926 as Radames, and in 1928 joined the Munich Opera where he remained as leading tenor until 1945 when he joined the Vienna Opera. Though he made occasional guest appearances abroad, and was a greatly admired Florestan and Hoffmann at Covent Garden between 1951-4, he preferred to remain a member of a permanent ensemble, singing a large variety of roles in French, Italian and Russian opera as well as the German-language repertoire. He was a fine Mozart tenor who was equally at home in operetta, or Wagner's *Lohengrin* or Pfitzner's *Palestrina.* His qualities of musicianship were more responsible for his success than his not unattractive but oddly plangent voice.

Pauvre Matelot, Le *(The Poor Sailor).* Opera in 3 acts by Milhaud. Libretto by Jean Cocteau. First performed Paris, 16 Dec 1927.

The sailor (ten.) returns home after an absence of fifteen years, and tests the fidelity of his wife (sop.) (who does not recognize him) by pretending to be a wealthy friend of her husband, and showing her jewels as proof. As he lies sleeping, the wife murders him for the jewels with which she intends to

Peter Pears in the title-role of Britten's *Peter Grimes* which he created at Sadler's Wells in 1945.

pay for the return of her husband for whom she still longs. Though in 3 acts, the opera plays for less than an hour, and is usually performed with another work.

Pavarotti, Luciano, b. Modena, 12 Oct 1935. Italian tenor. He made his début in 1961 in Reggio Emilia as Rodolfo in *La Bohème,* first sang at Covent Garden in 1963 in the same role, and made his American début in 1967. He has sung frequently at the Met since 1968. Possessor of a large and incisive voice produced in an open, Italian manner, he is heard at his best in the *verismo* operas. His lack of acting ability, perhaps exacerbated by his large size, militates against his success as an artist, but the enthusiasm of his singing combines with an ebullient personality and, be it admitted, the services of high-powered public relations consultants, to make him the most widely talked-about tenor since Caruso. In 1982, he starred in a Hollywood film, *Yes, Giorgio.* His most effective roles in opera are Puccini's Rodolfo and Cavaradossi, and Enzo Grimaldo in Ponchielli's *La Gioconda.*

Pears, (Sir) Peter, b. Farnham, 22 June 1910. English tenor. He sang in the Glyndebourne chorus in 1938, and made his solo début in opera as Hoffmann in London in 1942. From 1943-6 he was a member of the Sadler's Wells company, with whom in 1945 he created the title-role in Britten's *Peter Grimes.* A close friend of the composer, he created the tenor roles in all of Britten's operas, which were written with his particular talents in mind. At Covent Garden, he sang in Britten's *Peter Grimes, Billy Budd, Gloriana, A Midsummer Night's Dream, Owen Wingrave* and *Death in Venice,* as well as in Walton's *Troilus and Cressida,* Mozart's *Die Zauberflöte,* Wagner's *Die Meistersinger* (as David) and Smetana's *The Bartered Bride* (Vašek). He made a belated Met début in 1974 in *Death in Venice,* and was knighted in 1978. He was the co-founder, with Britten, of the Aldeburgh Festival.

Pêcheurs de Perles, Les *(The Pearl Fishers).* Opera in 3 acts by Bizet. Libretto by Eugène Cormon and Michel Carré. First performed Paris, 30 Sept 1863.

In ancient Ceylon, the fishermen Zurga (bar.) and Nadir (ten.), who had once fallen in love with the same Brahmin priestess, renew their old oath of friendship. When a new priestess arrives to offer prayers for the fishermen, Nadir recognizes her as Leïla (sop.), over whom he and Zurga had once fought. He and Leïla reaffirm their love for each other, but are overheard by the high priest, Nourabad (bass) who denounces them. The penalty for their sacrilege is death, but they are saved by Zurga who, although jealous of their love for each other, discovers that Leïla had, many years ago when she was a child, saved his life. In effecting the escape of Nadir and Leïla, Zurga is killed.

Pedrell, Felipe, b. Tortosa, 19 Feb 1841; d. Barcelona, 19 Aug 1922. Spanish composer. His ambition was to be a Spanish equivalent of Wagner, but his earliest operas, *El Último Abencerraje,* written in 1868 and revised on several later occasions, and *Quasimodo,* staged in Barcelona in 1875, were not particularly successful. For a time he turned to the composition of *zarzuelas,* three of which were produced in Madrid in 1881, while two, *Eda* (1884) and *Little Carmen* (1885), were written for and produced in New York. He returned to operatic composition with the Wagnerian trilogy, *Los Pirineos,* which he composed in 1890-1 but which was not staged in its entirety until 1902 in Barcelona.

Pedrillo (ten.). Belmonte's servant, in love with Blonde, in Mozart's *Die Entführung aus dem Serail.*

Peerce, Jan, b. New York, 3 June 1904. American tenor. He began his career as a violinist in dance bands, then became a popular singer on the radio before turning to opera. He sang in broadcasts and recordings of opera under Toscanini before making his stage début in Baltimore in 1938 as the Duke of Mantua in *Rigoletto.* He joined the Met in 1941 and remained a member of the company until 1968. He had a sturdy voice with a ringing top, and was greatly admired in the middle-period Verdi operas. After leaving the Met, he continued to sing in synagogues and concert halls, and in 1971 made his Broadway début as Tevye in *The Fiddler on the Roof.* In his seventies he was still able to give pleasure as a singer of popular songs and arias.

Pelléas et Mélisande. Opera in 5 acts by Debussy. Libretto from the play of the same title (1892) by Maurice Maeterlinck. First performed Paris, 30 Apr 1902.

Mélisande (sop.) is found weeping in a forest by Golaud (bar.), grandson of King Arkel (bass) of Allemonde. Golaud marries her, and takes her back to the court of Arkel, although she will disclose nothing about herself. Love blossoms between Mélisande and Golaud's half-brother, Pelléas (ten.). While talking with Pelléas, Mélisande loses her wedding-ring, and at that same moment Golaud meets with an accident. Mélisande nurses Golaud back to health. Golaud's child, Yniold (sop.), the son of a former marriage, unwittingly confirms his father's growing suspicions of the relationship between Pelléas and Mélisande. Finally, the lovers agree to part. They meet for the last time, but the jealous Golaud kills Pelléas. After she has given birth to a child, Mélisande dies.

Pelletier, Wilfrid, b. Montreal, 20 June 1896; d. New York, 9 Apr 1982. Canadian conductor. He studied in Paris, became a coach and later assistant conductor at the Met in 1917, and from 1932 was principal conductor of the Met's French repertory, a post he filled until 1950. He initiated the annual Metropolitan Auditions of the Air, and after leaving the Met became head of the Quebec Conservatorium of Music and Drama which he had organized for the Quebec government in 1943. He married the soprano Rose Bampton in 1937.

Penderecki, Krzysztof, b. Dębica, 23 Nov 1933. Polish composer. His first opera, *The Devils of Loudon,* created widespread interest when it was first staged in Hamburg in 1969, and subsequently performed by a number of leading international opera houses. A powerful expressionist study of religious and sexual obsession, it was followed by *Paradise Lost,* its libretto a condensation by Christopher Fry of Milton's epic poem. *Paradise Lost,* commissioned by the Lyric Opera of Chicago, was first performed in Chicago in 1978. In 1980 the composer authorized in Trieste the staging as an opera of his 1965 oratorio, *The Passion According to St Luke,* a work whose musical language is somewhat more restrained than that of the two operas.

Pénélope. Opera in 3 acts by Fauré. Libretto by René Fauchois. First performed Monte Carlo, 4 Mar 1913.

The libretto is based on the story in Homer's *Odyssey,* in which Penelope (sop.), the wife of Odysseus (ten.), is besieged by suitors while her husband is away during the Trojan War. Odysseus returns and slays all the suitors.

The opera *Penelope* by Liebermann, first performed in Salzburg in 1954, adapts the legend to fit the details of an actual incident of World War II in which Penelope (sop.), her husband missing and believed dead, has married the Marchése Ercole (ten.), only to discover that her first husband Ulisse (bass) is alive and is shortly to return home, a released prisoner-of-war. The libretto of Liebermann's opera is by Heinrich Strobel.

Pepusch, Johann Christoph, b. Berlin, 1667; d. London, 20 July 1752. German composer. A Prussian court musician, he settled in London around 1700, became a viola player and harpsichordist at Drury Lane Theatre, and produced a series of masques and operas there, among them *Venus and Adonis* (1715, text by Colley Cibber) and *The Prophetess* (1724), an opera with spoken dialogue. He arranged and partly composed the music of *The Beggar's Opera,* to a text by John Gay. First performed at the Lincoln's Inn Fields Theatre in 1728, *The Beggar's Opera* was so enormous a success that Pepusch and Gay published a sequel, *Polly,* the following year. Censorship prevented the performance of *Polly* until a quarter of a century after the death of Pepusch.

Perfect Fool, The. Opera in 1 act by Holst. Libretto by the composer. First performed London, 14 May 1923.

A parody in which a Princess (sop.) is wooed by a Verdian Troubadour (ten.) and a Wagnerian Traveller (bass), but gives her heart to a Fool (speaking part) who is not interested in her.

Pergolesi, Giovanni Battista, b. Iesi, 4 Jan 1710; d. Pozzuoli, 16 Mar 1736. Italian composer. One of the leading composers of Italian comic opera in the early 18th c. he began his career with an *opera seria, Salustia,* which was a failure when first performed in Naples in 1732. His most famous comedy,

La Serva Padrona, was composed to be performed as an intermezzo between the acts of his *opera seria, Il Prigionier Superbo,* in Naples in 1733. He enjoyed only limited success during his lifetime, but his fame became so great shortly after his death that many comic works were wrongly attributed to him, among them *Il Maestro di Musica,* the music of which is probably by Auletta.

Peri, Jacopo, b. Rome, 20 Aug 1561; d. Florence, 12 Aug 1633. A member of the Florentine group of musicians and intellectuals known as the Camerata, he is the composer of *Dafne* (1597) which is generally considered to have been the first opera. Peri himself probably sang the role of Apollo in the first performance of the work, most of the music of which is now lost. He took the role of Orpheus in the first performance of his second opera, *Euridice,* at the Palazzo Pitti in Florence in 1600. He composed a further five operas, none of which achieved the success of *Euridice.*

Périchole, La. Operetta in 3 acts by Offenbach. Libretto by Henri Meilhac and Ludovic Halévy, based on the play, *Le Carrosse du Saint-Sacrement* (1829) by Prosper Mérimée. First performed Paris, 6 Oct 1868.

The action takes place in Lima, Peru, and concerns two down-at-heel street-singers, La Périchole (sop.) and Piquillo (ten.), who are in love, and want to marry. While Piquillo is away attempting to earn enough money to enable the wedding to take place, La Périchole attracts the attention of Don Andrès (bar.), the Viceroy of Peru, and accepts an equivocal position as a lady-in-waiting in his entourage. It is only after many complications that the two lovers are reunited, with the blessing of the Viceroy.

Perlea, Jonel, b. Ograda, 13 Dec 1900; d. New York, 29 July 1970. Romanian conductor. He studied in Munich and Leipzig, became musical director of the Bucharest Opera in 1934, and spent most of World War II in a German internment camp. He conducted at La Scala and other Italian theatres from 1945-8, and then made a successful Met début in 1949 with *Tristan und Isolde.* He remained at the Met for only one season, not finding favour with the new general manager, Rudolf Bing, who was

appointed in 1950. He conducted opera in Italy in the 1950s, but also taught conducting at the Manhattan School of Music in New York until shortly before his death. He made a strong impression when he conducted *Tosca* in Boston in 1967.

Pertile, Aureliano, b. Montagnana, 9 Nov 1885; d. Milan, 11 Jan 1952. Italian tenor. He made his début in Vicenza in 1911 as Lionel in Flotow's *Martha,* and after appearing in other Italian theatres reached La Scala in 1916. He became famous in 1922 for his performance as Faust in Boito's *Mefistofele* at La Scala under Toscanini, and remained a leading tenor at La Scala until 1937, his most acclaimed roles including Lohengrin, Andrea Chénier, Radames, Canio and Don Alvaro *(La Forza del Destino).* Said to have been Toscanini's favourite singer during his Scala years, he continued to sing until 1945 and then taught at the Milan Conservatorium until shortly before his death. He sang at the Met only during the 1921-2 season, but was heard at Covent Garden between 1927-31, as Manrico, Radames, Rodolfo, Canio, Des Grieux and Cavaradossi.

Peter Grimes. Opera in 3 acts by Britten. Libretto by Montagu Slater, based on the poem, *The Borough* (1810), by George Crabbe. First performed London, 7 June 1945.

Set in a small fishing-village in East Anglia, the opera tells of the fisherman, Peter Grimes (ten.), a recluse who has lost his apprentice at sea. At the inquest, a verdict of accidental death is brought in, but Grimes is warned not to take another child apprentice. He does, however, purchase a boy from the workhouse, and the local schoolmistress, Ellen Orford (sop.) helps Grimes to look after the lad. She quarrels with Grimes when she discovers he has ill-treated the boy. By this time local feeling against Grimes has risen to such a pitch that the villagers march on Grimes's hut. In leaving the hut with Grimes, the boy falls to his death from a cliff. Grimes disappears but returns sometime later at night in a state of mental exhaustion and is told by his old friend Captain Balstrode (bar.) to sail his fishing-boat out to sea and sink it. Grimes does as he is told, and as a new day dawns the people of the village go about their business, having already forgotten about him.

Peter Ibbetson. Opera in 3 acts by Taylor. Libretto by the composer and Constance Collier, after Constance Collier's play based on the novel of that title (1892) by George du Maurier. First performed New York, 7 Feb 1931.

Peter Ibbetson (ten.) murders his uncle, Colonel Ibbetson (bar.), and is condemned to life imprisonment. In prison, in his dream life, he recalls the past and his sweetheart, Mary (sop.). When, after forty years in prison, he learns that she has died, he too dies. He and Mary are reunited after death.

Peters, Roberta, b. New York, 4 May 1930. American soprano. After studying in New York, she was engaged by the Met at the age of twenty, with no previous stage experience, and made her début in 1950 as Zerlina in *Don Giovanni* A lyric soprano with coloratura agility, she sang with the company for more than a quarter of a century, her most admired roles including Gilda, Lucia di Lammermoor, and Rosina in *Il Barbiere di Siviglia*. She appeared at Covent Garden in 1951 in *The Bohemian Girl,* and was a highly successful Queen of Night in *Die Zauberflöte* at Salzburg in 1963.

Petrassi, Goffredo, b. Zagarolo, nr Palestrina, 16 July 1904. Italian composer. One of the most important Italian composers of his generation, he was the director of the Teatro La Fenice, Venice, from 1937-40. He composed two operas, both of them 1-act pieces. *Il Cordovano* was staged in Milan in 1949, and *Morte dell'Aria,* based on the true-life incident of a man who, attempting to fly, plunged to his death from the Eiffel Tower, was performed in Rome in 1950.

Petrov, Ivan, b. Irkutsk, 29 Feb 1920. Russian bass. He studied in Moscow, and joined the Bolshoi Theatre in 1943. With the Bolshoi and other Russian companies, he sang most of the leading bass roles in the Russian repertory, and was for many years a greatly admired interpreter of Godunov, and Ruslan in Glinka's *Ruslan and Ludmilla.* He sang extensively in Eastern and Western European opera houses, and created a great impression at the Paris Opéra in 1954 as Boris.

Pfitzner, Hans, b. Moscow, 5 May 1869; d. Salzburg, 22 May 1949. German composer. One of the last of the German late-romantic composers, he began his career with two operas which were heavily indebted to Wagner: *Der arme Heinrich,* staged in Mainz in 1895, and *Die Rose vom Liebesgarten,* staged in Elberfeld in 1901. A more individual work, which is still performed in Germany though it has not been thought of great interest elsewhere, is *Palestrina,* which was first performed in 1917 in Munich. Dealing with the life of the 16th-c. composer, it is suitably antiquated in musical style. A later opera, *Das Herz,* produced simultaneously in Berlin and Munich in 1931, failed to repeat the great success of *Palestrina.*

Philidor, François-André, b. Dreux, 7 Sept 1726; d. London, 31 Aug 1795. Known in his own lifetime as a chess player, he was one of the most talented composers of French *opéra comique* in the second half of the 18th c. Of his twenty-seven works for the stage, only a handful are tragedies, the most successful of which is *Ernelinde, Princesse de Norvège,* produced in Paris in 1767. His *opéras comiques* were admired for their attractive melody, expressive and subtle harmony and effective orchestration. The best, *Tom Jones* (based on Fielding's novel, and staged in Paris in 1765) is also the most innovative of his comedies. Accusations that he plagiarized Gluck damaged Philidor's reputation in the 19th c., but cannot detract from the charm and originality of *Tom Jones* and *Ernelinde,* and the dramatic force of two later tragedies, *Persée* (1780) and *Thémistocle* (1785).

Philippe II (bass). Philip II of Spain appears as a leading character in Verdi's *Don Carlos.*

Piave, Francesco Maria, b. Murano, 18 May 1810; d. Milan, 5 Mar 1876. Italian librettist. Although he provided libretti for Mercadante, Pacini, Ponchielli and other composers, it is as Verdi's librettist that he is remembered. His collaboration with Verdi began with *Ernani,* produced at the Teatro La Fenice, Venice, in 1844. The two men became friends, and Piave went on to provide the libretti of nine Verdi operas, more than any other of the composer's favoured librettists. They include *Macbeth, Rigoletto, La Traviata, Simon Boccanegra* and *La Forza del Destino,* as well as such less

Francesco Piave. A friend of Verdi, he wrote the libretti for nine of his operas.

frequently performed works as *I Due Foscari, Il Corsaro* and *Stiffelio*. Piave was not the most elegant versifier among Verdi's collaborators, but he had a sound theatrical sense and was always ready to defer to the composer's wishes, and indeed to write to his instructions.

Piccaver, Alfred, b. Long Sutton, Lincs, 25 Feb 1884; d. Vienna, 23 Sept 1958. English tenor. He was brought up in New York where he studied. In 1907 he auditioned for and was accepted by Prague Opera, and made his début in Prague in that year as Roméo in Gounod's *Roméo et Juliette*. In 1910 he became a leading tenor with Vienna Staatsoper Opera, and remained a member of the company until 1937, specializing in such Italian and French roles as Radames, Andrea Chénier, Canio, Faust, Des Grieux and Don José, though he also ventured into Wagnerian territory with Lohengrin and Walther. Between 1923-25 he made some appearances outside central Europe, singing in the United States for the first time in Chicago in 1923, and at Covent Garden in 1924 as Cavaradossi and the Duke of Mantua. From 1937-55 he lived in London and taught singing. He returned to Vienna in 1955 as an honoured guest at the re-opening of the Staatsoper, and taught in Vienna until his death.

Picchi, Mirto, b. San Mauro, Florence, 15 Mar 1915; d. Florence, 25 Sept 1980. Italian tenor. He studied in Florence, and made his début in Milan in 1946 as Radames. Though he sang the usual dramatic tenor roles in the Italian repertory in Great Britain, Austria, Switzerland and South America (his first appearances in London were as the Duke of Mantua, Cavaradossi and Rodolfo in 1947-8), in Italy he became known as a specialist in contemporary opera. He was Captain Vere in the first Italian production of Britten's *Billy Budd,* and also sang Peter Grimes, the Drum Major in Berg's *Wozzeck* and Tom Rakewell in Stravinsky's *The Rake's Progress*. He was a much finer musician than Italian tenors are usually expected to be, and a convincing actor.

Piccinni, Niccolò, b. Bari, 16 Jan 1728; d. Passy, nr Paris, 7 May 1800. Italian composer. After studying in Naples, he began his career in Naples and Rome as a composer of opera buffa. *La Buona Figliuola,* staged in Rome in 1760, established him as the leading composer of comic opera, and he continued to produce works of this kind in Italy until 1776 when he moved to Paris. There he found himself set up as a rival to Gluck, and although his tragic operas, among them *Roland* (1778) and *Atys* (1780), were reasonably successful he was unable to compete against the greater composer. At the time of the French Revolution he returned to Naples and again began to write Italian operas. Political events caused him to move back to France but he was unable to regain his former success there. *Didon* (1783), perhaps the most substantial of his French tragic operas, continued to be performed until well into the 19th c.

Piccolo Marat, Il *(The Little Marat).* Opera in 3 acts by Mascagni. Libretto by Giovacchino Forzano and Giovanni Targioni-Tozzetti. First performed Rome, 2 May 1921.

In order to free his mother from prison during the French Revolution, the young Prince Jean-Charles de Fleury (ten.) joins the revolutionary forces and becomes known, for his zeal, as 'the little Marat'. With the aid of his lover Mariella (sop.) and the Carpenter (bar.) he outwits the President of the Revolutionary Council (bass) and effects his mother's escape.

Pierné, Gabriel, b. Metz, 16 Aug 1863; d. Ploujean, Finistère, 17 July 1937. French composer. After studying in Paris, he took up a career as a conductor, and succeeded Édouard Colonne as conductor of the Colonne concerts, remaining in that post until his retirement in 1934. He composed eight operas of which the most successful were *La Coupe Enchantée,* staged in Paris in 1905 though composed a good ten years earlier; *On ne Badine pas avec l'Amour,* a setting of de Musset's comedy, staged in Paris in 1910; and *Sophie Arnould,* a 1-act piece based on events in the life of the 18th-c. French soprano, composed in 1927 but apparently not performed.

Pietra del Paragone, La *(The Touchstone).* Opera in 2 acts by Rossini. Libretto by Luigi Romanelli. First performed Milan, 26 Sept 1812.

The wealthy Count Asdrubale (bar.) tests the sincerity of three women who hope to marry him, by pretending to have been dispossessed of his fortune. Clarice (mezzo-sop.), who survives the test, then turns the tables on Asdrubale by impersonating her twin brother who objects to their union. All ends happily.

Pilarczyk, Helga, b. Schöningen, nr Brunswick, 12 Mar 1925. German soprano. She studied in Brunswick and Hamburg, and made her début in Brunswick in 1951 in Lortzing's *Der Waffenschmied.* She was a member of the Hamburg Opera between 1954-67, and specialized in contemporary opera, becoming identified with such roles as Berg's Marie and Lulu, Renata in Prokofiev's *The Fiery Angel,* the Woman in Schoenberg's *Erwartung* and Jocasta in Stravinsky's *Oedipus Rex.* She made her American operatic début in *Erwartung* in Washington in 1960, and in 1965 sang Marie in *Wozzeck* at the Met in English. She appeared at Covent Garden in 1959 as Strauss's Salome. She was an extremely intelligent and effective interpreter.

Pilgrim's Progress, The. 'Morality' in 4 acts by Vaughan Williams. Libretto by the composer, derived from the allegory of the same title (1678;1684) by John Bunyan. First performed London, 26 Apr 1951.

A series of scenes depicts the adventures of the Pilgrim (bar.) on his journey through life to the Celestial City. An episode in Act IV, concerning the Pilgrim's meeting with the Shepherds of the Delectable Mountains, had been composed thirty years earlier and performed separately, before being incorporated in the longer work.

Pimen (bass). A monk, engaged in writing the history of Russia, in Mussorgsky's *Boris Godunov.*

Pinkerton (ten.). The American naval Lieutenant in Puccini's *Madama Butterfly,* who becomes Cio-Cio-San's lover.

Pinza, Ezio, b. Rome, 18 May 1892; d. Stamford, Conn., 9 May 1957. Italian bass. He studied in Bologna, and made his début in Soncino (Cremona) in 1914 as Oroveso in *Norma.* He sang at La Scala under Toscanini between 1922-4, and created the role of Tigellino in Boito's *Nerone* there in 1924. He made his first appearance at the Met in 1926 in Spontini's *La Vestale,* and sang with the company for twenty-two consecutive years in fifty roles. Possessor of a fine, incisive bass voice and a handsome presence, he became a great favourite in a wide variety of roles ranging from Bellini and Verdi to Mozart and to Mussorgsky's Boris which he sang in Italian at the Met. During the 1930s he sang also at Covent Garden and Salzburg, and was a greatly admired Don Giovanni and Figaro (in *Le Nozze di Figaro*). After leaving the Met and operatic roles in 1948, he began a second career in Broadway musicals (*South Pacific* in 1949; *Fanny* in 1954) and Hollywood films (among them *Mr Imperium* and *Slightly Dishonourable* in 1951, and *Tonight We Sing,* in which he portrayed the Russian bass, Chaliapin, in 1953).

Pirata, Il *(The Pirate).* Opera in 2 acts by Bellini. Libretto by Felice Romani, based on the play *Bertram, ou Le Pirate* by 'Raimond' (pseudonym of Isidore J.S. Taylor) (1826), which in turn was based on Charles Robert Maturin's tragedy, *Bertram, or The Castle of Saint Aldobrand* (1816). First performed Milan, 27 Oct 1827.

Gualtiero (ten.), ex-Count of Montalto but now an exile and head of the Aragonese pirates, returns to find that his beloved Imogene (sop.) has married his enemy, Ernesto, Duke of Caldora (bar.). When he surprises his wife in a secret rendezvous with her former lover, Ernesto challenges Gualtiero to a duel. He is killed by Gualtiero, who is then arrested and condemned to death. When this is revealed to her, Imogene loses her reason.

Pirates of Penzance, The. Operetta in 2 acts by Sullivan. Libretto by W.S. Gilbert. First performed Paignton, 30 Dec 1879.

Apprenticed, by a mistake on the part of his nurse Ruth (contr.), to a gang of pirates, Frederic (ten.) leaves them on his twenty-first birthday, only to discover that he was born in a leap year on 29 February and that his apprenticeship thus has many more years to run. In love with Mabel (sop.), one of the daughters of Major-General Stanley (bar.), he is nevertheless forced by honour to help the pirates defeat the forces of law and order. All is happily resolved when a successful appeal is made to the patriotism of the pirates who turn out to be 'noblemen who have gone astray'.

Pizarro (bar.). The prison governor who imprisons and attempts to murder Florestan in Beethoven's *Fidelio*.

Pizzetti, Ildebrando, b. Parma, 20 Sept 1880; d. Rome, 13 Feb 1968. Italian composer. One of the most conservative Italian composers of his generation, he composed more than a dozen operas, the earliest of which to be successfully staged being *Fedra*, based on D'Annunzio's version of the classical Greek tragedy, and performed in Milan in 1915. Pizzetti himself wrote the libretti of most of his later operas, which include *Debora e Jaele* (1922), *Fra Gherardo* (1928), *Lo Straniero* (1930) and *L'Oro* (1947). Of his later operas, the only ones to have been successfully performed outside Italy are *La Figlia di Jorio* (1954), its libretto an abridgment by the composer of a play by D'Annunzio, and *Assassinio nella Cattedrale* (1958), based on T.S. Eliot's *Murder in the Cathedral*. In most of these works, Pizzetti's musical style is a flexible, continuous arioso.

Planché, James Robinson, b. London, 27 Feb 1796; d. London, 29 May 1880. English librettist and translator. He translated a number of operas for performance in English, wrote scripts for pantomimes, and was the librettist of operas by Bishop, Wallace and others. He wrote the libretto of *Oberon,* Weber's only English-language opera, which was performed at Covent Garden in 1826. He also wrote *A History of British Costume* (1834) and a two-volume work, *Recollections and Reflections* (1872), which contains much interesting information regarding the theatrical life in England at that time.

Plançon, Pol, b. Fumay, Ardennes, 12 June 1854; d. Paris, 11 Aug 1914. French bass. He studied in Paris, and made his début in Lyons in 1877 as St Bris in *Les Huguenots*. From 1883-93 he sang at the Paris Opéra, and made his Covent Garden début in 1891 as Gounod's Méphistophélès. He became a favourite with the London public, and returned to Covent Garden every season until 1904, and even created a role in English: Friar Francis in Stanford's *Much Ado About Nothing* in 1901. At the Met, where he first appeared in 1893 as Jupiter in Gounod's *Philémon et Baucis,* he sang in most seasons until 1908. His voice had unusual flexibility for a bass, and he was one of the most elegant and accomplished operatic artists of his time.

Planquette, Robert, b. Paris, 31 July 1848; d. Paris, 28 Jan 1903. French composer. He composed more than twenty operettas, the most successful of which was *Les Cloches de Corneville,* which ran for more than four hundred consecutive performances when it was first produced in Paris in 1877, and had reached one thousand performances within ten years. Three of his later works were written for London theatres: *Rip Van Winkle* (1882), based on Washington Irving's novel; *Nell Gwynne* (1884); and *Captain Thérèse* (1891). None achieved the success of *Les Cloches de Corneville.* The best of his later operettas was *Mam'zelle Quat'sous* (1897) which was liked in France, but received few productions abroad. In general, Planquette's operettas lacked the melodic spontaneity of the best of his rivals, though he was a conscientious craftsman.

Plishka, Paul, b. Old Forge, Penn., 28 Aug 1941. American bass. He studied with Armen Boyajian, director of the Paterson Lyric Opera, and first appeared in opera with this company. In 1965 he joined the

Met's National Opera Company, on tour, singing Mozart's Bartolo and Colline in *La Bohème,* and at the end of the tour was invited to join the company in New York. He made his début there as the Monk in *La Gioconda* in 1967. He soon undertook major roles ranging from Leporello in *Don Giovanni* to King Mark in *Tristan und Isolde* and the great Verdi bass roles, and is still a leading bass at the Met, although he makes frequent guest appearances elsewhere in the United States (he was a superb Zaccaria in *Nabucco* in San Francisco in 1982) and abroad since 1974 when he made his début at La Scala in *La Damnation de Faust.* In the controversial Peter Hall production of *Macbeth* at the Met in 1982, he was a Banquo of impressive authority. He has a mellow voice of great power, and a fine sense of style.

Plowright, Rosalind, b. Worksop, Northants, 21 May 1949. British soprano. She studied in Manchester and London, and made her professional début in 1975 with Glyndebourne Touring Opera as Agathe in *Der Freischütz.* In the same year she made her first appearance with English National Opera, as Herod's Page in *Salome.* She was a touching Fennimore in Delius's *Fennimore and Gerda* at the Camden Festival, London, in 1979. She sang the title-role in *Manon Lescaut* in Torre del Lago in 1980, and in the same year also undertook Aida in Frankfurt and Ariadne in Stauss's *Ariadne auf Naxos* in Berne. Since then, she has sung frequently abroad. Her beautiful voice (though not her diction, which was unclear) was widely admired when she sang Desdemona in the English National Opera's *Otello.* She made her United States début in 1982 when she sang Medora in Verdi's *Il Corsaro* in San Diego. She is one of the best of the younger generation of Verdi sopranos.

Pogner (bass). Eva's father, the goldsmith, in Wagner's *Die Meistersinger.*

Poisoned Kiss, The. Opera in 3 acts by Vaughan Williams. Libretto by Evelyn Sharp, after the story 'The Poison Maid' by Richard Garnett, in the volume *The Twilight of the Gods* (1888). First performed Cambridge, 12 May 1936.

A fairy tale with spoken dialogue between the musical numbers, in which the sorcerer Dipsicus (bass) feeds his daughter, Tormentilla (sop.), on poisons so that, when she kisses Amaryllus (ten.), the son of Dipsicus's rival, the Empress Persicaria (contr.), she will kill him. However, the prince has been fed on antidotes since childhood, and he recovers. He and Tormentilla find that their love survives the unfortunate first kiss, and the opera ends happily, even for Dipsicus and Persicaria who also discover that they love each other.

Poliuto. Opera in 3 acts by Donizetti. Libretto by Salvatore Cammarano, based on the tragedy *Polyeucte* (1640) by Corneille. Composed in 1838 for production in Naples, but suppressed by censorship. Revised in 4 acts, with French text by Eugène Scribe, as *Les Martyrs,* and first performed Paris, 10 Apr 1840. The original 3-act Italian version first performed, post-humously, Naples, 30 Nov 1848.

The Roman Poliuto (ten.) becomes a secret convert to Christianity. When, in order to save the life of the Christian leader Nearco (bass), he reveals that he is now a Christian, he is condemned to death. His wife Paolina (sop.) is still in love with the Roman Proconsul Severo (bar.) whom she had thought dead before she married Poliuto, but who has now returned. However, moved by Poliuto's refusal to renounce his new faith, she decides to embrace the Christian religion and shares his martyrdom.

Pollak, Anna, b. Manchester, 1 May 1912. English mezzo-soprano of Austrian parentage. She studied singing with Joan Cross, after having begun her career in plays and musical comedy. She made her début with Sadler's Wells Opera in London in 1945 as Dorabella in *Così Fan Tutte,* and remained with the company until 1961, singing a wide variety of parts. She created a number of roles in new English operas, sang Cherubino at Covent Garden in 1952, and Dorabella at Glyndebourne in 1952-3, and was a much admired Orlovsky in the Sadler's Wells production of *Die Fledermaus.* Especially adept at travesty roles, she was a fine Hänsel in *Hänsel und Gretel.*

Pollione (ten.). The Roman Proconsul in love with the Druid priestess, Adalgisa, in Bellini's *Norma.*

Polly. Opera in 3 acts arranged, adapted, and partly composed by Pepusch. Libretto by John Gay. First performed London, 19 June 1777. Written in 1729 as a sequel to *The Beggar's Opera,* its performance was banned by the Lord Chamberlain, and it was not staged until nearly half a century later, when six songs by Samuel Arnold were added to the score.

Pomo d'Oro, Il *(The Golden Apple).* Opera in a prologue and five acts by Cesti. Libretto by Francesco Sbarra. First performed Vienna, during the Carnival season, 1667. Said to have been the most elaborate opera production ever staged, it was performed in a theatre built for the purpose in the Hofburg, seating two thousand, by Lodovico Burnacini, who also designed the twenty-one separate stage sets.

The opera is based on the myth of Paris and the Golden Apple, and the occasion of its first performance was the wedding of Leopold I, Emperor of Austria, to the Spanish Infanta, Margherita. The music for the final act no longer exists.

Ponchielli, Amilcare, b. Paderno Fasolaro (now re-named Paderno Ponchielli), nr Cremona, 31 Aug 1834; d. Milan, 17 Jan 1886. Italian composer. After Verdi, he was the most important Italian composer of opera in the mid- 19th c. He studied at the Milan Conservatorium, and later became a professor there and the teacher of Puccini and Mascagni. Of his ten operas, by far the finest, and indeed the only one to have endured, is *La Gioconda,* first produced at La Scala in 1876. His earlier works, with the exception of *I Promessi Sposi* (1856) which was reasonably successful when revived in 1872, are of little interest, and the two operas which followed *La Gioconda, Il Figliuol Prodigo* (1880) and *Marion Delorme* (1885), lacked sufficient individuality to survive in the new period of *verismo. La Gioconda,* a romantic melodrama with a cleverly constructed libretto by Arrigo Boito, (who wrote it under the anagram of 'Tobia Gorrio'), reveals Ponchielli's gifts for warm melody and effective orchestration at their highest level.

Ponnelle, Jean-Pierre, b. Paris, 19 Feb 1932. French designer and producer. His career in opera began when he was invited by Henze to design the first production of *Boulevard Solitude* in Hanover in 1952. He designed operas in France, Germany and in San Francisco, and in 1962 began to produce opera, beginning with *Tristan und Isolde* in Düsseldorf. He has become a leading producer, and invariably designs his own productions, which have included *Così Fan Tutte, Le Nozze di Figaro* and *Il Barbiere di Siviglia* in Salzburg, *Don Carlos* and *La Cenerentola* at La Scala; *L'Italiana in Algeri* at the Met, *Don Pasquale* at Covent Garden, and *Pelléas et Mélisande* in Munich.

Pons, Lily, b. Draguignan, nr Cannes, 16 Apr 1898; d. Dallas 13 Jan 1976. French, later American soprano. She studied piano and voice in Paris, and made her opera début in Mulhouse in 1928 as Lakmé. After singing in other French provincial theatres, she made her Met début in 1931 as Lucia. A sensational success, she sang with the Met until 1961, specializing in the lyric-coloratura repertory. Lucia remained one of her most popular roles, in which she had no rivals in the United States until the emergence of Joan Sutherland. Her other roles at the Met included Gilda, Amina in *La Sonnambula,* Marie in *La Fille du Régiment,* and Lakmé. She sang Rosina in *Il Barbiere di Siviglia* at Covent Garden, and starred in a number of musical films in Hollywood beginning in 1935 with *I Dream Too Much.* Her voice was of appealing quality and her technique exceptionally secure. She made many gramophone records, several conducted by André Kostelanetz to whom she was married from 1938-58.

Ponselle, Rosa, b. Meriden, Conn., 22 Jan 1897; d. Baltimore, 25 May 1981. American soprano of Italian parentage. She began singing in vaudeville theatres with her elder sister Carmela, a mezzo-soprano, and then studied in New York. Her coach brought her to the attention of Caruso who recommended her to the Met where she made her opera début, opposite Caruso, in *La Forza del Destino* in 1918. She sang with the Met for nineteen seasons, her roles including Norma, Violetta, Elvira in *Ernani* and the title-role in *La Gioconda.* She sang at Covent Garden, 1929-31, as Norma, Violetta, Leonora in *La Forza del Destino* and

Rosa Ponselle as Norma.

the title-role in *Fedra,* an opera by her singing teacher, Romano Romani. At the Florence Maggio Musicale in 1933 she sang Giulia in Spontini's *La Vestale.* She retired prematurely in 1937 after an altercation with the management of the Met. She was the possessor of a voice of rare beauty and a perfect technique. After her retirement she taught, and became artistic director of the Baltimore Civic Opera in 1954.

Popp, Lucia, b. Bratislava, 12 Nov 1939. Austrian soprano of Czech birth. She studied in Bratislava and she made her début there as Queen of Night in *Die Zauberflöte* while still a student. This led to her being invited to join the Vienna Staatsoper, and her first appearance in Vienna in 1963 was as Queen of Night in *Die Zauberflöte.* She has become one of the most admired lyric sopranos of her time in the Mozart and Strauss roles, and has now moved from her first role in *Die Zauberflöte* to Pamina. Susanna in *Le Nozze di Figaro* is one of her finest characterizations, as is Sophie in *Der Rosenkavalier.* She has a most attractive voice and a winning stage personality. She first appeared at Covent Garden in 1966 as Oscar in *Un Ballo in Maschera* and made her Met début the following year as the Queen of Night. She was acclaimed as an almost perfect Eva in *Die Meistersinger* at Covent Garden in 1982.

Porgy and Bess. Opera in 3 acts by Gershwin. Libretto by Du Bose Heyward and Ira Gershwin, based on the play, *Porgy,* by Du Bose and Dorothy Heyward (1927) which in turn was based on Du Bose Heyward's novel, *Porgy* (1925). First performed Boston, 30 Sept 1935.

In the negro community of Catfish Row in Charleston, South Carolina, the crippled Porgy (bar.) and the tough stevedore Crown (bar.) compete for the love of Bess (sop.). Crown is killed by Porgy, who then sets out to follow Bess to New York, whither she has been lured by Sportin' Life (ten.), a dope peddler.

Porpora, Nicola, b. Naples, 17 Aug 1686; d. Naples, 3 Mar 1768. Italian composer and teacher of singing. Internationally famous in his lifetime as the composer of more than fifty operas which were staged in London and Vienna as well as several Italian cities, he

is remembered now as a great singing teacher. His remarkable knowledge of the voice led him to write effective arias, but his operas are thought to have lacked dramatic impetus. His first opera, *Agrippina,* was produced in Naples in 1708, but his best period was between 1718-42. His London operas included *Arianna in Nasso* (1733), *Enea nel Lazio* (1734) and *Mitridate* (1736).

posse. Its literal meaning is 'farce'. The terms *Posse, Posse mit Gesang* and *Zauberposse* came to be used in Vienna to describe the comedies with songs, sometimes on magical themes, which were popular in 19th-c. Vienna. The most famous writers of these plays were Raimund and Nestroy, and the composers who wrote music for them included Wenzel Müller, Adolf Müller, Ferdinand Kauer and Franz von Suppé.

Postillon de Longjumeau, Le *(The Postilion of Longjumeau).* Opera in 3 acts by Adam. Libretto by Adolphe de Leuven and Léon Brunswick. First performed Paris, 13 Oct 1836.

Chappelou (ten.), a postilion, leaves his bride Madeleine (sop.) on their wedding night, having received an offer from the Marquis de Courcy (bar.) to sing at the Paris Opéra. Ten years later, now a celebrated tenor, Chappelou falls in love with Mme de Latour who turns out to be his deserted wife. After several complications, the truth is revealed, but Madeleine forgives her errant husband, and all ends happily.

Poulenc, Francis, b. Paris, 7 Jan 1899; d. Paris, 30 Jan 1963. French composer. Arguably the most distinguished French composer since Ravel, he wrote incidental music for a nonsense play, *Le Gendarme Incompris,* by Cocteau and Raymond Radiguet in 1921, but withdrew his score soon afterwards and did not arrive at the composition of real opera until 1944 when he set Apollinaire's play, *Les Mamelles de Tirésias.* A comic opera with moments of lyrical beauty, it was a huge success when staged in Paris in 1947. Poulenc's second opera, *Dialogues des Carmélites,* by contrast is a serious, indeed moving study of character and emotion among a group of Carmelite nuns condemned to the guillotine during the French Revolution. First produced in Milan and Paris in 1957, it has been frequently revived in France and abroad. His final work for the stage, *La Voix Humaine* (1959), is a 1-act piece for solo soprano and orchestra, a 40-minute telephone conversation between a woman and lover who is breaking off his relationship with her. It, too, is an effective and affecting piece of music theatre.

Powers, Marie, b. Mount Carmel, Pa., c.1910; d. New York, 28 Dec 1973. American contralto. Although she appeared in Europe in the 1930s under the name of Maria Crescentini, and in the United States on tour, it was when she created roles in two of Menotti's operas, *The Medium* (in the title-role) in 1947 and *The Consul* (as the Mother) in 1950 that her unique qualities as a singing actress became widely recognized. She sang in a number of productions of *The Medium,* including the London production of 1948. She also sang Fricka in *Die Walküre* at the Paris Opéra in 1951, and Mistress Quickly in *Falstaff* at the Opéra-Comique in 1952.

Pré aux Clercs, Le *(The Meadow of the Clerks).* Opera in 3 acts by Hérold. Libretto by François de Planard, based on Prosper Merimée's novel, *Chronique du Règne de Charles IX* (1829). First performed Paris, 15 Dec 1832.

The marriage between Isabelle de Béarn (sop.) and the Baron de Mergy (ten.) is brought about by Marguerite de Valois (mezzo-sop.). The Baron de Mergy defeats his rival for the hand of Isabelle, on the field known as Le Pré aux Clercs.

prelude. When used in an operatic context, the term denotes an orchestral piece played before the curtain rises. A prelude performs the same function as an overture, but is generally shorter, and simpler in form.

Prêtre, Georges, b. Waziers, 14 Aug 1924. French conductor. He studied in Paris, and made his début with Lalo's *Le Roi d'Ys* in Marseilles in 1946. After ten years in various French provincial opera houses, he first

Clara sings 'Summertime' at the beginning of Gershwin's *Porgy and Bess* in a performance by Houston Grand Opera in Paris.

appeared in Paris in 1956, at the Opéra-Comique conducting the first Paris performance of Strauss's *Capriccio*. He remained with the Opéra-Comique for three years, and was then engaged by the Opéra. In 1959 he conducted the première of Poulenc's *La Voix Humaine*. A highly respected interpreter of 19th-c. French opera, he made his first American appearance with Chicago Lyric Opera in 1959, and first conducted at the Met in 1964. He made his Covent Garden début the following year conducting *Tosca* with Callas. He made a highly admired gramophone recording of *Carmen* with Callas and Gedda in 1963, and conducted exciting performances of *Samson et Dalila* at Covent Garden in 1983.

Previtali, Fernando, b. Adria, 16 Feb 1907. Italian conductor. He studied in Turin and began his career as a cellist in the opera orchestra in Turin. In 1928 he moved to Florence to assist Vittorio Gui at the Teatro Comunale. He became known as an interpreter of contemporary scores, conducted opera frequently in Buenos Aires from 1959, and was appointed principal conductor at the Teatro San Carlo, Naples, in 1972, later becoming artistic director of the opera in Turin and Genoa. He made his American opera début in Dallas in 1975 with Donizetti's *Anna Bolena*.

Prey, Hermann, b. Berlin, 11 July 1929. German baritone. He studied in Berlin and made his début in Wiesbaden in 1952 as Second Prisoner in *Fidelio*. The following year he became leading baritone at the Hamburg Staatsoper, and by the end of the 1950s was regularly singing with the Vienna and Munich companies. Since 1959 he has also frequently appeared at the Salzburg Festival where he is highly prized in such Mozart roles as Papageno, Guglielmo in *Così Fan Tutte* and the Count in *Le Nozze di Figaro*. He also sings Figaro both in *Le Nozze di Figaro* and in *Il Barbiere di Siviglia*, and has sung the latter role with particular success at La Scala. He made his Met début in 1960 as Wolfram in *Tannhäuser,* and his Bayreuth début in the same role in 1965. He first appeared at Covent Garden in 1973 as Rossini's *Figaro,* and later appeared there as Papageno, Guglielmo, and as Eisenstein in *Die Fledermaus*. He has a warm, mellifluous baritone voice of wide range, and is an actor

of engaging charm. At Bayreuth in 1981, he undertook for the first time the role of Beckmesser in *Die Meistersinger*.

Preziosilla (mezzo-sop.). The gipsy girl and camp-follower in Verdi's *La Forza del Destino*.

Přibyl, Vilém, b. Náchod, 10 Apr 1925. Czech tenor. Originally an engineer, he began singing as an amateur. After studying in Czech provincial towns and accepting engagements with various opera companies, he became leading tenor in Brno in 1961, and later sang with the Prague National Theatre. He first sang abroad in 1964, in Edinburgh, with the Prague company as Smetana's Dalibor, and subsequently was engaged by Covent Garden as Florestan in *Fidelio*. In 1969 he took up a teaching post in Brno. The leading Czech tenor of the 1960s, his repertoire included Radames, Otello and Lohengrin.

Price, Leontyne, b. Laurel, Miss., 10 Feb 1927. American soprano. She studied in New York at the Juilliard School where she sang Alice Ford in *Falstaff* as a student. In 1952 she appeared in a revival of Virgil Thomson's *Four Saints in Three Acts* in New York, and from 1952-4 was engaged as Bess on a world tour of *Porgy and Bess*. After she sang Aida in 1958 in Verona, Vienna and Covent Garden, she was acclaimed as a Verdi soprano of the highest quality. In Vienna and Salzburg she was a great success as Donna Anna, Leonora in *Il Trovatore* and several other roles. Her Met début in 1961 was as Leonora. She is generally recognized as the finest Verdi soprano of her time, by virtue of her beautiful voice, assured technique, and unique understanding of the middle-period Verdi roles. At the opening of the new Met in 1966, she sang Cleopatra in Barber's *Antony and Cleopatra*. In her mid-fifties, in San Francisco in November 1981, she was still a superb Aida.

Price, Margaret, b. Blackwood, 13 Apr 1941. Welsh soprano. She studied in London, and made her début in 1962 with Welsh National Opera as Cherubino, a role she sang the following year at Covent Garden when she replaced an indisposed Teresa Berganza. In 1968 she sang Constanze in *Die Entführung aus dem Serail* at

Margaret Price (right) as Aida and Stefania Toczyska as Amneris in Verdi's *Aida* in San Francisco in 1981.

Glyndebourne. She became one of the most highly regarded Mozart sopranos of the 1970s, was acclaimed as Donna Anna in Vienna, and has sung a number of roles there and at Salzburg Festivals. Her first appearance in the United States was as Pamina in San Francisco in 1969. She has an impressive and agile voice, and a fine musical instinct. In 1983 in Munich, she sang the Marschallin in *Der Rosenkavalier*. Her continued neglect by British Opera houses is inexplicable.

Prigioniero, Il *(The Prisoner)*. Opera in 1 act by Dallapiccola. Libretto by the composer, based on *La Torture par Espérance* by Villiers de l'Isle Adam (1883), and Charles de Coster's *La Légende d'Eulenspiegel et de Lamme Goedzac*. First performed Florence, 20 May 1950.

A prisoner (bar.) of the Spaniards in the 17th-c Netherlands is treated in kindly fashion by his gaoler (ten.). Finding his cell door open, the prisoner escapes into the open-air, only to find he is in an enclosed garden where he is awaited by the Grand Inquisitor (ten.). He has been tortured by having been allowed to hope.

Prima Donna. Opera in 1 act by Benjamin. Libretto by Cedric Cliffe. First performed London, 23 Feb 1949.

A satire on the foibles of two rival prima donnas, set in 18th-c. Venice.

prima donna. Literally 'first lady', the term is used to describe the leading female singer in an opera. The male equivalent, *primo uomo*, is less commonly used outside Italy.

Prima la Musica e Poi le Parole *(First the music, and then the words)*. Opera in 1 act by Salieri. Libretto by Giovanni Battista Casti. First performed Vienna, 7 Feb 1786, together with Mozart's *Der Schauspieldirektor*.

A witty discussion between a composer and a poet on the subject of the relative importance of words and music in opera, its argument is used, and its title quoted, in Clemens Krauss's libretto for Richard Strauss's 20th-c. opera, *Capriccio*.

Prince Igor (Russian title, *Knyaz Igor*). Opera in a prologue and 4 acts by Borodin. Libretto by the composer, based on an outline by Vladimir Stasov. First performed St Petersburg, 4 Nov 1890. The opera was left unfinished by Borodin, and was completed and partly orchestrated by Rimsky-Korsakov and Glazunov.

In 12th-c. Russia, Prince Igor (bar.) and his son Vladimir (ten.) go to war against the Polovtsians who have invaded their country, leaving Igor's wife Yaroslavna (sop.) in the care of her brother Prince Galitzky (bass). Igor and Vladimir are captured by the Polovtsian leader, Khan Konchak (bass). Offered his freedom if he agrees not to fight the Polovtsians again, Igor refuses and escapes to rejoin his wife. Vladimir remains behind, and marries Konchakovna (mezzo-sop.), daughter of Konchak.

Prinz von Homburg, Der. Opera in 3 acts by Henze. Libretto by Ingeborg Bachmann, based on the play, *Prinz Friedrich von Homburg* (1821) by Heinrich von Kleist. First performed Hamburg, 22 May 1960.

Prince Friedrich (bar.), a cavalry general in the forces of the Elector of Brandenburg (ten.), dreams that he will win the battle and the hand of the Elector's niece Natalie (sop.). He attacks before the order is given and, although his forces are victorious, he is condemned to death for insubordination. He comes to accept the justice of this decision, but is then pardoned and reunited with Natalie, almost as in his dream.

Pritchard, (Sir) John, b. London, 5 Feb 1921. English conductor. He began his professional career as coach, chorus master, and assistant conductor at Glyndebourne in 1947, and made his début as a conductor of opera with *Don Giovanni* in 1949. He remained associated with Glyndebourne for many years, and from 1969-78 was musical director. He first appeared at Covent Garden in 1952 with *Un Ballo in Maschera,* and later conducted the premières there of Britten's *Gloriana* and Tippett's *Midsummer Marriage* and *King Priam*. He became chief conductor of Cologne Opera in 1978, and music director of the Belgium National

A scene from Prokofiev's *Love for Three Oranges* directed by András Békés at the State Opera House, Budapest in 1975.

Opera in 1981. His performances are capable, though lacking in dramatic flair, and his musical gifts are most clearly revealed in his handling of difficult modern scores. He was knighted in 1983.

Prodigal Son, The. Church parable in 1 act by Britten. Libretto by William Plomer, derived from the parable in the Gospel According to St Luke (Ch. 15, verses 11-32). First performed Orford, 10 June 1968.

The parable is performed as by a medieval Abbot and his monks, the Abbot taking the role of the Tempter (ten.) who lures the Younger Son (ten.) away from working in the fields with the Father (bass-bar.) and the Elder Son (bar.). The Younger Son takes his inheritance, and is robbed of it in the city. He returns home to be welcomed by his father and, eventually, reconciled with his brother.

Prokofiev, Sergei, b. Sontsovka, Ekaterinoslav district, 23 Apr 1891; d. Moscow, 5 Mar 1953. Russian composer. He composed his first opera, *The Giant,* at the age of nine, but it remained unperformed, and even unorchestrated. After four further youthful attempts at opera, none of them performed (except the last, *Maddalena,* which was broadcast by the BBC in 1979 and again in 1983), he wrote his first successful opera, *The Gambler,* between 1915-17. It was eventually performed in 1929, by which time *The Love for Three Oranges,* composed in 1919, had been staged in Chicago (in 1921). After the Russian Revolution, Prokofiev lived mainly in the United States and later in Paris, but returned to the Soviet Union in 1936 and stayed there for the remainder of his life. *The Fiery Angel,* which he had composed abroad between 1919-23, was not staged until eighteen months after his death, but the operas he composed after his return to the Soviet Union were all produced there. *Semyon Kotko* (1940), based on a novel by Valentin Katayev about the closing stages of the Revolution in the Ukraine, is still in the repertory of Soviet opera houses, though it is of too purely parochial interest to find favour abroad. *Betrothal in a Monastery* (composed in 1940-1 but not staged until 1946), based on Sheridan, is a work of lyrical charm. Prokofiev's operatic masterpiece, *War and Peace,* a setting of scenes from Tolstoy's

novel, was composed in 1941-2 and given an abridged performance in Leningrad in 1946. (It was staged, almost complete, in Moscow in 1957.) Although he began two other operas, Prokofiev completed only one more, *The Story of a Real Man,* which, written in 1947-8 to please the Soviet authorities, failed to do so, and was not staged until 1960.

Prophète, Le *(The Prophet).* Opera in 5 acts by Meyerbeer. Libretto by Eugène Scribe. First performed Paris, 16 Apr 1849.

The opera is based on the historical episode of the rising of the Münster Anabaptists in the 16th c. The Anabaptists are led by John of Leyden (ten.) whose rival for the hand of Bertha (sop.) is Count Oberthal (bar.). Oberthal threatens to put John's mother, Fidès (contr.) to death unless John surrenders Bertha to him. On learning that John is the Anabaptist prophet, Bertha kills herself. Oberthal and his troops set fire to the palace at Münster where John had had himself crowned king. Fidès joins her son, and both die in the flames.

Puccini, Giacomo, b. Lucca, 22 Dec 1858; d. Brussels, 29 Nov 1924. Italian composer. Verdi's successor, and the last of the great composers of Italian opera, Puccini came of a long line of composers for the church in Lucca, and began his own musical studies in Lucca before entering Milan Conservatorium. His first opera, *Le Villi* (1884), was successful enough when produced in Milan to win him a contract with the leading Italian music publisher, Ricordi, but *Edgar* (1889) met with a disappointing reception. It was with his third opera, *Manon Lescaut* (1893), that Puccini became internationally known.

His next three operas were all successful, and established Puccini as the leading opera composer of his generation. *La Bohème* (1896), *Tosca* (1900) and *Madama Butterfly* (1904) are among the most popular operas ever written, and in the repertory of virtually every opera house. If *Tosca* is musically not the equal of the other two, its tautly constructed melodramatic plot and its composer's gift for writing memorable tunes has made it no less popular.

The operas Puccini composed between *Madama Butterfly* (1904) and his final work, *Turandot,* have made their way to popular acceptance more slowly. *La Fanciulla del*

West, set in a Californian mining-camp in the mid-19th c., is, however, one of the most fascinating of Puccini's operas for the subtlety of its orchestration and the modernity of its harmonies, as well as for its Wild West plot, derived from David Belasco's play, *The Girl of the Golden West. La Rondine* (1917), which was commissioned by Viennese impresarios as an operetta, is in fact a light opera of considerable charm which does not merit the disdain lavished upon it by critics. *Il Trittico,* a trilogy of three 1-act operas first performed at the Met in 1918, has survived only uneasily as a complete entity. The central opera, *Suor Angelica,* is generally thought to be the weakest of the three and is performed less frequently than the other two: *Il Tabarro,* an effective piece of realistic melodrama, and *Gianni Schicchi,* a somewhat thin but not unamusing comedy.

Puccini did not live to complete his final opera, *Turandot,* whose last pages were composed by Franco Alfano. Posthumously staged at La Scala in 1926, it quickly established itself as the composer's masterpiece, and it remains, more than half a century later, the most recent Italian opera to have achieved worldwide popularity. At its première, Alfano's ending was performed in a truncated version. It was heard complete for the first time in a concert performance in London in 1982.

Though he encompassed a narrower range than his great predecessor, Verdi, and was a less conscientious artist, Puccini is, after Verdi, the most popular of the opera composers. Many of his arias, especially his somewhat self-pitying outbursts for his tenors, are known through gramophone records to millions who have never been inside an opera house.

Purcell, Henry, b. London, 1659; d. London, 21 Nov 1695. English composer. One of the great composers of the baroque period, he composed music for a number of masques or semi-operas, among them Dryden's *King Arthur* (1691) and *The Indian Queen* (1695), and composed the earliest opera in English, *Dido and Aeneas,* which was first performed at Josias Priest's School for Young Ladies, in Chelsea, in 1689.

Puritani, I *(The Puritans).* Opera in 3 acts by Bellini. Libretto by Carlo Pepoli, based

Giacomo Puccini

on the play, *Têtes Rondes et Cavaliers* (1833), by Jacques-Arsène Ancelot and Joseph-Xavier-Boniface Saintine. First performed Paris, 25 Jan 1835.

The opera is set in and around Plymouth near the end of the English Civil Wars in the mid-17th c. Arturo (ten.), a Stuart partisan or Cavalier, is about to marry Elvira (sop.), daughter of the Puritan Giorgio, Lord Walton (bass), but, finding that Queen Henrietta (mezzo-sop.), widow of Charles I, is being held prisoner in Walton's fortress, Arturo helps her to escape. Thinking that her bridegroom has deserted her for another woman, Elvira loses her reason. She recovers only when she is reunited with Arturo who is pardoned by Cromwell.

Q

Quadri, Argeo, b. Como, 23 Feb 1911. Italian conductor. A capable interpreter of the popular Italian repertory, he has conducted at the major Italian houses, and at Covent Garden where he appeared in 1956, conducting *Rigoletto* with Tito Gobbi and *Tosca* with Zinka Milanov. From 1957-75 he was engaged in Vienna, conducting numerous Italian operas at the Staatsoper and the Volksoper. In recent years he has been active in Italy. His *L'Elisir d'Amore* with Rome Opera in 1979 revealed a sound appreciation of Donizettian style.

Quattro Rusteghi, I *(The Four Boors).* Opera in 4 acts by Wolf-Ferrari. Libretto by Giuseppe Pizzolato, based on the play *I Rusteghi* (1760) by Carlo Goldoni. First performed Munich, 19 Mar 1906. In one of its English translations the opera is known as *The School for Fathers.*

Four wives of boorish husbands attempt to teach the men a lesson by interfering in the arrangements for the marriage to each other of two of their offspring. A comedy of sexual conflict ensues, and the opera ends with the men's acceptance of the fact that women will always meddle.

Queen of Night (sop.). Pamina's mother, and the embodiment of evil, in Mozart's *Die Zauberflöte.*

Queen of Shemakhan, The, (sop.). Cause of King Dodon's downfall in Rimsky-Korsakov's *Le Coq d'Or*.

Queen of Spades (Russian title, *Pikovaya Dama*). Opera in 3 acts by Tchaikovsky. Libretto by the composer and his brother Modest Tchaikovsky after the story of that title (1834) by Pushkin. First performed St Petersburg, 19 Dec 1890.

Hermann (ten.), a young officer in love with Lisa (sop.), is also obsessed by the secret of winning at cards which is said to be possessed by the old Countess (mezzo-sop.), Lisa's grandmother. He goes to the Countess's bedroom at night to persuade her to give up her secret, but frightens her to such an extent that she dies without speaking. Later, Hermann imagines that the ghost of the Countess appears to him, to reveal the winning cards. Lisa, realizing that Hermann no longer loves her and is close to makness, drowns herself. Hermann stakes everything on the cards the ghost of the Countess revealed to him, but loses. He see the ghost mocking him, and stabs himself.

Quickly, Mistress (mezzo-sop.). Friend of Mistress Ford and Mistress Page in Verdi's *Falstaff,* she delivers the wives' messages to Falstaff.

Quiet Flows the Don (Russian title, *Tikhiy Don*). Opera in 4 acts by Dzerzhinsky. Libretto by the composer's brother Leonid Dzerzhinsky, based on the first two volumes of the novel of the same title (1928) by Mikhail Sholokhov.

A story of love and war, set at the time of the Russian Revolution, the opera reveals how Gregor Melekhov (ten.) returns home from fighting at the Austrian front, kills the seducer of his former sweetheart, and then goes off to join the Russian revolutionary forces. The libretto is so simplified a version of Sholokhov's novel that it amounts to a falsification.

Quilico, Louis, b. Montreal, 14 Jan 1929. Canadian baritone. He studied in New York and Rome, and made his début with the New York City Opera in 1955 as Germont in *La Traviata*. He went to Europe in 1959, and sang at Covent Garden between 1960-3. His début role there was Germont in *La Traviata*. He achieved a great success as

Rigoletto and undertook such other roles as Scarpia, Amonasro and Sharpless in *Madama Butterfly*. In recent years he has sung mostly in Canada and the United States.

Quinault, Philippe, b. Paris, 3 June 1635; d. Paris, 26 Nov 1688. French dramatist and librettist. He wrote a number of libretti for Lully, with whom he helped to lay the foundations of French opera. The operas on which they collaborated include *Cadmus et Hermione* (1673), *Alceste* (1674), *Proserpine* (1680), *Phaéton* (1683), *Amadis* (1684) and *Armide et Renaud* (1686).

R

Rabaud, Henri, b. Paris, 10 Nov 1873; d. Paris, 11 Sept 1949. French composer. He studied composition with Massenet at the Paris Conservatoire, and was himself director of the Conservatoire from 1922-4. The earliest of his six operas, *La Fille de Roland* (1904), was considered a piece of dry academicism. His first success as a writer for the stage came with *Mârouf* (1914), a somewhat Wagnerian work which was received with enthusiasm both in France and abroad. *L'Appel de la Mer,* based on Synge's *Riders to the Sea,* was staged in 1924. Rabaud's later operas, conservative in musical language, were not conspicuously successful. They are *Rolande et le Mauvais Garçon* (1933), *Martine* (1947), and *Le Jeu de l'Amour et du Hasard* (1948).Left unfinished, the last opera was completed by Henri Busser and Max d'Ollone, and staged in Monte Carlo in 1955.

Rachel (sop.). The eponymous heroine of Halévy's *La Juive*.

Rachmaninov, Sergei, b. Semyonovo, 1 Apr 1873; d. Beverly Hills, Calif., 28 Mar 1943. Russian composer. One of the finest pianists of his day, as a composer he was the last of the Russian late-romantics. His greatest achievements were in piano and orchestral music, but he achieved some success with his first opera, *Aleko,* a 1-act piece composed as a student exercise in 1892 and staged at the Bolshoi Theatre, Moscow, the following year. After completing two more short operas, *The Miserly Knight* and

Francesca da Rimini, which were performed together at the Bolshoi in 1906, he never completed another opera, though he began one, *Monna Vanna,* and planned a second, *Salammbô,* in 1906-7.

Radames (ten.). The leader of the Egyptian forces, in love with the Ethiopian slave, Aida, in Verdi's *Aida.*

Radford, Robert, b. Nottingham, 13 May 1874; d. London, 3 Mar 1933. English bass. He studied in London, and made his opera début at Covent Garden in 1904 as the Commendatore in *Don Giovanni.* He became a leading bass with the British National Opera Company, and was the first performer of Boris Godunov in English.

Raimondi, Gianni, b. Bologna, 13 Apr 1923. Italian tenor. He made his début in Bologna in 1947 as the Duke of Mantua in *Rigoletto,* first appeared in London in the same role in 1953, and went on to become a leading dramatic tenor in the 1950-60s. He made his Met début in 1965 as Rodolfo in *La Bohème.* He was still singing in Italian provincial opera houses in the early 1980s.

Raimondi, Ruggero, b. Bologna, 3 Oct 1941. Italian bass. He studied in Rome, and made his début in Spoleto in 1964 as Colline in *La Bohème.* A fine *basso cantante* with a baritone-like quality reminiscent of Ezio Pinza, he made his British stage début at Glyndebourne in 1969 as Don Giovanni, and appeared at the Met for the first time the following year as Silva in *Ernani.* He first sang at Covent Garden in 1972 as Fiesco in *Simon Boccanegra.* Moses in Rossini's *Mosè in Egitto* and Boris Godunov are other roles in which he has had success. In 1982, his portrayal of the title-role in *Don Quichotte* in Venice was considered masterly.

Raimund, Ferdinand, b. Vienna, 1 June 1790; d. Pottenstein, 5 Sept 1836. Austrian dramatist. He wrote a number of popular plays and satires for Viennese theatres, many with music by such composers as Wenzel Müller, Conradin Kreutzer and Joseph Drechsler. These include *Der König und der Menschenfeind* (1828) and *Das Mädchen aus der Feenwelt* (1826). The melody, 'Bruderlein fein', from the latter play is by Raimund himself.

Rake's Progress, The. Opera in 3 acts and an epilogue by Stravinsky. Libretto by W.H. Auden and Chester Kallman. First performed Venice, 11 Sept 1951.

The plot of the opera was suggested by the engravings of William Hogarth. When he is brought news of an unexpected legacy by Nick Shadow (bass), Tom Rakewell (ten.) leaves his fiancée, Anne Trulove (sop.), and sets out for London. Nick acts as Tom's servant, and encourages him in acts of profligacy. He arranges Tom's marriage to a bearded lady, Baba the Turk (mezzo-sop.), and later reveals himself in his true colours as the Devil. Tom lapses into madness, and is committed to Bedlam. Anne visits him there, but he does not recognize her. In an epilogue, the principal singers step out of character to deliver the moral, a laconic statement of the protestant work ethic: 'For idle hands/And hearts and minds/The Devil finds/A work to do'.

Ralf, Torsten, b. Malmö 2 Jan 1901; d. Stockholm, 27 Apr 1954. Swedish tenor. He studied in Stockholm and Berlin, and made his début at Stettin in Germany, in 1930, as Cavaradossi. He joined the Dresden Staatsoper in 1935, and remained a member until 1944. In Dresden he created the role of Apollo in Richard Strauss's *Daphne* in 1938. He was heard at Covent Garden in several of the Wagner roles between 1935-9, and returned in 1948 to sing Radames in *Aida.* Between 1945-8 he sang at the Met in the Wagner roles, and also as Radames and Verdi's *Otello.*

Rameau, Jean-Philippe, b. Dijon, 25 Sept 1683; d. Paris, 12 Sept 1764. French composer. The leading composer of his day in France, he wrote more than thirty works for the stage. Though he composed comedies as well, his tragedies represent him at his finest. *Hippolyte et Aricie* (1733), *Castor et Pollux* (1737) and *Dardanus* (1739) are his earliest and best *tragédies lyriques.* The opera-ballet *Les Indes Galantes* (1735) is the earliest and best of his works in that genre, while *Platée* (1745) is an excellent example of his comic style. His music possessed not only the gracefulness characteristic of its period but also an unusual poignancy. He brought advances in harmony and a new power and excitement to French classical opera.

Kevin Langan as Trulove, Dennis Bailey as Tom Rakewell and Diana Soviero as Anne Trulove in Stravinsky's *The Rake's Progress* in San Francisco in 1982.

Ramerrez (ten.). The bandit who, under the name of Dick Johnson, wins the love of Minnie, in Puccini's *La Fanciulla del West*.

Ramey, Samuel, b. Kolby, Kans., 18 May 1940. American bass. He studied in Wichita and New York, and made his début with New York City Opera in 1973 in the small role of Zuniga in *Carmen*. He has sung with several other American opera companies, excelling as Mozart's Don Giovanni and Figaro, as Méphistophélès in *Faust* and Escamillo in *Carmen*. He made his European début at Glyndebourne in 1976 as Mozart's Figaro, and returned there in 1977 and 1978 as Nick Shadow in *The Rake's Progress*. Figaro was the role of his débuts at La Scala (1981), Vienna Staatsoper (1981) and Covent Garden (1982), and Covent Garden heard him as Don Giovanni in 1983. His voice has a lyrical, baritone-like timbre, and he is a lively actor.

Ramfis (bass). The High Priest in Verdi's *Aida*.

Rance, Jack (bar.). The sheriff, in love with Minnie, in Puccini's *La Fanciulla del West*.

Rankl, Karl, b. Gaaden, nr Vienna, 1 Oct 1898; d. Salzburg, 6 Sept 1968. Austrian, later British, conductor and composer. He studied composition in Vienna with Schoenberg and Webern, and conducted at a number of German and Austrian opera houses. In Prague in 1938 he conducted the première of Krenek's *Karl V*. At the outbreak of World War II he moved to England and became a British citizen. He was appointed musical director of the new opera company set up at Covent Garden in 1946, and gathered together a company of singers to perform opera in English. He resigned in 1951, and in 1958 accepted the post of director of the proposed Sydney

Opera House, but the building was not completed until 1973, by which time Rankl had died. His opera, *Deirdre of the Sorrows,* won a prize offered by the Arts Council of Great Britain in 1951 in connection with the Festival of Britain, but has not been performed.

Rape of Lucretia, The. Opera in 2 acts by Britten. Libretto by Ronald Duncan, based on the play *Le Viol de Lucrèce* (1931) by André Obey, which in turn is based on Shakespeare's poem *The Rape of Lucrece* (1594). First performed Glyndebourne, 12 July 1946.

A male (ten.) and female (sop.) Chorus frame the story of the ruler of Rome, Tarquinius (bar.) who, told that Lucretia (contr.), wife of Collatinus (bass), is the only officer's wife to be above suspicion of infidelity, 'decides to put her to the test. Tarquinius visits her at night and, when she does not respond to his advances, rapes her. The next morning, overcome with shame, Lucretia sends for her husband and stabs herself, dying in his arms. The male and female chorus then inappositely draw a Christian moral from the pagan tale.

Raskin, Judith, b. New York, 21 June 1932. American soprano. She studied in Northampton, Mass., and made her opera début in 1957 as Susanna in *Le Nozze di Figaro* at Ann Arbor, Mich. In 1959 she sang Despina in *Così Fan Tutte* with New York City Opera, and in 1962 made her Met début as Susanna. Specializing in Mozart, she first appeared at Glyndebourne in 1963 as Pamina. She continued to sing in opera throughout the 1960s but later concentrated more on concert and recital work.

Ravel, Maurice, b. Ciboure, Basses Pyrénées, 7 Mar 1875; d. Paris, 28 Dec 1937. French composer. An innovator in his music for the piano, and an orchestrator of genius, he composed only two operas, both short works but each in its way unique. *L'Heure Espagnole,* his first opera, was composed between 1907-9, and first performed in 1911. He worked intermittently between 1906-14 on a project to adapt Hauptmann's play, *Die versunkene Glocke,* but did not write any music for it. The composition of his second opera, *L'Enfant et les Sortilèges,* which he wrote in collabora-tion with the novelist Colette, whose libretto imaginatively recreated a magical childhood world, occupied Ravel for several years. He began work on the opera in 1918, but it was not completed until 1925, in which year it was staged in Monte Carlo. In his last years he planned two large-scale operatic projects, an opera-oratorio on the subject of Joan of Arc, and an opera-ballet on a story from *Thousand and One Nights.* Neither project was brought to completion.

Reardon, John, b. New York, 8 Apr 1930. American baritone. He studied in New York and made his début in 1954 with New York City Opera as Falke in *Die Fledermaus.* He first sang at the Met in 1965 as Tomsky in *The Queen of Spades,* and was also heard as Mandryka in *Arabella* in his first season there. One of the most intelligent and versatile of artists, he has sung a wide variety of roles in opera and operetta with many American companies, and is noted for his acting ability as well as for his firmly placed lyric baritone voice. He has a repertoire of more than one hundred parts and has created roles in several new American operas, among them Douglas Moore's *The Wings of the Dove* and Marvin David Levy's *Mourning Becomes Electra.* He sang Pelléas in Debussy's opera at the Spoleto Festival in 1966, the Count in *Le Nozze di Figaro* with the Met in Paris in the same year, and also appeared at the Teatro La Fenice, Venice, but his career has been largely confined to the United States. In 1981 he contributed an impressive Iago to Sarah Caldwell's production of *Otello* in Boston.

recitative. A style of writing for the voice in which the rhythms and variations in pitch of the speaking voice are imitated. The early operas were written largely in recitative. In *recitativo secco,* the voice is accompanied usually only by a keyboard instrument and perhaps also a cello. *Recitativo stromentato* or accompanied recitative has more instruments, usually a full orchestra, accompanying the voice. In eighteenth-century opera most of the plot was advanced in recitative, the aria or ensemble being used to convey the feelings of the characters.

Regina. Opera in 3 acts by Blitzstein. Libretto by the composer, based on the play

The Little Foxes (1939) by Lilian Hellman. First performed New York, 31 Oct 1949.

The story is widely known because of the film version of the play, with Bette Davis. It tells of the machinations of the domineering Regina Giddens (sop.) as she attempts to control the Giddens family business in a small town in the southern United States.

Reiner, Fritz, b. Budapest, 19 Dec 1888; d. New York, 15 Nov 1963. Hungarian conductor. He studied in Budapest, became a coach at the Budapest Opera and made his conducting début there with *Carmen* in 1909. The following year he became conductor at the Landestheater in Laibach (now Ljubliana), and in 1914 was appointed principal conductor at the Dresden Staatsoper. He moved to the United States in 1922, and conducted mainly at concerts until he appeared at Covent Garden in 1936 with *Tristan und Isolde,* on the occasion of Kirsten Flagstad's London début. He was engaged at the Met between 1948-53 and conducted *Der Rosenkavalier* at the Vienna Staatsoper during its re-opening celebrations in 1955. He was noted for his tautly controlled performances of the Wagner and Strauss operas.

Reinhardt, Delia, b. Elberfeld, 27 Apr 1892; d. Arlesheim, 3 Oct 1974. German soprano. She studied in Frankfurt and made her début in Breslau in 1913. In 1916 she was engaged by Bruno Walter for the Munich Opera where she remained until 1923, and was greatly admired in a number of Mozart roles. After leaving Munich, she sang regularly at the Berlin Staatsoper until 1938, her roles including the Empress in *Die Frau ohne Schatten,* the Composer in *Ariadne auf Naxos,* and Wagner's Elsa, Elisabeth and Eva. She sang at Covent Garden during the 1920s, and was Octavian in a famous series of performances of *Der Rosenkavalier* with Lotte Lehmann, Elisabeth Schumann and Richard Mayr, conducted by Bruno Walter. She sang at the Met between 1922-4.

Reinhardt, Max, b. Baden, nr Vienna, 9 Sept 1873; d. New York, 31 Oct 1943. Austrian producer. Renowned for his work as a producer of plays, Reinhardt began his career as an actor in Salzburg. He commissioned scores from several composers for his spectacular productions, but his own productions of operas were few. He staged Offenbach's *Orphée aux Enfers* in Berlin in 1906, and the same composer's *La Belle Hélène* in Venice in 1911. His most important and influential opera production was the première of Strauss's *Der Rosenkavalier* in Dresden in 1911, with sets and costumes by Alfred Roller. In 1912 he staged the première of the original version of *Ariadne auf Naxos* in Stuttgart. Together with Strauss and Hofmannsthal he was one of the founders of the annual Salzburg Festival in 1920, and he remained active in the Festival until 1937 when he emigrated to America. In 1930 he produced *Die Fledermaus* in Berlin, and in 1931 *Les Contes d'Hoffmann* in Salzburg, his final opera production.

Reining, Maria, b. Vienna, 7 Aug 1903. Austrian soprano. She studied in Vienna, and made her début at the Staatsoper in 1931, remaining with the company for two seasons before making appearances in several German opera houses. She returned to the Vienna Staatsoper in 1937, and sang regularly in Vienna until 1958. An elegant performer with a beautiful voice, she excelled in the Strauss, Wagner and Mozart roles, and was especially admired as Eva in *Die Meistersinger,* the Countess in *Le Nozze di Figaro* and the Marschallin in *Der Rosenkavalier.* She sang at several Salzburg Festivals between 1937-53, was heard at Covent Garden in 1938 as Elsa in *Lohengrin,* and in the same year made her American début in Chicago where she sang Eva, and the title-role in *Madama Butterfly.* In 1949 she was heard in New York when she appeared with New York City Opera as the Marschallin in *Der Rosenkavalier* and Ariadne in *Ariadne anf Naxos.*

Reizen, Mark, b. Zaitsevo, nr Lugansk, 3 July 1895. Russian bass. He studied in Kharkov, and made his début there in 1921 as Pimen in *Boris Godunov.* He sang in Leningrad from 1925-30 when he joined the company of the Bolshoi Theatre, Moscow, with whom he remained until 1954. He sang all the leading Russian bass roles, was considered the finest Boris Godunov of his day, and a superb King Philip in *Don Carlos.* He was a compelling actor, as well as the possessor of a voice of great range and tonal beauty.

Remedios, Alberto, b. Liverpool, 27 Feb 1935. English tenor. He studied in London, and made his début as Tinca in *Il Tabarro* at Sadler's Wells Theatre in 1957. He became the Sadler's Wells Opera's leading dramatic tenor, and sang Walther in their English-language production of *Die Meistersinger* in 1968. He sang both Siegmund and Siegfried in the company's *Ring* in the 1970s. He made his Covent Garden début in 1965 as Dmitri in *Boris Godunov,* and in 1976 sang Bacchus in *Ariadne auf Naxos* at the Met. Though his voice is not a naturally beautiful one, it has an individual timbre, and carries well over a Wagnerian orchestra.

Renato (bar.). Husband of Amelia in Verdi's *Un Ballo in Maschera.* When the opera is staged in its original Swedish setting, the character's name is Ankarstroem.

Renaud, Maurice, b. Bordeaux, 24 July 1861; d. Paris, 16 Oct 1933. French baritone. He studied in Paris and Brussels, and made his début in Brussels in 1883. Between 1890-1914 he sang in Paris, not only in French opera but also as Don Giovanni, Wolfram, and in a number of Italian roles. He also appeared at Covent Garden and the Met, and was considered one of the leading French baritones of his time.

Rennert, Günther, b. Essen, 1 Apr 1911; d. Salzburg, 31 July 1978. German producer. After producing opera in several German towns between 1935-42 he became chief producer at the Berlin Städtische Oper. He was in charge of Hamburg Opera between 1946-56 and between 1959-67, he was connected with Glyndebourne Festival Opera for whom he directed several productions. In 1967 he became director of the Munich Opera. He was particularly admired for his productions of 20th-c. operas.

Resnik, Regina, b. New York, 30 Aug 1922. American mezzo-soprano. She studied in New York, and began her career as a soprano, her début role being Lady Macbeth, with the New Opera Company, New York. She first appeared at the Met in 1944 as Leonora in *Il Trovatore* and was a leading soprano with the company for the next ten years, appearing at Bayreuth in 1953 as Sieglinde. In 1955 she began to sing mezzo-soprano roles, made a Covent Garden début in 1957 as Carmen, and appeared with success in several other roles at Covent Garden, most notably as Klytemnestra in *Elektra* in 1965. She also appeared frequently in Vienna and Salzburg, and in recent years she has turned to producing operas, both in the United States and Europe.

Respighi, Ottorino, b. Bologna, 9 July 1879; d. Rome, 18 Apr 1936. Italian composer. Best known for his orchestral music, he also composed nine operas. The first, *Rè Enzo,* was staged in Bologna in 1905. *Semirama* followed five years later. His later operas include *Belfagor,* produced in Milan in 1923; *Maria Egiziaca,* first per-

Ottorino Respighi

formed in both New York and Venice in 1932; and *Lucrezia,* completed by the composer's wife Elsa, and staged posthumously in 1937. The most captivating of his works for the stage is *La Bella Dormente nel Bosco,* a version of the Sleeping Beauty story, originally conceived for puppets in 1922, adapted for child mimes in 1934, and revised in a version for adult singers by Respighi's pupil Gianluca Tocchi in 1966.

Retablo de Maese Pedro, El (*Master Peter's Puppet Show*). Opera in 1 act by Falla. Libretto by the composer, based on an incident in *Don Quixote* by Cervantes (1615). First performed Seville (concert performance), 23 Mar 1923. First stage performance, Paris, 25 June 1923.

Master Peter (treble) introduces his puppets who perform to an audience which includes Don Quixote (bass). Thinking that the puppets are human beings who need his help, Don Quixote intervenes in the performance, thereby ruining it.

Rethberg, Elisabeth, b. Schwarzenburg, 22 Sept 1894; d. Yorktown Heights, N.Y., 6 June 1976. German soprano. She studied in Dresden, and made her début there in 1915 as Arsena in *Der Zigeunerbaron.* She remained with the Dresden company for seven years, singing a wide variety of roles in operas by, among others, Mozart, Strauss, Puccini and Wagner. In 1922 she made her Met début as Aida, and was a popular artist with the Met for the next twenty years, singing a number of Verdi and Mozart roles as well as Wagner's Elsa, Eva, Elisabeth and Sieglinde. In Dresden in 1928 she created the title-role in *Die Ägyptische Helena* by Strauss, sang at Covent Garden for the first time in 1925 in the title-role of *Madama Butterfly,* and was heard there again between 1934-39 in *La Bohème* (as Mimi), *Lohengrin, Prince Igor, Shvanda the Bagpiper, Aida, Der Rosenkavalier* (the Marschallin), *Die Walküre* (Sieglinde) and *Don Giovanni* (Donna Anna). A fine musician with a most beautiful voice, she was equally at home in Italian and German opera.

Reutter, Hermann, b. Stuttgart, 17 June 1900. German composer. Also a pianist, he accompanied a number of singers in recitals of Lieder, and composed six operas in a conservative style in which his feeling for the human voice is readily apparent. His earliest opera, *Saul,* was staged in Baden-Baden in 1928, and the last, *Die Brücke von San Luis Rey* (based on Thornton Wilder's novel) was first performed in Essen in 1954. The most successful was *Doktor Johannes Faustus,* which was first staged in Frankfurt in 1936, and revised for a production in Stuttgart in 1955.

Revisor, Der (*The Government Inspector*). Opera in 5 acts by Egk. Libretto by the composer, based on Gogol's *The Government Inspector* (1836). First performed Schwetzingen, 9 May 1957.

Klestakov (ten.), a penniless civil servant, is mistaken for the Government Inspector, and entertained lavishly by the Mayor (bass) and his family.

Reyer, Ernest, b. Marseilles, 1 Dec 1823; d. Le Lavandou, 15 Jan 1909. French composer. Largely self-taught, he composed five operas, the comparatively youthful works *Maître Wolfram* (1854), *La Statue* (1861) and *Erostrate* (1862) being of less interest than *Sigurd,* whose subject matter is Wagnerian, though its musical style owes more to Weber and Berlioz. *Sigurd* (1884) and *Salammbô* (1890) were first produced in Brussels. Though he admired Wagner, he refused to visit Germany after the 1870 Franco-Prussian War, and never went to Bayreuth. He did, however, travel to Cairo for the première of *Aida* in 1871, of which he wrote an interesting account.

Reznicek, Emil Nikolaus von, b. Vienna, 4 May 1860; d. Berlin, 2 Aug 1945. Austrian composer. He earned his living as a conductor, and it was while he was a military bandmaster in Prague that he composed his most popular opera, *Donna Diana,* which was first staged in Prague in 1894. Though the work is now rarely staged, its sparkling overture is still well known. His earliest work for the stage was *Die Jungfrau von Orleans,* based on Schiller's Joan of Arc play, and staged in Prague in 1887. Most of his operas are comedies, and the last, a 1-act piece, *Tenor und Bass,* was performed in Stockholm in 1934.

Rheingold, Das (*The Rhine Gold*). Opera in 1 act by Wagner, the first of the four works comprising *Der Ring des Nibelungen.*

Libretto by the composer. First performed Munich, 22 Sept 1869. First performance at Bayreuth as part of the complete *Ring*, 13 Aug 1876.

The Nibelung dwarf Alberich (bass-bar.), spurned by the Rhinemaidens, steals from them the gold under the Rhine which they have been guarding. From it he forges a magic ring with the aid of which he hopes to become master of the world. Meanwhile, on their mountain summit, the god Wotan (bass-bar.) and his spouse Fricka (mezzo-sop.) are obliged to offer Freia (sop.), goddess of eternal youth, to the giants Fasolt (bass) and Fafner (bass) in return for the giants having built Valhalla, a castle for the gods. Loge (ten.), god of fire and cunning, accompanies Wotan to Nibelheim where they steal from Alberich, including the ring his treasure on which he places a curse, and a magic helmet or Tarnhelm. Freia is ransomed from the giants with the gold, but the giants immediately quarrel over the ring, and Fasolt is killed by Fafner. As the gods ascend into their fortress, the voices of the Rhinemaidens can be heard lamenting the loss of their gold.

Ricci, Federico, b. Naples, 22 Oct 1809; d. Conegliano, 10 Dec 1877. Italian composer. He began his career with a comedy, *Il Colonello,* composed jointly with his brother Luigi and staged in Milan in 1835, and then had a huge success with a serious opera, *La Prigione di Edimburgo,* which he wrote alone. Based on Sir Walter Scott's *The Heart of Midlothian,* it was first performed in Trieste in 1838. An even greater success was *Corrado d'Altamura* (1841), based on the same plot as Verdi's *Oberto.* His best-known opera collaboration with his brother was the comedy, *Crispino e la Comare* (Venice, 1850). His operas are in the style of Bellini and Donizetti, as are those of his brother.

Ricci, Luigi, b. Naples, 8 July 1805; d. Prague, 31 Dec 1859. Italian composer. His comic operas in the manner of Donizetti were popular, though none has survived into the modern repertory. With his brother Federico he composed four operas, of which the best known is *Crispino e la Comare,* first performed in Venice in 1850.

Ricciarelli, Katia, b. Rovigo, 16 Jan 1946. Italian soprano. She studied in Venice, and made her début in 1969 in Mantua, as Mimi. Possessor of an attractive *spinto* voice with some agility in coloratura, she has had a number of successes in Verdi roles. She made her American début in Chicago in 1972 as Lucrezia in Verdi's *I Due Foscari,* and first appeared at Covent Garden in 1974 as Mimi in *La Bohème.* She was greatly admired in the title-role of *Luisa Miller* at Covent Garden in 1978. In 1983 at Covent Garden she sang Leonora in *Il Trovatore.*

Richard, Coeur de Lion *(Richard the Lion-heart).* Opera in 3 acts by Grétry. Libretto by Jean Michel Sedaine. First performed Paris, 21 Oct 1784.

Blondel (ten.), a minstrel disguised as a blind begger searches for, and eventually finds and rescues, his master, King Richard I (bar.) who had been imprisoned while on his way back from the third crusade.

Richter, Hans, b. Györ, 4 Apr 1843; d. Bayreuth, 5 Dec 1916. Austro-Hungarian conductor. He studied in Vienna, and began his career as horn-player in the orchestra of the Kärntnertor Theater. It is as an associate and interpreter of Wagner that he is remembered. He became a friend of the composer while in his twenties, conducted the first complete performance of *Der Ring des Nibelungen* at Bayreuth in 1876, and was a leading conductor at Bayreuth until 1912. At the Theatre Royal, Drury Lane, London, in 1882 he conducted the first British performances of *Tristan und Isolde* and *Die Meistersinger von Nürnberg.* In 1909 at Covent Garden he conducted the first English-language *Ring.*

Ridderbusch, Karl, b. Recklinghausen, 29 May 1932. German bass. He studied in Essen, and made his début in Münster in 1961. He quickly established himself as an effective performer of the Wagner bass roles, making his first Bayreuth appearances in 1967 as Heinrich in *Tannhäuser,* Titurel in *Parsifal* and Fasolt in *Das Rheingold.* In the same year he made his Met début as Hunding in *Die Walküre,* and was first heard at Covent Garden in 1971 as Fasolt, Hunding and Hagen. He also sings Ochs in *Der Rosenkavalier,* and Boris Godunov, as well as some of the Verdi bass roles, though he is internationally renowned primarily as a Wagner singer.

Rienzi. Opera in 5 acts by Wagner. Libretto by the composer, based on the novel of that title (1835) by Edward Bulwer-Lytton. First performed Dresden, 20 Oct 1842. (The full title of the opera is *Cola Rienzi, der letzte der Tribunen: Cola Rienzi, Last of the Tribunes.*)

The opera is set in Rome in the mid-14th c. The patrician Orsini (bass) and his followers attempt to abduct Irene (sop.), sister of Rienzi (ten.), but are foiled by Colonna (bass) whose son, Adriano (mezzo-sop.), succeeds in freeing Irene. The populace joins in the fight between the two noble families of Orsini and Colonna, and order is restored only with the appearance of Rienzi, who tells Adriano of his plans to seize power from the nobles and make Rome a free city. Because he is in love with Irene, Adriano agrees to support Rienzi.

In Act II, the nobles having been defeated, Orsini attempts to kill Rienzi during the triumphal celebrations. Orsini and Colonna are condemned to death, but Rienzi agrees to spare them. In Act III the populace is moved to anger by the patricians, who have again gathered an army together. When Colonna is killed, Adriano blames Rienzi and swears revenge. Magnanimously, Rienzi prevents the people from attacking Adriano.

Adriano plots against Rienzi in Act IV, and in the final act the people themselves, in exasperation and fury, rise against Rienzi. The Capitol is set on fire and, when Adriano attempts to enter it to rescue Rienzi and Irene, all three perish in the flames.

Rigoletto. Opera in 3 acts by Verdi. Libretto by Francesco Maria Piave, based on the play *Le Roi s'Amuse* (1832) by Victor Hugo. First performed Venice, 11 Mar 1851.

Anne-Marie Owens, Dennis O'Neill, Patricia O'Neill and Jonathan Summers in Verdi's *Rigoletto* in Jonathan Miller's modern dress production for English National Opera in 1982.

At the court of the licentious Duke of Mantua (ten.), the Duke's jester, the hunchback Rigoletto (bar.), insults Monterone (bar.), a nobleman whose daughter had been seduced by the Duke. The Duke and Rigoletto are in turn cursed by Monterone. Disguised as a student, the Duke has also been paying court to Gilda (sop.), Rigoletto's daughter whom her father keeps hidden in his house, away from the court. The courtiers, most of whom have felt the lash of the jester's tongue, trick Rigoletto into helping them to abduct Gilda, whom they carry off to the Duke's palace.

By the time Rigoletto finds his daughter at the palace, she has been violated by the Duke. Rigoletto hires an assassin, Sparafucile (bass), to kill the Duke, but Sparafucile is persuaded by his sister, Maddalena (mezzo-sop.), to spare the Duke and kill instead the first stranger to enter their inn. Overhearing this, Gilda sacrifices her life for the Duke, whom she still loves. When Rigoletto arrives to claim the body of the Duke, he is horrified to discover that it is his own daughter who has been assassinated. He remembers Monterone's curse as he collapses across Gilda's lifeless body.

Rimsky-Korsakov, Nikolai, b. Tikhvin, 18 Mar 1844; d. St Peterburg, 21 June 1908. Russian composer. His fourteen operas are by far the most important part of his *oeuvre,* although he also composed much orchestral and chamber music and a large number of songs. His first opera, *The Maid of Pskov,* was composed between 1868-72 at the same time that his friend Mussorgsky was beginning work on *Boris Godunov.* During one winter, the two composers shared a small room and a piano, Mussorgsky working on his opera in the mornings and Rimsky-Korsakov on his in the afternoons. Rimsky-Korsakov's opera was successfully produced in St Petersburg in 1873, though he was to make two later revisions of it. His second opera, in a simpler melodic style based on Glinka, was *May Night,* staged in St Petersburg in 1880. Like most of his later operas, it blended fairy-tale and legend with supernatural elements, enabling him to indulge his gift for colourful instrumentation. *Snow Maiden* (1882), *Christmas Eve* (1895) and *Sadko* (1898) were followed by two more realistic works, the 1-act *Mozart and Salieri,* (1898) which plays with the theory that Mozart was poisoned by his rival Salieri, and *The Tsar's Bride* (1899). With *Tsar Saltan* (1901), however, Rimsky-Korsakov returned to the world of fairy-tale and fantasy, which he was to continue to explore in *The Legend of the Invisible City of Kitezh* (1907) and *The Golden Cockerel* which was staged posthumously in 1909. He helped many other composers to orchestrate their works. It is his rewritten and reorchestrated version of Mussorgsky's *Boris Godunov,* on which he worked at various periods between 1888-1907, which first established Mussorgsky's opera as a masterpiece.

Rinaldo. Opera in 3 acts by Handel. Libretto by Giacomo Rossi, based on a scenario by Aaron Hill, after Tasso's *Gerusalemme Liberata* (1581). First performed London, 24 Feb 1711.

Handel's first and very successful London opera, it tells a story of love and sorcery set in the Holy Land during the First Crusade.

Ring des Nibelungen, Der *(The Nibelung's Ring).* Operatic tetralogy, comprising *Das Rheingold, Die Walküre, Siegfried* and *Götterdämmerung,* by Wagner. The first two operas had already been performed separately in Munich, in 1869 and 1870, when the work was performed in its entirety for the first time, at Bayreuth, between 13-17 August 1876. The operas are still sometimes performed apart, especially *Die Walküre.* (See separate entries for each work.)

Rinuccini, Ottavio, b. Florence, 20 Jan 1562; d. Florence, 28 Mar 1621. Italian librettist. He was associated with members of the Florentine Camerata group from whose experiments the earliest operas emerged. He wrote the libretto of Peri's *Dafne* in 1597, and of *Euridice* which was set both by Peri (1600) and by Caccini (1602). He also wrote *Arianna,* set by both Peri and Monteverdi, in 1608.

Rip Van Winkle. Opera in 3 acts by George Frederick Bristow. Libretto by Jonathan Howard Wainwright, based on Washington Irving's story of the same title (1819). First performed New York, 27 Sept 1855. Described as a 'Grand Romantic Opera', it was the first by an American composer on an American subject.

Rip Van Winkle is a henpecked husband who escapes from his wife by wandering off with his dog to the Catskill Mountains, just before the American War of Independence. After drinking with a group of dwarfs, Rip falls asleep for twenty years, and returns home to find his wife dead, his daughter married, and the portrait of King George replaced by one of George Washington. Although Bristow's subject–matter was American, his musical style was European, and it was somewhat in the style of Mendelssohn.

Risurrezione *(Resurrection)*. Opera in 4 acts by Alfano. Libretto by Cesare Hanau, based on Tolstoy's novel of the same title (1900). First performed Turin, 30 Nov 1904.

The plot is a simplification, if not a distortation, of that of Tolstoy's novel. Prince Dmitri (ten.) has seduced Katusha (sop.), and later abandoned her. When she is convicted of killing a man, and sent to Siberia, he recognizes that he bears a certain moral responsiblilty for her predicament, follows her to Siberia, and obtains a pardon for her. He asks her to marry him, but she rejects him in favour of a fellow convict, Simonson (bar.).

Rita. Opera in 1 act by Donizetti. Libretto by Gustave Vaëz. First performed Paris, 7 May 1860. Written in 1841, the opera was never staged in its composer's lifetime.

When Gasparo (bar.), the first husband of his wife Rita (sop.), arrives unexpectedly, having been presumed dead, the henpecked Peppe (ten.) suggests a game, the winner being the one to lose Rita. The opera ends with Peppe reconciled to his wife who promises to mend her ways.

Ritorno d'Ulisse in Patria, Il *(The Return of Ulysses to his Country)*. Opera in a prologue and 5 acts by Monteverdi. Libretto by Giacomo Badoaro. First performed Venice, Feb 1641.

Penelope laments the continued absence of her husband, Ulysses. After a discussion between the gods Jove and Neptune on the subject of the sins of mankind, Ulysses is put ashore while he is asleep. He is promised by Minerva that he will return home and reclaim his palace from those who have taken possession of it. Disguised as a beggar, Ulysses returns to his palace where he is

Nikolai Rimsky-Korsakov

mocked by the suitors of Penelope. After he wins a trial of strength with the three suitors by being the only one to be able to draw his bow, he transfixes each of the suitors with an arrow. Penelope is at first unwilling to believe that he is really Ulysses, but she is persuaded by Ericlea, her nurse, and the opera ends with the joyful reunion of Ulysses and Penelope.

The distribution of the voices varies with the several editions used in modern performance. In Dallapiccola's arrangement, first performed in Florence in 1942, Ulysses is sung by a tenor, and Penelope by a contralto. In Raymond Leppard's version, first performed at Glyndebourne in 1972, Ulysses is a baritone.

Robert le Diable *(Robert the Devil)*. Opera in 5 acts by Meyerbeer. Libretto by Eugène Scribe and Germain Delavigne. First performed Paris, 21 Nov 1831.

In 13th-c. Sicily, Robert, Duke of Normandy (ten.), offspring of the Devil and a mortal woman, falls in love with Isabella, Princess of Sicily (sop.). Disguised as a mortal and using the name Bertram, the Devil (bass) attempts to gain the soul of Robert by preventing him from winning the hand of Isabella in a tournament and then offering to help him in exchange for his soul. At a midnight orgy with the ghosts of nuns who, in life, were unfaithful to their vows, Robert accepts the aid of witchcraft to help him effect an entrance into Isabella's chamber, but then yields to her entreaties and rejects the Devil. Eventually, Robert and Isabella are married, and the Devil defeated, returns to Hell.

Roberto Devereux. Opera in 3 acts by Donizetti. Libretto by Salvatore Cammarano, based on François Ancelot's tragedy. *Élisabeth d'Angleterre* (1832) and on Felice Romani's libretto for Mercadante's *Il Conte d'Essex* (1833). First performed Naples, 28 Oct 1837.

Queen Elizabeth I (sop.) is in love with Roberto (ten.), Earl of Essex. Roberto, however loves Sara (mezzo-sop.), wife of the Duke of Nottingham. Roberto is arrested on a charge of treason, and Elizabeth finally signs the warrant for his execution. A message that would have

saved him arrives too late, for which the jealous Queen blames Sara.

Robin, Mado, b. Yseures-sur-Creuse, 29 Dec 1918; d. Paris, 10 Dec 1960. French soprano. She studied in Paris and made her opera début there in 1945 as Gilda. Possessor of a lyric-coloratura voice of great agility and phenomenal range, she sang such roles as Lucia, the Queen of Night, and Lakmé to great acclaim. Her appearances in opera were confined mainly to France and Belgium, though she sang in San Francisco between 1954-6, making her début there as Gilda. She was said to have been able to sing the highest note ever emitted by a singer, the 'C' an octave above the note usually referred to as 'high C'. She died prematurely while at the height of her career.

Robin Hood. Opera in 3 acts by George MacFarran. Libretto by John Oxenford. First performed London, 11 Oct 1860.

There have been several operas on the subject of the legendary outlaw of Sherwood Forest. MacFarren's was popular in its day, but is no longer performed. *Robin Hood* by the American Reginald de Koven (1859-1920), an opera first heard in Chicago in 1890, and performed in London in the same year under the title of *Maid Marian* (perhaps to avoid confusion with MacFarren's work), contains the ballad 'Oh, promise me', which became widely known as a concert song. (De Koven wrote a sequel to *Robin Hood,* actually called *Maid Marian,* produced in Philadelphia in 1901.)

Robinson, Faye, b. Houston, 2 Nov 1943. American soprano. She studied in Houston and New York, and made her début with New York City Opera in 1972 as Micaëla in *Carmen.* She has sung in a number of European opera houses, and in 1980 had a great success at the Teatro Colón, Buenos Aires, when she sang all three leading soprano roles in Tito Capobianco's production of *Les Contes d'Hoffmann.* She made her first appearance at the Vienna Staatsoper in 1982 as Constanze in *Die Entführung aus dem Serail.*

Rocca, Lodovico, b. Turin, 29 Nov 1895. Italian composer. Although he composed five operas, his fame rests on his extremely successful third opera, *Il Dibuk,* based on the

1916 play by Shelomoh An-Ski. The opera was staged at La Scala in 1934. A difficult, oddly heterogeneous work, it is very effective in performance. *Monte Ivnor* (1939) is less compelling. From 1940-66 Rocca was director of the Turin Conservatorium, during which period he composed another opera, *L'Uragano,* based on Ostrovsky's *The Storm,* and staged at La Scala in 1952.

Rocco (bass). The gaoler, and Marzelline's father, in Beethoven's *Fidelio.*

Rodelinda. Opera in 3 acts by Handel. Libretto by Antonio Salvi, altered by Nicola Haym. First performed London, 24 Feb 1725.

Bertarido (mezzo-sop.), King of Lombardy, returns home having been believed dead, to find his throne occupied by a usurper, Grimaldo (ten.), who is trying to force Bertarido's wife Rodelinda (sop.) into marriage. When Bertarido saves Grimaldo's life, Grimaldo gives up the throne, and the rightful King rules again with his Queen.

Rodolfo (ten.). The poet, in love with Mimi, in Puccini's *La Bohème.*

Rodrigue (bar.). The Marquis of Posa, friend of Don Carlos in Verdi's *Don Carlos.* When the opera is performed in its Italian translation, he is known as Rodrigo.

Roi David, Le *(King David).* Opera in 2 parts by Honegger. Libretto by René Morax. First performed Mézières, 11 June 1921.

Honegger's first dramatic work, it tells the Old Testament story as found in the Book of Samuel.

Roi de Lahore, Le *(The King of Lahore).* Opera in 5 acts by Massenet. Libretto by Louis Gallet. First performed Paris, 27 Apr 1877.

Based on an episode in the Hindu poem, *Mahabharata,* the opera tells the story of Sita (sop.) who is loved both by King Alim (ten.) and by his minsiter, Scindia (bar.). Scindia kills the King, who is allowed to return to earth as a beggar, but Sita kills herself in order to be with Alim in paradise.

Roi d'Ys, Le *(The King of Ys).* Opera in 3 acts by Lalo. Libretto by Édouard Blau.

First performed Paris, 7 May 1888.

Based on the same Breton legend drawn on by Debussy for his piano prelude, 'La Cathédrale Engloutie', the opera tells the story of the King's daughter, Margared (mezzo-sop.) who, in love with Mylio (ten.) who is to be married to her sister Rozenn (sop.), opens the floodgates on their wedding night, and lets in the sea to drown the entire town. As the water mounts, she becomes repentent. Announcing that the flood waters will not recede until they have claimed their rightful victim, she throws herself into the sea. The waters recede, and the citizens give thanks to their patron saint for having delivered them.

Roi L'a Dit, Le *(The King has Commanded it)*. Opera in 3 acts by Delibes. Libretto by Edmond Godinet. First performed Paris, 24 May 1873.

A comedy concerning the difficulties brought upon himself by the Marquis de Moncontour (bar.) when, having claimed to have a son, he is forced to engage a young peasant (ten.) to impersonate the non-existent youth.

Roi Malgré Lui, Le *(The King against his Will)*. Opera in 3 acts by Chabrier. Libretto by Émile de Najac and Paul Burani. First performed Paris, 18 May 1887.

About to be crowned King of France, Henri de Valois (bar.) discovers from Minka (sop.), to whom he is betrothed, that there is a plot against his life. By disguising himself as his friend De Nangis, he succeeds in joining the conspirators. This results in De Nangis (ten.) being mistaken for the King. The plot is foiled and Henri is crowned.

Roller, Alfred, b. Vienna, 10 Feb 1864; d. Vienna, 21 June 1935. Austrian designer. He designed a number of operas for Vienna, at the period when Gustav Mahler was director of the Opera. Their most famous collaboration was on a production of *Tristan und Isolde* in 1903. Roller also designed the first productions of Richard Strauss's *Der Rosenkavalier* (Dresden, 1911) and *Die Frau ohne Schatten* (Vienna, 1919). A member of the Viennese Secession group of artists, which he helped to found, he was chief designer at the Vienna Hofoper (later re-named the Staatsoper) from 1903-9, and from 1918-34.

Roman, Stella, b. Cluj, 23 Sept 1904. Romanian soprano. She studied in Bucharest, Milan and Rome, and made her début in Piacenza in 1932. Between 1936-40 she sang in Rome where she created the role of Cordelia in Alberto Ghislanzoni's *Rè Lear* in 1937. Her period of greatest success occurred at the Met where she made her début as Aida in 1941 and shared with Zinka Milanov the leading Italian dramatic soprano roles until 1950. She was especially admired in *Il Trovatore, Un Ballo in Maschera* and *Tosca*. During this period she also appeared in Chicago and San Francisco.

romance, romanza. In opera the term, whether in English or Italian, generally refers to a song or aria of tender or passionate character which is simple and direct, and lacking in display or ornamentation of any kind.

Romanelli, Luigi, b. 21 July 1751; d. Milan, 1 Mar 1839. Italian librettist. He wrote more than sixty libretti for Italian operas, among them Rossini's *La Pietra del Paragone,* Mercadante's *Elisa e Claudio* and Pacini's *La Vestale*. He was principal librettist at La Scala for more than thirty years, and from 1816-31 was Professor of Rhetoric and literature at Milan Conservatorium.

Romani, Felice, b. Genoa, 31 Jan 1788; d. Moneglia, 28 Jan 1865. Italian librettist. The most highly regarded librettist of his time, he began by providing two libretti for his friend Simone Mayr. These were for the operas *La Rosa Bianca e la Rosa Rossa* and *Medea in Corinto,* both performed in 1813. He became editor of a newspaper in Turin, but continued to write libretti, often as many as eight in a single year. He collaborated with all the leading Italian composers of the early 19th c. For Rossini he wrote *Aureliano in Palmira, Bianca e Faliero* and *Il Turco in Italia;* for Donizetti *L'Elisir d'Amore, Anna Bolena, Parisina d'Este* and *Lucrezia Borgia;* and for Bellini, with whom his name is most closely associated, *Il Pirata, La Straniera, Zaira, I Capuleti ed i Montecchi, La Sonnambula, Norma,* and *Beatrice di Tenda*. His only libretto for a Verdi opera was *Un Giorno di Regno,* but this was first written not in 1840 for Verdi but in 1818, as *Il Finto Stanislao,* for Adalbert Gyrowetz.

Romani retired in 1855, after writing *Cristina di Svezia* for the pianist-composer Sigismond Thalberg. He was praised usually for the elegance of his verses as well as for his dramatic sense, and was an intellectual cut above the average librettist of the Italian *ottocento*.

Romani, Pietro, b. Rome, 29 May 1791; d. Florence, 11 Jan 1877. Italian composer. He wrote two operas, *Il Qui Pro Quo,* which was staged in Rome in 1817, and *Carlo Magno,* staged in Florence in 1823. He is remembered, however, for one bass aria, 'Manca un foglio', which he wrote for insertion into Rossini's *Il Barbiere di Siviglia* for its performances in Florence in November 1816, when the singer who performed the role of Bartolo, one Paolo Rosich, found his aria, 'A un dottor della mia sorte', too difficult for him. Occasionally, and presumably for the same reason, Romani's aria is heard in present-day performances of Rossini's opera.

Romberg, Sigmund, b. Nagykanizsa, 29 July 1887; d. New York, 9 Nov 1951. Hungarian, later American, composer. He studied composition with Heuberger in Vienna, but emigrated to the United States in 1909, where he worked in New York as a pianist and dance-band leader, and began to compose songs and dances for revues. He became a leading composer of operettas, in the Viennese style he had known in Austria and Hungary. His most popular works, all of them first performed on Broadway and then produced throughout the world, include *Maytime* (1917), *Blossom Time,* based on the life of Schubert many of whose melodies it utilized (1921), *The Student Prince* (1924), *The Desert Song* (1926), *Rosalie* (1928) and *The New Moon* (1928). In the early 1930s he moved to Hollywood to write film scores. Many of his operettas were also filmed in the 1930-40s. His last two works to be produced on Broadway were *Up in Central Park* (1945) and *The Girl in Pink Tights* (1954): they were described not as operettas, but as musical comedies.

Roméo et Juliette. Opera in 5 acts by Gounod. Libretto by Jules Barbier and Michel Carré, after the play *Romeo and Juliet* by Shakespeare (1594). First performed Paris, 27 Apr 1867.

Sylvia Sass as Juliette, Neil Shicoff as Romeo and Peter Meven as Friar Lawrence in a scene from Gounod's *Roméo et Juliette* at the Paris Opéra in 1982.

Although it necessarily shortens Shakespeare's text, the libretto follows the plot of the play quite closely. The disposition of the voices is as follows: Romeo (ten.), Juliet (sop.), Tybalt (ten.), Mercutio (bar.), Friar Lawrence (bass).

Romeo und Julia. Opera in 2 acts by Sutermeister. Libretto by the composer, based on the Schlegel translation of Shakespeare's *Romeo and Juliet* (1594). First performed Dresden, 13 Apr 1940.

The opera concentrates on the young lovers, using a very much shortened version of the text of the play. Romeo (ten.), Juliet (sop.), the Nurse (mezzo-sop.), Capulet (bar.), Lady Capulet (mezzo-sop.), and Friar Lawrence (bass) are the leading characters.

Rondine, La *(The Swallow).* Opera in 3 acts by Puccini. Libretto by Giuseppe Adami, based on a German-language libretto by Alfred Maria Willner and Heinz Reichert. First performed Monte Carlo, 27 Mar 1917.

Set in Paris and on the Riviera at the time of the French Second Empire, the opera portrays the emotional life of Magda (sop.), mistress of the wealthy Parisian banker Rambaldo (bar.), who finds a chance for true love when she meets Ruggero (ten.), a young man from the provinces. She leaves Rambaldo to live with Ruggero, but comes to realize that her lover's family would never be able to accept her into their respectable bourgeois circle, and resolves to return to Rambaldo. A sub-plot involves the relationship of Magda's maid Lisette (sop.) with Prunier (ten.), a poet.

Rosalinde (sop.). Wife of Eisenstein, who disguises herself as a Hungarian countess at Prince Orlofsky's party, in Johann Strauss's *Die Fledermaus.*

Rosbaud, Hans, b. Graz, 22 July 1895; d. Lugano, 29 Dec 1962. Austrian conductor. His career lay mainly in concerts, with an emphasis on contemporary music. He conducted several Mozart operas at the Aix-en-Provence Festival between 1948-59, and also conducted the première performances of Schoenberg's *Moses und Aron,* for Hamburg radio in 1954, and at the Zurich Opera in 1957. At the 1958 Holland Festival,

he was highly praised for his double-bill of Schoenberg's *Erwartung* and *Von Heute auf Morgen.*

Rosenkavalier, Der *(The Knight of the Rose).* Opera in 3 acts by Richard Strauss. Libretto by Hugo von Hofmannsthal. First performed Dresden, 26 Jan 1911.

In the absence of her husband the Field-Marshal, the Marschallin (sop.) is having an affair with young Count Octavian (sop.). When the Marschallin's cousin, the boorish Baron Ochs (bass), arrives to inform her of his engagement to marry Sophie (sop.), Octavian dresses himself as one of the Marschallin's maids in order to prevent discovery, but is immediately ogled by Ochs. A Cavalier is required to take the traditional silver rose to Ochs's intended bride, and the Marschallin undertakes to find one. She entrusts the task to Octavian.

When Octavian presents the rose to Sophie, he and the young girl fall in love at first sight. Sophie is distressed by Ochs's oafish behaviour, and Octavian quarrels with him, and then hatches a plot to discredit the Baron.

Disguised again as the maid, Octavian accepts an assignation with Ochs at a seedy tavern. By arrangement, Sophie and her father, Von Faninal (bar.), and eventually the Marschallin, all arrive at the tavern, where Ochs has been attempting to seduce the 'maid'. Embarrassed and ridiculed, Ochs withdraws, and the Marschallin gives her blessing to Octavian and Sophie.

Rosenstock, Joseph, b. Cracow, 27 Jan 1895. Polish conductor. He studied in Cracow and Vienna, and conducted at several German opera houses in the 1920s. He was invited to become conductor of the German repertoire at the Met in 1929, but after a year in New York suffered a nervous breakdown and returned to Germany. Forced to leave Germany again in 1936, he conducted in Japan where he spent the war years in captivity. He was artistic director of New York City Opera from 1951-5, and returned to the Met in 1961 to conduct *Elektra* and *Tristan und Isolde.*

Rosina (mezzo-sop.). The ward of Dr Bartolo, she is the heroine of Rossini's *Il Barbiere di Siviglia.*

Rosing, Vladimir, b. St Petersburg, 23 Jan 1890; d. Los Angeles, 24 Nov 1963. Russian tenor. He made his opera début in St Petersburg in 1912 as Lensky in *Eugene Onegin,* and in 1915 sang Hermann in the English première of *Queen of Spades.* In 1927 he founded the American Opera Company which toured the United States performing opera in English. In 1936, in collaboration with Albert Coates, he founded the British Music-Drama Opera Company which survived at Covent Garden for only one season. He returned to America in 1939, and founded the Californian Opera Association. After 1943 he directed opera for the New York City Center Opera (now the New York City Opera).

Rossellini, Renzo, b. Rome, 2 Feb 1908; d. Monte Carlo, 13 May 1982. Italian composer. He composed six operas, among them *La Guerra* (Naples, 1956); *Uno Squardo dal Ponte* (Rome, 1961), based on Arthur Miller's play, *A View from the Bridge;* and *L'Annonce faite à Marie* (Paris, 1970), based on Paul Claudel's play of the same title.

Rossi, Gaetano, b. Verona, 18 May 1774; d. Verona, 25 Jan 1855. Italian librettist. He wrote more than 120 libretti for such composers as Mayr, Rossini *(Tancredi* and *Semiramide),* Meyerbeer, Mercadante *(Il Giuramento),* Donizetti *(Linda di Chamounix),* Gabussi, Nicolai, Nicolini, Pacini, the Ricci brothers, Vaccai and Zingarelli.

Rossi-Lemeni, Nicola, b. Istanbul, 6 Nov 1920. Italian-Russian bass. A pupil of his mother, a Russian singing teacher, he made his début in Venice in 1946 as Varlaam in *Boris Godunov.* He sang a number of leading roles at La Scala between 1947-60, his imposing stage presence making him an admired Boris, Philip II in *Don Carlos* and Méphistophélès in *Faust.* Though his voice declined prematurely, he gave fine dramatic performances in contemporary roles for some years, until he turned to directing operas. He sang Boris Godunov at Covent Garden in 1952, and Méphistophélès at the Met in 1953. He is married to the soprano Virginia Zeani.

Rossini, Gioacchino, b. Pesaro, 29 Feb 1792; d. Passy, nr Paris, 13 Nov 1868. Italian composer. The most famous composer of Italian opera in the first half of the 19th c. he wrote his first opera, *Demetrio e Polibio,* while he was a student and still in his teens. The first to be performed, however, was *La Cambiale di Matrimonio,* a 1-act piece which was staged in Venice in 1810. The earliest Rossini opera of any importance, *Tancredi,* based on a tragedy by Voltaire, was highly acclaimed at its première in Venice in 1813, and three months later the twenty-one-year-old composer had an even greater success with his comic opera, *L'Italiana in Algeri.* Now famous throughout Italy, he was invited to write operas for La Scala, but his next real success came in Naples in 1815 with *Elisabetta, Regina d'Inghilterra.*

For Rome, in the following year, Rossini composed in less than two weeks the opera generally regarded as his comic masterpiece, *Il Barbiere di Siviglia,* based on the famous play by Beaumarchais. He then began to turn out operas in quick succession. *Otello* (1816), which held the stage in Italy until Verdi's opera of the same title in 1887 dealt it a death blow, was followed by *La Cenerentola,* a comic opera based on the Cinderella fairy-tale, and a work of enduring wit and charm. *Mosè in Egitto* (1818) is among the finest of Rossini's serious works, *La Donna del Lago* (1819) and *Maometto II* (1820) are more uneven, and *La Gazza Ladra* (1817) is a curious work combining elements of both serious and comic opera. Of his remaining four Italian operas, *Semiramide* (1823) is the most important. After visits to Vienna, where he met Beethoven, and London, where he led a lively social life and even sang duets with George IV, he settled in Paris as director of the Théâtre Italien, the theatre where operas were given in Paris in the Italian language. But, with his sights set on the Paris Opéra, Rossini produced French-language versions of *Maometto II (Le Siège de Corinthe,* 1826) and *Mosè (Moïse et Pharaon,*1827), forerunners of Meyerbeerian grand opera, and then turned again to *opéra comique* with *Le Comte Ory,* an elegant comedy. His most influential opera for Paris, however, was also his final work for the stage, *Guillaume Tell,* based on Schiller's play about the Swiss patriot. A large-scale work of great originality and power, *Guillaume Tell* was staged at the Paris Opéra in 1829, and came

Gioacchino Rossini

Gioacchino Rossini

in due course to influence an entire generation of French composers. Only thirty-seven years of age, Rossini wrote no more works for the stage, and very little new music of any kind, although he lived on to the age of seventy-six.

Roswaenge, Helge, b. Copenhagen, 29 Aug 1897; d. Munich, 19 June 1972. Danish tenor. He made his début in Neustrelitz in 1921 as Don José, and after engagements at various German opera houses was engaged by the Berlin Staatsoper in 1930. He remained a member of the company until 1944, and returned in 1949. He continued to appear in Berlin and Vienna until the late 1960s. His repertoire embraced the leading Verdi and Puccini roles, as well as Beethoven's Florestan and Mozart's Tamino. In the mid-1930s he sang Parsifal at Bayreuth. His only Covent Garden appearance was in 1938 as Florestan, and his only American appearance was in concert in New York in 1962. He had a voice of great warmth and brilliance: his Alvaro in *La Forza del Destino* in Berlin when he was past sixty still had an impressive authority.

Rota, Nino, b. Milan, 3 Dec 1911; d. Rome, 10 Apr 1979. Italian composer. Internationally known as a composer of film scores, he also composed ten operas in a popular and tuneful style. The earliest to be performed was *Ariodante* (Parma, 1942), but by far the most successful was *Il Capello di Paglia di Firenze* (Palermo, 1955), based on the 1851 farce *Un Chapeau de Paille d'Italie (An Italian Straw Hat)* by Eugène Labiche. Of slight musical interest, it is nevertheless an extremely amusing and exhilarating work. Rota's last works for the stage were *La Visita Meravigliosa* (Palermo, 1970) and *Napoli Milionaria* (Spoleto, 1978).

Rothenberger, Anneliese, b. Mannheim, 19 June 1924. German soprano. She studied in Mannheim and made her début in Koblenz in small roles, graduating soon to leading parts such as Gilda. From 1946-56 she was a member of the Hamburg Staatsoper, where her roles included Cherubino, Musetta, and Oscar in *Un Ballo in Maschera*. After 1955 she sang regularly in Munich. Her repertoire embraced not only the lyric soprano roles of Mozart and Strauss but also modern works such as the

title-roles in Berg's *Lulu,* and in Sutermeister's *Madame Bovary* which she created in Zurich in 1967. She first appeared at the Met in 1960 as Zdenka in *Arabella,* and was a charming Sophie in *Der Rosenkavalier* in Salzburg in 1959 and 1960, and in Lotte Lehmann's staging of the opera at the Met in 1962. A charming artist with an attractive voice and personality, she was also at home in Viennese operetta.

Rothmüller, Marko, b. Trnjani, Croatia, 31 Dec 1908. Yugoslav baritone. He studied in Zagreb and Vienna, and made his début in Hamburg in 1932 as Ottokar in *Der Freischütz.* Forced to leave Germany in 1933 because of his Jewish birth, he sang with the Zurich Opera from 1935-47, being especially successful in the Verdi roles. He sang Krushina in *The Bartered Bride* under Beecham at Covent Garden in 1939, and returned to London in 1947 to sing Rigoletto with the New Opera Company. Recognized then as one of the finest actor-singers of his time, he was invited to join the newly formed company at Covent Garden. He was a greatly admired Wozzeck, Scarpia and Rigoletto at Covent Garden, and at Glyndebourne between 1949-55 appeared as Guglielmo, the Count in *Le Nozze di Figaro,* Don Carlo in *La Forza del Destino,* Macbeth, and Stravinsky's Nick Shadow. He made his New York début with City Opera in 1948, and later appeared at the Met. In 1962 he took up a teaching post at Indiana University, Bloomington.

Rouleau, Joseph, b. Matane, Quebec, 28 Feb 1929. Canadian bass. He studied in Montreal and made his début there in 1955 as Philip in *Don Carlos.* He first appeared at Covent Garden in 1957 as Colline in *La Bohème,* and sang a large number of roles with the company throughout the 1960-70s. In Toronto in 1967, he created the role of Bishop Taché in Harry Somers's *Louis Riel.* In 1983 at Covent Garden, he was an effective Inquisitor in *Don Carlos.*

Rousseau, Jean-Jacques, b. Geneva, 28 June 1712; d. Ermenonville, 2 July 1778. Swiss philosopher, author and composer. He composed seven works for the stage, one of which, *Le Devin du Village,* a 1-act comedy staged at Fontainebleau in 1752, had an enormous success. A work of simple charm, it greatly influenced the early romantic composers. He is best known as the author of *Confessions,* an autobiography, and *Le Contrat Social,* a treatize on the origins and organization of government and the rights of citizens.

Roussel, Albert, b. Tourcoing, 5 Apr 1869; d. Royan, 23 Aug 1937. French composer. His major stage work is the opera-ballet, *Padmâvatî,* based on a Hindu legend, and first staged in Paris in 1923. His comic opera, *Le Testament de la Tante Caroline* (Olomouc, 1936), was a failure. His style was highly eclectic: in *Padmâvatî* he succeeded in writing music of greater power than in his other stage-works which were, for the most part, ballet scores.

Roux, Michel, b. Angoulême, 1 Sept 1924. French baritone. He studied in Paris, and made his début there in 1948 in *Lakmé.* He sang in Paris in opera, and later operetta, for many years, and was heard frequently at Glyndebourne between 1956-69 as the Count in *Le Nozze di Figaro,* Golaud, Don Alfonso in *Così Fan Tutte* and Macrobio in *La Pietra del Paragone.* He now teaches in Paris.

Rozhdestvensky, Gennady, b. Moscow, 4 May 1931. Russian conductor. He studied in Moscow, and made his début while still a student at the age of twenty, conducting the ballet, *Nutcracker,* at the Bolshoi Theatre. He was appointed to the conducting staff of the Bolshoi in 1961, and from 1964-70 was principal conductor, during which time he conducted the Bolshoi première of Prokofiev's *War and Peace* (1959) and the Russian première of Britten's *A Midsummer Night's Dream* (1965). He made his Covent Garden début with *Boris Godunov* in 1970. In 1974 he became music director of an experimental group, the Moscow Chamber Musical Theatre.

Rubini, Giovanni Battista, b. Romano, nr Bergamo, 7 Apr 1794; d. Romano, 3 Mar 1854. Italian tenor. He studied in Bergamo and Naples, and made his début in Generali's *Le Lagrime di una Vedova* in Pavia in 1814. He became the leading tenor of his day, famous throughout Europe. He created the tenor roles in four of Bellini's operas, the last of which, Arturo in *I Puritani,* was

composed with Bellini and Rubini lodging together, the composer trying out each piece with the tenor as it was written. It was for Rubini's forceful intensity of expression and phenomenally high range that Bellini included a 'high F' for him in the last scene of *I Puritani,* a note which Rubini was able to produce excitingly, using a highly developed and fully supported falsetto. Between 1831-43 the tenor divided his time between the opera houses of Paris and London. He retired in 1845.

Rubinstein, Anton, b. Vikhvatinets, Podolsk district, 28 Nov 1829; d. Peterhof, 20 Nov 1894. Russian pianist and composer. One of the greatest pianists of the 19th c., he was also a prolific composer. Of his eighteen operas, some composed to Russian libretti and some to German, the only one to achieve popularity was *The Demon,* a melodramatic work based on a story by Lermontov in which a demon and an angel fight over the soul of a beautiful woman. It was first produced in St Petersburg in 1875 and within the next few years was heard in a number of countries. Rubinstein's other operas, cosmopolitan rather than Russian in style, include *Das verlorene Paradies* (based on Milton's *Paradise Lost),* composed in 1856 and staged in Düsseldorf in 1875; *Kalashnikov the Merchant,* first performed in St Petersburg in 1880; and *Moses,* first performed in Prague in 1892.

Ruddigore. Operetta in 2 acts by Sullivan. Libretto by W.S. Gilbert. First performed London, 22 Jan 1887.

A satire on the Gothic novel, it tells of the curse placed on the Murgatroyd family by one of the victims of Sir Rupert Murgatroyd, the first Baronet. Each member of the family must either commit at least one deadly crime daily, or perish in agony. Robin (bar.), the latest baronet, finds an ingenious way to comply with the terms of the curse while at the same time dissipating it for ever, and in doing so he wins the hand of his beloved Rose Maybud (sop.).

Rudel, Julius, b. Vienna, 6 Mar 1921. Austrian, later American conductor. He began his studies in Vienna but emigrated to the United States at the age of seventeen, and continued his musical studies in New York. He joined City Opera as a rehearsal pianist in 1943, and made his conducting début the following year with *Der Zigeunerbaron*. He became artistic director of the company in 1957, and was also Music Director of the Kennedy Center, Washington for its first four seasons from 1971. With City Opera he has conducted a wide range of operas from Handel to Ginastera, and has also made guest appearances with European companies.

Ruffo, Tita, b. Pisa, 9 June 1877; d. Florence, 6 July 1953. Italian baritone. He studied in Rome and Milan, and made his début in Rome in 1898 as the Herald in *Lohengrin*. He appeared at Covent Garden in 1903 as Enrico in *Lucia di Lammermoor* and Rossini's Figaro, but created so fine an impression at the dress rehearsal of *Rigoletto* with Melba as Gilda, that Melba insisted on his removal from the cast, claiming that he was too young to play her father. (Ruffo never again sang at Covent Garden, but had his revenge elsewhere some years later, when he was famous enough to be able to object to Melba as his Gilda on the grounds that she was too old to play his daughter.) He became one of the most popular baritones of his day in the Verdi roles, bringing a new and vigorous, if somewhat unpolished, style into their interpretation. He first appeared in the United States in 1912 in Philadelphia, and was also greatly admired in Chicago and in New York where he sang with the Met from 1922-9. He retired in 1931.

Rusalka. Opera in 3 acts by Dvořák. Libretto by Jaroslav Kvapil. First performed Prague, 31 Mar 1901.
Having fallen in love with a Prince (ten.), the water nymph Rusalka (sop.) desires to become human. She enlists the aid of the witch Ježibaba (mezzo-sop.) who imposes conditions, one of which is that, should the Prince be unfaithful to her, both will be damned for ever. When the Prince abandons Rusalka for the Foreign Princess (sop.), both he and Rusalka die, although his repentence ensures the water nymph a human soul.

Ruslan and Lyudmila. Opera in 5 acts by Glinka. Libretto by Valeryan Fyodorovich Shirkov, with additions by N. Kukolnik, M.A. Gedeonov, N. Markevich and the composer, based on Pushkin's poem (1820).

First performed St Petersburg, 9 Dec 1842.
In his search for Lyudmila (sop.) who has been kidnapped by a dwarf, Ruslan (bar.) is aided by Finn (ten.), a good fairy, and impeded by Naina (mezzo-sop.), a wicked fairy.

Rysanek, Leonie, b. Vienna, 14 Nov 1926. Austrian soprano. She studied in Vienna and made her début in Innsbruck in 1949 as Agathe in *Der Freischütz*. Her Sieglinde at the first post-war Bayreuth Festival in 1951 created a sensation, and she was compared to Lotte Lehmann, the great Sieglinde of the 1920-30s. Rysanek immediately became much sought after in the lyric-dramatic roles in Wagner and Strauss, and has been a leading soprano of the Munich and Vienna companies for more than thirty years. She is also an exciting interpreter of such Verdi roles as Lady Macbeth, Amelia in *Un Ballo in Maschera*, and Aida. First heard at Covent Garden in 1953 with the Munich company as Danae in Strauss's *Die Liebe der Danae*, she returned in the following two seasons as Chrysothemis in *Elektra*, and as Sieglinde. She made her American début in San Francisco in 1956 as Senta and Sieglinde, and first sang at the Met in 1959 when she replaced Callas who had withdrawn from a production of *Macbeth*. She has a voice of rich, creamy beauty, and is a performer of warm and impulsive temperament. Among her most successful roles are Elisabeth in *Tannhäuser*, the Empress in *Die Frau ohne Schatten*, and Salome. She appeared with Australian Opera in Sydney in 1983 as *Tosca*.

S

Sacchini, Antonio, b. Florence, 14 June 1730; d. Paris, 6 Oct 1786. Italian composer. A leading composer of *opera seria* in the late 18th c., he began his career with a number of comic operas in Italy. In 1772 he moved to London where he remained for nearly ten years. His first operas for London, *Il Cid* and *Tamerlano* (both 1773), won him great popularity, and a further fifteen operas, some of them adaptations of his Italian successes, were produced in London. His final operas, staged in Paris where he lived after 1781, were *Dardanus* (1784), *Oedipe à*

Colone (1786) and *Arvire et Evelina*, staged posthumously in 1788, having been completed by Jean-Baptiste Rey.

Sachs Hans (Bar.). Cobbler hero of Wagner's *Die Meistersinger*.

Sack, Erna, b. Berlin, 6 Feb 1898; d. Wiesbaden, 2 Mar 1972. German soprano. She studied in Prague and Berlin, began her career as a mezzo-soprano in small parts, and in 1930 in Bielefeld changed to coloratura-soprano roles. She joined the Dresden Staatsoper in 1935, in which year she created the role of Isotta in Richard Strauss's *Die schweigsame Frau*. With the Dresden company at Covent Garden in 1936 she sang Zerbinetta in *Ariadne auf Naxos*, conducted by the composer. In 1937 she sang Rosina in *Il Barbiere di Siviglia* and in the title-role of *Lucia di Lammermoor* with great success. She had a lyric-coloratura voice of limited colour but phenomenal range. After World War II, she sang no opera, but gave recitals in many countries.

Sadko. Opera in 7 scenes by Rimsky-Korsakov. Libretto by the composer and Vladimir Ivanovich Belsky. First performed Moscow, 7 Jan 1898.

Sadko (ten.) is promised by Volkhova (sop.), the Sea Princess, that he will be able to catch the golden fish in the sea. He succeeds, but his ships are becalmed because he has failed to pay tribute to the Sea King (bass). Sadko is set adrift on a raft which sinks to the sea bed where he is offered the hand of Volkhova in marriage. However, the opera ends with Volkhova transformed into a river, and Sadko back on shore.

Saint of Bleecker Street, The. Opera in 3 acts by Menotti. Libretto by the composer. First performed New York, 27 Dec 1954.

Anninia (sop.), who lives in Bleecker Street, Greenwich Village, is considered a saint by her Catholic neighbours, but is nevertheless the indirect cause of her brother, Michele (ten.), murdering his sweetheart, Desideria (mezzo-sop.).

Saint-Georges, Jules Henri Vernoy de, b. Paris, 7 Nov 1799; d. Paris, 23 Dec 1875. French librettist. He wrote more than eighty libretti, many in collaboration, for French composers, among them Auber, Bizet and

Hérold. His most important work was his libretto for Bizet's *La Jolie Fille de Perth* which he wrote in collaboration with Jules Adenis.

Saint-Saëns, Camille, b. Paris, 9 Oct 1835; d. Algiers, 16 Dec 1921. French composer. A fluent and prolific composer, he wrote thirteen operas, of which the only one to achieve international success was *Samson et Dalila*, which Saint-Saëns initially conceived as an oratorio. First staged in Weimar in 1877, it is still frequently performed. *Henry VIII*, produced at the Paris Opéra in 1883, has a principal theme based on a traditional English tune which the composer discovered in the library at Buckingham Palace, London. Though generally considered deficient in theatrical effect, at least two of Saint-Saëns's other operas, *Etienne Marcel* (1879) and *Ascanio* (1890), contain much agreeable music. His final opera, *Déjanire*, was staged in Monte Carlo in 1911.

Salammbô. Opera in 5 acts by Reyer. Libretto by Camille du Locle, based on the novel of the same title (1862) by Flaubert. First performed Brussels, 10 Feb 1890.

The opera is set in ancient Carthage, where Salammbô (sop.), a priestess in love with Matho (ten.), kills herself rather than carry out the execution of Matho, condemned to die by her hand. Matho stabs himself and dies.

Salieri, Antonio, b. Legnano, 18 Aug 1750; d. Vienna, 7 May 1825. Italian composer. He was taken to Vienna at the age of sixteen, where, in 1774, he became court composer and conductor of the Italian opera. He composed more than forty operas, most of them to Italian texts, the majority of which were performed in Vienna. The earliest was *Le Donne Letterate* (1770). *Prima la Musica e Poi le Parole* was written for a performance at Schoenbrunn in 1786 in honour of visiting royalty. *Tarare*, composed for Paris in 1786, was one of his greatest successes, as was *Falstaff*, staged in Vienna in 1799. A competent, conventional composer, he may well have been jealous of his great contemporary, Mozart; there is, however, no evidence to support the rumour, current in Vienna at the time of Mozart's death in 1791, that he had been poisoned by Salieri.

Salmhofer, Franz, b. Vienna, 22 Jan 1900; d. Vienna, 22 Sept 1975. Austrian composer and conductor. He wrote music for more than three hundred plays while he was music director at the Burg Theater, Vienna, from 1929-39. He was director of the Vienna Staatsoper company from 1945-55, and of the Volksoper from 1955-63. He composed four operas in a conservative Viennese romantic idiom: *Dame in Traum* (1935) and *Ivan Tarassenko* (1938), both staged at the Staatsoper; *Das Werbekleid*, produced in Salzburg in 1943; and *Dreikönig*, composed in 1945 but not performed until 1970, in Vienna.

Salome. Opera in 1 act by Richard Strauss. Libretto an abridgment in German translation by Hedwig Lachmann of Oscar Wilde's *Salome* (1893). First performed Dresden, 9 Dec 1905.

In Wilde's version of the biblical story, which Strauss set without any alteration other than the omission of certain passages,

Jochanaan or John the Baptist (bar.), imprisoned by Herod (ten.), rejects the advances of Herod's depraved step-daughter, Salome (sop.). During a banquet in the palace, when Herod asks Salome to dance for him, she agrees on condition that he will give her whatever she asks in return. After her Dance of the Seven Veils, she demands the head of Jochanaan. When, finally, Herod gives in to her demand, and the prophet's head is brought in on a silver tray, Salome fondles it erotically and kisses it until a disgusted Herod commands his soldiers to crush her beneath their shields.

Sammarco, Mario, b. Palermo, 13 Dec 1868; d. Milan, 24 Jan 1930. Italian baritone. He studied in Palermo and Milan, and made his début in Palermo in 1888 as Valentin in *Faust*. At La Scala in 1896 he created the role of Gérard in *Andrea Chénier*, and in 1904 he made his Covent Garden début as Scarpia. He appeared frequently at Covent Garden until 1914. Between 1907-13 he sang in the

A scene from Saint-Saens's *Samson et Dalila* at Covent Garden in 1983, with Jon Vickers as Samson and Shirley Verrett as Dalila.

United States, in New York, Boston, Chicago and Philadelphia. In Philadelphia in 1911 he created the role of Alvardo in Victor Herbert's *Natoma*. An impressive actor, he was vocally most suited to the *verismo* roles he sang, such as Gérard, Scarpia, and Tonio in *Pagliacci*.

Samson et Dalila. Opera in 3 acts by Saint-Saëns. Libretto by Ferdinand Lemaire, based on the biblical story in the Book of Judges, Chapters 14-16. First performed Weimar, 2 Dec 1877, in German. First performed in French, Brussels, 5 May 1878, in concert form. First staged performance, in French, Rouen, 3 Mar 1890.

The Hebrew warrior Samson (ten.) leads a revolt against the Philistine overlords. At the instigation of the High Priest of Dagon (bar.), the Philistine Dalila (mezzo-sop.) seduces Samson, and robs him of his great strength by cutting off his hair. Samson is taken prisoner and blinded, but recovers his strength through prayer. At a Philistine bacchanalia at the Temple of Dagon, whither he has been led to be mocked by his captors, he succeeds in pulling down the pillars, and destroying the temple and its occupants.

Sanjust, Filippo, b. Rome, 9 Sept 1925. Italian designer and producer. One of his earliest engagements was to design, in collaboration with Luchino Visconti, a production of *Don Carlos* at Covent Garden in 1958. Subsequently he designed operas in a number of European cities. In 1968 he began also to produce operas, his first being *Die Zauberflöte* in Frankfurt.

Santi, Nello, b. Adria, 22 Sept 1931. Italian conductor. He studied in Padua, and made his début there in 1951 with *Rigoletto*. He has conducted in the leading opera houses, making his Covent Garden début in 1960 with *La Traviata* when Joan Sutherland sang Violetta. He first conducted at the Met in 1962. A compliant accompanist in the popular Italian operas, he has always been more popular with singers than with critics.

Santini, Gabriele, b. Perugia, 20 Jan 1886; d. Rome, 13 Nov 1964. Italian conductor. He studied in Perugia and Bologna, made his début in 1906, and from 1925-9 was assistant to Toscanini at La Scala. He

conducted at the Rome Opera from 1929-32, and from 1944-62 was music director there. He also conducted in Buenos Aires, and Rio de Janeiro. He made a number of gramophone recordings of opera which were generally admired, among them *Gianni Schicchi* with Tito Gobbi.

Santley, (Sir) Charles, b. Liverpool, 28 Feb 1834; d. London, 22 Sept 1922. English baritone. He studied in London and Milan, and made his début in Pavia in 1857 as Dr Grenvil in *La Traviata*. In 1859 he made his British stage début as Hoël in Meyerbeer's *Dinorah* at Covent Garden, and remained with the company there until 1863, creating a number of roles in operas by Balfe, Wallace and Benedict. In 1863 he sang Valentin in the first British performances of *Faust* with such success that Gounod wrote the aria, 'Even Bravest Heart' especially for him to sing in the following year's performances. He was knighted in 1907, and retired from opera in 1911.

Sanzogno, Nino, b. Venice, 13 Apr 1911. Italian conductor. He became resident conductor at La Fenice, Venice, in 1937, first conducted at La Scala in 1939, and in 1955 inaugurated the Piccola Scala company to perform small-scale operas. He is especially admired for his performances of modern works, but is also an elegant interpreter of 18th-c. opera.

Sapho. Opera in 5 acts by Massenet. Libretto by Henri Cain and Arthur Bernède, based on the novel of the same title (1884) by Alphonse Daudet. First performed Paris, 27 Nov 1897.

The 'Sapho' of the title is not the poetess of ancient Greece, but a model, Fanny Legrand (sop.), who has been posing as Sappho for an artist. The opera tells of her unhappy love affair with Jean (ten.), a country youth.

Sarastro (bass). High priest of Isis and Osiris, in Mozart's *Die Zauberflöte*.

Sardinero, Vicente, b. Barcelona, 12 Jan 1937. Spanish baritone. He studied in Barcelona, and made his début there in operettas and *zarzuelas*. Germont in *La Traviata* was his first role in opera in Barcelona in 1964. He made a successful début at La Scala, Milan, in 1967 as Enrico in *Lucia di Lammermoor*, and now sings a number of Mozart, Rossini, Donizetti and Verdi roles at most of the leading European opera houses. His New York opera début was in 1970 with City Opera as Tonio in *Pagliacci*, and he was first heard at Covent Garden in 1976 as Marcello in *La Bohème*. An elegant lyric baritone, he is at his best in bel canto roles.

Šárka. Opera in 3 acts by Fibich. Libretto by Anežka Schulzová. First performed Prague, 28 Dec 1897.

The opera is based on an incident in Czech mythology. (It shares its subject with an opera of the same title by Janáček.) Šárka (sop.), leader of the Council of Women after the death of Libuše, falls in love with her opponent Ctirad (ten.).

Sarti, Giuseppe, b. Faenza, baptized 1 Dec 1729; d. Berlin, 28 July 1802. Italian composer. A leading figure in 18th-c. opera, he spent many years as court composer in Denmark and in Russia. He composed more than eighty operas, but is remembered now because a phrase from one of them, *Fra i due litiganti il terzo gode* (first performed in Milan in 1782), is quoted in the Act II supper scene in Mozart's *Don Giovanni*.

Sass, Sylvia, b. Budapest, 12 July 1951. She studied in Budapest, and made her début there in 1971 as Frasquita in *Carmen*. She came to international attention when she sang Giselda in *I Lombardi* in 1973, and began to appear in opera houses throughout Europe. Her British début was with Scottish Opera in 1975 as Desdemona, and she first appeared at Covent Garden the following year in *I Lombardi*. She made her Met début in 1977 as Tosca. Though an erratic vocalist, she possesses a fine soprano voice capable of undertaking lyric-dramatic roles, and is an actress of great presence. In Brussels in 1982, she undertook the title-role in Gluck's *Alceste*.

Satie, Erik, b. Honfleur, 17 May 1866; d. Paris, 1 July 1925. French composer. Remembered mainly as the composer of a number of slight and inconsequential piano pieces with bizarre titles, he also composed for the ballet, most notably for the Massine-Cocteau ballet, *Parade*, in 1917.

Geneviève de Brabant is a miniature opera for puppets, composed in 1899; *Pousse l'amour* an operetta performed in Monte Carlo in 1913; and *Le Piège de Méduse* a play with words and music by Satie, written in 1913.

Sauguet, Henri, b. Bordeaux, 18 May 1901. French composer. The earliest of his six operas was a comic piece in 1 act, *Le Plumet de Colonel*, both text and music of which were written by Sauguet. Most of his subsequent theatre music was composed for ballet, but a 2-act comic opera, *La Contrebasse* (1930), a trivial piece revived in Bordeaux in 1981, was followed by *La Chartreuse de Parme*, a full-length opera based on Stendhal's novel, the composition of which occupied Sauguet for some years. Staged in Paris in 1939, it is generally regarded as his most successful opera. *La Gageure Imprévue* (1942) was staged in Paris in 1944, and *Les Caprices de Marianne*, based on the play by Alfred de Musset, was produced in Aix-en-Provence in 1954. Sauguet spent some years in the 1960-70s writing *Le Pain des Autres*, a 2-act opera based on a story by Turgenev.

Saul og David. Opera in 4 acts by Nielsen. Libretto by Einar Christiansen, based on the Biblical story in the First Book of Samuel. First performed Copenhagen, 28 Nov 1902.

David (ten.) falls in love with Michal (sop.), daughter of Saul (bar.). Jonathan (ten.) brings news of the defeat of the Philistines. The opera ends with David becoming King.

Sylvia Sass

Saunders, Arlene, b. Cleveland, Ohio, 5 Oct 1935. American soprano. She studied in New York, and made her début in 1958 with the Met on tour, as Rosalinde in *Die Fledermaus*. She first appeared at the Met in New York in 1962, and in 1963 joined Hamburg Opera and was successful there in a wide range of roles. She made her Covent Garden début in 1980 as Minnie in *La Fanciulla del West*, when she gave a memorable interpretation of the role. In 1982, she sang the title-role of *Manon Lescaut* for English Opera North.

Sāvitri. Opera in 1 act by Holst. Libretto by the composer, based on an episode in the *Mahabharata*, the epic poem of ancient India. First performed London, 5 Dec 1916.

When Death (bass) comes to take her husband, Satyavān (ten.), Sāvitri (sop.) successfully pleads for him to be spared.

Savoy Operas. The operettas of Gilbert and Sullivan are frequently referred to as the Savoy operas, as many (though not all) of them were first performed at the Savoy Theatre, London, a theatre built by the impresario Richard d'Oyly Carte on the profits from earlier operettas in the series.

Sawallisch, Wolfgang, b. Munich, 26 Aug 1923. German conductor. He studied in Munich and made his début in Augsburg conducting *Hänsel und Gretel* in 1947. After working in several German opera houses, he became the youngest conductor to be engaged at Bayreuth when he made his début there in 1957 with *Tristan und Isolde*. In 1971 he became general music director of the Bavarian Staatsoper, with which company he first appeared at Covent Garden the following year.

Sayão, Bidu, b. Rio de Janeiro, 11 May 1902. Brazilian soprano. She studied in Rio and Nice, and made her début in Rio in 1925 as Rosina in *Il Barbiere di Siviglia*. She made a successful début at the Met as Manon in 1937, and sang regularly with the company until 1951, in such roles as Gilda, Mélisande, Juliette in Gounod's *Roméo et Juliette*, Violetta, Mimi, Susanna, and Adina in *La Sonnambula*. She was a delightful artist with an attractive lyric soprano voice. She retired in 1958, after farewell performances in Rio as Mimi, Mélisande and Juliette.

Scala di Seta, La *(The Silken Ladder).* Opera in 1 act by Rossini. Libretto by Giuseppe Foppa, after the play *L'Échelle de Soie* by François Antoine Eugène de Planard. First performed Venice, 9 May 1812.

Giulia (sop.) has occasion to keep her marriage to Dorvil (ten.) a secret from her guardian Dormont (bass), and so Dorvil is forced to use a silken ladder to enter his wife's apartment in the Dormont house.

Scarlatti, Alessandro, b. Palermo, 2 May 1660; d. Naples, 22 Oct 1725. Italian composer. One of the most important figures in operatic history, he composed well over one hundred operas, approximately seventy of which have survived though they are now rarely performed. His first opera, *Gli Equivoci nel Sembiante*, was staged in Rome in 1679, after which he composed operas at the rate of two or three a year until 1721 when he seems to have retired from active composition. Only one of the surviving operas, *Il Trionfo dell' Onore* (1718), is a comic piece, for Scarlatti's major contribution was to establish the classical *opera seria* in Italy. He developed the *da capo* aria, a three-part aria with an opening allegro, a middle andante, and a repeat of the allegro; and also the form of the overture, from which the classical symphony was later to grow. *Il Mitridate Eupatore*, produced in Venice in 1707, is regarded as one of his finest dramas. Exceptionally it is in five acts: most of Scarlatti's operas are in three.

Scarlatti, Domenico, b. Naples, 26 Oct 1685; d. Madrid, 23 July 1757. Italian composer. The son (one of ten children) of Alessandro Scarlatti, he is one of the greatest 18th-c. composers for the keyboard. He composed more than a dozen operas at the beginning of his career, but most have been lost. The majority of them were written for the Roman court of Maria Casimira, Queen of Poland, whose service Scarlatti entered in 1709. They include *Silvia* (1710), *Orlando* (1711) and *Ifigenia in Tauri* (1713).

Scarpia (bar.). The villainous Roman chief of police, in Puccini's *Tosca*.

Schalk, Franz, b. Vienna, 27 May 1863; d. Edlach, 3 Sept 1931. Austrian conductor. A

Domenico Scarlatti by Nicolas Largillière.

pupil of Bruckner, he made his début as a conductor in Liberec in 1886, and was appointed conductor at the Vienna Opera in 1900 by Gustav Mahler. In 1918 he became, with Richard Strauss, joint director of the company, and in 1919 conducted the première of Strauss's *Die Frau ohne Schatten*. After Strauss's resignation in 1924, Schalk remained sole director of the Vienna Opera until 1929. He conducted at the Met during the 1898-9 season, and at Covent Garden in 1898 (*Lohengrin*), 1907 (*Die Walküre, Tannhäuser*, and *The Bartered Bride*), and 1911 when he conducted all the operas in the autumn season which consisted of three complete *Ring* cycles, *Tannhäuser, Tristan und Isolde* and Humperdinck's *Königskinder*.

Schaunard (bar.). A musician, one of the four young bohemians in Puccini's *La Bohème*.

Schauspieldirektor, Der *(The Impresario)*. Singspiel in 1 act by Mozart. Libretto by Gottlieb Stephanie Jr. First performed Vienna, 7 Feb 1786.

At a theatre in Salzburg, the impresario Frank (speaking role) is auditioning singers and actors. The actors and actresses perform in interpolated scenes from various plays. Mozart's music is utilized when two rival prima donnas sing audition arias, and a quarrel breaks out between them. The rival sopranos are Madame Herz and Mademoiselle Silberklang, both sopranos. A tenor, Herr Vogelsang, tries in vain to keep the peace. When the work is performed now, the text is drastically shortened and most of the non-singing roles eliminated.

Schenk, Otto, b. Vienna, 12 June 1930. Austrian producer and actor. He studied acting and production in Vienna, and began his career first as an actor and then as a producer of plays. His first opera production, *Die Zauberflöte*, for the Landestheater in Salzburg in 1957, was successful enough for him to be invited to direct opera at the Vienna Staatsoper. His production of Berg's *Lulu* for the Vienna Festival in 1962 was much admired, and he has been chief producer at the Staatsoper since 1965. He made his Met début with *Fidelio* in 1970, and his Covent Garden début with *Un Ballo in*

Maschera in 1975. His productions are sensitive, imaginative, and faithful to the spirit of the work.

Schikaneder, Emanuel, b. Straubing, 1 Sept 1751; d. Vienna, 21 Sept 1812. Austrian dramatist, theatre manager, actor and singer. He became an actor in his early twenties, and later managed his own touring company. When he was in charge of a Viennese suburban theatre, the Theater auf der Wieden, he commissioned Mozart to write music for a play he had written for himself and his company to perform. This was *Die Zauberflöte*, at whose first performances in 1791, Schikaneder himself played and sang the role of Papageno. In 1801, he opened a new theatre, the Theater an der Wien, in the vicinity of the Theater auf der Wieden, and produced plays and operas in it until 1806. He was one of the most talented men of the theatre of his time, several of whose comedies continued to be performed in Vienna until well into the 19th c., influencing such later popular dramatists as Raimund and Nestroy. Other Viennese composers provided music for Schikaneder's plays, though he himself was capable of composing his own music when necessary.

Schillings, Max von, b. Düren, 19 Apr 1868; d. Berlin, 24 July 1933. German composer and conductor. He began his career at Bayreuth in 1892 as an assistant stage manager, and became chorus master there in 1902. From 1911 he was general music director of the opera at Stuttgart, and from 1919-25 was in charge of the Berlin Opera. He composed four operas. *Ingwelde*, staged in Karlsruhe in 1894, was gloomily Wagnerian in style and content; *Der Pfeifertag* (Schwerin, 1899), by contrast, was a comedy, but still Wagnerian in treatment. *Moloch* (Dresden, 1906) is said to have impressed Mahler. Schillings's only completely successful opera was *Mona Lisa*, staged in Stuttgart in 1915. It quickly became one of the most popular of modern German operas, and Schillings conducted a number of performances of it, among them the Met performances in 1923.

Schipa, Tito, b. Lecce, 2 Jan 1888; d. New York, 16 Dec 1965. Italian tenor. He studied in Lecce and Milan, and made his début in Vercelli in 1910 as Alfredo in *La Traviata*. In

1917 in Monte Carlo he created the role of Ruggero in Puccini's *La Rondine*. He became one of the most admired lyric tenors of his time, specializing in the more graceful bel canto roles and in such French roles as Massenet's Des Grieux and Werther. He made his American début in 1919 with the Chicago Opera, and continued to appear regularly with the Chicago company until 1932, after which he sang at the Met for three consecutive seasons, and again in 1941. His voice was not large but its timbre was distinctive, and he was a superb stylist. As Verdi's Alfredo and Duke of Mantua, Rossini's Almaviva, or as Ernesto in *Don Pasquale*, he had few, if any, equals. He never sang in opera in England. His final appearances in opera were in his home town of Lecce, in 1954, as Nemorino in *L'Elisir d'Amore*, but he continued to give recitals for some years.

Schippers, Thomas, b. Kalamazoo, Mich., 9 Mar 1930; d. New York, 16 Dec 1977. American conductor. He studied in Philadelphia, and made his début conducting the Lemonade Opera Company in New York in 1948. In 1950 he conducted Menotti's *The Consul* shortly after its première, and began an association with the composer which led to his conducting later Menotti operas and becoming music director of the Festival of Two Worlds at Spoleto. In 1963 he conducted *Die Meistersinger* at Bayreuth, and in 1966 conducted Barber's *Antony and Cleopatra* at the opening of the new Met in Lincoln Center.

Schlusnus, Heinrich, b. Braubach, 6 Aug 1888; d. Frankfurt, 18 June 1952. German baritone. He studied in Frankfurt and Berlin, and made his début in Hamburg in 1915 as the Herald in *Lohengrin*. He sang leading roles at the Berlin Staatsoper from 1917-45. He possessed of a voice of beautiful timbre, and he was greatly admired in Germany in the Verdi baritone roles. His only American appearances were in Chicago in 1927-8, and his only Bayreuth role was Amfortas in 1933. His last appearance in opera was as Rigoletto in Frankfurt in 1948.

Schneider-Siemssen, Günther, b. Augsburg, 7 June 1926. Austrian designer, of German birth. He began to design opera in Munich, encouraged by the conductor Clemens Krauss. In 1954 he became chief designer in Bremen, where he designed the first of his *Ring* productions. After collaborating with Herbert von Karajan on *Pelléas et Mélisande* in Vienna in 1960, he became Karajan's favourite designer, and has worked with him on a number of occasions, most memorably at the Salzburg Summer and Easter Festivals, where he has designed *Boris Godunov* (1965), the *Ring* (1967-70), *Fidelio* (1971), *Tristan und Isolde* (1972) and several other operas. He made his Covent Garden début in 1962 with Schoenberg's *Erwartung*, and then designed Hans Hotter's Covent Garden production of the *Ring* (1962-4). He makes great use of light in his semi-abstract designs for the Wagner operas.

Schoeck, Othmar, b. Brunnen, 1 Sept 1886; d. Zurich, 8 Mar 1957. Swiss composer. He composed nine operas, the earliest in a late-romantic style, the later ones somewhat more modern. They include *Don Ranudo de Colibrados* (Zurich, 1919), a comic opera; *Penthesilea* (Dresden, 1927) which is generally considered to be his finest work; and *Das Schloss Dürande* (Berlin, 1943).

Schoeffler, Paul, b. Dresden, 15 Sept 1897; d. Amersham, Bucks, 21 Nov 1977. Austrian baritone of German birth. He studied in Dresden, Berlin and Milan, and made his début in Dresden in 1925 as the Herald in *Lohengrin*. He remained a member of the Dresden company until 1938, and then joined the Vienna Staatsoper from 1938-65. His roles ranged from the Count in *Le Nozze di Figaro* to Verdi's Iago and Puccini's Scarpia. He was also renowned as Hans Sachs in *Die Meistersinger*, the role of his Bayreuth début in 1943. At Salzburg in 1952 he created the role of Jupiter in Strauss's *Die Liebe der Danae*. He sang at Covent Garden in the 1930s and again between 1949-53, and appeared at the Met during the 1950s. A genial and intelligent performer, he brought distinction even to the small roles he sang in Vienna towards the end of his career.

Schoenberg, Arnold, b. Vienna, 13 Sept 1874; d. Los Angeles, 13 July 1951. Austrian

composer. Famous as the first composer to develop the serial method of composition, he wrote four operas spanning the greater part of his creative life. *Erwartung*, composed in 1909 but not performed until 1924 in Prague, is a 1-act monodrama for soprano and orchestra. *Die glückliche Hand*, written immediately after *Erwartung* and in a similar musical style, also remained unperformed until 1924. *Von Heute auf Morgen* (1930) is a comedy, utilizing the twelve-tone technique. Schoenberg embarked upon his only full-length opera, *Moses und Aron*, in 1930, but abandoned it after completing two of its projected three acts, though to the end of his life he spoke of his intention of returning to the work. An opera of great intensity and power, it was first performed after the composer's death.

Schorr, Friedrich, b. Nagyvárad, 2 Sept 1888; d. Farmington, Conn., 14 Aug 1953. Hungarian, later American, bass-baritone. He studied in Vienna, and first sang in opera in small parts with the Chicago Opera in 1912, during a holiday visit to the United States. He made his official début in Graz in 1912 as Wotan in *Die Walküre*, remained with the Graz company until 1916, and then sang in various German opera houses, establishing himself as a leading Wagner singer. He joined the Berlin Staatsoper in 1923, and also sang Wotan at Bayreuth each season from 1925-31. He made his first appearance at Covent Garden in 1924 as Wotan in *Das Rheingold*, and sang most of his Wagner roles there. At the Met, he was first heard in 1924 as Wolfram, and sang there every season until 1943. Wotan and Hans Sachs were considered his greatest roles, to which he brought not only a beautiful voice but also great authority.

Schreier, Peter, b. Meissen, 29 July 1935. German tenor. He studied in Leipzig and Dresden, and made his début in Dresden in 1961 as the First Prisoner in *Fidelio*. Possessor of an attractive lyric tenor voice, he was soon singing Mozart roles at the Berlin Staatsoper, and in 1967 made his Met début as Tamino. He appears regularly in Vienna, Salzburg and Munich, and in 1970 made his début as a conductor with the Berlin Staatskapelle. His David in *Die Meistersinger* in Munich in 1982 was widely admired.

Schreker, Franz, b. Monaco, 23 Mar 1878; d. Berlin, 21 Mar 1934. Austrian composer. He composed nine operas, the first of which, *Flammen*, a 1-act piece, was performed only in a concert version in Vienna in 1902 with the composer playing the orchestral accompaniment on the piano. He made his reputation with *Der ferne Klang* (1912), a work which impressed many composers of his own generation, among them Schoenberg and Berg. *Das Spielwerk und die Prinzessin* (1913) was less successful, but *Die Gezeichneten* (1918) and *Der Schatzgräber* (1920) caused him to be considered one of the leading composers of German-language opera, and in 1920 he accepted the directorship of the Berlin Hochschule für Musik. With the rise of Naziism, he came under attack as a Jew, and was obliged to cancel the première of his seventh opera, *Christophorus*, which remained unperformed. *Der singende Teufel* (1928) and *Der Schmied von Gent* (1932) were staged in Berlin, but the latter work met with Nazi demonstrations. Schreker was forced to resign from the Hochschule, and shortly afterwards suffered a severe heart attack. His operas disappeared from the German stage during the Nazi period, but there have been post-war revivals of *Der ferne Klang* and *Der Schatzgräber*.

Schröder-Devrient, Wilhelmine, b. Hamburg, 6 Dec 1804; d. Coburg, 26 Jan 1860. German soprano. The finest dramatic soprano of her day, she studied singing in Vienna, and made her début there in 1821 as Pamina. Weber thought her the finest performer of Agathe in his opera *Der Freischütz*, and she was coached by Beethoven when she sang Leonore in his *Fidelio* in 1822. It was her performance in *Fidelio* which Richard Wagner claimed had inspired him to become a composer of opera. She later created roles in three Wagner operas: Adriano in *Rienzi*, Senta in *Der fliegende Holländer* and Venus in *Tannhäuser*. Most accounts of her performances assert that, despite vocal deficiencies, she was a great singing-actress.

Schröder-Feinen, Ursula, b. Gelsenkirchen, 21 July 1936. German soprano. She studied in Gelsenkirchen, joined the chorus of the opera company there in 1958, and made her solo début in 1961 in *Der*

Vogelhändler. Her roles included Aida, Beethoven's Leonore, Strauss's Salome, and Puccini's Turandot. A dramatic soprano of warmth and great strength, her voice was heard at its best in the Wagner roles which she sang at Bayreuth during the 1970s. She made her Met début in 1970, and her British début in 1975 as Salome at the Edinburgh Festival.

Schubert, Franz, b. Vienna, 31 Jan 1797; d. Vienna, 19 Nov 1828. Austrian composer. One of the greatest of the Viennese composers, he is renowned primarily for his songs, symphonies and piano and chamber music. He also composed or began sixteen works for the stage, the failure of which is generally attributed to their weak libretti. Though it is true that he was hampered by poor libretti, it is also undeniable that Schubert's genius was essentially lyrical, rather than dramatic, and that, although his operas and Singspiels are full of music of great beauty, they all lack dramatic impetus and any but the most rudimentary skill in dramatic characterization. He completed only the overture and one act of his first work for the stage, *Der Spiegelritter*, at the age of fifteen. In the following year, 1813, he composed a 3-act opera, *Des Teufels Lustschloss*, and in 1815, now aged eighteen and hopeful of beginning a career as a composer of opera, completed four Singspiels: *Der vierjährige Posten*, *Fernando*, *Claudine von Villa Bella* and *Die Freunde von Salamanka*. The first of his works to be staged, however, was *Die Zwillingsbrüder*, whose moderate success at the Kärntnertor Theater in June, 1820, led to a commission from the Theater an der Wien to compose music for a 3-act play, *Die Zauberharfe*. Schubert completed his score in two weeks, and the play was presented in August. Although he was to compose his three most important works for the stage between 1821-3, *Die Zwillingsbrüder* remains the only opera by Schubert to achieve production during the composer's lifetime. The works he completed after 1821 are *Alfonso und Estrella*, his most attractive and lyrical opera; *Die Verschworenen* (after the *Lysistrata* of Aristophanes); and *Fierabras*. In the autumn of 1823, he composed more incidental music for a play, this time for a production of *Rosamunde* by Hermine von Chézy. There have been occasional performances of some of the operas and Singspiels in the late 19th c. and the 20th c. but there is little likelihood that any will enter the repertoire. The best hope for them lies in festival productions or concert performances.

Schuller, Gunther, b. New York, 22 Nov 1925. American composer. Entirely self-taught in composition, though influenced by American jazz, he has also drawn on the techniques of such great contemporary composers as Stravinsky and Schoenberg. He has composed two operas. The first, *The Visitation*, based on Kafka's *The Trial*, was produced in Hamburg in 1966. The second, *The Fisherman and his Wife*, is a 1-act children's opera, with a libretto by the American novelist, John Updike, based on a Grimm fairy tale. It was produced in Boston in 1970.

Schumann, Elisabeth, b. Merseburg, 13 June 1885; d. New York, 23 Apr 1952. German soprano. She studied in Dresden, Berlin and Hamburg, and made her début in Hamburg as the Shepherd in *Tannhäuser* in 1909. She remained with the Hamburg company until 1919 when Richard Strauss persuaded her to join the Vienna Staatsoper. She became a great favourite in Vienna, until the Anschluss in 1938 caused her to emigrate to the United States where she gave recitals and taught. She had a delightful stage manner, and a silvery lyric soprano voice of great charm. Her most successful roles included Mozart's Susanna and Zerlina, Sophie in Richard Strauss's *Der Rosenkavalier* which she often sang in London and Vienna with her friend Lotte Lehmann as the Marschallin, and Adele in *Die Fledermaus*.

Schumann, Robert, b. Zwickau, 8 June 1810; d. Endenich, nr Bonn, 29 July 1856. German composer. A central figure in the German romantic movement, he began to write an opera, *Der Corsar*, based on Byron's poem, *The Corsair*, in 1844, but abandoned the project after composing a chorus and sketching an aria. His only completed opera, *Genoveva*, produced in Leipzig in 1850, contains much beautiful music, but its effect as an opera is vitiated by Schumann's lack of genuine dramatic talent. There is virtually no characterization, and the intended dramatic points are made so poorly that they pass virtually unnoticed.

Schumann-Heink, Ernestine, b. Lieben, nr Prague, 15 June 1861; d. Hollywood, 17 Nov 1936. Austrian, later American, contralto. She studied in Graz and Dresden, and made her début in 1878 in Dresden as Azucena in *Il Trovatore*. After four seasons at Dresden, she joined the company at Hamburg, where she remained from 1883-98. She first appeared in London in 1892 with the Hamburg Opera conducted by Gustav Mahler, when she was acclaimed as Erda, Fricka and Brangäne. Until 1893 when she married the actor Paul Schumann, she sang as Ernestine Heink. From 1896-1914 she was a popular performer at Bayreuth, and in 1899 she made her first appearance at the Met, as Ortrud. She sang frequently at the Met for four seasons, after which she began a series of concert tours of the United States which over the years was to make her a popular figure there. In 1909 in Dresden she created the role of Klytemnestra in *Elektra*. She continued to sing at the Met from time to time until her farewell appearance as Erda in *Das Rheingold* and *Siegfried* in 1932, when she was in her seventy-first year. She sang on the radio and in films until shortly before her death. She was an impressive artist with a rich and flexible voice, and a strong personality.

Schwarzkopf, Elisabeth, b. Jarotschin, nr Posen (now Poznań), 9 Dec 1915. German soprano. She studied in Berlin, and made her début there in 1938 as a Flowermaiden in *Parsifal*. She quickly graduated to leading roles, and first sang abroad during World War II with a Berlin company in Paris, as Adele in *Die Fledermaus*. In 1942 she joined the Vienna Staatsoper, with whom she first appeared at Covent Garden in 1947. She then became a member of the newly formed company at Covent Garden, remaining there until 1951, in which year she created the role of Anne in Stravinsky's *The Rake's Progress*. She became a celebrated Lieder singer, confining her operatic roles to those few which her husband, Walter Legge, considered best suited to her talents: the Marschallin, the Countess in *Le Nozze di Figaro*, Fiordiligi, Donna Elvira, and the Countess in *Capriccio*. She made her Met début as the Marschallin in 1963. She was admired in Mozart and Strauss, especially in Vienna and Salzburg during the 1960s. In 1972 she gave her farewell stage perform-

Renato Scotto acknowledging the applause after singing Lucia in Donizetti's *Lucia di Lammermoor* at La Scala in 1967.

ance in Brussels, as the Marschallin. The illusion of spontaneity played little part in her art, but her studied and elegant artificiality made her a superb Countess in Strauss's *Capriccio*, a role in which she had particular success in Vienna. After her retirement she became a noted teacher.

Schweigsame Frau, Die *(The Silent Woman)*. Opera in 3 acts by Richard Strauss. Libretto by Stefan Zweig, based on Ben Jonson's play *Epicoene* (1609). First performed Dresden, 24 June 1935.

Sir Morosus (bass), a retired English admiral with an obsessive hatred of noise, bemoans his bachelor state, and his barber (bar.) undertakes to find him a silent wife. Sir Morosus's nephew Henry arrives with his troupe of actors one of whom, Aminta (sop.), is Henry's wife. When Sir Morosus refuses to acknowledge Aminta as his niece, the barber and the actors work out a plan to trick the old man into compliance. This involves persuading him into marrying a timid girl who is, in fact, Aminta in disguise. A mock ceremony is performed by the actors, after which the new wife becomes loudly shrewish, to the great distress of Sir Morosus. Eventually the plot is disclosed, Sir Morosus reinstates his nephew in his affections, and returns to his state of former and unmarried contentment.

Sciutti, Graziella, b. Turin, 17 Apr 1932. Italian soprano. She studied in Rome, and made her début at Aix-en-Provence in 1951 as Lucy in Menotti's *The Telephone*. She excelled in such roles as Mozart's Susanna, Zerlina and Despina, Norina in *Don Pasquale*, and Nannetta in Verdi's *Falstaff*. In 1954 she made her British début as Rosina in *Il Barbiere di Siviglia* at Glyndebourne, and in 1956 sang Oscar in *Un Ballo in Maschera* at Covent Garden. From 1958-66 she was a great favourite in her Mozart roles at the Salzburg Festival, and in 1961 made her American début in San Francisco as Susanna. In recent years, while continuing her singing career, she has begun to produce opera. She is the possessor of a delightful lyric soprano voice, a highly attractive stage presence, and a fine musical intelligence.

Scotti, Antonio, b. Naples, 25 Jan 1866; d. Naples, 26 Feb 1936. Italian baritone. He studied in Naples, and made his début there in 1889 as Cinna in Spontini's *La Vestale*. He became a leading interpreter of the Verdi roles, Mozart's Giovanni, and Tonio in Leoncavallo's *Pagliacci*. It was as Giovanni that he first appeared at Covent Garden in 1899, which was also the year of his Met début. He was London and New York's first Scarpia in *Tosca*. He continued to sing at the Met until 1933, his great ability as an actor compensating for a deterioration in the quality of his voice in later years.

Scotto, Renata, b. Savona, 24 Feb 1934. Italian soprano. She studied in Milan, where she made her début in 1953 as Violetta. She was immediately recognized as an outstanding lyric-coloratura soprano, and sang at La Scala such roles as Lucia, Adina in *L'Elisir d'Amore*, Amina in *La Sonnambula* and the title-role in *Madama Butterfly*. She made her London début in 1957 as Mimi, and first appeared at the Met in 1965 as Butterfly. In recent years she has undertaken more dramatic roles, such as Bellini's Norma and Donizetti's Anna Bolena. In 1982 she sang Lady Macbeth at the Met in Sir Peter Hall's new production of Verdi's *Macbeth*. She had, in the earlier stages of her career, an attractive voice of great agility, and she later became a dramatic soprano of intelligence and a persuasive actress.

Scribe, Eugène, b. Paris, 24 Dec 1791; d. Paris, 20 Feb 1861. French librettist. He was one of the most successful dramatists of his time, and enormously prolific. A skilled theatrical craftsman of no great imaginative insight, he was adept at turning out well-made scripts, the demand for which was so great that he was usually obliged to work with collaborators. As a librettist he is remembered mainly for his work with Meyerbeer for whom he provided five libretti, including those of *L'Africaine*, *Les Huguenots* (with Émile Deschamps) and *Le Prophète*. He wrote libretti for most of the leading French composers of his time, among them Adam, Auber, Boïeldieu, Gounod, Halévy (six operas, including *La Juive*) and Hérold. He also collaborated with Italian composers, among them Donizetti and Verdi. For Verdi he provided the libretto of *Les Vêpres Siciliennes*. Antonio Somma's libretto for Verdi's *Un Ballo in Maschera* was based on Scribe's *Gustave III ou Le Bal Masqué*, which he wrote for Daniel Auber.

Searle, Humphrey, b. Oxford, 26 Aug 1915; d. London, 12 May 1982. English composer. A pupil of Webern, he was the best-known British exponent of serialism as a technique of composition. He wrote three operas. *The Diary of a Madman*, a 1-act setting of a Gogol story, was performed in Berlin in 1958. According to the composer there are electronic effects in the score, but these were omitted from the Berlin première, conducted by Hermann Scherchen. *The Photo of the Colonel*, based on a story by Eugène Ionesco, was first performed on BBC Radio in 1964, and given its stage première in Frankfurt later that year. Searle's only full-length opera, *Hamlet*, was performed in Hamburg in 1968 and at Covent Garden the following year. Although the composer's libretto followed Shakespeare closely, his music was disappointingly unmemorable, and amounted to little more than an unnecessary musical commentary on the play.

Sebastian, Georges, b. Budapest, 17 Aug 1903. Hungarian conductor. A pupil of Bruno Walter, he joined the music staff of the Munich Opera in 1922 while Walter was director, and worked at the Met in 1923-4. He conducted in Hamburg, Leipzig and Berlin between 1924-31, after which he conducted no opera until 1944 in San Francisco. He was chief conductor of the Paris Opéra from 1947-73, and was most highly regarded for his performances of the German repertory, especially Strauss and Wagner.

Sedaine, Michel-Jean, b. Paris, 4 July 1719; d. Paris, 17 May 1797. French librettist. He made his name as a librettist for Monsigny, but also provided texts for Philidor, Grétry and others. His best-known libretti are those for Grétry's *Richard Coeur de Lion*, Monsigny's *Le Roi et le Fermier* and *Le Déserteur* and Philidor's *Le Diable à Quatre*.

Seefried, Irmgard, b. Köngetried, Swabia, 9 Oct 1919. Austrian soprano. She studied in Augsburg, and began her career in Aachen in 1939, making her début as the off-stage voice of the Priestess in *Aida*. She joined the Vienna Staatsoper in 1943 and was chosen by Strauss to sing the role of the Composer in a special performance of *Ariadne auf Naxos* in 1944 for his eightieth birthday. She remained a member of the Staatsoper until her retirement, and was greatly admired as Susanna in *Le Nozze di Figaro*, Zerlina, Fiordiligi, Pamina, and Octavian in *Der Rosenkavalier*. She first appeared at Covent Garden in 1947 with the Vienna company, and made her Met début in 1953. She had a lyric soprano voice of great beauty, and was a most engaging actress. She was also a distinguished singer of Lieder, especially of Schubert. She made her farewell appearance at the Vienna Staatsoper in 1976 in *Katya Kabanova*.

Seinemeyer, Meta, b. Berlin, 5 Sept 1895; d. Dresden, 19 Aug 1929. German soprano. She studied in Berlin, and made her début there in 1918 in Offenbach's *Orphée aux Enfers*. In 1923-4 she toured the United States with Sol Hurok's German Opera Company, her performance as Eva in *Die Meistersinger* in New York being highly acclaimed. She became a member of the Dresden company in 1925, and was renowned for her performances of such Verdi roles as Leonora in *La Forza del Destino*, Aida, and Amelia in *Un Ballo in Maschera*. In the spring of 1929 she appeared as Covent Garden as Sieglinde, Eva and Elsa, but died of leukaemia two months later. She had a most beautiful voice and a fine understanding of Verdian style.

Selika (sop.). A slave in love with the navigator Vasco da Gama, she is the eponymous heroine of Meyerbeer's *L'Africaine*.

Sembrich, Marcella, b. Wiśniewczyk, 15 Feb 1858; d. New York, 11 Jan 1935. Polish soprano. She studied in Vienna, and made her début in Athens in 1877 as Elvira in *I Puritani*. She made her first appearance at

Irmgard Seefried (left) as Susanna in Mozart's *Le Nozze di Figaro* in her début at the Met in 1953. She was the most enchanting Susanna of her generation.

A scene from Handel's *Semele* at Covent Garden in 1982. It marked the 250th anniversary of the first theatre on the Covent Garden site.

Covent Garden in 1880 as Lucia, and at the Met in the same role in 1883. She sang at the Met in most seasons until her retirement in 1909, her repertoire of more than thirty roles including Violetta, Elvira in *Ernani*, Elsa, Eva and Mimi. She was regarded as one of the finest coloratura sopranos of her time, and became a distinguished teacher in New York after her retirement from opera.

Semele. Secular oratorio in 3 acts by Handel. Libretto by William Congreve. First performed London, 10 Feb 1744, as an oratorio. First stage production, Cambridge, 10 Feb 1925.

Semele (sop.) makes the mistake of insisting that her lover, Jupiter (ten.), appears to her in his full god-like splendour. When he does so, Semele dies from the effect of his radiance.

Semiramide. Opera in 2 acts by Rossini. Libretto by Gaetano Rossi, based on the play, *Sémiramis* (1748) by Voltaire. First performed Venice, 3 Feb 1823.

Semiramide, Queen of Babylon (sop.), and her lover, Assur (bar.), murder the King, but Semiramide then falls in love with and intends to marry Arsace (mezzo-sop.) who, before the ceremony can take place, is revealed to be her own son. Defending himself against an attack by Assur, Arsace accidentally kills Semiramide. Arsace is proclaimed King and hailed as the avenger of his father's murder.

Senta (sop.). Daland's daughter, she is in love with the legend of the Flying Dutchman, in Wagner's *Der fliegende Holländer*. Her love redeems the Dutchman when she kills herself as he sails away.

Serafin, Tullio, b. Rottanova di Cavarzere, Venice, 1 Sept 1878; d. Rome, 2 Feb 1968. Italian conductor. He studied in Milan, and began his career as a violinist in the orchestra of La Scala. He made his début as a conductor in Ferrara in 1898, first appeared at Covent Garden in 1907 conducting *La Bohème, Carmen, La Gioconda* and *Tosca,* and became principal conductor at La Scala in 1909. For the next half-century, he conducted a wide range of operas in Europe and America, advising and encouraging many important singers at the outset of their careers, among them Rosa Ponselle, Maria Callas and Joan Sutherland. From 1934-43 he was artistic director of Rome Opera. His last appearances at Covent Garden, more than fifty years after his first, were made in 1959 and 1960 when he coached Joan Sutherland for her first Lucia, and conducted the performances. He was an authoritative interpreter of the bel canto operas, but also an enthusiast for contemporary works, giving the first Italian performances of *Wozzeck* and *Peter Grimes.*

Sereni, Mario, b. Perugia, 25 Mar 1928. Italian baritone. He studied in Rome and Siena, and made his début in Florence in 1953 in Lualdi's *Il Diavolo nel Campanile.* He soon became a popular performer of the leading Italian baritone roles, and made his first appearance at the Met in 1957 as Gérard in *Andrea Chénier.* He has sung also at La Scala, the Vienna Staatsoper, and the Teatro Colón, Buenos Aires, with great success. His Belcore in *L'Elisir d'Amore* in Chicago in 1981 was stylishly sung.

Serse. Opera in 3 acts by Handel. Libretto by Niccolò Minato, originally written for Cavalli in 1654. First performed London, 26 Apr 1738.
Serse, or Xerxes (contr.), King of Persia, falls in love with Romilda (sop.), his brother's fiancée. This is the opera which contains the aria 'Ombra mai fù', a satirical serenade addressed to a tree, which has become famous in countless arrangements, often with religious texts substituted for the original words, as 'Handel's Largo'.

Serva Padrona, La *(The Maid as Mistress).* Opera in 2 parts by Pergolesi. Libretto by Gennaro Antonio Federico. First performed Naples, 28 Aug 1733, as an intermezzo

between the acts of Pergolesi's *Il Prigionier Superbo.*
Uberto (bass) is tricked by his serving-maid, Serpina (sop.), into marrying her.

Shacklock, Constance, b. Sherwood, Nottingham, 16 Apr 1913. English mezzo-soprano. She studied in London, and made her début there in 1947 as Mercédès in *Carmen.* She sang leading roles with the Covent Garden company until 1956, and was particularly admired as Octavian in *Der Rosenkavalier* and Amneris in *Aida.* After her retirement from opera, she sang in the first London production of *The Sound of Music* in 1961 as the Abbess.

Shaporin, Yuri, b. Glukhov, 8 Nov 1887; d. Moscow, 9 Dec 1966. Russian composer. The composer of a large number of cantatas and oratorios on Soviet themes, his only opera was *The Decembrists* on which he worked from 1920 until 1953. An incomplete version was performed in Leningrad in 1925 as *Paulina Goebbel,* but the completed work was not performed until 1953. It remains in the Soviet repertoire, but has not found favour abroad.

Sharpless (bar.). The American Consul in Puccini's *Madama Butterfly.*

Shaw, Glen Byam, b. London, 13 Dec 1904. English producer. After a distinguished career as a producer of plays, he began to produce opera only when he was appointed director of productions for the Sadler's Wells company (subsequently English National Opera). His productions at Sadler's Wells Theatre and at the London Coliseum have ranged from *Die Fledermaus* to Wagner's *Ring.*

Shebalin, Vissarion Yakovlevich, b. Omsk, 11 June 1902; d. Moscow, 28 May 1963. Russian composer. Primarily a composer of orchestral and chamber music, he wrote two operas, and one musical comedy, *The Embassy Bridegroom,* which was staged in 1942. His first opera, *Sun over the Steppe,* was written over a period of many years and given a concert performance in Moscow in 1958. His most successful work for the stage is *The Taming of the Shrew,* a setting of the Shakespeare play, first performed in Moscow in 1957.

Sheridan, Margaret, b. Castlebar, 15 Oct 1889; d. Dublin, 16 Apr 1958. Irish soprano. She studied in London and Milan, and made her début in Rome in 1918 as Mimi. The following year she appeared at Covent Garden as Mimi, and also sang the title-role in the first London performance of Mascagni's *Iris*. She returned to Covent Garden on several occasions, but sang mainly in Italy in the 1920s, making her début at La Scala in 1921. She retired in 1931 and taught in Dublin.

Shield, William, b. Swalwell, 5 Mar 1748; d. London, 25 Jan 1829. English composer. He played the violin in provincial theatres, and joined the orchestra of the King's Theatre in London in 1772, first as a violinist and then as leader of the violas. He remained there for eighteen years, and soon began to compose songs and pieces for the violin. He composed more than fifty operas, most of them comic pieces with spoken dialogue between the musical numbers, the majority of which were staged at Covent Garden. His earliest opera, *The Flitch of Bacon*, was produced in 1778, and his last, *Two Faces under one Hood*, in 1807. The only opera by Shield which has survived with its orchestral parts intact is *Rosina* (1782).

Shirley, George, b. Indianapolis, 18 Apr 1934. American tenor. He made his début as Eisenstein in *Die Fledermaus* in Woodstock, N.Y., in 1959, sang Rodolfo in *La Bohème* at the Teatro Nuovo, Milan, in 1960, and first appeared at the Met in 1961 as Ferrando in *Così Fan Tutte*. He made his British début in 1966 at Glyndebourne as Tamino. He returned frequently to Glyndebourne and Covent Garden, and was much admired at Covent Garden as Loge in *Das Rheingold*. He has an individual voice, somewhat baritonish in timbre, and is an expressive actor. In 1982, he sang the title-role in Cavalli's *L'Egisto* at the Dominion Theatre, London.

Shirley-Quirk, John, b. Liverpool, 28 Aug 1931. English bass-baritone. He studied in London and made his début at Glyndebourne in 1962 as the Doctor in *Pelléas et Mélisande*. He has sung with the leading British opera companies, created a number of roles in operas of Britten. He sang all seven baritone roles in *Death in Venice* in 1973, and made his Met début in those same roles in 1974. He created Lev in Tippett's *The Ice Break* in 1977.

Shostakovich, Dmitri, b. St Petersburg, 25 Sept 1906; d. Moscow, 9 Aug 1975. Russian composer. The last of the great symphonic composers, he composed only two operas. *The Nose*, a satirical comedy, was produced in Leningrad in 1930. *Lady Macbeth of the Mtsensk District* was generally admired when first performed in Leningrad in 1934, but savage criticism in *Pravda* in 1936 forced it off the Soviet stage for many years. *Pravda* described the music as, 'quacks, grunts and growls...love is smeared all over the opera in the most vulgar manner.' In the 1950s Shostakovich revised it as *Katerina Ismailova*, under which title it was produced in Moscow in 1963 and at several opera houses abroad. *Moskva, Cheremushki*, a musical comedy, was staged in Moscow in 1959. In 1956, he was awarded Russia's highest honour – the order of Lenin.

Shuard, Amy, b. London, 19 July 1924; d. London, 18 Apr 1975. English soprano. She studied in London, and made her début in Johannesburg in 1949 as Aida. Later that year she joined Sadler's Wells Opera, remaining with the company until 1954. She then joined the Covent Garden opera company where she sang many of the Verdi dramatic soprano roles such as Aida, Amelia and Lady Macbeth. She was also a greatly admired Turandot. An unsubtle artist with a strong and capable voice, she was a reliable performer of the standard repertory. She was admired in the operas of Puccini.

Shuisky (ten.). A scheming Boyar, in Mussorgsky's *Boris Godunov*.

Shvanda the Bagpiper (Czech title, *Švanda Dudák*). Opera in 2 acts by Weinberger. Libretto by Miloš Kareš. First performed Prague, 27 Apr 1927.

Based on a Czech folk-tale, the opera describes the adventures of the bagpiper Shvanda (bar.), persuaded by the robber Babinsky (ten.) to seek out the Queen Iceheart (mezzo-sop.). He finds himself in hell, but is rescued by Babinsky who plays cards with the Devil (bass) and cheats. Finally breaking free of the influence of Babinsky, Shvanda returns home to his wife, Dorotka (sop.).

Siebel (mezzo-sop.). A youth in love with Marguerite, in Gounod's *Faust*.

Siegfried. Opera in 3 acts by Wagner. Libretto by the composer. First performed Bayreuth, 16 Aug 1876, as part of the first complete performance of the tetralogy, *Der Ring des Nibelungen*.

Siegfried is the third of the four *Ring* operas. In Act I the young Siegfried (ten.), son of Siegmund and Sieglinde, who has been brought up in a cave in the forest by Mime (ten.), is told by Mime the story of his birth, and of the sword, Nothung. Wotan,

Siegfried holding up the newly forged sword, from a painting by F. Leeke, 1909.

disguised as a Wanderer (bass-bar.), questions Mime while Siegfried is absent, and prophesies that the sword will be forged again only by a hero who knows no fear. When Siegfried returns, Mime makes a futile attempt to kill him, but the fearless hero succeeds in forging the sword.

In Act II Siegfried rouses Fafner (bass) who, in the form of a dragon, has been guarding the gold. Siegfried kills Fafner, and then goes in search of the sleeping Brünnhilde (sop.), pausing only to kill Mime, against whom he has been warned by a Woodbird (sop.). In the last act, Siegfried forces his way past the Wanderer, symbolically shattering the god's spear with Nothung, his sword, and makes his way through the magic fire to Brünnhilde, whom he awakens, and claims as his bride.

Sieglinde (sop.). The sister and incestuous lover of Siegmund, in Wagner's *Die Walküre*.

Siegmund (ten.). The brother and lover of Sieglinde, in Wagner's *Die Walküre*.

Siepi, Cesare, b. Milan, 10 Feb 1923. Italian bass. Self-taught, he made his début in Schio, Veneto, in 1941 as Sparafucile in *Rigoletto*. His career was interrupted by the war, and he resumed it in Verona in 1945 as Zaccaria in *Nabucco*. He first appeared at Covent Garden in 1950 with a company from La Scala, as Colline in *La Bohème*, and made his Met début later the same year as Philip II in *Don Carlos*. He was a member of the Met company for twenty-four years, and also sang regularly in European opera houses. His Don Giovanni at Salzburg in 1953 and subsequently in Vienna was greatly admired. It was a role for which his strikingly handsome presence and his warm, lyrical bass voice rendered him well equipped, and his Salzburg performance has been captured on film. He was still singing leading roles in the early 1980s, his Basilio in *Il Barbiere di Siviglia* in San Francisco in 1982 revealing him to be an adept comedian.

Silja, Anja, b. Berlin, 17 Apr 1940. German soprano. She studied with her grandfather, Egon van Rijn, and made her opera début in Berlin in 1956 as Rosina in *Il Barbiere di Siviglia*. In 1960 she appeared at Bayreuth as Senta, and was encouraged by Wieland

Wagner to undertake other Wagner roles which were clearly too heavy for her essentially lyrical voice. She made her London début in 1963 with Frankfurt Opera in the title-role of *Fidelio*, and first sang in the United States in 1968 in Chicago as Senta. Though her voice understandably became prematurely affected by wear and tear, she was able to continue her career because of her striking ability as an operatic actress. She is heard at her best in roles such as Berg's Marie (in *Wozzeck*) and Lulu in which intelligent and compelling characterization is more important than beautiful vocalizing. She was still singing Marie in 1982.

Sills, Beverly, b. Brooklyn, N.Y., 25 May 1929. American soprano. She studied in New York, and made her opera début in Philadelphia in 1947 as Micaëla in *Carmen*. She became a leading soprano with New York City Opera in 1955, but her international fame resulted from her performance as Cleopatra in Handel's *Giulio Cesare* for City Opera in 1966. A lyric coloratura with a strikingly individual voice, she undertook a number of Donizetti roles with the company, and was also an affecting Manon in Massenet's opera. She made her Covent Garden début in *Lucia di Lammermoor* in 1970, and her Met début in Rossini's *Le Siège de Corinthe* in 1975. She retired from singing in 1979, and became director of the New York City Opera. She was a fine singing-actress, a commanding Elizabeth I in *Roberto Devereux*, and a captivating Rosina in *Il Barbiere di Siviglia*.

Anja Silja in Shostakovich's *Lady Macbeth of Mtsensk* in San Francisco in 1981.

Silva (bass). The Spanish grandee and rival of Ernani in Verdi's *Ernani*.

Silveri, Paolo, b. Ofena, nr Aquila, 28 Dec 1913. Italian baritone. He studied in Florence, and made his début in Rome in 1939 as Schwarz (a bass role) in *Die Meistersinger*. He first appeared in London in 1946 with a company from Naples, as Marcello, and sang with the newly formed Covent Garden company from 1947-9, undertaking such roles as Rigoletto, Escamillo and Boris Godunov in English. Between 1950-3 he sang at the Met. In 1959 in Dublin he appeared in the tenor role of Otello in Verdi's opera, but the following year reverted to baritone roles. Since 1970 he has taught in Rome.

Silvio (bar.). The young villager in love with Canio's wife, Nedda, in Leoncavallo's *Pagliacci*.

Simionato, Giulietta, b. Forlì, 12 May 1910. Italian mezzo-soprano. She studied in Rovigo, and made her début in Florence in 1935, in the première of Pizzetti's *Orsèolo*. She sang small parts throughout the 1930s, but was a leading singer at La Scala from 1939-66. She was popular at Covent Garden, where she made her first appearances in 1953 as Adalgisa, Amneris and Azucena, all with Callas. She made her American début in Chicago in 1954, and sang at the Met from 1959-63. She was greatly admired in Vienna in the Verdi roles, especially Amneris which she sang opposite the Aida of Leontyne Price. She retired in 1966. She had a warm mezzo-soprano voice of individual timbre, and was a fine musician and a most convincing actress.

Simon Boccanegra. Opera in a prologue and 3 acts by Verdi. Libretto by Francesco Maria Piave, based on the play *Simón Boccanegra* by Antonio García Gutiérrez. First performed Venice, 12 Mar 1857. Revised by the composer, with the libretto revised by Arrigo Boito, it was performed in Milan, 24 Mar 1881.

In the opera's prologue, the sea-adventurer Simon Boccanegra (bar.), who has had a child by Maria, daughter of the patrician Fiesco (bass), learns simultaneously that he has been elected Doge of Genoa, and that Maria has died. Twenty-five years later,

Fiesco, who has brought up the child, Amelia (sop.), but kept her in ignorance of her parentage, plots against the Doge, with the help of Gabriele Adorno (ten.) who is in love with Amelia. Boccanegra discovers Amelia's identity, and he and his daughter are reunited. Gabriele, misunderstanding the nature of their relationship, intends to kill the Doge, but when he learns the truth joins Boccanegra's faction. Boccanegra is poisoned by his disaffected henchman, Paolo (bar.). As he dies, he and Fiesco are reconciled. Boccanegra blesses the union of his daughter and Gabriele, and proclaims Gabriele as his successor.

Simoneau, Léopold, b. Quebec, 3 May 1918. Canadian tenor. He studied in Montreal, and made his début there in 1941 as Hadji in *Lakmé*. He sang in Paris in the late 1940s and early 1950s, and became renowned for his Mozart performances at Aix-en-Provence in 1950 and at Glyndebourne from 1951. He was Tom in the first French production of *The Rake's Progress* in 1953. He had a voice of beautiful timbre, and was a fine Mozart stylist. After his retirement he taught in Montreal, helped to found the Quebec Opera in 1971, and became its first artistic director. He resigned shortly after the company opened, and moved to San Francisco in 1972, but in recent years has coached students in Vancouver at the annual Shawnigan Summer School's Opera Center whose artistic director is his wife, the soprano, Pierrette Alarie.

Singspiel. This German term ('sing-play') is used to describe a play with musical numbers, the German equivalent of a French *opéra comique*. Mozart's *Die Entführung aus dem Serail*, its musical numbers separated by dialogue, is a Singspiel. So, theoretically, is *Die Zauberflöte*, though it so transcends the form that it is rarely referred to as such. The Singspiel paved the way to 19th-c. German romantic opera, notably to Weber.

Sinopoli, Giuseppe, b. Venice, 2 Nov 1946. Italian conductor and composer. He studied composition in Venice and conducting with Hans Swarowsky in Vienna. Although he began his career as a specialist in contemporary music, since 1978 when he conducted *Aida* in Venice he has come to be regarded as an authoritative interpreter of Verdi. In 1980 he conducted *Macbeth* in Berlin, *Aida* in Hamburg and *Attila* in Vienna. The following year, his *Luisa Miller* in Hamburg was greatly acclaimed, as was his *Macbeth* in Vienna in 1982. He made his Covent Garden début in 1983 with *Manon Lescaut*. His opera, *Lou Salome*, was performed in Munich in May, 1981, conducted by Sinopoli himself.

Sir John in Love. Opera in 4 acts by Vaughan Williams. Libretto selected by the composer from Shakespeare's *The Merry Wives of Windsor* (1600-01). First performed London, 21 Mar 1929.

The plot follows closely that of Shakespeare's play.

Slezak, Leo, b. Schönberg, Moravia, 18 Aug 1873; d. Egern am Tegernsee, 1 June 1946. Austrian tenor. He studied in Paris, and made his début in 1896 in Brno as Lohengrin. His début at Covent Garden in the same role on 18 May 1900 was ruined by the pandemonium that broke out in the auditorium after Act II when the relief of Mafeking was announced. He was engaged by Mahler for the Vienna Opera in 1901 and remained one of the most popular singers in Vienna until his final appearance in *Pagliacci* in 1933. He made his Met début in 1909 as Otello, and sang with the company for four seasons. A superb Wagnerian tenor, he possessed one distinctly un-Wagnerian attribute, an irrepressible sense of fun. At a performance of *Aida* at the Met, he is said to have so convulsed the chorus that they were fined by the management. (Slezak paid the fine.) After his retirement from opera, he undertook comic roles in German-language films in Austria. He also wrote six volumes of autobiography and reminiscence between 1922-46.

Slobodskaya, Oda, b. Vilna, 28 Nov 1888; d. London, 29 July 1970. Russian soprano. She studied in St Petersburg, and made her début there in 1919 as Lisa in Tchaikovsky's *Queen of Spades*. In 1922 in Paris she created the role of Parasha in Stravinsky's *Mavra*, and in 1931 first appeared in London, at the Lyceum Theatre, with Chaliapin in Dargomyzhsky's *Rusalka*. She made her Covent Garden début the following year as Venus in *Tannhäuser*. Though she sang at La Scala in

Bedřich Smetana in 1881.

1933 and the Teatro Colón, Buenos Aires, in 1936, her subsequent career was based on London where she lived for the remainder of her life. She continued to sing as a recitalist, and to make gramophone recordings, until her mid-seventies, and taught in London until shortly before her death.

Smareglia, Antonio, b. Pola, 5 May 1854; d. Grado, 15 Apr 1929. Italian composer. He composed nine operas, the first of which, *Preziosa*, was produced in Milan in 1880, and the last, *Abisso*, also in Milan, in 1914. Two of his operas were given for the first time in German translation in prestigious conditions: *Il Vassallo di Szigeth* in Vienna in 1889, and *Cornil Schut* in Dresden in 1893. His operas reveal a strong influence of the early Wagner, though from *Nozze Istriane* (Trieste, 1895) onwards they are closer in style to Italian *verismo*.

Smetana, Bedřich, b. Litomyšl, 2 Mar 1824; d. Prague, 12 May 1884. Czech composer. The first major Czech nationalist composer, he composed eight operas which led to his being considered as the father of modern Czech music. The first, *The Brandenburgers in Bohemia*, performed in Prague in 1866, won its composer the chief conductorship of the Provisional Theatre, a post he held for eight years. Later in 1866, his second opera, *The Bartered Bride*, was staged. It soon became a riotous success, was revised by Smetana on three occasions, achieving its definitive form in 1870, and has remained the most popular Czech opera, and the only opera by Smetana to achieve world-wide popularity. A cheerful comedy of village life, it was followed in 1868 by the serious and heroic *Dalibor*, and in 1881 by the intensely patriotic *Libuse*, performed at the opening of the new National Theatre. Three operas composed between *Dalibor* and the première of *Libuse* were more domestic in style and subject, and have not been successful outside Czechoslovakia. They are *The Two Widows* (1874), *The Kiss* (1876) and *The Secret* (1878). Smetana's final opera, *The Devil's Wall*, a parody of romantic opera, was staged in 1882. Smetana began work on *Viola*, based on Shakespeare's *Twelfth Night*, but had only sketched 365 bars of music when he died.

Smyth, (Dame) Ethel, b. London, 22 Apr 1858; d. Woking, 9 May 1944. English composer. She composed six operas, the first three of which were given their premières in Germany, where she studied composition. *Fantasio*, a comedy based on a play by Alfred de Musset, was staged in Weimar in 1898, but later suppressed by the composer. *Der Wald*, a symbolist drama, was first staged in Berlin in 1902, but aroused little interest when it was performed later the same year at Covent Garden. Ethel Smyth's third and most ambitious opera, *The Wreckers*, was composed to her own French text (based on a Cornish play) in the expectation of a production in Brussels. This failed to materialize, and the opera first reached the stage in German translation, as *Strandrecht*, in Leipzig in 1906. After the first performance, dismayed at unauthorized cuts in the final act the composer stole into the orchestra pit, collected her score and all the orchestral parts, and made off for Prague where she had been promised a production. *The Wreckers* was first performed in English in London in 1909. It is a work of some dramatic strength and musical interest, despite the influence of Wagner in the love music and Sullivan in the choruses. *The Boatswain's Mate* (1916) was liked when it was first performed in London, though it has rarely been revived. Ethel Smyth's remaining operas are 1-act pieces, *Fête Galante* (1923) and *Entente Cordiale* (1925).

Snow Maiden, The (Russian title, *Snegur-ochka*). Opera in a prologue and 4 acts by Rimsky-Korsakov. Libretto by the composer, based on the play (1873) by Alexsandr Nikolayevich Ostrovsky. First performed St Petersburg, 10 Feb 1882.

The Snow Maiden (sop.), the child born of Spring (mezzo-sop.) and Winter, is adopted by the mortals Bobil (ten.) and Bobilicka (mezzo-sop.). A wealthy youth, Misgir (bar.), falls in love with her. The intervention of Tsar Berendey (ten.) leads to tragedy for the Snow Maiden who melts away when her heart is warmed by love.

Söderström, Elisabeth, b. Stockholm, 7 May 1927. Swedish soprano. She studied in Stockholm and made her début in 1947 at Drottningholm as Bastienne in Mozart's *Bastien und Bastienne*. She has sung leading roles with Swedish Royal Opera since 1950,

Elisabeth Söderström in Janáček's *Jenůfa*.

and has made guest appearances in most of the leading European opera houses. She first sang in opera in Great Britain at Glyndebourne in 1957 as the Composer in *Ariadne auf Naxos*. She made her Met début in 1959 as Sophie in *Der Rosenkavalier*, and in the same year also sang the other leading roles in the same opera: Octavian at Glyndebourne, and the Marschallin in Stockholm. She is admired for her Mozart roles, especially the Countess in *Le Nozze di Figaro*. She is a sensitive musician and a convincing actress, with a lyric soprano voice of attractive timbre. Her Emilia in *The Makropoulos Affair* is a justly famous characterization. It was the role of her Australian début in Adelaide in 1982.

Soldaten, Die *(The Soldiers)*. Opera in 4 acts by Zimmermann. Libretto by the composer, based on the play (1776) by Jakob Michael Lenz. First performed Cologne, 15 Feb 1965.

Marie (sop.), a respectable middle-class girl engaged to Stolzius (bar.), is seduced by Baron Desportes (ten.), an aristocratic officer, and eventually becomes a common soldiers' whore.

Solera, Temistocle, b. Ferrara, 25 Dec 1815; d. Milan, 21 Apr 1878. Italian librettist and composer. His first and most important libretti were written for Verdi. He worked on the libretto of Verdi's first opera, *Oberto* (1839), revising Antonio Piazza's original text, and went on to produce four more libretti for Verdi: *Nabucco* (1842), *I Lombardi* (1843), *Giovanna d'Arco* (1845) and *Attila* (1846). He also wrote libretti for several minor composers. He composed four operas to his own texts between 1840-5.

Solti, (Sir) Georg, b. Budapest, 21 Oct 1912. Hungarian, later British, conductor. He made his début as a conductor in Budapest in 1938 with *Le Nozze di Figaro*, escaped to Switzerland during the war, and in 1942 won a piano competition in Geneva. He returned to conducting in 1946 when he was appointed music director of the Bavarian Staatsoper in Munich, moving to a similar post in Frankfurt in 1952. He was music director at Covent Garden from 1961-71. He is at his best as a conductor of the Strauss operas, but was chosen to conduct the 1983 production of Wagner's *Der Ring des Nibelungen* at Bayreuth.

Somers, Harry, b. Toronto, 11 Sept 1925. Canadian composer. The leading Canadian composer of his generation, he has written two operas, the second of which, *Louis Riel*, was favourably received at its première in Toronto in 1967.

Sondheim, Stephen, b. New York, 22 Mar 1930. American composer. He wrote the lyrics for a number of Broadway musicals, among them Bernstein's *West Side Story* and Jule Styne's *Gypsy*, and is the composer and lyricist of several musicals, including *A Funny Thing Happened on the Way to the Forum* (1962), *A Little Night Music* (1973) and *Pacific Overtures* (1976). His major work

is *Sweeney Todd* which, though it was first presented on Broadway in 1979 as a musical, is of operatic stature.

Sonnambula, La *(The Female Sleepwalker)*. Opera in 2 acts by Bellini. Libretto by Felice Romani. First performed Milan, 6 Mar 1831.

In a Swiss village in the early 19th c., Amina (sop.), foster-daughter of Teresa (sop.), owner of the village mill, celebrates her betrothal to Elvino (ten.), a young farmer. During the ceremony on the village green, a handsome stranger appears. He is Count Rodolfo (bass), returning to the village of his childhood after many years. The Count takes a room at the inn, whose proprietress is Lisa (sop.), who is also in love with Elvino.

Unknown to anyone else, Amina is a sleepwalker, and that evening she walks into the Count's room at the inn. The Count discreetly withdraws, but Amina's presence is discovered by Lisa and disclosed to Elvino who arrives as Amina awakens, unable to explain her presence in the Count's room. Elvino, thinking the worst, denounces Amina, and proposes marriage to Lisa. The Count attempts to explain matters, but the villagers have never heard of sonnambulism, and do not believe him. When Amina is seen sleepwalking on the roof of the mill house, the truth is clear. Amina awakes to find Elvino asking her forgiveness.

Sophie (sop.). Faninal's daughter, in love with Octavian, in Strauss's *Der Rosenkavalier*.

soprano. The highest category of female voice. In opera, the category is sub-divided into dramatic, lyric, light or coloratura, and spinto which has elements of both the lyric and dramatic. The male castrato's highest vocal category was also soprano.

Sorochintsy Fair (Russian title, *Sorochinskaya Yarmarka*). Opera in 3 acts by Mussorgsky. Libretto by the composer, based on a story by Gogol (1831-2). The opera was left unfinished by Mussorgsky. A performing version, based on editions by Anatoly Lyadov (1904) and Vyacheslav Karatygin (1912), was performed in Moscow, 21 Oct 1913. Other composers' versions of the opera were subsequently

Luciana Serra as Amina in Bellini's *La Sonnambula* at Covent Garden in 1982.

staged: Cui's in St Petersburg in 1917; Tcherepnin's in Monte Carlo in 1923; and Shebalin's in Leningrad in 1931.

Tcherevik (bass) takes his daughter Parassia (sop.) to the fair where she encounters her lover Gritzko (ten.), who asks Tcherevik for Parassia's hand in marriage. The old man agrees. Though Parassia's mother Khivria (mezzo-sop.) disapproves, her authority is weakened when it is discovered she has been having an affair with the son of the local priest. All ends happily for the young lovers.

Soyer, Roger, b. Paris, 1 Sept 1939. French bass. He studied in Paris, and made his début there in small roles in 1962. He was admired as Don Giovanni in Aix-en-Provence, and has sung leading roles at the Paris Opéra since 1973. They have included Méphistophélès in *Faust* and Procida in *Les Vêpres Siciliennes*.

Sparafucile (bass). The assassin hired to kill the Duke of Mantua in Verdi's *Rigoletto*.

Spiess, Ludovic, b. Cluj, 13 May 1938. Romanian tenor. He studied in Bucharest and Milan, and made his début in Braşov in 1962. He first sang at the Bucharest National Opera in 1966 as Cavaradossi, and began his international career when chosen by Karajan to sing Dmitri in *Boris Godunov* at Salzburg in 1967. He made his Covent Garden début in 1973 as Radames, a role he has also sung with success in Vienna and at the Met.

Spohr, Louis, b. Brunswick, 5 Apr 1784; d. Kassel, 22 Oct 1859. German composer and violinist. One of the leading composers of instrumental music in the early romantic period, he also composed ten operas. *Faust* (1813), his first important opera, is significant in that it made use of leading motifs, anticipating their use by Wagner.

Spohr developed his system of leading motifs more fully in *Zemire und Azor* (1819) and in his greatest operatic success, *Jessonda* (1823). He anticipated Wagner also in developing recitative into a melodic arioso. His later operas were less adventurous.

Spoletta (ten.). Scarpia's agent in Puccini's *Tosca*.

Spontini, Gasparo, b. Maiolati, 14 Nov 1774; d. Maiolati, 24 Jan 1851. Italian composer. The most important figure in French serious opera at the beginning of the 19th c., he composed nine Italian operas before moving to Paris, where he became, with *La Vestale* (1807), one of the leading composers of his day. He achieved even greater success with *Fernand Cortez* (1809) and *Olympie* (1819). From 1820-40 he was engaged as composer for and director of the Berlin Court Opera, where he produced his last important opera, *Agnes von Hohenstaufen*, in 1829.

Stabile, Mariano, b. Palermo, 12 May 1888; d. Milan, 11 Jan 1968. Italian baritone. He studied in Rome, and made his début in Palermo in 1909 as Amonasro in *Aida*. He was chosen by Toscanini to sing Falstaff at La Scala in 1921, and was so successful in the role that he became associated with it for the remainder of his career. He sang it at Covent Garden in 1926 when he also appeared as Iago and Don Giovanni. He appeared frequently at Covent Garden, and later at Glyndebourne, in the 1930s, and returned after the war to London to sing Falstaff, Scarpia and other roles between 1946-9. A singing actor of great elegance, he still delighted audiences as Falstaff in his seventies.

Stade, Frederica von, b. Somerville, N.J., 1 June 1945. American mezzo-soprano. She studied in New York and made her début at the Met in 1970 as the Third Boy in *Die Zauberflöte*. She made her Glyndebourne début in 1973 with a delightful and beautifully sung Cherubino, and first sang at Covent Garden in 1975 as Rosina. A tasteful performer, she is at her best in Mozart, but is also a most affecting Mélisande in Debussy's *Pelléas et Mélisande*. In 1982, she sang the title-role in Thomas's *Mignon* in Santa Fe.

Stanford, (Sir) Charles, b. Dublin, 30 Sept 1852; d. London, 29 Mar 1924. Irish composer. Primarily a composer of church music and oratorios, he wrote ten operas, the first two of which were produced in Germany: *The Veiled Prophet of Khorassan* (Hanover, 1881) and *Savonarola* (Hamburg, 1884). *The Canterbury Pilgrims* was staged in London in 1884, but his first real success came with *Shamus O'Brien*, given fifty performances in London in 1896. His later operas include *Much Ado About Nothing*, which had its première at Covent Garden in 1901; *The Critic* (1916); and *The Travelling Companion* (1926).

Steber, Eleanor, b. Wheeling, W. Va., 17 July 1916. American soprano. She studied in Boston and New York, and made her début at the Met in 1940 as Sophie in *Der Rosenkavalier*. She sang with the Met company for nearly thirty years, in such Mozart roles as the Countess, Fiordiligi and Donna Elvira, and also as Elsa in *Lohengrin* (which she sang at Bayreuth in 1953) and in the title-role of Strauss's *Arabella* which she sang in the first American performances at the Met in 1955. In 1958 she created the title-role in Barber's *Vanessa*. She sang Miss Wingrave in the American première of Britten's *Owen Wingrave* at Santa Fe in 1973.

Stevens, Risë, b. New York, 11 June 1913. American mezzo-soprano. She studied in New York and Salzburg, sang such roles as Mignon, Orpheus and Octavian in Prague and Vienna between 1936-8, then returned to New York and made her Met début in 1938 as Mignon. She sang at the Met until 1961, her best roles including Carmen, Octavian, Cherubino and Dorabella. She also appeared in Hollywood films, among them *The Chocolate Soldier* with Nelson Eddy (1941) and *Going My Way* with Bing Crosby (1944). She appeared at Glyndebourne in 1939 as Cherubino and Dorabella, and returned in 1955 as Cherubino. She was a singer with a warm, attractive voice, and a delightful personality.

Stewart, Thomas, b. San Saba, Tex., 29 Aug 1926. American baritone. He studied in New York, where he made his début as La Roche in Strauss's *Capriccio* in 1954 while still a student. He had an important European career, making his Berlin début as

Frederica von Stade in *La Donna del Lago.*

Escamillo in 1958, and appearing at Covent Garden in 1960 in the same role. Between 1960-76 he sang a number of Wagner roles at Bayreuth. He is married to the soprano Evelyn Lear, with whom he sang in *Eugene Onegin* in San Francisco in 1971. In 1981 he sang, with great success, the title-role in the American première of Reimann's *Lear* in San Francisco, and in 1982, he and Evelyn Lear sang in the world première of Robert Ward's *Minutes Till Midnight* in Miami.

Stitch-Randall, Teresa, b. West Hartford, Conn., 24 Dec 1927. American soprano. She studied in Hartford and New York, and made her début while still a student, as Gertrude Stein in the première of Virgil Thomson's *The Mother of Us All,* at Columbia University, N.Y., in 1947. She joined the Vienna Staatsoper in 1952, and was greatly admired in Vienna for her Mozart performances. She sang Gilda in Chicago in 1955, and made her Met début as Fiordiligi in 1961. In 1970 she sang Ariadne in Strauss's *Ariadne auf Naxos* in Lisbon, with great success, and in 1971 undertook the title-role in Bellini's *Norma* in Trier, Germany.

Stiedry, Fritz, b. Vienna, 11 Oct 1883; d. Zurich, 8 Aug 1968. Austrian conductor. He began his career in Dresden, conducted in Berlin and Vienna in the 1920s and early 1930s and, when forced to leave Germany, conducted opera and concerts in Russia from 1933-7. Between 1946-58 he conducted regularly at the Met, specializing in Wagner and Verdi. He made his Covent Garden début in 1953 with Wagner's *Ring.*

Stiffelio. Opera in 3 acts by Verdi. Libretto by Francesco Maria Piave, based on the play, *Le Pasteur* (1849) by Émile Souvestre and Eugène Bourgeois. First performed Trieste, 16 Nov 1850.

Stiffelio (ten.), a Protestant clergyman, discovers that his wife, Lina (sop.), has been unfaithful to him. In due course he forgives her, but not before his father-in-law, Stankar (bar.), has killed Lina's seducer, Raffaele (ten.), in a duel.

With its plot and characters transferred to England at the beginning of the 13th c., the opera was re-launched in 1857 as *Aroldo.*

Stignani, Ebe, b. Naples, 10 July 1904; d. Imola, 5 Oct 1974. Italian mezzo-soprano. She studied in Naples and made her début there in 1925 as Amneris. The following year Toscanini engaged her for La Scala where she sang the leading Verdi mezzo roles, as well as Adalgisa in *Norma,* Leonora in *La Favorite* and several French and German roles. She remained at La Scala until 1956. At Covent Garden, she first appeared in 1937 as Amneris, and returned on many occasions, on the last of which, in 1957, she sang Adalgisa to Callas's Norma. The following year she made a final opera appearance at Drury Lane as Azucena, perhaps her greatest role. She was an authoritative performer, with a rich and powerful voice.

Still, William Grant, b. Woodville, Miss., 11 May 1895; d. Los Angeles, 3 Dec 1978. American composer. Best known as the composer of the Afro-American Symphony (1939), he wrote eight operas, the earliest of which is *Blue Steel* (1935), and the last *Highway no.1 USA,* a 1-act piece which was first performed at the University of Miami in 1963. The attractively simple but haunting 3-act work, *A Bayou Legend,* which he wrote as early as 1941, seems not to have been staged until 1974 when Opera/South, an all-black company, gave a first-rate account of it in Jackson, Miss. The libretti of all of Still's operas were written by his wife, Verna Arvey.

Stilwell, Richard, b. St Louis, Miss., 6 May 1942. American baritone. He studied in New York, and made his début there in 1970 with City Opera as Pelléas, which was also the role of his Covent Garden début in 1974. He had first appeared in Great Britain the previous year, at Glyndebourne, as Ulisse in Monteverdi's *Il Ritorno d'Ulisse in Patria.* He has sung with most major American companies, and at several European opera houses. The possessor of a pleasant light baritone voice and an agreeable stage presence, he has been admired at Glyndebourne especially in Mozart roles, and was a first-rate Count in *Le Nozze di Figaro* at Covent Garden in 1982.

Stolze, Gerhard, b. Dessau, 1 Oct 1926; d. Garmisch-Partenkirchen, 11 Mar 1979. German tenor. He studied in Dresden and

Berlin, and made his début in Berlin in 1949 as Moser in *Die Meistersinger*. He specialized in such character roles as David in *Die Meistersinger*, Mime, which was a role he sang frequently at Bayreuth between 1957-69, and Herod in *Salome*. An intelligent singing actor, he also sang Oberon in Britten's *A Midsummer Night's Dream* and in Vienna was admired in the (baritone) title-role of *Wozzeck* which he sang with Irmgard Seefried as Marie.

Stracciari, Riccardo, b. Casalecchio de Reno, 26 June 1875; d. Rome, 10 Oct 1955. Italian baritone. He studied in Bologna and made his opera début there in 1898 as Marcello in *La Bohème*. He sang in the leading Italian opera houses until 1944, and was considered the finest Figaro in Rossini's opera in the 1920-30s. His only Covent Garden appearance was in 1905 as Amonasro, and at the Met he sang only between 1906-8. His mellow voice and elegant style were greatly admired in several Verdi roles. He was also admired as Rigoletto.

Stradella, Alessandro, b. 1 Oct 1644; d. Genoa, 25 Feb 1682. Italian composer. One of the most versatile composers of his day, he wrote music in most forms, and also led an extremely adventurous life, which ended with his murder by the brothers of his mistress. He composed five operas which are said to have influenced the Neapolitan school of the following generation. *La Forza dell'Amor Paterno* was performed in Genoa in 1678, and *Il Moro per Amore* in Rome in 1695.

Straniera, La *(The Foreign Woman)*. Opera in 2 acts by Bellini. Libretto by Felice Romani, based on a novel, *L'Étrangère*, by Victor-Charles Prévôt. First performed Milan, 14 Feb 1829.

Arturo (ten.), betrothed to Isoletta (sop.), falls in love with Alaide (sop.), a stranger in the locality who is suspected by the local inhabitants of being a witch. Seeing her embracing Valdeburgo (bar.), whom he does not realize is her brother, Arturo challenges his supposed rival to a duel, and Valdeburgo falls, wounded, into the lake. Thinking him dead, Alaide reveals to Arturo that Valdeburgo was her brother. When she is accused of his murder, Arturo confesses that he is the guilty one, and both

Johann Strauss (II)

are saved from execution only by the sudden appearance of Valdeburgo. Arturo and Isoletta, now apparently reconciled to each other, are about to marry when Arturo discovers that Alaide, with whom he is still in love, is in fact Agnese, whom the King of France had bigamously married. This proves too much for Arturo, who kills himself.

Stratas, Teresa, b. Toronto, 26 May 1938. Canadian soprano of Greek parentage. She studied in Toronto where, in 1959, she made her début as Mimi. She first appeared at the Met later the same year, as Poussette in *Manon*. She continues to sing at the Met, and in leading opera houses in Europe. Mimi was the role of her Covent Garden début in 1961, and she has been greatly admired there as Mozart's Susanna and as Nedda in *Pagliacci*. She is a most convincing actress, at her best in highly dramatic roles.

Straus, Oscar, b. Vienna, 6 Mar 1870; d. Bad Ischl, 11 Jan 1954. Austrian composer. He composed more than forty operettas, of which the most popular are *Ein Walzertraum*, first produced in Vienna in 1907; *Der Tapfere Soldat* (Vienna, 1908) known in English as *The Chocolate Soldier*, its plot taken from Shaw's *Arms and the Man*; and *Drei Walzer* (Zurich, 1935) which used music drawn from Johann Strauss I in Act I, Johann Strauss II in Act II, and Oscar Straus himself in Act III. After the Anschluss, Straus went to America, but returned to Austria in 1948. His post-war works for the stage proved less popular than his earlier operettas but he had a great success with the song which he composed for the film, *La Ronde*, in 1950.

Strauss, Johann (II), b. Vienna, 25 Oct 1825; d. Vienna, 3 June 1899. Austrian composer, conductor, and violinist. Son of Johann Strauss I, he became the most famous member of the celebrated family of composers of Viennese light music. *The Blue Danube*, *Tales from the Vienna Woods*, *Artists' Life* are the titles of his most famous waltzes. He is also the father of 19th-c. Viennese operetta, having been encouraged by Offenbach to write for the stage. He wrote sixteen operettas, most of which were

first performed in Vienna at the Theater an der Wien. The earliest, *Indigo und die vierzig Räuber*, was staged in 1871. The most famous of all was his third, *Die Fledermaus* (1874), a heady amalgam of gaiety, sentimentality and typically Viennese melancholy. Other successes included *Cagliostro in Wien* (1875), *Der lustige Krieg* (1882), *Eine Nacht in Venedig* (1883), *Der Zigeunerbaron* (1885), a romantic operetta which was second only to *Die Fledermaus* in popularity, and the more serious *Ritter Pázmán*, performed not at the Theater an der Wien but at the Opera House, in 1892. *Wiener Blut* (1899), first performed some months after Strauss's death, is a work put together by Adolf Müller Jnr. from existing Strauss compositions.

Strauss, Richard, b. Munich, 11 June 1864; d. Garmisch-Partenkirchen, 8 Sept 1949. German composer. The last of the great late-romantic composers of opera, he composed his earliest works for the stage under the influence of Wagner. *Guntram* was staged in Weimar in 1894, and *Feuersnot* in Dresden in 1901. The individual voice of Strauss was heard in the erotic violence of *Salome* (1905), which was followed by a finer work in the same style, *Elektra* (1909). *Elektra* was the first product of the composer's long collaboration with the Austrian poet and playwright Hugo von Hofmannsthal. Their next work, *Der Rosenkavalier* (1911), has proved to be

Richard Strauss

Strauss's most popular opera, an elegant and sumptuous picture of life in 18th-c. Vienna. After *Ariadne auf Naxos*, which was given in its definitive version in Vienna in 1916, and *Die Frau ohne Schatten* (1919), Strauss's later works are less successful, though the nostalgic *Arabella* (1933) can be remarkably effective in a really fine performance. For *Intermezzo*, (1924), a portrait of his stormy domestic life, Strauss wrote his own libretto. His other operas are *Die Ägyptische Helena* (1928); *Die schweigsame Frau*, its libretto by Stefan Zweig (1935); three operas with libretti by Josef Gregor, *Friedenstag*, *Daphne* (both 1938) and *Die Liebe der Danae* which reached dress rehearsal stage in 1944 but had to wait until 1952 for its first night; and a final work, *Capriccio* (libretto by the conductor Clemens Krauss) in which the seventy-eight-year-old Strauss recaptured something of his old flair, though the lyrical flame burned less brightly than it had done in his youth and maturity.

Stravinsky, Igor, b. Oranienbaum (now Lomonosov), 17 June 1882; d. New York, 6 Apr 1971. Russian composer, later of French and then American nationality. One of the greatest composers of the 20th c., he composed operas at all stages of his long career. He was a pupil of Rimsky-Korsakov, and his first opera, *The Nightingale*, begun in Russia in 1908 and finished in Switzerland in 1914, reveals something of the older composer's influence. *The Wedding*, composed between 1914–17, but not performed until 1923, is a kind of choral ballet, and *L'Histoire du Soldat* (1918) contains dancing and acting but no singing. This unconventional attitude to opera was continued with *Renard* (1922) in which the action was mimed by dancers, the singers (all male) being placed in the orchestra. More traditionally operatic was the comedy, *Mavra* (1922).

The first of Stravinsky's two major works for the stage, *Oedipus Rex* (1927) is an opera-oratorio which was first performed in Paris in 1927 as an oratorio, and staged in 1928 in Vienna as an opera. The sung text is in Latin, but a speaker, using the vernacular of the audience, introduces each of the work's six episodes. *Perséphone* (1934) is a melodrama for speaking voice, tenor, chorus, dancers and orchestra. With *The Rake's Progress* (1951) Stravinsky composed his operatic masterpiece, conventional in form and neo-classical in style. *The Flood*, composed for television using serial technique, was broadcast in 1962, and staged in Hamburg in 1963, an anti-climactic 1-act setting of parts of the medieval York and Chester miracle plays.

Strahler, Giorgio, b. Trieste, 14 Aug 1921. Italian producer. He began his career as a producer of plays, turning to opera with *La Traviata* at La Scala in 1947. Since 1965 he has produced a number of operas at the Salzburg Festival, but most of his work in opera has been at La Scala or the Piccolo Scala whose small-scale opera productions he helped to develop.

Streich, Rita, b. Barnaul, 18 Dec 1920. German soprano of Russian and German parentage. She studied in Berlin, and made her début in Aussig in 1943 as Zerbinetta. From 1946-51 she sang such roles as Gilda, Sophie, and Olympia in *Les Contes d'Hoffmann* at the Berlin Staatsoper, and in 1953 joined the Vienna Staatsoper. She first appeared in London in 1954 with the Vienna company, as Zerlina and Susanna, and made her American début in San Francisco in 1957 as Sophie. She was adept at lyric coloratura roles, and was a pert and charming actress. Since 1974 she has taught in Essen.

Suchoň, Eugen, b. Pezinok, Slovakia, 25 Sept 1908. Slovakian composer. He became known abroad after the production of his first opera, *The Whirlpool*, in 1949. A second opera, *Svätopluk*, which portrays events in the life of King Svätopluk, a powerful Moravian ruler, was successfully staged in Bratislava in 1960.

Sullivan, (Sir) Arthur, b. London, 13 May 1842; d. London, 22 Nov 1900. English composer. His first two operettas, the 1-act farce *Cox and Box* and *The Contrabandista* (both 1867), were written in collaboration with F.C. Burnand. He first collaborated with W.S. Gilbert to write *Thespis* (1871), but it was with their second work, the 1-act *Trial by Jury* (1875), unique in that it is the only Gilbert and Sullivan operetta to contain no dialogue, that their years of success commenced. Together they produced *The Sorcerer* (1877), *HMS Pinafore* (1878), *The Pirates of Penzance* (1879), *Patience* (1881),

Iolanthe (1882), *Princess Ida* (1884), *The Mikado* (1885), *Ruddigore* (1887), *The Yeomen of the Guard* (1888), and *The Gondoliers* (1889).

Sullivan then broke away to write a romantic opera, *Ivanhoe*, which opened the Royal English Opera House in London (now the Palace Theatre) in 1891, and took another collaborator, Sidney Grundy, for his next operetta, *Haddon Hall* (1892). He had quarrelled with Gilbert, but a reconciliation was effected, and they collaborated again on *Utopia Limited* (1893) and *The Grand Duke* (1896), without achieving the success of their earlier works. Sullivan went on to write *The Beauty Stone* (1898) with Sir Arthur Pinero and Comyns Carr, and *The Rose of Persia* (1899) and *The Emerald Isle* with Basil Hood. He did not live to finish the latter work, which was completed by Edward German and staged in 1901.

Suor Angelica *(Sister Angelica)*. Opera in 1 act by Puccini. Libretto by Giovacchino Forzano. First performed New York, 14 Dec 1918, with *Il Tabarro* and *Gianni Schicchi*, as part of *Il Trittico*.

Sister Angelica (sop.), a girl of good family, has become a nun in order to expiate the sin of having given birth to an illegitimate child. When her aunt, the Princess (contr.), visits Angelica to make her sign away her inheritance in favour of her younger sister who is about to marry, she informs Angelica that her child has been dead for two years. Angelica kills herself, but at the moment of death receives a sign of heavenly forgiveness when the Virgin and Child appear to her in a vision.

Supervia, Conchita, b. Barcelona, 9 Dec 1895; d. London, 30 Mar 1936. Spanish mezzo-soprano. She had received little musical training when she made her début in a small role in Stiattesi's *Blanca de Beaulieu* at the Teatro Colón, Buenos Aires, in 1910, and she was only in her sixteenth year when she sang Octavian in the first Italian performances of *Der Rosenkavalier* in Rome in 1911. She became famous in the coloratura-mezzo roles in Rossini's operas, especially *Il Barbiere di Siviglia*, *La Cenerentola* and *L'Italiana in Algeri*. She sang these roles, and Carmen, at Covent Garden in 1934-5, and was greatly admired for her virtuosity and the richness of her voice.

Suppé, Franz von, b. Spalato (now Split, Yugoslavia) 18 Apr 1819; d. Vienna, 21 May 1895. Austrian composer of Belgian descent. He worked as a conductor in Viennese theatres, conducting at the Theater an der Wien from 1845-62, and wrote a vast number of musical farces and operettas for Vienna. Among the operettas are *Die schöne Galatea* (1865), *Die leichte Kavallerie* (1866), *Fatinitza* (1876), and his masterpiece, *Boccaccio* (1879). *Lohengelb, oder Die Jungfrau von Dragant* (1870) was an operetta parody of Wagner's *Lohengrin*.

Susanna (sop.). The Countess Almaviva's maid, and Figaro's bride, in Mozart's *Le Nozze di Figaro*.

Sutermeister, Heinrich, b. Feuerthalen, 12 Aug 1910. Swiss composer. Concerned to write operas which were comprehensible to audiences rather than merely to other composers, and claiming the last works of Verdi as his models, he became known in the 1940s with operas of tunefulness and dramatic impact. *Romeo und Julia* (1940) was widely admired, *Die Zauberinsel* (1942), based on Shakespeare's *The Tempest*, was dramatically effective though musically less persuasive than the earlier Shakespeare opera, while *Niobe* (1946) and *Raskolnikoff* (1948) were less successful. *Die schwarze Spinne*, which Sutermeister had written for radio in 1936, was revised for the stage in 1948. *Titus Feuerfuchs*, performed in Basel in 1958, and *Madame Bovary* (1967) are the most interesting of the later operas.

Sutherland, (Dame) Joan, b. Sydney, 7 Nov 1926. Australian soprano. She studied in Sydney and made her stage début in the title-role of Goossens's *Judith* at Sydney Conservatorium in 1951. She first appeared at Covent Garden in 1952, as First Lady in *Die Zauberflöte*, and sang a variety of leading roles, among them Amelia in *Un Ballo in Maschera*, the Countess in *Le Nozze di Figaro*, Agathe in *Der Freischütz*, Micaëla in *Carmen*, Gilda, Desdemona, and all three soprano roles in *Les Contes d'Hoffmann*, before her performance in 1959 as Lucia in Donizetti's *Lucia di Lammermoor* brought her world fame and a concentration on the dramatic coloratura roles in the bel canto operas of Bellini and Donizetti. In recent years, though she continues to sing such roles (her Lucia at the Met in December 1982 was as beautifully sung as ever), she has begun to expand her repertoire, most notably in the field of 19th-c. French opera. She also commands the style for such operetta roles as Rosalinde in *Die Fledermaus* and the title-role in *The Merry Widow* which she has sung with great success in Sydney. Her voice is a dramatic coloratura of great volume, beauty of tone, and agility. She is married to the conductor, Richard Bonynge, who has played a large part in shaping her career.

Suzuki (mezzo-sop.). The heroine's faithful servant, in Puccini's *Madama Butterfly*.

Svanholm, Set, b. Västeras, 2 Sept 1904; d. nr Stockholm, 2 Oct 1964. Swedish tenor. He studied in Stockholm and made his début there in 1930 as a baritone, singing the role of Silvio in *Pagliacci*. After six years in baritone roles, he made a second début as Radames, and then began to concentrate on the Wagner roles. He sang such roles as Siegmund, Parsifal and Tristan, in Salzburg and Vienna between 1938-42, and was Bayreuth's Siegfried in 1942. He first appeared at the Met in 1946 as Siegfried, and made his Covent Garden début in 1948. In 1956 he became Director of the Royal Opera in Stockholm.

Szell, George, b. Budapest, 7 June 1897; d. Cleveland, 29 July 1970. Hungarian, later American, conductor. He conducted at several German opera houses in the 1920s, was in charge of the German Opera in Prague from 1929-37, and conducted at the Met between 1942-6. In his later years, he concentrated on concerts, though he also made a number of appearances at Salzburg where he conducted the première performances of Liebermann's *Penelope* (1954) and Egk's *Irische Legende* (1955). At the Met, his performances of Strauss and Wagner were much admired.

Szymanowski, Karol, b. Timoshovka, 6 Oct 1882; d. Lausanne, 29 Mar 1937. Polish composer. An important figure in Polish music in the first half of the 20th c., he composed an operetta and two operas, one of which, *King Roger*, first performed in Warsaw in 1926, is still quite frequently performed. It has also been admired outside

Poland for its romantic intensity of expression.

T

Tabarro, Il *(The Cloak)*. Opera in 1 act by Puccini. Libretto by Giuseppe Adami, based on the play *La Houppelande* (1910) by Didier Gold. First performed New York, 14 Dec 1918, with *Suor Angelica* and *Gianni Schicchi*, as part of *Il Trittico*.

The Seine bargee, Michele (bar.), accidentally discovers that his wife, Giorgetta (sop.), is being unfaithful to him with the young stevedore, Luigi (ten.). Michele kills Luigi on the barge deck, and, when he hears his wife approaching, quickly draws Luigi's body within the folds of his cloak. He invites Giorgetta to nestle close to him, inside his cloak. As she does so, Michele flings the cloak open, revealing the dead body of her lover.

Taddei, Giuseppe, b. Genoa, 26 June 1916. Italian baritone. He studied in Rome and made his début there in 1936 as the Herald in *Lohengrin*. He sang in Rome until 1942 when his career was interrupted first by conscription and then by imprisonment by the Germans. A concert he gave for the American forces in Vienna led to his being engaged by the Vienna Staatsoper for two seasons, after which he embarked upon an international career as a specialist in Mozart and Verdi roles. In 1947 he sang Scarpia and Rigoletto in London, and in 1948 appeared

Joan Sutherland as Violetta in Verdi's *La Traviata* at Covent Garden in 1975. This was one of her most successful roles.

at the Salzburg Festival for the first time, as Mozart's Figaro. A compelling actor, he gave memorable performances of such roles as Iago, Leporello and Macbeth, in London and Vienna, and became a notable Falstaff, a role which he was still able to portray superbly in his mid-sixties in Karajan's 1981 Salzburg production.

Tagliabue, Carlo, b. Mariano Comense, 13 Jan 1898; d. Monza, 5 Apr 1978. Italian baritone. He made his début in Lodi in 1922 as Amonasro, and in the 1930-40s sang frequently at La Scala and other Italian theatres in the Italian repertory, and also in Wagner roles. He first appeared at the Met in 1937 as Amonasro, sang at Covent Garden the following year as Rigoletto, and returned there in 1946 as Germont. He was last heard in London in 1953 as a stylish and dramatic Don Carlo in *La Forza del Destino*. He retired in 1960.

Tagliavini, Ferrucio, b. Reggio Emilia, 14 Aug 1913. Italian tenor. He studied in Parma and Florence, and made his début in Florence in 1938 as Rodolfo. His international career began after World War II, when he began an association of several seasons at the Met in 1946, and sang a mellifluous Nemorino in *L'Elisir d'Amore* at Covent Garden in 1950. He often appeared in Italian theatres with his wife, the soprano Pia Tassinari. Elvino in *La Sonnambula*, the Duke in *Rigoletto,* and Werther in Massenet's opera were among his finest roles. He made his last appearance in opera in Venice in 1965, as Werther.

Tajo, Italo, b. Pinerolo, Piedmont, 25 Apr 1915. Italian bass. He studied in Turin, and made his début there in 1935 as Fafner in *Das Rheingold*. In the summer of that year, he understudied at Glyndebourne, and during the next ten years established himself in Italy as a fine Mozart performer. He first sang in London in 1947 as Don Basilio in *Il Barbiere di Siviglia*, Leporello, and Don Pasquale. He had made his American début in Chicago in 1946 as Ramfis in *Aida*, and first sang at the Met in 1948. In the 1950s he appeared in Broadway musicals and films, but continued to sing in opera. In the early 1980s in the United States he was active as a producer, and was still heard in small operatic roles.

Talich, Václav, b. Kroměříž, 28 May 1883; d. Brno, 16 Mar 1961. Czech conductor. He was in charge of the opera company at the National Theatre, Prague, from 1935 until the closure of the theatre in 1944. After the war, he conducted opera in Prague only briefly, during the 1947-8 season. He was the leading conductor of the Czech operatic repertory of his time.

Talvela, Martti, b. Hiitola, 4 Feb 1935. Finnish bass. He studied in Stockholm, and made his début there in 1961 as Sparafucile. At Bayreuth between 1962-70 he sang such roles as Titurel, Fasolt, Hunding, Hagen and Daland. He first appeared at the Met in 1968, and sang Boris in the original version of *Boris Godunov* there in 1974. He has appeared on several occasions at Covent Garden since 1970, and was especially admired there as Gurnemanz in *Parsifal* in 1973. A large man with a powerful voice, he is heard at his best in Wagner. He became director of the Savonlinna Festival in Finland in 1972, and sang Sarastro to great acclaim at Savonlinna in 1973.

Tamagno, Francesco, b. Turin, 28 Dec 1850; d. Varese, 31 Aug 1905. Italian tenor. A leading dramatic tenor of his day, he is remembered as the creator of the title-role in Verdi's *Otello* in 1887, having been chosen by the composer. His other Verdi roles included Ernani, Don Carlos, Radames, and Gabriele which he sang in the revised *Simon Boccanegra* in 1881. He repeated his performance of Otello in London in 1889, and in Chicago and New York in 1890. His voice, as revealed by gramophone records of excerpts from *Otello*, had a virile quality well suited to the role, and he was said to have been a forceful actor.

Tamino (ten.). The hero of Mozart's *Die Zauberflöte* who, accompanied by Papageno, sets out to rescue Pamina.

Tancredi. Opera in 2 acts by Rossini. Libretto by Gaetano Rossi, based on Voltaire's *Tancrède* (1760). First performed Venice, 6 Feb 1813.

Tancredi (contr.) returns from his exile in Sicily in time to prevent the marriage of his beloved Amenaide (sop.) to Orbazzano (bar.). Orbazzano has Amenaide arrested on a false charge of treason, for which she is to

Title-page of Rossini's *Tancredi*

be executed unless a champion appears and fights to defend her honour. Though he believes her guilty, Tancredi offers himself as her defender, and wins. He leads a successful expedition against the Sicilians, the truth is revealed, and he and Amenaide are reunited.

For the opera's second production, in Ferrara some weeks after the Venice première, the libretto was altered to accord more closely to Voltaire, and the opera ended with the death of Tancredi, who had been wounded in battle. Rossini composed new music for this version, but audiences disliked the tragic ending, and the original version was used for subsequent productions.

Tannhäuser. Opera in 3 acts by Wagner. Libretto by the composer. First performed Dresden, 19 Oct 1845. Revised version first performed Paris, 13 Mar 1861.

The knight Tannhäuser (ten.) has been enjoying a prolonged sojourn with Venus (sop.), goddess of love, in the Venusberg.

However, tiring of the delights of love, he invokes the Virgin Mary, and the Venusberg immediately disappears. Tannhäuser now finds himself in the valley of the Wartburg where he encounters his friend Wolfram (bar.), in company with the Landgrave (bass). Tannhäuser decides to return with them when they describe how unhappy Elisabeth (sop.), the Landgrave's niece, has been during his absence.

Tannhäuser competes in a song contest for the hand of Elisabeth, but his song of carnal love, in praise of Venus, so offends everyone present that he is banished, to seek absolution for his sins from the Pope. He joins a group of pilgrims making their way to Rome.

Several months later Tannhäuser returns in despair, the Pope having said that not until his holy staff sprouted leaves would Tannhäuser find forgiveness. A funeral procession approaches. It is that of Elisabeth who has died of a broken heart. Tannhäuser falls dead by Elisabeth's body, and pilgrims arrive from Rome bearing the Pope's staff, which has blossomed as a sign that God has forgiven Tannhäuser.

Tatiana (sop.). The heroine of Tchaikovsky's *Eugene Onegin*, in love with Onegin.

Tauber, Richard, b. Linz, 16 May 1891; d. London, 8 Jan 1948. Austrian, later British, tenor. He studied in Freiburg, and made his début in Chemnitz in 1913 as Tamino. He was immediately engaged by the Dresden Opera, and was a member of the company there from 1913–26. From 1926–38 he was a leading lyric tenor with the Vienna Staatsoper. His beautiful and individual voice, his musicianship and his highly personal style of singing made him a popular favourite in Mozart as well as in a number of French and Italian roles, and he reached a much wider public with his recordings of popular songs. He was also a fine interpreter of German Lieder. From the mid-1920s he began to appear in the operettas of his friend Franz Lehár, whose later works were written for Tauber. His British stage début was in Lehár's *Das Land des Lächelns (The Land of Smiles)* at Drury Lane in 1931. He first appeared at Covent Garden in 1938 as Belmonte in *Die Entführung aus dem Serail* and Tamino, and the following year as Ottavio in *Don Giovanni* and Hans in the German version of Smetana's *The Bartered Bride.* In 1947, although seriously ill and within weeks of his death, he sang Ottavio again with his old colleagues of the Vienna Staatsoper when that company visited Covent Garden. He was still the superb Mozart stylist that he had always been. He was also an accomplished composer of operettas, songs and orchestral music, and starred in a number of musical films in Germany and England.

Taylor, Deems, b. New York, 22 Dec 1885; d. New York, 3 July 1966. American composer and critic. An authoritative music critic, he wrote four operas, of which the first two, *The King's Henchman*, staged in 1927, and *Peter Ibbetson*, staged in 1931, both at the Met, were the most successful. *Ramuntcho*, produced in Philadelphia in 1942, and a 1-act piece, *The Dragon* (New York, 1958), aroused less interest.

Tchaikovsky, Pyotr, b. Kamsko-Votkinsk, 7 May 1840; d. St Petersburg, 6 Nov

Kiri Te Kanawa in the title-role of Strauss's *Arabella* at Covent Garden.

1893. Russian composer. Though Western-orientated and not a part of the nationalist movement, he was the dominant figure in 19th-c. Russian music. A great symphonic composer, he also composed ten operas (and began several more). He destroyed *The Voyevoda*, his first completed opera, some years after its Bolshoi première of 1869, but the work was later reconstructed from the surviving orchestral parts and other material. He used much of its music again in *The Oprichnik*, performed in St Petersburg in 1874. *Vakula the Smith* (1876) is somewhat more personal in style: it was later revised as *The Slippers*, and performed at the Bolshoi in 1887.

Tchaikovsky's next opera was his masterpiece, *Eugene Onegin*, which he wrote at a time (1877–8) when his ill-advised marriage had brought him close to nervous collapse. It drew from him some of his most lyrical and most heart-felt music. The opera was produced in Moscow in 1879. *The Maid of Orleans* (1881) is a less personal work, a setting of Schiller's Joan of Arc play in which the character of Joan somehow fails to come to life, despite the melodic richness and beauty of Tchaikovsky's score. *Mazeppa* (1884) is a work of dramatic power, but *The Sorceress* (1887) is only partially successful. Much finer are the composer's last two operas, *Queen of Spades* (1890), a study of psychotic obsession, and *Iolanta* (1892), a 1-act piece which contains some of Tchaikovsky's most passionate music. Though most of his operas are performed from time to time in the Soviet Union, only *Eugene Onegin* and *Queen of Spades* have proved popular abroad.

Te Kanawa, Kiri, b. Gisborne, Auckland, 6 Mar 1944. New Zealand soprano, of Maori parentage. She studied in London and made her début there in 1969 as Elena in a semi-professional production of Rossini's *La Donna del Lago.* Her first appearance at Covent Garden was in 1970 as a Flowermaiden in *Parsifal.* An attractive woman with a voice of warm timbre, she soon established herself as a lyric soprano in opera houses in Europe and America, though she has also continued to sing frequently at Covent Garden. Her first

major role was the Countess in *Le Nozze di Figaro* which she sang in San Francisco in 1972 and at Glyndebourne in 1973. She made her Met début in 1974 as Desdemona. Other Covent Garden roles have included Amelia in *Simon Boccanegra*, Mimi, Donna Elvira, Fiordiligi, and, less successfully, Strauss's Arabella. In 1983 she sang the title-role in *Manon Lescaut* for the first time, at Covent Garden. Not a very interesting or individual interpreter, she is popular because of the beauty of her voice and her appearance.

Tear, Robert, b. Barry, 8 Mar 1939. Welsh tenor. He studied in Cambridge, sang with the English Opera Group from 1963-71, and first appeared at Covent Garden in the première performances of Tippett's *The Knot Garden* in 1970. He has since sung a number of roles there, among them Paris in Tippett's *King Priam*, Matteo in *Arabella*, and Orlovsky in *Die Fledermaus*. In 1982 he was Jupiter in the new production of Handel's *Semele* to celebrate the 250th anniversary of the first theatre on the Covent Garden site. His lyric tenor voice is of somewhat wiry timbre, but he is an intelligent interpreter.

Tebaldi, Renata, b. Pesaro, 1 Feb 1922. Italian soprano. She studied in Parma and made her début in Rovigo in 1944 as Elena in *Mefistofele*. She first sang at La Scala in the 1946-7 season as Mimi, and appeared there regularly between 1949-54. She made her London début with the Scala company in 1950 as Desdemona, became the leading Italian soprano of her day in the Verdi and Puccini repertory, and appeared frequently

Robert Tear as Jupiter with Valerie Masterson as Semele in Handel's *Semele* at Covent Garden in 1982.

in the United States in the 1950-60s. Tosca, Mimi, Aida, and Desdemona were among her best roles. She was a poor actress, but this was more than compensated for by the beauty of her voice.

Telemann, Georg Philipp, b. Magdeburg, 14 Mar 1681; d. Hamburg, 25 June 1767. German composer. A contemporary of Bach, he was widely regarded as the leading German composer in his lifetime. Though he was immensely prolific, he composed comparatively few operas, the best known of which is *Pimpinone* (1725), a comic intermezzo. His greatest success *Socrates* (1721), which contains elements of both comic and serious opera.

Telephone, The. Opera in 1 act by Menotti. Libretto by the composer. First performed New York, 18 Feb 1947.

Ben (bar.) visits Lucy (sop.) and attempts to propose marriage to her, but finds her so intrigued with her newly installed telephone that he cannot engage her attention. In desperation, he leaves and calls her from the nearest public telephone.

Telramund (bar.). Husband of Ortrud and opponent of Lohengrin in Wagner's *Lohengrin*.

tenor. The highest category of male voice, with a range of approximately two octaves upwards from C in the bass clef. The various types of tenor voice include the heroic tenor, who undertakes such roles as Wagner's Siegfried and Verdi's Otello and Radames; the lyric tenor (the Mozart roles, Donizetti's Nemorino); the spinto, incorporating elements of both dramatic and lyric, the kind of voice for which most of Verdi's tenor roles were written; and the tenorino, a lyric tenor of limited size and volume.

Tetrazzini, Luisa, b. Florence, 29 June 1871; d. Milan, 28 Apr 1940. She studied in Florence, and made her début there in 1890 as Inez in *L'Africaine.* She became one of the leading lyric coloratura sopranos of her day, and made a sensational Covent Garden début in 1907 as Violetta in *La Traviata,* repeating her success in the same role the following year in New York. Her agile technique and attractive timbre made her a fine performer of such roles as Lucia di

Lammermoor, Elvira in *I Puritani* and Marie in *La Fille du Régiment.* She continued to sing until 1934.

Teyte, (Dame) Maggie, b. Wolverhampton, 17 Apr 1888; d. London, 26 May 1976. English soprano. She studied in London and Paris, and made her début in Monte Carlo in 1907 before being engaged for the Paris Opéra-Comique where she appeared between 1907-11, and where in 1908, coached by Debussy, she sang Mélisande in *Pelléas et Mélisande.* Between 1911-14 she sang in Chicago, where her parts included the title-role in Massenet's *Cendrillon.* She was a member of the company in Boston between 1914-17, and she was especially admired there as Puccini's Mimi. (It was not until 1948, when she sang the role with New York City Opera, that America heard her as Mélisande.) She sang occasionally at Covent Garden, making her first appearance there in 1910 as Mozart's Cherubino and her last in 1938 as Puccini's Butterfly. She made her final appearances in opera in London in 1951 as Belinda in *Dido and Aeneas,* with Kirsten Flagstad as Dido.

Thaïs. Opera in 3 acts by Massenet. Libretto by Louis Gallet, based on the novel (1890) by Anatole France. First performed Paris, 16 Mar 1894.

In 4th-c. Alexandria, the monk Athanaël (bar.) converts the courtesan Thaïs (sop.), who becomes a nun. Athanaël, however, becomes enamoured of her, and attempts to address her passionately as she lies dying. As she dies Thaïs has a vision of the heavens opening to receive her soul.

Thebom, Blanche, b. Monessen, Pa., 19 Sept 1918. American mezzo-soprano, of Swedish parentage. She studied in New York, and made her début at the Met as Fricka in *Die Walküre* in 1944. She was a member of the Met company until 1967, and sang a wide variety of roles. She first appeared in England at Glyndebourne in 1950 as Dorabella in *Così Fan Tutte,* and was Dido in Berlioz's *Les Troyens* at Covent Garden in 1957.

Thill, Georges, b. Paris, 14 Dec 1897. French tenor. He studied in Paris and Naples, and made his début at the Paris Opéra in 1924 as Nicias in *Thaïs.* He remained a leading tenor in Paris for nearly thirty years, in Italian and German roles as well as the French repertory. He sang at Covent Garden in 1928 as Samson in Saint-Saëns's *Samson et Dalila*, and appeared at the Met in the 1931-2 season. The most distinguished French tenor of his day, he sang an exemplary Canio in *Pagliacci* at his farewell performance at the Paris Opéra-Comique in 1953.

Thomas, Ambroise, b. Metz, 5 Aug 1811; d. Paris, 12 Feb 1896. French composer. He composed twenty operas, the earliest of which, a 1-act piece, *La Double Échelle*, was staged in Paris in 1837. His greatest successes were *Mignon* (1866) and *Hamlet* (1868). By 1894, *Mignon*, one of the most popular operas of its day, had been given more than 1,000 performances at the Opéra-Comique. Both *Mignon* and *Hamlet* are still occasionally performed.

Thomas, Arthur Goring, b. Ratton Park, Sussex, 20 Nov 1850; d. London 20 Mar 1892. English composer. He wrote four operas, of which the most successful was *Esmeralda* (1883), based on Victor Hugo's novel, *Notre-Dame de Paris*. *Nadeshda* (1885) contains attractive music, though it is lacking in dramatic impetus. Thomas's style was not individual enough to ensure the survival of either work into the 20th c.

Thomas, Jess, b. Hot Springs, S. Dak., 2 Aug 1927. American tenor. He studied singing while a student of psychology at Stanford University, and made his opera début in San Francisco in 1957 as Malcolm in *Macbeth*. He was with the opera company in Karlsruhe from 1958-61, where he sang thirty-eight roles in as many months. He undertook leading Wagner and Strauss roles in Munich, Bayreuth and Vienna in the 1960s, and first appeared at the Met in 1962 as Walther in *Die Meistersinger*. Walther was also the role of his Covent Garden début in 1969.

Thomas, John Charles, b. Meyersdale, Va., 6 Sept 1891; d. Apple Valley, Calif., 13 Dec 1960. American baritone. He studied in Baltimore and first appeared in operetta and musical comedy before turning to recitals and eventually to opera. He sang fifteen major roles in Brussels between 1925-28,

and sang at the Met from 1934-43. An ebullient performer with a fine voice, he was heard at his best in such roles as Rossini's Figaro, Verdi's Rigoletto and Tonio in Leoncavallo's *Pagliacci*. His Valentin in *Faust* at Covent Garden in 1928, when Chaliapin sang Méphistophélès, received greater praise than the Russian bass's performance, but nonetheless he never sang again in opera in London.

Thomson, Virgil, b. Kansas City, 25 Nov 1896. American composer and critic. He composed three operas, two of which, written to libretti by Gertrude Stein, excited much critical comment. They are *Four Saints in Three Acts* (1934) and *The Mother of Us All* (1947). His most ambitious work, with a stronger musical and emotional content than the Stein operas, is *Lord Byron*, first performed in New York in 1972.

Thorborg, Kerstin, b. Venjan, 19 May 1896; d. Falun, 12 Apr 1970. Swedish mezzo-soprano. She studied in Stockholm, and made her début there in 1924 as Ortrud in *Lohengrin*. She sang in Berlin, Vienna and Salzburg in the 1930s, and was generally considered to be one of the finest exponents of the Wagner mezzo roles of her time. She appeared in Wagner operas at Covent Garden between 1936-9, when she was acclaimed as a great singing-actress. Her Met début was in 1936, as Fricka in *Die Walküre,* and she appeared regularly at the Met until 1950.

Tibbett, Lawrence, b. Bakersfield, Calif., 16 Nov 1896; d. New York, 15 July 1960. American baritone. He studied in New York, and made his début at the Met in a minor role in *Boris Godunov*. He became the leading American baritone of his day, and sang many Verdi roles at the Met until his retirement in 1950, as well as creating a number of roles in American operas. At Covent Garden in 1937, he created the title-role in Goossens's *Don Juan de Mañara,* and was also admired for the beauty of his voice and the dramatic vigour of his interpretations, as Amonasro, Iago and Scarpia during the same season.

Tiefland *(Lowland).* Opera in a prologue and 3 acts by D'Albert. Libretto by Rudolf Lothar, based on a Catalan play, *Terra Baixa*

Sir Michael Tippett in 1980

(1896) by Angel Guimerá. First performed Prague, 15 Nov 1903.

Martha (sop.), mistress of Sebastiano (bar.) against her will, is given by him as bride to Pedro (ten.) A tale of passion and misunderstanding concludes with the murder of Sebastiano by Pedro.

Tinsley, Pauline, b. Wigan, 27 Mar 1928. English soprano. She studied in Manchester and London, and made her début in London in 1961 as Desdemona in Rossini's *Otello*. She has sung a number of Verdi roles with British companies and, after appearing in a number of small roles at Covent Garden, sang Santuzza in *Cavalleria Rusticana* there in 1976. She appeared at Santa Fe in 1969 as Anna Bolena in Donizetti's opera, and has performed with other American companies. For Welsh National Opera in 1978, she sang the title-role in *Elektra* with steely tone and a fierce intensity. In Gelsenkirchen in 1982, she sang Isolde for the first time.

Tippett, (Sir) Michael, b. London, 2 Jan 1905. English composer. The most successful 20th-c. British composer of opera after Benjamin Britten, he composed four major operas, as well as one or two minor pieces in the 1930s. *The Midsummer Marriage,* first performed at Covent Garden in 1955, remains his most successful work for the stage, though *King Priam* (1962) has also been successfully revived. His later works, *The Knot Garden* (1970) and *The Ice Break* (1977), remain more problematical, due to some extent to the unsatisfactory libretti by the composer himself, though *The Knot Garden* is musically fascinating.

Titus, Alan, b. New York, 28 Oct 1945. American baritone. He studied in Denver and New York, and made his début in Washington in 1969 as Marcello in *La Bohème*. He became known internationally in 1971 when he created the role of the Celebrant in Bernstein's *Mass* at the opening of the Kennedy Center. He made his European début as Pelléas in Amsterdam in 1973, and first sang at the Met in 1976 as Harlequin in *Ariadne auf Naxos*. He is an engaging performer with a pleasant high lyric baritone voice. He appeared at Glyndebourne in 1983 as Storch in Strauss's *Intermezzo*.

Tomova-Sintow, Anna, b. Stara Zagora, 22 Sept 1941. Bulgarian soprano. She studied in Sofia and made her début in Stara Zagora in 1965 as Tatiana in *Eugene Onegin*. She sings in the leading European and American opera houses in Mozart, Strauss and Wagner roles, and was a fine Desdemona to the Otello of Placido Domingo in Verdi's opera at the Bregenz Festival, 1981.

Tonio (bar.). The clown who informs Canio of his wife's infidelity in Leoncavallo's *Pagliacci*.

Tosca. Opera in 3 acts by Puccini. Libretto by Giuseppe Giacosa and Luigi Illica, based on the play *La Tosca* (1887) by Victorien Sardou. First performed Rome, 14 Jan 1900.

Cavaradossi (ten.), an artist and a republican, helps Angelotti (bass), consul of the former Roman Republic, who has escaped from prison. Playing on the jealousy of Cavaradossi's mistress, the singer Floria Tosca (sop.), the corrupt chief of police Baron Scarpia (bar.) tricks Tosca into revealing the whereabouts of Angelotti and the involvement of Cavaradossi in his escape. Scarpia offers to save her lover from execution if Tosca will give herself to him. Tosca agrees, and Scarpia assures her that he will arrange a mock execution for Cavaradossi. When he attempts to embrace her, Tosca stabs Scarpia. She hurries to inform Cavaradossi of the plans for his escape, but the execution turns out to be real, and the painter is shot by a firing squad. Pursued by Scarpia's men who have discovered the police chief's body, Tosca kills herself by jumping from the battlements of the Castello Sant' Angelo.

Toscanini, Arturo, b. Parma, 25 Mar 1867; d. New York, 16 Jan 1957. Italian conductor. He conducted the first performances of *Pagliacci* (1892) and *La Bohème* (1896), and became the leading Italian conductor of opera of his time. He conducted frequently at La Scala, and was artistic director there from 1892-1902 and again in the 1920s until distaste for the Fascist regime led him to leave in 1929. A fine interpreter of Puccini, and of some Verdi operas, he became the first non-German conductor at Bayreuth in 1930 and 1931. Later he conducted frequently at the Salzburg Festival. He had first appeared in the United States when he conducted at the Met between 1908-15, and New York became the centre of his activities for the last twenty-five years of his career. Though he did not conduct in the opera house during this time, he gave a number of concert performances of Verdi operas in New York between 1944-54. In his later years his interpretations became somewhat rigid and inhumane, and his behaviour a caricature of the ill-tempted autocratic maestro.

Tote Stadt, Die *(The Dead City)*. Opera in 3 acts by Korngold. Libretto by Paul Schott, after the novel *Bruges-la-morte* (1892) by Georges Rodenbach. First performed simultaneously in Hamburg and Cologne, 4 Dec 1920.

Paul (ten.), who mourns his dead wife Marie, (sop.) finds her image in the dancer, Marietta (sop.). Marietta proves unfaithful, and in his dream Paul strangles her with her own long hair.

Tottola, Leone Andrea, b. Naples, second half of the 18th c. d. Naples, 15 Sept 1831. Italian librettist. He wrote libretti for Bellini, Donizetti, Rossini, Pacini, Mercadante, Mayr and others. His most important work was his libretto for Rossini's *Mosè in Egitto* (1818).

Tourel, Jennie, b. ? Russia, 26 June 1899; d. New York, 23 Nov 1973. American mezzo-soprano, probably of Russian birth. She studied in Paris, and made her début there in 1931 as a Polovtsian maiden in *Prince Igor*. At the Opéra-Comique from 1933 she sang Carmen, Mignon, Charlotte in *Werther* and the title-role in Bizet's *Djamileh*. She made her Met début in 1937 as Mignon, and created the role of Baba the Turk in *The Rake's Progress* in Venice in 1951. She later taught in New York.

Tozzi, Giorgio, b. Chicago, 8 Jan 1923. American bass. He made his opera début in

The Rape of Lucretia in New York in 1948. He first sang at the Met in 1955, and has appeared in a number of leading opera houses in Europe in such roles as Boris Godunov, Philip II, Méphistophélès, and Mozart's Figaro. He provided the singing voice for the actor Rossano Brazzi in the film of *South Pacific*, the Richard Rodgers musical, in 1958. He still sings with regional companies in America.

Traubel, Helen, b. St Louis, 20 June 1899; d. Santa Monica, 28 July 1972. American soprano. She began her career in concerts, and first appeared in opera at the Met in Walter Damrosch's *The Man Without a Country* (1937). She became a leading dramatic soprano in Wagner roles during the war years, and remained at the Met until 1953. She later sang in night-clubs, and appeared in films and on television.

Traviata, La *(The Woman Gone Astray).* Opera in 3 acts by Verdi. Libretto by Francesco Maria Piave, based on the play *La Dame aux Camélias* (1852) by Alexandre Dumas *fils*. First performed Venice, 6 Mar 1853.

Alfredo (ten.) falls in love with Violetta (sop.), a high-class Parisian courtesan who, unknown to him, is dying of consumption. She goes to live with him in the country, but leaves him at the request of his father, Germont (bar.), in order not to bring scandal upon the family. She returns to her former protector, but is publicly insulted at a party by Alfredo, who fights a duel with his rival. Alfredo returns to Violetta when he learns the truth about her sacrifice, but arrives only a short time before she dies.

Treigle, Norman, b. New Orleans, 6 Mar 1927; d. New Orleans, 16 Feb 1975. American bass. He studied in New Orleans, and made his début there in 1947 as Lodovico in *Otello*. He was a leading bass with New York City Opera from 1953, and was highly regarded as a singing-actor in such roles as Boris Godunov, Don Giovanni, and all four villains in *Les Contes d'Hoffmann*. He made his only Covent Garden appearance in 1974 as Méphistophélès in *Faust*.

Tristan und Isolde. Opera in 3 acts by Wagner. Libretto by the composer, drawn

Arturo Toscanini

from several versions of the old legend. First performed Munich, 10 June 1865.

Tristan (ten.) is bringing Isolde (sop.) from Ireland to Cornwall to be the bride of King Mark (bass). Holding Tristan responsible for the death of her betrothed, and unable to admit to herself her love for him, Isolde orders her attendant Brangäne (mezzo-sop.) to prepare a death potion for her and for Tristan. Brangäne substitutes a potion which will release inhibited feelings, and when Tristan and Isolde drink it they realize that they love each other.

In Cornwall they are discovered in a midnight *rendezvous* by King Mark. Tristan is attacked by Melot (ten.), one of Mark's retinue, and allows himself to be wounded. He is taken to his castle in Brittany by his retainer, Kurwenal (bar.), to recuperate, but in his fever he can think only of Isolde. She arrives, but only at the moment of Tristan's death. A second ship brings King Mark and Melot, and Kurwenal dies in killing Melot unaware that their intention is to pardon Tristan. Isolde dies by Tristan's body.

Trittico, Il *(The Triptych)*. Puccini's three 1-act operas, *Il Tabarro, Suor Angelica* and *Gianni Schicchi*, first performed together at the Met, 14 Dec 1918, but now frequently performed separately.

Troilus and Cressida. Opera in 3 acts by Walton. Libretto by Christopher Hassall, based on Chaucer's poem *(c.* 1385). First performed London, 1954.

Troilus (ten.) and Cressida (sop.) swear eternal loyalty to each other. In an exchange of prisoners during the Trojan War, Cressida is taken by the Greeks, and agrees to marry Diomede (bar.). While fighting Diomede, Troilus is stabbed in the back. Cressida kills herself over his body, rather than become a harlot in the Greek camp.

Trovatore, Il *(The Troubadour)*. Opera in 4 acts by Verdi. Libretto by Salvatore Cammarano, based on the play *El Trovador* (1836) by Antonio García Gutiérrez. First performed Rome, 19 Jan 1853.

In 15th-c. Spain, during a period of civil war, the royalist Count di Luna (bar.) and Manrico, a troubadour (ten.) and a rebel leader, are rivals for the hand of Leonora (sop.), who gives her love to Manrico. Di Luna and Manrico are unaware that they are brothers. Manrico has been brought up by Azucena (mezzo-sop.) a gipsy whom he believes to be his mother. She has periods in which her mind wanders, during one of which she reveals that her own mother had been burned as a witch by the present Count di Luna's father. She recalls how, in her madness, intending to throw the Count's brother into the flames she had killed her own child by mistake.

Leonora, believing Manrico killed in battle, is about to enter a convent when Di Luna attempts to abduct her. He is foiled by the sudden arrival of Manrico. Preparations for the marriage of Leonora and Manrico are in hand, when Manrico learns that Azucena, whom he still thinks is his mother, has been captured by Di Luna. He rushes off to save her, and is imprisoned by the Count.

In order to procure the release of Manrico, Leonora offers herself to Di Luna, and then takes poison rather than submit to him. When Manrico learns the price of his freedom, he curses Leonora, but realizes he has wronged her when she collapses and dies in his arms. The Count orders Manrico's

Kirsten Flagstad in her début in *Tristan und Isolde* at Covent Garden in 1936.

execution. As he dies, Azucena announces to the Count that he has killed his own brother. At last, she has avenged her mother's death, though at a cruel cost to herself, for she loved Manrico as though he were her son.

Troyanos, Tatiana, b. New York, 9 Dec 1938. American mezzo-soprano. She studied in New York, and made her début there as Hippolyta in *A Midsummer Night's Dream* in 1963. She first appeared at Covent Garden in 1969 as Octavian in *Der Rosenkavalier*, and made her Scala début in 1977 as Adalgisa. She is a performer of fiery temperament, with an effective and wide-ranging voice. At San Francisco in 1982, she sang the title-role of Handel's *Giulio Cesare* with success.

Troyens, Les *(The Trojans)*. Opera in 5 acts by Berlioz. Libretto by the composer, after Virgil's *Aeneid*. In order to secure a performance, Berlioz was obliged to divide the work into two parts. Part 1, *La Prise de Troie (The Capture of Troy)*, consists of Acts 1 and II of the complete opera. Part II, *Les Troyens à Carthage (The Trojans at Carthage)*, consists of the remaining three acts. *Les Troyens à Carthage* was first performed in Paris, 4 Nov 1863; *La Prise de Troie* was first performed in Karlsruhe, 6 Dec 1890; the first complete performance of *Les Troyens* was given in Karlsruhe in 1890, spread over two evenings, 6 and 7 Dec.

In Part I, Cassandra (sop.) forecasts the fall of Troy, and Aeneas (ten.) makes his escape from the city, as the Greeks rush in and the women of Troy stab themselves. In Part II, Aeneas arrives at the court of Queen Dido (mezzo-sop.) at Carthage. They become lovers. When Aeneas eventually leaves her, to fulfil his destiny and found the city of Rome, Dido kills herself.

Tsar's Bride, The (Russian title, *Tsarskaya Nevesta*). Opera in 4 acts by Rimsky-Korsakov. Libretto by the composer and I.F. Tyumenev, based on the play (1849) by Lev Aleksandrovich Mey. First performed Moscow, 3 Nov 1899.

Gryaznoy (bar.) and Lykov (bass) are both in love with Marfa (sop.) who is chosen

as his bride by the Tsar, Ivan the Terrible. Gryaznoy tries to win Marfa with a love potion, but his mistress Lyubasha (mezzo-sop.) substitutes poison. Lykov is executed for the crime, and on learning this Marfa loses her reason before dying in the Kremlin. Gryaznoy kills Lyubasha.

Tucker, Richard, b. Brooklyn N.Y., 28 Aug 1913; d. Kalamazoo, Mich., 8 Jan 1975. American tenor. He studied in New York and made his début there in 1943 as Alfredo. He first appeared at the Met in 1945, and sang more than thirty Italian and French roles there until his death. A fine Verdi stylist, he was also much admired as Enzo in *La Gioconda*, and as Eléazar in *La Juive* which he sang, late in his career, in New Orleans in 1973. He had an exciting dramatic tenor voice. His only appearance at Covent Garden was in 1958 as Cavaradossi in *Tosca*.

Turandot. Opera in 3 acts by Puccini. Libretto by Giuseppe Adami and Renato Simoni, based on the play *Turandot* (1762) by Carlo Gozzi. Left unfinished by Puccini, the last act was completed by Franco Alfano, and the opera was first performed in Milan, 25 Apr 1926.

In ancient China, the cruel Princess Turandot (sop.) poses three riddles for intending suitors to answer. Those who fail are beheaded. An unknown Prince, Calaf (ten.), succeeds in answering the riddles, but agrees to forfeit his life if Turandot can discover his name by the next dawn. Turandot tortures Liu (sop.), a slave girl who loves Calaf, but Liu kills herself rather than betray her master. Calaf reveals his name, and Turandot, at last realizing the nature of true love, accepts him as her husband.

Turco in Italia, Il *(The Turk in Italy).* Opera in 2 acts by Rossini. Libretto by Felice Romani. First performed Milan, 14 Aug 1814.

The poet Prosdocimo (bar.) manipulates an intrigue involving Selim (bass), the Turk of the title, Donna Fiorilla (sop.), the wife of Don Geronio (bass), and the poet Narciso (ten.), Fiorilla's admirer.

Turiddu (ten.). The young soldier whose affair with Lola, wife of Alfio, leads to tragedy, in Mascagni's *Cavalleria Rusticana*.

A scene from Houston Grand Opera's performance of Puccini's *Turandot* in 1982.

Turn of the Screw, The. Opera in a prologue and 2 acts by Britten. Libretto by Myfanwy Piper, based on the novella (1898) by Henry James. First performed Venice, 14 Sept 1954.

A Governess (sop.), sent to look after two children, Miles (treble) and Flora (sop.), in a manor house run by a housekeeper, Mrs Grose (sop.), comes to realize that the children are in the clutches of the spirits of two former servants who had died, Peter Quint (ten.) and Miss Jessel (sop.). She fights Quint for the souls of the children, and wins, but her victory is an empty one for it leads to the death of the boy, Miles.

Turner, (Dame) Eva, b. Oldham, 10 Mar 1892. English soprano. She studied in London, and joined the chorus of the Carl Rosa company in 1916, making her solo début as a Page in *Tannhäuser*. She was engaged by Toscanini to sing Freia in *Das Rheingold* at La Scala in 1924, and established herself as a leading dramatic soprano, singing Aida, the *Trovatore* Leonora, and other roles with an Italian company touring Germany. She first sang the title-role in *Turandot* in Brescia in 1926, only months after the opera's première at La Scala, and became closely associated with it for the next twenty years. At Covent Garden in the 1930s, in addition to Turandot, she was heard as Aida, Santuzza, Sieglinde, Isolde, Agathe (in *Der Freischütz*) and Amelia (in *Un Ballo in Maschera*). She had a powerful dramatic soprano voice and an impressive stage personality.

U

Uhde, Hermann, b. Bremen, 20 July 1914; d. Copenhagen, 10 Oct 1965. German baritone. He studied in Bremen, and made his début there in the bass role of Titurel in *Parsifal* in 1936. He began his international career after the war when he scored a huge success as Mandryka in *Arabella* at Covent Garden in 1953. He sang at the Met between 1955-60, making a strong impression in the Wagner roles and also as Wozzeck, a role he sang at the Met in English.

Ulfung, Ragnar, b. Oslo, 28 Feb 1927. Norwegian tenor. He studied in Oslo and Milan, and made his stage début in Oslo in 1952 as the Magician in *The Consul*. In 1958 he joined the Swedish Royal Opera, and soon began to sing leading roles abroad. He created the title-role in Maxwell Davies's *Taverner* at Covent Garden in 1972, and the following year made his Met début as Mime. He has produced opera in Stockholm, Oslo, and in the United States. In 1982 at Santa Fe, he sang Basilio in *Le Nozze di Figaro* and Pollux in *Die Liebe der Danae*.

Ulrica (mezzo-sop.). The fortune-teller in Verdi's *Un Ballo in Maschera*. When the opera is performed in its original Swedish setting, she is given her real name, Madame Arvidson.

Uppman, Theodor, b. Palo Alto, Calif., 12 Jan 1920. American baritone. He studied in Philadelphia and California, and made his début in a concert performance of *Pelléas et Mélisande* in San Francisco in 1947, in which he sang Pelléas to the Mélisande of Maggie Teyte. At Covent Garden in 1951 he created the title-role in Britten's *Billy Budd*, and in 1953 he made his Met début as Pelléas. At the Met he was popular as Papageno, Guglielmo in *Così Fan Tutte*, Eisenstein in *Die Fledermaus* and a variety of other roles. With American companies he has created

Ralph Vaughan Williams

several roles in new operas. In April 1983 in Geneva, he performed all the baritone roles in Britten's *Death in Venice*.

Ursuleac, Viorica, b. Czernowitz, 26 Mar 1894. Romanian soprano. She studied in Vienna, and made her début in Zagreb in 1922 as Charlotte in *Werther*. She married the conductor Clemens Krauss, and created the leading soprano roles in Richard Strauss's *Arabella*, (1933) *Friedenstag* (1938) and *Capriccio* (1942), whose premières were conducted by her husband. She appeared at Covent Garden in 1934 in *Arabella, Shvanda the Bagpiper* and *Otello*. She never sang in the United States.

V

Vaccai, Nicola, b. Tolentino. 15 Mar 1790; d. Pesaro, 6 Aug 1848. Italian composer and teacher of singing. After the success of his first opera, *I Solitari di Scozia*, in Naples in 1815, he was discouraged by the failure in Venice of *Malvina* (1816) and *Il Lupo di Ostenda* (1818), but became a prestigious teacher of singing. He returned to composition with several operas, one of which, *Giulietta e Romeo* (1825), was enormously successful: after 1832, its final act was often substituted for Bellini's in performances of the latter composer's *I Capuleti ed i Montecchi*. The advent of Bellini, however, led to a decline in Vaccai's fortunes as a composer, and he returned to teaching. His last opera, the somewhat Donizettian *Virginia* (Milan, 1846), is not without interest.

Valentin (bar.). Marguerite's brother, in Gounod's *Faust*.

Valentine (sop.). The daughter of St Bris, in Meyerbeer's *Les Huguenots*.

Valentini-Terrani, Lucia, b. Padua, 28 Sept 1948. Italian contralto. She studied in Padua, and made her début in Brescia in 1969 in the title-role of Rossini's *La Cenerentola*. At La Scala and in leading opera houses throughout Europe she has been acclaimed in the Rossini coloratura roles. She made her Met début in 1975 as Isabella in *L'Italiana in Algeri*. In 1983 at La Scala she sang Eboli in the French-language performances of Verdi's *Don Carlos* conducted by Claudio Abbado.

Valetti, Cesare, b. Rome, 18 Dec 1922. Italian tenor. He studied in Rome, and made his début in Bari in 1947 as Alfredo in *La Traviata*. He first appeared at Covent Garden in 1950 as Fenton in *Falstaff*. In 1953 he made his American début in San Francisco as Werther, and sang frequently at the Met between 1953-62. He was a graceful lyric tenor, at his best in the bel canto roles. He retired in 1968,.

Vallin, Ninon, b. Montalieu-Vercien, 8 Sept 1886; d. Lyons 22 Nov 1961. French soprano. She studied in Lyons and Paris, and made her opera début in Paris in 1912 as Micaëla. She became the leading Manon, Louise (in Charpentier's *Louise*) and Charlotte (in *Werther*) of her day. She appeared frequently in Buenos Aires between 1916-36. At the age of sixty she was still singing well, as the Countess in *Le Nozze di Figaro* in Paris, and continued to give recitals for several more years.

Vampyr, Der *(The Vampire)*. Opera in 2 acts by Marschner. Libretto by Wilhelm August Wohlbrück. First performed Leipzig, 29 Mar 1828.

Lord Ruthven (ten.), a Scottish vampire, kills two victims, Janthe (sop.), and Emmy (sop.), and almost claims a third, Malvina (sop.), before being destroyed.

Van Allan, Richard, b. Chipston, Notts, 28 May 1935. English bass. He studied in Birmingham, and began his career in 1964 in the chorus at Glyndebourne. His solo début there was in *Die Zauberflöte* (1966) in which he played a Priest and the First Armed Man. In 1971 he joined The Royal Opera at Covent Garden where he sang such roles as Leporello, Don Alfonso (in *Così Fan Tutte*) and Figaro (in *Le Nozze di Figaro*). In 1976 he sang Baron Ochs in *Der Rosenkavalier* for the first time, in San Diego. He is excellent in character roles such as Wurm in *Luisa Miller* which he sang first at Covent Garden and, in 1982, in Brussels.

Van Dam, José, b. Brussels, 25 Aug 1940. Belgian bass. He studied in Brussels, and

began his career at the Paris Opéra in 1961 in minor roles. In timbre and range his voice is capable of encompassing both bass and baritone roles, and he has become a highly acclaimed Figaro (in Mozart's opera). Prince Igor, and Rangoni (in *Boris Godunov*) in several European opera houses. One of his best roles is Escamillo in *Carmen*, with which he made his Covent Garden début in 1973. In Paris in 1982 he undertook the title-role of *Don Giovanni*.

Vanzo, Alain, b. Monte Carlo, 2 Apr 1928. French tenor. He studied in Aix-les-Bains, and made his début at the Paris Opéra in 1954 as a pirate in *Oberon*. He has sung much of the French tenor repertory in France and Belgium, and appeared at Covent Garden in 1961 as Edgardo in *Lucia di Lammermoor* and in 1963 as Rodolfo in *La Bohème*. In 1982 in Avignon, he was still an effective Gérald in *Lakmé*.

Varady, Julia, b. Oradea, 1 Sept 1941. Romanian soprano. She studied in Bucharest, and joined the company at Cluj in Transylvania in 1962, where she remained in leading dramatic soprano roles for ten years. In 1972 she joined the Munich company, and has since appeared at a number of European houses. She is much admired as Strauss's Arabella, and in the title-role of Gluck's *Alceste* which she sang with Scottish Opera in 1974. In 1982 she had a great success at the Deutsche Oper, Berlin, as Leonora in *La Forza del Destino*.

Varlaam (bass). The drunken monk in Mussorgsky's *Boris Godunov*.

Varnay, Astrid, b. Stockholm, 25 Apr 1918. Austro-Hungarian, later American, soprano. Her father was an Austrian singer and producer and her mother a Hungarian soprano who emigrated to the United States in 1920. She studied with her mother, and with Hermann Weigert whom she later married. She made her début at the Met in 1941, substituting for an indisposed Lotte Lehmann, and remained a leading dramatic soprano at the Met until 1957, specializing in Strauss and Wagner roles. From 1951-67 she sang regularly at Bayreuth, where her roles included Brünnhilde, Isolde, Kundry and Senta. She first appeared at Covent Garden in 1948 as Brünnhilde, and returned on several occasions until 1968, when she sang the Kostelnička in *Jenůfa*. She was an exciting singer and actress, and continued to appear in opera in less demanding roles, in her sixties.

Varviso, Silvio, b. Zurich, 20 June 1924. Swiss conductor. He studied in Zurich and Vienna, and made his début in St Gallen in 1944 with *Die Zauberflöte*. He has conducted at most of the leading European and American opera houses, and became musical director of the Paris Opéra in 1981. Though he conducts a wide range of operas, he is particularly admired in Rossini, Bellini and Donizetti. His *Pelléas et Mélisande* at Covent Garden in 1982 was exemplary.

Vasco da Gana (ten.). Hero of Meyerbeer's *L'Africaine*.

Vašek (ten.). The shy and stuttering son of Micha in Smetana's *The Bartered Bride*.

· **Vaughan,** Elizabeth, b. Llanfyllin, 12 Mar 1937. Welsh soprano. She studied in London, and made her début with Welsh National Opera in Cardiff in 1960, as Abigaille in *Nabucco*. She joined the Royal Opera at Covent Garden in 1961, and sang such roles as Mimi, Liu (*Turandot*), Gilda, Violetta, and Teresa (*Benvenuto Cellini*). She made her Met début in 1972 as Donna Elvira. With Welsh National Opera in Cardiff (1981) and London (1982) she was an affecting Leonora in *La Forza del Destino*.

Vaughan Williams, Ralph, b. Down Ampney, Gloucs., 12 Oct 1872; d. London, 26 Aug 1958. English composer. The most important English symphonic composer of his generation, he wrote five operas, all of which contain music of much gentle charm and attractiveness, though none has been completely successful in dramatic terms. *Hugh the Drover* was completed in 1914, but not performed until 1924. *Sir John in Love* (1929), a relaxed and unexciting setting of *The Merry Wives of Windsor*, was followed by *The Poisoned Kiss* and *Riders to the Sea*, both written in the 1920s but not performed until 1936 (*The Poisoned Kiss*) and 1937 (*Riders to the Sea*). The opera closest to its composer's heart was *The Pilgrim's Progress*, first performed at Covent Garden in 1951, which incorporated a shorter piece, *The*

Josephine Veasey as Dido in 1969

Shepherds of the Delectable Mountains, which he had composed as early as 1921. An uneven and slow-moving work, *The Pilgrim's Progress* was final proof that his great talent was not for dramatic music.

Veasey, Josephine, b. London, 10 July 1930. English mezzo-soprano. She studied in London, and joined the Covent Garden chorus in 1949. She left in 1950 to sing solo roles with the Art Council's touring company, Opera for All, and then returned to Covent Garden where she sang mezzo roles from 1955-82, among them Octavian, Eboli, Dido (in *Les Troyens*) and Dorabella (*Così Fan Tutte*). A dependable artist with a fine voice, she was especially effective as Fricka in *Die Walküre*, a role which she sang under Karajan in 1968 both at Salzburg and at the Met. She retired in 1982.

Venus (sop.). The goddess of Love, in Wagner's *Tannhäuser*.

Vêpres Siciliennes, Les (*The Sicilian Vespers*). Opera in 5 acts by Verdi. Libretto by Eugène Scribe and Charles Duveyrier. First performed Paris, 13 June 1855.

A fictional plot, involving the love of Hélène (sop.), a Sicilian patriot, for Henri (ten.) who, unknown to her, is the son of Montfort (bar.), the French govenor of Sicily, is set against the historical events of 1282 when the Sicilians rose against the French in an act of wholesale slaughter. The opera ends with the massacre, known as the Sicilian Vespers because the signal for attack was given by the ringing of the vesper bell.

Verdi, Giuseppe, b. Le Roncole, 10 Oct 1813; d. Milan, 27 Jan 1901. Italian composer. The greatest composer of Italian opera, he began his career with *Oberto* (1839) which combined Bellinian delicacy with what was soon to be recognized as Verdian vigour and humanity. His second opera, *Un Giorno di Regno* (1840), failed to please its audience, but with *Nabucco* (1842) he produced his first masterpiece, and the earliest of his operas to contain scenes which enabled Italian audiences to consider them as symbolizing their own situation and their aspirations to freedom from foreign rule.

I Lombardi (1843) and *Ernani* (1844)

Giuseppe Verdi

towards dramatic truth and a musical style combining psychological depth with a continuing abundance of that prolific and individual melodic gift which was never to desert him.

With *Luisa Miller* (1849), Verdi's great middle period begins. *Stiffelio* (1850; later to be revised as *Aroldo*, 1857) is followed by his three most popular works, *Rigoletto* (1851), *Il Trovatore* (1853) and *La Traviata* (1853), operas in which a high level of inspiration is sustained throughout. *Les Vêpres Siciliennes* (1855), composed for the Paris Opéra, was followed by *Simon Boccanegra* (1857) which did not achieve its definitive form until revived in 1881. *Un Ballo in Maschera* (1859), a work of almost seamless perfection, contrasts with *La Forza del Destino* (1862) which is anything but flawless but contains great riches, both musical and dramatic: a sprawling essay on the respective values of the contemplative and the active life.

Verdi's second opera for Paris, *Don Carlos* (1867), is a complex work which makes politics and religion into viable and interesting operatic subjects. His final three operas, recognized from their first performances as masterpieces, are *Aida* (1871), *Otello* (1887) and *Falstaff* (1893). *Aida*, for all its public scenes, is the most intimate of grand operas; *Otello* and *Falstaff* are even greater works than the Shakespeare plays on which they are based. In *Falstaff*, which Verdi composed when he was approaching eighty, there is almost too much to admire, especially the extraordinary pace of the entire opera which seems to last no longer than one sudden flash of inspiration.

continue Verdi's development towards more expressive use of the orchestra and greater dramatic thrust, and *I Due Foscari* (1844) sounds the melancholy note which would be heard frequently in mature Verdi. Looking back later, Verdi referred to the period after 1844 as his years in the galleys, and it is true that, in those years, he produced operas in quick succession (though nowhere near the pace of most purveyors of Italian opera at that time). *Giovanna d'Arco* and *Alzira* (both 1845), *Attila* (1846), *I Masnadieri* (1847), *Il Corsaro* (1848) and *La Battaglia di Legnano* (1849) are all uneven, though there is not one of them which does not contain much exciting music. But, in 1847, Verdi had produced another masterpiece, his first Shakespearian opera, *Macbeth*, in which he moved further

verismo. Literally 'realism', the term is used to describe the realistic or, more correctly, naturalistic school of Italian opera which flourished in the late-19th and early-20th c. The subjects were modern, and tended to be not just slices of life but slices of low life, as in Mascagni's *Cavalleria Rusticana* which, together with Leoncavallo's *Pagliacci*, is one of the earliest and highest peaks of *verismo*. The movement corresponds to the realistic school in French literature as exemplified by Émile Zola. The only French composer to contribute significantly to *verismo* was Massenet, with *La Navarraise*. Giordano, Zandonai, and to a certain extent Puccini, are the other major Italian composers of *verismo*.

Véronique. Operetta in 3 acts by Messager. Libretto by Albert van Loo and Georges Duval. First performed Paris, 10 Dec 1898.

Hélène (sop.), about to be married, by order of the King, to Florestan (ten.) whom she has never met, overhears Florestan describing her unfavourably, and decides to teach him a lesson. Pretending to be Véronique, a flower-girl, she wins his love, which she then realizes she reciprocates. After many complications, all ends happily for the two lovers.

Verrett, Shirley, b. New Orleans, 31 May 1931. American mezzo-soprano. She studied in Los Angeles, and made her opera début in Yellow Springs, Ohio, in 1957 as Lucretia in Britten's *Rape of Lucretia*. Carmen in Bizet's opera was the role of her débuts in Spoleto (1962), at the Bolshoi Theatre, Moscow (1963), La Scala (1966) and the Met (1968). She first appeared at Covent Garden as Ulrica in *Un Ballo in Maschera* in 1966, and returned on many occasions as Carmen, Amneris, Eboli, Azucena, and Gluck's Orfeo. She has a rich mezzo-soprano voice of great range, and she is able to undertake certain soprano roles. At Covent Garden in 1981 and again in 1983 she was a superb Dalila in *Samson et Dalila*.

Verstovsky, Alexei, b. Seliverstovo, 1 Mar 1799; d. Moscow, 17 Nov 1862. Russian composer. He composed six operas which were popular in Russia. His first, *Pan Twardowski* (1828), was unsuccessful, but *Vadim* (1832) and, in particular, *Askold's Grave* (1835), enjoyed enormous popularity. (In 1869 it became the first Russian opera to be performed in America, when produced by a Russian company in New York.) His later operas were *Longing for the Homeland* (1839), *Chur Valley* (1841) and *Gromoboy* (1858).

Vestale, La *(The Vestal Virgin)*. Opera in 3 acts by Spontini. Libretto by Étienne de Jouy. First performed Paris, 16 Dec 1807.

The vestal virgin Giulia (sop.) and the Roman captain Licinio (ten.) are lovers. When Licinio visits Giulia during her vigil in the temple, she allows the sacred flame to be extinguished. Sentenced to be buried alive for this impious dereliction of duty, she is saved when the flame is rekindled by a flash of lightning.

Vickers, Jon, b. Prince Albert, 29 Oct 1926. Canadian tenor. He studied in Toronto, and made his début there in 1954 as the Duke of Mantua. He first appeared at Covent Garden in 1957 as Riccardo in *Un Ballo in Maschera* when his huge voice and authoritative performance caused something of a sensation. He sang at Covent Garden a wide range of roles including Aeneas in *Les Troyens*, Radames, Otello, Don Carlos, Florestan in *Fidelio*, Canio, Don José, Peter Grimes, and several Wagner roles. He first sang at Bayreuth in 1958, and made his Met début in 1960 as Canio. His Samson in *Samson et Dalila* at Covent Garden in 1981 and 1983 was highly impressive.

Vida Breve, La *(Brief Life)*. Opera in 2 acts by Falla. Libretto by Carlos Fernández Shaw. First performed Nice, 1 Apr 1913.

Salud (sop.) is in love with Paco (ten.) who secretly plans to marry Carmela (mezzo-sop.). At his wedding, Salud curses Paco and dies broken-hearted.

Vie Parisienne, La *(Parisian Life)*. Operetta in 5 acts (later reduced to 4 acts) by Offenbach. Libretto by Henri Meilhac and Ludovic Halévy. First performed Paris, 31 Oct 1866.

A satirical picture of Parisian life in the 1860s, it describes the adventures of a number of visitors to Paris, among them a Swedish baron (bar.) and baroness (sop.), and their involvement with two young Parisians, Raoul (ten.) and Bobinet (bar.) who are both in love with the *demi-mondaine* Metella (sop.).

Village Romeo and Juliet, A. Opera in a prologue and 3 acts by Delius. Libretto by the composer, based on the story *Romeo und Juliet aus dem Dorfe* (1856) by Gottfried Keller. First performed Berlin, 21 Feb 1907, in German. First performance in English, London, 22 Feb 1910.

Encouraged by the mysterious Dark Fiddler (bar.), two lovers, Sali (ten.) and Vreli (sop.), children of rival farmers, find that their only chance of happiness together will be after death. They drown themselves in a barge that sinks as it floats downstream.

Villa-Lobos, Heitor, b. Rio de Janeiro, 5 Mar 1887; d. Rio de Janeiro, 17 Nov 1959. Brazilian composer. He composed two

Shirley Verrett as Dalila and Jon Vickers as Samson at Covent Garden in 1983.

operas. *Izath*, written in 1912-14, was not staged until 1958. *Yerma*, based on a play by Lorca, was composed in 1955-6 and performed at Santa Fe in 1971. Villa-Lobos had a greater success with his one musical comedy, *Magdalena*, which opened in Los Angeles in 1948 and also had a run on Broadway.

Villi, Le *(The Witch-dancers)*. Opera in 1 act (later revised in 2 acts) by Puccini. Libretto by Ferdinando Fontana. First performed, Milan, 31 May 1884. Two-act version first performed Turin, 26 Dec 1884.

Puccini's first opera, it tells the story of Roberto (ten.) who leaves his village sweetheart Anna (sop.) when he inherits wealth, and leads a life of dissipation in the city. Anna dies of grief, and when Roberto returns he finds her transformed into one of those spirits of forsaken maidens who return from their graves to lure faithless lovers into dancing until they drop dead.

Vinay, Ramón, b. Chillán, 31 Aug 1912. Chilean tenor and baritone. He studied in Mexico City, and made his début there in 1931 in the baritone role of Alfonso in *La Favorite*. After singing baritone roles for several years, he made a second début in Mexico City as a tenor in 1943, as Don José in *Carmen*. He sang at the Met from 1946-61 in Wagner roles and became a renowned interpreter of the title-role of Verdi's *Otello*, which he also sang at La Scala, Salzburg and Covent Garden. In 1962, he reverted to baritone roles, among them Telramund in *Lohengrin*, Scarpia and Iago. He performed always with intelligence and musical artistry, though his voice revealed signs of strain in later years.

Violetta (sop.). The heroine of Verdi's *La Traviata*.

Visconti, Luchino, b. Milan, 2 Nov 1906; d. Rome, 17 Mar 1976. Italian producer and designer. His first opera productions were at La Scala, from 1954: *La Vestale*, *La Sonnambula*, *La Traviata*, *Anna Bolena* and *Iphigénie en Tauride*, with Maria Callas in the leading roles. In 1958 he staged and designed *Don Carlos* at Covent Garden, returning there to produce *Il Trovatore, Der Rosenkavalier* and *La Traviata*.

Vishnevskaya, Galina, b. Leningrad, 25 Oct 1926. Russian soprano. She studied in Leningrad, and made her début there in operetta in 1944. From 1952-74 she was a leading soprano at the Bolshoi, where she undertook such roles as Aida, Violetta, Butterfly and Tosca, as well as the Russian lyric soprano repertory. A distinguished Tatiana in *Eugene Onegin*, she has also sung modern Russian roles. It was as Aida that she made her Met (1961) and Covent Garden (1962) débuts. Her performances are intensely dramatic, though not always impeccably sung.

Vivaldi, Antonio, b. Venice, 4 Mar 1678; d. Vienna, 28 July 1741. The most important Italian composer of his generation, and extremely influential in the development of the concerto and of programme music, he also wrote nearly fifty operas. Most were hastily composed, and they are not generally considered to be important in Vivaldi's total *oeuvre*. The earliest, *Ottone in Villa*, was staged in Vicenza in 1713, and the last, *Feraspe*, in Venice in 1739. The scores of no more than twenty-one of the operas have survived.

Vogel, Siegfried, b. Chemnitz, 6 Mar 1937. German bass. He studied in Dresden, and began his career in small roles with the Dresden Staatsoper. He joined the Berlin Staatsoper in 1965, and was acclaimed for his Mozart performances, especially Figaro, Leporello and Alfonso. His Rocco in *Fidelio* at the Paris Opéra in 1982 was much admired.

Voix Humaine, La *(The Human Voice)*. Opera in 1 act by Poulenc. Libretto by Jean Cocteau. First performed Paris, 6 Feb 1959. In this 45-minute scena for solo soprano and orchestra, a young woman converses on the telephone with her lover who is leaving her. The role was created by Denise Duval, for whom Poulenc composed it, and who has performed it in a number of countries.

Völker, Franz, b. Neu-Isenburg, 31 Mar 1899; d. Darmstadt 4 Dec 1965. German tenor. He studied in Frankfurt where he began his career in 1926, and later became a

333

leading dramatic tenor in Berlin, Munich and Vienna. A Wagner specialist, he sang at Bayreuth between 1933–42. He made his Covent Garden début in 1934 as Florestan in *Fidelio* with Lotte Lehmann in the title-role, and also sang Siegmund to Lehmann's Sieglinde. He returned to Covent Garden in 1937 as Siegmund. He never sang in the United States, though he continued to sing opera in the post-war years, principally in Munich from 1945-52.

Volo di Notte *(Night Flight).* Opera in 1 act by Dallapiccola. Libretto by the composer after the novel *Vol de Nuit* (1931) by Antoine de Saint-Exupéry. First performed Florence, 18 May 1940.

The opera is set in the control room of an airport. Rivière (bass-bar.), director of the airline, a radio-telephonist (ten.) and the wife (sop.) of a pilot on a night flight, anxiously await the plane's arrival.

Von Heute auf Morgen *(From Day to Day).* Opera in 1 act by Schoenberg. Libretto by Max Blonda (pseudonym of the composer's wife). First performed Frankfurt, 1 Feb 1930.

Schoenberg's only comic opera, it describes the successful attempt of a wife (sop.) to keep her marriage from disintegrating. The other characters are her husband (bar.), a singer (ten.) and his female companion (sop.) with whom the husband is infatuated.

W

Waechter, Eberhard, b. Vienna, 9 July 1929. Austrian baritone. He studied in Vienna and made his début there in 1953 as Silvio in *Pagliacci*. He has been a member of the Vienna Staatsoper since 1954, his most successful roles including Don Giovanni, the Count in *Le Nozze di Figaro*, Renato in *Un Ballo in Maschera*, Eisenstein in *Die Fledermaus* and Amfortas in *Parsifal*. He first appeared at Covent Garden in 1956 in *Le Nozze di Figaro*, and made his Met début in 1961 as Wolfram in *Tannhäuser*. In 1981 he sang Eisenstein in Lisbon, in the first-ever performance in Portugal of a Johann Strauss operetta. He is an engaging lyric baritone, with a fine presence. His son, Franz

Richard Wagner

Waechter, also sings baritone roles in Vienna.

Wagner, Richard, b. Leipzig, 22 May 1813; d. Venice, 13 Feb 1883. German composer. The greatest 19th-c. German composer, he began his career as a conductor of opera in Würzburg, Magdeburg and Riga. While he was still chorus master in Würzburg he composed his first opera, *Die Feen*, which was not staged during his lifetime. *Das Liebesverbot*, based on Shakespeare's *Measure for Measure*, was a failure when produced in Magdeburg in 1836, and it was not until the production of *Rienzi* in Dresden in 1842 that Wagner had his first taste of success. He had by this time completed both the libretto (he was always to write his own) and the music of *Der fliegende Holländer,* the earliest of his operas still to be regularly performed. The first opera in which Wagner's genius shines forth unencumbered, *Der fliegende Holländer*, was well received at its Dresden première in 1843. A month later, its composer was appointed Kapellmeister to the Dresden Court.

Wagner spent the next six years in Dresden, during which time *Tannhäuser* was completed and produced (1845) and *Lohengrin* was composed. *Tannhäuser* is a curiously slow and stately work, given that its subject is the relationship of sacred to profane love, but *Lohengrin*, first performed under Liszt at Weimar in 1850, marks a real advance for its composer, anticipating the direction he was to take in his next completed work, *Tristan und Isolde.* Though it was poorly received in Munich in 1865, *Tristan und Isolde* is now accepted as one of the great peaks of 19th-c. romanticism, and the masterpiece of Wagner's mature years. The score's heavily sensuous chromaticism and the ecstatic richness of its orchestration combine to give *Tristan und Isolde* a curious psychological strength. It was in this opera that Wagner discovered how simultaneously to reach his audience's conscious and sub-conscious responses.

For a production of *Tannhäuser* in Paris in 1861 Wagner had made changes to his score to incorporate the obligatory ballet. It is this version which is generally performed now.

Wagner's next opera, *Die Meistersinger von Nürnberg*, staged in Munich in 1868, was

intended to be a light comedy but turned out to be a hymn to artistic compromise with, in its final scene, an irrelevant aside appealing to the baser aspects of nationalism.

The composition of *Der Ring des Nibelungen* was spread over more than twenty years. Though the first two works in the tetralogy, *Das Rheingold* and *Die Walküre*, were first performed separately in Munich in 1869 and 1870, the first complete performances of *Der Ring* were given in 1876 in Bayreuth, in a theatre of the composer's own design in which, though it was intended only as a temporary structure, the annual Wagner Festival performances are still given. For all its unevenness and disproportionate length, the *Ring* is Wagner's most important work and also the one on which most critical estimates of the composer are based. Such is its scale that it can be interpreted in terms of sociology, politics, history, psychology or moral philosophy.

Wagner composed his final opera, *Parsifal* (first performed in Bayreuth, 1882), as a sacred Christian music-drama. Others have described it as an attempt to give aesthetic validity to his own racial prejudice, or even as a celebration of high-minded, ascetic homosexuality. Whatever else it may be, *Parsifal* is a complex work of art, and musically an advance even upon the harmonic language of *Tristan und Isolde*.

Wagner, Siegfried, b. Triebschen, nr Lucerne, 6 June 1869; d. Bayreuth, 4 Aug 1930. German composer and conductor. The son of Richard Wagner, he composed fifteen operas in the style of his father, several of which were staged in Germany, but none of which has merited revival. The first, *Der Bärenhäuter*, was produced in Munich in 1899, and the last, *Der Schmied von Marienburg*, was performed in Rostock in 1923. He was artistic director of the Wagner Festival at Bayreuth from 1908-30.

Wagner, Wieland, b. Bayreuth, 5 Jan 1917; d. Munich, 17 Oct 1966. German producer. Son of Siegfried Wagner, and grandson of Richard, he was, with his brother Wolfgang, artistic director of the Bayreuth Festival from its reopening in 1951 until his death. His abstract stagings of the Wagner operas, based on the ideas of Adolphe Appia, influenced an entire generation of German opera producers.

Wagner, Wolfgang, b. Bayreuth, 30 Aug 1919. Grandson of Richard, and son of Siegfried, he became artistic director of the Bayreuth Festival in 1951 together with his brother Wieland, and since Wieland's death in 1966 has been sole director. His productions of Wagner's operas, which are more conventional in style than those of his brother Wieland's, are given authority by virtue of his relationship to the composer.

Wagner-Régeny, Rudolf, b. Szász-Régen, Transylvania, 28 Aug 1903; d. Berlin, 18 Sept 1969. Hungarian, later German, composer. He composed seven operas, of which *Der Günstling* (Dresden, 1935) and *Die Bürger von Calais* (Berlin, 1939) aroused most interest when they were first produced. *Das Bergwerk zu Falun*, performed at the 1961 Salzburg Festival, was generally considered insipid.

Walküre, Die *(The Valkyrie).* Opera in 3 acts by Wagner. Libretto by the composer. First performed Munich, 26 June 1870. First performed as part of the complete cycle of *Der Ring des Nibelungen*, Bayreuth, 14 Aug 1876.

Fleeing from his enemies, Siegmund (ten.) stumbles into Hunding's hut, where Sieglinde (sop.), Hunding's wife, finds him. The two feel strangely attracted to each other, and Sieglinde shows him a sword left embedded in a tree-trunk by Wotan (bass-bar.), which can only be withdrawn by a hero. Siegmund succeeds in wresting the sword from the trunk. Discovering that they are brother and sister, Siegmund and Sieglinde embrace incestuously, and rush away together. When Siegmund and Hunding (bass) meet to fight, Fricka (mezzo-sop.) forces Wotan to side with Hunding. However, Brünnhilde (sop.), the Valkyrie warrior and Wotan's favourite daughter, senses her father's true sympathies, and supports Siegmund. Wotan intervenes, and both Siegmund and Hunding are killed. Brünnhilde helps the pregnant Sieglinde to safety, and entrusts the shattered pieces of Siegmund's sword to her care. For her disobedience, Brünnhilde is reluctantly punished by Wotan, who puts her to sleep on a rock, surrounded by fire so that she will be discovered and awakened only by a true hero, who will make his way through the magic fire to claim her.

Wallace, Vincent, b. Waterford, 11 Mar 1812; d. Vieuzos, Hautes-Pyrénées, 12 Oct 1865. Irish composer. He led an adventurous life, performing as pianist and violinist in Australia, India, South America and elsewhere. He composed six operas, of which the first and most successful was *Maritana*, an immediate success on its first production at Drury Lane Theatre, London, in 1845. The best of his other operas, *Lurline*, was composed in 1847 though not staged until 1860 at Covent Garden. *Maritana* is still occasionally performed by amateur operatic societies.

Wallman, Margherita, b. Vienna, 22 June 1904. Austrian producer. She began her career as a dancer and choreographer, and produced her first opera, *Orfeo ed Euridice*, in Salzburg in 1937 at the invitation of Bruno Walter. Since 1952 she has produced many operas at La Scala, and has also produced for the Met and Covent Garden, as well as other leading theatres in Europe. In 1983 she returned to Covent Garden to re-stage her 1958 production of Poulenc's *Dialogues des Carmelites.*

Wally, La. Opera in 4 acts by Catalani. Libretto by Luigi Illica, based on the novel *Die Geyer-Wally* (1875) by Wilhelmine von Hillern. First performed Milan, 20 Jan 1892.

The action takes place in a village in the Tyrol in 1800. Wally (sop.) is in love with Hagenbach (ten.), and resists her father's attempt to make her marry Gellner (bar.). Thinking, mistakenly, that Hagenbach has insulted her, Wally asks Geller to kill him. Gellner pushes Hagenback off the side of a mountain into a ravine, but Wally, now repentant, rescues him. Hagenbach encounters her on a mountain-top, and they confess their love. They perish in an avalanche.

Walter, Bruno, b. Berlin, 15 Sept 1876; d. Los Angeles, 17 Feb 1962. German, later American, conductor. A protegé of Gustav Mahler, he worked with Mahler in Vienna from 1901. After conducting at many German opera houses, among them Munich

Gwyneth Jones as Brünnhilde and Jeannine Altmeyer as Sieglinde in a scene from Act III of Wagner's *Die Walküre* at Bayreuth.

Bruno Walter

(where he was general music director from 1913-22) and Berlin, he became a principal conductor at the Salzburg Festival and again in Vienna. He left Austria at the Anschluss, and conducted at the Met frequently between 1941-59. He was renowned especially for his performances of the Mozart, Wagner and Strauss operas, which were characterized by a humane, lyrical approach. He first appeared at Covent Garden in 1910, and conducted there on many occasions in the 1920s. His performances of *Der Rosenkavalier*, with Lotte Lehmann as the Marschallin, and of *Die Fledermaus*, with Lehmann as Rosalinde, were greatly admired at Covent Garden.

Walther von Stolzing (ten.). The knight who wins the singing contest and the hand of Eva in *Die Meistersinger von Nürnberg*.

Walton, (Sir) William, b. Oldham, 29 Mar 1902; d. Ischia, 8 Mar 1983. English composer. A noted composer of orchestral music, he wrote only two operas. *Troilus and Cressida*, staged at Covent Garden in 1954, is almost Puccinian in its approach. It was followed by a 1-act comedy, *The Bear* (1967), based on a Chekov story.

Wanderer, The (bass-bar.). The name by which Wotan is known in Wagner's *Siegfried*.

War and Peace (Russian title, *Voyna i mir*). Opera in 13 scenes by Prokofiev. Libretto by the composer and Mira Mendelson-Prokofieva, after the novel (1869) by Tolstoy. First performed Leningrad, 12 June 1946; first performance of revised version, Leningrad, 31 Mar 1955.

The opera is a setting of selected scenes from Tolstoy's panoramic novel. Prince Andrey Bolkonsky (bar.) meets Natasha Rostova (sop.) at a ball. Prince Anatol Kuragin (ten.) endears himself to Natasha, but Pierre Bezukhov (ten.) reveals to Natasha that Anatol is already married. Napoleon (bar.) invades Russia. General Kutuzov (bass) retreats, and Moscow is taken, Natasha finds Andrey dying among the wounded. Finally the French army retreats but the city is set alight by the inhabitants from the country, and the Russians are victorious.

Ward, David, b. Dumbarton, 3 July 1922. Scottish bass. He studied in London and Munich, and made his début in London with

Sadler's Wells Opera in 1953 as the Old Bard in Boughton's *The Immortal Hour*. He first appeared at Covent Garden in 1960 as Pogner in *Die Meistersinger*, and sang leading bass roles there until his retirement. He was especially admired in Wagner and Verdi, and was a notable Wotan. He made his Met début in 1964 as Sarastro. His final role at Covent Garden was the Grand Inquisitor in *L'Africaine* in 1978.

Warren, Leonard, b. New York, 21 Apr 1911; d. New York, 4 Mar 1960. American baritone. He studied in New York and made his début at the Met in 1939 as Paolo in *Simon Boccanegra*. He became the Met's leading Verdi baritone until his death, which occurred during a performance of *La Forza del Destino*. His voice was powerful and of great range.

Watson, Claire, b. New York, 3 Feb 1927. American soprano. She studied in New York with Elisabeth Schumann and in Vienna with Otto Klemperer, and made her début in Graz in 1951 as Desdemona. She was a leading soprano with the Munich Opera from 1958 until her retirement in 1976, and sang mainly in Mozart, Strauss and Wagner roles. She made her Covent Garden début in 1958 as the Marschallin. She was a sensitive artist with a most sympathetic stage presence.

Weber, Carl Maria von, b. Eutin, ?18 Nov 1786; d. London, 5 June 1826. German composer. One of the leading figures of the Romantic movement in Germany, he composed, apart from fragmentary and unfinished pieces, eight operas of which the earliest to be performed was *Das Waldmädchen* (Freiberg, 1800), which was reworked as *Silvana* and staged again in Frankfurt in 1810. *Peter Schmoll und seine Nachbarn* (Augsburg, 1803) reveals the teenage composer's already developing gift for melody, and *Abu Hassan* (Munich, 1811) is a delightful 1-act comedy. Weber's masterpiece, *Der Freischütz*, produced in Berlin in 1821, achieved an immediate popularity by virtue of its romantic atmosphere and its feeling for German nature and myth. The composer seemed to lose his direction and his confidence after *Der Freischütz*. He abandoned *Die drei Pintos*, which was performed in a version completed and edited

by Gustav Mahler in 1888; he was hampered by a naive and undramatic libretto in *Euryanthe* (Vienna, 1823); and although *Oberon* (London, 1826) is full of musical riches it too is vitiated by the mould into which it was forced by Planché's English-language text and its conventions.

Weber, Ludwig, b. Vienna, 29 July 1899; d. Vienna, 9 Dec 1974. Austrian bass. He studied in Vienna and made his début there in 1920 as Fiorello in *Il Barbiere di Siviglia*. He was a leading bass in Munich from 1932-45, and in Vienna from 1945 till his retirement in 1960. He was regarded as one of the finest Wagner basses of the century, and was also a distinguished Baron Ochs, and Rocco. He sang at Covent Garden frequently between 1936-9 and again after the war, and appeared regularly in the post-war Bayreuth seasons from 1951.

Weill, Kurt, b. Dessau, 2 Mar 1900; d. New York, 3 Apr 1950. German composer. His first operas were 1-act pieces, *Der Protagonist* (Dresden, 1926), *Royal Palace* (Berlin, 1927) and *Der Zar lässt sich photographieren* (Leipzig, 1928), but it was with *Die Dreigroschenoper*, which he wrote in collaboration with Bertolt Brecht, that he achieved his first popular success, in Berlin in 1928. A number of other works with Brecht followed, didactic in intent and deliberately simple in musical style: *Happy End* (Berlin, 1929), *Aufstieg und Fall der Stadt Mahagonny* (Leipzig, 1930), and *Der Jasager* (Berlin, 1930). When their political ideas began to diverge (Brecht remained a hard-line communist), Weill turned to other librettists. *Die Bürgschaft*, its libretto by Caspar Neher, was staged in Berlin in 1932, and *Der Silbersee* (its text by Georg Kaiser) in Leipzig in 1933. Forced to leave Germany as a Jew, Weill renewed his partnership with Brecht briefly in *Die sieben Todsünden* (Paris, 1933), then made his way via London to New York where, in due course, he became a celebrated Broadway composer, adapting his German style, and something of his old intent, to the requirements of the American musical, to which he made important contributions with such works as *Johnny Johnson* (1936), *Knickerbocker Holiday* (1938), *Lady in the Dark* (1941), *One Touch of Venus* (1943), *Street Scene* (1947), *Down in the Valley* (an opera for college performance,

1948), and *Lost in the Stars* (1949). With Maxwell Anderson, who had written the libretti of *Knickerbocker Holiday* and *Lost in the Stars*, Weill was at work on a musical play, *Huckleberry Finn* (based on Mark Twain), when he died.

Weinberger, Jaromír, b. Prague, 8 Jan 1896; d. St Petersburg, Florida, 8 Aug 1967. Czech composer. He achieved a great success with his opera, *Shvanda the Bagpiper*, which was first staged in Prague in 1927, and soon afterwards translated into German, Slovenian, Hungarian, Croatian, Finnish, Lettish, Bulgarian, French, Danish and Polish, and produced in a great many countries. It remains the most popular Czech opera after Smetana's *Bartered Bride*. Weinberger composed three more operas (one of them a setting of Bret Harte's *The Outcasts of Poker Flat*) and four operettas, none of which achieved a comparable success.

Weingartner, Felix von, b. Zara, Dalmatia, 2 June 1863; d. Winterthur, 7 May 1942. Austrian conductor and composer. A leading conductor of opera in German and Austrian theatres between 1884-1939, he conducted *Parsifal* and *Tannhäuser* at Covent Garden in 1939. He composed nine operas, all but one of which were performed, though without great success.

Welitsch, Ljuba, b. Borisovo, 10 July 1913. Austrian soprano of Bulgarian birth. She studied in Vienna, and made her début in Sofia in a small role in *Louise* in 1934. From 1940-64 she was a member of the Vienna Staatsoper, with whom she made her London début in 1947 as Salome, her most famous role, which she had first sung at a special performance in Vienna in 1944 for its composer's eightieth birthday. A singer of exciting temperament with a beautiful dramatic soprano voice, she excelled as Donna Anna, Aida, Tosca, and Musetta. After an illness in the mid-1950s her voice lost much of its sheen and its carrying power, but she continued to sing in small roles in opera and operetta in Vienna.

Welting, Ruth, b. Memphis, Tenn. 11 May 1949. American soprano. She studied in New York, Rome and Paris, and made her début in 1970 with New York City Opera as

Blondchen in *Die Entführung aus dem Serail*. She sings such lyric coloratura roles as Norina in *Don Pasquale*, Zerbinetta in *Ariadne auf Naxos*, and Adele in *Die Fledermaus*, and made her first appearance at Covent Garden in 1975 as Rosina in *Il Barbiere di Siviglia*. She made her Met début the following year as Zerbinetta, and has sung there frequently, her Olympia in *Les Contes d'Hoffmann* in 1982 being acclaimed.

Werther. Opera in 4 acts by Massenet. Libretto by Édouard Blau, Paul Milliet and Georges Hartmann, based on the novel *Die Leiden des jungen Werthers* (1774) by Goethe. First performed Vienna, 16 Feb 1892, in German. First performed in French, Geneva, 27 Dec 1892.

Werther (ten.) loves Charlotte (mezzo-sop.) who is engaged to Albert (bar.). He travels in the hope of forgetting her, but when he returns to find her married to Albert, he kills himself.

White, Willard, b. Jamaica, 10 Oct 1946. West Indian bass. He studied in New York, and made his début with New York City Opera in 1974 as Colline in *La Bohème*. He has sung with a number of American and

Ljuba Welitsch as Salome in 1947

European opera companies, and in 1976 made his London opera début with English National Opera as Seneca in Monteverdi's *L' Incoronazione di Poppea*, having appeared in London earlier in the same year as Porgy in a concert performance of *Porgy and Bess*. He sang the King in Prokofiev's *Love for Three Oranges* at Glyndebourne in 1982.

Widdop, Walter, b. Norland, nr Halifax, 19 Apr 1892; d. London, 6 Sept 1949. English tenor. He made his début with the British National Opera Company in 1923 as Radames, and performed major Wagner roles at Covent Garden in the 1920-30s. He sang Lohengrin's Farewell at a Promenade concert in London the night before he died.

Williamson, Malcolm, b. Sydney, 21 Nov 1931. Australian composer. Of his nine operas, written in an accessible if eclectic style, the most successful are *Our Man in Havana* (based on Graham Greene's novel), staged in London in 1963; *The Violins of Saint-Jacques* (London, 1966); and *Lucky Peter's Journey* (London, 1969). He was appointed Master of the Queen's Music in 1975.

Windgassen, Wolfgang, b. Annemasse, France, 26 June 1914; d. Stuttgart, 5 Sept 1974. German tenor. His parents were singers, and he studied with his father, Fritz Windgassen. He made his début in Pforzheim in 1941 as Alvaro in *La Forza del Destino*. From 1945-72 he sang leading roles with the Stuttgart Opera, and became the leading Wagner tenor of the 1950-60s. He sang at Bayreuth each season from 1951, when he made his début as Parsifal, to 1970, and appeared at most of the leading European opera houses. He first sang at Covent Garden in 1955, and at the Met in 1957. Although his voice was somewhat light for such roles as Siegfried and Tristan, he was a fine musician and a conscientious artist, and his performances invariably gave great pleasure.

Wixell, Ingvar, b. Luleå, 7 May 1931. Swedish baritone. He studied in Stockholm, and made his opera début there in 1955 as Papageno. He first appeared at Covent Garden in 1960 as Ruggiero in *Alcina* with the Royal Swedish Opera. He became a leading Verdi baritone, and first returned to Covent Garden in 1972 in the title-role of *Simon Boccanegra*, making his Met début the following year as Rigoletto. He has a high baritone voice of impressive timbre, and a powerful stage personality. He is, however, almost as renowned for cancelling his scheduled performances as for singing them. In 1982 he sang Scarpia in Paris with great success.

Wolf, Hugo, b. Windischgraz, Styria, 13 Mar 1860; d. Vienna 22 Feb 1903. Austrian composer. Renowned for his Lieder, he began an opera, *Konig Alboin*, when he was sixteen, but wrote no more than twenty-one bars. His only completed opera, *Der Corregidor*, was staged in Mannheim in 1896. A slow-moving and undramatic work, into which the composer inserted two of his songs, it is rarely performed. In 1897 Wolf began a third opera, *Manuel Venegas*, of which he completed five scenes which were given a concert performance in Mannheim in 1903.

Wolf-Ferrari, Ermanno, b. Venice, 12 Jan 1876; d. Venice, 21 Jan 1948. German-Italian composer. Born of a German father and an Italian mother, he studied art in Rome and Munich, intending to become a painter, with music as a part-time activity. His operas, though all but one are written to Italian libretti, reveal the influence of German romanticism and specifically of Wagner. His earliest success was with his fourth opera, *Le Donne Curiose*, staged in Munich in 1903. Both it and his next opera, *I Quattro Rusteghi* (Munich, 1906), are based on Goldoni comedies. *Il Segreto di Susanna* (Munich, 1909), a 1-act comedy, became his most popular work, but his incursion into *verismo* drama with *I Gioielli della Madonna* (Berlin, 1911) was less successful. After World War I, which had a profound psychological effect on him, Wolf-Ferrari composed little for several years. He worked from 1917-25 on *Das Himmelskleid*, a failure when it was produced in Munich in 1927, and made an unsuccessful attempt to recapture his earlier flair for comedy with *Sly* (Milan, 1927) and *La Vedova Scaltra* (Rome, 1931). His final three operas were equally unsuccessful.

Wolfram (bar.). A minstrel and friend of Tannhäuser, in Wagner's *Tannhäuser*.

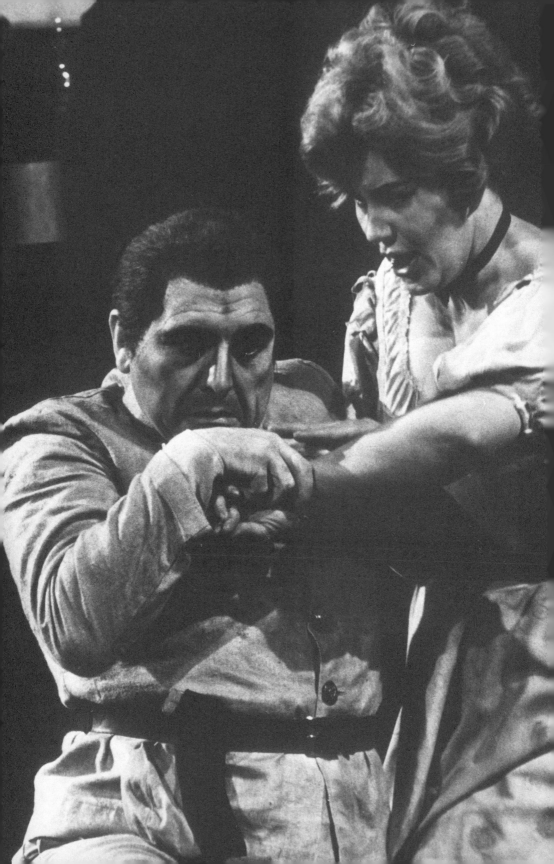

Geraint Evans in the title-role of Berg's *Wozzeck* at Covent Garden.

Wotan (bass-bar.). The ruler of the gods, in Wagner's *Der Ring des Nibelungen*.

Wozzeck. Opera in 3 acts by Berg. Libretto by the composer after the play *Woyzeck* (1836) by Georg Büchner. First performed Berlin, 14 Dec 1925.

From Büchner's twenty-six scenes, Berg chose fifteen, dividing them into three acts each of five scenes. The simple-minded soldier, Wozzeck (bar.), is patronized by his Captain (ten.), experimented upon by a neurotic doctor (bass), and betrayed by his mistress, Marie (sop.), who allows herself to be seduced by a Drum Major (ten.). In a fit of jealousy, Wozzeck stabs Marie, near a lake in the forest. He returns later to dispose of the knife which he has left by Marie's body, but wades into the lake and drowns. In the final scene of the opera, children are playing, among them Marie's little boy. Other children rush in with the news that Marie has been found murdered, but the child continues uncomprehendingly to play on his hobby-horse.

Wranitzky, Paul, b. Nová Říše, Moravia, 30 Dec 1756; d. Vienna, 26 Sept 1808. Austrian composer. He composed several operas and operettas which were performed in Vienna between 1789-1805, the best known of which is the earliest, *Oberon, König der Elfen* (Vienna, 1789), a Singspiel which has been revived in recent years in Vienna. The enthusiastic reception of *Oberon* in 1789 prompted Schikaneder to conceive *Die Zauberflöte*. Mozart's setting of Schikaneder's text bears certain resemblances to Wranitzky's *Oberon* score.

Wreckers, The. Opera in 3 acts by Smyth. Libretto by the composer, originally written in French as *Les Naufrageurs*, based on a play by Henry Brewster. First performed (in German, as *Strandrecht*), Leipzig, 11 Nov 1906. First stage performance in English (in a translation by the composer and Alma Strettell), London, 22 June 1909.

The inhabitants of a Cornish fishing village make their living by scavenging ships wrecked off their shore. Thirza (mezzo-sop), married to the local preacher Pascoe (bass-bar.) but in love with the young fisherman, Mark (ten.), helps Mark to light a bonfire to warn ships. Pascoe is suspected of having lit the fire, but Mark confesses. Avis (sop.), in love with Mark, tries to save him by claiming that he had spent the night with her, but no one believes her. Thirza and Mark are condemned to death by drowning.

Wunderlich, Fritz, b. Kusel, 26 Sept 1930; d. Heidelberg, 17 Sept 1966. German tenor. He studied in Freiburg, made his début there as Tamino in a student production of *Die Zauberflöte* in 1954, and his professional début the following year in Stuttgart in the same role. He quickly became Germany's leading lyric tenor, joined the Munich Opera in 1960, and from 1962 also performed regularly in Vienna. He sang not only the Mozart roles but also Ernesto in *Don Pasquale*, Alfredo in *La Traviata* and Lensky in *Eugene Onegin* with mellifluous tone and sensitive musicianship. He sang Don Ottavio in *Don Giovanni* to great acclaim at Covent Garden in 1965. His death at the age of thirty-six the following year was the result of an accident.

Xenia (sop.). Daughter of Tsar Boris, in Mussorgsky's *Boris Godunov*.

Xyndas, Spyridon, b. Corfu, ?1812; d. Athens, 12 Nov 1896. Greek composer. He studied in Corfu and Naples, and composed six operas which were popular in Greece in the second half of the 19th c. *The Parliamentary Candidate* (in Greek: *Oypopsifios vouleftis*), first performed in Corfu in 1867, was the first opera to be composed to a Greek libretto.

Yakar, Rachel, b. Lyons, 3 Mar 1938. French soprano. She studied in Paris, and began her career in Strasbourg in 1963, later singing leading roles in Paris and elsewhere in France, Belgium, Germany and Austria. She is admired especially for her Mozart

Alexander Young (right) in the title-role of Rossini's *Count Ory* at Sadler's Wells in 1963.

roles, among them Donna Elvira in *Don Giovanni* and Celia in *Lucio Silla*. She sang the title-role in *Jenůfa* at the Paris Opéra in 1980, and the Marschallin in *Der Rosenkavalier* at Glyndebourne in 1980 and 1982.

Yaroslavna (sop.). Igor's wife, in Borodin's *Prince Igor*.

Yeomen of the Guard, The. Operetta in 2 acts by Sullivan. Libretto by W.S. Gilbert. First performed London, 3 Oct 1888.

Under sentence of death, Colonel Fairfax (ten.) undergoes a form of marriage with Elsie (sop.), to the dismay of Elsie's admirer, the jester Jack Point (bar.). When all ends happily for Fairfax and his bride, Jack Point dies of a broken heart.

Yniold (sop. or boy treble). Golaud's young son, in Debussy's *Pelléas et Mélisande*.

Young, Alexander, b. London, 18 Oct 1920. English tenor. He studied in London, joined the Glyndebourne chorus in 1948, and made his solo début with the Glyndebourne company at the 1950 Edinburgh Festival, as Scaramuccio in *Ariadne auf Naxos*. He has sung a wide range of lyric tenor roles with British companies, among them Tom Rakewell in the British première of *The Rake's Progress* (Glyndebourne, 1953), Count Ory, Almaviva (in *Il Barbiere di Siviglia*) and Eisenstein (in *Die Fledermaus*) for Sadler's Wells Opera, and Matteo in *Arabella* at Covent Garden. He sang David in *Die Meistersinger* in San Francisco in 1965, with conspicuous success. Though in recent years he has concentrated on teaching, he was heard in the role of Bajazet in two operas: in 1977 in Iain Hamilton's *Tamburlaine* on BBC radio, and in 1978 at Hammersmith, London, in Handel's *Tamerlano*.

Z

Zaccaria (bass). Hebrew high priest in Verdi's *Nabucco*.

Zaïde. Opera in 2 acts (unfinished) by Mozart. Libretto by Johann Andreas Schachtner, after an earlier libretto written by Franz Joseph Sebastiani, *Das Serail* (1779). First performed Frankfurt, 27 Jan 1866.

Zaïde (sop.) and Gomatz (ten.) attempt to escape from the Sultan Soliman (ten.), with the help of Allazim (bass), overseer of the Sultan's slaves. They are recaptured, and the opera ends at the point where Zaïde, Gomatz and Allazim beg for the Sultan's mercy.

Zandonai, Riccardo, b. Sacco di Rovereto, 30 May 1883; d. Pesaro, 5 June 1944. Italian composer. The publisher Ricordi hoped to launch him as the successor of Puccini, but of his thirteen operas only four were reasonably successful when first staged. *Conchita* (1911) was followed by his finest opera, *Francesca da Rimini* (1914), which is still quite frequently performed in Italy and appears in the Met 1983-4 programme. *Giulietta e Romeo* (1922) and *I Cavalieri di Ekebù* (1925) contain incidental musical delights, but neither has managed to hold the stage.

Zar und Zimmermann *(Tsar and Carpenter)*. Opera in 3 acts by Lortzing. Libretto by the composer, based on the play (1818) by Anne Honoré Joseph Mélesville, Jean Toussaint Merle, and Eugène Cantiran de Boirie. First performed Leipzig, 22 Dec 1837.

Peter the Great (bar.), working in the Saardam shipyards under a pseudonym, befriends Peter Ivanov (ten.), a fellow Russian and a deserter from the Tsar's army. A confusion of indentities between the two Peters ends happily for both. They return to Russia, the Tsar promising Peter Ivanov a safe conduct.

zarzuela. A type of Spanish romantic operetta, or opera with dialogue between the numbers, which has flourished in Spain since the 17th c.

Zauberflöte, Die *(The Magic Flute)*. Opera in 2 acts by Mozart. Libretto by Emanuel Schikaneder, derived from a number of sources. First performed Vienna, 30 Sept 1791.

Tamino (ten.) sets out to rescue Pamina (sop.), daughter of the Queen of Night (sop.), from the clutches of Sarastro (bass),

345

A scene from Houston Grand Opera's staging of *Die Zauberflöte* in 1980.

with the help of a magic flute. He is accompanied, reluctantly, by the birdcatcher, Papageno (bar.). Tamino becomes convinced that Sarastro is, in fact, a high priest of benevolence and wisdom, and he and Pamina undergo tests before being initiated into Sarastro's brotherhood. Meanwhile Papageno has been searching for a soulmate, Papagena (sop.), whom he eventually acquires. The Queen of Night and her attendants are vanquished by the radiance of the sun, and the opera ends with a hymn of praise to Isis and Osiris.

Zaza. Opera in 4 acts by Leoncavallo. Libretto by the composer, based on a French play by Pierre Berton and Charles Simon. First performed Milan, 10 Nov 1900.

Zaza (sop.), a music-hall performer, has an affair with Milio Dufresne (ten.), but returns to her former lover, Cascart (bar.) when she considers Dufresne has treated her unfairly by not revealing the existence of his wife and child.

Zdenka (sop.). Arabella's sister, in Richard Strauss's *Arabella*.

Zeani, Virginia, b. Solovastru, 25 Oct 1928. Romanian soprano. She studied in Bucharest and Milan, and made her début in Bologna in 1948 as Violetta in *La Traviata*. This was also the role of her first appearances in London (1953), Vienna (1957), New York (1966) and Moscow (1969). Acclaimed in bel canto operas, she began in 1970 to undertake more dramatic roles such as Aida and Tosca. She is married to the bass, Nicola Rossi-Lemeni.

Zeffirelli, Franco, b. Florence, 12 Feb 1923. Italian producer and designer. He began as a designer, working with Luchino Visconti. His first major opera production was *La Cenerentola* at La Scala in 1953, after which he worked mainly in opera for several years, his best-known productions including *Lucia di Lammermoor* (1959) at Covent Garden with Joan Sutherland, *Tosca* (1964) at Covent Garden with Callas and Gobbi, and Barber's *Antony and Cleopatra* (1966) at the opening of the new Met in Lincoln Center in 1966.

Zeller, Karl, b. St. Peter in der Au, 19 June; d. Baden, nr Vienna, 17 Aug 1898. Austrian composer. He composed seven comic operas and operettas, most of which were produced in Vienna, from 1876 to the end of his life. His two greatest successes were *Der Vogelhändler* (1891), which is still popular in Austria, and *Der Obersteiger* (1894), which is less frequently revived but from which one song, *'Sei nicht bös'* (Don't be cross), is widely known.

Zemlinsky, Alexander von, b. Vienna, 14 Oct 1871; d. Larchmont, N.Y., 15 Mar 1942. Austrian composer and conductor. He conducted opera in Vienna, Prague and Berlin between 1906-32 and then again in Vienna from 1933 until the Anschluss when he fled to the United States. He composed eight operas, all but the last of which were successfully staged in Austria and Germany. They include *Es war einmal* (Vienna, 1900), *Kleider machen Leute* (Vienna, 1910), *Eine florentinische Tragödie* (Stuttgart, 1917), and *Der Zwerg* (Cologne, 1922).

Zenatello, Giovanni, b. Verona, 22 Feb 1876; d. New York, 11 Feb 1949. Italian tenor. He began his career in Belluno in 1898 in the baritone role of Silvio in *Pagliacci,* and the following year made a fresh start in Naples, in the same opera but in the tenor role of Canio. He first appeared at Covent Garden in 1905 as Riccardo in *Un Ballo in Maschera*. He was a famous Otello in Verdi's opera, performing the role more than three hundred times. He was instrumental in launching the annual performances at the Arena in Verona, and was manager there for several seasons.

Zerbinetta (sop.). The leader of the troupe of *commedia dell' arte* players, in Strauss's *Ariadne auf Naxos*.

Zerlina (sop.). The peasant girl, the bride of Masetto, whom Giovanni attempts to seduce on her wedding day, in Mozart's *Don Giovanni*.

Zigeunerbaron, Der *(The Gipsy Baron).* Operetta in 3 acts by Johann Strauss. Libretto by Ignaz Schnitzer, based on a story, *Saffi,* by Maurus Jókai. First performed Vienna, 24 Oct 1885.

The complex plot tells of Sandor

Barinkay (ten.) who returns to claim his ancestral lands only to find them occupied by gipsies, with one of whom, Saffi (sop.), he falls in love. It is subsequently discovered that Saffi is of noble birth, which puts her out of Sandor's reach until, after he has distinguished himself in the war with Spain, he is ennobled, and decides to claim the title of Gipsy Baron.

Zingarelli, Niccolò Antonio, b. Naples, 4 Apr 1752; d. Torre del Greco, nr Naples, 5

May 1837. Italian composer. The last major composer of *opera seria*, he wrote more than forty operas, of which the best known is *Giulietta e Romeo*, based on Shakespeare and first performed in Milan in 1796. He composed no operas after 1811, believing that he had been eclipsed by the emergence of Rossini.

Zweig, Stefan, b. Vienna, 28 Nov 1881; d. Petropolis, nr Rio de Janeiro, 22 Feb 1942. Austrian writer. For his friend Richard

Franco Zeffirelli

Strauss he wrote the libretto of *Die schweigsame Frau*. As Zweig was Jewish, the opera's première in Dresden in 1935 was attended by demonstrations. Zweig's ideas for future libretti were entrusted by Strauss to Joseph Gregor to write. They became, in due course, *Friedenstag* and *Daphne*. Another idea by Zweig became the basis of *Capriccio*, written by Clemens Krauss.

Zylis-Gara, Teresa, b. Landvarov, nr Vilnius, 23 Jan 1935. Polish soprano. She studied in Lódź and made her début in Cracow in 1956 in the title-role of Moniuszko's *Halka*. Her international career began in Munich in 1960, and she became a much sought-after performer of such roles as Violetta, the Countess in *Le Nozze di Figaro*, Desdemona, Tosca and the Marschallin. She has an attractive and well-produced voice and is a dignified actress. She first appeared in Great Britain in 1965, at Glyndebourne (as Octavian) and at Covent Garden (as Violetta). In the same year she made her Met début as Donna Elvira. She was highly acclaimed in Geneva in 1982, as Lisa in Tchaikovsky's *Queen of Spades*.

Leading Opera Houses

BARCELONA: Teatro Liceo

Though the opera house in Barcelona is known internationally as the Teatro Liceo, the Catalan form of its full name is Gran Teatro del Liceu. First built in 1847, destroyed by fire in 1861, and rebuilt and reopened in the following year, it is a handsome theatre with a seating capacity of 3,000. The first opera in the Catalan language, actually a one-act operetta, *A la Voreta del Mar (On the Seashore)* by Juan Goula, was performed at the Liceo in July 1881. A concert performance of excerpts from Falla's *Atlántida* was given on 24 November 1961, seven months before the opera's stage première at La Scala, Milan.

By the terms of its charter, the Teatro Liceo must stage at least one Spanish opera each year. Its international reputation is higher than that of the opera house in Spain's capital city, Madrid, and its regular winter seasons of opera extend from November until March, with performances two or three times a week. Occasionally, guest performances are given by visiting companies from abroad, and even in the Liceo's own productions guest singers from abroad play a predominant part. Distinguished Spanish singers of world fame also appear frequently at the Liceo, among them Montserrat Caballé, José Carreras and Giacomo Aragall. In addition to the Italian and French repertoire, the operas of Wagner are popular in Barcelona and are regularly staged at the Liceo.

BAYREUTH: Wagner Festival Theatre

Since 1876, opera in this small German town of about 70,000 inhabitants has meant Wagner. (A century earlier, however, more varied operatic fare was provided in the beautiful baroque Markgräfliches Opernhaus which opened in 1748 with an opera by Hasse. Nowadays this theatre is used only for occasional performances, as often as not by students.) The Wagner Festival Theatre, a temporary structure of wood and brick which opened in 1876 with the first complete performance of *Der Ring des Nibelungen*, is still in use for the annual Wagner Festival which takes place in the summer. Only operas by Wagner are performed, and only those Wagner operas which the composer's descendants consider to be the works of the composer's maturity. *Die Feen, Das Liebesverbot* and *Rienzi* have never been staged at Bayreuth.

After Wagner's death in 1883, control of the theatre passed to his widow, Cosima. Their son, Siegfried, was in charge from 1909-30, and Siegfried's widow, the English-born Winifred Wagner, assumed direction of the theatre and the Festival from 1930 until the closure of all German theatres in 1944. Due mainly to Winifred's enthusiastic espousal of the Nazi cause, it was not until 1951 that the Bayreuth Festival could be launched again.

In this post-war period, the Wagner grandsons, Wieland and Wolfgang, were in control, and Wolfgang has continued as sole director since the death of his brother in 1966. Wieland's productions favoured an abstract, simpler kind of staging rather than the old naturalistic Bayreuth style. In recent years there has been a considerable amount of experimentation by younger directors. The centenary production of *Der Ring* in 1976 by Patrice Chéreau outraged half of its audience, while it delighted the other half. It was replaced in 1983 by a new production by Sir Peter Hall, to commemorate the hundredth anniversary of the death of Richard Wagner.

EAST BERLIN: Staatsoper

The Berlin Staatsoper, in the Unter den Linden which now finds itself in East Berlin, is the city's oldest opera house. Known as the Hofoper or Court Opera, the first theatre on the site, designed by Georg von Knobelsdorff, opened on 7 December 1742, with Graun's *Cleopatra e Cesare*. Closed for repairs in 1786, the theatre reopened in 1788 with Reichardt's *Andromeda*. It was closed again during the two years of French occupation in 1806-7. On the night of 18 August 1843, the opera house burned down. Modernized (with gas lighting), it opened again on 7 December 1844, with Meyerbeer's *Ein Feldlager in Schlesien* in which Jenny Lind made her Berlin début.

In the late-19th-early-20th c., though few new works of importance were produced in the theatre, the level of performance reached great heights under such conductors as Weingartner and Richard Strauss. After World War I and the collapse of the German monarchy, the now re-named Staatsoper became one of Europe's leading opera houses. During the 1930-40s its company contained virtually all of Germany's finest singers. When the theatre was destroyed by bombs in 1945, the company transferred to the Admiralspalast. In 1955, having been rebuilt to Knobelsdorff's original 18th-c. designs, the Staatsoper reopened in a now-divided Berlin. It is now one of East Berlin's two opera houses, performing a fairly conventional repertory with less impressive casts than in the past. (More controversial works and productions are to be found in East Berlin's Komische Oper.)

WEST BERLIN: Deutsche Oper

The present opera house on the Bismarck-strasse opened on 24 September 1961 with a production of Mozart's *Don Giovanni*. The theatre which it replaced had been built in 1912, as an addition to an undivided city's already thriving operatic life, and had opened its doors in November of that year with *Fidelio*. At that time it was known as the Deutsches Opernhaus. In 1925, the city administration took it over and renamed it the Städtische Oper (Civic Opera). Its performances in the 1920s conducted by Bruno Walter began to rival those at the Staatsoper in the Unter den Linden. With the rise to power of the Nazis, Goebbels took the theatre over and as a state theatre it became the Deutsches Opernhaus again. After the house was destroyed by bombs in 1942 the company moved first to the Admiralspalast and then, in September 1945, to the Theater des Westens in Kantstrasse. At this time it reverted to its title of Städtische Oper. Between 1945-61 when it was able to move back into the reconstructed opera house on the Bismarckstrasse, the company expanded its repertory and staged the premières of several new German operas.

The present Deutsche Oper maintains a large repertory, and performs seven nights a week throughout the year, with a summer break of several weeks in July-August. Though German singers and conductors predominate, international artists frequently appear as guests.

BRUSSELS: Théâtre Royal de la Monnaie

The first Théâtre Royal de la Monnaie was built in 1700. Throughout the 18th c. its repertoire was dominated by French operas, especially those of Lully, Campra, and the *opéras comiques* of Favart. A riot in the theatre during a performance of Auber's *La Muette de Portici* on 25 August 1830 helped to spark off the revolution which led to the creation of the modern state of Belgium. The theatre's most successful period was between 1875-89 during which time the premières of Massenet's *Hérodiade* (1881), Reyer's *Sigurd* (1884), Chabrier's *Gwendoline* (1886) and Godard's *Jocelyn* (1888) were given. Melba made her opera début at the Monnaie in 1887 as Gilda in *Rigoletto*. During World War I, the occupying Germans organized opera seasons, which included *Der Rosenkavalier* conducted by its composer, Richard Strauss. In 1963, for financial reasons, the city of Brussels relinquished ownership of the theatre, and it became a national responsibility. The theatre's recent operatic history has been undistinguished, the emphasis in the 1960s having been on ballet with the foundation of Maurice Béjart's Ballet du XXème Siècle. However, a new administration hopes to restore the opera house to its former international standard.

BUDAPEST: Állami Operaház

Regular performances of opera in the Hungarian capital city date from the late-18th c. A national Hungarian opera slowly developed during the 19th c., though the most popular operas continued to be Italian until the emergence of the Hungarian composer Sándor Erkel. The former Hungarian Royal Opera House is now called the Magyar Állami Operaház or Hungarian State Opera House. Designed by Miklós Ybl, it has a seating capacity of approximately 1,400. The theatre's foundation stone was laid in September 1875, but financial difficulties prevented much work being done until 1882. It opened on 27 September 1884, and boasted of having the first hydraulic sinkable stage on the Asphaleia system in Europe. The entire building cost a mere £43,000. The opera company has had a number of distinguished chief conductors, among them Gustav Mahler (1888-91), Artur Nikisch (1893-5), and Otto Klemperer, a Mahler protégé (1947-51). The present company contains some excellent singers, among them the sopranos Sylvia Sass and Eva Marton who have also made distinguished international careers. (Budapest's second opera house, where smaller-scale works and modern Hungarian operas are performed, is the former Civic Theatre known since 1951 as the Erkel Theatre.)

BUENOS AIRES: Teatro Colón

The focus of operatic activity in Argentina is at the Teatro Colón in Buenos Aires. The original Teatro Colón opened on 25 April 1857 with a performance of Verdi's *La Traviata*, and soon became the centre of the country's operatic life, performing a predominantly Italian repertory. After the theatre's destruction in 1889, operas were performed in a smaller theatre until the present Colón, seating nearly 2,500 with standing room for a further 1,000, opened on 25 May 1908 with Verdi's *Aida*. The repertory was widened to include German, Czech and Russian opera, and in 1922 a complete *Ring* with German artists, including Lotte Lehmann as Sieglinde, was conducted by Weingartner. In 1931, when the Colón became a municipally owned theatre, the season included several operas conducted by Klemperer, among them his last complete *Ring* in any opera house. Standards were low during the Perón regime, but after 1955 the theatre began to regain its former traditions. The change of government in 1973 led to an upheaval in the administration, since when the Colón has been undergoing difficulties. World-famous singers are still to be heard there from time to time, though as often as not in productions which are less than first-rate.

CHICAGO: Civic Opera House

The first opera to be performed in Chicago, Illinois, was Bellini's *La Sonnambula* in 1850. The Crosby Opera House, opened in 1865, was destroyed in the great fire of 1871, but a second opera house, the Auditorium, in which opera is still occasionally performed, was opened in 1889 with *Roméo et Juliette*. In 1910 the Chicago Grand Opera Company was formed. Mary Garden, who sang Mélisande in Debussy's opera on the second evening (4 November 1910), became an important figure in Chicago opera, singing with the company until 1932 and for the 1921-2 season also acting as general director. It was during that season that Prokofiev's *The Love For Three Oranges* was given its world première in Chicago. After 1922, the company was known as the Chicago Civic

GLYNDEBOURNE: Opera House

The annual summer festival of opera in the theatre attached to the country house of the Christie family in Sussex was begun by John Christie in 1934 as a Mozart festival, primarily in order to allow his wife, the soprano Audrey Mildmay, to sing such roles as Susanna and Zerlina. The theatre at first seated no more than 300: its present capacity is 800. In 1938 Verdi's *Macbeth* entered the repertoire, which was further extended in the post-war years. Although Mozart remains staple fare at Glyndebourne, the other major composers of opera, with the exception of Wagner, are now also represented. In the 1930s and again in 1950-1, Fritz Busch was chief conductor, and the producer of the operas was Carl Ebert. After Busch's death in 1951, Carl Ebert continued as producer (until 1959) and Vittorio Gui, who introduced Rossini into the repertory, became chief conductor. Since 1960, a number of conductors and producers have been associated with Glyndebourne, among them John Pritchard, Raymond Leppard, Bernard Haitink, Günther Rennert, John Cox and Peter Hall. The post-war singers at Glyndebourne have included Janet Baker, Ileana Cotrubas, Sena Jurinac, Elisabeth Söderström, Richard Lewis and George Shirley. Performances and productions continue to be of high standard, mainly due to the time taken in preparing and rehearsing the musical and dramatic presentation of the operas. Usually five operas are given each summer, the season running from late May to early August.

Opera, and in 1929 it moved into a newly-built Civic Opera House. The depression caused performances to be mounted only on an *ad hoc* basis, and it was not until 1954 that the present company, now known as the Lyric Opera of Chicago, came into existence. Under the artistic direction of Carol Fox, the company achieved an enviable standard, staging regular yearly seasons with international singers. The present music director and chief conductor is Bruno Bartoletti. The company continues to perform in the Civic Opera House, a handsome, huge auditorium seating 3,600, which opened on 4 November 1929, with a performance of *Aida*. Operas are given in the winter months with internationally famous singers. A second opera company gives spring or summer seasons in the Auditorium, with new young American singers and conductors.

LONDON: Royal Opera House, Covent Garden

The first theatre on the Covent Garden site opened on 7 December 1732 with Congreve's play, *The Way of the World*. Several of Handel's operas were performed there, but the theatre was never exclusively an opera house. It was destroyed by fire in 1808, and the second theatre opened the following year. Weber's *Oberon,* specially written for the theatre, was given its première there in 1826, and in 1847 the name became the Royal Italian Opera. It, too, was destroyed by fire in 1856, and the present theatre opened on 15 May 1858 with a performance of Meyerbeer's *Les Huguenots.*

Since 1858, there have been seasons of opera every year with the exception of periods during both World Wars. Between 1858-1939, the world's most famous singers and conductors appeared at Covent Garden, in a varied repertoire. Until the late-19th c., all operas were given in Italian. It later became the custom to perform most operas in the original languages, except for special seasons with mainly British artists when performances were in English. The period between the wars, 1919-1939, found Covent Garden at its peak, with operas performed by such singers as Melchior, Lehmann, Leider, Schorr, Tauber, Kipnis, Martinelli, Supervia and Flagstad, and conductors who included Walter, Beecham, Furtwängler and Weingartner.

The theatre was used as a dance hall during World War II, but became an opera house again in 1946 when a permanent company was installed to perform opera in English. The first music director, from 1946-51, was the Austrian Karl Rankl. He was succeeded by Rafael Kubelik, Georg Solti and Colin Davis. Over the years, it gradually became the custom to perform operas in their original languages. A number of new British operas, mainly by Britten and Tippett, have been staged, and although the company suffers from the lack of an artistic director, and from having to share the theatre with The Royal Ballet, it has continued to maintain its standards. Among distinguished productions in the post-war years have been *Otello* with Ramon Vinay and, later, James McCracken; *Lucia di Lammermoor* with Joan Sutherland; Visconti's *Don Carlos* conducted by Giulini, with Vickers, Brouwenstijn, Gobbi, Christoff and Barbieri; *Boris Godunov* with Christoff; *Falstaff* with Gobbi; *Fidelio,* conducted by Klemperer, with Jurinac and Vickers; *Eugene Onegin* with Mazurok and Gedda; *Arabella* with Della Casa and Fischer-Dieskau; and *Peter Grimes* with Peter Pears. Hans Hotter's Wotan dominated the productions of Wagner's *Ring* until his retirement, and some fine Wagner singers in recent years have included Gwyneth Jones, Peter Hoffmann and René Kollo. Colin Davis, who has been Music Director since 1971, has conducted a number of fine performances, especially of works by Mozart.

MILAN: Teatro alla Scala

The theatre familiarly known as La Scala was designed by Giuseppe Piermarini, built on the site of the demolished church of Santa Maria alla Scala, and opened in 1778. (Although *scala* is the Italian word for staircase or ladder, neither the theatre nor the church has anything to do with ladders. The church had been built in the first place by Regina della Scala, wife of one of the ruling family of Visconti in the fourteenth century.) The opening opera was Salieri's *Europa Riconosciuta*, played before the Austrian Archduke Ferdinand and his wife Princess Maria Ricciarda Beatrice d'Este.

La Scala quickly became the main social, intellectual and political meeting place of Milan, and the leading opera house in Italy. All the great Italian composers wrote operas which were first staged there. Rossini's *La Pietra del Paragone* (1812), *Aureliano in Palmira* (1813), *Il Turco in Italia* (1814), *La Gazza Ladra* (1817) and *Bianca e Falliero* (1819) were given their premières at La Scala; six operas by Donizetti, among them *Lucrezia Borgia* (1833) and *Maria Stuarda* (1835) were first performed there; so were Bellini's *Il Pirata* (1827), *La Straniera* (1829) and *Norma* (1831). Verdi's first four operas, *Oberto* (1839), *Un Giorno di Regno* (1840), *Nabucco* (1842) and *I Lombardi* (1843) were first staged at La Scala. Later, Italy's greatest composer professed himself dissatisfied with the standards of production and performance at La Scala, and boycotted the theatre for a quarter of a century! After *Giovanna d'Arco* (1845), the only other Verdi operas to be given their premières at La Scala were his final two masterpieces, *Otello* (1887) and *Falstaff* (1893). Three operas by Puccini were given their premières at La Scala: *Edgar* (1889), *Madama Butterfly* (1904) and *Turandot* (1926).

In the 20th c., La Scala continued to be regarded as the leading Italian opera house until well after World War II. Under Toscanini in the 1920s, with such singers as Toti dal Monte, Gilda dalla Rizza, Conchita Supervia, Aureliano Pertile, Tancredi Pasero and Mariano Stabile, high standards were maintained. Again, in the 1950s, with Callas, Gobbi, Tebaldi, Corelli, Di Stefano, and Simionato, a number of fine performances were to be heard there. The theatre's musical standards are still high, as one would expect with Claudio Abbado as artistic director. But, like most other Italian opera houses, La Scala has fallen victim to Italian political chicanery, and its artists and staff sometimes work under conditions in which the art of opera is pushed into second place. The elegant auditorium bides its time.

MOSCOW: Bolshoi Theatre

Opera was first heard in Moscow when Italian troupes visited Russia in 1731, but the first opera house to be constructed in the city opened in 1742 with Mozart's *La Clemenza di Tito*. In the 19th c., there were two principal theatres in Moscow, the Bolshoi (which means big) and the Maly (small). The Bolshoi Theatre of today has undergone renovation on several occasions, but is basically as it was when reconstructed after a fire in 1853 had virtually destroyed the building. The new theatre, with a seating capacity of 2,000, was opened in 1856 as a home for both opera and ballet.

After the Russian Revolution, the distinguished Russian tenor Leonid Sobinov was in charge of the Bolshoi for a brief period.

Over the years, the Bolshoi has become renowned for its performances of the classics of Russian opera and ballet. Though its ballet company is better known abroad than its opera ensemble, the Bolshoi is the goal of Russian singers. All operas are performed in Russian, and very few singers from outside the Soviet Union appear there. Productions tend to be conventional, and the repertoire is firmly based on Tchaikovsky, Mussorgsky, Rimsky-Korsakov, Borodin, Glinka and Prokofiev. Smaller-scale productions, sometimes more adventurous than those of the Bolshoi, are to be found at the Maly, and productions on an even larger and more lavish scale than those of the Bolshoi are sometimes mounted in the modern Palace of Congresses within the Kremlin.

MUNICH: Staatsoper

There are, at present, four opera houses in Munich, three of which are used. The oldest of the four is the Residenztheater, designed by Cuvilliés in the 1750s and known familiarly as the Cuvilliéstheater. A tiny rococo jewel of a theatre, it housed the première of Mozart's *Idomeneo* in 1781 and is still used for Mozart and for such Strauss operas as *Intermezzo* and *Capriccio*. The Theater am Gärtnerplatz is an attractive 19th-c. theatre where operas and operettas are given in German. It bears the same relationship to Munich's leading opera house, the Staatsoper, as the Vienna Volksoper does to that city's Staatsoper. The Prinzregententheater, intended mainly for Wagner performances and opened in 1901 with *Die Meistersinger*, was used as the city's leading opera house between 1945-63, while the Staatsoper, which had been destroyed by bombs, was awaiting reconstruction.

The Staatsoper, which reopened in 1963, is a completely new building on the same site as the old Hof und National Theater which stood from 1825-1943. It is the home of the Bavarian State Opera, which is probably Germany's most prestigious opera company. Performances are given throughout most of the year, and an annual summer festival presents operas by Strauss, Mozart and Wagner.

NAPLES: Teatro di San Carlo
The San Carlo was first constructed in 1737, and opened with Domenico Sarro's *Achille in Sciro*. It was destroyed by fire in February 1816, and replaced by the present theatre which was designed by Antonio Nicolini and which opened on 12 January 1817. Several operas by Rossini were first performed there, among them *Armida, Mosè, La Donna del Lago* and *Otello*. Bellini's *Bianca e Fernando* had its première at the San Carlo in 1826 and Donizetti's *Lucia di Lammermoor* in 1835. Verdi composed *Alzira* (1845) and *Luisa Miller* (1849) for the theatre, and intended *Un Ballo in Maschera* also for the San Carlo. (Censorship problems resulted in the opera having its première in Rome.)

The stage of the theatre was modernized in 1929, and a new foyer was added. During World War II, the theatre came under the management of the British forces, and was much frequented by British and American troops. A number of new Italian operas have been staged at the San Carlo in recent years, though none of any importance. The standard of performance is variable, but the somewhat shabby elegance of the theatre itself adds considerably to the pleasure of seeing opera at the San Carlo.

NEW YORK: Metropolitan Opera House

The old Metropolitan Opera House, familiarly known as the Met, a name which has passed to its successor, stood on Broadway between 39th and 40th streets, in the middle of New York's theatre district. A huge theatre with a seating capacity of 3,615, it opened on 22 October 1883 with a performance of Gounod's *Faust*. From the very beginning it was a theatre where great singers were valued above all else. Superb conductors did, of course, appear at the Met, among them Mahler, Toscanini and Bruno Walter; but until the appointment of James Levine as music director of the new Met in 1975, the artistic direction of the Met was more often than not in the hands of administrators, men like Gatti-Casazza or Rudolf Bing, and they in turn worshipped famous and expensive voices.

In the early days of the Met, the administration favoured German opera, and even non-German operas were sung in German. Later, under Gatti-Casazza, Italian opera became as important. Puccini's *La Fanciulla del West* had its première at the Met in 1910, and the same composer's *Trittico* was unveiled there in 1918. Among the most popular singers to appear there were Galli-Curci, Gigli, Ponselle, Muzio, Pinza, Jeritza, Rethberg, Leider, Lehmann, Melchior, Grace Moore, Lily Pons, Flagstad and Lawrence Tibbett. During the period from 1935-50 when the Canadian tenor Edward Johnson was the company's general manager, more young American singers were encouraged. Leonard Warren, Dorothy Kirsten, Richard Tucker, Jan Peerce, Helen Traubel, Patrice Munsel and Blanche Thebom all emerged at this time.

In the post-war years, the Met maintained its reputation as an opera house in which, whatever the quality of the stage production, one was certain to hear fine singing. Milanov, Callas, Tebaldi, Gedda, Di Stefano, Corelli, Björling, Bergonzi and Siepi appeared together with a new generation of American artists. In 1955 Marian Anderson became the first black singer to appear in a leading role at the Met, and it was not long before she was followed by Leontyne Price, Shirley Verrett, Mattiwilda Dobbs, Reri Grist, Grace Bumbry and many others.

The company moved to its new home in Lincoln Center in 1966, and the old Met was demolished. The new Met, even bigger than the old one, with a seating capacity of 3,800, opened with an opera specially commissioned for the occasion, *Antony and Cleopatra* by Samuel Barber. In recent years its productions have been more frequently worthy of an international opera house than they were in the past, and under James Levine the standard of musical preparation is remarkably high. Though the Lincoln Center building is still young, already it begins to inspire that affection which used to be lavished on the golden horseshoe of Broadway and 39th.

PARIS: Opéra

Before the French Revolution, there were several opera houses in Paris. The official title of the Opéra, both the opera house itself and the company performing in it, was Académie Royale (or Imperiale) de Musique. Public theatres proliferated to such an extent in the early days of the Revolution that Napoleon in 1807 was led to reduce the total number of theatres to eight, only three of which were musical theatres: the Opéra, the Opéra-Comique and the Odéon. The Opéra had already occupied several other theatres when, in 1821, it moved to its new premises in the rue Le Peletier where, the following year, the introduction of gas lighting revolutionized stage effects. This was the opera house in which the grand operas of Meyerbeer were staged, and for which Verdi composed *Les Vêpres Siciliennes* (1855) and *Don Carlos* (1867). It was destroyed by fire on 29 October 1873.

The new theatre, the present opera house, was designed by Charles Garnier, and is familiarly known as the Palais Garnier. When it opened on 5 January 1875 it was thought to be one of the grandest and most sumptuous opera houses in existence. It still is, and its ceremonial staircase in the foyer is as impressive now as it was in 1875. In this theatre, a number of Wagner's operas were belatedly introduced to Paris: *Lohengrin* (1891), the *Ring*, slowly, opera by opera, between 1893 (*Das Rheingold*) and 1908 (*Götterdämerung*), *Die Meistersinger* (1897) and *Parsifal* (1911). German operas made their way to Paris with great caution. Strauss's *Elektra* did not reach the Opéra until 1933.

Even *Der Rosenkavalier* had to wait until 1927, sixteen years after its Dresden première. *Wozzeck* was not performed at the Opéra until 1965.

The operas of Gounod and Massenet were staged at the Opéra, and its standards were high until the advent of World War II. In the 1920-30s, such singers as Ninon Vallin, Georges Thill and Marjorie Lawrence were to be heard there. The German occupation of Paris of course made a difference: the most important new production during the war years was of Pfitzner's *Palestrina* in 1942. After the war, the Opéra went through a bad period. In the 1950s, when Vienna, New York and London were able to present operas with a new generation of first-rate artists, Paris was unable to produce French singers of comparable standard, even though all productions at the Opéra were at this time sung in French. It was not until 1971, with the appointment of Rolf Liebermann as administrator, that the Paris Opéra emerged from the doldrums. French singers were still slow in coming forward, so that for the leading roles in, for instance, such masterpieces of the French lyric theatre as *Orphée, Les Contes d'Hoffmann* and *Faust*, the Opéra turned to a distinguished foreign tenor, Nicolai Gedda. With the closure of the Opéra-Comique in 1972 for several years, spoken dialogue was admitted for the first time at the Opéra. The Liebermann régime came to an end in 1980. Since then, the Opéra has seemed to lack a sense of identity, although individual productions have often been impressive. In 1982, Massimo Bogianckino became the administrator.

PRAGUE: National Theatre
Czechoslovakia's Národni Divadlo, or
National Theatre, came into being as the
result of a movement which began in 1850
and which, in 1862, produced a Provisional
Theatre, directed for some years by the
composer Smetana. The building of the
permanent theatre began in 1868, to designs
by Josef Zítek, and the theatre opened in
1881 with the première of Smetana's *Libuše*,
only to be destroyed by fire two months
later. Within four weeks sufficient funds had
been collected by donation to rebuild, and
the new theatre was opened in 1883 again
with *Libuše*. The reconstruction was super-
vised by the architect Josef Schulz who improved on Zítek's original designs. The
technical equipment and decorations were
also considered superior to those of the first
building. The theatre now seats 1,598.

Many important Czech operas of the 19th
c. and 20th c. have had their premières at the
National Theatre, among them Dvořák's
Rusalka (1901), Janáček's *Mr Brouček's
Excursion to the Moon* (1920) and Martinů's
Juliette (1938). The theatre is shared by the
national opera and theatre companies.

ROME: Teatro dell' Opera

The Teatro Costanzi was built by Domenico Costanzi, the rich owner of a firm of builders, and designed by Achille Sfondrini. Seating nearly 2,300, it opened on 27 November 1880 with a performance of Rossini's *Semiramide*. It was here that Mascagni's *Cavalleria Rusticana* was given its première in May 1890, and Puccini's *Tosca* in January 1900. From 1911-25 the soprano Emma Carelli managed the theatre which, in 1926, was taken over by the city of Rome, enlarged and renovated. Renamed the Teatro Reale dell' Opera (the name it still bears today, with the 'Reale' or 'Royal' omitted), it reopened on 28 February 1928 with Boito's *Nerone*. The distinguished conductor Tullio Serafin was both chief conductor and artistic director from 1934-43, and during this period many singers were enticed away from Milan's La Scala to the Rome Opera, as Mussolini wanted it to be the best in Italy. During the German occupation, Serafin managed to stage Berg's *Wozzeck* with Tito Gobbi, despite the fact that the opera was banned in Nazi Germany.

Since the end of World War II, the Rome Opera has seen many changes in management and artistic direction. It continues to challenge La Scala, though it remains a less attractive theatre with a considerably less distinguished past than that of its northern rival.

SALZBURG: Grosses Festspielhaus

The first opera performance north of the Alps was given in Salzburg in 1618. Here Mozart was born in 1756 and Herbert von Karajan in 1908. The first Mozart festivals in Salzburg were held between 1877-1910, and in 1906 Mahler conducted *Le Nozze di Figaro* and *Don Giovanni* in productions designed by Alfred Roller. The first of the annual summer festivals was given in 1922, when four Mozart operas were staged with casts which included Rethberg, Tauber and Elisabeth Schumann. The new Festspielhaus was opened in that year, but the operas were staged in the city's older theatre, and the new Festspielhaus was not used for opera until 1927 when Lotte Lehmann appeared there in *Fidelio*.

In 1960, a second Festspielhaus, now known as the Large Festival Theatre or Grosses Festspielhaus to distinguish it from the smaller 1922 Kleines Festspielhaus, was opened with *Der Rosenkavalier*. It seats 2,160, and its stage is the largest in the world. It is used for the more lavish Salzburg Festival productions of opera, which are generally those conducted by Herbert von Karajan who, since 1966, has also directed an annual Easter Festival devoted primarily to Wagner.

SAN FRANCISCO: War Memorial Opera House

In San Francisco's great days as a boom town in the mid-19th c., operas were performed in eleven theatres, mainly by visiting companies. In 1852, the Pellegrini company performed *La Sonnambula, Norma* and *Ernani*. By the end of the century, the Met was including San Francisco in its tours, offering in 1890 Tamagno in *Otello* and Patti in *Semiramide, Traviata* and other operas, and in 1900 a complete *Ring*. Caruso sang Don José in *Carmen* in San Francisco the evening before the famous earthquake of 1906, and was seen rushing from the foyer of the Palace Hotel at 5 a.m. when the first tremors were felt, clutching his silver-framed, signed photograph of Theodore Roosevelt, and muttering to himself in terror, 'Vesuvius!'

The San Francisco Opera was founded in 1923, and gave its first annual seasons in the Civic Auditorium, until in 1932 the War Memorial Opera House, a huge theatre seating 3,200, opened with Claudia Muzio in *Tosca*. The company still performs in this attractive theatre with its pleasant air of spaciousness and its excellent acoustics. It engages the best of American and international singers, and many European artists have made their American débuts in San Francisco, among them Giulietta Simionato, Renata Tebaldi, Mario del Monaco and Tito Gobbi. In the Wagner seasons of the 1930s, Lehmann, Melchior, Schorr and Flagstad were to be heard.

The company performs in the autumn and winter, and in recent years has added a summer festival season of four or five operas. In 1961 a Spring Opera Company was founded to give performance opportunities to new young American singers.

STOCKHOLM: Royal Opera House

The first opera performances in Stockholm were given during the reign of Queen Christina in the mid-17th c. By the middle of the following century opera was firmly established there, and a theatre (which is still used) was built at Drottningholm, near Stockholm. In 1782, Gustav III opened the first Royal Opera House. Ironically, it was here that, in 1792, he was assassinated: an event portrayed in Verdi's opera, *Un Ballo in Maschera*.

Gustav's opera house was demolished in 1890, and the present theatre was erected on the site. A building with a seating capacity of approximately 1,300, it opened in 1898.

Throughout the 20th c., many world-famous singers have emerged from Sweden and from the training they received at the Royal Swedish Opera and its school. The earlier years of the century produced a fine group of Swedish Wagnerians, among them Kerstin Thorborg, Nanny Larsen-Todsen, Karin Branzell, Set Svanholm, Carl Martin Ochmann and Gertrud Wettergren, and of course the non-Wagnerian Jussi Björling. The post-World War II years produced Birgit Nilsson, Nicolai Gedda, Elisabeth Söderström, Kerstin Meyer, Ingvar Wixell and others.

The company of the Swedish Royal Opera appears for most of the year in the Opera House in Stockholm. A number of performances are given during the summer at Drottningholm where the 18th-c. stage machinery is still in working condition.

SYDNEY: Opera House

Until well after World War II, Australia did not have a permanent, professional opera company. Sydney, the largest city in the country, and the one with the most cosmopolitan population, had to make do with occasional visits from companies which toured to Australia from abroad. In the mid-1950s, the nucleus of a company was assembled, and the New South Wales government announced an international competition for the design of an opera house. This was won by the Danish architect, Joern Utzon, whose building is certainly a work of art, though it has its drawbacks as an opera house. It is a structure which contains three auditoria, and the architect's intention was, of course, that the largest of the three would be used for opera. However, during the construction of the building, it became clear that the principal user of the largest auditorium wanted it to be a concert hall, and so opera was relegated to the medium-sized auditorium. (Asked if he thought the orchestra pit adequate, Benjamin Britten replied: 'Well, if the players are all Japanese and playing piccolos . . .').

Australian Opera, which plays two seasons yearly in the opera house, and even manages to mount some of its productions in the concert hall, opened the building in 1973 with Prokofiev's *War and Peace*, the Australian opera commissioned for the opening not being ready. (It was never completed.) Richard Bonynge is now Australian Opera's music director, and Australia's most famous soprano, Joan Sutherland, frequently appears with the company.

VENICE: Teatro La Fenice

Named Fenice (Phoenix) because it arose from the ashes of the Teatro San Benedetto which was destroyed by fire in 1773 (though in another part of Venice), the theatre opened on 16 May 1792 with Paisiello's *I Giuochi d'Agrigento*. Among operas which were given their premières there were Rossini's *Tancredi* and *Semiramide*, Bellini's *Beatrice di Tenda* and Donizetti's *Belisario*. This theatre, too, was destroyed by fire, in December 1836. It was quickly rebuilt, and the present Fenice opened one year later, on 26 December 1837. Verdi's close association with the theatre began with the commissioning of *Ernani* which had its première at the Fenice in 1844. Other Verdi operas first performed there are *Attila, Rigoletto, La Traviata* and *Simon Boccanegra*.

In 1854 the theatre was closed for eight months for redecoration, and reopened in December of that year, looking much as it does today. Its annual seasons now run from December to May. The auditorium seats 1,500, and its blue, cream and gold decoration makes it one of the most beautiful theatres in the world.

VIENNA: Staatsoper

It was during the reign of Ferdinand III, Habsburg Emperor and composer, that opera was first performed in Vienna. Francesco Bonacossi's *Adriana Abbandonata* was staged there in 1641, and Francesco Cavalli's *Egisto* in 1643. Under Leopold I (1658–1705), opera continued to flourish. Leopold himself, another Habsburg composer, contributed some of the music to Cesti's *Il Pomo d'Oro*, a lavishly staged entertainment written to celebrate Leopold's marriage. It was for the performance of *Il Pomo d'Oro* in 1666 that Vienna's first important opera house was constructed. Designed by Burnacini, it stood in the main square of the Imperial palace or Hofburg until, under the threat of Turkish attacks on Vienna, it was demolished in 1683. In the 18th c., opera houses proliferated in Vienna and in the royal palaces in the surrounding country. Three of Mozart's operas, *Die Entführung aus dem Serail, Le Nozze di Figaro* and *Così Fan Tutte*, were first performed at the Burgtheater. One, *Die Zauberflöte*, had its première at the suburban Theater auf der Wieden. In 1801, the enchanting little Theater an der Wien was opened. It was here that Beethoven's *Fidelio* was first staged, and later in the 19th c. the operettas of Johann Strauss, and even later, in the 20th c., those of Franz Lehár.

When the centre of Vienna underwent extensive rebuilding in the mid-19th c., and the great circular road, the Ring, was constructed, it was decided to build a new Imperial and Royal Opera House at the corner of the Ring and the Kärntnerstrasse. Designed by Eduard van der Nüll and August Siccard von Siccardsburg in 1860–1, the opera house was opened in 1869 with a performance of Mozart's *Don Giovanni*. The problems encountered during the construction of the building, and the carping of the Viennese, drove Van der Nüll to suicide before the opening. Von Siccardsburg had a stroke and died, heartbroken, a few months later.

Under Gustav Mahler (1897–1907), the company at the Hofoper reached its greatest heights: the enormous reputation which the Vienna Opera still enjoys can be traced directly back to the Mahler period. With the fall of the Habsburgs and the end of the Austro-Hungarian Empire after World War II, the Hofoper or Court Opera was renamed Staatsoper or State Opera. It continued until the beginning of the 1939–45 war to have the best opera ensemble in Europe, with such singers as Lotte Lehmann, Maria Jeritza, Elisabeth Schumann, Richard Tauber, Alfred Piccaver, and Vera Schwarz, and conductors of the calibre of Bruno Walter, Josef Krips and Clemens Krauss.

Its stage and auditorium almost completely gutted by bombs in 1945, the Staatsoper was rebuilt, and opened again in 1955 with Beethoven's *Fidelio* conducted by Karl Böhm. The exterior walls of the theatre, the original foyer and the principal staircase still remain, and Rodin's bust of Mahler is to be found in the upstairs foyer. Performances are given every night of the week for ten months of the year, with a break in July and August during most of which the theatre's orchestra, the Vienna Philharmonic, is busy playing for the opera in Salzburg.

Illustration Acknowledgments

The publishers would like to thank the following for permission to reproduce photographs:

J. Allan Cash, 363
Catherine Ashmore, 47, 83
Austrian National Tourist Office, 373
Clive Barda, 67, 92, 118, 278, 302, 315, 319, 332
BBC Copyright, 138, 163
Belgian Embassy, 254
Bildarchiv Preussischer Kulturbesitz, 351, 352
Camera Press, 9 (Photo: J. R. Roustan), 31, 40, 41, 44, 67, 70, 81, 91, 97, 98, 115, 145, 154, 170, 172, 181, 202, 225, 226 (Photo: Mander & Mitchenson Collection), 280, 335, 348, 361, 375
Czechoslovak News Agency, 32, 299
Dallas Opera, 292, 316, 329
Zoë Dominic, 27, 30, 55, 58, 76, 185, 200, 210, front jacket UK Drottingholms Teatermuseum, 377
English National Opera, 152, 159, 194 (Photo: Reg Wilson), 237, 264 (Photo: Clive Barda)
E. T. Archive, 10, 23, 49, 73
Festspielleitung, Bayreuth, 337
Hamlyn Group Picture Library, 15, 190, 207, 214, 216, 228, 255, 261, 267, 273, 282, 285, 295, 307, 326, 330, 342, 350, 379
Houston Grand Opera, 192, 219 (Photo: Jim Caldwell), 232 (Photo: Jim Caldwell), 304 (Photo: Jim Caldwell), 346
Istituto Italiano di cultura, 371
Interfoto MTI, 148
John Topham Picture Library, 356, 357, 380
Keystone, 21, 35, 87, 125, 131, 141, 166, 187, 249, 252, 289, 321, 338, 370, 378
Kungl Teatern, Stockholm, 300
Iveagh Bequest, back jacket

Lyric Opera, Chicago, 357 (Photo: Weidenfeld & Nicolson Archive)
Mansell Collection, 13, 37, 74
Metropolitan Opera House, 367
New York City Opera, 65 (Photo: Gerry Goodstein)
Novosti, 51, 102, 110, 127, 168, 362
Popperfoto, 63, 104, 162, 179, 183, 270, 291, 308, 353, 355, 360, 365
Rainbird, 26 (Photo: Roger Viollet)
Roger Viollet, 369
Royal Opera House, London, 188, 220, 242, 247, 313, 323, 358
San Francisco Opera, 213 (Photo: Ira Nowinski), 222 (Photo: David Powers), 251 (Photo: David Powers), 296 (Photo: Ira Nowinski)
Donald Southern (Photos), 340, 344
Scottish Opera, 196 (Photo; Eric Thorburn), 209 (Photo: Eric Thorburn)
Stuart-Liff Collection, 205
Syndication International, 12, 107, 311
Wiener Festwochen, 129
Reg Wilson, 101, 112, 117
Axel Zeininger, 231